CCNA Cybersecurity Operations
Companion Guide

Cisco Press

CCNA Cybersecurity Operations Companion Guide

Copyright © 2018 Cisco Systems, Inc.

Published by:
Cisco Press

Library of Congress Control Number: 2018939878

ISBN-13: 978-1-58713-439-5
ISBN-10: 1-58713-439-X

1   18

Warning and Disclaimer

This book is designed to provide information about the Cisco Networking Academy CCNA Cybersecurity Operations course. Every effort has been made to make this book as complete and as accurate as possible, but no warranty or fitness is implied.

The information is provided on an "as is" basis. The authors, Cisco Press, and Cisco Systems, Inc. shall have neither liability nor responsibility to any person or entity with respect to any loss or damages arising from the information contained in this book or from the use of the discs or programs that may accompany it.

The opinions expressed in this book belong to the author and are not necessarily those of Cisco Systems, Inc.

Editor-in-Chief
Mark Taub

Alliances Manager, Cisco Press
Arezou Gol

Executive Editor
Mary Beth Ray

Managing Editor
Sandra Schroeder

Development Editor
Ellie C. Bru

Senior Project Editor
Tonya Simpson

Copy Editor
Bill McManus

Technical Editor
Patrick Gargano

Editorial Assistant
Vanessa Evans

Cover Designer
Chuti Prasertsith

Composition
codemantra

Indexer
Lisa Stumpf

Proofreader
Jeanine Furino

cisco.

Trademark Acknowledgments

All terms mentioned in this book that are known to be trademarks or service marks have been appropriately capitalized. Cisco Press or Cisco Systems, Inc., cannot attest to the accuracy of this information. Use of a term in this book should not be regarded as affecting the validity of any trademark or service mark.

Special Sales

For information about buying this title in bulk quantities, or for special sales opportunities (which may include electronic versions; custom cover designs; and content particular to your business, training goals, marketing focus, or branding interests), please contact our corporate sales department at corpsales@pearsoned.com or (800) 382-3419.

For government sales inquiries, please contact governmentsales@pearsoned.com.

For questions about sales outside the U.S., please contact intlcs@pearson.com.

Feedback Information

At Cisco Press, our goal is to create in-depth technical books of the highest quality and value. Each book is crafted with care and precision, undergoing rigorous development that involves the unique expertise of members from the professional technical community.

Readers' feedback is a natural continuation of this process. If you have any comments regarding how we could improve the quality of this book, or otherwise alter it to better suit your needs, you can contact us through email at feedback@ciscopress.com. Please make sure to include the book title and ISBN in your message.

We greatly appreciate your assistance.

Americas Headquarters	Asia Pacific Headquarters	Europe Headquarters
Cisco Systems, Inc.	Cisco Systems (USA) Pte. Ltd.	Cisco Systems International BV Amsterdam,
San Jose, CA	Singapore	The Netherlands

Cisco has more than 200 offices worldwide. Addresses, phone numbers, and fax numbers are listed on the Cisco Website at www.cisco.com/go/offices.

Cisco and the Cisco logo are trademarks or registered trademarks of Cisco and/or its affiliates in the U.S. and other countries. To view a list of Cisco trademarks, go to this URL: www.cisco.com/go/trademarks. Third party trademarks mentioned are the property of their respective owners. The use of the word partner does not imply a partnership relationship between Cisco and any other company. (1110R)

About the Contributing Author

Allan Johnson entered the academic world in 1999 after 10 years as a business owner/operator to dedicate his efforts to his passion for teaching. He holds both an MBA and an M.Ed in training and development. He taught CCNA courses at the high school level for seven years and has taught both CCNA and CCNP courses at Del Mar College in Corpus Christi, Texas. In 2003, Allan began to commit much of his time and energy to the CCNA Instructional Support Team providing services to Networking Academy instructors worldwide and creating training materials. He now works full time for Cisco Networking Academy as Curriculum Lead.

Contents at a Glance

Contents

Command Syntax Conventions

The conventions used to present command syntax in this book are the same conventions used in the IOS Command Reference. The Command Reference describes these conventions as follows:

- **Boldface** indicates commands and keywords that are entered literally as shown. In actual configuration examples and output (not general command syntax), boldface indicates commands that are manually input by the user (such as a **show** command).

- *Italic* indicates arguments for which you supply actual values.

- Vertical bars (|) separate alternative, mutually exclusive elements.

- Square brackets ([ ]) indicate an optional element.

- Braces ({ }) indicate a required choice.

- Braces within brackets ([{ }]) indicate a required choice within an optional element.

Introduction

CCNA Cybersecurity Operations Companion Guide is the official supplemental textbook for the Cisco Networking Academy CCNA Cybersecurity Operations v1.x course. Cisco Networking Academy is a comprehensive program that delivers information technology skills to students around the world. The curriculum emphasizes real-world practical application, while providing opportunities for you to gain the skills needed to successfully handle the tasks, duties, and responsibilities of an associate-level cybersecurity analyst working in a Security Operations Center (SOC).

As a textbook, this book provides a ready reference to explain the same concepts, technologies, protocols, and tools as the online curriculum. You can use the online curriculum as directed by your instructor and then use this *Companion Guide*'s study tools to help solidify your understanding of all the topics.

Who Should Read This Book

The book, as well as the course, is designed as an introduction to cybersecurity operations for those pursuing careers as a cybersecurity analyst. Topics are presented concisely, starting with the most fundamental concepts and progressing to a comprehensive understanding of security monitoring, intrusion analysis, and incident response. The content of this book provides preparation for the CCNA Cyber Ops certification exams (SECFND and SECOPS).

Book Features

The educational features of this book focus on supporting topic coverage, readability, and practice of the course material to facilitate your full understanding of the course material.

Topic Coverage

The following features give you a thorough overview of the topics covered in each chapter so that you can make constructive use of your study time:

- **Objectives:** Listed at the beginning of each chapter, the objectives reference the core concepts covered in the chapter. The objectives match the objectives stated in the corresponding chapters of the online curriculum; however, the question format in the *Companion Guide* encourages you to think about finding the answers as you read the chapter.

- **Notes:** These are short sidebars that point out interesting facts, time-saving methods, and important safety issues.

- **Chapter summaries:** At the end of each chapter is a summary of the chapter's key concepts. It provides a synopsis of the chapter and serves as a study aid.

- **Practice:** At the end of chapter there is a full list of all the labs, class activities, and Packet Tracer activities to refer back to for study time.

Readability

The following features assist your understanding of the networking vocabulary:

- **Key terms:** Each chapter begins with a list of key terms, along with a page number reference from inside the chapter. The terms are listed in the order in which they are explained in the chapter. This handy reference allows you to find a term, flip to the page where the term appears, and see the term used in context. The Glossary defines all the key terms.

- **Glossary:** This book contains an all new Glossary with almost 400 terms.

Practice

Practice makes perfect. This *Companion Guide* offers you ample opportunities to put what you learn into practice. You will find the following features valuable and effective in reinforcing the instruction that you receive:

- **Check Your Understanding questions and answer key:** Review questions are presented at the end of each chapter as a self-assessment tool. These questions match the style of questions that you see in the online course. Appendix A, "Answers to the 'Check Your Understanding' Questions," provides an answer key to all the questions and includes an explanation of each answer.

- **Labs and activities:** Throughout each chapter, you will be directed back to the online course to take advantage of the activities created to reinforce concepts. In addition, at the end of each chapter, there is a practice section that collects a list of all the labs and activities to provide practice with the topics introduced in that chapter.

- **Page references to online course:** After headings, you will see, for example, (1.1.2.3). This number refers to the page number in the online course so that you can easily jump to that spot online to view a video, practice an activity, perform a lab, or review a topic.

About Packet Tracer Software and Activities

Interspersed throughout the chapters you'll find a few Cisco Packet Tracer activities. Packet Tracer allows you to create networks, visualize how packets flow in the network, and use basic testing tools to determine whether the network would work. When you see this icon, you can use Packet Tracer with the listed file to perform a task suggested in this book. The activity files are available in the course. Packet Tracer software is available only through the Cisco Networking Academy website. Ask your instructor for access to Packet Tracer.

How This Book Is Organized

This book corresponds closely to the Cisco Networking Academy CCNA Cybersecurity Operations v1 course and is divided into 13 chapters, one appendix, and a glossary of key terms:

- **Chapter 1, "Cybersecurity and the Security Operations Center":** This chapter examines why networks and data are attacked and how to prepare for a career in cybersecurity operations.

- **Chapter 2, "Windows Operating System":** This chapter discusses the features and characteristics of the Windows operating system, including its operation and how to secure Windows endpoints.

- **Chapter 3, "Linux Operating System":** This chapter discusses the features and characteristics of the Linux operating system, including basic operation in the Linux shell, basic administrative tasks, and basic security-related tasks on a Linux host.

- **Chapter 4, "Network Protocols and Services":** This chapter discusses the operation of network protocols and services, including network operations, Ethernet and IP, common testing utilities, address resolution, transport functionality, and applications that provide network services.

- **Chapter 5, "Network Infrastructure":** This chapter discusses network infrastructure, including wired and wireless networks, network security devices, and network topologies.

- **Chapter 6, "Principles of Network Security":** This chapter discusses the various types of network attacks, including how networks are attacked and the various types of threats and attacks.

- **Chapter 7, "Network Attacks: A Deeper Look":** This chapter dives deeper into network attacks, including how to identify attacks using network monitoring tools. Also, the vulnerabilities of TCP/IP and network applications are discussed.

- **Chapter 8, "Protecting the Network":** This chapter discusses methods to prevent malicious access to networks, hosts, and data, including approaches to network security defense, access control methods, and using various intelligence sources to locate current security threats.

- **Chapter 9, "Cryptography and the Public Key Infrastructure":** This chapter discusses the impact of cryptography on network security monitoring, including tools to encrypt and decrypt data and the public key infrastructure (PKI).

- **Chapter 10, "Endpoint Security and Analysis":** This chapter discusses how to investigate endpoint vulnerabilities and attacks, including malware analysis and endpoint vulnerability assessment.

- **Chapter 11, "Security Monitoring":** This chapter discusses how to identify network security alerts, including how network security technologies affect security monitoring and the type of log files used in security monitoring.

- **Chapter 12, "Intrusion Data Analysis":** This chapter discusses how to analyze network intrusion data to verify potential exploits, including the process of evaluating alerts, determining the source of an alert, and the handling of evidence to ensure proper attack attribution.

- **Chapter 13, "Incident Response and Handling":** This chapter discusses how to apply incident response models to manage security incidents. Response models include the Cyber Kill Chain, the Diamond Model of intrusion, the VERIS schema, and NIST 800-61r2 standards.

- **Appendix A, "Answers to the 'Check Your Understanding' Questions":** This appendix lists the answers to the "Check Your Understanding" review questions that are included at the end of each chapter.

- **Glossary:** The Glossary provides you with definitions for all the key terms identified in each chapter.

## CHAPTER 1

Cybersecurity and the Security Operations Center

Objectives

Upon completion of this chapter, you will be able to answer the following questions:

- What are some features of examples of cybersecurity incidents?

- What are the motivations of the threat actors behind specific security incidents?

- What is the potential impact of network security attacks?

- What is the mission of the Security Operations Center (SOC)?

- What are some resources available to prepare for a career in cybersecurity operations?

Key Terms

This chapter uses the following key terms. You can find the definitions in the Glossary.

Introduction (1.0)

In this chapter, you will learn about the who, what, and why of cyberattacks. Different people commit cybercrime for different reasons. Security Operations Centers (SOC) work to combat cybercrime. People prepare for work in a SOC by earning certifications, seeking formal education, and by using employment services to gain internship experience and jobs.

Class Activity 1.0.1.2: Top Hacker Shows Us How It is Done

In this class activity, you will view a TED Talk video that discusses various security vulnerabilities. You will also research one of the vulnerabilities mentioned in the video.

The Danger (1.1)

In this section, you will learn some common war stories in the cybersecurity arena as well as some of the major *threat actors* and threat impacts.

War Stories (1.1.1)

In this topic, you will learn about three types of victims in cybercrime: individuals, organizations, and nations.

Hijacked People (1.1.1.1)

Sarah stopped by her favorite coffee shop to grab her afternoon drink. She placed her order, paid the clerk, and waited while the baristas worked furiously to fulfill the backup of orders. Sarah pulled out her phone, opened the wireless client, and connected to what she assumed was the coffee shop's free wireless network.

However, sitting in a corner of the store, a hacker had just set up an open "rogue" wireless hotspot posing as the coffee shop's wireless network. When Sarah logged onto her bank's website, the hacker hijacked her session, and gained access to her bank accounts.

View the following video posted in 2008 to see a demonstration of how one wireless network was vulnerable to hacking:

https://www.youtube.com/watch?v=zcmmFQGxMNU

In this course, you will learn about security technologies that easily prevent this type of attack.

Ransomed Companies (1.1.1.2)

Rashid, an employee in the finance department of a major, publicly held corporation, receives an email from his CEO with an attached PDF. The PDF is about the company's third-quarter earnings. Rashid does not remember his department creating the PDF. His curiosity is peaked, so he opens the attachment.

The same scenario plays out across the organization as dozens of other employees are successfully enticed to click the attachment. When the PDF opens, *ransomware* is installed on the employees' computers and begins the process of gathering and encrypting corporate data. The goal of the attackers is financial gain, because they hold the company's data for ransom until they are paid.

View the following video to see a dramatization of how this ransomware attack could happen:

https://www.youtube.com/watch?v=4gR562GW7TITargeted

Nations (1.1.1.3)

Some of today's *malware* is so sophisticated and expensive to create that security experts believe only a nation state or group of nations could possibly have the influence and funding to create it. Such malware can be targeted to attack a nation's vulnerable infrastructure, such as the water system or power grid.

This was the purpose of the Stuxnet worm, which infected USB drives. These drives were carried by five Iranian component vendors, with the intention of infiltrating nuclear facilities supported by the vendors. Stuxnet was designed to infiltrate Windows operating systems and then target Step 7 software. Step 7 was developed by Siemens for their programmable logic controllers (PLC). Stuxnet was looking for a specific model of the Siemens PLCs that controls the centrifuges in nuclear facilities. The worm was transmitted from the infected USB drives into the PLCs and eventually damaged many of these centrifuges.

Zero Days, a film released in 2016, attempts to document the development and deployment of the Stuxnet targeted malware attack. Search the Internet for a web location where you can view the film.

Lab 1.1.1.4: Installing the CyberOps Workstation Virtual Machine

In this lab, you will install VirtualBox on your personal computer. You will then download and install the CyberOps Workstation Virtual Machine (VM).

Lab 1.1.1.5: Cybersecurity Case Studies

In this lab, you will analyze the given cases and answer questions about them.

Threat Actors (1.1.2)

In this topic, you will learn about the motivations of the threat actors behind specific security incidents.

Amateurs (1.1.2.1)

Threat actors include, but are not limited to, amateurs, *hacktivists*, organized crime groups, state-sponsored and terrorist groups. Threat actors are individuals or a group of individuals who perform cyberattacks against another individual or organization. Cyberattacks are intentional, malicious acts meant to negatively impact another individual or organization.

Amateurs, also known as *script kiddies*, have little or no skill. They often use existing tools or instructions found on the Internet to launch attacks. Some are just curious, while others try to demonstrate their skills by causing harm. Even though they are using basic tools, the results can still be devastating.

Hacktivists (1.1.2.2)

Hacktivists are hackers who protest against a variety of political and social ideas. Hacktivists publicly protest against organizations or governments by posting articles and videos, leaking sensitive information, and disrupting web services with illegitimate traffic in *distributed denial of service (DDoS)* attacks.

Financial Gain (1.1.2.3)

Much of the hacking activity that consistently threatens our security is motivated by financial gain. These cybercriminals want to gain access to our bank accounts, personal data, and anything else they can leverage to generate cash flow.

Trade Secrets and Global Politics (1.1.2.4)

The past several years have seen many stories about nation states hacking other countries, or otherwise interfering with internal politics. Nation states are also interested in using cyberspace for industrial espionage. The theft of intellectual property can give a country a significant advantage in international trade.

Defending against the fallout from state-sponsored cyberespionage and cyberwarfare will continue to be a priority for cybersecurity professionals.

How Secure Is the Internet of Things? (1.1.2.5)

The Internet of Things (IoT) is all around us and quickly expanding. We are just beginning to reap the benefits of the IoT. New ways to use connected things are being developed daily. The IoT helps individuals connect things to improve their quality of life. For example, many people are now using connected wearable devices to track their fitness activities. How many devices do you currently own that connect to your home network or the Internet?

How secure are these devices? For example, who wrote the firmware? Did the programmer pay attention to security flaws? Is your connected home thermostat vulnerable to attacks? What about your DVR? If security vulnerabilities are found, can firmware in the device be patched to eliminate the vulnerability? Many devices on the Internet are not updated with the latest firmware. Some older devices were not even developed to be updated with patches. These two situations create opportunity for threat actors and security risks for the owners of these devices.

In October 2016, a DDoS attack against the domain name provider Dyn took down many popular websites. The attack came from a large number of webcams, DVRs, routers, and other IoT devices that had been compromised by malicious software. These devices formed a "botnet" that was controlled by hackers. This botnet was used to create an enormous DDoS attack that disabled essential Internet services. Dyn has posted a blog here to explain the attack and their reaction to it.

Avi Rubin, Professor of Computer Science at Johns Hopkins University and Technical Director of the JHU Information Security Institute, highlights the dangers of not securing all our connected devices. Search the Internet to view his TED talk.

Lab 1.1.2.6: Learning the Details of Attacks

In this lab, you will research and analyze IoT application vulnerabilities.

Threat Impact (1.1.3)

In this topic, you will learn about the potential impact of network security attacks.

PII and PHI (1.1.3.1)

The economic impact of cyberattacks is difficult to ascertain with precision; however, according to an article in *Forbes*, it is estimated that businesses lose $400 billion annually to cyberattacks.

Personally identifiable information (PII) is any information that can be used to positively identify an individual. Examples of PII include:

- Name
- Social security number
- Birthdate
- Credit card numbers

- Bank account numbers

- Government issued ID

- Address information (street, email, phone numbers)

One of the more lucrative goals of cybercriminals is obtaining lists of PII that can then be sold on the dark web. The dark web can only be accessed with special software and is used by cybercriminals to shield their activities. Stolen PII can be used to create fake accounts, such as credit cards and short-term loans.

A subset of PII is *protected health information (PHI)*. The medical community creates and maintains electronic medical records (EMR) that contain PHI. In the United States, handling of PHI is regulated by the Health Insurance Portability and Accountability Act (HIPAA). The equivalent regulation in the European Union is called Data Protection.

Most hacks on companies and organizations reported in the news involved stolen PII or PHI. In only three months in 2016, the following attacks occurred:

- In March 2016, a data breach at a health care provider exposed the personal information of 2.2 million patients.

- In April 2016, a laptop and portable drives were stolen from a government agency that included personal information for as many as 5 million people.

- In May 2016, a data breach at a payroll company exposed the payroll, tax, and benefits information of over 600,000 companies.

Lost Competitive Advantage (1.1.3.2)

Companies are increasingly worried about corporate espionage in cyberspace. An additional major concern is the loss of trust that comes when a company is unable to protect its customers' personal data. The loss of competitive advantage may come from this loss of trust rather than another company or country stealing trade secrets.

Politics and National Security (1.1.3.3)

It is not just businesses that get hacked. In February 2016, a hacker published the personal information of 20,000 U.S. Federal Bureau of Investigation (FBI) employees and 9,000 U.S. Department of Homeland Security (DHS) employees. The hacker was apparently politically motivated.

The Stuxnet worm was specifically designed to impede Iran's progress in enriching uranium that could be used in a nuclear weapon. Stuxnet is a prime example of a network attack motivated by national security concerns. Cyberwarfare is a serious possibility. State-supported hacker warriors can cause disruption and destruction of vital services and resources within an enemy nation. The Internet has become essential as a medium for commercial and financial activities. Disruption of these activities can devastate a nation's economy. Controllers, similar to those attacked by Stuxnet, also are used to control the flow of water at dams and the switching of electricity on the power grid. Attacks on such controllers can have dire consequences.

 Lab 1.1.3.4: Visualizing the Black Hats

In this lab, you will research and analyze cybersecurity incidents to create scenarios of how organizations can prevent or mitigate an attack.

Fighters in the War Against Cybercrime (1.2)

In this section, you will learn about the *Security Operations Center (SOC)* and how to become a defender in the cybersecurity arena.

The Modern Security Operations Center (1.2.1)

In this topic, you will learn about the people, processes, and technologies in an SOC.

Elements of an SOC (1.2.1.1)

Defending against today's threats requires a formalized, structured, and disciplined approach, which is executed by professionals at SOCs. SOCs provide a broad range of services, from monitoring and management, to comprehensive threat solutions and hosted security that can be customized to meet customer needs. SOCs can be wholly in-house, owned and operated by a business, or elements of an SOC can be contracted out to security vendors, such as Cisco's Managed Security Services.

The major elements of an SOC, shown in Figure 1-1, are people, processes, and technology.

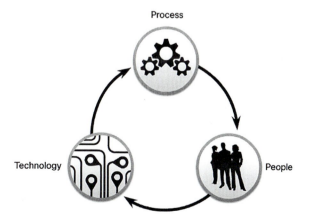

Figure 1-1   Elements of a Security Operations Center

People in the SOC (1.2.1.2)

The SANS Institute (https://www.sans.org) classifies the roles people play in a SOC into four job titles:

- *Tier 1 Alert Analyst*: These professionals monitor incoming alerts, verify that a true incident has occurred, and forward tickets to Tier 2, if necessary.

- *Tier 2 Incident Responder*: These professionals are responsible for deep investigation of incidents and advise remediation or action to be taken.

- *Tier 3 Subject Matter Expert (SME)/Hunter*: These professionals have expert-level skill in network, endpoint, threat intelligence, and malware reverse engineering. They are experts at tracing the processes of the malware to determine its impact and how it can be removed. They are also deeply involved in hunting for potential threats and implementing threat detection tools.

- *SOC Manager*: This professional manages all the resources of the SOC and serves as the point of contact for the larger organization or customer.

This course offers preparation for a certification suitable for the position of Tier 1 Alert Analyst, also known as Cybersecurity Analyst.

Figure 1-2 graphically represents how these roles interact with each other.

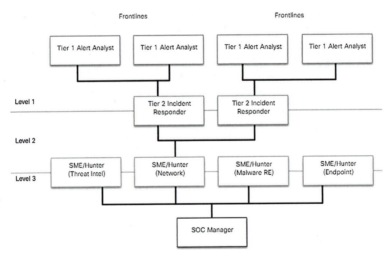

Figure 1-2   Roles of the People in a Security Operations Center

Process in the SOC (1.2.1.3)

The day of a Tier 1 Analyst begins with monitoring security alert queues. A ticketing system is frequently used to allow analysts to select alerts from a queue to investigate. Because the software that generates alerts can trigger false alarms, one job of the Tier 1 Analyst might be to verify that an alert represents a true security incident. When verification is established, the incident can be forwarded to investigators or other security personnel to be acted upon, or resolved as a false alarm.

If a ticket cannot be resolved, the Tier 1 Analyst will forward the ticket to a Tier 2 Analyst for deeper investigation and remediation. If the Tier 2 Analyst cannot resolve the ticket, she will forward it to a Tier 3 Analyst with in-depth knowledge and threat hunting skills.

Figure 1-3 summarizes the roles of Tier 1, Tier 2, and Tier 3 analysts.

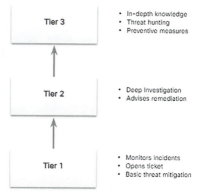

Figure 1-3   Threat Incident Escalation Process

Technologies in the SOC (1.2.1.4)

As shown in Figure 1-4, a SOC needs a *security information and event management system (SIEM)*, or its equivalent. This system combines data from multiple technologies. SIEM systems are used for collecting and filtering data, detecting and classifying threats, analyzing and investigating threats, and managing resources to implement preventive measures and address future threats. SOC technologies include one or more of the following:

- Event collection, correlation, and analysis
- Security monitoring
- Security control
- Log management
- Vulnerability assessment
- Vulnerability tracking
- Threat intelligence

Figure 1-4 is a simplified representation of an SOC monitoring system. Information about network traffic, network flows, system logs, endpoint data, intelligence threat feeds, security events, and identifying asset context are all fed into the SIEM system.

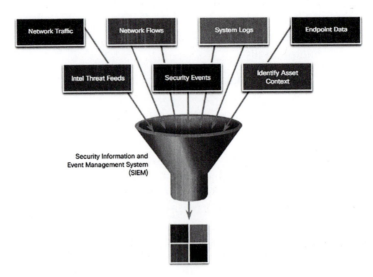

Figure 1-4 SOC Monitoring System

Enterprise and Managed Security (1.2.1.5)

For medium and large networks, the organization will benefit from implementing an enterprise-level SOC. The SOC can be a complete in-house solution. However, many larger organizations will outsource at least part of the SOC operations to a security solutions provider.

Cisco has a team of experts who help ensure timely and accurate incident resolution. Cisco offers a wide range of incident response, preparedness, and management capabilities:

- Cisco Smart Net Total Care Service
- Cisco Product Security Incident Response Team (PSIRT)
- Cisco Computer Security Incident Response Team (CSIRT)
- Cisco Managed Services
- Cisco Tactical Operations (TacOps)
- Cisco's Safety and Physical Security Program

Security vs. Availability (1.2.1.6)

Most enterprise networks must be up and running at all times. Security personnel understand that for the organization to accomplish its priorities, network availability must be preserved.

Each business or industry has a limited tolerance for network downtime. That tolerance is usually based upon a comparison of the cost of the downtime in relation to the cost of ensuring against downtime. For example, in a small retail business with only one location, it may be tolerable to have a router as a single point of failure. However, if a large portion of that business's sales are from online shoppers, then the owner may decide to provide a level of redundancy to ensure that a connection is always available.

Preferred uptime is often measured in the number of down minutes in a year, as shown in Table 1-1. For example, a "five nines" uptime means that the network is up 99.999% of the time or down for no more than 5 minutes a year. "Four nines" would be a downtime of 53 minutes a year.

Table 1-1   Availability and Downtime

Availability %	Downtime
99.8%	17.52 hours
99.9% ("three nines")	8.76 hours
99.99% ("four nines")	52.56 minutes
99.999% ("five nines")	5.256 minutes
99.9999% ("six nines")	31.5 seconds
99.99999% ("seven nines")	3.15 seconds

However, security cannot be so strong that it interferes with the needs of employees or business functions. It is always a tradeoff between strong security and permitting efficient business functioning.

Interactive Graphic

Activity 1.2.1.7: Identify the SOC Terminology

Refer to the online course to complete this Activity.

Becoming a Defender (1.2.2)

In this topic, you will learn about the available certifications, degrees, and opportunities for gaining experience in cybersecurity operations.

Certifications (1.2.2.1)

A variety of cybersecurity certifications that are relevant to careers in SOCs are available from several different organizations.

Cisco CCNA Cyber Ops

The CCNA Cyber Ops certification provides a valuable first step in acquiring the knowledge and skills needed to work with a SOC team. It can be a valuable part of a career in the exciting and growing field of cybersecurity operations.

CompTIA Cybersecurity Analyst Certification

The CompTIA Cybersecurity Analyst (CSA+) certification is a vendor-neutral IT professional certification. It validates knowledge and skills required to configure and use threat detection tools, perform data analysis, and interpret the results to identify vulnerabilities, threats, and risks to an organization. The end goal is the ability to secure and protect applications and systems within an organization.

(ISC)^2 Information Security Certifications

(ISC)^2 is an international non-profit organization that offers the highly acclaimed CISSP certification. (ISC)^2 offers a range of other certifications for various specialties in cybersecurity.

Global Information Assurance Certification (GIAC)

GIAC, which was founded in 1999, is one of the oldest security certification organizations. It offers a wide range of certifications in seven categories.

Other Security-Related Certifications

Search for "cybersecurity certifications" to find information about other vendor and vendor-neutral certifications.

Further Education (1.2.2.2)

Degrees

Anyone considering a career in the cybersecurity field, should seriously consider pursuing a technical degree or bachelor's degree in computer science, electrical engineering, information technology, or information security. Many educational institutions offer security-related specialized tracks and certifications.

Python Programming

Computer programming is an essential skill for anyone who wishes to pursue a career in cybersecurity. If you have never learned how to program, then Python might be the first language to learn. Python is an open-source, object-oriented language that is routinely used by cybersecurity analysts. It is also a popular programming language for Linux-based systems and software-defined networking (SDN).

Sources of Career Information (1.2.2.3)

A variety of websites and mobile applications advertise information technology jobs. Each site targets a variety of job applicants and provides different tools for candidates to research their ideal job position. Many sites are job site aggregators. Job site aggregators gather listings from other job boards and company career sites and display them in a single location.

Indeed.com

Advertised as the world's #1 job site, Indeed.com attracts over 180 million unique visitors every month from over 50 different countries. Indeed.com is truly a worldwide job site. It helps companies of all sizes hire the best talent and offers the best opportunity for job seekers.

CareerBuilder.com

CareerBuilder serves many large and prestigious companies. As a result, this site attracts specific candidates that typically have more education and higher credentials. The employers posting on CareerBuilder commonly get more candidates with college degrees, advanced credentials, and industry certifications.

USAJobs.gov

The United States federal government posts any openings on USAJobs:

https://www.usajobs.gov

Salary Information

The website glassdoor.com provides salary information for different job types, companies, and locations. Search for "cyber security analyst" to see salaries and requirements for current job openings.

Getting Experience (1.2.2.4)

There are variety of ways to get experience. The following are a few ideas.

Internships

Internships are an excellent method for gaining entry into the cybersecurity field. Sometimes, internships turn into an offer of full-time employment. However, even a temporary internship allows you the opportunity to gain experience in the inner workings of a cybersecurity organization. The contacts you make during an internship can also prove to be a valuable resource as you continue your career.

Search the Internet for a *Forbes* article titled "The 10 Best Websites For Finding An Internship."

Cisco Cybersecurity Scholarship

To help close the security skills gap, Cisco introduced the Global Cybersecurity Scholarship program in 2016. Cisco is motivated to increase the pool of talent with critical cybersecurity proficiency. Registration opens in spring and awards are announced in late fall. Visit the following website to learn more about the scholarship:

https://mkto.cisco.com/Security-Scholarship

Temporary Agencies

If you are having difficulty finding your first job, a temporary agency can be a great place to start. Most temporary agencies will help you polish your resume and make recommendations on additional skills you may need to obtain to make yourself more attractive to potential employers.

Many organizations use temporary agencies to fill job openings for the first 90 days. Then, if the employee is a good match, the organization may offer to buy the contract from the temporary agency, converting the employee to a full-time, permanent position.

Your First Job

If you have no experience in the cybersecurity field, then you will most likely look for a company that is willing to train you for a position similar to a Tier 1 Analyst. Working for a call center or support desk may be your first step into gaining the experience you need to move ahead in your career.

How long should you stay in your first job? Generally, you want to make it through a full review cycle before leaving a company. That is, you typically want to make it past 18 months. Potential employers will normally want to know if you met or exceeded expectations in your current or past jobs.

Lab 1.2.2.5: Becoming a Defender

In this lab, you will research and analyze what it takes to become a network defender.

Summary (1.3)

In the beginning of the chapter you learned that people, companies, and even nations can all fall victim to cyberattacks. There are various types of attackers, including amateurs who attack for fun and prestige, hacktivists who hack to further a political cause, and professional hackers who attack for profit. In addition, nations may attack other nations to gain economic advantage through the theft of intellectual property, or to damage or destroy the assets of another country. The networks that are vulnerable to attack are not just business networks of PCs and servers, but also the thousands of devices on the Internet of Things.

SOCs are responsible for preventing, detecting, and responding to cybercrime. SOCs consist of people following processes to use technologies to respond to threats. There are four main roles in the SOC. Tier 1 Analysts verify security alerts using network data. Tier 2 Incident Responders investigate verified incidents and decide on how to act. Tier 3 SMEs/Hunters are experts and are able to investigate threats at the highest level. The fourth role is the SOC Managers. They manage the resources of the center and communicate with customers. Customers can be internal or external. A SOC may be operated by a single company or may provide services to many companies. Finally, although network security is extremely important, it cannot interfere with the ability of the company and its employees to fulfill the mission of an organization.

In order to work in an SOC, you learned that you can study to earn certifications that are offered by a number of different organizations. In addition, you can pursue degrees in higher education that are relevant to cyberoperations, and learn other skills such as programming in Python. Job leads can be found at a number of employment websites, and agencies can help you to find temporary jobs, internships, or permanent employment.

Practice

The following activities provide practice with the topics introduced in this chapter. The Labs and Class Activities are available in the companion *CCNA Cybersecurity Operations Lab Manual* (ISBN 9781587134388).

 Class Activities

Class Activity 1.0.1.2: Top Hacker Shows Us How It is Done

Labs

Lab 1.1.1.4: Installing the CyberOps Workstation Virtual Machine

Lab 1.1.1.5: Cybersecurity Case Studies

Lab 1.1.2.6: Learning the Details of Attacks

Lab 1.1.3.4: Visualizing the Black Hats

Lab 1.2.2.5: Becoming a Defender

Check Your Understanding

Complete all the review questions listed here to test your understanding of the topics and concepts in this chapter. The appendix "Answers to the 'Check Your Understanding' Questions" lists the answers.

1. A computer is presenting a user with a screen requesting payment before the user data is allowed to be accessed by the same user. What type of malware is this?

    A. A type of virus

    B. A type of logic bomb

    C. A type of ransomware

    D. A type of worm

2. What is cyberwarfare?

    A. It is an attack only on military targets.

    B. It is an attack on a major corporation.

    C. It is an attack that only involves robots and bots.

    D. It is an attack designed to disrupt, corrupt, or exploit national interests.

3. How can a security information and event management system in an SOC be used to help personnel fight against security threats?

    A. By collecting and filtering data

    B. By filtering network traffic

    C. By authenticating users to network resources

    D. By encrypting communications to remote sites

4. Which three technologies should be included in an SOC security information and event management system? (Choose three.)

    A. Proxy service

    B. User authentication

    C. Threat intelligence

    D. Security monitoring

    E. Intrusion prevention

    F. Event collection, correlation, and analysis

5. What name is given to hackers who hack for a political or social cause?

    A. White hat

    B. Hacker

    C. Hacktivist

    D. Blue hat

6. Which organization is an international nonprofit organization that offers the CISSP certification?

    A. $(ISC)^2$

    B. IEEE

    C. GIAC

    D. CompTIA

7. After a security incident is verified in a SOC, an incident responder reviews the incident but cannot identify the source of the incident and form an effective mitigation procedure. To whom should the incident ticket be escalated?

    A. A cyberoperations analyst for help

    B. An SME for further investigation

    C. An alert analyst for further analysis

    D. The SOC manager to ask for other personnel to be assigned

8. The term Alert Analyst refers to which group of personnel in an SOC?

    A. Tier 1 personnel

    B. Tier 2 personnel

    C. Tier 3 personnel

    D. SOC managers

9. What is a rogue wireless hotspot?

    A. It is a hotspot that was set up with outdated devices.

    B. It is a hotspot that does not encrypt network user traffic.

    C. It is a hotspot that does not implement strong user authentication mechanisms.

    D. It is a hotspot that appears to be from a legitimate business but was actually set up by someone without the permission from the business.

## CHAPTER 2

Windows Operating System

Objectives

Upon completion of this chapter, you will be able to answer the following questions:

- What is the history of the Windows operating system?
- What is the architecture of Windows and its operation?
- How do you configure and monitor Windows?
- How is Windows kept secure?

Key Terms

This chapter uses the following key terms. You can find the definitions in the Glossary.

Introduction (2.0)

From its humble beginnings over 30 years ago in 1985, the Windows operating system has seen many iterations; from Windows 1.0 to today's current desktop version, Windows 10, and server version, Windows Server 2016.

This chapter covers some of the basic concepts of Windows, including how the operating system works and the tools used to secure Windows endpoints.

Class Activity 2.0.1.2: Identify Running Processes

In this lab, you will use TCP/UDP Endpoint Viewer, a tool in Sysinternals Suite, to identify any running processes on your computer.

Windows Overview (2.1)

In this section, you will learn about Window's history, architecture, and operations.

Windows History (2.1.1)

In this topic, you will learn about the beginnings of Windows, the history of Windows versions, the Windows graphical user interface (GUI), and Windows vulnerabilities.

Disk Operating System (2.1.1.1)

The first computers did not have modern storage devices such as hard drives, optical drives, or flash storage. The first storage methods used punch cards, paper tape, magnetic tape, and even audio cassettes.

Floppy disk and hard disk storage requires software to read from, write to, and manage the data that they store. A *Disk Operating System (DOS)* is an operating system that the computer uses to enable these data storage devices to read and write files. The DOS provides a file system which organizes the files in a specific way on the disk. *MS-DOS* is a DOS created by Microsoft. MS-DOS used a command line as the interface for people to create programs and manipulate data files, as shown in Figure 2-1.

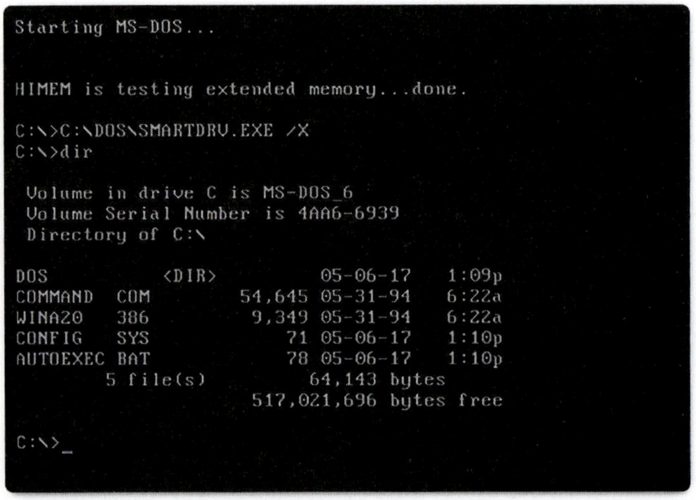

```
Starting MS-DOS...


HIMEM is testing extended memory...done.

C:\>C:\DOS\SMARTDRV.EXE /X
C:\>dir

 Volume in drive C is MS-DOS_6
 Volume Serial Number is 4AA6-6939
 Directory of C:\

DOS          <DIR>            05-06-17    1:09p
COMMAND  COM          54,645 05-31-94    6:22a
WINA20   386           9,349 05-31-94    6:22a
CONFIG   SYS              71 05-06-17    1:10p
AUTOEXEC BAT              78 05-06-17    1:10p
         5 file(s)        64,143 bytes
                      517,021,696 bytes free


C:\>_
```

Figure 2-1   MS-DOS 6.3

With MS-DOS, the computer had a basic working knowledge of how to access the disk drive and load the operating system files directly from the disk as part of the boot process. When it was loaded, MS-DOS could easily access DOS because it was built into the operating system.

Early versions of Windows consisted of a GUI that ran over MS-DOS, with the first being Windows 1.0 in 1985. The disk operating system still controlled the computer and its hardware. A modern operating system like Windows 10 is not considered a disk operating system. It is built on Windows NT, which stands for "New Technology." The operating system itself is in direct control of the computer and its hardware. NT is an OS with support for multiple user processes. This is much different than the single-process, single-user MS-DOS.

Today, anything that used to be accomplished through the command line interface of MS-DOS can be accomplished in the Windows GUI. You can still experience what it was like to use MS-DOS by opening a command window, but what you see is no longer MS-DOS, it is a function of Windows. To experience a little of what it was like to work in MS-DOS, open a command window by typing **cmd** in Windows Search and pressing **Enter**. These are some commands that you can use:

- **dir:** Shows a listing of all the files in the current directory (folder)
- **cd** *directory*: Changes the directory to the indicated directory
- **cd..:** Changes the directory to the directory above the current directory
- **cd\:** Changes the directory to the root directory (often C:)
- **copy:** Copies files to another location

- **del:** Deletes one or more files

- **find:** Searches for text in files

- **mkdir:** Creates a new directory

- **ren:** Renames a file

- **help:** Displays all the commands that can be used, with a brief description

- **help** *command*: Displays extensive help for the indicated command

Windows Versions (2.1.1.2)

Since 1993, there have been more than 20 releases of Windows that are based on the NT operating system. Most of these versions were for use by the general public and businesses because of the file security offered by the file system that was used by the NT OS. Businesses also adopted NT OS-based Windows operating systems. This is because many editions were built specifically for the workstation, professional, server, advanced server, and datacenter server, to name just a few of the many purpose-built versions.

Beginning with Windows XP, a 64-bit edition was available. The 64-bit operating system was an entirely new architecture. It had a 64-bit address space instead of a 32-bit address space. This is not simply twice the amount of space because these bits are binary numbers. While 32-bit Windows can address a little less than 4 GB of RAM, 64-bit Windows can theoretically address 16.8 million terabytes. When the OS and the hardware all support 64-bit operation, extremely large data sets can be used. These large data sets include very large databases, scientific computing, and manipulation of high-definition digital video with special effects. In general, 64-bit computers and operating systems are backward-compatible with older, 32-bit programs, but 64-bit programs cannot be run on older, 32-bit hardware.

With each subsequent release of Windows, the operating system has become more refined by incorporating more features. Windows 7 was offered with six different editions, Windows 8 was offered with as many as four different editions, and Windows 10 is offered with eight different editions! Each edition not only offers different capabilities, but also different price points. Microsoft has said that Windows 10 is the last version of Windows, that Windows has become a service rather than just an OS. They say that rather than purchasing new operating systems, users will just update Windows 10 instead.

Table 2-1 lists the popular modern versions of Windows.

Table 2-1   Modern Windows Versions

OS Version	Editions
Windows 7	Starter, Home Basic, Home Premium, Professional, Enterprise, Ultimate
Windows Server 2008 R2	Foundation, Standard, Enterprise, Datacenter, Web Server, HPC Server, Itanium-Based Systems
Windows Home Server 2011	None
Windows 8	Windows 8, Windows 8 Pro, Windows 8 Enterprise, Windows RT
Windows Server 2012	Foundation, Essentials, Standard, Datacenter
Windows 8.1	Windows 8.1, Windows 8.1 Pro, Windows 8.1 Enterprise, Windows RT 8.1
Windows Server 2012 R2	Foundation, Essentials, Standard, Datacenter
Windows 10	Home, Pro, Pro Education, Enterprise, Education, IoT Core, Mobile, Mobile Enterprise
Windows Server 2016	Essentials, Standard, Datacenter, Multipoint Premium Server, Storage Server, Hyper-V Server

Windows GUI (2.1.1.3)

Windows has a graphical user interface (GUI) for users to work with data files and software. The GUI has a main area that is known as the Desktop, shown in Figure 2-2. The Desktop can be customized with various colors and background images. Windows supports multiple users, so each user can customize the Desktop to their liking. The Desktop can store files, folders, shortcuts to locations and programs, and applications. The Desktop also has a recycle bin icon, where files are stored when the user deletes them. Files can be restored from the recycle bin or the recycle bin can be emptied of files, which truly deletes them.

At the bottom of the desktop is the Task Bar. The Task Bar has three areas that are used for different purposes. At the left is the Start menu. It is used to access all of the installed programs, configuration options, and the search feature. At the center of the Task Bar, users place quick launch icons that run specific programs or open specific folders when they are clicked. Finally, on the right of the Task Bar is the notification area. The notification area shows, at a glance, the functionality of many different programs and features. For example, a blinking envelope icon may indicate new email, or a network icon with a red "x" may indicate a problem with the network.

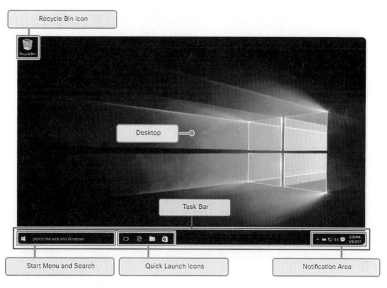

Figure 2-2   Windows 10 GUI

Often, right-clicking an icon will bring up additional functions that can be used. This list is known as a Context Menu, shown in Figure 2-3. There are Context Menus for the icons in the notification area, and also for quick launch icons, system configuration icons, and for files and folders. The Context Menu provides many of the most commonly used functions by just clicking. For example, the Context Menu for a file will contain such items as Copy, Delete, Share, and Print. To open folders and manipulate files, Windows uses Windows File Explorer, also shown in Figure 2-3.

Figure 2-3   Windows File Explorer

Windows File Explorer is a tool used to navigate the entire file system of a computer, including multiple storage devices and network locations. Using Windows

File Explorer, you can easily create folders, copy files and folders, and move them around to different locations and devices. Basically, the tool has two main windows. The one on the left allows quick navigation to storage devices, parent folders, and child folders. The one on the right shows the content of the location that is selected in the left pane.

Operating System Vulnerabilities (2.1.1.4)

Operating systems consist of millions of lines of code. Installed software can also contain millions of lines of code. With all this code comes vulnerabilities. A *vulnerability* is some flaw or weakness that can be exploited by an attacker to reduce the viability of a computer's information. To take advantage of an operating system vulnerability, the attacker must use a technique or a tool to exploit the vulnerability. The attacker can then use the vulnerability to get the computer to act in a fashion outside of its intended design. In general, the goal is to gain unauthorized control of the computer, change permissions, or manipulate data.

These are some common Windows OS security recommendations:

- **Virus or malware protection:** By default, Windows uses *Windows Defender*. Windows Defender provides a suite of protection tools built into the system. If Windows Defender is turned off, the system becomes more vulnerable to attacks and malware.

- **Unknown or unmanaged services:** There are many services that run behind the scenes. It is important to make sure that each service is identifiable and safe. With an unknown service running in the background, the computer can be vulnerable to attack.

- *Encryption*: When data is not encrypted, it can easily be gathered and exploited. This is important not only for desktop computers, but especially mobile devices.

- **Security policy:** A good security policy must be configured and followed. Many settings in the Windows Security Policy control can prevent attacks.

- *Firewall*: By default, Windows uses Windows Firewall to limit communication with devices on the network. Over time, rules may no longer apply. For example, a port may be left open that should no longer be readily available. It is important to review firewall settings periodically to ensure that the rules are still applicable and remove any that no longer apply.

- **File and share permissions:** These permissions must be set correctly. It is easy to just give the "Everyone" group Full Control, but this allows all people to do what they want to all files. It is best to provide each user or group with the minimum necessary permissions for all files and folders.

- **Weak or no password:** Many people choose weak passwords or do not use a password at all. It is especially important to make sure that all accounts, especially the Administrator account, have a very strong password.

- **Login as Administrator:** When a user logs in as an administrator, any program that they run will have the privileges of that account. It is best to log in as a Standard User and only use the Administrator password to accomplish certain tasks.

Windows Architecture and Operations (2.1.2)

In this topic, you will learn about the Windows hardware abstraction layer, user mode, kernel mode, file system, boot process, startup, shutdown, processes, threads, services, memory allocation, handles, and registry.

Hardware Abstraction Layer (2.1.2.1)

Windows computers use many different types of hardware. The operating system can be installed on a computer off of the shelf, or a computer built from the ground up. When the operating system is installed, it must be isolated from differences in hardware. The basic Windows architecture is shown in Figure 2-4. A *hardware abstraction layer (HAL)* is code that handles all of the communication between the hardware and the *kernel*. The kernel is the core of the operating system and has control over the entire computer. It handles all of the input and output requests, memory, and all of the peripherals connected to the computer.

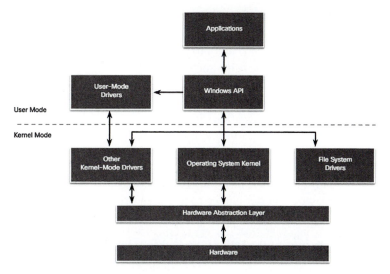

Figure 2-4 Basic Windows Architecture

In some instances, the kernel still communicates with the hardware directly, so it is not completely independent of the HAL. The HAL also needs the kernel to perform some functions.

User Mode and Kernel Mode (2.1.2.2)

There are two different modes in which a CPU operates when the computer has Windows installed: user mode and kernel mode. Installed applications run in user mode, and operating system code runs in kernel mode. Code that is executing in kernel mode has unrestricted access to the underlying hardware and is capable of executing any CPU instruction. Kernel mode code also can reference any memory address directly. Generally reserved for the most trusted functions of the OS, crashes in code running in kernel mode stop the operation of the entire computer. Conversely, programs such as user applications run in user mode and have no direct access to hardware or memory locations. User mode code must go through the operating system to access hardware resources. Because of the isolation provided by user mode, crashes in user mode are restricted to the application only and are recoverable. Most of the programs in Windows run in user mode. Device drivers, pieces of software that allow the operating system and a device to communicate, may run in either kernel or user mode, depending on the driver.

All of the code that runs in kernel mode uses the same address space. Kernel-mode drivers have no isolation from the operating system. If an error occurs with the driver running in kernel mode, and it writes to the wrong address space, the operating system or another kernel-mode driver could be adversely affected. In this respect, the driver might crash, causing the entire operating system to crash.

When user mode code runs, it is granted its own restricted address space by the kernel, along with a process created specifically for the application. The reason for this functionality is mainly to prevent applications from changing operating system code that is running at the same time. By having its own process, that application has its own private address space, rendering other applications unable to modify the data in it. This also helps to prevent the operating system and other applications from crashing if that application crashes.

Windows File Systems (2.1.2.3)

A file system is how information is organized on storage media. Some file systems may be a better choice to use than others, depending on the type of media that will be used. These are the file systems that Windows supports:

- *File Allocation Table (FAT)*: This is a simple file system supported by many different operating systems. FAT has limitations to the number of partitions, partition sizes, and file sizes that it can address, so it is not usually used for hard drives (HDs) or solid state drives (SSDs) anymore. Both FAT16 and FAT32 are available to use, with FAT32 being the most common because it has many fewer restrictions than FAT16.

- *Extended FAT (exFAT)*: This is an extended version of FAT that has even fewer restrictions than FAT32, but is not supported very well outside of the Windows ecosystem.

- *Hierarchical File System Plus (HFS+)*: This file system is used on macOS X computers and allows much longer filenames, file sizes, and partition sizes than previous file systems. Although it is not supported by Windows without special software, Windows is able to read data from HFS+ partitions.

- *Extended File System (EXT)*: This file system is used with Linux-based computers. Although it is not supported by Windows, Windows is able to read data from EXT partitions with special software.

- *New Technology File System (NTFS)*: This is the most commonly used file system when installing Windows. All versions of Windows and Linux support NTFS, while macOS X computers can only read an NTFS partition (they can write to an NTFS partition after installing special drivers).

NTFS is the most widely used file system for Windows for many reasons. NTFS supports very large files and partitions; it is very compatible with other operating systems. NTFS is also very reliable and supports recovery features. Most importantly, it supports many security features. Data access control is achieved through security descriptors. These security descriptors contain file ownership and permissions all the way down to the file level. NTFS also tracks many timestamps to track file activity. Sometimes referred to as MACE, the timestamps Modify, Access, Create, and Entry Modified are often used in forensic investigations to determine the history of a file or folder. NTFS also supports file system encryption to secure the entire storage media.

Alternate Data Streams

NTFS stores files as a series of attributes, such as the name of the file, or a timestamp. The data which the file contains is stored in the attribute $DATA, and is known as a data stream. By using NTFS, you can connect *Alternate Data Streams (ADSs)* to the file. This is sometimes used by applications that are storing additional information about the file. The ADS is an important factor when discussing malware. This is because it is easy to hide data in an ADS. An attacker could store malicious code within an ADS that can then be called from a different file.

In the NTFS file system, a file with an ADS is identified after the filename and a colon, for example, Testfile.txt:ADSdata. This filename indicates an ADS called ADSdata is associated with the file called Testfile.txt. An example of ADS is shown in Example 2-1.

Example 2-1   Alternate Data Stream

```
C:\ADS> echo "Alternative Data Here" > Textfile.txt:ADS


C:\ADS> dir
 Volume in drive C is OS
 Volume Serial Number is F244-E247


 Directory of C:\ADS


12/27/2017   03:03 PM      <DIR>          .
12/27/2017   03:03 PM      <DIR>          ..
12/27/2017   03:03 PM                   0 Textfile.txt
              1 File(s)            0 bytes
              2 Dir(s)   402,725,310,464 bytes free

C:\ADS> more < Testfile.txt:ADS
"Alternative Data Here"


C:\ADS> dir /r
 Volume in drive C has no label.
 Volume Serial Number is F244-E247
 Directory of C:\ADS


12/27/2017   03:03 PM      <DIR>          .
12/27/2017   03:03 PM      <DIR>          ..
12/27/2017   03:03 PM                   0 Textfile.txt
                                       24 Textfile.txt:ADS:$DATA
              1 File(s)            0 bytes
              2 Dir(s)   402,725,310,464 bytes free


C:\ADS>
```

- The first command places the text "Alternate Data Here" into an ADS of the file Testfile.txt called "ADS".

- The next command, **dir**, shows that the file was created, but the ADS is not visible.

- The next command shows that there is data in the Testfile.txt:ADS data stream.

- The last command shows the ADS of the Testfile.txt file because the **r** switch was used with the **dir** command.

Before a storage device such as a disk can be used, it must be formatted with a file system. In turn, before a file system can be put into place on a storage device, the device needs to be partitioned. A hard drive is divided into areas called partitions. Each partition is a logical storage unit that can be formatted to store information, such as data files or applications. During the installation process, most operating systems automatically partition and format the available drive space with a file system such as NTFS.

NTFS formatting creates important structures on the disk for file storage, and tables for recording the locations of files:

- *Partition Boot Sector*: This is the first 16 sectors of the drive. It contains the location of the Master File Table. The last 16 sectors contain a copy of the boot sector.

- *Master File Table (MFT)*: This table contains the locations of all the files and directories on the partition, including file attributes such as security information and timestamps.

- *System Files*: These are hidden files that store information about other volumes and file attributes.

- **File Area:** The main area of the partition where files and directories are stored.

> **Note**
>
> When formatting a partition, the previous data may still be recoverable because not all the data is completely removed. The free space can be examined and files can be retrieved, which can compromise security. It is recommended to perform a secure wipe on a drive that is being reused. The secure wipe will write data to the entire drive multiple times to ensure there is no remaining data.

Windows Boot Process (2.1.2.4)

Many actions occur between the time when the computer power button is pressed and Windows is fully loaded, as shown in Figure 2-5.

Two types of computer firmware exist: *Basic Input-Output System (BIOS)* and *Unified Extensible Firmware Interface (UEFI)*. BIOS firmware was created in the early 1980s and works in the same way it did when it was created. As computers evolved, it became difficult for BIOS firmware to support all the new features requested by users. UEFI was designed to replace BIOS and support the new features.

In BIOS firmware, the process begins with the BIOS initialization phase. This is when hardware devices are initialized and a power-on self-test (POST) is performed to make sure all of these devices are communicating. When the system disk is discovered, the POST ends. The last instruction in the POST is to look for the *master boot record (MBR)*.

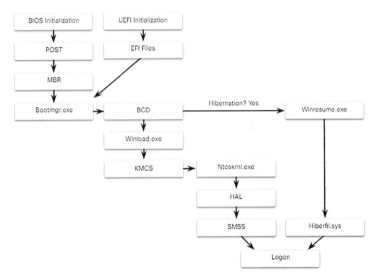

Figure 2-5   Windows Boot Process

The MBR contains a small program that is responsible for locating and loading the operating system. The BIOS executes this code and the operating system starts to load.

In contrast to BIOS firmware, UEFI firmware has a lot of visibility into the boot process. UEFI boots by loading EFI program files, stored as .efi files in a special disk partition, known as the EFI System Partition (ESP).

Note

A computer that uses UEFI stores boot code in the firmware. This helps to increase the security of the computer at boot time because the computer goes directly into protected mode.

Whether the firmware is BIOS or UEFI, after a valid Windows installation is located, the Bootmgr.exe file is run. Bootmgr.exe switches the system from real mode to protected mode so that all of the system memory can be used.

Bootmgr.exe reads the *Boot Configuration Database (BCD)*. The BCD contains any additional code needed to start the computer, along with an indication of whether the computer is coming out of hibernation, or if this is a cold start. If the computer is coming out of hibernation, the boot process continues with Winresume.exe. This allows the computer to read the Hiberfil.sys file, which contains the state of the computer when it was put into hibernation.

If the computer is being booted from a cold start, then the Winload.exe file is loaded. The Winload.exe file creates a record of the hardware configuration in the registry. The registry is a record of all of the settings, options, hardware, and software the computer has. The registry will be explored in depth later in this chapter. Winload.exe also uses *Kernel Mode Code Signing (KMCS)* to make sure that all drivers are digitally signed. This ensures that the drivers are safe to load as the computer starts.

After the drivers have been examined, Winload.exe runs Ntoskrnl.exe, which starts the Windows kernel and sets up the HAL. Finally, the *Session Manager Subsystem (SMSS)* reads the registry to create the user environment, start the Winlogon service, and prepare each user's desktop as they log on.

Windows Startup and Shutdown (2.1.2.5)

There are two important registry items that are used to automatically start applications and services:

- **HKEY_LOCAL_MACHINE:** Several aspects of Windows configuration are stored in this key, including information about services that start with each boot.

- **HKEY_CURRENT_USER:** Several aspects related to the logged-in user are stored in this key, including information about services that start only when the user logs on to the computer.

Different entries in these registry locations define which services and applications will start, as indicated by their entry type. These types include Run, RunOnce, RunServices, RunServicesOnce, and Userinit. These entries can be manually entered into the registry, but it is much safer to use the Msconfig.exe tool. This tool is used to view and change all of the startup options for the computer. Use the search box to find and open the **Msconfig** tool.

There are five tabs which contain the configuration options:

- **General:** Three different startup types can be chosen here. Normal loads all drivers and services. Diagnostic loads only basic drivers and services. Selective allows the user to choose what to load on startup. The General tab is shown in Figure 2-6.

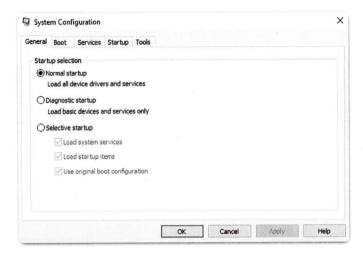

Figure 2-6   General Tab of System Configuration

■ **Boot:** Any installed operating system can be chosen here to start. There are also options for Safe boot, which is used to troubleshoot startup. The Boot tab is shown in Figure 2-7.

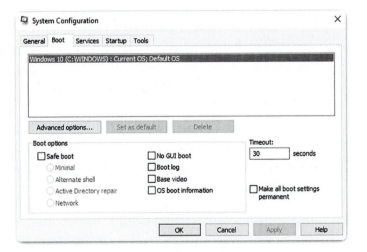

Figure 2-7   Boot Tab of System Configuration

■ **Services:** All the installed services are listed here so that they can be chosen to start at startup. The Services tab is shown in Figure 2-8.

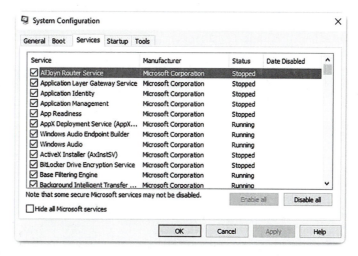

Figure 2-8   Services Tab of System Configuration

- **Startup:** All the applications and services that are configured to automatically begin at startup can be enabled or disabled by opening Task Manager from this tab. The Startup tab is shown in Figure 2-9.

Figure 2-9   Startup Tab of System Configuration

- **Tools:** Many common operating system tools can be launched directly from this tab. The Tools tab is shown in Figure 2-10.

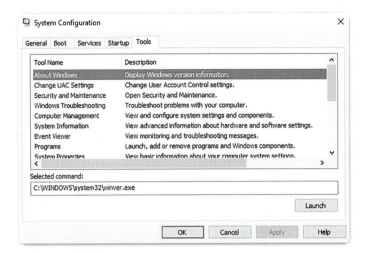

Figure 2-10   Tools Tab of System Configuration

Shutdown

It is always best to perform a proper shutdown to turn off the computer. Files that are left open, services that are closed out of order, and applications that hang can all be damaged if the power is turned off without first informing the operating system. The computer needs time to close each application, shut down each service, and record any configuration changes before power is lost.

During shutdown, the computer will close user mode applications first, followed by kernel mode processes. If a user mode process does not respond within a certain amount of time, the OS will display notification and allow the user to wait for the application to respond, or forcibly end the process. If a kernel mode process does not respond, the shutdown will appear to hang, and it may be necessary to shut down the computer with the power button.

There are several ways to shut down a Windows computer: Start menu power options, the command line command **shutdown**, and using **Ctrl-Alt-Delete** and clicking the power icon. There are three different options from which to choose when shutting down the computer: Shutdown, which turns the computer off, Restart, which reboots the computer from scratch, and Hibernate, which records the current state of the computer and user environment and stores it in a file. Hibernation allows the user to pick up right where they left off very quickly with all their files and programs still open.

Processes, Threads, and Services (2.1.2.6)

A Windows application is made up of *processes*. The application can have one or many processes dedicated to it. A process is any program that is currently executing.

Each process that runs is made up of at least one *thread*. A thread is a part of the process that can be executed. The processor performs calculations on the thread. To configure Windows processes, search for **Task Manager**. The Processes tab of Task Manager is shown in Figure 2-11.

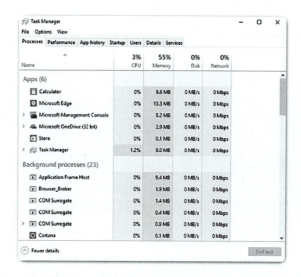

Figure 2-11   Windows Task Manager Processes Tab

All of the threads dedicated to a process are contained within the same address space. This means that these threads may not access the address space of any other process. This prevents corruption of other processes. Because Windows multi-tasks, multiple threads can be executed at the same time. The number of threads that can be executed at the same time is dependent on how many processors the computer has.

Some of the processes that Windows runs are *services*. These are programs that run in the background to support the operating system and applications. They can be set to start automatically when Windows boots or they can be started manually. They can also be stopped, restarted, or disabled. Services provide long-running functionality, such as wireless or access to an FTP server. To configure Windows Services, search for **services**. The Windows Services control panel applet is shown in Figure 2-12. Be very careful when manipulating the setting of these services. Some programs rely on one or more services to operate properly. Shutting down a service may adversely affect applications, or other services.

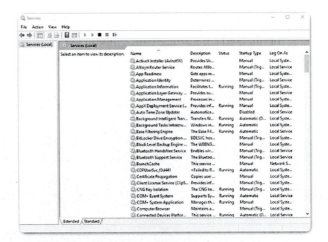

Figure 2-12   Windows Services Control Panel Applet

Memory Allocation and Handles (2.1.2.7)

A computer works by storing instructions in RAM until the CPU processes them. The virtual address space for a process is the set of virtual addresses that the process can use. The virtual address is not the actual physical location in memory, but an entry in a page table that is used to translate the virtual address into the physical address.

Each process in a 32-bit Windows computer supports a virtual address space that enables addressing up to 4 gigabytes. Each process in a 64-bit Windows computer supports a virtual address space of 8 terabytes.

Each user space process runs in a private address space, separate from other user space processes. When the user space process needs to access kernel resources, it must use a process handle. This is because the user space process is not allowed to directly access these kernel resources. The process handle provides the access needed by the user space process without a direct connection to it.

One of the more powerful tools we use to view memory allocation is Sysinternals RamMap, shown in Figure 2-13.

The Windows Registry (2.1.2.8)

Windows stores all of the information about hardware, applications, users, and system settings in a large database known as the *registry*. The ways that these objects interact are also recorded, such as what files an application opens and all of the property details of folders and applications. The registry is a hierarchical database where the highest level is known as a hive, below which are keys, followed by subkeys. Values, which store data, are stored in keys and subkeys. The registry key can be up to 512 levels deep.

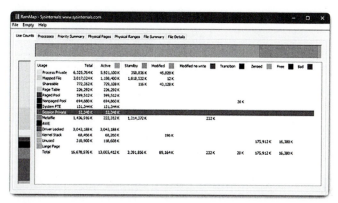

Figure 2-13   Sysinternals RamMap

These are the five hives of the Windows registry:

- **HKEY_CURRENT_USER (HKCU):** Holds data concerning the currently logged-in user

- **HKEY_USERS (HKU):** Holds data concerning all the user accounts on the host

- **HKEY_CLASSES_ROOT (HKCR):** Holds data about object linking and embedding (OLE) registrations

- **HKEY_LOCAL_MACHINE (HKLM):** Holds system-related data

- **HKEY_CURRENT_CONFIG (HKCC):** Holds data about the current hardware profile

New hives cannot be created. The registry keys and values in the hives can be created, modified, or deleted by an account with administrative privileges. As shown in Figure 2-14, the tool regedit.exe is used to modify the registry. Be very careful when using this tool. Minor changes to the registry can have massive or even catastrophic effects.

Navigation in the registry is very similar to navigation in Windows File Explorer. Use the left panel to navigate the hives and the structure below it, and use the right panel to see the contents of the highlighted item in the left panel. With so many keys and subkeys, the key path can become very long. The path is displayed at the bottom of the window for reference. Because each key and subkey is essentially a container, the path is represented much like a folder in a file system. The backslash (\) is used to differentiate the hierarchy of the database.

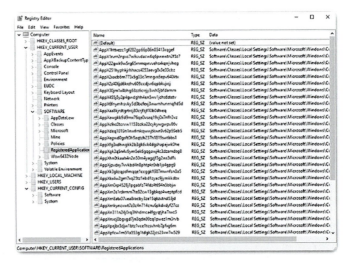

Figure 2-14   Windows Registry Editor

Registry keys can contain either a subkey or a value. These are the different values that keys can contain:

- **REG_BINARY:** Numbers or Boolean values

- **REG_DWORD:** Numbers greater than 32 bits or raw data

- **REG_SZ:** String values

Because the registry holds almost all the operating system and user information, it is critical to make sure that it does not become compromised. Potentially malicious applications can add registry keys so that they start when the computer is started. During a normal boot, the user will not see the program start because the entry is in the registry and the application displays no windows or indication of starting when the computer boots. A keylogger, for example, would be devastating to the security of a computer if it were to start at boot without the user's knowledge or consent. When performing normal security audits, or remediating an infected system, review the application startup locations within the registry to ensure that each item is known and safe to run.

The registry also contains the activity that a user performs during normal day-to-day computer use. This includes the history of hardware devices, including all devices that have been connected to the computer, identified by name, manufacturer, and serial number. Other information, such as what documents a user and program have opened, where they are located, and when they were accessed, is stored in the registry. This is all very useful information when a forensic investigation needs to be performed.

Interactive Graphic

Activity 2.1.2.9: Identify the Windows Registry Hive

Refer to the online course to complete this Activity.

Lab 2.1.2.10: Exploring Processes, Threads, Handles, and Windows Registry

In this lab, you will explore the processes, threads, and handles using Process Explorer in Sysinternals Suite. You will also use the Windows registry to change a setting.

Windows Administration (2.2)

In this section, you will learn about Windows configuration, monitoring, and security.

Windows Configuration and Monitoring (2.2.1)

In this topic, you will learn about Windows configuration management, including running applications as the Administrator, configuring local users and domains, and working with the command line interface (CLI), PowerShell, and Windows Management Instrumentation (WMI). You will also learn how to monitor Windows using the **net** command, Task Manager, Resource Monitor, and networking tools.

Run as Administrator (2.2.1.1)

As a security best practice, it is not advisable to log on to Windows using the Administrator account or an account with administrative privileges. This is because any program that is executed while logged on with those privileges will inherit them. Malware that has administrative privileges has full access to all the files and folders on the computer.

Sometimes, it is necessary to run or install software that requires the privileges of the Administrator. To accomplish this, there are two different ways to install it:

- **Run as Administrator:** Right-click the command in Windows File Explorer and choose **Run as administrator** from the Context Menu, shown in Figure 2-15.

- **Administrator Command Prompt:** Search for **command**, right-click the executable file, and choose **Run as administrator** from the Context Menu, shown in Figure 2-16. Every command that is executed from this command line will be carried out with administrative privileges, including installation of software.

Figure 2-15   Run as Administrator from Windows File Explorer

Figure 2-16   Run as Administrator Using Administrator Command Prompt

Local Users and Domains (2.2.1.2)

When you start a new computer for the first time, or you install Windows, you will be prompted to create a user account. This is known as a local user. This account will contain all of your customization settings, access permissions, file locations, and many other user-specific data. There are also two other accounts that are present: Guest and Administrator. Both of these accounts are disabled by default.

As a security best practice, do not enable the Administrator account and do not give standard users administrative privileges. If a user needs to perform any function that requires administrative privileges, the system will ask for the Administrator password and allow only that task to be performed as an administrator. By entering the Administrator password, this protects the computer by preventing any software that is not authorized from installing, executing, or accessing files.

The Guest account should not be enabled. The Guest account does not have a password associated with it because it is created when a computer is going to be used by many different people who do not have accounts on the computer. Each time the Guest account logs on, a default environment is provided to them with limited privileges.

To make administration of users easier, Windows uses groups. A group will have a name and a specific set of permissions associated with it. When a user is placed into a group, the permissions of that group are given to that user. A user can be placed into multiple groups to be provided with many different permissions. When the permissions overlap, certain permissions, like "explicitly deny," will override the permission provided by a different group. There are many different user groups built in to Windows that are used for specific tasks. For example, the Performance Log Users group allows members to schedule logging of performance counters and collect logs either locally or remotely. Local users and groups are managed with the lusrmgr.msc control panel applet, as shown in Figure 2-17.

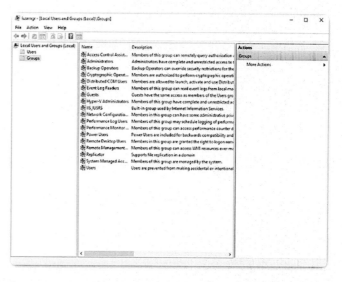

Figure 2-17   lusrmgr.msc

In addition to groups, Windows can also use domains to set permissions. A *domain* is a type of network service where all of the users, groups, computers, peripherals, and security settings are stored on and controlled by a database. This database is stored on special computers or groups of computers called *domain controllers (DCs)*. Each user and computer on the domain must authenticate against the DC to log on and access network resources. The security settings for each user and each computer are set by the DC for each session. Any setting supplied by the DC defaults to the local computer or user account setting.

CLI and PowerShell (2.2.1.3)

The Windows *command line interface (CLI)* can be used to run programs, navigate the file system, and manage files and folders. In addition, files called batch files can be created to execute multiple commands in succession, much like a basic script. To open the Windows CLI, search for **cmd.exe** and click the program. Remember that right-clicking the program provides the option to Run as Administrator, giving much more power to the commands that will be used.

The prompt displays the current location within the file system. These are a few things to remember when using the CLI:

- The filenames and paths are not case sensitive, by default.

- Storage devices are assigned a letter for reference. The letter, followed by a backslash (\), indicates the root of the device. Folder and file hierarchy on the device is indicated by separating them with the backslash. For example, C:\Users\Jim\Desktop\file.txt is the file called file.txt in the Desktop folder within the Jim folder within the Users folder on the device C:.

- Commands that have optional switches use the forward slash (/) to delineate between the command and each switch.

- You can use the Tab key to auto-complete commands when directories or files are referenced.

- Windows keeps a history of the commands that were entered during a CLI session. Access historical commands by using the Up Arrow and Down Arrow keys.

- To switch between storage devices, type the letter of the device, followed by a colon, and then press Enter.

Even though the CLI has many commands and features, it cannot work together with the core of Windows or the GUI. Another environment, called the Windows *PowerShell*, can be used to create scripts to automate tasks that the regular CLI is unable to create. PowerShell also provides a CLI for initiating commands. PowerShell is an integrated program within Windows and can be opened by clicking **Start**, searching for **PowerShell**, and clicking the program. Like the CLI, PowerShell can also be run with administrative privileges.

These are the types of commands that PowerShell can execute:

- **Cmdlets:** These commands perform an action and return an output or object to the next command that will be executed.

- **PowerShell scripts:** These are files with a .ps1 extension that contain PowerShell commands that are executed.

- **PowerShell functions:** These are pieces of code that can be referenced in a script.

To see more information about Windows PowerShell and get started using it, type **help** in PowerShell, as shown in Example 2-2. You will be provided with much more information and resources to start using PowerShell.

Example 2-2   Windows PowerShell Help

```
PS C:\Windows\System32> help

TOPIC
    Windows PowerShell Help System

SHORT DESCRIPTION
    Displays help about Windows PowerShell cmdlets and concepts.

LONG DESCRIPTION
    Windows PowerShell Help describes Windows PowerShell cmdlets,
    functions, scripts, and modules, and explains concepts, including
    the elements of the Windows PowerShell language.

    Windows PowerShell does not include help files, but you can read the
    help topics online, or use the Update-Help cmdlet to download help files
    to your computer and then use the Get-Help cmdlet to display the help
    topics at the command line.

    You can also use the Update-Help cmdlet to download updated help files
    as they are released so that your local help content is never obsolete.

    Without help files, Get-Help displays auto-generated help for cmdlets,
    functions, and scripts.


  ONLINE HELP
    You can find help for Windows PowerShell online in the TechNet Library
    beginning at http://go.microsoft.com/fwlink/?LinkID=108518.
```

```
    To open online help for any cmdlet or function, type:

       Get-Help <cmdlet-name> -Online

UPDATE-HELP
    To download and install help files on your computer:

       1. Start Windows PowerShell with the "Run as administrator" option.
       2. Type:

          Update-Help

    After the help files are installed, you can use the Get-Help cmdlet to
    display the help topics. You can also use the Update-Help cmdlet to
    download updated help files so that your local help files are always
    up-to-date.

    For more information about the Update-Help cmdlet, type:

       Get-Help Update-Help -Online

-- More   --
```

There are four levels of help in Windows PowerShell:

- **get-help** *PS command*: Displays basic help for a command

- **get-help** *PS command* [-*examples*]: Displays basic help for a command with examples

- **get-help** *PS command* [-*detailed*]: Displays detailed help for a command with examples

- **get-help** *PS command* [-*full*]: Displays all help information for a command with examples in greater depth

Windows Management Instrumentation (2.2.1.4)

Windows Management Instrumentation (WMI) is used to manage remote computers. It can retrieve information about computer components, display hardware and software statistics, and monitor the health of remote computers. You can open WMI control by searching for and opening **Computer Management**, and then right-clicking the **WMI Control** entry under **Services and Applications** and choosing **Properties**. The WMI Control Properties window is shown in Figure 2-18.

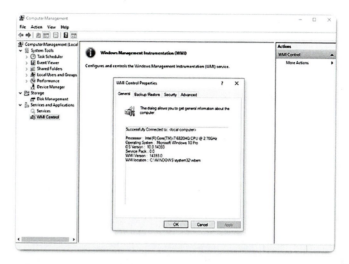

Figure 2-18   WMI Control Panel Properties Window

These are the four tabs in the WMI Control Properties window:

- **General:** Summary information about the local computer and WMI

- **Backup/Restore:** Allows manual backup of statistics gathered by WMI

- **Security:** Settings to configure who has access to different WMI statistics

- **Advanced:** Settings to configure the default namespace for WMI

Some attacks today use WMI to connect to remote systems, modify the registry, and run commands. WMI helps them to avoid detection because it is common traffic, most often trusted by the network security devices, and the remote WMI commands do not usually leave evidence on the remote host. Because of this, WMI access should be strictly limited.

The net Command (2.2.1.5)

Windows has many commands that can be entered at the command line. One important command is the **net** command, used in the administration and maintenance of the OS. The **net** command supports many other commands that follow the **net** command and can be combined with switches to focus on specific output.

To see a list of the many **net** commands, type **net help** at the command prompt. Example 2-3 shows the commands that the **net** command can use. To see verbose help about any of the **net** commands, type **net help** *command*.

Example 2-3   Net Commands

```
C:\Users> net help
The syntax of this command is:

NET HELP
command
      -or-
NET command /HELP


  Commands available are:


  NET ACCOUNTS              NET HELPMSG              NET STATISTICS
  NET COMPUTER              NET LOCALGROUP           NET STOP
  NET CONFIG                NET PAUSE                NET TIME
  NET CONTINUE              NET SESSION              NET USE
  NET FILE                  NET SHARE                NET USER
  NET GROUP                 NET START                NET VIEW
  NET HELP


  NET HELP NAMES explains different types of names in NET HELP syntax lines.
  NET HELP SERVICES lists some of the services you can start.
  NET HELP SYNTAX explains how to read NET HELP syntax lines.
  NET HELP command | MORE displays Help one screen at a time.


C:\Users>
```

These are some common net commands:

- **net accounts:** Sets password and logon requirements for users

- **net session:** Lists or disconnects sessions between a computer and other computers on the network

- **net share:** Creates, removes, or manages shared resources

- **net start:** Starts a network service or lists running network services

- **net stop:** Stops a network service

- **net use:** Connects, disconnects, and displays information about shared network resources

- **net view:** Shows a list of computers and network devices on the network

Task Manager and Resource Monitor (2.2.1.6)

There are two very important and useful tools to help an administrator to under-stand the many different applications, services, and processes that are running on a Windows computer. These tools also provide insight into the performance of the computer, such as CPU, memory, and network usage. These tools are especially use-ful when investigating a problem where malware is suspected. When a component is not performing the way that it should be, these tools can be used to determine what the problem might be.

Task Manager

Task Manager, shown in Figure 2-19, provides a lot of information about what is running, and general performance of the computer.

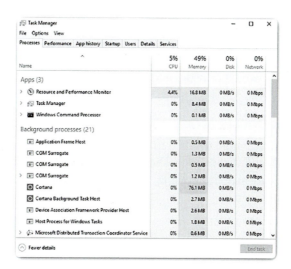

Figure 2-19   Windows 10 Task Manager

There are seven tabs in Task Manager:

- **Processes:** All of the programs and processes that are currently running are shown here. The CPU, memory, disk, and network utilization of each process is displayed in columns. You can examine the properties of any of these processes, or end a process that is not behaving properly or has stalled.

- **Performance:** A view of all the performance statistics provides a useful overview of the CPU, memory, disk, and network performance. Clicking each item in the left pane will show detailed statistics of that item in the right pane.

- **App history:** The use of resources by applications over time provides insight into applications that are consuming more resources than they should be. Click **Options** and **Show history for all processes** to see the history of every process that has run since the computer was started.

- **Startup:** All of the applications and services that start when the computer is booted are shown in this tab. To disable a program from starting at startup, right-click the item and choose **Disable**.

- **Users:** All of the users that are logged on to the computer are shown in this tab. Also shown are all the resources that each user's applications and processes are using. From this tab, an administrator can disconnect a user from the computer.

- **Details:** Similar to the Processes tab, this tab provides additional management options for processes such as setting a priority to make the processor devote more or less time to a process. CPU affinity can also be set, which determines which core or CPU a program will use. Also, a useful feature called Analyze Wait Chain shows any process for which another process is waiting. This feature helps to determine if a process is simply waiting, or is stalled.

- **Services:** All the services that are loaded are shown in this tab. The process ID (PID) and a short description are also shown along with the status of either Running or Stopped. At the bottom, there is a button to open the Services console, which provides additional management of services.

Resource Monitor

When more detailed information about resource usage is needed, you can use *Resource Monitor*, shown in Figure 2-20. When searching for the reason a computer may be acting erratically, Resource Monitor can help to find the source of the problem.

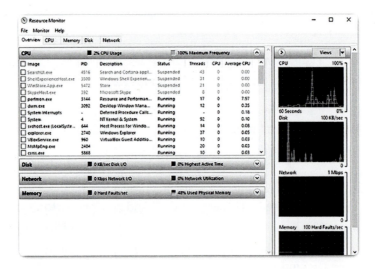

Figure 2-20   Windows 10 Resource Monitor

Resource Monitor has five tabs:

- **Overview:** General usage for each resource is shown in this tab. If you select a single process, it will be filtered across all of the tabs to show only that process's statistics.

- **CPU:** The PID, number of threads, which CPU the process is using, and the average CPU usage of each process are shown in this tab. Additional information about any services that the process relies on, and the associated handles and modules, can be seen by expanding the lower rows.

- **Memory:** All of the statistical information about how each process uses memory is shown in this tab. Also, an overview of usage of all the RAM is shown below the Processes row.

- **Disk:** All of the processes that are using a disk are shown in this tab, with read/write statistics and an overview of each storage device.

- **Network:** All of the processes that are using the network are shown in this tab, with read/write statistics. Most importantly, the current TCP connections are shown, along with all of the ports that are listening. This tab is very useful when trying to determine which applications and processes are communicating over the network. It makes it possible to tell if an unauthorized process is accessing the network, listening for a communication, and the address with which it is communicating.

Networking (2.2.1.7)

One of the most important features of any operating system is the ability for the computer to connect to a network. Without this feature, there is no access to network resources or the Internet. To configure Windows networking properties and test networking settings, the Network and Sharing Center, shown in Figure 2-21, is used. The easiest way to run this tool is to search for **Network and Sharing Center** and click it in the search results.

The initial view shows an overview of the active network. This view shows whether there is Internet access and if the network is private, public, or guest. The type of network, either wired or wireless, is also shown. From this window, you can see the HomeGroup the computer belongs to, or create one if it is not already part of a HomeGroup. This tool can also be used to change adapter settings, change advanced sharing settings, set up a new connection, or troubleshoot problems.

To configure a network adapter, choose **Change adapter settings** to show all of the network connections that are available. Right-click the adapter you wish to configure and choose **Properties**, as shown in Figure 2-22.

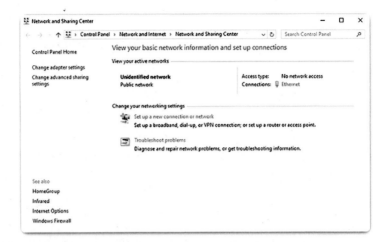

Figure 2-21   Windows 10 Network and Sharing Center

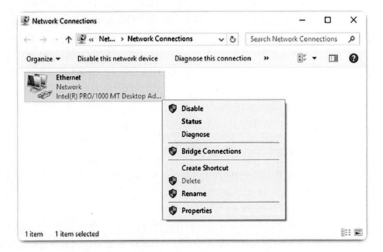

Figure 2-22   Windows 10 Network Connections

This connection uses the following items: box, highlight **Internet Protocol Version 4 (TCP/IPv4)** or **Internet Protocol Version 6 (TCP/IPv6)** depending on which version you wish to use (see Figure 2-23). Click **Properties** to configure the adapter.

In the Properties dialog box, shown in Figure 2-24, you can choose to **Obtain an address automatically** if there is a DHCP server available on the network. If you wish to configure addressing manually, you can fill in the address, subnet, default gateway, and DNS servers to configure the adapter. Click **OK** to accept the changes.

Figure 2-23   Windows 10 IPv4 Properties

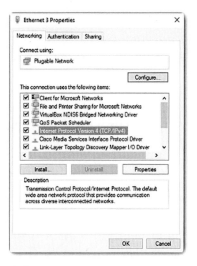

Figure 2-24   Windows 10 Ethernet Properties

You can also use the **netsh.exe** tool to configure networking parameters from a command prompt. This program can display and modify the network configuration. Type **netsh /?** at the command prompt to see a list of all the switches that can be used with this command.

After the network configuration is complete, there are some basic commands that can be used to test connectivity to the local network, and the Internet. The most basic test is performed with the **ping** command. To test the adapter itself, type **ping 127.0.0.1** at the command prompt, as shown in Example 2-4. This will make sure that the adapter is able to send and receive data. It also confirms that the TCP/IP protocol suite is properly installed in the computer. The 127.0.0.1 address is known as the loopback address.

Example 2-4   Pinging the Loopback Address

```
C:\Users> ping 127.0.0.1

Pinging 127.0.0.1 with 32 bytes of data:
Reply from 127.0.0.1: bytes=32 time<1ms TTL=128
Reply from 127.0.0.1: bytes=32 time<1ms TTL=128
Reply from 127.0.0.1: bytes=32 time<1ms TTL=128
Reply from 127.0.0.1: bytes=32 time<1ms TTL=128

Ping statistics for 127.0.0.1:
    Packets: Sent = 4, Received = 4, Lost = 0 (0% loss),
Approximate round trip times in milli-seconds:
    Minimum = 0ms, Maximum = 0ms, Average = 0ms

C:\Users>
```

Next, ping any host on the network. If you do not know any IP addresses of other hosts on the network, you can ping the default gateway. To find the address of the default gateway, type **ipconfig** at the command prompt, as shown in Example 2-5.

Example 2-5   The **ipconfig** Command

```
C:\Users> ipconfig

Windows IP Configuration


Ethernet adapter Ethernet:

    Connection-specific DNS Suffix  . :
    Link-local IPv6 Address . . . . . : fe80::1074:d6c8:f89d:43ad%17
    IPv4 Address. . . . . . . . . . . : 10.10.10.4
    Subnet Mask . . . . . . . . . . . : 255.255.255.0
    Default Gateway . . . . . . . . . : 10.10.10.1
Ethernet adapter VirtualBox Host-Only Network:

    Connection-specific DNS Suffix  . :
    Link-local IPv6 Address . . . . . : fe80::1c12:a86f:b858:77ac%11
    IPv4 Address. . . . . . . . . . . : 192.168.56.1
    Subnet Mask . . . . . . . . . . . : 255.255.255.0
    Default Gateway . . . . . . . . . :
```

```
Tunnel adapter Local Area Connection* 14:

   Connection-specific DNS Suffix . . :
   IPv6 Address. . . . . . . . . . . : 2001:0:4137:9e76:c5c:17ab:bd3b:e62c
   Link-local IPv6 Address . . . . . : fe80::c5c:17ab:bd3b:e62c%4
   Default Gateway . . . . . . . . . : ::

C:\Users>
```

This command will return basic network information including the IP address of the host, the subnet mask, and the default gateway. You can also ping hosts on other connected networks to make sure that you have connectivity to those networks. The **ipconfig** command has many switches that are helpful when troubleshooting network issues. Type **ipconfig /?** to see a list of all the switches that can be used with this command.

When the **ping** command is issued, it will send four ICMP echo request messages to the indicated IP address. If there is no reply, there may be a problem with the network configuration. It is also possible that the intended host blocks ICMP echo requests. In this case, try to ping a different host on the network. Most often, there are four replies to the requests, showing the size of each request, the time it took to travel, and the time to live (TTL). TTL is the number of hops a packet takes along the path to its destination.

Domain Name System (DNS) should also be tested because it is used very often to find the address of hosts by translating it from a name. Use the **nslookup** command to test DNS. Type **nslookup cisco.com** at the command prompt to find the address of the Cisco web server. When the address is returned, you know that DNS is functioning correctly. You can also check to see what ports are open, where they are connected, and what their current status is. Type **netstat** at the command line to see details of active network connections, as shown in Example 2-6. The **netstat** command will be examined further later in this chapter.

Example 2-6   The **netstat** Command

```
C:\Users> netstat

Active Connections

   Proto  Local Address          Foreign Address        State
   TCP    10.10.10.4:50008       bn3sch020022361:https  ESTABLISHED
   TCP    10.10.10.4:56145       a23-204-181-116:https  ESTABLISHED
   TCP    10.10.10.4:56630       a23-0-224-158:https    ESTABLISHED
   TCP    10.10.10.4:57101       162.125.8.4:https      CLOSE_WAIT
   TCP    10.10.10.4:57102       162.125.8.4:https      CLOSE_WAIT

C:\Users>
```

Accessing Network Resources (2.2.1.8)

Like other operating systems, Windows uses networking for many different applications such as web, email, and file services. Originally developed by IBM, Microsoft aided in the development of the *Server Message Block (SMB)* protocol to share network resources. SMB is mostly used for accessing files on remote hosts. The Universal Naming Convention (UNC) format is used to connect to resources, for example:

```
\\servername\sharename\file
```

In the UNC, *servername* is the server that is hosting the resource. This can be a DNS name, a NetBIOS name, or simply an IP address. The *sharename* is the root of the folder in the file system on the remote host, while the *file* is the resource that the local host is trying to find. The file may be deeper within the file system and this hierarchy will need to be indicated.

When sharing resources on the network, the area of the file system that will be shared will need to be identified. Access control can be applied to the folders and files to restrict users and groups to specific functions such as read, write, or deny. There are also special shares that are automatically created by Windows. These shares are called administrative shares. An administrative share is identified by the dollar sign ($) that comes after the share name. Each disk volume has an administrative share, represented by the volume letter and the $ such as C$, D$, or E$. The Windows installation folder is shared as admin$, the printers folder is shared as print$, and there are other administrative shares that can be connected. Only users with administrative privileges can access these shares.

The easiest way to connect to a share is to type the UNC of the share into Windows File Explorer, in the box at the top of the screen which shows the breadcrumb listing of the current file system location. When Windows tries to connect to the share, you will be asked to provide credentials for accessing the resource. Remember that because the resource is on a remote computer, the credentials need to be for the remote computer, not the local computer.

Besides accessing shares on remote hosts, you can also log in to a remote host and manipulate that computer as if it were local, to make configuration changes, install software, or troubleshoot an issue with the computer. In Windows, this function is known as the Remote Desktop Protocol (RDP). When investigating security incidents, a security analyst uses RDP often to access remote computers. To start RDP and connect to a remote computer, search for **Remote Desktop** and click the application. The Remote Desktop Connection window is shown in Figure 2-25.

Windows Server (2.2.1.9)

Most Windows installations are performed as desktop installation on desktops and laptops. There is another edition of Windows that is mainly used in data centers called Windows Server. This is a family of Microsoft products that began with Windows Server 2003. Today, the latest release is Windows Server 2016. Windows Server hosts many different services and can fulfill different roles within a company.

Figure 2-25   Windows Remote Desktop Connection

Note

Although there is a Windows Server 2000, it is considered a client version of Windows NT 5.0. Windows Server 2003 is a server based on NT 5.2 and begins a new family of Windows Server versions.

These are some of the services that Windows Server hosts:

- **Network Services:** DNS, DHCP, Terminal services, Network Controller, and Hyper-V Network virtualization

- **File Services:** SMB, NFS, and DFS

- **Web Services:** FTP, HTTP, and HTTPS

- **Management:** Group policy and Active Directory domain services control

Lab 2.2.1.10: Create User Accounts

In this lab, you will create and modify user accounts in Windows.

Lab 2.2.1.11: Using Windows PowerShell

The objective of this lab is to explore some of the functions of PowerShell.

Lab 2.2.1.12: Windows Task Manager

In this lab, you will explore Task Manager and manage processes from within Task Manager.

Lab 2.2.1.13: Monitor and Manage System Resources in Windows

In this lab, you will use administrative tools to monitor and manage system resources.

Windows Security (2.2.2)

In this topic, you will learn about Windows security tools, including **netstat**, Event Viewer, Windows Update, Local Security Policy, Windows Defender, and Windows Firewall.

The netstat Command (2.2.2.1)

When malware is present in a computer, it will often open communication ports on the host to send and receive data. The *netstat* command can be used to look for inbound or outbound connections that are not authorized. When used on its own, the **netstat** command will display all of the active TCP connections that are available.

By examining these connections, it is possible to determine which of the programs are listening for connections that are not authorized. When a program is suspected of being malware, a little research can be performed to determine its legitimacy. From there, the process can be shut down with Task Manager, and malware removal software can be used to clean the computer.

To make this process easier, you can link the connections to the running processes in Task Manager. To do this, open a command prompt with administrative privileges and use the command **netstat -abno**, as shown in Example 2-7.

Example 2-7   The netstat -abno Command

```
C:\WINDOWS\system32> netstat -abno

Active Connections

  Proto   Local Address          Foreign Address        State           PID
  TCP     0.0.0.0:135            0.0.0.0:0              LISTENING       1128
  RpcSs
 [svchost.exe]
  TCP     0.0.0.0:445            0.0.0.0:0              LISTENING       4
Can not obtain ownership information
  TCP     0.0.0.0:2869           0.0.0.0:0              LISTENING       4
```

```
Can not obtain ownership information
  TCP     0.0.0.0:5357            0.0.0.0:0           LISTENING    4
Can not obtain ownership information
  TCP     0.0.0.0:6646            0.0.0.0:0           LISTENING    5992
[MMSSHOST.EXE]
  TCP     0.0.0.0:8019            0.0.0.0:0           LISTENING    4828
[QBCFMonitorService.exe]
  TCP     0.0.0.0:18800           0.0.0.0:0           LISTENING    20020
[Amazon Music Helper.exe]
  TCP     0.0.0.0:49664           0.0.0.0:0           LISTENING    924
Can not obtain ownership information
  TCP     0.0.0.0:49665           0.0.0.0:0           LISTENING    1520
  EventLog
[svchost.exe]
  TCP     0.0.0.0:49666           0.0.0.0:0           LISTENING    2484
  Schedule
[svchost.exe]
  TCP     0.0.0.0:49689           0.0.0.0:0           LISTENING    364
[lsass.exe]
  TCP     0.0.0.0:49735           0.0.0.0:0           LISTENING    4772
[spoolsv.exe]
  TCP     0.0.0.0:49828           0.0.0.0:0           LISTENING    1012
Can not obtain ownership information
  TCP     10.10.10.4:139          0.0.0.0:0           LISTENING    4
Can not obtain ownership information
<output omitted>

C:\WINDOWS\system32>
```

By examining the active TCP connections, an analyst should be able to determine
if there are any suspicious programs that are listening for incoming connections on
the host. You can also trace that process to Task Manager and cancel the process.
There may be more than one process listed with the same name. If this is the case,
use the PID to find the correct process. Each process running on the computer has
a unique PID. To display the PIDs for the processes in Task Manager, open Task
Manager, right-click the table heading, and select **PID**.

Event Viewer (2.2.2.2)

Windows *Event Viewer*, shown in Figure 2-26, logs the history of application, security, and system events. These log files are a valuable troubleshooting tool because
they provide information necessary to identify a problem. To open Event Viewer,
search for it and click the program icon.

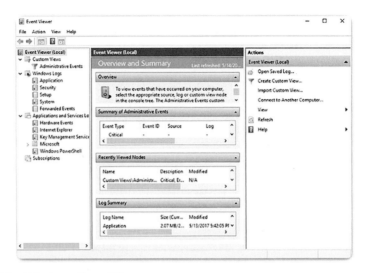

Figure 2-26   Windows Event Viewer

Windows includes two categories of event logs: Windows Logs, and Application and Services Logs. Each of these categories has multiple log types. Events that are displayed in these logs have a level: information, warning, error, or critical. They also have the date and time that the event occurred, along with the source of the event and an ID which relates to that type of event.

It is also possible to create a custom view. This is useful when looking for certain types of events, finding events that happened during a certain time period, displaying events of a certain level, and many other criteria. There is a built-in custom view called Administrative Events that shows all critical, error, and warning events from all of the administrative logs. This is a good view to start with when trying to troubleshoot a problem.

Windows Update Management (2.2.2.3)

No software is perfect, and the Windows operating system is no exception. Attackers are constantly coming up with new ways to compromise computers and exploit bad code. Some of these attacks come so quickly that there is no defense against them. These are called zero-day exploits. Microsoft and security software developers are always trying to stay ahead of the attackers, but they are not always successful. To ensure the highest level of protection against these attacks, always make sure Windows is up to date with the latest service packs and security patches.

Patches are code updates that manufacturers provide to prevent a newly discovered virus or worm from making a successful attack. From time to time, manufacturers combine patches and upgrades into a comprehensive update application called a service pack. Many devastating virus attacks could have been much less severe if more users had downloaded and installed the latest service pack.

Windows routinely checks the Windows Update website for high-priority updates that can help protect a computer from the latest security threats. These updates include security updates, critical updates, and service packs. Depending on the setting you choose, Windows automatically downloads and installs any high-priority updates that your computer needs or notifies you as these updates become available. To configure the settings for Windows Update, search for **Windows Update** and click the application.

The Update status, shown in Figure 2-27, allows you to check for updates manually and see the update history of the computer. There are also settings for indicating the hours during which the computer will not automatically restart, for example during regular business hours. You can also choose when to restart the computer after an update, if necessary, with the Restart options. Advanced options are also available to choose how updates are installed and get updates for other Microsoft products.

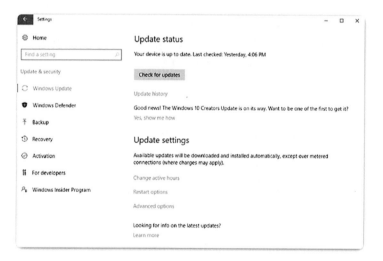

Figure 2-27   Windows Update Status

Local Security Policy (2.2.2.4)

A security policy is a set of objectives that ensures the security of a network, the data, and the computer systems in an organization. The security policy is a constantly evolving document based on changes in technology, business, and employee requirements.

In most networks that use Windows computers, Active Directory is configured with domains on a Windows Server. Windows computers join the domain. The administrator configures a Domain Security Policy that applies to all computers that join the domain. Account policies are automatically set when a user logs in to a computer that is a member of a domain. Windows Local Security Policy, shown in Figure 2-28, can be used for stand-alone computers that are not part of an Active Directory domain. To open the Local Security Policy applet, search for **Local Security Policy** and click the program.

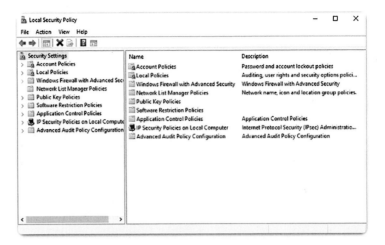

Figure 2-28   Windows Local Security Policy

Password guidelines are an important component of a security policy. Any user that must log on to a computer or connect to a network resource should be required to have a password. Passwords help prevent theft of data and malicious acts. Passwords also help to confirm that the logging of events is valid by ensuring that the user is the person they say that they are. Password Policy is found under Account Policies, and defines the criteria for the passwords for all of the users on the local computer.

Use the Account Lockout Policy in Account Policies to prevent brute-force login attempts. You can set the policy to allow the user to enter a wrong username and/or password five times. After five attempts, the account is locked out for 30 minutes. After 30 minutes, the number of attempts is reset to zero and the user can attempt to log in again.

It is important to make sure that computers are secure when users are away. A security policy should contain a rule about requiring a computer to lock when the screen saver starts. This will ensure that after a short time away from the computer, the screen saver will start and then the computer cannot be used until the user logs in.

If the Local Security Policy on every stand-alone computer is the same, then use the Export Policy feature. Save the policy with a name, such as workstation.inf. Copy the policy file to an external media or network drive to use on other stand-alone computers. This is particularly helpful if the administrator needs to configure extensive local policies for user rights and security options.

The Local Security Policy applet contains many other security settings that apply specifically to the local computer. You can configure user rights, firewall rules, and even the ability to restrict the files that users or groups are allowed to run with AppLocker.

Windows Defender (2.2.2.5)

Malware includes viruses, worms, Trojan horses, keyloggers, spyware, and adware. These are designed to invade privacy, steal information, damage the computer, or corrupt data. It is important that you protect computers and mobile devices using reputable antimalware software. The following types of antimalware programs are available:

- **Antivirus protection:** This program continuously monitors for viruses. When a virus is detected, the user is warned, and the program attempts to quarantine or delete the virus.

- **Adware protection:** This program continuously looks for programs that display advertising on your computer.

- **Phishing protection:** This program blocks the IP addresses of known phishing websites and warns the user about suspicious sites.

- **Spyware protection:** This program scans for keyloggers and other spyware.

- **Trusted/untrusted sources:** This program warns you about unsafe programs about to be installed or unsafe websites before they are visited.

It may take several different programs and multiple scans to completely remove all malicious software. Run only one malware protection program at a time.

Several reputable security organizations, such as McAfee, Symantec, and Kaspersky, offer all-inclusive malware protection for computers and mobile devices. Windows has built-in virus and spyware protection called Windows Defender, shown in Figure 2-29. Windows Defender is turned on by default, providing real-time protection against infection.

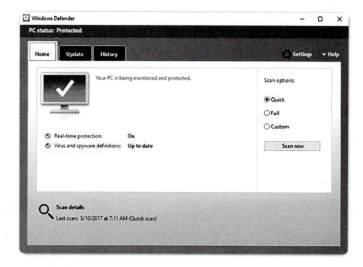

Figure 2-29   Windows Defender

To open Windows Defender, search for it and click the program. Although Windows Defender works in the background, you can perform manual scans of the computer and storage devices. You can also manually update the virus and spyware definitions in the **Update** tab. Also, to see all of the items that were found during previous scans, click the **History** tab.

Windows Firewall (2.2.2.6)

A firewall selectively denies traffic to a computer or network segment. Firewalls generally work by opening and closing the ports used by various applications. By opening only the required ports on a firewall, you are implementing a restrictive security policy. Any packet not explicitly permitted is denied. In contrast, a permissive security policy permits access through all ports, except those explicitly denied. In the past, software and hardware were shipped with permissive settings. As users neglected to configure their equipment, the default permissive settings left many devices exposed to attackers. Most devices now ship with settings as restrictive as possible, while still allowing easy setup.

To allow program access through Windows Firewall, search for **Windows Firewall**, click its name to run it, and click **Allow an app or feature through Windows Firewall**, as shown in Figure 2-30.

If you wish to use a different software firewall, you will need to disable Windows Firewall. To disable Windows Firewall, click **Turn Windows Firewall on or off**.

Many additional settings can be found under **Advanced settings**, as shown in Figure 2-31. Here you can create inbound or outbound traffic rules based on different criteria. You can also import and export policies or monitor different aspects of the firewall.

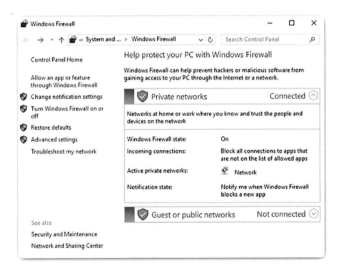

Figure 2-30   Windows Firewall

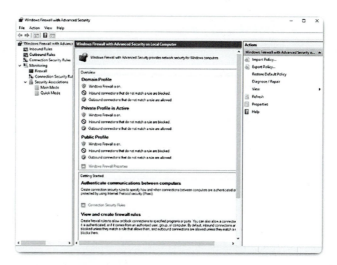

Figure 2-31   Windows Firewall Advanced Settings

Activity 2.2.2.7: Identify the Windows Command

Refer to the online course to complete this Activity.

Activity 2.2.2.8: Identify the Windows Tool

Refer to the online course to complete this Activity.

Summary (2.3)

In this chapter, you learned about the history and architecture of the Windows operating system. There have been over 40 versions of Windows desktop, Windows server, and Windows mobile operating systems.

HAL handles all the communication between the hardware and the kernel. The CPU can operate in two separate modes: kernel mode and user mode. Applications that are installed are run in user mode, and operating system code runs in kernel mode.

NTFS formats the disk into four important data structures:

- Partition Boot Sector
- Master File Table (MFT)
- System Files
- File Area

Applications are generally made up of many processes. A process is any program that is currently executing. Each running process is made up of at least one thread. A thread is a part of the process that can be executed. Some of the processes that Windows runs are services. These are programs that run in the background to support the operating system and applications.

Each process in a 32-bit Windows computer supports a virtual address space that enables addressing up to 4 GB. Each process in a 64-bit Windows computer supports a virtual address space of up to 8 TB.

Windows stores all of the information about hardware, applications, users, and system settings in a large database known as the registry. The registry is a hierarchical database where the highest level is known as a hive. These are the five hives of the Windows registry:

- HKEY_CURRENT_USER (HKCU)
- HKEY_USERS (HKU)
- HKEY_CLASSES_ROOT (HKCR)
- HKEY_LOCAL_MACHINE (HKLM)
- HKEY_CURRENT_CONFIG (HKCC)

In this chapter, you also learned how to configure, monitor, and keep Windows secure. To do this normally requires that you run programs as Administrator. As Administrator, you can create users and groups, disable access to the Administrator and Guest accounts, and use a variety of administrator tools, including

- All commands available via the CLI and PowerShell
- Remote computer management using WMI and Remote Desktop
- Task Manager and Resource Monitor
- Networking configuration

As Administrator, you will also have the ability to use all the Windows security tools, including

- The **netstat** command to look for inbound and outbound connections that are not authorized
- Event Viewer for access to logs that document the history of application, security, and system events
- Windows Update configuration and scheduling
- Windows Local Security Policy to secure stand-alone computers that are not part of an Active Directory domain
- Windows Defender configuration for built-in virus and spyware protection
- Windows Firewall configuration to fine-tune the default settings

As a cybersecurity analyst, you need a basic understanding of how Windows operates and what tools are available to help keep Windows endpoints secure.

Practice

The following activities provide practice with the topics introduced in this chapter. The Labs and Class Activities are available in the companion *CCNA Cybersecurity Operations Lab Manual* (ISBN 9781587134388).

Class Activities

Class Activity 2.0.1.2: Identify Running Processes

Labs

Lab 2.1.2.10: Exploring Processes, Threads, Handles, and Windows Registry

Lab 2.2.1.10: Create User Accounts

Lab 2.2.1.11: Using Windows PowerShell

Lab 2.2.1.12: Windows Task Manager

Lab 2.2.1.13: Monitor and Manage System Resources in Windows

Check Your Understanding

Complete all the review questions listed here to test your understanding of the topics and concepts in this chapter. The appendix "Answers to 'Check Your Understanding' Questions" lists the answers.

1. What contains information on how hard drive partitions are organized?

   A. CPU

   B. MBR

   C. BOOTMGR

   D. Windows Registry

2. Which **net** command is used on a Windows PC to establish a connection to a shared directory on a remote server?

   A. **net use**

   B. **net start**

   C. **net share**

   D. **net session**

3. Which type of startup must be selected for a service that should run each time the computer is booted?

   A. Boot

   B. Manual

   C. Automatic

   D. Start

   E. Startup

4. A user creates a file with a .ps1 extension in Windows. What type of file is it?

   A. PowerShell cmdlet

   B. PowerShell function

   C. PowerShell documentation

   D. PowerShell script

5. When a user makes changes to the settings of a Windows system, where are these changes stored?

   A. Control panel

   B. Registry

   C. win.ini

   D. boot.ini

6. Which Windows version was the first to introduce a 64-bit Windows operating system?

    A. Windows NT

    B. Windows XP

    C. Windows 7

    D. Windows 10

7. Two pings were issued from a host on a local network. The first ping was issued to the IP address of the default gateway of the host and it failed. The second ping was issued to the IP address of a host outside the local network and it was successful. What is a possible cause for the failed ping?

    A. The default gateway device is configured with the wrong IP address.

    B. The TCP/IP stack on the default gateway is not working properly.

    C. The default gateway is not operational.

    D. Security rules are applied to the default gateway device, preventing it from processing ping requests.

8. Which command is used to manually query a DNS server to resolve a specific hostname?

    A. net

    B. tracert

    C. nslookup

    D. ipconfig /displaydns

9. What is the purpose of the **cd** command?

    A. changes directory to the previous directory

    B. changes directory to the root directory

    C. changes directory to the next highest directory

    D. changes directory to the next lower directory

10. How much RAM is addressable by a 32-bit version of Windows?

    A. 4 GB

    B. 8 GB

    C. 16 GB

    D. 32 GB

11. How can a user prevent specific applications from accessing a Windows computer over a network?

    A. Enable MAC address filtering.

    B. Disable automatic IP address assignment.

    C. Block specific TCP or UDP ports in Windows Firewall.

    D. Change default usernames and passwords.

12. What utility is used to show the system resources consumed by each user?

    A. Task Manager

    B. User Accounts

    C. Device Manager

    D. Event Viewer

## CHAPTER 3

Linux Operating System

Objectives

Upon completion of this chapter, you will be able to answer the following questions:

- Why are Linux skills essential for network security monitoring and investigation?

- How do you use the Linux shell to manipulate text files?

- How do client-server networks function?

- How does a Linux administrator locate and manipulate security log files?

- How do you manage the Linux file system and permissions?

- What are the basic components of the Linux GUI?

- What tools can you use to detect malware on a Linux host?

Key Terms

This chapter uses the following key terms. You can find the definitions in the Glossary.

Introduction (3.0)

Linus Torvalds released the first *Linux* kernel in 1991 under the open source model. Originally developed for the Intel x86 chip architecture, Linux has grown to incorporate many different hardware configurations.

In this chapter, you learn how to perform basic Linux operations as well as administrative and security-related tasks.

Linux Overview (3.1)

In this section, you will learn Linux basics including the Linux shell and the role of Linux servers and clients.

Linux Basics (3.1.1)

In this topic, you will learn what Linux is, its value, its role in a Security Operations Center (SOC), and some of the more important Linux tools.

What is Linux? (3.1.1.1)

Linux is an operating system created in 1991. Linux is open source, fast, reliable, and small. It requires very little hardware resources to run, and is highly customizable. Unlike other operating systems such as Windows and macOS X, Linux was created, and is currently maintained, by a community of programmers. Linux is part of several platforms and can be found on devices anywhere from "wristwatches to supercomputers."

Another important aspect of Linux is that it is designed to be connected to the network, which makes it much simpler to write and use network-based applications. Because Linux is open source, any person or company can get the kernel's source code, inspect it, modify it, and recompile it at will. They are also allowed to redistribute the program with or without charges.

A Linux distribution is the term used to describe packages created by different organizations. Linux distributions (or *distros*) include the Linux kernel with customized tools and software packages. While some of these organizations may charge for their Linux distribution support (geared toward Linux-based businesses), the majority of them also offer their distribution for free without support. Debian, Red Hat, Ubuntu, CentOS, and SUSE are just a few examples of Linux distributions.

The Value of Linux (3.1.1.2)

Linux is often the operating system of choice in the SOC. These are some of the reasons to choose Linux:

- **Linux is open source:** Any person can acquire Linux at no charge and modify it to fit specific needs. This flexibility allows analysts and administrators to tailor-build an operating system specifically for security analysis.

- **The Linux CLI is very powerful:** While a GUI makes many tasks easier to perform, it adds complexity and requires more computer resources to run. The Linux command line interface (CLI) is extremely powerful and enables analysts to perform tasks not only directly on a terminal, but also remotely because the CLI requires very few resources.

- **The user has more control over the OS:** The administrator user in Linux, known as the root user, or *superuser*, has absolute power over the computer. Unlike other operating systems, the root user can modify any aspect of the computer with a few keystrokes. This ability is especially valuable when working with low-level functions such as the network stack. It allows the root user to have precise control over the way network packets are handled by the operating system.

- **It allows for better network communication control:** Control is an inherent part of Linux. Because the OS can be tweaked and adjusted in practically every aspect, it is a great platform for creating network applications. This is the same reason why many great network-based software tools are available for Linux only.

Linux in the SOC (3.1.1.3)

The flexibility provided by Linux is a great feature for the SOC. The entire operating system can be tailored to become the perfect security analysis platform. For example, administrators can add only the necessary packages to the OS, making it lean and efficient. Specific software tools can be installed and configured to work in conjunction, allowing administrators to build a customized computer that fits perfectly in the workflow of an SOC.

These are a few tools that are often found in an SOC:

- **Network packet capture software:** This software is used for network packet captures. This is a crucial tool for an SOC analyst as it makes it possible to observe and understand every detail of a network transaction. Figure 3-1 shows a screenshot of Wireshark, a popular packet capture tool.

- **Malware analysis tools:** In the case of new malware detection, these tools allow analysts to safely run and observe malware execution without the risk of compromising the underlying system.

- *Intrusion detection systems (IDSs):* These tools are used for real-time traffic monitoring and inspection. If any aspect of the currently flowing traffic matches any of the established rules, a predefined action is taken.

- **Firewalls:** This software is used to specify, based on predefined rules, whether traffic is allowed to enter or leave the network.

- **Log managers:** Log files are used to record events. Because a large network can generate a very large number of events log entries, log managers are employed to facilitate log monitoring.

- **Security information and event management (SIEM):** SIEM systems provide real-time analysis of alerts and log entries generated by network appliances such as IDSs and firewalls.

- **Ticketing systems:** Ticket assignment, editing, and recording is done through a ticket management system.

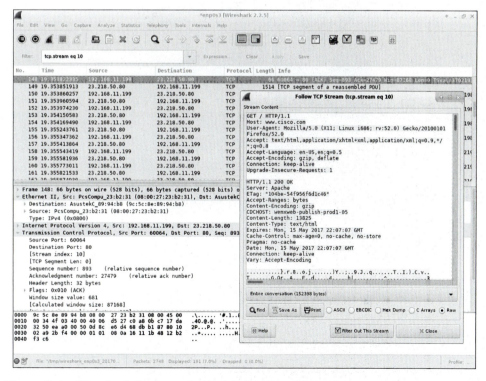

Figure 3-1   Wireshark Capture of a Web Page Request

Linux Tools (3.1.1.4)

In addition to SOC-specific tools, Linux computers used in the SOC often contain penetration testing tools. Also known as pentesting, *penetration testing* is the process of looking for vulnerabilities in a network or computer by attacking it. Packet generators, port scanners, and proof-of-concept exploits are examples of penetration testing tools.

Kali Linux is a Linux distribution created to group many penetration tools. Kali contains a great selection of penetration testing tools. Figure 3-2 shows a screenshot of Kali Linux. Notice all the major categories of penetration testing tools.

Figure 3-2   Kali Linux Tool Categories

Working in the Linux Shell (3.1.2)

In this topic, you will learn about the Linux shell, including common commands used in the CLI and working with text files.

The Linux Shell (3.1.2.1)

In Linux, the user communicates with the OS by using the CLI or the GUI. Linux often boots into the GUI by default, hiding the CLI from the user. One way to access the CLI from the GUI is through a *terminal emulator* application. These applications provide user access to the CLI and are often named as some variation of the word "terminal." In Linux, popular terminal emulators are Terminator, eterm, xterm, konsole, and gnome-terminal.

To experience the Linux CLI in your web browser, go to the following website:

https://bellard.org/jslinux/

Type the **ls** command to list the current directory content. Keep the tab open if you would like to try out some of the other commands discussed in this chapter.

Figure 3-3 shows gnome-terminal, a popular Linux terminal emulator.

Note

The terms shell, console, console window, CLI terminal, and terminal window are often used interchangeably.

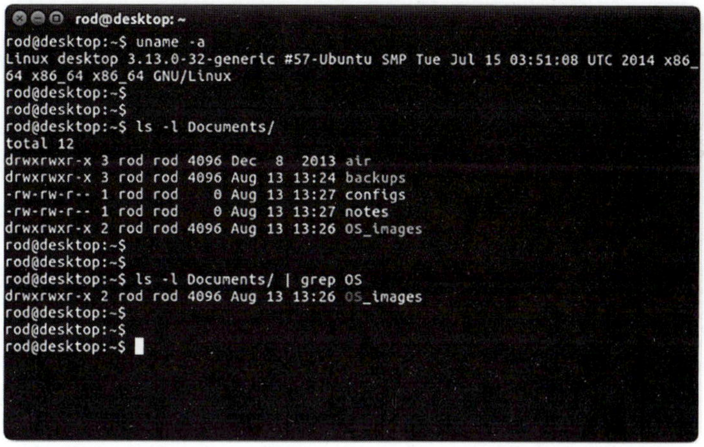

Figure 3-3   Gnome Terminal

Basic Commands (3.1.2.2)

Linux commands are programs created to perform a specific task. Use the **man** command (short for manual) to obtain documentation about commands. As an example, **man ls** provides documentation about the **ls** command from the user manual.

Because commands are programs stored on the disk, when a user types a command, the shell must find it on the disk before it can be executed. The shell will look for user-typed commands in specific directories and attempt to execute them. The list of directories checked by the shell is called the path. The path contains many directories commonly used to store commands. If a command is not in the path, the user must specify its location or the shell will not be able to find it. Users can easily add directories to the path, if necessary.

To invoke a command via the shell, simply type its name. The shell will try to find it in the system path and execute it.

Table 3-1 shows a list of some basic Linux commands and their functions.

Table 3-1   Basic Linux Commands

Command	Description
mv	Used to move or rename files and directories.
chmod	Used to modify file permissions.
chown	Used to change the ownership of a file.
dd	Used to copy data from an input to an output.
pwd	Used to display the name of the current directory.
ps	Used to list the processes currently running on the system.
su	Used to simulate a login as another user or to become a superuser.
sudo	Used to run a command as another user.
grep	Used to search for specific strings of characters within a file or other commands' outputs. To search through the output of a previous command, **grep** must be piped at the end of the previous command.
ifconfig	Used to display or configure network card–related information. If issued without parameters, **ifconfig** will display the configuration of the current network card(s).
apt-get	Used to install, configure, and remove packages on Debian and its derivatives. Note: **apt-get** is a user-friendly command line front end for **dpkg**, Debian's package manager. The combo **dpkg** and **apt-get** is the default package manager system in all Debian Linux derivatives, including Raspbian.
iwconfig	Used to display or configure wireless network card–related information. Similar to **ifconfig**, **iwconfig** will display wireless information when issued without parameters.
shutdown	Used to shut down the system. **shutdown** can be instructed to perform a number of shutdown-related tasks, including restart, halt, put to sleep, or kick out all currently connected users.

Command	Description
passwd	Used to change the password. If no parameters are provided, **passwd** changes the password for the current user.
cat	Used to list the contents of a file and expects the filename as the parameter. The **cat** command is usually used on text files.
man	Used to display the documentation for a specific command.

> **Note**
>
> The text here assumes the user has the proper permissions to execute the command. File permissions in Linux are covered later in this chapter.

File and Directory Commands (3.1.2.3)

Many command line tools are included in Linux by default. To adjust the command operation, users can pass parameters and switches along with the command. Table 3-2 shows a few of the most common commands related to files and directories.

Table 3-2   Common File and Directory Commands

Command	Description
ls	Displays the files inside a directory
cd	Changes the current directory
mkdir	Creates a directory under the current directory
cp	Copies files from source to destination
mv	Moves files to a different directory
rm	Removes files
grep	Searches for specific strings of characters within a file or other commands' outputs
cat	Lists the contents of a file and expects the filename as the parameter

Working with Text Files (3.1.2.4)

Linux has many different text editors, with various features and functions. Some text editors include graphical interfaces while others are command line–only tools. Each text editor includes a feature set designed to support a specific type of task. Some text editors focus on the programmer and include features such as syntax highlighting, brackets, parentheses, checks, and other programming-focused features.

While graphical text editors are convenient and easy to use, command line–based text editors are very important for Linux users. The main benefit of command line–based text editors is that they allow for text file editing from a remote computer.

Consider the following scenario: a user must perform administrative tasks on a Linux computer but is not sitting in front of that computer. Using Secure Shell (SSH), the user starts a remote shell to the remote computer. Under the text-based remote shell, the graphical interface is not available, which makes it impossible to rely on tools such as graphical text editors. In this type of situation, text-based programs are crucial.

Figure 3-4 shows nano (or GNU nano), a popular command-line text editor. The administrator is editing firewall rules. Text editors are often used for system configuration and maintenance in Linux.

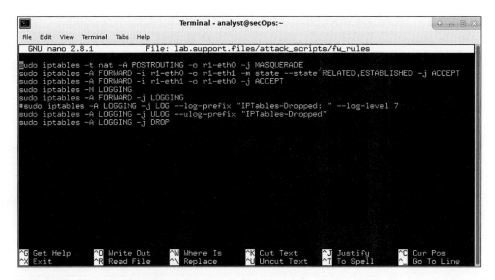

Figure 3-4   The nano Text Editor

Due to the lack of graphical support, nano can only be controlled with the keyboard. For example, **CTRL-O** saves the current file; **CTRL-W** opens the search menu. GNU nano uses a two-line shortcut bar at the bottom of the screen, where commands for the current context are listed. Press **CTRL-G** for the help screen and a complete list of commands.

The Importance of Text Files in Linux (3.1.2.5)

In Linux, everything is treated as a file, including the memory, the disks, the monitor, the files, and the directories. For example, from the operating system standpoint, showing information on the display means to write to the file that represents the display device. It should be no surprise that the computer itself is configured through files. Known as configuration files, they are usually text files used to store adjustments and settings for specific applications or services. Practically everything in Linux relies on configuration files to work. Some services have not one but several configuration files.

Users with proper permission levels can use text editors to change the contents of configuration files. After the changes are made, the file is saved and can be used by the related service or application. Users are able to specify exactly how they want any given application or service to behave. When launched, services and applications check the contents of specific configuration files to adjust their behavior accordingly.

In Figure 3-5, the administrator opened the host configuration file in nano for editing. Only the superuser can change the host file.

Figure 3-5   Editing a Text File in nano

Note

The administrator used the command **sudo nano /etc/hosts** to open the file. The command **sudo** (short for "superuser do") invokes the superuser privilege to use the nano text editor to open the host file.

Lab 3.1.2.6: Working with Text Files in the CLI

In this lab, you will get familiar with Linux command-line text editors and configuration files.

 Lab 3.1.2.7: Getting Familiar with the Linux Shell

In this lab, you will use the Linux command line to manage files and folders and perform some basic administrative tasks.

Linux Servers and Clients (3.1.3)

In this topic, you will learn about Linux client-server communications.

An Introduction to Client-Server Communications (3.1.3.1)

Servers are computers with software installed that enables them to provide services to clients. There are many types of services. Some provide resources such as files, email messages, or web pages to clients upon request. Other services run maintenance tasks such as log management, memory management, disk scanning, and more. Each service requires separate server software. For example, the server in Figure 3-6 requires file server software to provide clients with the ability to retrieve and submit files.

Client-server communications is discussed in more detail later in the course.

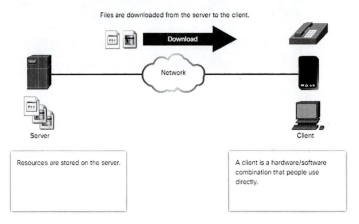

Figure 3-6   Server Sending Files to Client

Servers, Services, and Their Ports (3.1.3.2)

For a computer to be the server for multiple services, ports are used. A *port* is a reserved network resource used by a service. A server is said to be "listening" on a port when it has associated itself to that port.

While the administrator can decide which port to use with any given service, many clients are configured to use a specific port by default. To make it easier for the client, it is common practice to leave the service running in its default port. Table 3-3 shows a few commonly used ports and their services. These are also called "well-known ports."

Ports and their uses in network communications are discussed in more detail later in the course.

Table 3-3   Common Port Numbers and Services

Port Number	Service
21	File Transfer Protocol (FTP)
22	Secure Shell (SSH)
23	Telnet remote login service
25	Simple Mail Transfer Protocol (SMTP)
53	Domain Name System (DNS)
80	Hypertext Transfer Protocol (HTTP)
110	Post Office Protocol version 3 (POP3)
123	Network Time Protocol (NTP)
161	Internet Message Access Protocol (IMAP)
161	Simple Network Management Protocol (SNMP)
443	HTTP Secure (HTTPS)

Clients (3.1.3.3)

Clients are programs or applications designed to communicate with a specific server. Also known as client applications, clients use a well-defined protocol to communicate with the server. Web browsers are web clients used to communicate with web servers via the Hypertext Transfer Protocol (HTTP). The File Transfer Protocol (FTP) client is software used to communicate with an FTP server. Figure 3-7 shows a client uploading files to a server.

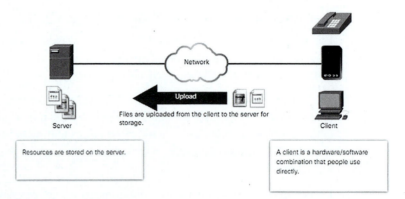

Figure 3-7   Client Uploading File to Server

Lab 3.1.3.4: Linux Servers

In this lab, you will use the Linux command line to identify servers running on a given computer.

Linux Administration (3.2)

In this section, you will learn about basic Linux server administration and the Linux file system.

Basic Server Administration (3.2.1)

In this topic, you will learn about Linux server configuration files, hardening Linux servers, and monitoring Linux services.

Service Configuration Files (3.2.1.1)

In Linux, services are managed using *configuration files*. Common options are port number, location of the hosted resources, and client authorization details. When the service starts, it looks for its configuration files, loads them into memory, and adjusts itself according to the settings in the files. Configuration file modifications often require restarting the service before the changes take effect.

Because services often require superuser privileges to run, service configuration files often require superuser privileges for editing.

Example 3-1 shows a portion of the configuration file for Nginx, a lightweight web server for Linux.

Example 3-1   Nginx Web Server Configuration File

```
[analyst@secOps ~]$ cat /etc/nginx/nginx.conf

#user html;
worker_processes  1;

#error_log  logs/error.log;
#error_log  logs/error.log  notice;
#error_log  logs/error.log  info;

#pid          logs/nginx.pid;


events {
    worker_connections  1024;
}


http {
    include       mime.types;
    default_type  application/octet-stream;

    #log_format  main  '$remote_addr - $remote_user [$time_local] "$request" '
    #                  '$status $body_bytes_sent "$http_referer" '
    #                  '"$http_user_agent" "$http_x_forwarded_for"';

    #access_log  logs/access.log  main;

    sendfile        on;
    #tcp_nopush     on;

    #keepalive_timeout  0;
    keepalive_timeout  65;

    #gzip  on;

<output omitted>

[analyst@secOps ~]$
```

Example 3-2 shows the configuration file for the Network Time Protocol, NTP.

Example 3-2 NTP Configuration File

```
[analyst@secOps ~]$ cat ls /etc/ntp.conf
cat: ls: No such file or directory
# Please consider joining the pool:
#
#     http://www.pool.ntp.org/join.html
#
# For additional information see:
# - https://wiki.archlinux.org/index.php/Network_Time_Protocol_daemon
# - http://support.ntp.org/bin/view/Support/GettingStarted
# - the ntp.conf man page


# Associate to Arch's NTP pool
server 0.arch.pool.ntp.org
server 1.arch.pool.ntp.org
server 2.arch.pool.ntp.org
server 3.arch.pool.ntp.org


# By default, the server allows:
# - all queries from the local host
# - only time queries from remote hosts, protected by rate limiting and kod
restrict default kod limited nomodify nopeer noquery notrap
restrict 127.0.0.1
restrict ::1


# Location of drift file
driftfile /var/lib/ntp/ntp.drift
[analyst@secOps ~]$
```

Example 3-3 shows the configuration file for *Snort*, a Linux-based intrusion detection system (IDS).

Example 3-3 Snort Configuration File

```
[analyst@secOps ~]$ cat /etc/snort/snort.conf
#-------------------------------------------------
#   VRT Rule Packages Snort.conf
#
#   For more information visit us at:
#     http://www.snort.org                Snort Website
#     http://vrt-blog.snort.org/     Sourcefire VRT Blog
#
#     Mailing list Contact:      snort-sigs@lists.sourceforge.net
```

```
#      False Positive reports:     fp@sourcefire.com
#      Snort bugs:                 bugs@snort.org
#
#      Compatible with Snort Versions:
#      VERSIONS : 2.9.9.0
#
#      Snort build options:
#      OPTIONS : --enable-gre --enable-mpls --enable-targetbased --enable-ppm
  --enable-perfprofiling --enable-zlib --enable-active-response --enable-normalizer
  --enable-reload --enable-react --enable-flexresp3
#
#      Additional information:
#      This configuration file enables active response, to run snort in
#      test mode -T you are required to supply an interface -i <interface>
#      or test mode will fail to fully validate the configuration and
#      exit with a FATAL error
#--------------------------------------------------


###################################################
# This file contains a sample snort configuration.
# You should take the following steps to create your own custom configuration:
#
#  1) Set the network variables.
#  2) Configure the decoder
#  3) Configure the base detection engine
#  4) Configure dynamic loaded libraries
#  5) Configure preprocessors
#  6) Configure output plugins
#  7) Customize your rule set
#  8) Customize preprocessor and decoder rule set
#  9) Customize shared object rule set
###################################################


###################################################
# Step #1: Set the network variables.  For more information, see README.variables
###################################################

# Setup the network addresses you are protecting
###ipvar HOME_NET any
###ipvar HOME_NET [192.168.0.0/24,192.168.1.0/24]
ipvar HOME_NET [209.165.200.224/27]
```

```
# Set up the external network addresses. Leave as "any" in most situations
ipvar EXTERNAL_NET any

# List of DNS servers on your network
###ipvar DNS_SERVERS $HOME_NET
ipvar DNS_SERVERS 209.165.200.236

# List of SMTP servers on your network
###ipvar SMTP_SERVERS $HOME_NET
ipvar SMTP_SERVERS 209.165.200.236

# List of web servers on your network
###ipvar HTTP_SERVERS $HOME_NET
ipvar HTTP_SERVERS 209.165.200.235

# List of sql servers on your network
###ipvar SQL_SERVERS $HOME_NET
ipvar SQL_SERVERS 209.165.200.235

# List of telnet servers on your network
###ipvar TELNET_SERVERS $HOME_NET
ipvar TELNET_SERVERS 209.165.200.236

# List of ssh servers on your network
###ipvar SSH_SERVERS $HOME_NET
ipvar SSH_SERVERS 209.165.200.236

<output omitted>
[analyst@secOps ~]$
```

There is no rule for a configuration file format; it is the choice of the service's developer. However, the **option = value** format is often used. In Example 3-3, variable **ipvar** is configured with several options. The first option, HOME_NET, has the value 209.165.200.224/27.

Hardening Devices (3.2.1.2)

Device hardening involves implementing proven methods of securing the device and protecting its administrative access. Some of these methods involve maintaining passwords, configuring enhanced remote login features, and implementing SSH. Defining administrative roles in terms of access is another important aspect of securing infrastructure devices because not all information technology personnel should have the same level of access to the infrastructure devices.

Depending on the Linux distribution, many services are enabled by default. Some of these features are enabled for historical reasons, but are no longer required. Stopping such services and ensuring they do not automatically start at boot time is another device hardening technique.

OS updates are also extremely important to maintaining a hardened device. New vulnerabilities are discovered every day. OS developers create and issue fixes and patches regularly. An up-to-date computer is less likely to be compromised.

The following list provides a few basic recommended steps for device hardening:

- Ensure physical security.
- Minimize installed packages.
- Disable unused services.
- Use SSH and disable the root account login over SSH.
- Keep the system updated.
- Disable USB auto-detection.
- Enforce strong passwords.
- Force periodic password changes.
- Keep users from reusing old passwords.
- Review logs regularly.

Many other steps exist and are often service- or application-dependent.

Monitoring Service Logs (3.2.1.3)

Log files are the records that a computer stores to keep track of important events. Kernel, services, and applications events are all recorded in log files. It is very important for an administrator to periodically review the logs of a computer to keep it healthy. By monitoring Linux log files, an administrator gains a clear picture of the computer's performance, security status, and any underlying issues. Log file analysis allows an administrator to guard against upcoming issues before they occur.

In Linux, log files can be categorized as

- Application logs
- Event logs
- Service logs
- System logs

Some logs contain information about daemons that are running in the Linux system. A *daemon* is a background process that runs without the need for user interaction. For example, the System Security Services Daemon (SSSD) manages remote access and authentication for single sign-on capabilities. The following are a few popular Linux log files and their functions:

- **/var/log/messages:** This directory contains generic computer activity logs. It is mainly used to store informational and noncritical system messages. In Debian-based computers, the /var/log/syslog directory serves the same purpose.

- **/var/log/auth.log:** This file stores all authentication-related events in Debian and Ubuntu computers. Anything involving the user authorization mechanism can be found in this file.

- **/var/log/secure:** This directory is used by Red Hat and CentOS computers instead of /var/log/auth.log. It also tracks sudo logins, SSH logins, and other errors logged by SSSD.

- **/var/log/boot.log:** This file stores boot-related information and messages logged during the computer startup process.

- **/var/log/dmesg:** This directory contains kernel ring buffer messages. Information related to hardware devices and their drivers is recorded here. It is very important because, due to their low-level nature, logging systems such as syslog are not running when these events take place and, therefore, are often unavailable to the administrator in real time.

- **/var/log/kern.log:** This file contains information logged by the kernel.

- **/var/log/cron:** Cron is a service used to schedule automated tasks in Linux and this directory stores its events. Whenever a scheduled task (also called a cron job) runs, all its relevant information including execution status and error messages are stored here.

- **/var/log/mysqld.log or /var/log/mysql.log:** This is the MySQL log file. All debug, failure, and success messages related to the mysqld process and mysqld_ safe daemon are logged here. Red Hat, CentOS, and Fedora store MySQL logs under /var/log/mysqld.log, while Debian and Ubuntu maintain the log in the /var/log/mysql.log file.

Example 3-4 shows a portion of the /var/log/syslog log file. Each line represents a logged event. The timestamps at the beginning of the lines mark the moment the event took place.

Example 3-4 Output of /var/log/syslog

```
[analyst@secOps]$ cat /var/log/syslog
Nov 15 09:17:13 secOps kernel: [    0.000000] Linux version 4.10.10-1-ARCH
  (builduser@tobias) (gcc versi
on 6.3.1 20170306 (GCC) ) #1 SMP PREEMPT Wed Apr 12 19:10:48 CEST 2017
Nov 15 09:17:13 secOps kernel: [    0.000000] ------------[ cut here ]------------
Nov 15 09:17:13 secOps kernel: [    0.000000] WARNING: CPU: 0 PID: 0 at arch/x86/
  kernel/fpu/xstate.c:595
  fpu__init_system_xstate+0x465/0x7b2
Nov 15 09:17:13 secOps kernel: [    0.000000] XSAVE consistency problem, dumping
  leaves
Nov 15 09:17:13 secOps kernel: [    0.000000] Modules linked in:
Nov 15 09:17:13 secOps kernel: [    0.000000] CPU: 0 PID: 0 Comm: swapper Not
  tainted 4.10.10-1-ARCH #1
Nov 15 09:17:13 secOps kernel: [    0.000000] Call Trace:
Nov 15 09:17:13 secOps kernel: [    0.000000]  dump_stack+0x58/0x74
Nov 15 09:17:13 secOps kernel: [    0.000000]  __warn+0xea/0x110
Nov 15 09:17:13 secOps kernel: [    0.000000]  ? fpu__init_system_xstate+0x465/0x7b2
Nov 15 09:17:13 secOps kernel: [    0.000000]  warn_slowpath_fmt+0x46/0x60
Nov 15 09:17:13 secOps kernel: [    0.000000]  fpu__init_system_xstate+0x465/0x7b2
Nov 15 09:17:13 secOps kernel: [    0.000000]  fpu__init_system+0x18c/0x1b1
Nov 15 09:17:13 secOps kernel: [    0.000000]  early_cpu_init+0x110/0x113
Nov 15 09:17:13 secOps kernel: [    0.000000]  setup_arch+0xe4/0xbb6
Nov 15 09:17:13 secOps kernel: [    0.000000]  start_kernel+0x8f/0x3ce
Nov 15 09:17:13 secOps kernel: [    0.000000]  i386_start_kernel+0x91/0x95
Nov 15 09:17:13 secOps kernel: [    0.000000]  startup_32_smp+0x16b/0x16d
Nov 15 09:17:13 secOps kernel: [    0.000000] ---[ end trace c61a827435bb526d ]---
<output omitted>
[analyst@secOps]$
```

Lab 3.2.1.4: Locating Log Files

In this lab, you will get familiar with locating and manipulating Linux log files.

The Linux File System (3.2.2)

In this topic, you will learn about Linux file system types, Linux roles and file permissions, and creating hard and symbolic links.

The File System Types in Linux (3.2.2.1)

There are many different kinds of file systems, varying in properties of speed, flexibility, security, size, structure, logic, and more. It is up to the administrator to decide which file system type best suits the operating system and the files it will store. Below are a few file system types commonly found and supported by Linux:

- *ext2* **(second extended file system):** ext2 was the default file system in several major Linux distributions until supplanted by ext3. Almost fully compatible with ext2, ext3 also supports journaling (see below). ext2 is still the file system of choice for flash-based storage media because its lack of a journal increases performance and minimizes the number of writes. Because flash memory devices have a limited number of write operations, minimizing write operations increases the device's lifetime. However, contemporary Linux kernels also support ext4, an even more modern file system, with better performance and which can also operate in a journal-less mode.

- *ext3* **(third extended file system):** ext3 is a journaled file system designed to improve the existing ext2 file system. A *journal*, the main feature added to ext3, is a technique used to minimize the risk of file system corruption in the event of sudden power loss. The file system keeps a log (or journal) of all the file system changes about to be made. If the computer crashes before the change is complete, the journal can be used to restore or correct any eventual issues created by the crash. The maximum file size in ext3 file systems is 32 TB.

- *ext4* **(fourth extended file system):** Designed as a successor of ext3, ext4 was created based on a series of extensions to ext3. While the extensions improve the performance of ext3 and increase supported file sizes, Linux kernel developers were concerned about stability issues and were opposed to adding the extensions to the stable ext3. The ext3 project was split in two; one kept as ext3 and its normal development and the other, named ext4, incorporated the mentioned extensions.

- *NFS* **(Network File System):** NFS is a network-based file system, allowing file access over the network. From the user standpoint, there is no difference between accessing a file stored locally or on another computer on the network. NFS is an open standard which allows anyone to implement it.

- *CDFS* **(Compact Disc File System):** CDFS was created specifically for optical disk media.

- *Swap file system*: The swap file system is used by Linux when it runs out of RAM. Technically, it is a swap partition that does not have a specific file system but it is relevant to the file system discussion. When this happens, the kernel moves inactive RAM content to the swap partition on the disk. While swap partitions (also known as swap space) can be useful to Linux computers with a limited amount of memory, they should not be considered as a primary solution. A swap partition is stored on disk, which has much lower access speeds than RAM.

- **HFS Plus or *HFS+* (Hierarchical File System Plus):** Primary file system used by Apple in its Macintosh computers. The Linux kernel includes a module for mounting HFS+ for read-write operations.

- **Master boot record (MBR):** Located in the first sector of a partitioned computer, the MBR stores all the information about the way in which the file system is organized. The MBR quickly hands over control to a loading function, which loads the OS.

Mounting is the term used for the process of assigning a directory to a partition. After a successful mount operation, the file system contained on the partition is accessible through the specified directory. In this context, the directory is called the mounting point for that file system. Windows users may be familiar with a similar concept: the drive letter.

Example 3-5 shows the output of the **mount** command issued in the Cisco CyberOPS VM.

Example 3-5   The Output of **mount** in the CyberOPS VM

```
[analyst@secOps ~]$ mount
proc on /proc type proc (rw,nosuid,nodev,noexec,relatime)
sys on /sys type sysfs (rw,nosuid,nodev,noexec,relatime)
dev on /dev type devtmpfs (rw,nosuid,relatime,size=511056k,nr_inodes=127764,
  mode=755)
run on /run type tmpfs (rw,nosuid,nodev,relatime,mode=755)
/dev/sda1 on / type ext4 (rw,relatime,data=ordered)
securityfs on /sys/kernel/security type securityfs (rw,nosuid,nodev,noexec,relatime)
tmpfs on /dev/shm type tmpfs (rw,nosuid,nodev)
devpts on /dev/pts type devpts (rw,nosuid,noexec,relatime,gid=5,mode=620,ptmxmode=000)
tmpfs on /sys/fs/cgroup type tmpfs (ro,nosuid,nodev,noexec,mode=755)
cgroup on /sys/fs/cgroup/systemd type cgroup
  (rw,nosuid,nodev,noexec,relatime,xattr,release_agent=/usr/lib/systemd/
  systemd-cgroups-agent,name=systemd)
pstore on /sys/fs/pstore type pstore (rw,nosuid,nodev,noexec,relatime)
cgroup on /sys/fs/cgroup/perf_event type cgroup (rw,nosuid,nodev,noexec,relatime,
  perf_event)
cgroup on /sys/fs/cgroup/freezer type cgroup (rw,nosuid,nodev,noexec,relatime,freezer)
cgroup on /sys/fs/cgroup/net_cls type cgroup (rw,nosuid,nodev,noexec,relatime,net_cls)
cgroup on /sys/fs/cgroup/cpuset type cgroup (rw,nosuid,nodev,noexec,relatime,cpuset)
cgroup on /sys/fs/cgroup/devices type cgroup (rw,nosuid,nodev,noexec,relatime,devices)
cgroup on /sys/fs/cgroup/blkio type cgroup (rw,nosuid,nodev,noexec,relatime,blkio)
cgroup on /sys/fs/cgroup/pids type cgroup (rw,nosuid,nodev,noexec,relatime,pids)
cgroup on /sys/fs/cgroup/cpu,cpuacct type cgroup (rw,nosuid,nodev,noexec,relatime,
  cpu,cpuacct)
cgroup on /sys/fs/cgroup/memory type cgroup (rw,nosuid,nodev,noexec,relatime,memory)
systemd-1 on /proc/sys/fs/binfmt_misc type autofs (rw,relatime,fd=28,pgrp=1,
  timeout=0,minproto=5,maxproto=5,direct)
hugetlbfs on /dev/hugepages type hugetlbfs (rw,relatime)
tmpfs on /tmp type tmpfs (rw,nosuid,nodev)
```

```
mqueue on /dev/mqueue type mqueue (rw,relatime)
debugfs on /sys/kernel/debug type debugfs (rw,relatime)
configfs on /sys/kernel/config type configfs (rw,relatime)
tmpfs on /run/user/1000 type tmpfs (rw,nosuid,nodev,relatime,size=102812k,mode=700,
   uid=1000,gid=1000)
[analyst@secOps ~]$
```

When issued with no options, **mount** returns the list of file systems currently mounted in a Linux computer. While many files systems shown are out of the scope of this course, notice the root file system (highlighted). The root file system is represented by the "/" symbol and holds all files in the computer by default. It is also shown in Example 3-5 that the root file system was formatted as ext4 and occupies the first partition of the first drive (/dev/sda1).

Linux Roles and File Permissions (3.2.2.2)

In Linux, most system entities are treated as files. In order to organize the system and reinforce boundaries within the computer, Linux uses file permissions. File permissions are built into the file system structure and provide a mechanism to define permissions on every file. Every file in Linux carries its file permissions, defining the actions that the owner, the group, and others can do with the file. The possible permission rights are Read, Write, and Execute. The **ls** command with the **-l** parameter lists additional information about the file. Consider the output of the **ls -l** command in Example 3-6.

Example 3-6   Viewing Permissions for a Linux File

```
[analyst@secOps ~]$ ls -l space.txt
-rwxrw-r-- 1 analyst staff 253 May 20 12:49 space.txt
[analyst@secOps ~]$
```

The output provides a lot of information about the file space.txt.

The first field of the output displays the permissions associated to space.txt (**-rwxrw-r--**). File permissions are always displayed in the User, Group, and Other order, so you can interpret the first field as follows:

- The dash (-) means that this is a file. For directories, the first dash would be a "d" instead.

- The first set of characters is for user permissions (**rwx**). The user, **analyst**, who owns the file can Read, Write, and eXecute the file.

- The second set of characters is for group permissions (**rw-**). The group, **staff**, who owns the file can Read and Write to the file.

- The third set of characters is for any other user or group permissions (**r--**). Any other user or group on the computer can only Read the file.

The second field defines the number of hard links to the file (the number **1** after the permissions). A hard link creates another file with a different name linked to the same place in the file system (called an inode). This is in contrast to a symbolic link, which is discussed next.

The third and fourth field display the user (**analyst**) and group (**staff**) who own the file, respectively.

The fifth field displays the file size in bytes. The **space.txt** file has 253 bytes.

The sixth field displays the date and time of the last modification.

The seventh field displays the filename.

Figure 3-8 shows a breakdown of file permissions in Linux.

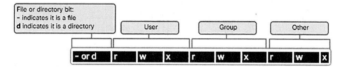

Figure 3-8   File Permissions

Table 3-4 shows how to interpret the octal values for permissions.

Table 3-4   Octal Values for Permissions

Binary	Octal	Permission	Description
000	0	---	No access
001	1	--x	Execute only
010	2	-w-	Write only
011	3	-wx	Write and Execute
100	4	r--	Read only
101	5	r-x	Read and Execute
110	6	rw-	Read and Write
111	7	rwx	Read, Write, and Execute

File permissions are a fundamental part of Linux and cannot be broken. A user has as much rights to a file as the file permissions allow. The only user that can override file permission on a Linux computer is the root user. Because the root user has the power to override file permissions, the root user can write to any file. Because everything is treated as a file, the root user has full control over a Linux computer. Root access is often required before performing maintenance and administrative tasks.

Hard Links and Symbolic Links (3.2.2.3)

A *hard link* is another file that points to the same location as the original file. Use the command **ln** to create a hard link. The first argument is the existing file and the second argument is the new file. The file **space.txt** is linked to **space.hard.txt** in Example 3-7 and the link field now shows 2.

Example 3-7   Creating Hard Links in Linux

```
[analyst@secOps ~]$ ln space.txt space.hard.txt
[analyst@secOps ~]$ ls -l space*
-rwxrw-r-- 2 analyst staff 253 May 20 14:41 space.hard.txt
-rwxrw-r-- 2 analyst staff 253 May 20 14:41 space.txt
[analyst@secOps ~]$ echo "Testing hard link" >> space.txt
[analyst@secOps ~]$ ls -l space*
-rwxrw-r-- 2 analyst staff 273 May 20 14:41 space.hard.txt
-rwxrw-r-- 2 analyst staff 273 May 20 14:41 space.txt
[analyst@secOps ~]$ rm space.hard.txt
[analyst@secOps ~]$ more space.txt
"Space is big. Really big. You just won't believe how vastly, hugely, mindbog-
  glingly big it is. I mean, you may think it's a long way down the road to the
  chemist, but that's just peanuts in space."
--Douglas Adams, The Hitchhiker's Guide to the Galaxy


Testing hard link
[analyst@secOps ~]$
```

Both files point to the same location in the file system. If you change one file, the other is changed, as well. The **echo** command is used to add some text to **space.txt**. Notice that the file size for both **space.txt** and **space.hard.txt** increased to 273 bytes. If you delete the space.hard.txt file with the **rm** command (remove), the **space.txt** file still exists, as verified with the **more space.txt** command.

A *symbolic link*, also called a symlink or soft link, is similar to a hard link in that applying changes to the symbolic link will also change the original file. As shown in Example 3-8, use the **ln** command option **-s** to create a symbolic link. Notice that adding a line of text to **test.txt** also adds the line to **mytest.txt**. However, unlike a hard link, deleting the original **test.txt** file means that **mytest.txt** is now linked to a file that no longer exists, as shown with the **more mytest.txt** and **ls -l mytest.txt** commands.

Example 3-8   Creating Symbolic Links in Linux

```
[analyst@secOps ~]$ echo "Hello World!" > test.txt
[analyst@secOps ~]$ ln -s test.txt mytest.txt
[analyst@secOps ~]$ echo "It's a lovely day!" >> mytest.txt
[analyst@secOps ~]$ more test.txt
Hello World!
It's a lovely day!
[analyst@secOps ~]$ more mytest.txt
Hello World!
It's a lovely day!
[analyst@secOps ~]$ rm test.txt
[analyst@secOps ~]$ more mytest.txt
more: stat of mytest.txt failed: No such file or directory
[analyst@secOps ~]$ ls -l mytest.txt
lrwxrwxrwx 1 analyst staff 8 May 20 15:15 mytest.txt -> test.txt
[analyst@secOps ~]$
```

Although symbolic links have a single point of failure (the underlying file), symbolic links have several benefits over hard links:

- Locating hard links is more difficult. Symbolic links show the location of the original file in the **ls -l** command, as shown in the last line of output in Example 3-8 (**mytest.txt -> test.txt**).

- Hard links are limited to the file system in which they are created. Symbolic links can link to a file in another file system.

- Hard links cannot link to a directory because the system itself uses hard links to define the hierarchy of the directory structure. However, symbolic links can link to directories.

 Lab 3.2.2.4: Navigating the Linux Filesystem and Permission Settings

In this lab, you will familiarize yourself with Linux filesystems.

Linux Hosts (3.3)

In this section, you will learn about working with Linux hosts through the GUI and the CLI.

Working with the Linux GUI (3.3.1)

In this topic, you will learn about the Linux GUI.

X Window System (3.3.1.1)

The graphical interface present in most Linux computers is based on the *X Window System*. Also known as X or X11, X Window is a windowing system designed to provide the basic framework for a GUI. X includes functions for drawing and moving windows on the display device and interacting with a mouse and keyboard.

X works as a server and, as such, allows a remote user to use the network to connect, start a graphical application, and have the graphical window open on the remote terminal. While the application itself runs on the server, the graphical aspect of it is sent by X over the network and displayed on the remote computer.

Notice that X does not specify the user interface, leaving it to other programs such as window managers to define all the graphical components. This abstraction allows for great flexibility and customization as graphical components such as buttons, fonts, icons, window borders, and color scheme are all defined by the user application. Because of this separation, the Linux GUI varies greatly from distribution to distribution. Examples of window managers are Gnome and KDE, as shown in Figures 3-9 and 3-10, respectively. While the look and feel of window managers vary, the main components are still present.

Figure 3-9   Gnome Window Manager

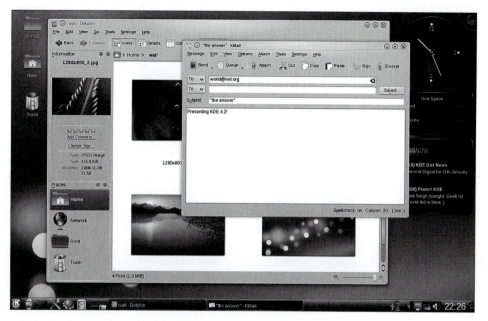

Figure 3-10   KDE Window Manager

For more information on Gnome, visit the following website:

https://www.gnome.org/

For more information on KDE, visit the following website:

https://www.kde.org/

The Linux GUI (3.3.1.2)

Although an operating system does not require a GUI to function, GUIs are considered more user-friendly than the CLI. The Linux GUI as a whole can be easily replaced by the user. As a result of the large number of Linux distributions, this chapter focuses on Ubuntu when covering Linux because it is a very popular and user-friendly distribution.

Ubuntu Linux uses Unity as its default GUI. Unity's goal is to make Ubuntu even more user-friendly. The main UI components of Unity include:

- **Top Menu Bar:** This multipurpose menu bar contains the currently running application. It includes the maximize, minimize, and exit buttons of the application in focus, as well as the system toggles including settings, logout, and shutdown, clock, and other notifications.

- **Launcher:** This is a dock on the left side of the screen that serves as the application launcher and switcher. Click to launch an application and when the application is running, click again to switch between running applications.

If more than one instance of an application is running, Launcher will display all instances.

■ **Quicklist:** Right-click any application hosted on the Launcher to access a short list of tasks the application can perform.

■ **Dash Search Box:** This holds the Search tool and a list of recently used applications. Dash includes Lenses at the bottom of the Dash area which allow the user to fine-tune Dash search results. To access Dash, click the Ubuntu button on the top of the Launcher.

■ **System and Notification Menu:** Many important functions are located in the indicator menu, located at the top right corner of the screen. Use the indicator menu to switch users, shut down your computer, control the volume level, or change network settings.

Figure 3-11 shows a breakdown of the Ubuntu Unity Desktop.

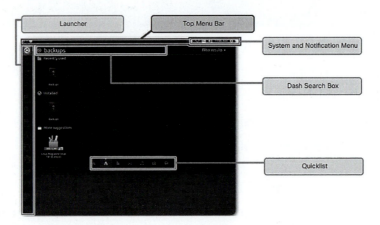

Figure 3-11   Ubuntu Unity GUI

To experience Unity desktop in your web browser, visit the following website:

http://tour.ubuntu.com/en/

Working on a Linux Host (3.3.2)

In this topic, you will learn how to install and run Linux applications, keep your system up to date, and guarding against malware on a Linux host.

Installing and Running Applications on a Linux Host (3.3.2.1)

Many end-user applications are complex programs written in compiled languages. To aid in the installation process, Linux often includes programs called package managers. A package is the term used to refer to a program and all its supported files. By using a package manager to install a package, all the necessary files are placed in the correct file system location.

There are several package managers. For this course, we will use the Advanced Packaging Tool (apt) package manager. Example 3-9 shows the output of a few **apt** commands. The **apt-get update** command is used to fetch the package list from the package repository and update the local package database. The **apt-get upgrade** command is used to update all currently installed packages to their latest versions.

Example 3-9   The Advanced Packaging Tool (APT) Package Manager

```
analyst@cuckoo:~$ sudo apt-get update
[sudo] password for analyst:
Hit:1 http://us.archive.ubuntu.com/ubuntu xenial InRelease
Get:2 http://us.archive.ubuntu.com/ubuntu xenial-updates InRelease [102 kB]
Get:3 http://security.ubuntu.com/ubuntu xenial-security InRelease [102 kB]
Get:4 http://us.archive.ubuntu.com/ubuntu xenial-backports InRelease [102 kB]
Get:5 http://us.archive.ubuntu.com/ubuntu xenial-updates/main amd64 Packages [534 kB]
<output omitted>
Fetched 4,613 kB in 4s (1,003 kB/s)
Reading package lists... Done
analyst@cuckoo:~$
analyst@cuckoo:~$ sudo apt-get upgrade
Reading package lists... Done
Building dependency tree
Reading state information... Done
Calculating upgrade... Done
The following packages have been kept back:
 linux-generic-hwe-16.04 linux-headers-generic-hwe-16.04
  linux-image-generic-hwe-16.04
The following packages will be upgraded:
 firefox firefox-locale-en gir1.2-javascriptcoregtk-4.0 gir1.2-webkit2-4.0
  libjavascriptcoregtk-4.0-18
 libwebkit2gtk-4.0-37 libwebkit2gtk-4.0-37-gtk2 libxen-4.6 libxenstore3.0 linux-
  libc-dev logrotate openssh-client
 qemu-block-extra qemu-kvm qemu-system-common qemu-system-x86 qemu-utils snapd
  ubuntu-core-launcher zlib1g
 zlib1g-dev
21 upgraded, 0 newly installed, 0 to remove and 3 not upgraded.
Need to get 85.7 MB of archives.
After this operation, 1,576 kB of additional disk space will be used.
Do you want to continue? [Y/n]
```

Keeping the System Up to Date (3.3.2.2)

Also known as *patches*, OS updates are released periodically by OS companies to address any known vulnerabilities in their operating system. While companies have update schedules, the release of unscheduled OS updates can happen when a major vulnerability is found in the OS code. Modern operating systems will alert the user when updates are available for download and installation but the user can check for updates at any time.

To update the local package metadata database using the CLI, use the **apt-get update** command.

To upgrade all the currently installed packages using the CLI, use the **apt-get upgrade** command.

To manually check and install updates on Linux using the GUI, click **Dash Search Box**, type **software updater**, and click the **Software Updater** icon, as shown in Figure 3-12.

Figure 3-12   The Ubuntu GUI-Based Software Updater

Processes and Forks (3.3.2.3)

A process is a running instance of a computer program. Multitasking operating systems can execute many processes at the same time.

Forking is a method that the kernel uses to allow a process to create a copy of itself. Processes need a way to create new processes in multitasking operating systems. The fork operation is the only way of doing so in Linux.

Forking is important for many reasons. One of them relates to process scalability. Apache, a popular web server, is a good example. By forking itself, Apache is able to serve a large number of requests with fewer system resources than a single-process-based server.

When a process calls fork, the caller process becomes the parent process, with the newly created process referred to as its child. After the fork, the processes are, to some extent, independent processes; they have different process IDs but run the same program code.

The following are a few commands used to manage processes:

- **ps:** This command is used to list the processes running on the computer at the time it is invoked. **ps** can be instructed to display running processes that belong to the current user or other users. While listing processes does not require root privileges, killing or modifying other users' processes does.

- **top:** This command is also used to list running processes, but unlike **ps**, **top** keeps displaying running processes dynamically. Press **q** to exit **top**.

- **kill:** This command is used to modify the behavior of a specific process. Depending on the parameters, **kill** will remove, restart, or pause a process. In many cases, the user will run **ps** or **top** before running **kill**. This is done so the user can learn the PID of a process before running **kill**.

Example 3-10 shows the output of the **top** command on a Linux computer.

Example 3-10   Output of the **top** Command

```
top - 12:37:51 up 28 min,  1 user,  load average: 0.07, 0.02, 0.02
Tasks:  99 total,  1 running, 98 sleeping,  0 stopped,  0 zombie
%Cpu0  :  2.8/0.7    3[|||                                               ]
GiB Mem : 94.6/0.981    [                                                ]
GiB Swap: 0.0/0.000     [                                                ]

  PID USER      PR  NI    VIRT    RES %CPU %MEM     TIME+ S COMMAND
    1 root      20   0    8.9m   3.8m  0.0  0.4   0:00.70 S systemd
  173 root      20   0   70.6m   2.4m  0.0  0.2   0:00.06 S `- systemd-journal
  205 root      20   0   15.0m   1.8m  0.0  0.2   0:00.09 S `- systemd-udevd
  270 root      20   0    5.5m   0.3m  0.0  0.0   0:00.09 S `- ovsdb-server
  272 root      20   0    5.7m   0.9m  0.0  0.1   0:00.00 S `- start_pox.sh
  281 root      20   0   42.0m   8.2m  0.7  0.8   0:03.47 S   `- python2.7
  274 root      20   0   23.2m   1.6m  0.0  0.2   0:00.00 S `- rsyslogd
  276 root      20   0    7.0m   1.3m  0.0  0.1   0:00.00 S `- systemd-logind
```

```
277 dbus        20   0    6.4m   2.0m   0.0   0.2   0:00.18 S   `- dbus-daemon
283 systemd+    20   0   16.6m   0.5m   0.0   0.1   0:00.00 S   `- systemd-network
284 root        20   0    7.5m   1.2m   0.0   0.1   0:00.00 S   `- ovs-vswitchd
297 root        20   0   29.3m   1.5m   0.0   0.2   0:00.19 S   `- VBoxService
314 root        20   0    5.2m   0.7m   0.0   0.1   0:00.00 S   `- vsftpd
317 root        20   0    7.6m   0.9m   0.0   0.1   0:00.00 S   `- sshd
320 root        20   0   35.3m   6.7m   0.0   0.7   0:00.04 S   `- lightdm
332 root        20   0  164.3m  61.5m   2.6   6.1   0:05.76 S      `- Xorg
385 root        20   0   31.2m   2.9m   0.0   0.3   0:00.01 S      `- lightdm
396 analyst     20   0    5.5m   1.0m   0.0   0.1   0:00.00 S        `- sh
416 analyst     20   0   75.7m  26.8m   0.0   2.7   0:00.07 S
`- xfce4-session
426 analyst     20   0   60.0m  28.9m   0.0   2.9   0:00.41 S
`- xfwm4
427 analyst     20   0   57.6m  25.6m   0.0   2.6   0:00.06 S
`- Thunar
428 analyst     20   0   70.3m  31.9m   0.0   3.2   0:00.28 S
`- xfce4-panel
459 analyst     20   0   56.7m  26.0m   0.0   2.6   0:00.08 S
`- panel-6-systray
462 analyst     20   0   57.9m  25.5m   0.0   2.5   0:00.09 S
`- panel-2-actions
432 analyst     20   0   90.2m  33.6m   0.0   3.3   0:00.57 S
`- xfdesktop
444 analyst     20   0   78.5m  25.9m   0.0   2.6   0:00.06 S
`- polkit-gnome-au
329 root        20   0    7.5m   0.5m   0.0   0.1   0:00.00 S   `- nginx
330 http        20   0    8.8m   1.3m   0.0   0.1   0:00.00 S      `- nginx
333 root        20   0   38.0m   2.8m   0.0   0.3   0:00.03 S   `- accounts-daemon
340 polkitd     20   0   71.2m  10.3m   0.0   1.0   0:00.07 S   `- polkitd
391 analyst     20   0    8.9m   1.8m   0.0   0.2   0:00.00 S   `- systemd
392 analyst     20   0   12.2m   1.1m   0.0   0.1   0:00.00 S      `- (sd-pam)
408 analyst     20   0    6.4m   1.8m   0.0   0.2   0:00.02 S      `- dbus-daemon
420 analyst     20   0   10.2m   2.4m   0.0   0.2   0:00.01 S      `- xfconfd
671 analyst     20   0   42.9m   6.4m   0.0   0.6   0:00.01 S
`- at-spi-bus-laun
423 analyst     20   0    4.7m   0.2m   0.0   0.0   0:00.00 S   `- ssh-agent
425 analyst     20   0   23.3m   0.2m   0.0   0.0   0:00.02 S   `- gpg-agent
430 analyst     20   0   67.9m  26.3m   0.0   2.6   0:00.03 S   `- xfsettingsd
440 analyst     20   0   80.0m  26.6m   0.0   2.6   0:00.08 S   `- xfce4-power-man
448 analyst     20   0   79.8m  26.5m   0.0   2.6   0:00.02 S   `- xfce4-power-man
463 root        20   0   52.6m   2.5m   0.0   0.2   0:00.02 S   `- upowerd
478 analyst     20   0   15.2m   0.3m   0.0   0.0   0:00.00 S   `- VBoxClient
487 analyst     20   0   17.4m   0.4m   0.7   0.0   0:01.78 S      `- VBoxClient
479 analyst     20   0   15.2m   0.3m   0.0   0.0   0:00.00 S   `- VBoxClient
484 analyst     20   0   16.9m   0.4m   0.0   0.0   0:00.01 S      `- VBoxClient
```

Malware on a Linux Host (3.3.2.4)

Linux malware includes viruses, Trojan horses, worms, and other types of malware that can affect the operating system. Due to a number of design components such as file system structure, file permissions, and user account restrictions, Linux operating systems are generally regarded as better protected against malware.

While arguably better protected, Linux is not immune to malware. Many vulnerabilities have been found and exploited in Linux. These range from server software to kernel vulnerabilities. Attackers are able to exploit these vulnerabilities and compromise the target. Due to the open source nature of Linux, fixes and patches are often made available within hours of the discovery of such problems.

If a malicious program is executed, it will cause damage, regardless of the platform. A common Linux attack vector is its services and processes. Vulnerabilities are frequently found in server and process code running on computers connected to the network. An outdated version of the Apache web server could contain an unpatched vulnerability which can be exploited by an attacker, for example. Attackers often probe open ports to assess the version and nature of the server running on that port. With that knowledge, attackers can research if there are any known issues with that particular version of that particular server to support the attack. As with most vulnerabilities, keeping the computer updated and closing any unused services and ports is a good way to reduce the opportunities for attack in a Linux computer.

Example 3-11 shows an attacker using the **telnet** command to probe the nature and version of a web server. The attacker has learned that the server in question is running nginx version 1.12.0. The next step would be to research known vulnerabilities in the nginx 1.12.0 code.

> **Note**
>
> You will learn more about this attack later in the course.

Example 3-11   Using **telnet** to Probe a Web Server

```
[analyst@secOps ~]$ telnet 209.165.200.224 80
Trying 209.165.200.224...
Connected to 209.165.200.224.
Escape character is '^]'.
type anything to force an HTTP error response
HTTP/1.1 400 Bad Request
Server: nginx/1.12.0
Date: Wed, 17 May 2017 14:27:30 GMT
Content-Type: text/html
Content-Length: 173
Connection: close
```

```
<html>
<head><title>400 Bad Request</title></head>
<body bgcolor="white">
<center><h1>400 Bad Request</h1></center>
<hr><center>nginx/1.12.0</center>
</body>
</html>
Connection closed by foreign host.
[analyst@secOps ~]$
```

Rootkit Check (3.3.2.5)

A *rootkit* is a set of software tools designed to increase a user's privileges, or grant access to portions of the software that should not normally be allowed. Rootkits are also often used to secure a backdoor to a compromised computer.

The installation of a rootkit can be automated (done as part of an infection) or an attacker can manually install it after compromising a computer. A rootkit is destructive because it changes kernel code and its modules, changing the most fundamental operations of the OS itself. With such a deep level of compromise, rootkits can hide the intrusion, remove any installation tracks, and even tamper with troubleshooting and diagnostics tools so that their output now hides the presence of the rootkit. While a few Linux vulnerabilities through history have allowed rootkit installation via regular user accounts, the vast majority of rootkit compromises require root or administrator access.

Because the very nature of the computer is compromised, rootkit detection can be very difficult. Typical detection methods often include booting the computer from trusted media such as a diagnostics operating system live CD. The compromised drive is mounted and, from the trusted system toolset, trusted diagnostic tools can be launched to inspect the compromised file system. Inspection methods include behavioral-based methods, signature scanning, difference scanning, and memory dump analysis.

Rootkit removal can be complicated and often impossible, especially in cases where the rootkit resides in the kernel; reinstallation of the operating system is usually the only real solution to the problem. Firmware rootkits usually require hardware replacement.

chkrootkit is a popular Linux-based program designed to check the computer for known rootkits. It is a shell script that uses common Linux tools such as strings and **grep** to compare the signatures of core programs. It also looks for discrepancies as it traverses the /proc file system comparing the signatures found there with the output of the **ps** command For more information about **chkrootkit**, visit the following website:

http://www.chkrootkit.org/

While helpful, keep in mind that programs to check for rootkits are not 100% reliable.

Example 3-12 shows the output of **chkrootkit** on Ubuntu Linux.

Example 3-12   Output of the **chkrootkit** Command

```
analyst@cuckoo:~$ sudo ./chkrootkit
[sudo] password for analyst:
ROOTDIR is `/'
Checking `amd'... not found
Checking `basename'... not infected
Checking `biff'... not found
Checking `chfn'... not infected
Checking `chsh'... not infected
Checking `cron'... not infected
Checking `crontab'... not infected
Checking `date'... not infected
Checking `du'... not infected
Checking `dirname'... not infected
Checking `echo'... not infected
Checking `egrep'... not infected
Checking `env'... not infected
Checking `find'... not infected
Checking `fingerd'... not found
Checking `gpm'... not found
Checking `grep'... not infected
Checking `hdparm'... not infected
Checking `su'... not infected
Checking `ifconfig'... not infected
Checking `inetd'... not tested
Checking `inetdconf'... not found
Checking `identd'... not found
Checking `init'... not infected
Checking `killall'... not infected
Checking `ldsopreload'... not infected
Checking `login'... not infected
Checking `ls'... not infected
Checking `lsof'... not infected
Checking `mail'... not found
Checking `mingetty'... not found
Checking `netstat'... not infected
Checking `named'... not found
Checking `passwd'... not infected
Checking `pidof'... not infected
Checking `pop2'... not found
Checking `pop3'... not found
Checking `ps'... not infected
Checking `pstree'... not infected
Checking `rpcinfo'... not found
Checking `rlogind'... not found
Checking `rshd'... not found
```

```
Checking `slogin'... not infected
Checking `sendmail'... not found
Checking `sshd'... not infected
Checking `syslogd'... not tested
Checking `tar'... not infected
Checking `tcpd'... not infected
Checking `tcpdump'... not infected
Checking `top'... not infected
Checking `telnetd'... not found
Checking `timed'... not found
Checking `traceroute'... not found
Checking `vdir'... not infected
Checking `w'... not infected
Checking `write'... not infected
Checking `aliens'... no suspect files
Searching for sniffer's logs, it may take a while... nothing found
Searching for HiDrootkit's default dir... nothing found
Searching for t0rn's default files and dirs... nothing found
Searching for t0rn's v8 defaults... nothing found
Searching for Lion Worm default files and dirs... nothing found
Searching for RSHA's default files and dir... nothing found
Searching for RH-Sharpe's default files... nothing found
Searching for Ambient's rootkit (ark) default files and dirs... nothing found
Searching for suspicious files and dirs, it may take a while...
/usr/lib/debug/.build-id /lib/modules/4.8.0-36-generic/vdso/.build-id /lib/
    modules/4.8.0-52-generic/vdso/.build-id /lib/modules/4.8.0-49-generic/vdso/.build-id
/usr/lib/debug/.build-id /lib/modules/4.8.0-36-generic/vdso/.build-id /lib/
    modules/4.8.0-52-generic/vdso/.build-id /lib/modules/4.8.0-49-generic/vdso/.build-id
Searching for LPD Worm files and dirs... nothing found
Searching for Ramen Worm files and dirs... nothing found
Searching for Maniac files and dirs... nothing found
Searching for RK17 files and dirs... nothing found
Searching for Ducoci rootkit... nothing found
Searching for Adore Worm... nothing found
Searching for ShitC Worm... nothing found
Searching for Omega Worm... nothing found
Searching for Sadmind/IIS Worm... nothing found
Searching for MonKit... nothing found
Searching for Showtee... nothing found
Searching for OpticKit... nothing found
Searching for T.R.K... nothing found
Searching for Mithra... nothing found
Searching for LOC rootkit... nothing found
Searching for Romanian rootkit... nothing found
Searching for Suckit rootkit... nothing found
Searching for Volc rootkit... nothing found
Searching for Gold2 rootkit... nothing found
```

```
Searching for TC2 Worm default files and dirs... nothing found
Searching for Anonoying rootkit default files and dirs... nothing found
Searching for ZK rootkit default files and dirs... nothing found
Searching for ShKit rootkit default files and dirs... nothing found
Searching for AjaKit rootkit default files and dirs... nothing found
Searching for zaRwT rootkit default files and dirs... nothing found
Searching for Madalin rootkit default files... nothing found
Searching for Fu rootkit default files... nothing found
Searching for ESRK rootkit default files... nothing found
Searching for rootedoor... nothing found
Searching for ENYELKM rootkit default files... nothing found
Searching for common ssh-scanners default files... nothing found
Searching for Linux/Ebury - Operation Windigo ssh... not tested
Searching for 64-bit Linux Rootkit ... nothing found
Searching for 64-bit Linux Rootkit modules... nothing found
Searching for Mumblehard Linux ... nothing found
Searching for Backdoor.Linux.Mokes.a ... nothing found
Searching for Malicious TinyDNS ... nothing found
Searching for Linux.Xor.DDoS ... nothing found
Searching for Linux.Proxy.1.0 ... nothing found
Searching for suspect PHP files... nothing found
Searching for anomalies in shell history files... nothing found
Checking `asp'... not infected
Checking `bindshell'... not infected
Checking `lkm'... chkproc: nothing detected
chkdirs: nothing detected
Checking `rexedcs'... not found
Checking `sniffer'... enp0s3: PF_PACKET(/sbin/dhclient)
virbr0: not promisc and no PF_PACKET sockets
Checking `w55808'... not infected
Checking `wted'... chkwtmp: nothing deleted
Checking `scalper'... not infected
Checking `slapper'... not infected
Checking `z2'... user analyst deleted or never logged from lastlog!
Checking `chkutmp'...  The tty of the following user process(es) were not found
in /var/run/utmp !
! RUID          PID TTY    CMD
! analyst      2597 pts/5  bash
! root         3733 pts/5  sudo ./chkrootkit
! root         3734 pts/5  /bin/sh ./chkrootkit
! root         4748 pts/5  ./chkutmp
! root         4749 pts/5  sh -c ps ax -o "tty,pid,ruser,args"
! root         4750 pts/5  ps ax -o tty,pid,ruser,args
chkutmp: nothing deleted
Checking `OSX_RSPLUG'... not tested
analyst@cuckoo:~$
```

Piping Commands (3.3.2.6)

Although command line tools are usually designed to perform a specific, well-defined task, many commands can be combined to perform more complex tasks by a technique known as piping. Named after its defining character, the pipe (|), *piping* consists of chaining commands together, feeding the output of one command into the input of another.

For example, the **ls** command is used to display all the files and directories of a given directory. The **grep** command compares searches through a file or text looking for the specified string. If found, **grep** displays the entire contents of the folder where the string was found. The two commands, **ls** and **grep**, can be piped together to filter out the output of **ls**, as shown in Example 3-13 with the **ls -l | grep nimda** command.

Example 3-13   Output of the **grep** Command

```
[analyst@secOps ~]$ ls -l lab.support.files
total 584
-rw-r--r-- 1 analyst analyst    649 Jun 28  2017 apache_in_epoch.log
-rw-r--r-- 1 analyst analyst    126 Jun 28  2017 applicationX_in_epoch.log
drwxr-xr-x 4 analyst analyst   4096 Aug 24 12:36 attack_scripts
-rw-r--r-- 1 analyst analyst    102 Jul 20 09:37 confidential.txt
-rw-r--r-- 1 analyst analyst   2871 Dec 15  2016 cyops.mn
-rw-r--r-- 1 analyst analyst     75 May 24  2017 elk_services
-rw-r--r-- 1 analyst analyst    373 Feb 16  2017 h2_dropbear.banner
-rw-r--r-- 1 analyst analyst    147 Mar 21  2017 index.html
drwxr-xr-x 2 analyst analyst   4096 Aug 24 12:36 instructor
-rw-r--r-- 1 analyst analyst    255 May  2  2017 letter_to_grandma.txt
-rw-r--r-- 1 analyst analyst  24464 Feb  7  2017 logstash-tutorial.log
drwxr-xr-x 2 analyst analyst   4096 May 25  2017 malware
-rwxr-xr-x 1 analyst analyst    172 Jul 25 16:27 mininet_services
drwxr-xr-x 2 analyst analyst   4096 Feb 14  2017 openssl_lab
drwxr-xr-x 2 analyst analyst   4096 Aug 24 12:35 pcaps
drwxr-xr-x 7 analyst analyst   4096 Sep 20  2016 pox
-rw-r--r-- 1 analyst analyst 473363 Feb 16  2017 sample.img
-rw-r--r-- 1 analyst analyst     65 Feb 16  2017 sample.img_SHA256.sig
drwxr-xr-x 3 analyst analyst   4096 Aug 24 10:47 scripts
-rw-r--r-- 1 analyst analyst  25553 Feb 13  2017 SQL_Lab.pcap
[analyst@secOps ~]$ ls -l lab.support.files | grep ap
-rw-r--r-- 1 analyst analyst    649 Jun 28  2017 apache_in_epoch.log
-rw-r--r-- 1 analyst analyst    126 Jun 28  2017 applicationX_in_epoch.log
drwxr-xr-x 2 analyst analyst   4096 Aug 24 12:35 pcaps
-rw-r--r-- 1 analyst analyst  25553 Feb 13  2017 SQL_Lab.pcap
[analyst@secOps ~]$
```

Video Demonstration 3.3.2.7: Applications, Rootkits, and Piping Commands

Video

Refer to the online course to view this video.

Summary (3.4)

In this chapter, you learned how the Linux operation system is used in a SOC environment, including:

- Linux tools that are used for security monitoring and investigation
- How to use the Linux shell to work with directory and files and how to create, modify, copy, and move text files
- The difference between server and client applications

In this chapter, you also learned how to perform basic Linux administration tasks, including:

- How to view service configuration files
- What features need to be hardened on Linux devices
- The types and location of services logs used for monitoring purposes

You also learned about the various Linux file system types, including:

- ext2, ext3, and ext4
- NFS
- CDFS
- Swap file system
- HFS+
- Master boot record

You learned how roles and file permissions dictate which users or groups can access which files and whether those users or groups have Read, Write, or Execute permissions. You also learned how the root user or owner of a file can change permissions. These files can have hard links or symbolic links. A hard link is another file that points to the same location as the original file. A symbolic link, sometimes called a symlink or soft link, is similar to a hard link in that applying changes to the symbolic link will also change the original file.

Finally, in this chapter you learned how to perform basic security-related tasks on a Linux host, including:

- Installing and running applications from the command line
- Keeping the system up to date with **apt-get update** and **apt-get upgrade**
- Viewing the current processes and forks running in memory
- Using **chkrootkit** to check the computer for known rootkits

- Using piping to chain commands together, feeding one command output into the input of another command

As a cybersecurity analyst, you need a basic understanding of the features and characteristics of the Linux operating system and how Linux is used in a SOC environment.

Practice

The following activities provide practice with the topics introduced in this chapter. The Labs are available in the companion *CCNA Cybersecurity Operations Lab Manual* (ISBN 9781587134388).

Labs

Lab 3.1.2.6: Working with Text Files in the CLI

Lab 3.1.2.7: Getting Familiar with the Linux Shell

Lab 3.1.3.4: Linux Servers

Lab 3.2.1.4: Locating Log Files

Lab 3.2.2.4: Navigating the Linux Filesystem and Permission Settings

Check Your Understanding

Complete all the review questions listed here to test your understanding of the topics and concepts in this chapter. The appendix "Answers to 'Check Your Understanding' Questions" lists the answers.

1. What is the outcome when a Linux administrator enters the **man man** command?

   A. The **man man** command configures the network interface with a manual address.

   B. The **man man** command provides documentation about the **man** command.

   C. The **man man** command provides a list of commands available at the current prompt.

   D. The **man man** command opens the most recent log file.

2. What is a benefit of Linux being an open source operating system?

   A. Linux distributions are maintained by a single organization.

   B. Linux distributions must include free support without cost.

C. Linux distribution source code can be modified and then recompiled.

D. Linux distributions are simpler operating systems since they are not designed to be connected to a network.

3. Which types of files are used to manage services in a Linux system?

A. Device files

B. System files

C. Directory files

D. Configuration files

4. Which working environment is more user-friendly?

A. A CLI

B. A GUI

C. The command prompt

D. A hybrid GUI and CLI interface

5. Which Linux component would be used to access a short list of tasks the application can perform?

A. Launcher

B. Quicklist

C. Dash Search Box

D. System and Notification Menu

6. Which term is used to describe a running instance of a computer program?

A. Fork

B. Patch

C. Process

D. Package manager

7. Which type of tool is used by a Linux administrator to attack a computer or network to find vulnerabilities?

A. Firewall

B. PenTesting

C. Malware analysis

D. Intrusion detection system

8. Which method can be used to harden a computing device?

   A. Allow USB auto-detection.

   B. Force periodic password changes.

   C. Allow default services to remain enabled.

   D. Update patches on a strict annual basis irrespective of release date.

9. Consider the result of the **ls -l** command in the Linux output below. What are the group file permissions assigned to the analyst.txt file?

   ```
   ls -l analyst.txt
   -rwxrw-r-- sales staff 1028 May 28 15:50 analyst.txt
   ```

   A. Read only

   B. Read, write

   C. Full access

   D. Read, write, execute

## CHAPTER 4

Network Protocols and Services

Objectives

Upon completion of this chapter, you will be able to answer the following questions:

- What is the basic operation of data network communications?

- How do protocols enable network operations?

- How does Ethernet support network communication?

- How does the IPv4 protocol support network communications?

- How do IP addresses enable network communication?

- Which type of IPv4 addresses enable network communication?

- How does the default gateway enable network communications?

- How does the IPv6 protocol support network communications?

- How is ICMP used to test network connectivity?

- How do you use ping and traceroute utilities to test network connectivity?

- What are the roles of the MAC address and the IP address?

- What is the purpose of ARP?

- How do ARP requests impact network and host performance?

- How do transport layer protocols support network communication?

- How do the transport layer protocols operate?

- How do DHCP services enable network functionality?

- How do DNS services enable network functionality?

- How do NAT services enable network functionality?

- How do file transfer services enable network functionality?

- How do email services enable network functionality?

- How do HTTP services enable network functionality?

Key Terms

This chapter uses the following key terms. You can find the definitions in the Glossary.

network protocols   *page 123*

protocol suite   *page 124*

TCP/IP protocol suite   *page 126*

Domain Name System (DNS)   *page 126*

Bootstrap Protocol (BOOTP)   *page 126*

Dynamic Host Configuration Protocol (DHCP)   *page 126*

Introduction (4.0)

Cybersecurity analysts work to identify and analyze the traces of network security incidents. These traces consist of records of network events. These events, recorded in log files from various devices, are primarily composed of details of network protocol operations. Addresses identify which hosts connected to each other, within an organization, or to distant hosts on the Internet. Addresses held in log files also identify which hosts connected with, or attempted to connect with, hosts within an organization. Other traces, in the form of protocol addresses, identify what the network connections attempted to do, and whether this behavior was normal, suspicious, or damaging. Finally, network traces are recorded for the applications that enable us to receive and use information from the network. From all of these traces, cybersecurity analysts detect threats to the security of organizations and their data.

Cybersecurity analysts must understand the network on which normal data travels so that they can detect the abnormal behavior that is created by hackers, malevolent software, and dishonest users of the network. Protocols are at the heart of network communications, and network services support the tasks that we perform using the network. This chapter provides an overview of how networks normally behave through a discussion of the protocols in the TCP/IP suite of protocols, and associated services that enable us to accomplish tasks on computer networks.

Network Protocols (4.1)

In this section, you will learn how protocols enable network operations.

Network Communications Process (4.1.1)

In this topic, you will learn the basic operation of data network communications.

Views of the Network (4.1.1.1)

Networks come in all sizes. They can range from simple networks consisting of two computers to networks connecting millions of devices.

Home office networks and small office networks are often set up by individuals that work from a home or a remote office and need to connect to a corporate network or other centralized resources. Additionally, many self-employed entrepreneurs use home office and small office networks to advertise and sell products, order supplies and communicate with customers.

In businesses and large organizations, networks can be used on an even broader scale to provide consolidation, storage, and access to information on network servers. Networks also allow for rapid communication such as email, instant messaging, and collaboration among employees. In addition to internal benefits, many organizations use their networks to provide products and services to customers through their connection to the Internet.

The Internet is the largest network in existence. In fact, the term Internet means a "network of networks." The Internet is literally a collection of interconnected private and public networks.

Client-Server Communications (4.1.1.2)

All computers that are connected to a network and that participate directly in network communication are classified as hosts. Hosts are also called end devices, endpoints, or nodes. Much of the interaction between end devices is client-server traffic. For example, when you access a web page on the Internet, your web browser (the client) is accessing a server. When you send an email message, your email client will connect to an email server.

Servers are simply computers with specialized software. This software enables servers to provide information to other end devices on the network. A server can be single-purpose, providing only one service, such as web pages. A server can be multipurpose, providing a variety of services such as web pages, email, and file transfers.

Client computers have software installed, such as web browsers, email, and file transfer applications. This software enables them to request and display the information obtained from the server. A single computer can also run multiple types of client software. For example, a user can check email and view a web page while listening to Internet radio.

A Typical Session: Student (4.1.1.3)

A typical network user at school, at home, or in the office will normally use some type of computing device to establish many connections with network servers. Those servers could be located in the same room or around the world. Let's look at a few typical network communication sessions.

Terry is a high school student whose school has recently started a "bring your own device" (BYOD) program. Students are encouraged to use their cell phones or other devices such as tablets or laptops to access learning resources. Terry has just been given an assignment in language arts class to research the effects of World War I on the literature and art of the time. She enters the search terms she has chosen into a search engine app that she has opened on her cell phone.

Terry has connected her phone to the school Wi-Fi network. Her search is submitted from her phone to the school network wirelessly. Before her search can be sent, the data must be addressed so that it can find its way back to Terry. Her search terms are then represented as a string of binary data that has been encoded into radio waves.

Her search string is then converted to electrical signals that travel on the school's wired network until they reach the place at which the school's network connects to the Internet service provider's (ISP) network. A combination of technologies take Terry's search to the search engine website.

For example, Terry's data flows with the data of thousands of other users along a fiber-optic network that connects Terry's ISP with the several other ISPs, including the ISP that is used by the search engine company. Eventually, Terry's search string enters the search engine company's website and is processed by its powerful servers. The results are then encoded and addressed to Terry's school and her device.

All of these transitions and connections happen in a fraction of a second, and Terry has started on her path to learning about her subject.

A Typical Session: Gamer (4.1.1.4)

Michelle loves computer games. She has a powerful gaming console that she uses to play games against other players, watch movies, and play music. Michelle connects her game console directly to her network with a copper network cable.

Michelle's network, like many home networks, connects to an ISP using a router and modem. These devices allow Michelle's home network to connect to a cable TV network that belongs to Michelle's ISP. The cable wires for Michelle's neighborhood all connect to a central point on a telephone pole and then connect to a fiber-optic network. This fiber-optic network connects many neighborhoods that are served by Michelle's ISP.

All those fiber-optic cables connect to telecommunications services that provide access to the high-capacity connections. These connections allow thousands of users in homes, government offices, and businesses to connect Internet destinations around the world.

Michelle has connected her game console to a company that hosts a very popular online game. Michelle is registered with the company, and its servers keep track of Michelle's scores, experiences, and game assets. Michelle's actions in her game become data that is sent to the gamer network. Michelle's moves are broken up to groups of binary data that each consist of a string of zeros and ones. Information that identifies Michelle, the game she is playing, and Michelle's network location are added to the game data. The pieces of data that represent Michelle's game play are sent at high speed to the game provider's network. The results are returned to Michelle in the form of graphics and sounds.

All of this happens so quickly that Michelle can compete with hundreds of other gamers in real time.

A Typical Session: Surgeon (4.1.1.5)

Dr. Ismael Awad is an oncologist who performs surgery on cancer patients. He frequently needs to consult with radiologists and other specialists on patient cases. The hospital that Dr. Awad works for subscribes to a special service called a cloud. The cloud allows medical data, including patient X-rays and MRIs, to be stored in a central location that is accessed over the Internet. In this way, the hospital does not need to manage paper patient records and X-ray films.

When a patient has an X-ray taken, the image is digitized as computer data. The X-ray is then prepared by hospital computers to be sent to the medical cloud service. Because security is very important when working with medical data, the hospital uses network services that encrypt the image data and patient information. This encrypted data cannot be intercepted and read as it travels across the Internet to the cloud service provider's data centers. The data is addressed so that it can be routed to the cloud provider's data center to reach the correct services that provide storage and retrieval of high-resolution digital images.

Dr. Awad and the patient's care team can connect to this special service, meet with other doctors in audio conferences, and discuss patient records to decide on the best treatment that can be provided to the patient. Dr. Awad can work with specialists from diverse locations to view the medical images and other patient data and discuss the case.

All of this interaction is digital and takes place using networked services that are provided by the medical cloud service.

Tracing the Path (4.1.1.6)

We tend to think about the data networks we use in our daily lives as we think about driving a car. We do not really care what happens in the engine as long as the car takes us where we want to go. However, just like a car's mechanic knows the details of how a car operates, cybersecurity analysts need to have a deep understanding of how networks operate.

When we connect to a website to read social media or shop, we seldom care about how our data gets to the website and how data from the website gets to us. We are not aware of the many technologies that enable us to use the Internet. A combination of copper and fiber-optic cables that go over land and under the ocean carry data traffic. High-speed wireless and satellite technologies are also used. These connections connect telecommunications facilities and ISPs that are distributed throughout the world, as shown in Figure 4-1.

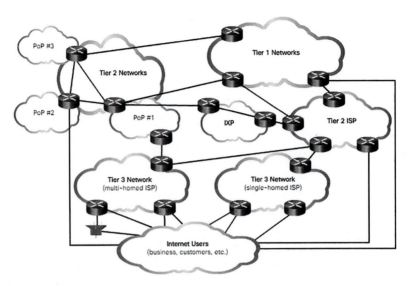

Figure 4-1   Tracing the Path

These global Tier 1 and Tier 2 ISPs connect portions of the Internet together, usually through an Internet Exchange Point (IXP). Larger networks will connect to Tier 2 networks through a Point of Presence (PoP), which is usually a location in the building where physical connections to the ISP are made. The Tier 3 ISPs connect homes and businesses to the Internet.

Because of different relationships between ISPs and telecommunications companies, traffic from a computer to an Internet server can take many paths. The traffic of a user in one country can take a very indirect path to reach its destination. The traffic might first travel from the local ISP to a facility that has connections to many other ISPs. A user's Internet traffic can go many hundreds of miles in one direction only to be routed in a completely different direction to reach its destination. Some of the traffic can take certain routes to reach the destination, and then take completely different routes to return.

Cybersecurity analysts must be able to determine the origin of traffic that enters the network, and the destination of traffic that leaves it. Understanding the path that network traffic takes is essential to this.

Lab 4.1.1.7: Tracing a Route

In this lab, you will use two route tracing utilities to examine the Internet pathway to destination networks. First, you will verify connectivity to a website. Second, you will use the traceroute utility on the Linux command line. Third, you will use a web-based traceroute tool.

Communications Protocols (4.1.2)

In this topic, you will learn how protocols enable network operations.

What Are Protocols? (4.1.2.1)

Simply having a wired or wireless physical connection between end devices is not enough to enable communication. For communication to occur, devices must know "how" to communicate. Communication, whether by face-to-face or over a network, is governed by rules called protocols. These protocols are specific to the type of communication method occurring.

For example, consider two people communicating face-to-face. Prior to communicating, they must agree on how to communicate. If the communication is using voice, they must first agree on the language. Next, when they have a message to share, they must be able to format that message in a way that is understandable. For example, if someone uses the English language but poor sentence structure, the message can easily be misunderstood.

Network protocol communication is the same way. Network protocols provide the means for computers to communicate on networks. *Network protocols* dictate the message encoding, formatting, encapsulation, size, timing, and delivery options, as shown in Figure 4-2. As a cybersecurity analyst, you must be very familiar with structure of protocols and how they are used in network communications.

Figure 4-2 Network Protocol Characteristics

Network Protocol Suites (4.1.2.2)

A *protocol suite* is a set of protocols that work together to provide comprehensive network communication services. A protocol suite may be specified by a standards organization or developed by a vendor.

For devices to successfully communicate, a network protocol suite must describe precise requirements and interactions. Networking protocols define a common format and set of rules for exchanging messages between devices. Some common networking protocols are Hypertext Transfer Protocol (HTTP), Transmission Control Protocol (TCP), and Internet Protocol (IP).

Note

IP in this course refers to both the IPv4 and IPv6 protocols. IPv6 is the most recent version of IP and will eventually replace the more common IPv4.

Figures 4-3 through 4-6 illustrate the role of networking protocols:

- How the message is formatted or structured, as shown in Figure 4-3

- The process by which networking devices share information about pathways with other networks, as shown in Figure 4-4

- How and when error and system messages are passed between devices, as shown in Figure 4-5

- The setup and termination of data transfer sessions, as shown in Figure 4-6

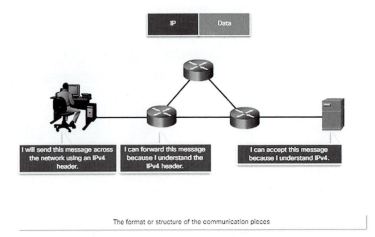

Figure 4-3   The Role of Protocols: Format and Structure

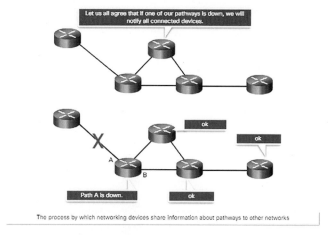

Figure 4-4   The Role of Protocols: Routers Sharing Path Information

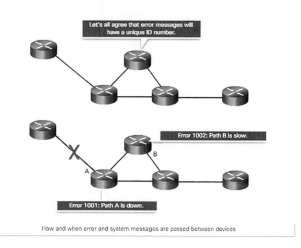

Figure 4-5   The Role of Protocols: Error Messages

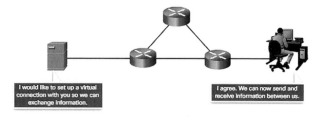

Figure 4-6   The Role of Protocols: Session Setup and Termination

The TCP/IP Protocol Suite (4.1.2.3)

Networks today use the *TCP/IP protocol suite*. Figure 4-7 shows the protocols of the TCP/IP protocol suite.

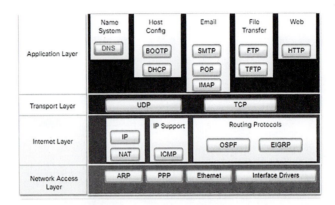

Figure 4-7 TCP/IP Protocol Suite and Communication Process

Table 4-1 lists a description of each protocol shown in Figure 4-7.

Table 4-1 TCP/IP Protocols and Standards Descriptions

Name	Acronym	Description
Domain Name System	*DNS*	Translates domain names, such as cisco.com, into IP addresses.
Bootstrap Protocol	*BOOTP*	Enables a diskless workstation to discover its own IP address, the IP address of a BOOTP server on the network, and a file to be loaded into memory to boot the machine. BOOTP is being superseded by DHCP.
Dynamic Host Configuration Protocol	*DHCP*	Dynamically assigns IP addresses to client stations at startup. Allows the addresses to be reused when no longer needed.
Simple Mail Transfer Protocol	*SMTP*	Enables clients to send email to a mail server. Enables servers to send email to other servers.
Post Office Protocol version 3	*POP3*	Enables clients to retrieve email from a mail server. Downloads email from the mail server to the desktop.
Internet Message Access Protocol	*IMAP*	Enables clients to access email stored on a mail server. Maintains email on the server.
File Transfer Protocol	*FTP*	Sets rules that enable a user on one host to access and transfer files to and from another host over a network. A reliable, connection-oriented, and acknowledged file delivery protocol.

Name	Acronym	Description
Trivial File Transfer Protocol	*TFTP*	A simple, connectionless file transfer protocol. A best-effort, unacknowledged file delivery protocol. Utilizes less overhead than FTP.
Hypertext Transfer Protocol	*HTTP*	Set of rules for exchanging text, graphic images, sound, video, and other multimedia files on the World Wide Web.
User Datagram Protocol	*UDP*	Enables a process running on one host to send packets to a process running on another host. Does not confirm successful datagram transmission.
Transmission Control Protocol	*TCP*	Enables reliable communication between processes running on separate hosts. Reliable, acknowledged transmissions that confirm successful delivery.
Internet Protocol	*IP*	Receives message segments from the transport layer. Packages messages into packets. Addresses packets for end-to-end delivery over an Internetwork.
Network Address Translation	*NAT*	Translates IP addresses from a private network into globally unique public IP addresses.
Internet Control Message Protocol	*ICMP*	Provides feedback from a destination host to a source host about errors in packet delivery.
Open Shortest Path First	*OSPF*	Link-state routing protocol. Hierarchical design based on areas. Open standard interior routing protocol.
Enhanced Interior Gateway Routing Protocol	*EIGRP*	Cisco proprietary routing protocol. Uses composite metric based on bandwidth, delay, load, and reliability.
Address Resolution Protocol	*ARP*	Provides dynamic address mapping between an IP address and a hardware address.
Point-to-Point Protocol	*PPP*	Provides a means of encapsulating packets for transmission over a serial link.
Ethernet		Defines the rules for wiring and signaling standards of the network access layer.
Interface Drivers		Provides instruction to a machine for the control of a specific interface on a network device.

The individual protocols are organized in layers using the TCP/IP protocol model: Application, Transport, Internet, and Network Access Layers. TCP/IP protocols are specific to the Application, Transport, and Internet layers. The network access layer protocols are responsible for delivering the IP packet over the physical medium, such as through a network cable or wireless signal.

The TCP/IP protocol suite is implemented on both the sending and receiving hosts to provide end-to-end delivery of messages over a network. TCP/IP has standardized the way the computers communicate, which has enabled the Internet as we know it today. Unfortunately, this widespread usage has attracted the attention of people who want to misuse networks. Much of the work of the cybersecurity analyst concerns analysis of the behavior of the TCP/IP suite of protocols.

Format, Size, and Timing (4.1.2.4)

Protocols define the format, size, and timing of different forms of messages.

Format

When you send an email, protocols of the TCP/IP protocol suite are used by your device to format your message for sending on the network. This is similar to you sending a letter in the mail. You place your letter in an envelope. The envelope has the address of the sender and receiver, each located at the proper place on the envelope. If the destination address and formatting are not correct, the letter is not delivered. The process of placing one message format (the letter) inside another message format (the envelope) is called encapsulation. De-encapsulation occurs when the process is reversed by the recipient and the letter is removed from the envelope.

Just as a letter is encapsulated in an envelope for delivery, so too are computer messages encapsulated. Each computer message is encapsulated in a specific format, called a frame, before it is sent over the network. The frame structure is discussed later in the chapter.

Size

Another rule of communication is size. When people communicate in person or over the phone, a conversation is usually made up of many smaller sentences to ensure that each part of the message is received and understood.

Likewise, when a long message is sent from one host to another over a network, it is necessary to break the message into many frames, as shown in Figure 4-8. Each frame will have its own addressing information. At the receiving host, the individual frames are reconstructed into the original message.

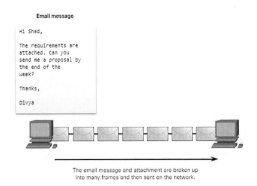

Figure 4-8   Breaking Up a Message

Timing

Timing includes the access method (when can a host send), flow control (how much information can a host send at one time), and response timeout (how long to wait for a response). This chapter will explore how network protocols manage these timing issues.

Unicast, Multicast, and Broadcast (4.1.2.5)

A message can be delivered in different ways. Sometimes, a person wants to communicate information to a single individual. At other times, the person may need to send information to a group of people at the same time, or even to all people in the same area.

Hosts on a network use similar delivery options to communicate.

A one-to-one delivery option is referred to as a *unicast*, meaning there is only a single destination for the message, as shown in Figure 4-9.

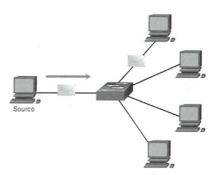

Figure 4-9   Unicast Message

When a host needs to send messages using a one-to-many delivery option, it is referred to as a *multicast*, as shown in Figure 4-10.

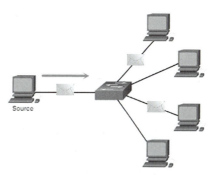

Figure 4-10   Multicast Message

If all hosts on the network need to receive the message at the same time, a *broadcast* may be used. Broadcasting represents a one-to-all message delivery option, as shown in Figure 4-11.

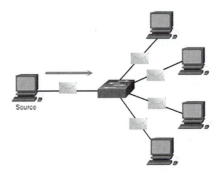

Figure 4-11   Broadcast Message

Reference Models (4.1.2.6)

As you learned earlier, the TCP/IP protocol suite is represented by a four-layer model: Application, Transport, Internet, and Network Access. Another popular reference model is the Open Systems Interconnection (OSI) model, which uses a seven-layer model, as shown Figure 4-12. In networking literature, when a layer is referred to by a number, such as Layer 4, then the reference is using the *Open Systems Interconnection (OSI) model*. Reference to layers in the TCP/IP model use the name of the layer, such as the transport layer.

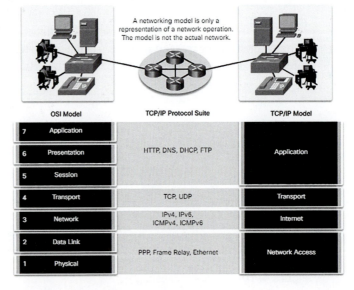

Figure 4-12   Comparing the OSI and TCP/IP Models

The OSI Reference Model

The OSI model provides an extensive list of functions and services that can occur at each layer. It also describes the interaction of each layer with the layers directly above and below. Table 4-2 describes each layer of the OSI model.

Table 4-2   Layers of the OSI Model

Number	Layer Name	Description
7	*Application*	The application layer contains protocols used for process-to-process communications.
6	*Presentation*	The presentation layer provides for common representation of the data transferred between application layer services.
5	*Session*	The session layer provides services to the presentation layer to organize its dialogue and to manage data exchange.
4	*Transport*	The transport layer defines services to segment, transfer, and reassemble the data for individual communications between the end devices.
3	*Network*	The network layer provides services to exchange the individual pieces of data over the network between identified end devices.
2	*Data Link*	The data link layer protocols describe methods for exchanging data frames between devices over a common media.
1	*Physical*	The physical layer protocols describe the mechanical, electrical, functional, and procedural means to activate, maintain, and deactivate physical connections for bit transmission to and from a network device.

The TCP/IP Protocol Model

The TCP/IP protocol model for internetwork communications was created in the early 1970s. As shown in Figure 4-13, it defines four categories of functions that must occur for communications to be successful.

Three Addresses (4.1.2.7)

Network protocols require that addresses be used for network communication. Addressing is used by the client to send requests and other data to a server. The server uses the client's address to return the requested data to the client that requested it.

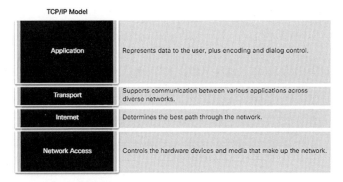

Figure 4-13   Layers of the TCP/IP Model

Protocols operate at layers. The OSI transport, network, and data link layers all use addressing in some form. The transport layer uses protocol addresses in the form of port numbers to identify network applications that should handle client and server data. The network layer specifies addresses that identify the networks that clients and servers are attached to and the clients and servers themselves. Finally, the data link layer specifies the devices on the local LAN that should handle data frames. All three addresses are required for client-server communication, as shown in Figure 4-14.

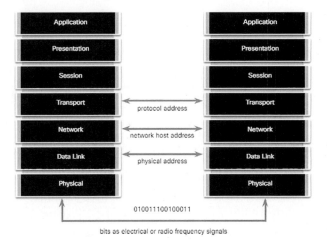

Figure 4-14   The Three Addresses and Layers

Encapsulation (4.1.2.8)

As you have seen, data is divided into smaller, more manageable pieces to send over the network. This division of data into smaller pieces is called segmentation. Segmenting messages has two primary benefits:

- *Segmentation* (Figure 4-15): This process increases the efficiency of network communications. If part of the message fails to make it to the destination, due to failure in the network or network congestion, only the missing parts need to be retransmitted.

- *Multiplexing* (Figure 4-16): By sending smaller individual pieces from source to destination, many different conversations can be interleaved on the network. This is called multiplexing.

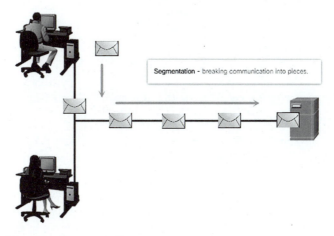

Figure 4-15   Message Segmentation

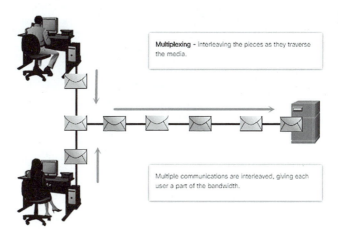

Figure 4-16   Message Multiplexing

In network communications, each segment of the message must be properly labeled to ensure that it gets to the correct destination and can be reassembled into the content of the original message, as shown in Figure 4-17.

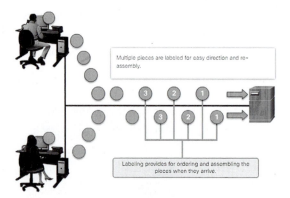

Figure 4-17   Labeling the Message

As application data is passed down the protocol stack on its way to be transmitted across the network media, it is encapsulated with various protocol information at each level.

The form that an encapsulated piece of data takes at any layer is called a *protocol data unit (PDU)*. Each succeeding layer encapsulates the PDU that it receives from the layer above in accordance with the protocol being used. At each stage of the process, a PDU has a different name to reflect its new functions. Although there is no universal naming convention for PDUs, in this course, the PDUs are named according to the protocols of the TCP/IP suite, as shown in the Figure 4-18.

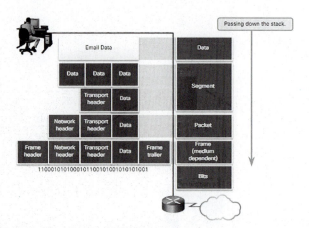

Figure 4-18   Encapsulation Down the Layers

When sending messages on a network, the encapsulation process works from top to bottom. At each layer, the upper layer information is considered data within the encapsulated protocol. For example, the TCP segment is considered data within the

IP packet. Figures 4-19 through 4-23 demonstrate the encapsulation process as a web server sends a web page to a web client.

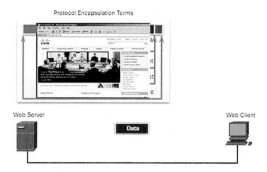

Figure 4-19 Encapsulation: Data

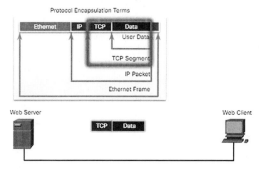

Figure 4-20 Encapsulation: TCP

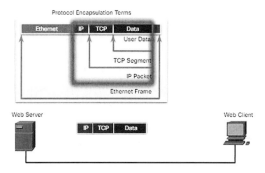

Figure 4-21 Encapsulation: IP

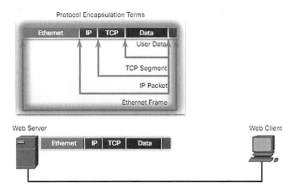

Figure 4-22   Encapsulation: Ethernet

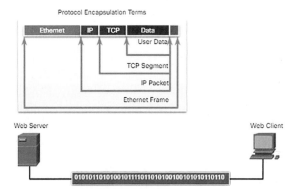

Figure 4-23   Encapsulation: Bits

Messages sent across the network are first converted into bits by the sending host. Each bit is encoded into a pattern of sounds, light waves, or electrical impulses depending on the network media over which the bits are transmitted. The destination host receives and decodes the signals in order to interpret the message.

This process is reversed at the receiving host, and is known as de-encapsulation. The data is de-encapsulated as it moves up the stack toward the end-user application. Figures 4-24 and 4-25 demonstrate the de-encapsulation process.

Scenario: Sending and Receiving a Web Page (4.1.2.9)

To summarize network communication processes and protocols, consider the scenario of sending and receiving a web page. Figure 4-26 lists some of the protocols used between a web server and a web client:

- **HTTP:** This application protocol governs the way a web server and a web client interact.

- **TCP:** This transport protocol manages individual conversations. TCP divides the HTTP messages into smaller pieces, called segments. TCP is also responsible for controlling the size and rate at which messages are exchanged between the server and the client.

- **IP:** This Internet protocol is responsible for taking the formatted segments from TCP, encapsulating them into packets, assigning them the appropriate addresses, and delivering them to the destination host.

- **Ethernet:** This network access protocol is responsible for taking the packets from IP and formatting them to be transmitted over the media.

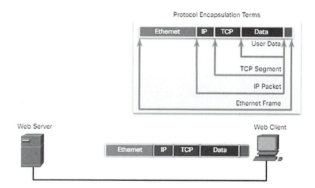

Figure 4-24   Receiving the Message

Figure 4-25   Displaying the Web Page

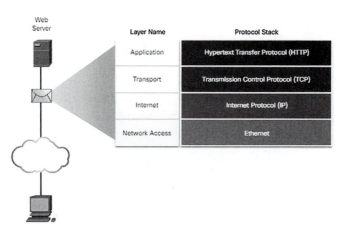

Figure 4-26 Interaction of Protocols

In the previously shown Figures 4-19 through 4-25 the complete communication process is demonstrated using an example of a web server transmitting data to a client and the client receiving the data:

1. The web server prepared the Hypertext Markup Language (HTML) page as data to be sent.

2. The application protocol HTTP header is added to the front of the HTML data. The header contains various information, including the HTTP version that the server is using and a status code indicating it has information for the web client.

3. The HTTP application layer protocol delivers the HTML-formatted web page data to the transport layer. TCP segments the data adding source and destination port numbers.

4. The IP information is added to the front of the TCP information. IP assigns the appropriate source and destination IP addresses. The TCP segment has now been encapsulated in an IP packet.

5. The Ethernet protocol adds information to both ends of the IP packet to create a frame. This frame is delivered through the network towards the web client.

6. The client receives the data link frames that contain the data. Each protocol header is processed and then removed in the opposite order it was added. The Ethernet information is processed and removed, followed by the IP protocol information, the TCP information, and finally the HTTP information.

7. The web page information is then passed on to the client's web browser software.

Cybersecurity analysts are adept at using tools to view the behavior of network protocols. For example, Wireshark captures all the details of the protocols encapsulated in packets and data that travels through the network. This course will focus on the use of Wireshark and the interpretation of Wireshark data.

Lab 4.1.2.10: Introduction to Wireshark

Wireshark is a software protocol analyzer, or "packet sniffer" application, used for network troubleshooting, analysis, software and protocol development, and education. Wireshark is used throughout the course to demonstrate network concepts. In this lab, you will use Wireshark to capture and analyze network traffic.

Ethernet and Internet Protocol (IP) (4.2)

In this section, you will learn how the Ethernet and IP protocols support network communication.

Ethernet (4.2.1)

In this topic, you will learn how Ethernet supports network communication.

The Ethernet Protocol (4.2.1.1)

Ethernet operates in the data link layer and the physical layer, as shown in Figure 4-27. It is a family of networking technologies that are defined in the IEEE 802.2 and 802.3 standards. Ethernet relies on the two separate sublayers of the data link layer to operate, the *Logical Link Control (LLC)* and the *Media Access Control (MAC)* sublayers.

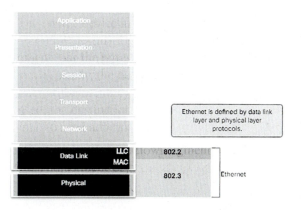

Figure 4-27   Ethernet

LLC is responsible for communication with the network layer. MAC is implemented by the computer's network interface card (NIC). The MAC sublayer has two primary responsibilities:

- **Data encapsulation:** Ethernet encapsulates the IP packet into a frame, adding timing information, destination and source MAC addresses, and an error checking feature.

- **Media access control:** Ethernet manages the process of converting the frame into bits and sending the frame out onto the network. In older wired networks, devices could not send and receive data at the same time. This is still the case for wireless networks. In such situations, Ethernet use a process to determine when a device can send and what to do if the data sent by two devices collides on the network. This process is discussed later in the chapter.

The Ethernet Frame (4.2.1.2)

The minimum Ethernet frame size is 64 bytes and the maximum is 1518 bytes. This includes all bytes from the Destination MAC Address field through the Frame Check Sequence (FCS) field. The Preamble field is not included when describing the size of a frame.

Any frame less than 64 bytes in length is considered a "collision fragment" or "runt frame." Frames with more than 1518 bytes are considered "jumbo frames" or "baby giant frames."

If the size of a transmitted frame is less than the minimum or greater than the maximum, the receiving device drops the frame. Dropped frames are likely to be the result of collisions or other unwanted signals and are therefore considered invalid.

Figure 4-28 shows the structure of the Ethernet II frame.

Figure 4-28   Ethernet II Frame Fields

Table 4-3 describes the function of each field in the Ethernet frame.

Table 4-3   Description of the Ethernet Frame Fields

Frame Field	Description
Preamble and Start Frame Delimiter fields	The Preamble field (7 bytes) and Start Frame Delimiter (SFD)—also called Start of Frame—field (1 byte) are used for synchronization between the sending and receiving devices. These first 8 bytes of the frame are used to get the attention of the receiving nodes. Essentially, the first few bytes tell the receivers to get ready to receive a new frame.
Destination MAC Address field	This 6-byte field is the identifier for the intended recipient. As you will recall, this address is used by Layer 2 to assist devices in determining if a frame is addressed to them. The address in the frame is compared to the MAC address in the device. If there is a match, the device accepts the frame. Can be a unicast, multicast, or broadcast address.
Source MAC Address field	This 6-byte field identifies the frame's originating NIC or interface. Must be a unicast address.
EtherType field	This 2-byte field identifies the upper layer protocol encapsulated in the Ethernet frame. Common values are, in hexadecimal, 0x800 for IPv4, 0x86DD for IPv6, and 0x806 for ARP.
Data field	This field (46–1500 bytes) contains the encapsulated data from a higher layer, which is a generic Layer 3 PDU, or more commonly, an IPv4 packet. All frames must be at least 64 bytes long. If a small packet is encapsulated, additional bits called a pad are used to increase the size of the frame to this minimum size.
Frame Check Sequence field	The Frame Check Sequence (FCS) field (4 bytes) is used to detect errors in a frame. It uses a cyclic redundancy check (CRC). The sending device includes the results of a CRC in the FCS field of the frame. The receiving device receives the frame and generates a CRC to look for errors. If the calculations match, no error occurred. Calculations that do not match are an indication that the data has changed; therefore, the frame is dropped. A change in the data could be the result of a disruption of the electrical signals that represent the bits.

MAC Address Format (4.2.1.3)

An Ethernet MAC address is a 48-bit binary value expressed as 12 hexadecimal digits (4 bits per hexadecimal digit). Hexadecimal digits use the numbers 0 to 9 and the letters A to F. Figure 4-29 shows the equivalent decimal and hexadecimal values for binary 0000 to 1111. Hexadecimal is commonly used to represent binary data. IPv6 addresses are another example of hexadecimal addressing.

Depending on the device and the operating system, you will see various representations of MAC addresses, as displayed in Figure 4-30.

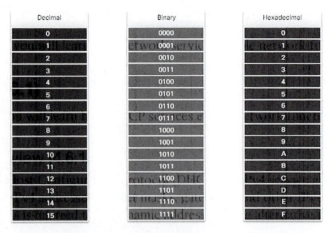

Figure 4-29   Decimal, Binary, and Hexadecimal Numbering Systems

Figure 4-30   Different Representations of MAC Addresses

All data that travels on the network is encapsulated in Ethernet frames. A cyber-security analyst should be able to interpret the Ethernet data that is captured by protocol analyzers and other tools.

Activity 4.2.1.4: Ethernet Frame Fields

Refer to the online course to complete this Activity.

IPv4 (4.2.2)

In this topic, you will learn how the IPv4 protocol supports network communications.

IPv4 Encapsulation (4.2.2.1)

As we know, Ethernet operates at the data link and physical layers of the OSI model. We will now focus on the network layer. Just as the data link layer encapsulates IP packets as frames, the network layer encapsulates segments from the transport layer into IP packets, as shown in Figure 4-31.

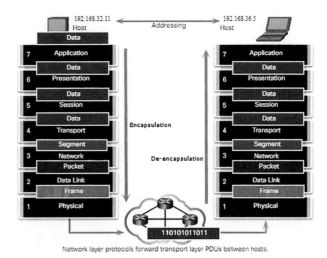

Figure 4-31   The Exchange of Data

IP encapsulates the transport layer segment by adding an IP header. This header includes information that is necessary to deliver the packet to the destination host.

Figure 4-32 illustrates how the transport layer PDU is then encapsulated by the network layer PDU to create an IP packet.

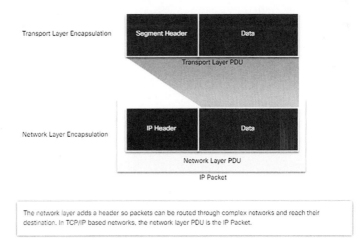

Figure 4-32   Network Layer PDU = IP Packet

IPv4 Characteristics (4.2.2.2)

The basic characteristics of IP, as shown in Figure 4-33, are

- **Connectionless:** No connection with the destination is established before sending data packets.

- **Best effort:** IP is inherently unreliable because packet delivery is not guaranteed.

- **Media independent:** Operation is independent of the medium (i.e., copper, fiber optic, or wireless) carrying the data.

Figure 4-33   Characteristics of the IP Protocol

Connectionless

IP is *connectionless*, meaning that no dedicated end-to-end connection is created before data is sent. As shown in Figure 4-34, connectionless communication is conceptually similar to sending a letter to someone without notifying the recipient in advance.

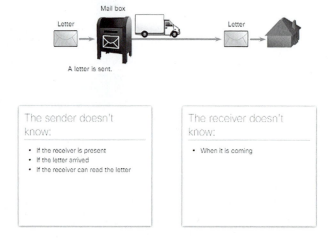

Figure 4-34   Connectionless Communication: Mail Analogy

Connectionless data communications work on the same principle. As shown in Figure 4-35, IP requires no initial exchange of control information to establish an end-to-end connection before packets are forwarded.

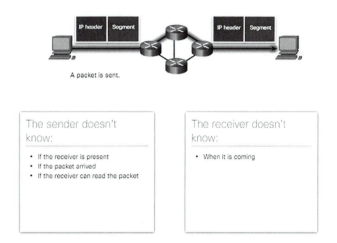

Figure 4-35   Connectionless Communication over Networks

IP also does not require additional fields in the header to maintain an established connection. This process greatly reduces the overhead of IP. However, with no pre-established end-to-end connection, senders are unaware whether destination devices are present and functional when sending packets, nor are they aware if the destination receives the packet, or if they are able to access and read the packet.

Best Effort

Figure 4-36 illustrates the unreliable, or best-effort, delivery characteristic of the IP protocol. The IP protocol does not guarantee that all packets that are delivered are, in fact, received.

Unreliable means that IP does not have the capability to manage and recover from undelivered or corrupt packets. This is because while IP packets are sent with information about the location of delivery, they contain no information that can be processed to inform the sender whether delivery was successful. Packets may arrive at the destination corrupted, out of sequence, or not at all. IP provides no capability for packet retransmissions if errors occur.

If out-of-order packets are delivered, or packets are missing, then upper layer services must resolve these issues. This allows IP to function very efficiently. In the TCP/IP protocol suite, reliability is the role of the transport layer, as we will discuss later in the chapter.

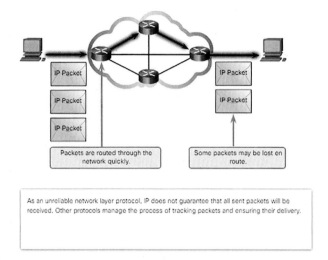

Figure 4-36   Best Effort Process

Media Independent

IP operates independently of the media that carry the data at lower layers of the protocol stack. As shown in Figure 4-37, IP packets can be sent as electronic signals over copper cable, as optical signals over fiber, or wirelessly as radio signals.

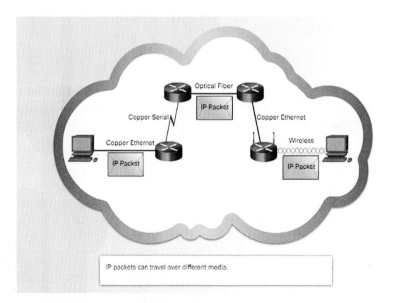

Figure 4-37   Media Independent Process

It is the responsibility of the data link layer to take an IP packet and prepare it for transmission over the communications medium. This means that the transport of IP packets is not limited to any particular medium.

There is, however, one major characteristic of the media that the network layer considers: the maximum size of the PDU that each medium can transport. This characteristic is referred to as the *maximum transmission unit (MTU)*. Part of the control communication between the data link layer and the network layer is the establishment of a maximum size for the packet. The data link layer passes the MTU value up to the network layer. The network layer then determines how large packets can be.

In some cases, an intermediate device, usually a router, must split up a packet when forwarding it from one medium to another medium with a smaller MTU. This process is called fragmenting the packet, or fragmentation.

Interactive Graphic

Activity 4.2.2.3: IPv4 Characteristics

Refer to the online course to complete this Activity.

The IPv4 Packet (4.2.2.4)

An IPv4 packet header consists of fields containing important information about the packet. These fields contain binary numbers which are examined by the Layer 3 process. The binary values of each field identify various settings of the IP packet. Protocol header diagrams, which are read left to right, and top down, provide a visual to refer to when discussing protocol fields. The IP protocol header diagram in Figure 4-38 identifies the fields of an IPv4 packet.

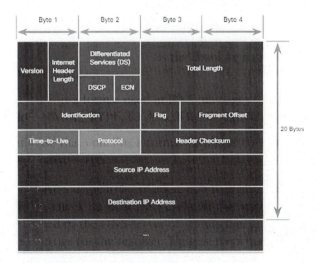

Figure 4-38 IPv4 Packet Headers

The fields in the IPv4 packet header are discussed in more detail later in the course.

The two most commonly referenced fields are the source and destination IP addresses. These fields identify where the packet is coming from and where it is going.

Cybersecurity analysts must have a firm grasp of the operation of IP and the meaning of IP data that is captured by protocol analyzers and other network devices. This data is mostly in the form of the information contained in IP packet headers.

Video

Video Demonstration 4.2.2.5: Sample IPv4 Headers in Wireshark

Refer to the online course to view this video.

IPv4 Addressing Basics (4.2.3)

In this topic, you will learn how IP addresses enable network communication.

IPv4 Address Notation (4.2.3.1)

An IPv4 address is simply a series of 32 binary bits (ones and zeros). It is very difficult for humans to read a binary IPv4 address. For this reason, the 32 bits are grouped into four 8-bit bytes called octets. Each *octet* is represented as its decimal value, separated by a decimal point or period. This is referred to as *dotted-decimal* notation.

When a host is configured with an IPv4 address, it is entered as a dotted-decimal number such as 192.168.10.10. The equivalent address in binary is 1100000.10101000. 00001010.00001010. The conversion to dotted-decimal is shown in Figure 4-39.

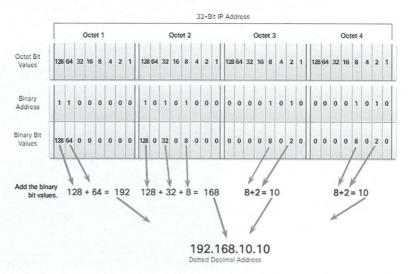

Figure 4-39   Converting Binary to Dotted-Decimal

> **Note**
>
> If you are new to binary-to-decimal conversion, search the Internet for tutorials. Some proficiency in binary will be helpful in your job as a cybersecurity analyst.

IPv4 Host Address Structure (4.2.3.2)

An IPv4 address is a hierarchical address that is made up of a network portion and a host portion. When determining the network portion versus the host portion, it is necessary to look at the 32-bit stream. Within the 32-bit stream, a portion of the bits identifies the network, and a portion of the bits identifies the host, as shown in Figure 4-40.

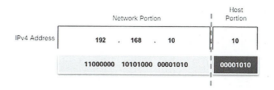

Figure 4-40   IPv4 Address Structure

The bits within the network portion of the address must be identical for all devices that reside in the same network. The bits within the host portion of the address must be unique to identify a specific host within a network. For example, if you look at the IPv4 addresses for various devices in your home network, you will most likely see the same network portion. Example 4-1 shows the IPv4 configuration for a Windows computer.

Example 4-1   Checking IP Configuration on a Windows PC

```
C:\> ipconfig

Windows IP Configuration

Ethernet adapter Ethernet:

   Connection-specific DNS Suffix   . :
   Link-local IPv6 Address . . . . . : fe80::1074:d6c8:f89d:43ad%18
   IPv4 Address. . . . . . . . . . . : 192.168.10.10
   Subnet Mask . . . . . . . . . . . : 255.255.255.0
   Default Gateway . . . . . . . . . : 192.168.10.1

<output omitted>

C:\>
```

Figure 4-41 shows the IPv4 address for an iPhone.

Figure 4-41   iPhone IPv4 Address

Figure 4-42 shows the IPv4 configuration for an Xbox One gaming console. Notice that all three devices share the same network address portion, 192.168.10, and that each device has a unique host portion, .10, .7, and .12, respectively.

Figure 4-42   Xbox One IPv4 Address

But how do hosts know which portion of the 32 bits identifies the network and which portion identifies the host? That is the job of the subnet mask.

IPv4 Subnet Mask and Network Address (4.2.3.3)

The subnet mask is logically ANDed with the host address to determine the network address. Logical AND is the comparison of 2 bits that produce the results shown in Figure 4-43. Note how only a 1 AND 1 produces a 1.

```
1 AND 1 = 1
0 AND 1 = 0
0 AND 0 = 0
1 AND 0 = 0
```

Figure 4-43 Logical AND Operation

To identify the network address of an IPv4 host, the IPv4 address is logically ANDed, bit by bit, with the subnet mask. ANDing between the address and the subnet mask yields the network address.

To illustrate how AND is used to discover a network address, consider a host with the IPv4 address 192.168.10.10 and a subnet mask of 255.255.255.0. Figure 4-44 displays the host IPv4 address and converted binary address.

IP address	192	.	168	.	10	.	10
Binary	11000000		10101000		00001010		00001010

Figure 4-44 Host IP Binary Address

The host subnet mask binary address is added in Figure 4-45.

IP address	192	.	168	.	10	.	10
Binary	11000000		10101000		00001010		00001010
Subnet mask	255	.	255	.	255	.	0
	11111111		11111111		11111111		00000000

Figure 4-45 Binary Address of 255.255.255.0

The yellow highlighted sections in Figure 4-46 identify the AND bits that produced a binary 1 in the AND Results row. All other bit comparisons produced binary 0s. Notice how the last octet no longer has any binary 1 bits.

Finally, Figure 4-47 displays the resulting network address 192.168.10.0 255.255.255.0. Therefore, host 192.168.10.10 is on network 192.168.10.0 255.255.255.0.

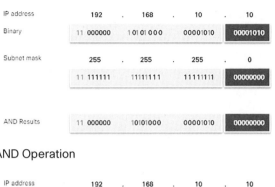

Figure 4-46   AND Operation

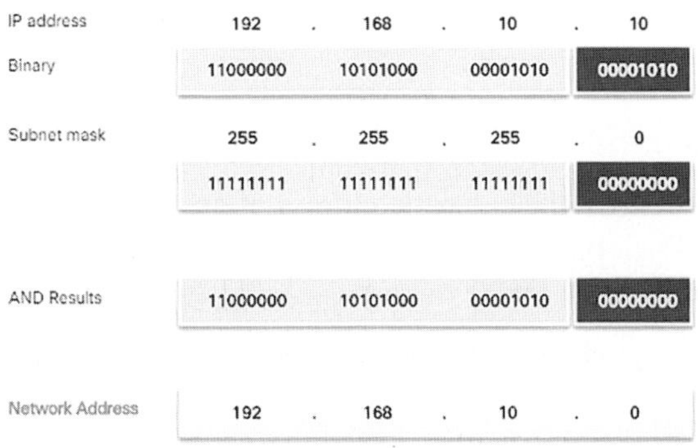

Figure 4-47   Resulting Network Address

Subnetting Broadcast Domains (4.2.3.4)

The 192.168.10.0/24 network can support 254 hosts. Larger networks, such as 172.16.0.0/16, can support many more host addresses (over 65,000). However, this can potentially create a larger broadcast domain. A problem with a large broadcast domain is that these hosts can generate excessive broadcasts and negatively affect the network. In Figure 4-48, LAN 1 connects 400 users that could each generate broadcast traffic. That much broadcast traffic can slow down network operations. It can also slow device operations because each device must accept and process each broadcast packet.

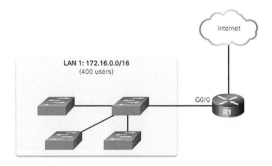

Figure 4-48   A Large Broadcast Domain

The solution is to reduce the size of the network to create smaller broadcast domains in a process called *subnetting*. These smaller network spaces are called subnets.

In Figure 4-49, for example, the 400 users in LAN 1 with network address 172.16.0.0/16 have been divided into two subnets of 200 users each: 172.16.0.0/24 and 172.16.1.0/24. Broadcasts are only propagated within the smaller broadcast domains. Therefore, a broadcast in LAN 1 would not propagate to LAN 2.

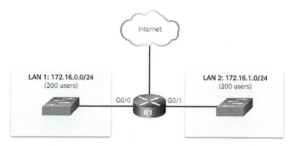

Figure 4-49   Communicating Between Networks

Notice how the prefix length has changed from a /16 to a /24. This is the basis of subnetting: using host bits to create additional subnets.

> **Note**
>
> The terms subnet and network are often used interchangeably. Most networks are a subnet of some larger address block.

Subnetting reduces overall network traffic and improves network performance. It also enables an administrator to implement security policies such as which subnets are allowed or not allowed to communicate together.

There are various ways of using subnets to help manage network devices. Network administrators can group devices and services into subnets that may be determined by a variety of factors:

- Location, such as floors in a building (Figure 4-50)
- Organizational unit (Figure 4-51)
- Device type (Figure 4-52)
- Any other division that makes sense for the network

A cybersecurity analyst does not need to know how to subnet. However, it is important to know the meaning of the subnet mask and that hosts with addresses on different subnets come from different places in a network.

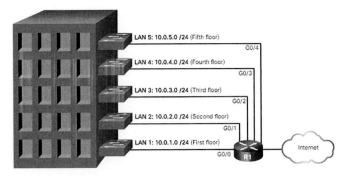

Figure 4-50 Subnetting by Location

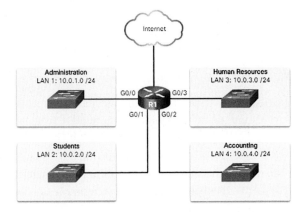

Figure 4-51 Communicating Between Networks

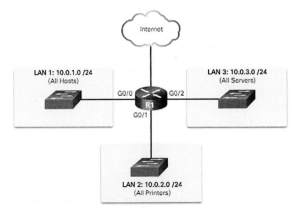

Figure 4-52 Subnetting by Device Type

Video

Video Demonstration 4.2.3.5: Network, Host, and Broadcast Addresses

Refer to the online course to view this video.

Types of IPv4 Addresses (4.2.4)

In this topic, you will learn the type of IPv4 addresses that enable network communication.

IPv4 Address Classes and Default Subnet Masks (4.2.4.1)

There are various types and classes of IPv4 addresses. While address classes are becoming less important in networking, they are still used and referred to commonly in network documentation.

Address Classes

In 1981, IPv4 addresses were assigned using classful addressing as defined in RFC 790. Customers were allocated a network address based on one of three classes, A, B, or C. The RFC divided the unicast ranges into specific classes:

- **Class A (0.0.0.0/8 to 127.0.0.0/8):** Designed to support extremely large networks with more than 16 million host addresses. It used a fixed /8 prefix with the first octet to indicate the network address and the remaining three octets for host addresses.

- **Class B (128.0.0.0/16 to 191.255.0.0/16):** Designed to support the needs of moderate to large size networks with up to approximately 65,000 host addresses. It used a fixed /16 prefix with the two high-order octets to indicate the network address and the remaining two octets for host addresses.

- **Class C (192.0.0.0/24 to 223.255.255.0/24):** Designed to support small networks with a maximum of 254 hosts. It used a fixed /24 prefix with the first three octets to indicate the network and the remaining octet for the host addresses.

> **Note**
>
> There is also a Class D multicast block consisting of 224.0.0.0 to 239.0.0.0 and a Class E experimental address block consisting of 240.0.0.0 to 255.0.0.0.

As shown in Figure 4-53, the classful system allocated 50% of the available IPv4 addresses to 128 Class A networks, 25% of the addresses to Class B, and then Class C shared the remaining 25% with Classes D and E. Although appropriate at the time, as the Internet grew it was obvious that this method was wasting addresses and depleting the number of available IPv4 network addresses.

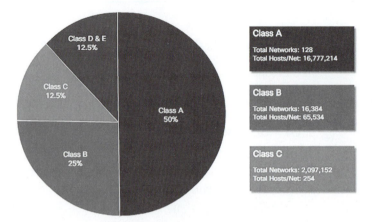

Figure 4-53   Summary of Classful Addressing

Classful addressing was abandoned in the late 1990s for the newer and current classless addressing system. However, as we will see later in this section, classless addressing was only a temporary solution to the depletion of IPv4 addresses.

Reserved Private Addresses (4.2.4.2)

Public IPv4 addresses are addresses which are globally routed between ISP routers. However, not all available IPv4 addresses can be used on the Internet. There are blocks of addresses called private addresses that are used by most organizations to assign IPv4 addresses to internal hosts.

In the mid-1990s, *private IPv4 addresses* were introduced because of the depletion of IPv4 address space. Private IPv4 addresses are not unique and can be used by any internal network.

These are the private address blocks:

- 10.0.0.0/8 or 10.0.0.0 to 10.255.255.255

- 172.16.0.0/12 or 172.16.0.0 to 172.31.255.255

- 192.168.0.0/16 or 192.168.0.0 to 192.168.255.255

It is important to know that addresses within these address blocks are not allowed on the Internet and must be filtered (discarded) by Internet routers. For example, as shown in Figure 4-54, users in networks 1, 2, and 3 are sending packets to remote destinations. The ISP routers would see that the source IPv4 addresses in the packets are from private addresses and would, therefore, discard the packets.

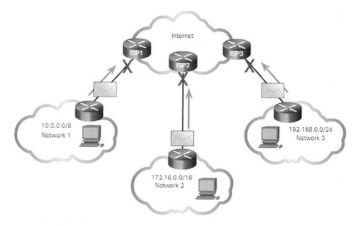

Figure 4-54   Private Addresses Cannot Be Routed Over the Internet

Most organizations use private IPv4 addresses for their internal hosts. However, these RFC 1918 addresses are not routable on the Internet and must be translated to a public IPv4 addresses. Network Address Translation (NAT) is used to translate between private IPv4 and public IPv4 addresses. This is usually done on the router that connects the internal network to the ISP's network.

Home routers provide the same capability. For instance, most home routers assign IPv4 addresses to their wired and wireless hosts from the private address of 192.168.1.0/24. The home router interface that connects to the Internet service provider (ISP) network is often assigned a public IPv4 address to use on the Internet.

The Default Gateway (4.2.5)

In this topic, you will learn how the default gateway enables network communication.

Host Forwarding Decision (4.2.5.1)

A host can send a packet to three types of destinations, as shown in Figure 4-55:

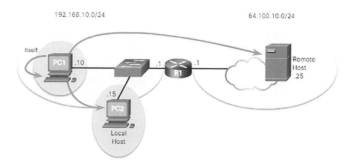

Figure 4-55   Three Types of Destinations

- **Itself:** A host can ping itself by sending a packet to a special IPv4 address of 127.0.0.1, which is referred to as the loopback interface. Pinging the loopback interface tests the TCP/IP protocol stack on the host.

- **Local host:** This is a host on the same local network as the sending host (from PC1 to PC2). The hosts share the same network address.

- **Remote host:** This is a host on a remote network. The hosts do not share the same network address. Notice that R1, a router, is in between PC1 and the remote host. R1 is the default gateway for PC1 and PC2. R1's job is to route any traffic destined for remote networks.

As we have seen, the subnet mask is used to determine to which network an IPv4 host address belongs. Whether a packet is destined for a local host or a remote host is determined by the IP address and subnet mask combination of the source device compared to the IP address and subnet mask combination of the destination device. PC 1 knows it is on the 192.168.10.0/24 network. Therefore, it knows that PC 2 is also on the same network and that the server, Remote Host, is not on the same network. When a source device sends a packet to a remote host, then the help of routers and routing is needed. Routing is the process of identifying the best path to a destination. The router connected to the local network segment is referred to as the default gateway.

Default Gateway (4.2.5.2)

As shown Figure 4-56, three dotted-decimal IPv4 addresses must be configured when assigning an IPv4 configuration to host:

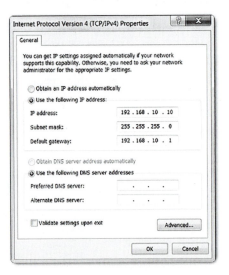

Figure 4-56   Checking Windows IPv4 Properties

- **IPv4 address:** Unique IPv4 address of the host

- *Subnet mask*: Used to identify the network/host portion of the IPv4 address

- *Default gateway*: Identifies the local gateway (i.e., local router interface IPv4 address) to reach remote networks

The default gateway is the network device that can route traffic to other networks. It is the router that can route traffic out of the local network.

If you use the analogy that a network is like a room, then the default gateway is like a doorway. If you want to get to another room or network, you need to find the doorway.

Alternatively, a PC or computer that does not know the IP address of the default gateway is like a person, in a room, that does not know where the doorway is. They can talk to other people in the room or network, but if they do not know the default gateway address, or there is no default gateway, then there is no way out.

Using the Default Gateway (4.2.5.3)

A host's routing table will typically include a default gateway. The host receives the IPv4 address of the default gateway either dynamically from Dynamic Host Configuration Protocol (DHCP) or configured manually. In Figure 4-57, PC1 and PC2 are configured with the default gateway's IPv4 address of 192.168.10.1. Having a default gateway configured creates a default route in the routing table of the PC. A default route is the route or pathway your computer will take when it tries to contact a remote network.

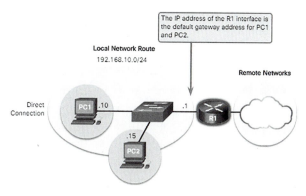

Figure 4-57   Host Default Gateway

The default route is derived from the default gateway configuration and is placed in the host computer's routing table. Both PC1 and PC2 will have a default route for sending all traffic destined to remote networks to R1, as shown in Figure 4-58.

192.168.10.0/24

Figure 4-58   Local Topology for PC1

You can view the routing table for a Windows host using either the **netstat -r** or **route print** command, as shown in Example 4-2.

Example 4-2   IPv4 Routing Table for PC1

```
C:\Users\PC1> netstat -r
<output omitted>


IPv4 Route Table
===========================================================================
Active Routes:
Network Destination        Netmask          Gateway       Interface  Metric
          0.0.0.0          0.0.0.0     192.168.10.1   192.168.10.10     25
        127.0.0.0        255.0.0.0         On-link         127.0.0.1    306
        127.0.0.1  255.255.255.255         On-link         127.0.0.1    306
  127.255.255.255  255.255.255.255         On-link         127.0.0.1    306
     192.168.10.0    255.255.255.0         On-link     192.168.10.10    281
    192.168.10.10  255.255.255.255         On-link     192.168.10.10    281
   192.168.10.255  255.255.255.255         On-link     192.168.10.10    281
        224.0.0.0        240.0.0.0         On-link         127.0.0.1    306
        224.0.0.0        240.0.0.0         On-link      192.168.10.1    281
  255.255.255.255  255.255.255.255         On-link         127.0.0.1    306
  255.255.255.255  255.255.255.255         On-link      192.168.10.1    281
===========================================================================
<output omitted>
C:\Users\PC1>
```

IPv6 (4.2.6)

In this topic, you will learn how the IPv6 protocol supports network communications.

Need for IPv6 (4.2.6.1)

The depletion of IPv4 address space has been the motivating factor for moving to IPv6. As Africa, Asia, and other areas of the world become more connected to the Internet, there are not enough IPv4 addresses to accommodate this growth. As shown in Figure 4-59, four out of the five Regional Internet Registries (RIRs) have run out of IPv4 addresses.

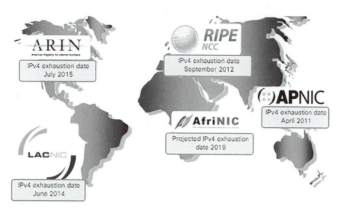

Figure 4-59   RIR IPv4 Exhaustion Dates

IPv4 has a theoretical maximum of 4.3 billion addresses. Private addresses in combination with Network Address Translation (NAT) have been instrumental in slowing the depletion of IPv4 address space. However, NAT breaks many applications and has limitations that severely impede peer-to-peer communications.

Note

NAT is discussed in more detail later in the chapter.

IPv6 Size and Representation (4.2.6.2)

IPv6 is designed to be the successor to IPv4. IPv6 has a 128-bit address space, providing for 340 undecillion addresses. (That is the number 340, followed by 36 zeros.) However, IPv6 is more than just a bigger pool of addresses. When the Internet Engineering Task Force (IETF) began its development of a successor to IPv4, it used this opportunity to fix the limitations of IPv4 and include additional enhancements. One example is Internet Control Message Protocol version 6 (ICMPv6), which includes address resolution and address auto-configuration not found in ICMP for IPv4 (ICMPv4).

IPv6 addresses are written as a string of hexadecimal values. Every 4 bits is represented by a single hexadecimal digit, for a total of 32 hexadecimal values. IPv6 addresses are not case-sensitive and can be written in either lowercase or uppercase.

As shown in Figure 4-60, the format for writing an IPv6 address is x:x:x:x:x:x:x:x, with each "x" consisting of four hexadecimal values.

When referring to 8 bits of an IPv4 address, we use the term octet. In IPv6, a *hextet* is the unofficial term used to refer to a segment of 16 bits or four hexadecimal values. Each "x" is a single hextet, 16 bits or four hexadecimal digits.

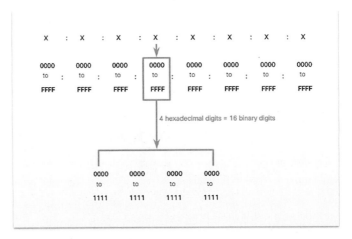

Figure 4-60   Hextets

IPv6 Address Formatting (4.2.6.3)

It is no problem for computers to read the new 128-bit IPv6 addressing. IPv6 just adds more ones and zeros to the source and destination addresses in the packet. For humans, though, the change from a 32-bit address written in dotted-decimal notation to an IPv6 address written as a series of 32 hexadecimal digits can be quite an adjustment. Techniques have been developed to compress the written IPv6 address into a more manageable format.

Compressing IPv6 Addresses

IPv6 addresses are written as a string of hexadecimal values. Every 4 bits is represented by a single hexadecimal digit for a total of 32 hexadecimal values. Table 4-4 shows a fully expanded IPv6 address and two methods of making it more easily readable.

Table 4-4   Compressing an IPv6 Address

Description	IPv6 Address
Fully expanded	2001:0DB8:0000:1111:0000:0000:0000:0200
No leading 0s	2001:DB8:0:1111:0:0:0:200
Compressed	2001:DB8:0:1111::200

There are two rules that help reduce the number of digits needed to represent an IPv6 address.

Rule 1: Omit Leading Zeros

The first rule to help reduce the notation of IPv6 addresses is to omit any leading 0s (zeros) in any 16-bit section. For example:

- 0DB8 can be represented as DB8.

- 0000 can be represented as 0.

- 0200 can be represented as 200.

Rule 2: Omit One "all zeros" Segment

The second rule to help reduce the notation of IPv6 addresses is that a double colon (::) can replace any group of consecutive segments that contain only zeros. The double colon (::) can only be used once within an address, otherwise there would be more than one possible resulting address.

IPv6 Prefix Length (4.2.6.4)

Recall that the prefix, or network portion, of an IPv4 address can be identified by a dotted-decimal subnet mask or prefix length (slash notation). For example, an IPv4 address of 192.168.1.10 with dotted-decimal subnet mask 255.255.255.0 is equivalent to 192.168.1.10/24.

IPv6 uses the prefix length to represent the prefix portion of the address. IPv6 does not use the dotted-decimal subnet mask notation. The prefix length is used to indicate the network portion of an IPv6 address using the IPv6 address/prefix length.

The prefix length can range from 0 to 128. A typical IPv6 prefix length for LANs and most other types of networks is /64, as shown in Figure 4-61. This means the prefix or network portion of the address is 64 bits in length, leaving another 64 bits for the interface ID (host portion) of the address.

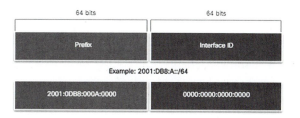

Figure 4-61 IPv6 Prefix Length

Activity 4.2.6.5: IPv6 Address Notation

Refer to the online course to complete this Activity.

Video

Video Tutorial 4.2.6.6: Layer 2 and Layer 3 Addressing
Refer to the online course to view this video.

Connectivity Verification (4.3)

In this section, you will learn how to use common testing utilities to verify and test network connectivity.

ICMP (4.3.1)

In this topic, you will learn how ICMP is used to test network connectivity.

ICMPv4 Messages (4.3.1.1)

Although IP is only a best-effort protocol, the TCP/IP suite does provide for messages to be sent in the event of certain errors. These messages are sent using the services of ICMP. The purpose of these messages is to provide feedback about issues related to the processing of IP packets under certain conditions, not to make IP reliable. ICMP messages are not required and are often not allowed within a network for security reasons.

ICMP is available for both IPv4 and IPv6. ICMPv4 is the messaging protocol for IPv4. ICMPv6 provides these same services for IPv6 but includes additional functionality. In this course, the term ICMP will be used when referring to both ICMPv4 and ICMPv6.

The types of ICMP messages and the reasons why they are sent, are extensive. We will discuss some of the more common messages.

ICMP messages common to both ICMPv4 and ICMPv6 include:

- Host confirmation
- Destination or Service Unreachable
- Time Exceeded
- Route Redirection

Host Confirmation

An ICMP Echo message can be used to determine if a host is operational. The local host sends an ICMP Echo Request to a host. If the host is available, the destination host responds with an Echo Reply. These ICMP Echo messages are the basis of the ping utility. Figure 4-62 shows an Echo Request message being sent from H1 to H2.

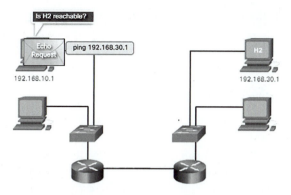

Figure 4-62   Ping to a Remote Host

Figure 4-63 shows an Echo Reply message being sent from H2 back to H1 confirming that H2 is on the network.

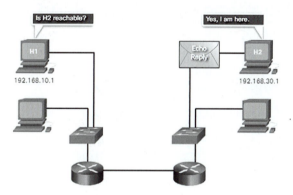

Figure 4-63   Reply from Remote Host

Destination or Service Unreachable

When a host or gateway receives a packet that it cannot deliver, it can use an ICMP Destination Unreachable message to notify the source that the destination or service is unreachable. The message will include a code that indicates why the packet could not be delivered.

These are some of the Destination Unreachable codes for ICMPv4:

- **0:** Net unreachable

- **1:** Host unreachable

- **2:** Protocol unreachable

- **3:** Port unreachable

ICMPv6 has similar but slightly different codes for Destination Unreachable messages.

Time Exceeded

An ICMPv4 Time Exceeded message is used by a router to indicate that a packet cannot be forwarded because the *Time to Live (TTL)* field of the packet was decremented to 0. If a router receives a packet and decrements the TTL field in the IPv4 packet to zero, it discards the packet and sends a Time Exceeded message to the source host.

ICMPv6 also sends a Time Exceeded message if the router cannot forward an IPv6 packet because the packet has expired. IPv6 does not have a TTL field; it uses the Hop Limit field to determine if the packet has expired.

ICMPv6 RS and RA Messages (4.3.1.2)

The informational and error messages found in ICMPv6 are very similar to the control and error messages implemented by ICMPv4. However, ICMPv6 has new features and improved functionality not found in ICMPv4. ICMPv6 messages are encapsulated in IPv6.

ICMPv6 includes four new protocols as part of the *Neighbor Discovery Protocol (ND or NDP)*.

Messaging between an IPv6 router and an IPv6 device:

- *Router Solicitation (RS)* message
- *Router Advertisement (RA)* message

Messaging between IPv6 devices:

- *Neighbor Solicitation (NS)* message
- *Neighbor Advertisement (NA)* message

ICMPv6 ND also includes the Redirect message, which has a similar function to the Redirect message used in ICMPv4.

Figure 4-64 shows an example of a PC and router exchanging Solicitation and Router Advertisement messages.

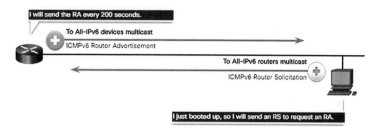

Figure 4-64   IPv6 RS and RA Messages

The host in Figure 4-64 is configured to obtain its addressing information automatically using *Stateless Address Autoconfiguration (SLAAC)*. So the host sends an RS message to the router requesting an RA message.

RA messages are sent by routers to provide addressing information to hosts using SLAAC. The RA message can include addressing information for the host such as the prefix, prefix length, DNS address, and domain name. The router in Figure 4-64 sends an RA message periodically or in response to an RS message. A host using SLAAC will set its default gateway to the link-local address of the router that sent the RA.

Neighbor Solicitation and Neighbor Advertisement messages are used for address resolution and *Duplicate Address Detection (DAD)*.

Address Resolution

Address resolution is used when a device on the LAN knows the IPv6 unicast address of a destination but does not know its Ethernet MAC address. To determine the MAC address for the destination, the device will send an NS message to the solicited node address. The message will include the known (targeted) IPv6 address. The device that has the targeted IPv6 address will respond with an NA message containing its Ethernet MAC address. Figure 4-65 shows two PCs exchanging NS and NA messages.

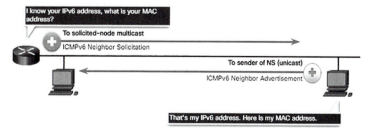

Figure 4-65   IPv6 NS and NA Messages

Duplicate Address Detection

When a device is assigned a global unicast or link-local unicast address, it is recommended that DAD is performed on the address to ensure that it is unique. To check the uniqueness of an address, the device will send an NS message with its own IPv6 address as the targeted IPv6 address, shown in Figure 4-66.

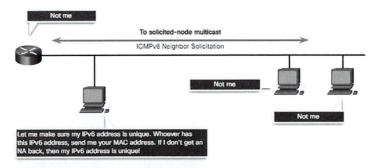

Figure 4-66   IPv6 Duplicate Address Detection

If another device on the network has this address, it will respond with an NA message. This NA message will notify the sending device that the address is in use. If a corresponding NA message is not returned within a certain period of time, the unicast address is unique and acceptable for use.

Note

DAD is not required, but RFC 4861 recommends that DAD is performed on unicast addresses.

Ping and Traceroute Utilities (4.3.2)

In this topic, you will learn how to use ping and traceroute utilities to test network connectivity.

Ping: Testing the Local Stack (4.3.2.1)

Ping is a testing utility that uses ICMP echo request and echo reply messages to test connectivity between hosts. Ping works with both IPv4 and IPv6 hosts.

To test connectivity to another host on a network, an echo request is sent to the host address using the **ping** command. If the host at the specified address receives the echo request, it responds with an echo reply. As each echo reply is received, ping provides feedback on the time between when the request was sent and when the reply was received. This can be a measure of network performance.

Ping has a timeout value for the reply. If a reply is not received within the timeout, ping provides a message indicating that a response was not received. This usually indicates that there is a problem, but could also indicate that security features blocking ping messages have been enabled on the network.

After all the requests are sent, the ping utility provides a summary that includes the success rate and average round-trip time to the destination.

Pinging the Local Loopback

There are some special testing and verification cases for which we can use ping. One case is for testing the internal configuration of IPv4 or IPv6 on the local host. To perform this test, we ping the local loopback address of 127.0.0.1 for IPv4 (::1 for IPv6). Testing the IPv4 loopback is shown in Figure 4-67.

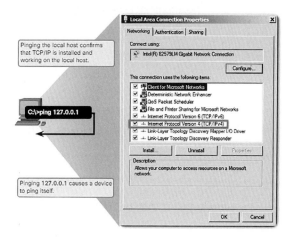

Figure 4-67   Testing the Local TCP/IP Stack

A response from 127.0.0.1 for IPv4, or ::1 for IPv6, indicates that IP is properly installed on the host. This response comes from the network layer. This response is not, however, an indication that the addresses, masks, or gateways are properly configured. Nor does it indicate anything about the status of the lower layer of the network stack. This simply tests IP down through the network layer of IP. An error message indicates that TCP/IP is not operational on the host.

Ping: Testing Connectivity to the Local LAN (4.3.2.2)

You can also use ping to test the ability of a host to communicate on the local network, as shown in Figure 4-68. This is generally done by pinging the IP address of the gateway of the host. A ping to the gateway indicates that the host and the router interface serving as the gateway are both operational on the local network.

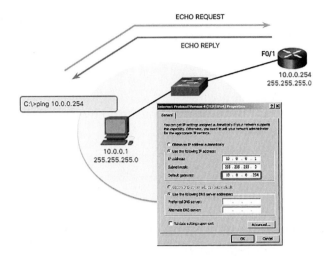

Figure 4-68   Testing IPv4 Connectivity to the Local Network

For this test, the gateway address is most often used because the router is normally always operational. If the gateway address does not respond, a ping can be sent to the IP address of another host on the local network that is known to be operational.

If either the gateway or another host responds, then the local host can successfully communicate over the local network. If the gateway does not respond but another host does, this could indicate a problem with the router interface serving as the gateway.

One possibility is that the wrong gateway address has been configured on the host. Another possibility is that the router interface may be fully operational but have security applied to it that prevents it from processing or responding to ping requests.

Ping: Testing Connectivity to Remote Host (4.3.2.3)

Ping can also be used to test the ability of a local host to communicate across an internetwork. The local host can ping an operational IPv4 host of a remote network because the router forwards the Echo Request, as shown in Figure 4-69.

When the remote host responds, the router forwards the Echo Reply back to the local host, as shown in Figure 4-70.

If this ping is successful, the operation of a large piece of the internetwork can be verified. A successful ping across the internetwork confirms communication on the local network. It also confirms the operation of the router serving as the gateway, and the operation of all other routers that might be in the path between the local network and the network of the remote host.

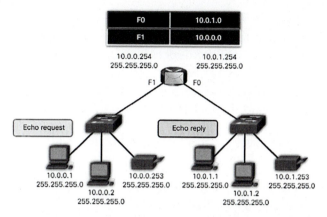

Figure 4-69   The Router Forwards the Echo Request out the F0 Interface

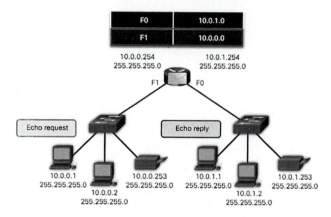

Figure 4-70   The Router Forwards the Echo Reply out the F1 Interface

Additionally, the functionality of the remote host can be verified. If the remote host could not communicate outside of its local network, it would not have responded.

<table>
<tr><td>**Note**</td></tr>
</table>

For security reasons, many network administrators limit or prohibit the entry of ICMP messages into the corporate network; therefore, the lack of a ping response could be due to security restrictions.

Traceroute: Testing the Path (4.3.2.4)

Ping is used to test connectivity between two hosts but does not provide information about the details of devices between the hosts. *Traceroute* (tracert) is a utility that generates a list of hops that were successfully reached along the path. This list can provide important verification and troubleshooting information. If the data reaches the destination, then the trace lists the interface of every router in the path between the hosts. If the data fails at some hop along the way, the address of the last router that responded to the trace can provide an indication of where the problem is, or where security restrictions are found.

Round-Trip Time (RTT)

Using traceroute provides round-trip time for each hop along the path and indicates if a hop fails to respond. The round-trip time is the time a packet takes to reach the remote host and for the response from the host to return. An asterisk (*) is used to indicate a lost or unacknowledged packet.

This information can be used to locate a problematic router in the path. If the display shows high response times or data losses from a particular hop, this is an indication that the resources of the router or its connections may be overloaded.

IPv4 TTL and IPv6 Hop Limit

Traceroute makes use of a function of the TTL field in IPv4 and the Hop Limit field in IPv6 in the Layer 3 headers, along with the ICMP time exceeded message.

Figures 4-71 through 4-78 demonstrate how traceroute takes advantage of TTL.

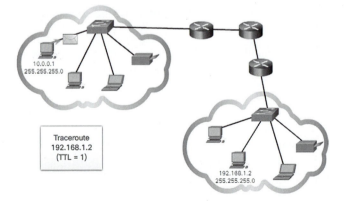

Figure 4-71   Traceroute with One Hop

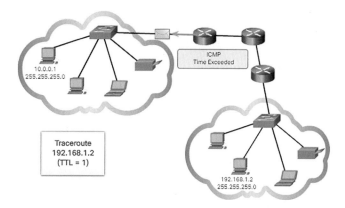

Figure 4-72   Time Exceeded Replay from First Hop

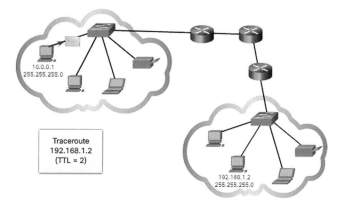

Figure 4-73   Traceroute with Two Hops

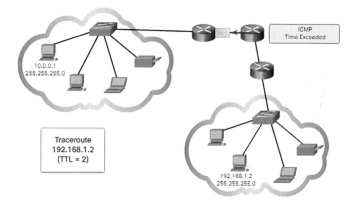

Figure 4-74   Time Exceeded Replay from Second Hop

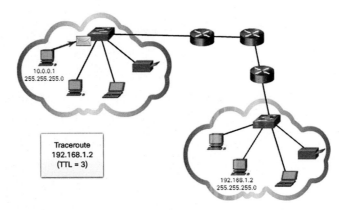

Figure 4-75 Traceroute with Three Hops

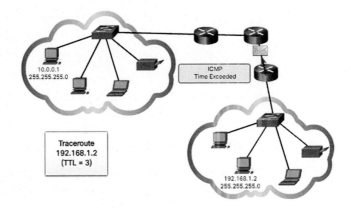

Figure 4-76 Time Exceeded Replay from Third Hop

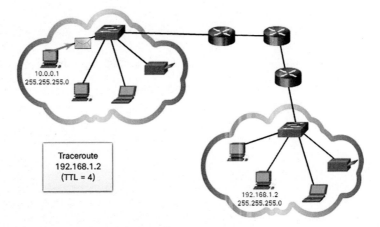

Figure 4-77 Traceroute with Four Hops

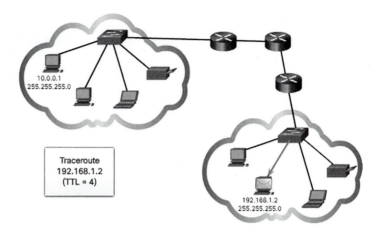

Figure 4-78 Traceroute Reaches Destination

The first sequence of messages sent from traceroute will have a TTL field value of 1 (Figure 4-71). This causes the TTL to time out the IPv4 packet at the first router. This router then responds with an ICMPv4 message (Figure 4-72). Traceroute now has the address of the first hop.

Traceroute then progressively increments the TTL field (2, 3, 4...) for each sequence of messages (Figures 4-73 through 4-76). This provides the trace with the address of each hop as the packets timeout further down the path. The TTL field continues to be increased until the destination is reached, or it is incremented to a predefined maximum.

After the final destination is reached, the host responds with either an ICMP port unreachable message or an ICMP echo reply message instead of the ICMP time exceeded message (Figures 4-77 and 4-78).

ICMP Packet Format (4.3.2.5)

ICMP is encapsulated directly into IP packets. In this sense, it is almost like a transport layer protocol, because it is encapsulated into a packet; however, it is considered to be a Layer 3 protocol. ICMP acts as a data payload within the IP packet. It has a special Header Data field, as shown in Figure 4-79.

ICMP uses message codes to differentiate between different types of ICMP messages. These are some common message codes:

- **0:** Echo reply (response to a ping)

- **3:** Destination Unreachable

- **5:** Redirect (use another route to your destination)

- **8:** Echo request (for ping)

- **11:** Time Exceeded (TTL became 0)

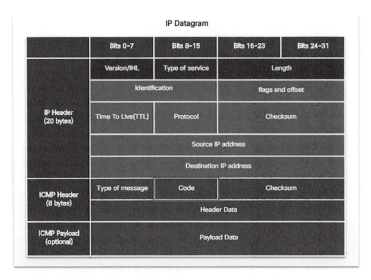

Figure 4-79   IPv4 Datagram

As you will see later in the course, a cybersecurity analyst knows that the optional ICMP Payload field can be used in an attack vector to exfiltrate data.

Address Resolution Protocol (4.4)

In this section, you will learn how the Address Resolution Protocol enables communication on a network.

MAC and IP (4.4.1)

In this topic, you will learn the roles of the MAC address and the IP address.

Destination on the Same Network (4.4.1.1)

There are two primary addresses assigned to a device on an Ethernet LAN:

- **Physical address (the MAC address):** This is used for Ethernet NIC to Ethernet NIC communications on the same network.

- **Logical address (the IP address):** This is used to send the packet from the original source to the final destination.

IP addresses are used to identify the address of the original source device and the final destination device. The destination IP address may be on the same IP network as the source or may be on a remote network.

Note

Most applications use DNS (Domain Name System) to determine the IP address when given a domain name such as www.cisco.com. DNS is discussed in a later chapter.

Layer 2 or physical addresses, like Ethernet MAC addresses, have a different purpose. These addresses are used to deliver the data link frame with the encapsulated IP packet from one NIC to another NIC on the same network. If the destination IP address is on the same network, the destination MAC address will be that of the destination device.

Figure 4-80 shows the Ethernet MAC addresses and IP address for PC A sending an IP packet to the file server on the same network.

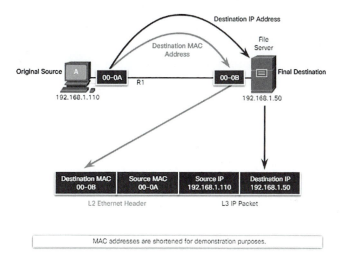

Figure 4-80   Communicating on a Local Network

The Layer 2 Ethernet frame contains:

- **Destination MAC address:** This is the MAC address of the file server's Ethernet NIC.

- **Source MAC address:** This is the MAC address of PC A's Ethernet NIC.

The Layer 3 IP packet contains:

- **Source IP address:** This is the IP address of the original source, PC A.

- **Destination IP address:** This is the IP address of the final destination, the file server.

Destination on a Remote Network (4.4.1.2)

When the destination IP address is on a remote network, the destination MAC address will be the address of the host's default gateway, which is the router's NIC, as shown in Figure 4-81.

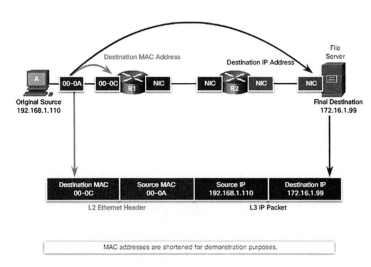

Figure 4-81   Communicating to a Remote Network

Using a postal analogy, this would be similar to a person taking a letter to their local post office. All they need to do is take the letter to the post office and then it becomes the responsibility of the post office to forward the letter on towards its final destination.

Figure 4-81 shows the Ethernet MAC addresses and IPv4 addresses for PC A sending an IP packet to a file server on a remote network. Routers examine the destination IPv4 address to determine the best path to forward the IPv4 packet. This is similar to how the postal service forwards mail based on the address of the recipient.

When the router receives the Ethernet frame, it de-encapsulates the Layer 2 information. Using the destination IP address, it determines the next-hop device, and then encapsulates the IP packet in a new data link frame for the outgoing interface. Along each link in a path, an IP packet is encapsulated in a frame specific to the particular data link technology associated with that link, such as Ethernet. If the next-hop device is the final destination, the destination MAC address will be that of the device's Ethernet NIC.

How are the IPv4 addresses of the IPv4 packets in a data flow associated with the MAC addresses on each link along the path to the destination? This is done through a process called Address Resolution Protocol (ARP).

ARP (4.4.2)

In this topic, you will learn the purpose of ARP.

Introduction to ARP (4.4.2.1)

Recall that every device with an IP address on an Ethernet network also has an Ethernet MAC address. When a device sends an Ethernet frame, it contains these two addresses:

- **Destination MAC address:** The MAC address of the Ethernet NIC, which will be either the MAC address of the final destination device or the MAC address of the router.

- **Source MAC address:** The MAC address of the sender's Ethernet NIC.

To determine the destination MAC address, the device uses ARP, as shown in Figure 4-82. ARP resolves IPv4 addresses to MAC addresses, and maintains a table of mappings.

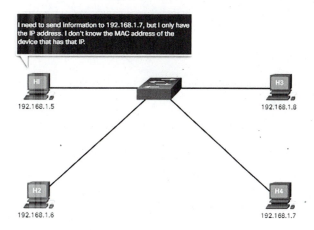

Figure 4-82   H1 Needs the MAC Address for H4

ARP Functions (4.4.2.2)

When a packet is sent to the data link layer to be encapsulated into an Ethernet frame, the device refers to a table in its memory to find the MAC address that is mapped to the IPv4 address. This table is called the ARP table or the ARP cache. The ARP table is stored in the RAM of the device.

The sending device will search its ARP table for a destination IPv4 address and a corresponding MAC address. If the packet's destination IPv4 address is on the same network as the source IPv4 address, the device will search the ARP table for the destination IPv4 address. If the destination IPv4 address is on a different network than the source IPv4 address, the device will search the ARP table for the IPv4 address of the default gateway.

In both cases, the search is for an IPv4 address and a corresponding MAC address for the device.

Each entry, or row, of the ARP table binds an IPv4 address with a MAC address. We call the relationship between the two values a map. It simply means that you can locate an IPv4 address in the table and discover the corresponding MAC address. The ARP table temporarily saves (caches) the mapping for the devices on the LAN.

If the device locates the IPv4 address, its corresponding MAC address is used as the destination MAC address in the frame. If no entry is found, then the device sends an ARP request, as shown in Figure 4-83.

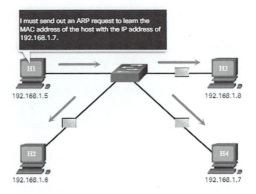

Figure 4-83   H1 Sends an ARP Request

The destination sends an ARP reply, as shown in Figure 4-84.

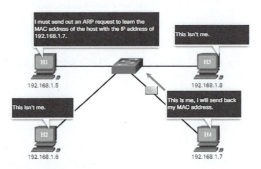

Figure 4-84   H4 Sends an ARP Reply

Video 4.4.2.3: ARP Operation – ARP Request

Video

Refer to the online course to view this video.

Video 4.4.2.4: ARP Operation – ARP Reply

Refer to the online course to view this video.

Video 4.4.2.5: ARP Role in Remote Communication

Refer to the online course to view this video.

Removing Entries from an ARP Table (4.4.2.6)

For each device, an ARP cache timer removes ARP entries that have not been used for a specified period of time. The times differ depending on the device's operating system. For example, some Windows operating systems store ARP cache entries for 2 minutes, as shown in Figure 4-85.

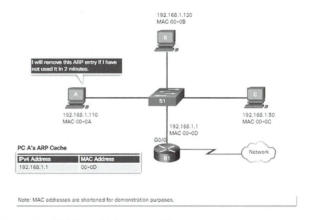

Figure 4-85   Removing MAC-to-IP Address Mappings

Commands may also be used to manually remove all or some of the entries in the ARP table. After an entry has been removed, the process for sending an ARP request and receiving an ARP reply must occur again to enter the map in the ARP table.

ARP Tables on Networking Devices (4.4.2.7)

Network hosts and routers keep ARP tables. ARP information is held in memory on these devices in what is commonly called the ARP cache. The table entries are held for a period of time until they "age out" and are automatically removed from the ARP cache. This ensures the accuracy of the mappings. Holding ARP tables in memory helps to improve network efficiency by decreasing ARP traffic.

The ARP table on a Windows PC can be displayed using the **arp -a** command, as shown in Example 4-3.

Example 4-3 Host ARP Table

```
C:\> arp -a

Interface: 192.168.1.67 --- 0xb
  Internet Address      Physical Address      Type
  192.168.1.254         64-0f-29-0d-36-91     dynamic
  192.168.1.255         ff-ff-ff-ff-ff-ff     static
  224.0.0.22            01-00-5e-00-00-16     static
  224.0.0.251           01-00-5e-00-00-fb     static
  224.0.0.252           01-00-5e-00-00-fc     static
  255.255.255.255       ff-ff-ff-ff-ff-ff     static

Interface: 10.82.253.91 --- 0x10
  Internet Address      Physical Address      Type
  10.82.253.92          64-0f-29-0d-36-91     dynamic
  224.0.0.22            01-00-5e-00-00-16     static
  224.0.0.251           01-00-5e-00-00-fb     static
  224.0.0.252           01-00-5e-00-00-fc     static
  255.255.255.255       ff-ff-ff-ff-ff-ff     static
C:\>
```

 Lab 4.4.2.8: Using Wireshark to Examine Ethernet Frames

In this lab, you will complete the following objectives:

- Part 1: Examine the Header Fields in an Ethernet II Frame
- Part 2: Use Wireshark to Capture and Analyze Ethernet Frames

ARP Issues (4.4.3)

In this topic, you will learn how ARP requests impact network and host performance.

ARP Broadcasts (4.4.3.1)

As a broadcast frame, an ARP request is received and processed by every device on the local network. On a typical business network, these broadcasts would probably have minimal impact on network performance. However, if a large number of devices were to be powered up and all start accessing network services at the same time, there could briefly be some reduction in performance, as shown in Figure 4-86. After the devices send out the initial ARP broadcasts and have learned the necessary MAC addresses, any impact on the network will be minimized.

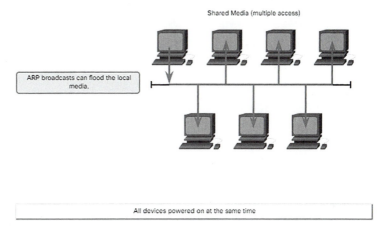

Figure 4-86   ARP Broadcasts and Security

ARP Spoofing (4.4.3.2)

In some cases, the use of ARP can lead to a potential security risk known as *ARP spoofing* or ARP poisoning. This is a technique used by an attacker to reply to an ARP request for an IPv4 address belonging to another device, such as the default gateway, as shown in Figure 4-87. The attacker sends an ARP reply with its own MAC address. The receiver of the ARP reply will add the wrong MAC address to its ARP table and send these packets to the attacker.

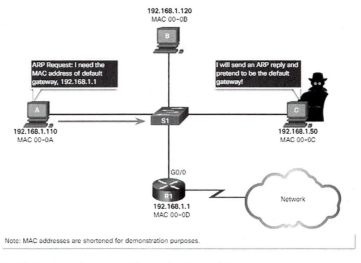

Figure 4-87   All Devices Powered On at the Same Time

ARP vulnerabilities will be discussed in more detail later in the course.

The Transport Layer (4.5)

In this section, you will learn how transport layer protocols support network functionality.

Transport Layer Characteristics (4.5.1)

In this topic, you will learn how transport layer protocols support network communication.

Transport Layer Protocol Role in Network Communication (4.5.1.1)

The transport layer is responsible for establishing a temporary communication session between two applications and delivering data between them. An application generates data that is sent from an application on a source host to an application on a destination host. This is without regard to the destination host type, the type of media over which the data must travel, the path taken by the data, the congestion on a link, or the size of the network. As shown in Figure 4-88, the transport layer is the link between the application layer and the lower layers that are responsible for network transmission.

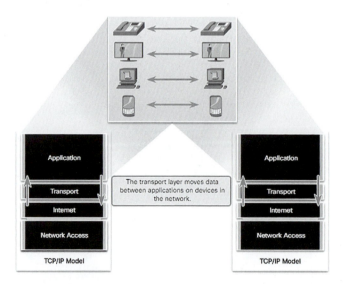

Figure 4-88   Enabling Applications on Devices to Communicate

Tracking Individual Conversations

At the transport layer, each set of data flowing between a source application and a destination application is known as a conversation (Figure 4-89). A host may have multiple applications that are communicating across the network simultaneously.

Each of these applications communicates with one or more applications on one or more remote hosts. It is the responsibility of the transport layer to maintain and track these multiple conversations.

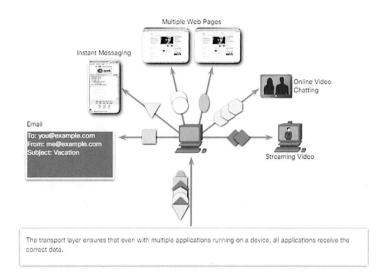

Figure 4-89   Transport Tracks Individual Conversations

Segmenting Data and Reassembling Segments

Data must be prepared to be sent across the media in manageable pieces. Most networks have a limitation on the amount of data that can be included in a single packet. Transport layer protocols have services that segment the application data into blocks that are an appropriate size. This service includes the encapsulation required on each piece of data. A header, used for reassembly, is added to each block of data. This header is used to track the data stream.

At the destination, the transport layer must be able to reconstruct the pieces of data into a complete data stream that is useful to the application layer. The protocols at the transport layer describe how the transport layer header information is used to reassemble the data pieces into streams to be passed to the application layer.

Identifying the Applications

To pass data streams to the proper applications, the transport layer must identify the target application. To accomplish this, the transport layer assigns each application an identifier called a port number. Each software process that needs to access the network is assigned a port number unique to that host.

Transport Layer Mechanisms (4.5.1.2)

Sending some types of data (for example, a streaming video) across a network, as one complete communication stream, can consume all of the available bandwidth. This will then prevent other communications from occurring at the same time. It would also make error recovery and retransmission of damaged data difficult.

Figure 4-90 shows that segmenting the data into smaller chunks enables many different communications, from many different users, to be interleaved (multiplexed) on the same network.

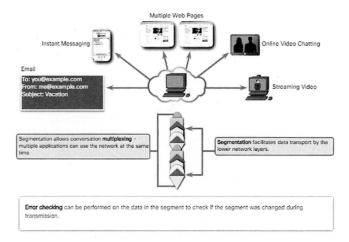

Figure 4-90   Transport Layer Services

To identify each segment of data, the transport layer adds a header containing binary data organized into several fields. It is the values in these fields that enable various transport layer protocols to perform different functions in managing data communication.

The transport layer is also responsible for managing reliability requirements of a conversation. Different applications have different transport reliability requirements.

IP is concerned only with the structure, addressing, and routing of packets. IP does not specify how the delivery or transportation of the packets takes place. Transport protocols specify how to transfer messages between hosts. TCP/IP provides two transport layer protocols, Transmission Control Protocol (TCP) and User Datagram Protocol (UDP), as shown in Figure 4-91. IP uses these transport protocols to enable hosts to communicate and transfer data.

TCP is considered a reliable, full-featured transport layer protocol, which ensures that all of the data arrives at the destination. However, this requires additional fields in the TCP header, which increases the size of the packet and also increases delay. In contrast, UDP is a simpler transport layer protocol that does not provide for reliability. It therefore has fewer fields and is faster than TCP.

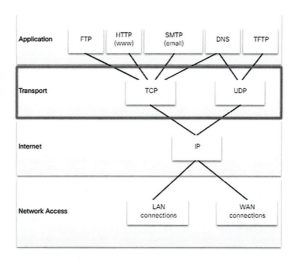

Figure 4-91   Two Transport Layer Protocols

TCP Local and Remote Ports (4.5.1.3)

The transport layer must be able to separate and manage multiple communications with different transport requirement needs. Users expect to be able to simultaneously receive and send email and instant messages, view websites, and conduct a VoIP phone call. Each of these applications is sending and receiving data over the network at the same time, despite different reliability requirements. Additionally, data from the phone call is not directed to the web browser, and text from an instant message does not appear in an email.

TCP and UDP manage these multiple simultaneous conversations by using header fields that can uniquely identify these applications. These unique identifiers are the port numbers.

The source port number is associated with the originating application on the local host, as shown in Figure 4-92. The destination port number is associated with the destination application on the remote host.

Source Port

The *source port* number is dynamically generated by the sending device to identify a conversation between two devices. This process allows multiple conversations to occur simultaneously. It is common for a device to send multiple HTTP service requests to a web server at the same time. Each separate HTTP conversation is tracked based on the source ports.

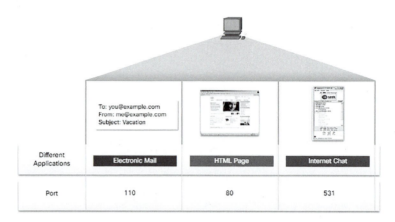

Figure 4-92   Port Number Examples

Destination Port

The client places a *destination port* number in the segment to tell the destination server what service is being requested, as shown in Figure 4-93.

For example, when a client specifies port 80 in the destination port, the server that receives the message knows that web services are being requested. A server can offer more than one service simultaneously such as web services on port 80 at the same time that it offers File Transfer Protocol (FTP) connection establishment on port 21.

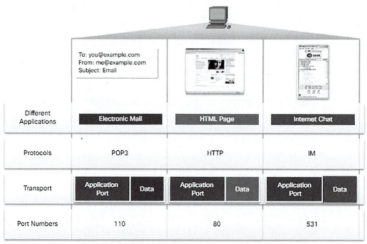

Data for different applications is directed to the correct application because each application has a unique port number.

Figure 4-93   Mapping Application Protocols to Port Numbers

Socket Pairs (4.5.1.4)

The source and destination ports are placed within the segment, as shown in Figure 4-94.

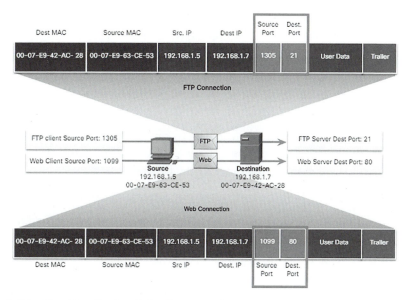

Figure 4-94   Tracking Socket Pairs Between Source and Destination

The segments are then encapsulated within an IP packet. The IP packet contains the IP address of the source and destination. The combination of the source IP address and source port number, or the destination IP address and destination port number, is known as a *socket*. The socket is used to identify the server and service being requested by the client. A client socket might look like this, with 1099 representing the source port number: 192.168.1.5:1099

The socket on a web server might be: 192.168.1.7:80

Together, these two sockets combine to form a socket pair: 192.168.1.5:1099, 192.168.1.7:80

Sockets enable multiple processes, running on a client, to distinguish themselves from each other, and multiple connections to a server process to be distinguished from each other.

The source port number acts as a return address for the requesting application. The transport layer keeps track of this port and the application that initiated the request so that when a response is returned, it can be forwarded to the correct application.

TCP vs. UDP (4.5.1.5)

For some applications, segments must arrive in a very specific sequence to be processed successfully. With other applications, all data must be fully received before any is considered useful. In both of these instances, TCP is used as the transport protocol. Application developers must choose which transport protocol type is appropriate based on the requirements of the applications.

For example, applications such as databases, web browsers, and email clients require that all data that is sent arrives at the destination in its original condition. Any missing data could cause a corrupt communication that is either incomplete or unreadable. These applications are designed to use TCP.

TCP transport is analogous to sending packages that are tracked from source to destination. If a shipping order is broken up into several packages, a customer can check online to see the order of the delivery.

With TCP, there are three basic operations of reliability:

- Numbering and tracking data segments transmitted to a specific host from a specific application

- Acknowledging received data

- Retransmitting any unacknowledged data after a certain period of time

Figures 4-95 through 4-98 demonstrate how TCP segments and acknowledgments are transmitted between sender and receiver.

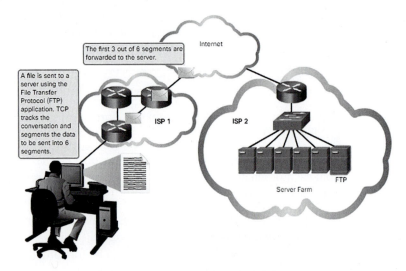

Figure 4-95   Sending Data Using a TCP Application: FTP

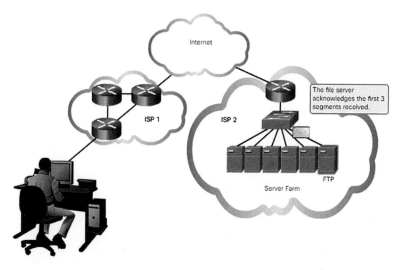

Figure 4-96   Acknowledging Receipt of TCP Application Data

In other cases, an application can tolerate some data loss during transmission over the network, but delays in transmission are unacceptable. UDP is the better choice for these applications because less network overhead is required. There is a trade-off between the value of reliability and the burden it places on network resources. Adding overhead to ensure reliability for some applications could reduce the usefulness of the application and can even be detrimental. In such cases, UDP is a better transport protocol. UDP is preferable for applications such as streaming live audio, live video, and Voice over IP (VoIP). Acknowledgments and retransmission would slow down delivery.

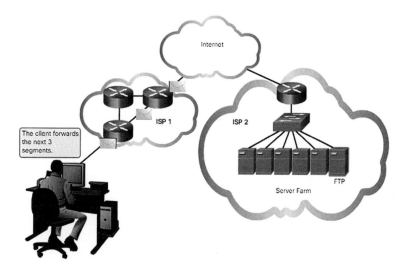

Figure 4-97   Sending More Data Using TCP

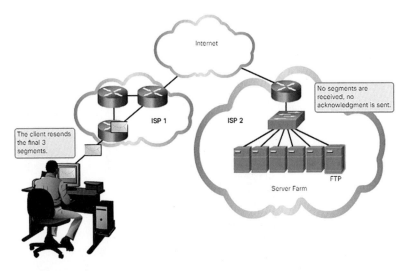

Figure 4-98   No Segments Received at Destination

For example, if one or two segments of a live video stream fail to arrive, it creates a momentary disruption in the stream. This may appear as distortion in the image or sound, but may not be noticeable to the user. If the destination device had to account for lost data, the stream could be delayed while waiting for retransmissions, therefore causing the image or sound to be greatly degraded. In this case, it is better to render the best media possible with the segments received, and forego reliability.

UDP provides the basic functions for delivering data segments between the appropriate applications, with very little overhead and data checking. UDP is known as a best-effort delivery protocol. In the context of networking, best-effort delivery is referred to as "unreliable" because there is no acknowledgment that the data is received at the destination. With UDP, there are no transport layer processes that inform the sender of a successful delivery.

UDP is similar to placing a regular, non-registered, letter in the mail. The sender of the letter is not aware of the availability of the receiver to receive the letter. Nor is the post office responsible for tracking the letter or informing the sender if the letter does not arrive at the final destination.

Figures 4-99 and 4-100 demonstrate how UDP segments are transmitted from sender to receiver.

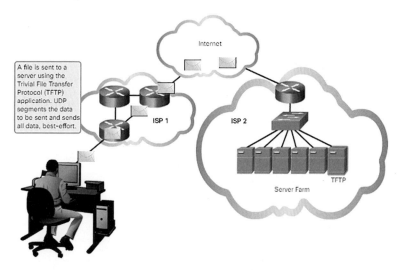

Figure 4-99   Sending Data Using a UDP Application: TFTP

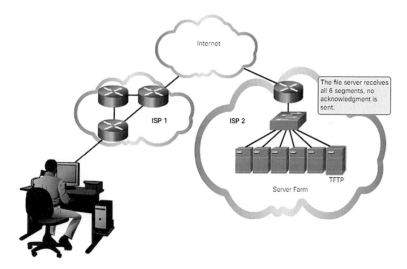

Figure 4-100   No Acknowledgments Sent by Destination

Figure 4-101 provides an overview and comparison of the features of TCP and UDP.

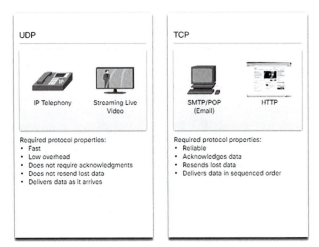

Figure 4-101   Comparing UDP and TCP

Applications that stream stored audio and video use TCP. For example, if your network suddenly cannot support the bandwidth needed to watch an on-demand movie, the application pauses the playback. During the pause, you might see a "buffering..." message while TCP works to re-establish the stream. When all the segments are in order and a minimum level of bandwidth is restored, your TCP session resumes and the movie continues to play.

TCP and UDP Headers (4.5.1.6)

TCP is a stateful protocol. A stateful protocol is a protocol that keeps track of the state of the communication session. To track the state of a session, TCP records which information it has sent and which information has been acknowledged. The stateful session begins with the session establishment and ends when closed with the session termination.

As shown in Figure 4-102, each TCP segment has 20 bytes of overhead in the header encapsulating the application layer data:

- **Source Port (16 bits) and Destination Port (16 bits):** These are used to identify the application.

- **Sequence Number (32 bits):** This is used for data reassembly purposes.

- **Acknowledgment Number (32 bits):** This indicates the data that has been received.

- **Header Length (4 bits):** This is known as "data offset." It indicates the length of the TCP segment header.

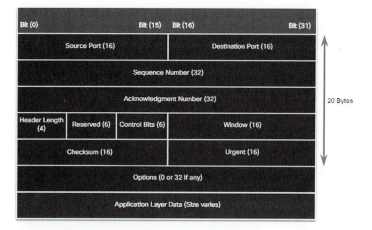

Figure 4-102 TCP Segment Headers

- **Reserved (6 bits):** This field is reserved for the future.

- **Control Bits (6 bits):** This includes bit codes, or flags, which indicate the purpose and function of the TCP segment.

- **Window (16 bits):** This indicates the number of bytes that can be accepted at one time.

- **Checksum (16 bits):** This is used for error checking of the segment header and data.

- **Urgent (16 bits):** This indicates if data is urgent.

There are 6 control bits:

- **URG:** This indicates that the segment should be classified as urgent.

- **ACK:** This indicates that the Acknowledgment Number field is significant. All segments in an established connection will have this bit set.

- **PSH:** This is the push function. It indicates that the segment should not be buffered but should be sent immediately to the receiving application.

- **RST:** This indicates that an unexpected condition has occurred and that the connection should be reset.

- **SYN:** This is used to initiate a connection. This should only be set in the initial segments in the connection establishment phase of data communication.

- **FIN:** This signals that no more data will be transferred and that the connection should be terminated.

UDP is a stateless protocol, meaning neither the client nor the server is obligated to keep track of the state of the communication session. If reliability is required when using UDP as the transport protocol, it must be handled by the application.

One of the most important requirements for delivering live video and voice over the network is that the data continues to flow quickly. Live video and voice applications can tolerate some data loss with minimal or no noticeable effect, and are perfectly suited to UDP.

The pieces of communication in UDP are called datagrams, as shown in Figure 4-103. These datagrams are sent as best-effort by the transport layer protocol. UDP has a low overhead of 8 bytes.

Figure 4-103   UDP Segment Headers

Activity 4.5.1.7: Compare TCP and UDP Characteristics

Refer to the online course to complete this Activity.

Transport Layer Operation (4.5.2)

In this topic, you will learn how transport layer protocols operate.

TCP Port Allocation (4.5.2.1)

Each application process running on a server is configured to use a port number, either by default or manually, by a system administrator. An individual server cannot have two services assigned to the same port number within the same transport layer services.

For example, a server running a web server application and a file transfer application cannot have both configured to use the same port (for example, TCP port 80). An active server application assigned to a specific port is considered to be open. This means that the transport layer running on the server accepts and processes segments addressed to that port. Any incoming client request addressed to the correct socket is accepted, and the data is passed to the server application. There can be many ports open simultaneously on a server, one for each active server application.

When establishing a connection with a server, the transport layer on the client establishes a source port to keep track of data sent from the server. Just as a server can have many ports open for server processes, clients can have many ports open for connections to multiple sockets. Local source ports are randomly allocated from a range of numbers that is usually from 49152 to 65535. Segments sent to the client from a server will use the client port number as the destination port for data from the socket.

Refer to Figures 4-104 through 4-108 to see the typical allocation of source and destination ports in TCP client-server operations.

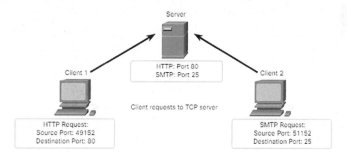

Figure 4-104   Clients Sending TCP Requests

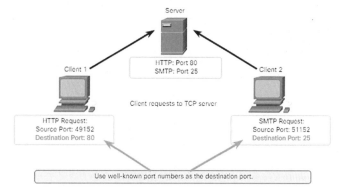

Figure 4-105   Request Destination Ports

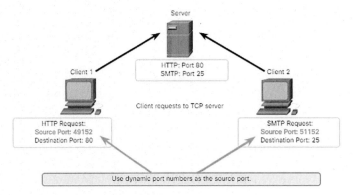

Figure 4-106   Request Source Ports

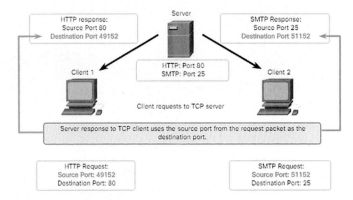

Figure 4-107   Response Destination Ports

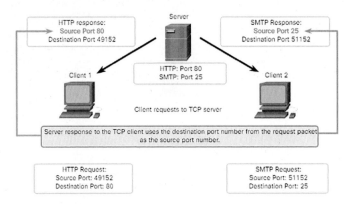

Figure 4-108   Response Source Ports

A TCP Session Part I: Connection Establishment and Termination (4.5.2.2)

In some cultures, when two persons meet, they often greet each other by shaking hands. The act of shaking hands is understood by both parties as a signal for a friendly greeting. Connections on the network are similar. In TCP connections, the host client establishes the connection with the server.

Connection Establishment

Hosts track each data segment within a session and exchange information about what data is received using the information in the TCP header. TCP is a full-duplex protocol, where each connection represents two one-way communication streams or sessions. To establish the connection, the hosts perform a three-way handshake. Control bits in the TCP header indicate the progress and status of the connection.

The three-way handshake accomplishes three things:

- It establishes that the destination device is present on the network.

- It verifies that the destination device has an active service and is accepting requests on the destination port number that the initiating client intends to use.

- It informs the destination device that the source client intends to establish a communication session on that port number.

A TCP connection is established in three steps, as shown in Figure 4-109:

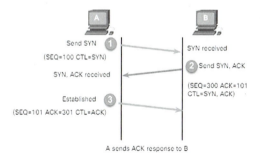

Figure 4-109 TCP Connection Establishment and Termination

1. The initiating client requests a client-to-server communication session with the server.

2. The server acknowledges the client-to-server communication session and requests a server-to-client communication session.

3. The initiating client acknowledges the server-to-client communication session.

Connection Termination

After the communication is completed, the sessions are closed, and the connection is terminated. The connection and session mechanisms enable TCP's reliability function.

To close a connection, the Finish (FIN) control flag must be set in the segment header. To end each one-way TCP session, a two-way handshake, consisting of a FIN segment and an Acknowledgment (ACK) segment, is used. Therefore, to terminate a single conversation supported by TCP, four exchanges are needed to end both sessions, as shown in Figure 4-110.

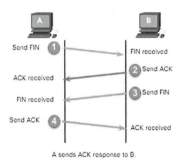

A sends ACK response to B.

Figure 4-110   TCP Session Termination (FIN)

Note

In this explanation, the terms client and server are used as a reference for simplicity, but the termination process can be initiated by any two hosts that have an open session:

1. When the client has no more data to send in the stream, it sends a segment with the FIN flag set.

2. The server sends an ACK to acknowledge the receipt of the FIN to terminate the session from client to server.

3. The server sends a FIN to the client to terminate the server-to-client session.

4. The client responds with an ACK to acknowledge the FIN from the server.

When all segments have been acknowledged, the session is closed.

The 6 bits in the Control Bits field (Figure 4-111) of the TCP segment header are also known as flags. A flag is a bit that is set to "on" or "off." For our purposes, four flags are important: SYN, ACK, FIN, and RST. The RST flag is used to reset a connection when an error or timeout occurs.

Video Demonstration 4.5.2.3: TCP 3-Way Handshake

Refer to the online course to view this video.

Video

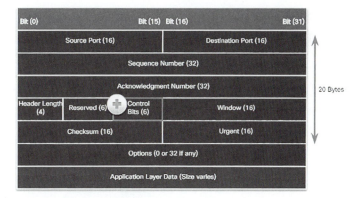

Figure 4-111   The Control Bits Field

Lab 4.5.2.4: Using Wireshark to Observe the TCP 3-Way Handshake

In this lab, you will complete the following objectives:

- Part 1: Prepare the Hosts to Capture the Traffic
- Part 2: Analyze the Packets Using Wireshark
- Part 3: View the Packets Using tcpdump

Interactive Graphic

Activity 4.5.2.5: TCP Connection and Termination Process

Refer to the online course to complete this Activity.

A TCP Session Part II: Data Transfer (4.5.2.6)

TCP Ordered Delivery

TCP segments may arrive at their destination out of order. For the original message to be understood by the recipient, the data in these segments is reassembled into the original order. Sequence numbers are assigned in the header of each packet to achieve this goal. The sequence number represents the first data byte of the TCP segment.

During session setup, an initial sequence number (ISN) is set. This ISN represents the starting value of the bytes for this session that is transmitted to the receiving application. As data is transmitted during the session, the sequence number is incremented by the number of bytes that have been transmitted. This data byte tracking enables each segment to be uniquely identified and acknowledged. Missing segments can then be identified.

Note

The ISN does not begin at 1 but instead is a random number. This is to prevent certain types of malicious attacks. For simplicity, we will use an ISN of 1 for the examples in this chapter.

Segment sequence numbers indicate how to reassemble and reorder received segments, as shown in Figure 4-112.

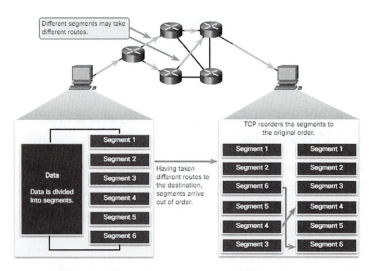

Figure 4-112   TCP Segments Are Reordered at the Destination

The receiving TCP process places the data from a segment into a receiving buffer. Segments are placed in the proper sequence order and passed to the application layer when reassembled. Any segments that arrive with sequence numbers that are out of order are held for later processing. Then, when the segments with the missing bytes arrive, these segments are processed in order.

Flow Control

TCP also provides mechanisms for *flow control*, which is the amount of data that the destination can receive and process reliably. Flow control helps maintain the reliability of TCP transmission by adjusting the rate of data flow between source and destination for a given session. To accomplish this, the TCP header includes a 16-bit field called the window.

Figure 4-113 shows an example of window size and acknowledgments.

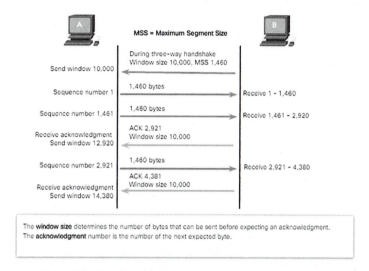

Figure 4-113   TCP Window Size Example

The *window size* is the number of bytes that the destination device of a TCP session can accept and process at one time. In this example, PC B's initial window size for the TCP session is 10,000 bytes. Starting with the first byte, byte number 1, the last byte PC A can send without receiving an acknowledgment is byte 10,000. This is known as PC A's send window. The window size is included in every TCP segment so the destination can modify the window size at any time depending on buffer availability.

Note

In Figure 4-113, the source is transmitting 1460 bytes of data within each TCP segment. This is known as the MSS (Maximum Segment Size).

The initial window size is agreed upon when the TCP session is established during the three-way handshake. The source device must limit the number of bytes sent to the destination device based on the destination's window size. Only after the source device receives an acknowledgment that the bytes have been received can it continue sending more data for the session. Typically, the destination will not wait for all the bytes for its window size to be received before replying with an acknowledgment. As the bytes are received and processed, the destination will send acknowledgments to inform the source that it can continue to send additional bytes.

The process of the destination sending acknowledgments as it processes bytes received and the continual adjustment of the source's send window is known as sliding windows.

If the availability of the destination's buffer space decreases, it may reduce its window size and inform the source to reduce the number of bytes it should send without receiving an acknowledgment.

A useful discussion of TCP sequence and acknowledgment numbers can be found here.

Video

Video Demonstration 4.5.2.7: Sequence Numbers and Acknowledgments

Refer to the online course to view this video.

Video

Video Demonstration 4.5.2.8: Data Loss and Retransmission

Refer to the online course to view this video.

A UDP Session (4.5.2.9)

Like segments with TCP, when UDP datagrams are sent to a destination, they often take different paths and arrive in the wrong order. UDP does not track sequence numbers the way TCP does. UDP has no way to reorder the datagrams into their transmission order.

Therefore, UDP simply reassembles the data in the order that it was received and forwards it to the application, as shown in Figure 4-114. If the data sequence is important to the application, the application must identify the proper sequence and determine how the data should be processed.

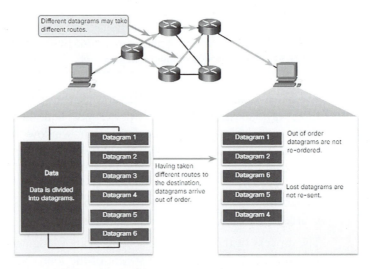

Figure 4-114   UDP Is Connectionless and Unreliable

Like TCP-based applications, UDP-based server applications are assigned well-known or registered port numbers, as shown in Figure 4-115.

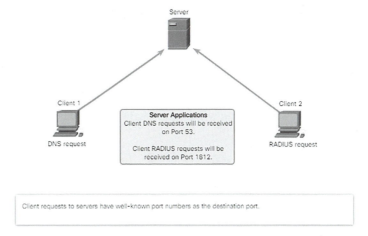

Figure 4-115   UDP Server Listening for Requests

When these applications or processes are running on a server, they accept the data matched with the assigned port number. When UDP receives a datagram destined for one of these ports, it forwards the application data to the appropriate application based on its port number.

Note

The Remote Authentication Dial-in User Service (RADIUS) server shown in Figure 4-115 provides authentication, authorization, and accounting services to manage user access.

As with TCP, client-server communication is initiated by a client application that requests data from a server process. The UDP client process dynamically selects a port number from the range of port numbers and uses this as the source port for the conversation. The destination port is usually the well-known or registered port number assigned to the server process.

After a client has selected the source and destination ports, the same pair of ports is used in the header of all datagrams used in the transaction. For the data returning to the client from the server, the source and destination port numbers in the datagram header are reversed.

Lab 4.5.2.10: Exploring Nmap

Port scanning is usually part of a reconnaissance attack. There are a variety of port scanning methods that can be used. We will explore how to use the Nmap utility. Nmap is a powerful network utility that is used for network discovery and security auditing.

Network Services (4.6)

In this section, you will learn how network services enable network functionality.

DHCP (4.6.1)

In this topic, you will learn how DHCP services enable network functionality.

DHCP Overview (4.6.1.1)

The Dynamic Host Configuration Protocol (DHCP) for IPv4 service automates the assignment of IPv4 addresses, subnet masks, gateways, and other IPv4 networking parameters. This is referred to as dynamic addressing. The alternative to dynamic addressing is static addressing. When using static addressing, the network administrator manually enters IP address information on hosts. DHCPv6 (DHCP for IPv6) provides similar services for IPv6 clients.

When an IPv4, DHCP-configured device boots up or connects to the network, the client broadcasts a DHCP discover (DHCPDISCOVER) message to identify any available DHCP servers on the network. A DHCP server replies with a DHCP offer (DHCPOFFER) message, which offers a lease to the client, as shown in Figure 4-116.

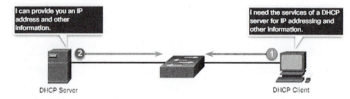

Figure 4-116 Dynamic Host Configuration Protocol (DHCP)

The offer message contains the IPv4 address and subnet mask to be assigned, the IPv4 address of the DNS server, and the IPv4 address of the default gateway. The lease offer also includes the duration of the lease.

The client may receive multiple DHCPOFFER messages if there is more than one DHCP server on the local network. Therefore, it must choose between them, and sends a DHCP request (DHCPREQUEST) message that identifies the explicit server and lease offer that the client is accepting. A client may also choose to request an address that it had previously been allocated by the server.

Assuming that the IPv4 address requested by the client, or offered by the server, is still available, the server returns a DHCP acknowledgment (DHCPACK) message that acknowledges to the client that the lease has been finalized. If the offer is no longer valid, then the selected server responds with a DHCP negative acknowledgment

(DHCPNAK) message. If a DHCPNAK message is returned, then the selection process must begin again with a new DHCPDISCOVER message being transmitted. After the client has the lease, it must be renewed prior to the lease expiration through another DHCPREQUEST message. Figures 4-117 and 4-118 illustrate the steps in DHCPv4 operation.

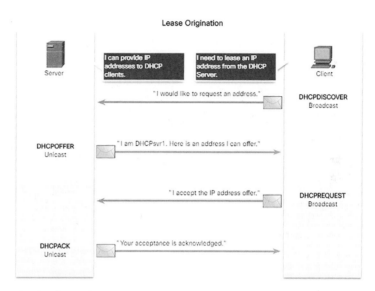

Figure 4-117 DHCPv4 Operation: Lease Origination

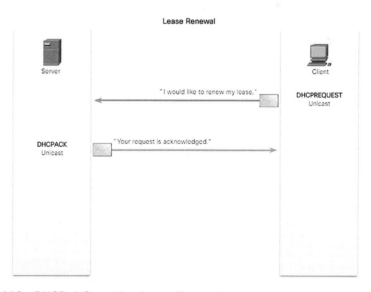

Figure 4-118 DHCPv4 Operation: Lease Renewal

The DHCP server ensures that all IP addresses are unique (the same IP address cannot be assigned to two different network devices simultaneously). Most Internet providers use DHCP to allocate addresses to their customers.

DHCPv6 has similar set of messages to those used for DHCP for IPv4. The DHCPv6 messages are SOLICIT, ADVERTISE, INFORMATION REQUEST, and REPLY.

DHCPv4 Message Format (4.6.1.2)

The DHCPv4 message format is used for all DHCPv4 transactions. DHCPv4 messages are encapsulated within the UDP transport protocol. DHCPv4 messages sent from the client use UDP source port 68 and destination port 67. DHCPv4 messages sent from the server to the client use UDP source port 67 and destination port 68.

Figure 4-119 shows the format of a DHCPv4 message with the following fields:

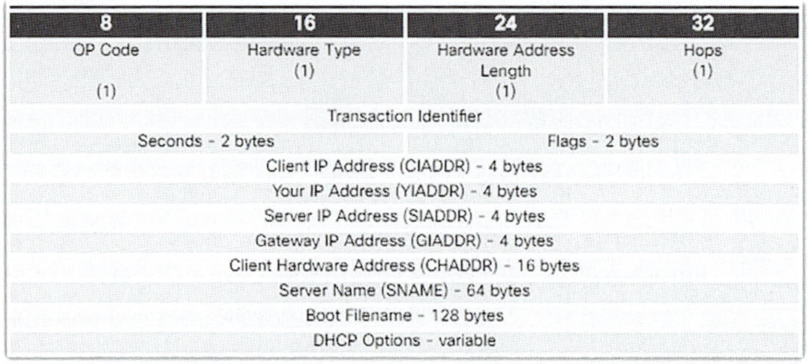

8	16	24	32
OP Code (1)	Hardware Type (1)	Hardware Address Length (1)	Hops (1)
Transaction Identifier			
Seconds – 2 bytes		Flags – 2 bytes	
Client IP Address (CIADDR) – 4 bytes			
Your IP Address (YIADDR) – 4 bytes			
Server IP Address (SIADDR) – 4 bytes			
Gateway IP Address (GIADDR) – 4 bytes			
Client Hardware Address (CHADDR) – 16 bytes			
Server Name (SNAME) – 64 bytes			
Boot Filename – 128 bytes			
DHCP Options – variable			

Figure 4-119   DHCPv4 Header Fields

- **Operation (OP) Code:** Specifies the general type of message. A value of 1 indicates a request message; a value of 2 is a reply message.

- **Hardware Type:** Identifies the type of hardware used in the network. For example, 1 is Ethernet, 15 is Frame Relay, and 20 is a serial line. These are the same codes used in ARP messages.

- **Hardware Address Length:** Specifies the length of the address.

- **Hops:** Controls the forwarding of messages. Set to 0 by a client before transmitting a request.

- **Transaction Identifier:** Used by the client to match the request with replies received from DHCPv4 servers.

- **Seconds:** Identifies the number of seconds elapsed since a client began attempting to acquire or renew a lease. Used by DHCPv4 servers to prioritize replies when multiple client requests are outstanding.

- **Flags:** Used by a client that does not know its IPv4 address when it sends a request. Only one of the 16 bits is used, which is the broadcast flag. A value of 1 in this field tells the DHCPv4 server or relay agent receiving the request that the reply should be sent as a broadcast.

- **Client IP Address:** Used by a client during lease renewal when the address of the client is valid and usable, not during the process of acquiring an address. The client puts its own IPv4 address in this field if and only if it has a valid IPv4 address while in the bound state; otherwise, it sets the field to 0.

- **Your IP Address:** Used by the server to assign an IPv4 address to the client.

- **Server IP Address:** Used by the server to identify the address of the server that the client should use for the next step in the bootstrap process, which may or may not be the server sending this reply. The sending server always includes its own IPv4 address in a special field called the Server Identifier DHCPv4 option.

- **Gateway IP Address:** Routes DHCPv4 messages when DHCPv4 relay agents are involved. The gateway address facilitates communications of DHCPv4 requests and replies between the client and a server that are on different subnets or networks.

- **Client Hardware Address:** Specifies the physical layer of the client.

- **Server Name:** Used by the server sending a DHCPOFFER or DHCPACK message. The server may optionally put its name in this field. This can be a simple text nickname or a DNS domain name, such as dhcpserver.netacad.net.

- **Boot Filename:** Optionally used by a client to request a particular type of boot file in a DHCPDISCOVER message. Used by a server in a DHCPOFFER to fully specify a boot file directory and filename.

- **DHCP Options:** Holds DHCP options, including several parameters required for basic DHCP operation. This field is variable in length. Both client and server may use this field.

DNS (4.6.2)

In this topic, you will learn how DNS services enable network functionality.

DNS Overview (4.6.2.1)

The web servers that we so often connect to using names like www.cisco.com are actually reached by assigning IP addresses to packets. On the Internet, these domain names are much easier for people to remember than 198.133.219.25, which is the actual numeric IP address for this server. If Cisco decides to change the numeric address of www.cisco.com, it is transparent to the user because the domain name remains the same. The new address is simply linked to the existing domain name and connectivity is maintained.

The Domain Name System (DNS) was developed to provide a reliable means of managing and providing domain names and their associated IP addresses. DNS consists of a global hierarchy of distributed servers that contain databases of name to IP address mappings. The client computer in Figure 4-120 will send a request to the DNS server to get the IP address for www.cisco.com.

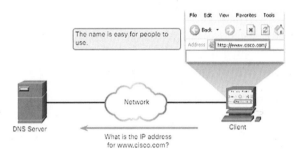

Figure 4-120   DNS Resolves Names to IP Addresses

A recent analysis of network security threats discovered that over 90% of the malicious software that is used to attack networks uses the DNS system to carry out attack campaigns. A cybersecurity analyst should have a thorough understanding of the DNS system and the ways in which malicious DNS traffic can be detected through protocol analysis and the inspection of DNS monitoring information.

The DNS Domain Hierarchy (4.6.2.2)

The DNS consists of a hierarchy of generic top-level domains (gTLDs) which consist of .com, .net, .org, .gov, .edu, and numerous country-level domains, such as .br (Brazil), .es (Spain), .uk (United Kingdom), etc. At the next level of the DNS hierarchy are second-level domains. These are represented by a domain name that is followed by a top-level domain. Subdomains are found at the next level of the DNS hierarchy and represent some division of the second-level domain. Finally, a fourth level can represent a host in a subdomain. Each element of a domain specification is sometimes called a label. The labels move from the top of the hierarchy downward from right to left. A dot (".") at the end of a domain name represents the root server at the top of the hierarchy. Figure 4-121 illustrates this DNS domain hierarchy.

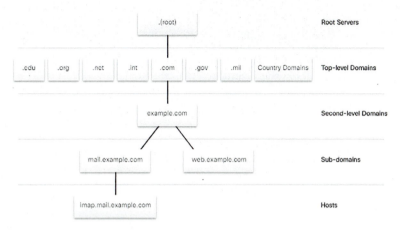

Figure 4-121 DNS Domain Hierarchy

The DNS Lookup Process (4.6.2.3)

To understand DNS, cybersecurity analysts should be familiar with the following terms:

- *Resolver*: A DNS client that sends DNS messages to obtain information about the requested domain name space.

- *Recursion*: The action taken when a DNS server is asked to query on behalf of a DNS resolver.

- *Authoritative server*: A DNS server that responds to query messages with information stored in Resource Records (RRs) for a domain name space stored on the server.

- *Recursive resolver*: A DNS server that recursively queries for the information asked in the DNS query.

- *FQDN*: A *fully qualified domain name* is the absolute name of a device within the distributed DNS database.

- *RR*: A *resource record* is a format used in DNS messages that is composed of the following fields: NAME, TYPE, CLASS, TTL, RDLENGTH, and RDATA.

- *DNS Zone*: A database that contains information about the domain name space stored on an authoritative server.

When attempting to resolve a name to an IP address, a user host, known in the system as a resolver, will first check its local DNS cache. If the mapping is not found there, a query will be issued to the DNS server or servers that are configured in the network addressing properties for the resolver. These servers may be present at an enterprise or ISP. If the mapping is not found there, the DNS server will query other higher-level DNS servers that are authoritative for the top-level domain in order to find the mapping. These are known as recursive queries.

Because of the potential burden on authoritative top-level domain servers, some DNS servers in the hierarchy maintain caches of all DNS records that they have resolved for a period of time. These caching DNS servers can resolve recursive queries without forwarding the queries to higher-level servers. If a server requires data for a zone, it will request a transfer of that data from an authoritative server for that zone. The process of transferring blocks of DNS data between servers is known as a zone transfer.

Figures 4-122 through 4-127 display the steps involved in DNS resolution.

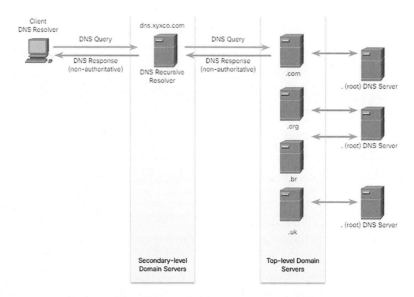

Figure 4-122   Example of the DNS Lookup Process

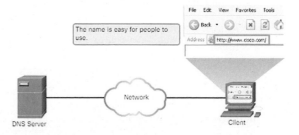

Figure 4-123   Resolving DNS Addresses: Step 1

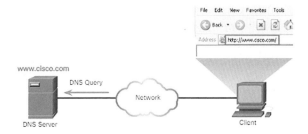

Figure 4-124   Resolving DNS Addresses: Step 2

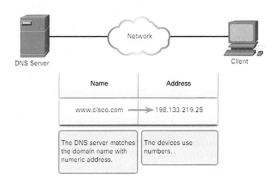

Figure 4-125   Resolving DNS Addresses: Step 3

Figure 4-126   Resolving DNS Addresses: Step 4

Figure 4-127   Resolving DNS Addresses: Step 5

DNS Message Format (4.6.2.4)

DNS uses UDP port 53 for DNS queries and responses. DNS queries originate at a client and responses are issued from DNS servers. If a DNS response exceeds 512 bytes, TCP port 53 is used to handle the message. It includes the format for queries, responses, and data. The DNS protocol communications use a single format called a message. This message format, shown in Figure 4-128, is used for all types of client queries and server responses, error messages, and the transfer of resource record information between servers.

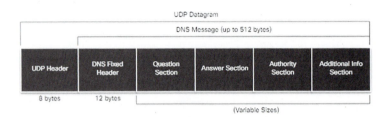

Figure 4-128   DNS Headers

The DNS server stores different types of RRs used to resolve names. These records contain the name, address, and type of record. Here is a list of some of these record types:

- **A:** An end device IPv4 address

- **NS:** An authoritative name server

- **AAAA:** An end device IPv6 address (pronounced quad-A)

- **MX:** A mail exchange record

When a client makes a query, the server's DNS process first looks at its own records to resolve the name. If it is unable to resolve the name using its stored records, it contacts other servers to resolve the name. After a match is found and returned to the original requesting server, the server temporarily stores the numbered address in the event that the same name is requested again.

The DNS Client service on Windows PCs also stores previously resolved names in memory. The **ipconfig /displaydns** command displays all of the cached DNS entries.

Dynamic DNS (4.6.2.5)

DNS requires registrars to accept and distribute DNS mappings from organizations that wish to register domain name and IP address mappings. After the initial mapping has been created, a process which can take 24 hours or more, changes to the IP address that is mapped to the domain name can be made by contacting the registrar or using an online form to the make the change. However, because of the time it takes for this process to occur and the new mapping to be distributed in DNS, the change can take hours before the new mapping is available to resolvers. In situations in which an ISP is using DHCP to provide addresses to a domain, it is possible that the address that is mapped to the domain could expire and a new address be granted by the ISP. This would result in a disruption of connectivity to the domain through

DNS. A new approach was necessary to allow organizations to make fast changes to the IP address that is mapped to a domain.

Dynamic DNS (DDNS) allows a user or organization to register an IP address with a domain name as in DNS. However, when the IP address of the mapping changes, the new mapping can be propagated through the DNS almost instantaneously. For this to occur, a user obtains a subdomain from a DDNS provider. That subdomain is mapped to the IP address of the user's server, or home router connection to the Internet. Client software runs on either the router or a host PC that detects a change in the Internet IP address of the user. When a change is detected, the DDNS provider is immediately informed of the change and the mapping between the user's subdomain and the Internet IP address is immediately updated, as shown in Figure 4-129.

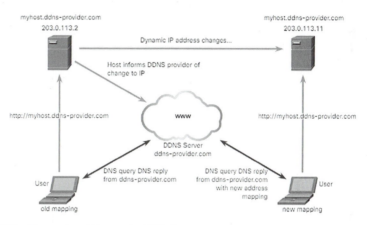

Figure 4-129   Example of Dynamic DNS Process

DDNS does not use a true DNS entry for a user's IP address. Instead, it acts as an intermediary. The DDNS provider's domain is registered with the DNS, but the subdomain is mapped to a totally different IP address. The DDNS provider service supplies that IP address to the resolver's second level DNS server. That DNS server, either at the organization or ISP, provides the DDNS IP address to the resolver.

The WHOIS Protocol (4.6.2.6)

WHOIS is a TCP-based protocol that is used to identify the owners of Internet domains through the DNS system. When an Internet domain is registered and mapped to an IP address for the DNS system, the registrant must supply information regarding who is registering the domain. The WHOIS application uses a query, in the form of an FQDN. The query is issued through a WHOIS service or application. The official ownership registration record is returned to the user by the WHOIS service. This can be useful for identifying the destinations that have been accessed by hosts on a network. WHOIS has limitations, and hackers have ways of hiding their identities. However, WHOIS is a starting point for identifying potentially dangerous Internet locations that may have been reached through the network. An Internet-based WHOIS service is maintained by ICANN and can be reached at https://whois.icann.org/, as shown in Figure 4-130. Other WHOIS services are maintained by Regional Internet Registries such as RIPE and APNIC.

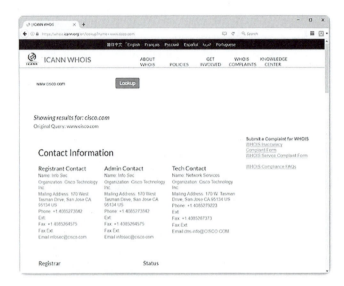

Figure 4-130   The ICANN WHOIS Website

Lab 4.6.2.7: Using Wireshark to Examine a UDP DNS Capture

In this lab, you will communicate with a DNS server by sending a DNS query using the UDP transport protocol. You will use Wireshark to examine the DNS query and response exchanges with the same server.

NAT (4.6.3)

In this topic, you will learn how NAT services enable network functionality.

NAT Overview (4.6.3.1)

There are not enough public IPv4 addresses to assign a unique address to each device connected to the Internet. Networks are commonly implemented using private IPv4 addresses, as defined in RFC 1918. Table 4-5 shows the range of addresses included in RFC 1918. It is very likely that the computer that you use to view this course is assigned a private address.

Table 4-5 Private IPv4 Addresses

Class	RFC 1918 Internal Address Range	CIDR Prefix
A	10.0.0.0 to 10.255.255.255	10.0.0.0/8
B	172.16.0.0 to 172.31.255.255	172.16.0.0/12
C	192.168.0.0 to 192.168.255.255	192.168.0.0/16

These private addresses are used within an organization or site to allow devices to communicate locally. However, because these addresses do not identify any single company or organization, private IPv4 addresses cannot be routed over the Internet. To allow a device with a private IPv4 address to access devices and resources outside of the local network, the private address must first be translated to a public address, as shown in Figure 4-131.

Figure 4-131 Translating Between Private and Public IPv4 Addresses

NAT-Enabled Routers (4.6.3.2)

NAT-enabled routers can be configured with one or more valid public IPv4 addresses. These public addresses are known as the NAT pool. When an internal device sends traffic out of the network, the NAT-enabled router translates the internal IPv4 address of the device to a public address from the NAT pool. To outside devices, all traffic entering and exiting the network appears to have a public IPv4 address from the provided pool of addresses.

A NAT router typically operates at the border of a stub network. A stub network is a network that has a single connection to its neighboring network, one way in and one way out of the network. In the example in Figure 4-132, R2 is a border router. As seen from the ISP, R2 forms a stub network.

When a device inside the stub network wants to communicate with a device outside of its network, the packet is forwarded to the border router. The border router performs the NAT process, translating the internal private address of the device to a public, outside, routable address.

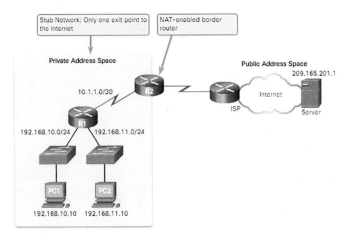

Figure 4-132   NAT Border

> **Note**
>
> The connection to the ISP may use a private address or a public address that is shared among customers. For the purposes of this chapter, a public address is shown.

Port Address Translation (4.6.3.3)

NAT can be implemented as one-to-one static mappings of private addresses to public addresses, or many internal addresses can be mapped to a single public address. This is known as *Port Address Translation (PAT)*. PAT is quite commonly used in home networks when an ISP provides a single public IP address to the home router. In most homes, multiple devices will require Internet access. PAT allows all of the network devices within the home network to share the single IP address that is provided by the ISP. In larger networks, PAT can be used to map many internal addresses to several public addresses as well.

With PAT, multiple addresses can be mapped to one or to a few addresses, because each private address is also tracked by a port number. When a device initiates a TCP/IP session, it generates a TCP or UDP source port value or a specially assigned query ID for ICMP, to uniquely identify the session. When the NAT router receives a packet from the client, it uses its source port number to uniquely identify the specific NAT translation. The PAT process also validates that the incoming packets were requested, thus adding a degree of security to the session.

Figure 4-133 illustrates the PAT process. PAT adds unique source port numbers to the inside global address to distinguish between translations.

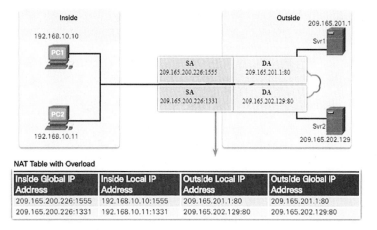

Figure 4-133   PAT Process

As R2 processes each packet, it uses a port number (1331 and 1555, in this example) to identify the device from which the packet originated. The source address (SA) is the inside local address with the TCP/IP assigned port number added. The destination address (DA) is the outside local address with the service port number added. In this example, the service port is 80, which is HTTP.

For the source address, R2 translates the private address (known as an inside local address) to an outside global public address with the port number added. The destination address is not changed, but is now referred to as the outside global IPv4 address. When the web server replies, the path is reversed.

NAT/PAT can complicate cyber-operations because it can hide addressing information in the log files created by network security and monitoring devices.

File Transfer and Sharing Services (4.6.4)

In this topic, you will learn how file transfer services enable network functionality.

FTP and TFTP (4.6.4.1)

FTP and TFTP are two commonly used file transfer protocols.

File Transfer Protocol (FTP)

FTP is another commonly used application layer protocol. FTP was developed to allow for data transfers between a client and a server. An FTP client is an application that runs on a computer that is used to push and pull data from an FTP server.

As Figure 4-134 illustrates, to successfully transfer data, FTP requires two connections between the client and the server, one for commands and replies, the other for the actual file transfer:

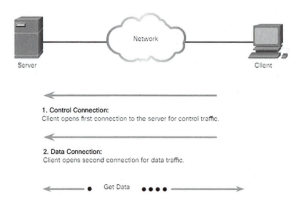

Figure 4-134 FTP Process

1. The client establishes the first connection to the server for control traffic using TCP port 21, consisting of client commands and server replies.

2. The client establishes the second connection to the server for the actual data transfer using TCP port 20. This connection is created every time there is data to be transferred.

The data transfer can happen in either direction. The client can download (pull) data from the server, or the client can upload (push) data to the server.

FTP was not designed to be a secure application layer protocol. For this reason, SSH File Transfer Protocol, which is a secure form of FTP that uses the Secure Shell protocol to provide a secure channel, is the preferred file transfer implementation.

Trivial File Transfer Protocol (TFTP)

TFTP is a simplified file transfer protocol that uses the well-known UDP port number 69. It lacks many of the features of FTP, such as the file management operations of listing, deleting, or renaming files. Because of its simplicity, TFTP has a very low network overhead and is popular for non-critical file transfer applications. It is fundamentally insecure, however, because it has no login or access control features. For this reason, TFTP needs to implemented carefully, and only when absolutely necessary.

SMB (4.6.4.2)

The *Server Message Block (SMB)* is a client/server file sharing protocol that describes the structure of shared network resources, such as directories, files, printers, and serial ports, as shown in Figure 4-135. It is a request-response protocol. All SMB messages share a common format. This format uses a fixed-sized header, followed by a variable-sized parameter and data component.

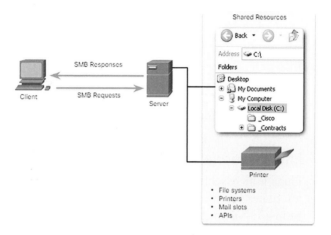

Figure 4-135   SMB Protocol

SMB messages can start, authenticate, and terminate sessions, control file and printer access, and allow an application to send or receive messages to or from another device.

SMB file sharing and print services have become the mainstay of Microsoft networking, as shown in Figure 4-136.

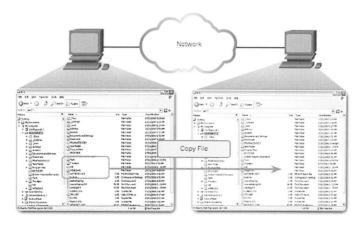

Figure 4-136   SMB File Sharing

Lab 4.6.4.3: Using Wireshark to Examine TCP and UDP Captures

In this lab, you will complete the following objectives:

- Identify TCP header fields and operation using a Wireshark FTP session capture

- Identify UDP header fields and operation using a Wireshark TFTP session capture

Email (4.6.5)

In this topic, you will learn how email services enable network functionality.

Email Overview (4.6.5.1)

Email is an essential network application. To run on a computer or other end device, it requires several applications and services, as shown in Figure 4-137. Email is a store-and-forward method of sending, storing, and retrieving electronic messages across a network. Email messages are stored in databases on mail servers.

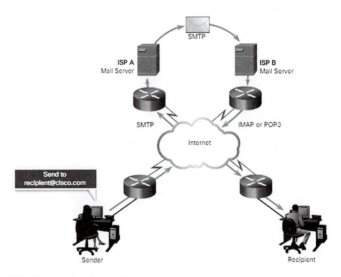

Figure 4-137 Example of the Email Process

Email clients communicate with mail servers to send and receive email. Mail servers communicate with other mail servers to transport messages from one domain to another. An email client does not communicate directly with another email client when sending email. Instead, both clients rely on the mail server to transport messages.

Email supports three separate protocols for operation: Simple Mail Transfer Protocol (SMTP), Post Office Protocol version 3 (POP3), and Internet Message Access Protocol (IMAP). The application layer process that sends mail uses SMTP. A client retrieves email, however, using one of the two application layer protocols: POP3 or IMAP.

SMTP (4.6.5.2)

SMTP message formats require a message header and a message body. While the message body can contain any amount of text, the message header must have a properly formatted recipient email address and a sender address.

When a client sends email, the client SMTP process connects with a server SMTP process on well-known port 25. After the connection is made, the client attempts to send the email to the server across the connection. When the server receives the message, it either places the message in a local account, if the recipient is local, or forwards the message to another mail server for delivery, as shown in Figure 4-138.

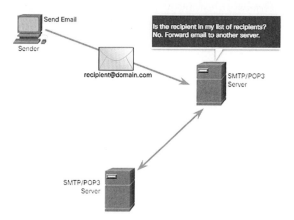

Figure 4-138   SMTP Process

The destination email server may not be online or may be busy when email messages are sent. Therefore, SMTP spools messages to be sent at a later time. Periodically, the server checks the queue for messages and attempts to send them again. If the message is still not delivered after a predetermined expiration time, it is returned to the sender as undeliverable.

POP3 (4.6.5.3)

POP3 is used by an application to retrieve mail from a mail server. With POP3, mail is downloaded from the server to the client and then deleted on the server, as shown in Figure 4-139.

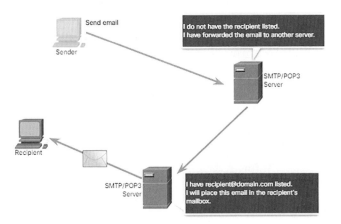

Figure 4-139 POP3 Process

The server starts the POP3 service by passively listening on TCP port 110 for client connection requests. When a client wants to make use of the service, it sends a request to establish a TCP connection with the server. When the connection is established, the POP3 server sends a greeting. The client and POP3 server then exchange commands and responses until the connection is closed or aborted.

With POP3, email messages are downloaded to the client and removed from the server, so there is no centralized location where email messages are kept. Because POP3 does not store messages, it is undesirable for a small business that needs a centralized backup solution.

IMAP (4.6.5.4)

IMAP is another protocol that describes a method to retrieve email messages, as shown in Figure 4-140.

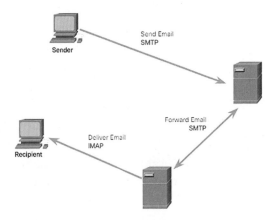

Figure 4-140 IMAP Process

Unlike POP3, when the user connects to an IMAP-capable server, copies of the messages are downloaded to the client application. The original messages are kept on the server until manually deleted. Users view copies of the messages in their email client software.

Users can create a file hierarchy on the server to organize and store mail. That file structure is duplicated on the email client as well. When a user decides to delete a message, the server synchronizes that action and deletes the message from the server.

HTTP (4.6.6)

In this topic, you will learn how HTTP services enable network functionality.

HTTP Overview (4.6.6.1)

To better understand how the web browser and web server interact, we can examine how a web page is opened in a browser. For this example, use the URL http://www.cisco.com, as shown in Figure 4-141.

Figure 4-141   HTTP Example Topology

First, the browser interprets the three parts of the URL:

- **http** (the protocol or scheme)

- **www.cisco.com** (the server name)

- **index.html** (the default home page is requested)

> **Note**
>
> Web servers typically display the home page, index.html, as the default page if no other page is specified. You do not need to enter the full path including the /index.html. If fact, you can simply enter cisco.com. Regardless of whether you enter cisco.com, www.cisco.com, or www.cisco.com/index.html, the web server will display the same home page, index.html.

As shown in Figure 4-142, the browser then checks with a name server to convert www.cisco.com into a numeric IP address, which it uses to connect to the server.

Using HTTP requirements, the browser sends a GET request to the server and asks for the index.html file. The server, as shown in Figure 4-143, sends the HTML code for this web page to the browser.

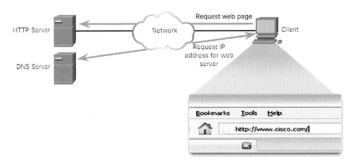

Figure 4-142   HTTP Process: Step 1

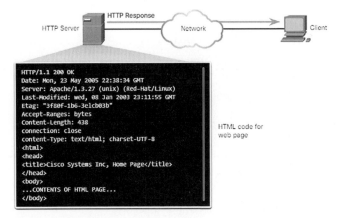

Figure 4-143   HTTP Process: Step 2

Finally, as shown in Figure 4-144, the browser deciphers the HTML code and formats the page for the browser window.

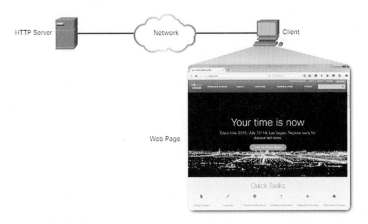

Figure 4-144   HTTP Process: Step 3

The HTTP URL (4.6.6.2)

An HTTP URL can also specify the port on the server that should handle the HTTP methods. In addition, it can specify a query string and fragment. The query string typically contains information that is not handled by the HTTP server process itself, but is instead handled by another process that is running on the server. Query strings are preceded by a "?" character and typically consist of a series of name and value pairs. A fragment is preceded by a "#" character. It refers to a subordinate part of the resource that is requested in the URL. For example, a fragment could refer to a named anchor in an HTML document. The URL will access the document and then move to the part of the document specified by the fragment if a matching named anchor link exists in the document. An HTTP URL that includes these parts is shown in Figure 4-145.

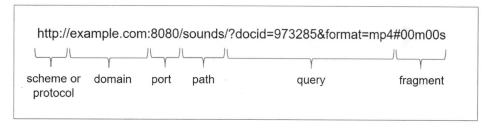

Figure 4-145   Parts of a URL

The HTTP Protocol (4.6.6.3)

HTTP is a request/response protocol that uses TCP port 80, although other ports can be used. When a client, typically a web browser, sends a request to a web server, it will use one of five methods that are specified by the HTTP protocol:

- **GET:** A client request for data. A client (web browser) sends the GET message to the web server to request HTML pages, as shown in Figure 4-146.

- **POST:** Submits data to be processed by a resource.

- **PUT:** Uploads resources or content to the web server such as an image.

- **DELETE:** Deletes the resource specified.

- **OPTIONS:** Returns the HTTP methods that the server supports.

- **CONNECT:** Requests that an HTTP proxy server forward the HTTP TCP session to the desired destination.

Although HTTP is remarkably flexible, it is not a secure protocol. The request messages send information to the server in plaintext that can be intercepted and read. The server responses, typically HTML pages, are also unencrypted.

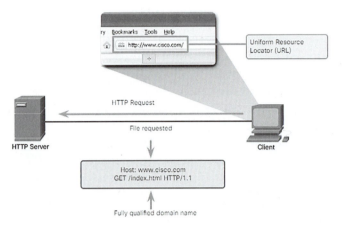

Figure 4-146 HTTP Using GET

Securing HTTP

For secure communication across the Internet, the HTTP Secure (HTTPS) protocol is used. HTTPS uses TCP port 443. HTTPS uses authentication and encryption to secure data as it travels between the client and server. HTTPS uses the same client request–server response process as HTTP, but the data stream is encrypted with Secure Sockets Layer (SSL), or Transport Layer Security (TLS), before being transported across the network. Although SSL is the predecessor to TLS, both protocols are often referred to as SSL.

Much confidential information, such as passwords, credit card information, and medical information, is transmitted over the Internet using HTTPS.

HTTP Status Codes (4.6.6.4)

The HTTP server responses are identified with various status codes that inform the host application of the outcome of client requests to the server. The codes are organized into five groups. The codes are numeric, with the first number in the code indicating the type of message. The five status code groups are:

- **1xx:** Informational
- **2xx:** Success
- **3xx:** Redirection
- **4xx:** Client Error
- **5xx:** Server Error

An explanation of some common status codes is shown in Table 4-6.

Table 4-6   Some Common HTTP Status Codes

Code	Status	Meaning
1xx - Informational		
100	Continue	The client should continue with request. Server has verified that the request can be fulfilled.
2xx - Success		
200	OK	The request completed successfully.
202	Accepted	The request has been accepted for processing, but processing is not completed.
4xx - Client Error		
403	Forbidden	The request is understood by the server, but the resource will not be fulfilled, possibly because the requester is not authorized to view the resource.
404	Not Found	The server cannot find the requested resource.

Lab 4.6.6.5: Using Wireshark to Examine HTTP and HTTPS Traffic

In this lab, you will complete the following objectives:

- Capture and view HTTP traffic
- Capture and view HTTPS traffic

Summary (4.7)

In this chapter, you learned the basic operation of network protocols and services. Networks come in all sizes, from small, home office networks to the Internet. Protocols are the rules for how traffic is sent across networks. Networking engineers use two models to understand and communicate the operation of protocols: the OSI model and the TCP/IP model. Regardless of the model used, the process of encapsulation describes how data is formatted for transmission across the network so that the destination can receive and de-encapsulate the data.

Ethernet operates at Layer 2 of the OSI model. Ethernet is responsible for encapsulating the upper layer data in a frame, which includes source and destination MAC addresses. MAC addresses are used on the LAN to locate either the destination or the default gateway.

IP operates at Layer 3 of the OSI model. IP comes in two versions: IPv4 and IPv6. Although IPv4 is being replaced by IPv6, IPv4 is still prevalent on today's networks. IPv4 uses a 32-bit address space represented in dotted-decimal format, such as 192.168.1.1. IPv6 uses a 128-bit address space represented in hexadecimal format. In IPv6, you can omit leading zeros in each hextet and omit one "all zeros" segment, such as 2001:0DB8:0000:1111:0000:0000:0000:0200 represented as 2001:DB8:0:1111::200.

ICMP is used primarily for testing end-to-end connectivity from source to destination. ICMP for IPv4 is different than ICMP for IPv6. ICMP for IPv6 includes router and neighbor solicitations, router and neighbor advertisements, and duplicate address detection. The ping and traceroute utilities both use a feature of ICMP. Ping is used to test connectivity between two hosts but does not provide information about the details of devices between the hosts. Traceroute (tracert) is a utility that generates a list of hops that were successfully reached along the path.

ARP operates between Layer 2 and Layer 3, mapping MAC addresses to IP addresses. Before a host can send traffic to a remote network, it must know the MAC address for the default gateway. The host already knows the IP address for the default gateway. For example, a host with an IP address 192.168.1.10 might have a default gateway configured of 192.168.1.1. The host uses an ARP request to ask "Who is 192.168.1.1?" The default gateway will reply with its own MAC address. At that point, the host has mapped the IP address to the default gateway's MAC address and can now construct the frame to send data to a remote network.

The transport layer is responsible for separating the data from the application layer into segments that can be sent down to the network layer. TCP is the transport layer protocol used when all the data must arrive at the destination in the correct order. UDP is the transport layer protocol used when the application can tolerate some data loss during transmission.

At the application layer, there are several important network services that the cybersecurity analysts should be aware of:

- **DHCP:** This automates the assignment of IPv4 addresses, subnet masks, gateways, and other IPv4 networking parameters.

- **DNS:** This provides a reliable means of managing and providing domain names and their associated IP addresses.

- **NAT:** This translates between private and public IPv4 addresses.

- **File Transfer:** Applications such as FTP, TFTP, and SMB can be used to transfer files from one host to another.

- **Email:** This requires several applications and services including POP3, IMAP, and SMTP.

- **HTTP:** This protocol is used to send and receive web pages.

Practice

The following activities provide practice with the topics introduced in this chapter. The Labs are available in the companion *CCNA Cybersecurity Operations Lab Manual* (ISBN: 9781587134388).

Labs

Lab 4.1.1.7: Tracing a Route

Lab 4.1.2.10: Introduction to Wireshark

Lab 4.4.2.8: Using Wireshark to Examine Ethernet Frames

Lab 4.5.2.4: Using Wireshark to Observe the TCP 3-Way Handshake

Lab 4.5.2.10: Exploring Nmap

Lab 4.6.2.7: Using Wireshark to Examine a UDP DNS Capture

Lab 4.6.4.3: Using Wireshark to Examine TCP and UDP Captures

Lab 4.6.6.5: Using Wireshark to Examine HTTP and HTTPS Traffic

Check Your Understanding

Complete all the review questions listed here to test your understanding of the topics and concepts in this chapter. The appendix "Answers to 'Check Your Understanding' Questions" lists the answers.

1. Which message does an IPv4 host use to reply when it receives a DHCPOFFER message from a DHCP server?

   A. DHCPACK

   B. DHCPREQUEST

   C. DHCPDISCOVER

   D. DHCPOFFER

2. What OSI layer is responsible for establishing a temporary communication session between two applications and ensuring that transmitted data can be reassembled in proper sequence?

   A. Session

   B. Transport

   C. Network

   D. Data link

3. PC1 and PC3 are on different networks separated by a router, RT1. PC1 issues an ARP request because it needs to send a packet to PC3. In this scenario, what will happen next?

   A. RT1 will forward the ARP request to PC3.

   B. RT1 will drop the ARP request.

   C. RT1 will send an ARP reply with its own MAC address.

   D. RT1 will send an ARP reply with the PC3 MAC address.

4. What addresses are mapped by ARP?

   A. Destination IPv4 address to the source MAC address

   B. Destination IPv4 address to the destination hostname

   C. Destination MAC address to the source IPv4 address

   D. Destination MAC address to a destination IPv4 address

5. Which statement is true about FTP?

   A. The client can download data from or upload data to the server.

   B. The client can choose if FTP is going to establish one or two connections with the server.

   C. FTP is a peer-to-peer application.

   D. FTP does not provide reliability during data transmission.

6. Which two OSI model layers have the same functionality as two layers of the TCP/IP model? (Choose two.)

   A. Session

   B. Transport

   C. Network

   D. Data link

   E. Physical

7. Which statement is true about the TCP/IP and OSI models?

   A. The TCP/IP transport layer and OSI Layer 4 provide similar services and functions.

   B. The TCP/IP network access layer has similar functions to the OSI network layer.

   C. The OSI Layer 7 and the TCP/IP application layer provide identical functions.

   D. The first three OSI layers describe general services that are also provided by the TCP/IP Internet layer.

8. What is the most compressed representation of the IPv6 address 2001:0000:0000:abcd:0000:0000:0000:0001?

   A. 2001::abcd::1

   B. 2001:0:abcd::1

   C. 2001::abcd:0:1

   D. 2001:0:0:abcd::1

   E. 2001:0000:abcd::1

9. What three application layer protocols are part of the TCP/IP protocol suite? (Choose three.)

   A. ARP

   B. DHCP

   C. DNS

   D. FTP

   E. NAT

   F. PPP

10. If the default gateway is configured incorrectly on the host, what is the impact on communications?

   A. The host is unable to communicate on the local network.

   B. There is no impact on communications.

   C. The host can communicate with other hosts on remote networks, but is unable to communicate with hosts on the local network.

   D. The host can communicate with other hosts on the local network, but is unable to communicate with hosts on remote networks.

11. Which message delivery option is used when all devices need to receive the same message simultaneously?

   A. Duplex

   B. Unicast

   C. Multicast

   D. Broadcast

## CHAPTER 5

Network Infrastructure

Objectives

Upon completion of this chapter, you will be able to answer the following questions:

- How do network devices enable network communication?

- How do wireless devices enable network communication?

- How are specialized devices used to enhance network security?

- How do network services enhance network security?

- How are network designs represented by interconnected symbols?

Key Terms

This chapter uses the following key terms. You can find the definitions in the Glossary.

Introduction (5.0)

The network infrastructure defines the way in which devices are connected together to achieve end-to-end communications. Just as there are many sizes of networks, there are also many ways to build an infrastructure. However, there are some standard designs that the network industry recommends to achieve networks that are available and secure.

This chapter covers the basic operation of network infrastructures, including wired and wireless networks, network security, and network designs.

Network Communication Devices (5.1)

In this section, you will learn how network devices enable wired and wireless network communication.

Network Devices (5.1.1)

In this topic, you will learn how network devices enable network communication.

End Devices (5.1.1.1)

End devices include computers, laptops, servers, printers, smart devices, and mobile devices. Individual end devices are connected to the network by *intermediary devices*. Intermediary devices not only connect the individual end devices to the network but also connect multiple individual networks to form an internetwork. These intermediary devices provide connectivity and ensure that data flows across the network. In Figure 5-1, a packet moves from an end device through intermediary devices to another end device.

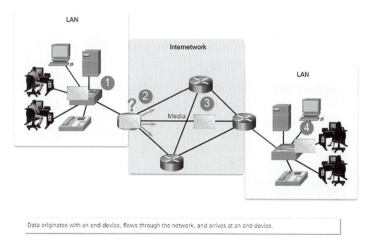

Data originates with an end device, flows through the network, and arrives at an end device.

Figure 5-1   Data Flowing Through the Internetwork

Intermediary devices use the destination end device address, in conjunction with information about the network interconnections, to determine the path that messages should take through the network. Examples of the more common intermediary devices are shown in Figure 5-2.

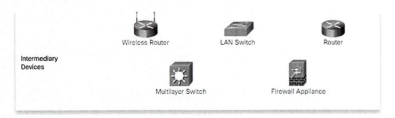

Figure 5-2   Intermediary Network Devices

Intermediary network devices perform some or all of these functions:

- Regenerate and retransmit data signals
- Maintain information about what pathways exist through the network and internetwork
- Notify other devices of errors and communication failures
- Direct data along alternate pathways when there is a link failure
- Classify and direct messages according to priorities
- Permit or deny the flow of data, based on security settings

Video Tutorial 5.1.1.2: End Devices

Video

Refer to the online course to view this video.

Routers (5.1.1.3)

Routers are devices that operate at the OSI network layer. They use the process of routing to forward data packets between networks, or subnetworks, as shown in Figure 5-3.

The routing process uses network routing tables, protocols, and algorithms to determine the most efficient path for forwarding an IP packet. Routers gather routing information and update other routers about changes in the network. Routers increase the scalability of networks by segmenting broadcast domains.

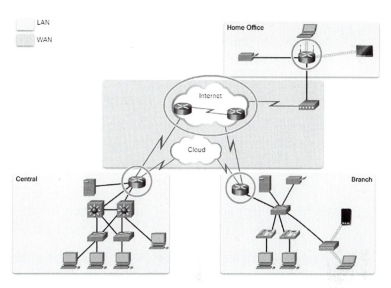

Figure 5-3   The Router Connection

Routers have two primary functions: *path determination* and *packet forwarding*. To perform path determination, each router builds and maintains a routing table, which is a database of known networks and how to reach them. The routing table can be built manually and contain static routes or can be built using a dynamic routing protocol.

Packet forwarding is accomplished by using a switching function. Switching is the process used by a router to accept a packet on one interface and forward it out of another interface. A primary responsibility of the switching function is to encapsulate packets in the appropriate data link frame type for the outgoing data link. Figure 5-4 shows R1 receiving a packet on one network and preparing to forward the packet out of another network toward the destination network.

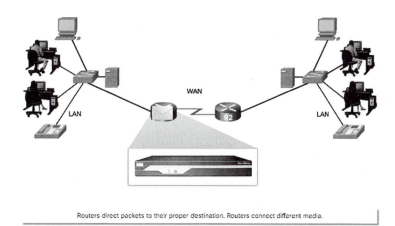

Routers direct packets to their proper destination. Routers connect different media.

Figure 5-4   Routers Connect

After the router has determined the exit interface using the path determination function, the router must encapsulate the packet into the data link frame of the outgoing interface.

What does a router do with a packet received from one network and destined for another network? The router performs the following three major steps:

1. It de-encapsulates the Layer 2 frame header and trailer to expose the Layer 3 packet.

2. It examines the destination IP address of the IP packet to find the best path in the routing table.

3. If the router finds a path to the destination, it encapsulates the Layer 3 packet into a new Layer 2 frame and forwards that frame out the exit interface.

As shown in Figure 5-5, devices have Layer 3 IPv4 addresses, while Ethernet interfaces have Layer 2 data link addresses.

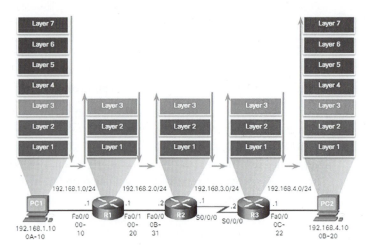

Figure 5-5   Encapsulating and De-Encapsulating Packets

The MAC addresses are shortened to simplify the illustration. For example, PC1 is configured with IPv4 address 192.168.1.10 and an example MAC address of 0A-10. As a packet travels from the source device to the final destination device, the Layer 3 IP addresses do not change. This is because the Layer 3 PDU does not change. However, the Layer 2 data link addresses change at every router on the path to the destination, as the packet is de-encapsulated and re-encapsulated in a new Layer 2 frame.

Interactive Graphic

Activity 5.1.1.4: Match Layer 2 and Layer 3 Addressing

Refer to the online course to complete this Activity.

Router Operation (5.1.1.5)

To increase scalability, networks can be divided into subnetworks, which are called subnets. Subnets create the network segments which support end devices and create a hierarchical structure. A primary function of a router is to determine the best path to use to send packets to each subnet. To determine the best path, the router searches its routing table for a network address that matches the destination IP address of the packet.

The routing table search results in one of three path determinations:

- **Directly connected network:** If the destination IP address of the packet belongs to a device on a network that is directly connected to one of the interfaces of the router, that packet is forwarded directly to the destination device. This means that the destination IP address of the packet is a host address on the same network as the interface of the router.

- **Remote network:** If the destination IP address of the packet belongs to a remote network, then the packet is forwarded to another router. Remote networks can only be reached by forwarding packets to another router.

- **No route determined:** If the destination IP address of the packet does not belong to either a connected or remote network, then the router determines if there is a Gateway of Last Resort available. A Gateway of Last Resort is set when a default route is configured or learned on a router. If there is a default route, the packet is forwarded to the Gateway of Last Resort. If the router does not have a default route, then the packet is discarded.

The logic flowchart in Figure 5-6 illustrates the router packet forwarding decision process.

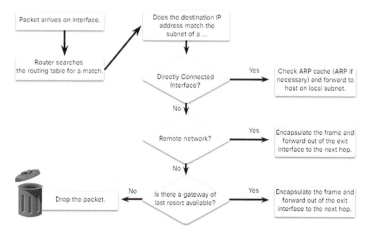

Figure 5-6   Packet Forwarding Decision Process

Because routers do not forward Ethernet broadcast frames, they separate a network into separate broadcast domains. This keeps broadcast traffic isolated to a given network attached to a router interface.

In Figure 5-7, PC1 is sending a packet to PC2.

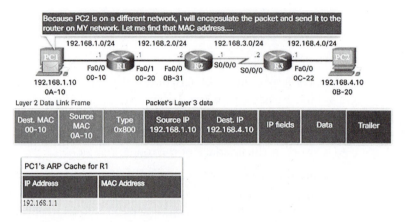

Figure 5-7   PC1 Builds a Packet to Send to PC2

PC1 must determine if the destination IPv4 address is on the same network. PC1 determines its own subnet by doing an AND operation on its own IPv4 address and subnet mask. This produces the network address to which PC1 belongs. Next, PC1 does this same AND operation using the packet destination IPv4 address and the PC1 subnet mask. The result tells PC1 that PC2 is not on the same network as PC1. Therefore, PC1 builds a packet to send to its default gateway, R1.

Routing Information (5.1.1.6)

The routing table of a router stores the following information:

- **Directly connected routes:** These routes come from the active router interfaces. Routers add a directly connected route when an interface is configured with an IP address and is activated.

- **Remote routes:** These are remote networks connected to other routers. Routes to these networks can either be statically configured or dynamically learned through dynamic routing protocols.

Specifically, a routing table is a data file in RAM that is used to store route information about directly connected and remote networks. The routing table contains network or next-hop associations. These associations tell a router that a particular destination can be optimally reached by sending the packet to a specific router that represents the next hop on the way to the final destination. The next-hop association can also be the outgoing or exit interface to the next destination.

Figure 5-8 identifies the directly connected networks and remote networks of router R1.

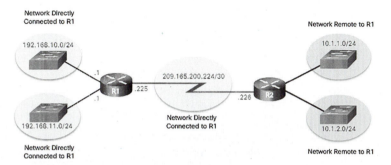

Figure 5-8   Directly Connected and Remote Network Routes

The destination network entries in the routing table can be added in several ways:

- **Local route interfaces:** These are added when an interface is configured and active. This entry is only displayed in IOS 15 or newer for IPv4 routes, and all IOS releases for IPv6 routes.

- **Directly connected interfaces:** These are added to the routing table when an interface is configured and active.

- *Static routes*: These are added when a route is manually configured and the exit interface is active.

- *Dynamic routing protocol*: This is added when routing protocols that dynamically learn about the network, such as EIGRP or OSPF, are implemented and networks are identified.

Dynamic routing protocols exchange network reachability information between routers and dynamically adapt to network changes. Each routing protocol uses routing algorithms to determine the best paths between different segments in the network, and updates routing tables with these paths.

Dynamic routing protocols have been used in networks since the late 1980s. One of the first routing protocols was the Routing Information Protocol (RIP). RIPv1 was released in 1988. As networks evolved and became more complex, new routing protocols emerged. The RIP protocol was updated to RIPv2 to accommodate growth in the network environment. However, RIPv2 still does not scale to the larger network implementations of today. To address the needs of larger networks, two advanced routing protocols were developed: Open Shortest Path First (OSPF) and Intermediate

System-to-Intermediate System (IS-IS). Cisco developed the Interior Gateway Routing Protocol (IGRP) and Enhanced IGRP (EIGRP), which also scales well in larger network implementations.

Additionally, there was the need to connect different internetworks and provide routing between them. The Border Gateway Protocol (BGP) is now used between Internet service providers (ISPs). BGP is also used between ISPs and their larger private clients to exchange routing information.

Table 5-1 classifies the protocols. Routers configured with these protocols will periodically send messages to other routers. As a cybersecurity analyst, you will see these messages in various logs and packet captures.

Table 5-1   Routing Protocol Classification

	Interior Gateway Protocols				Exterior Gateway Protocols
	Distance Vector		**Link-State**		**Path Vector**
IPv4	RIPv2	EIGRP	OSPFv2	IS-IS	BGP-4
IPv6	RIPng	EIGRP for IPv6	OSPFv3	IS-IS for IPv6	BGP-MP

Video

Video Tutorial 5.1.1.7: Static and Dynamic Routing

Refer to the online course to view this video.

Hubs, Bridges, LAN Switches (5.1.1.8)

The topology icons for hubs, bridges, and LAN switches are shown in Figure 5-9.

Figure 5-9   LAN Devices

An Ethernet hub acts as a multiport repeater that receives an incoming electrical signal (data) on a port. It then immediately forwards a regenerated signal out all other ports. Hubs use physical layer processing to forward data. They do not look at the source and destination MAC address of the Ethernet frame. Hubs connect the network into a star topology with the hub as the central connection point. When two or more end devices connected to a hub send data at the same time, an electrical collision takes place, corrupting the signals. All devices connected to a hub belong to the same collision domain. Only one device can transmit traffic at any given time on a collision domain. If a collision does occur, end devices use *CSMA/CD* logic to avoid transmission until the network is clear of traffic.

Bridges have two interfaces and are connected between hubs to divide the network into multiple collision domains. Each collision domain can have only one sender at a time. Collisions are isolated by the bridge to a single segment and do not impact devices on other segments. Just like a switch, a bridge makes forwarding decisions based on Ethernet MAC addresses.

LAN switches are essentially multiport bridges that connect devices into a star topology. Like bridges, switches segment a LAN into separate collision domains, one for each switch port. A switch makes forwarding decisions based on Ethernet MAC addresses. Figure 5-10 shows the Cisco series of 2960-X switches that are commonly used to connect end devices on a LAN.

Figure 5-10   Cisco 2960-X Series Switches

Switching Operation (5.1.1.9)

Switches use MAC addresses to direct network communications through the switch, to the appropriate port, and toward the destination. A switch is made up of integrated circuits and the accompanying software that controls the data paths through the switch. For a switch to know which port to use to transmit a frame, it must first learn which devices exist on each port. As the switch learns the relationship of ports to devices, it builds a table called a MAC address table, or *content addressable memory (CAM)* table. CAM is a special type of memory used in high-speed searching applications.

LAN switches determine how to handle incoming data frames by maintaining the MAC address table. A switch builds its MAC address table by recording the MAC address of each device connected to each of its ports. The switch uses the information in the MAC address table to send frames destined for a specific device out the port which has been assigned to that device.

The following two-step process is performed on every Ethernet frame that enters a switch.

Step 1. Learn: Examining the Source MAC Address

Every frame that enters a switch is checked for new information to learn. The switch does this by examining the frame's source MAC address and port number where the frame entered the switch. If the source MAC address does not exist, it is added to the table along with the incoming port number, as shown in Figure 5-11. If the source MAC address does exist, the switch updates the refresh timer for that entry. By default, most Ethernet switches keep an entry in the table for 5 minutes.

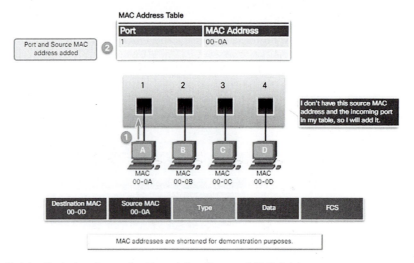

Figure 5-11   Switches Learn by Examining Source MAC Addresses

Note

If the source MAC address does exist in the table but on a different port, the switch treats this as a new entry. The entry is replaced using the same MAC address, but with the more current port number.

Step 2. Forward: Examining the Destination MAC Address

If the destination MAC address is a unicast address, the switch will look for a match between the destination MAC address of the frame and an entry in its MAC address table. If the destination MAC address is in the table, it will forward the frame out the specified port. If the destination MAC address is not in the table, the switch will forward the frame out all ports except the incoming port, as shown in Figure 5-12. This is called an unknown unicast.

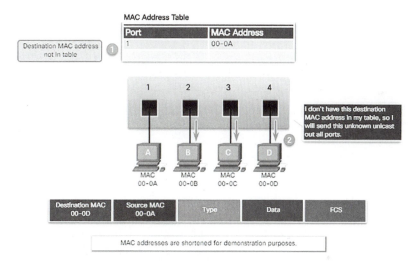

Figure 5-12   Switches Forward by Examining Destination MAC Address

> **Note**
>
> If the destination MAC address is a broadcast or a multicast, the frame is also flooded out all ports except the incoming port.

Video

Video Tutorial 5.1.1.10: MAC Address Tables on Connected Switches

Refer to the online course to view this video.

VLANs (5.1.1.11)

Within a switched internetwork, *virtual LANs (VLANs)* provide segmentation and organizational flexibility. VLANs provide a way to group devices within a LAN. A group of devices within a VLAN communicate as if they were connected to the same network segment. VLANs are based on logical connections, instead of physical connections.

VLANs allow an administrator to segment networks based on factors such as function, project team, or application, without regard for the physical location of the user or device, as shown in Figure 5-13.

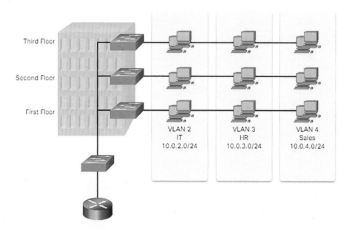

Figure 5-13   Defining VLAN Groups

Devices within a VLAN act as if they are in their own independent network, even if they share a common infrastructure with other VLANs. Any switch port can belong to a VLAN. Unicast, broadcast, and multicast packets are forwarded and flooded only to end devices within the VLAN where the packets are sourced. Each VLAN is considered a separate logical network. Packets destined for devices that do not belong to the VLAN must be forwarded through a device that supports routing.

A VLAN creates a logical broadcast domain that can span multiple physical LAN segments. VLANs improve network performance by separating large broadcast domains into smaller ones. If a device in one VLAN sends a broadcast Ethernet frame, all devices in the VLAN receive the frame, but devices in other VLANs do not.

VLANs also prevent users on different VLANs from snooping on each other's traffic. For example, even though HR and Sales are connected to the same switch in Figure 5-13, the switch will not forward traffic between the HR and Sales VLANs. This allows a router or another device to use access control lists (ACLs) to permit or deny the traffic. Access control lists are discussed in more detail later in the chapter. For now, just remember that VLANs can help limit the amount of data visibility on your LANs.

STP (5.1.1.12)

Network redundancy is a key to maintaining network reliability. Multiple physical links between devices provide redundant paths. The network can then continue to operate when a single link or port has failed. Redundant links can also share the traffic load and increase capacity.

Multiple paths need to be managed so that Layer 2 loops are not created. The best paths are chosen, and an alternate path is immediately available should a primary path fail. The *Spanning Tree Protocol (STP)* is used to maintain one loop-free path in the Layer 2 network, at any time.

Redundancy increases the availability of the network topology by protecting the network from a single point of failure, such as a failed network cable or switch. When physical redundancy is introduced into a design, loops and duplicate frames occur. Loops and duplicate frames have severe consequences for a switched network. STP was developed to address these issues.

STP ensures that there is only one logical path between all destinations on the network by intentionally blocking redundant paths that could cause a loop. A port is considered blocked when user data is prevented from entering or leaving that port. This does not include bridge protocol data unit (BPDU) frames that are used by STP to prevent loops. Blocking the redundant paths is critical to preventing loops on the network. The physical paths still exist to provide redundancy, but these paths are disabled to prevent the loops from occurring. If the path is ever needed to compensate for a network cable or switch failure, STP recalculates the paths and unblocks the necessary ports to allow the redundant path to become active.

In this example, all switches have STP enabled:

1. PC1 sends a broadcast out onto the network (Figure 5-14).

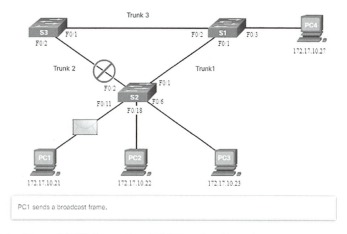

Figure 5-14   Normal STP Operation: PC1 Sends a Broadcast

2. S2 is configured with STP and has set the port for Trunk2 to a blocking state. The blocking state prevents ports from being used to forward user data, which prevents a loop from occurring. S2 forwards a broadcast frame out all switch ports (Figure 5-15), except the originating port from PC1 and the port for Trunk2.

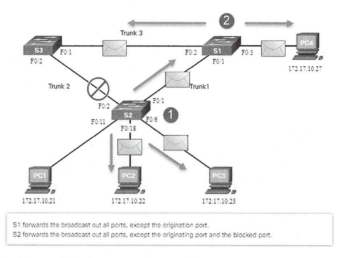

S1 forwards the broadcast out all ports, except the origination port.
S2 forwards the broadcast out all ports, except the originating port and the blocked port.

Figure 5-15 Normal STP Operation: S1 and S3 Forward the Broadcast

3. S1 receives the broadcast frame and forwards it out all of its switch ports, where it reaches PC4 and S3. S3 forwards the frame out the port for Trunk2 and S2 drops the frame (Figure 5-16). The Layer 2 loop is prevented.

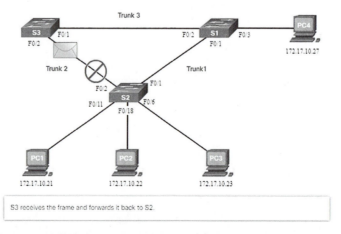

S3 receives the frame and forwards it back to S2.

Figure 5-16 Normal STP Operation: S3 Forwards Broadcast to S2

Figures 5-17 through 5-21 illustrate STP recalculation when a failure occurs.

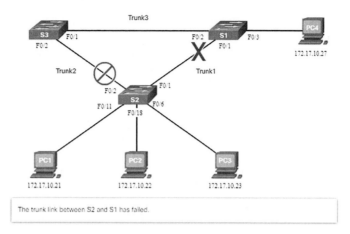

Figure 5-17 STP Detects a Link Failure

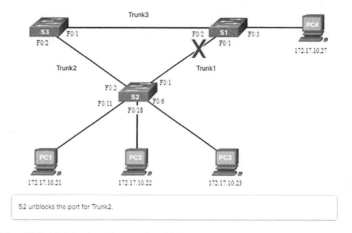

Figure 5-18 STP Unblocks Alternative Link

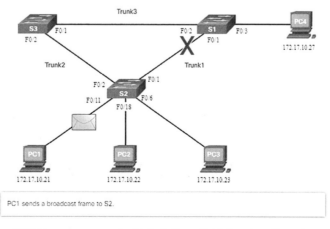

Figure 5-19 STP Compensates for Link Failure: PC1 Sends a Broadcast

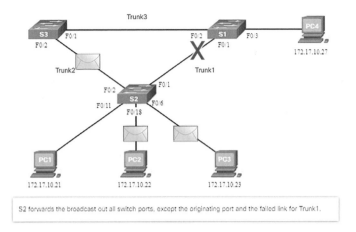

S2 forwards the broadcast out all switch ports, except the originating port and the failed link for Trunk1.

Figure 5-20 STP Compensates for Link Failure: S2 Forwards the Broadcast

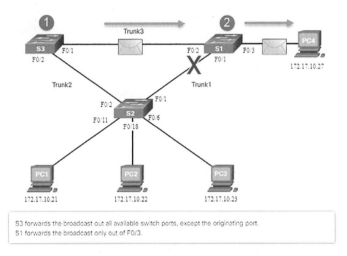

S3 forwards the broadcast out all available switch ports, except the originating port.
S1 forwards the broadcast only out of F0/3.

Figure 5-21 STP Compensates for Link Failure: S3 and S1 Forward the Broadcast

STP prevents loops from occurring by configuring a loop-free path through the network using strategically placed "blocking-state" ports. The switches running STP are able to compensate for failures by dynamically unblocking the previously blocked ports and permitting traffic to traverse the alternate paths.

STP generates traffic on the network. It will appear in some packet captures. Wireshark will recognize the traffic and identify the protocol as STP in the capture window.

Multilayer Switching (5.1.1.13)

Multilayer switches (also known as Layer 3 switches) not only perform Layer 2 switching, but also forward frames based on Layer 3 and 4 information. All Cisco Catalyst multilayer switches support the following types of Layer 3 interfaces:

- *Routed port*: A pure Layer 3 interface similar to a physical interface on a Cisco IOS router.

- *Switch virtual interface (SVI)*: A virtual VLAN interface for inter-VLAN routing. In other words, SVIs are the virtual-routed VLAN interfaces.

Routed Ports

A routed port is a physical port that acts similarly to an interface on a router (Figure 5-22).

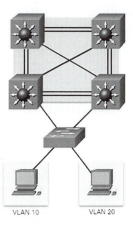

Figure 5-22   Routed Ports

Unlike an access port, a routed port is not associated with a particular VLAN. A routed port behaves like a regular router interface. Also, because Layer 2 functionality has been removed, Layer 2 protocols, such as STP, do not function on a routed interface. However, some protocols, such as LACP and EtherChannel, do function at Layer 3. Unlike Cisco IOS routers, routed ports on a Cisco IOS switch do not support subinterfaces.

Switch Virtual Interfaces

An SVI is a virtual interface that is configured within a multilayer switch, as shown in Figure 5-23.

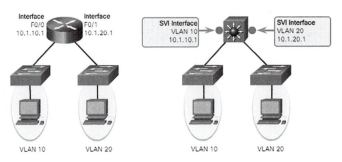

Figure 5-23   Switch Virtual Interface

Unlike the basic Layer 2 switches discussed above, a multilayer switch can have multiple SVIs. An SVI can be created for any VLAN that exists on the switch. An SVI is considered to be virtual because there is no physical port dedicated to the interface. It can perform the same functions for the VLAN as a router interface would, and can be configured in much the same way as a router interface (i.e., IP address, inbound/outbound ACLs, etc.). The SVI for the VLAN provides Layer 3 processing for packets to or from all switch ports associated with that VLAN.

Wireless Communications (5.1.2)

In this topic, you will learn how wireless devices enable network communication.

Video Tutorial 5.1.2.1: Wireless Communications

Refer to the online course to view this video.

Protocols and Features (5.1.2.2)

Wireless LANs (WLANs) use radio frequencies (RF) instead of cables at the physical layer and MAC sublayer of the data link layer. WLANs share a similar origin with Ethernet LANs. The IEEE has adopted the 802 LAN/MAN portfolio of computer network architecture standards. The two dominant 802 working groups are 802.3 Ethernet, which defined Ethernet for wired LANs, and 802.11, which defined Ethernet for WLANs. There are important differences between the two, as shown in Table 5-2.

Table 5-2 WLANs Versus LANs

Characteristic	802.11 Wireless LAN	802.3 Ethernet LANs
Physical Layer	Radio frequency (RF)	Cable
Media Access	Collision Avoidance	Collision Detection
Availability	Anyone with a radio NIC in range of an access point	Cable connection required
Signal Interference	Yes	Inconsequential
Regulation	Additional regulation by country authorities	IEEE standard dictates

WLANs also differ from wired LANs as follows:

- WLANs connect clients to the network through a *wireless access point (AP)* or wireless router, instead of an Ethernet switch.

- WLANs connect mobile devices that are often battery powered, as opposed to plugged-in LAN devices. Wireless NICs tend to reduce the battery life of a mobile device.

- WLANs support hosts that contend for access on the RF media (frequency bands). 802.11 prescribes collision avoidance (*CSMA/CA*) instead of collision detection (CSMA/CD) for media access to proactively avoid collisions within the media.

- WLANs use a different frame format than wired Ethernet LANs. WLANs require additional information in the Layer 2 header of the frame.

- WLANs raise more privacy issues because radio frequencies can reach outside the facility.

All Layer 2 frames consist of a header, payload, and FCS section as shown in Figure 5-24. The 802.11 frame format is similar to the Ethernet frame format, with the exception that it contains additional fields.

As shown in Figure 5-24, all 802.11 wireless frames contain the following fields:

- **Frame Control:** Identifies the type of wireless frame and contains subfields for Protocol Version, Frame Type, Address Type, Power Management, and Security Settings.

- **Duration:** Typically used to indicate the remaining time needed to receive the next frame transmission.

- **Address1:** Usually contains the MAC address of the receiving wireless device or AP.

- **Address2:** Usually contains the MAC address of the transmitting wireless device or AP.

- **Address3:** Sometimes contains the MAC address of the destination, such as the router interface (default gateway) to which the AP is attached.

- **Sequence Control:** Contains the Sequence Number and the Fragment Number subfields. The Sequence Number indicates the sequence number of each frame. The Fragment Number indicates the number of each frame sent of a fragmented frame.

- **Address4:** Usually empty because it is used only in ad hoc mode.

- **Payload:** Contains the data for transmission.

- **FCS:** Frame Check Sequence; used for Layer 2 error control.

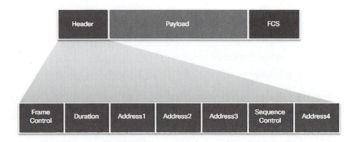

Figure 5-24   Content of Wireless 802.11 Frame Header

Wireless Network Operations (5.1.2.3)

For wireless devices to communicate over a network, they must first associate with an AP or wireless router. An important part of the 802.11 process is discovering a WLAN and subsequently connecting to it.

Management frames are used by wireless devices to complete the following three-stage process, as shown in Figure 5-25:

1. Discover new wireless AP.

2. Authenticate with AP.

3. Associate with AP.

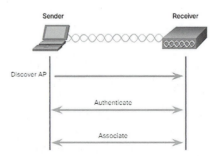

Figure 5-25   802.3 Wireless Association Is a Three-Stage Process

To associate with each other, a wireless client and an AP must agree on specific parameters. Parameters must be configured on the AP, as shown in Figure 5-26, and subsequently on the client to enable the negotiation of these processes.

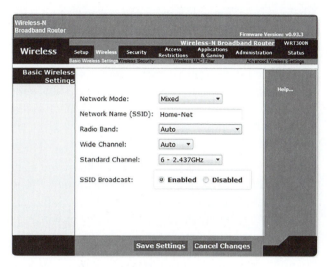

Figure 5-26   Basic Wireless Settings Example

Common configurable wireless parameters include

- **Network mode:** Refers to the 802.11 WLAN standards. APs and wireless routers can operate in a Mixed mode, as shown in Figure 5-26, which means that they can simultaneously use multiple standards.

- **SSID:** A *service set identifier (SSID)* is a unique identifier that wireless clients use to distinguish between multiple wireless networks in the same vicinity. If SSID broadcast is enabled, the SSID name appears in the list of available wireless networks on a client. Depending on the network configuration, several APs on a network can share an SSID. Names are usually 2 to 32 characters long. In Figure 5-26, the SSID is configured as Home-Net and SSID broadcast is enabled.

- **Channel settings:** Refers to the frequency bands being used to transmit wireless data. Wireless routers and APs can choose the channel setting or it can be set manually if there is interference with another AP or wireless device. In Figure 5-26, the channel is manually set to 6, which is the 2.437 GHz frequency.

- **Security mode:** Refers to the security parameter settings, such as WEP, WPA, or WPA2. Always enable the highest security level supported. For a home or small office, you would use WPA2 Personal.

- **Encryption:** WPA2 requires that you choose an encryption. Use AES whenever possible.

- **Password:** Required from the wireless client to authenticate to the AP. A password is sometimes called the security key. It prevents intruders and other unwanted users from accessing the wireless network.

Wireless devices must discover and connect to an AP or wireless router. Wireless clients connect to the AP using a scanning (probing) process. This process can be passive or active:

- **Passive mode:** The AP openly advertises its service by periodically sending broadcast beacon frames containing the SSID, supported standards, and security settings. The primary purpose of the beacon is to allow wireless clients to learn which networks and APs are available in a given area, thereby allowing them to choose which network and AP to use.

- **Active mode:** Wireless clients must know the name of the SSID. The wireless client initiates the process by broadcasting a Probe Request frame on multiple channels. The probe request includes the SSID name and standards supported. Active mode may be required if an AP or wireless router is configured to not broadcast beacon frames.

The 802.11 standard was originally developed with two authentication mechanisms:

- **Open authentication:** Fundamentally a NULL authentication where the wireless client says "authenticate me" and the AP responds with "yes." Open authentication provides wireless connectivity to any wireless device and should only be used in situations where security is of no concern.

- **Shared key authentication:** Technique is based on a key that is pre-shared between the client and the AP.

The Client to AP Association Process (5.1.2.4)

A wireless client goes through a three-stage process to associate with an AP. After the wireless client has associated with the AP, traffic is able to flow between the client and the AP.

Stage 1: Discovery

In the discovery phase, a wireless client locates the appropriate AP to first associate with. After the client has associated, other APs may be used if the client is roaming through the network.

Figure 5-27 illustrates how passive mode works with the AP broadcasting a beacon frame every so often.

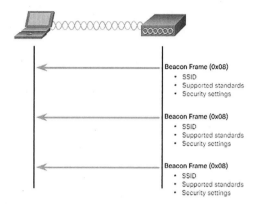

Figure 5-27   Client Devices Listen for an AP

Figure 5-28 illustrates how active mode works with a wireless client broadcasting a probe request for a specific SSID. The AP with that SSID responds with a probe response frame.

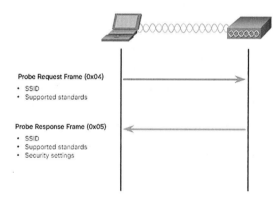

Figure 5-28   Active Mode Request and Response Probes

A wireless client could also send a probe request without an SSID name to discover nearby WLAN networks. APs configured to broadcast beacon frames would respond to the wireless client with a probe response and provide the SSID name. APs with the broadcast SSID feature disabled do not respond.

Stage 2: Authentication

Figure 5-29 provides a simple overview of the authentication process.

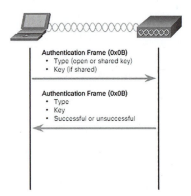

Figure 5-29   Client and AP Authenticate

However, in most shared key authentication installations, the exchange is as follows:

1. The wireless client sends an authentication frame to the AP.

2. The AP responds with a challenge text to the client.

3. The client encrypts the message using its shared key and returns the encrypted text back to the AP.

4. The AP then decrypts the encrypted text using its shared key.

5. If the decrypted text matches the challenge text, the AP authenticates the client. If the messages do not match, the wireless client is not authenticated and wireless access is denied.

After a wireless client has been authenticated, the AP proceeds to the association stage.

Stage 3: Association

The association stage finalizes settings and establishes the data link between the wireless client and the AP, as shown in Figure 5-30.

As part of this stage:

1. The wireless client forwards an Association Request frame that includes its MAC address.

2. The AP responds with an Association Response that includes the AP BSSID, which is the AP MAC address.

3. The AP maps a logical port known as the association identifier (AID) to the wireless client. The AID is equivalent to a port on a switch and allows the infrastructure switch to keep track of frames destined for the wireless client to be forwarded.

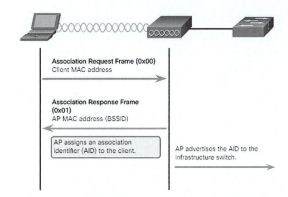

Figure 5-30 Client and AP Associate

Activity 5.1.2.5: Order the Steps in the Client and AP Association Process

Refer to the online course to complete this Activity.

Wireless Devices: AP, LWAP, WLC (5.1.2.6)

A common wireless data implementation is enabling devices to connect wirelessly via a LAN. In general, a wireless LAN requires wireless access points and clients that have wireless NICs. Home and small business wireless routers integrate the functions of a router, switch, and access point into one device, as shown Figure 5-31. Note that in small networks, the wireless router may be the only AP because only a small area requires wireless coverage. In larger networks, there can be many APs.

Figure 5-31 Cisco Wireless Router WRP500

All of the control and management functions of the APs on a network can be centralized into a *Wireless LAN Controller (WLC)*. When using a WLC, the APs no longer act autonomously, but instead act as *lightweight APs (LWAPs)*. LWAPs only forward data between the wireless LAN and the WLC. All management functions, such as defining SSIDs and authentication, are conducted on the centralized WLC rather than on each individual AP. A major benefit of centralizing the AP management functions in the WLC is simplified configuration and monitoring of numerous access points, among many other benefits.

Interactive Graphic

Activity 5.1.2.7: Identify the LAN Device

Refer to the online course to complete this Activity.

Network Security Infrastructure (5.2)

In this section, you will learn how devices and services are used to enhance network security.

Security Devices (5.2.1)

In this topic, you will learn how specialized devices are used to enhance network security.

Video

Video Tutorial 5.2.1.1: Security Devices

Refer to the online course to view this video.

Firewalls (5.2.1.2)

A firewall is a system, or group of systems, that enforces an access control policy between networks, as shown in Figure 5-32.

All firewalls share some common properties:

- Firewalls are resistant to network attacks.
- Firewalls are the only transit point between internal corporate networks and external networks because all traffic flows through the firewall.
- Firewalls enforce the access control policy.

- Allow traffic from any external address to the web server.
- Allow traffic to FTP server.
- Allow traffic to SMTP server.
- Allow traffic to internal IMAP server.

- Deny all inbound traffic with network addresses matching internal-registered IP addresses.
- Deny all inbound traffic to server from external addresses.
- Deny all inbound ICMP echo request traffic.
- Deny all inbound MS Active Directory queries.
- Deny all inbound traffic to MS SQL server queries.
- Deny all MS Domain Local Broadcasts.

Figure 5-32   Firewall Operation

There are several benefits of using a firewall in a network:

- They prevent the exposure of sensitive hosts, resources, and applications to untrusted users.
- They sanitize protocol flow, which prevents the exploitation of protocol flaws.
- They block malicious data from servers and clients.
- They reduce security management complexity by off-loading most of the network access control to a few firewalls in the network.

Firewalls also present some limitations:

- A misconfigured firewall can have serious consequences for the network, such as becoming a single point of failure.
- The data from many applications cannot be passed over firewalls securely.
- Users might proactively search for ways around the firewall to receive blocked material, which exposes the network to potential attack.
- Network performance can slow down.
- Unauthorized traffic can be tunneled or hidden as legitimate traffic through the firewall.

Firewall Type Descriptions (5.2.1.3)

It is important to understand the different types of firewalls and their specific capabilities so that the right firewall is used for each situation.

■ *Packet filtering (stateless) firewall*: Typically a router with the capability to filter some packet content, such as Layer 3 and sometimes Layer 4 information according to a set of configured rules (Figure 5-33).

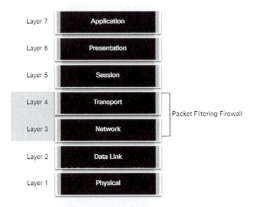

Figure 5-33   Packet Filtering Firewall

■ *Stateful firewall*: A stateful inspection firewall allows or blocks traffic based on state, port, and protocol. It monitors all activity from the opening of a connection until it is closed. Filtering decisions are made based on both administrator-defined rules as well as context, which refers to using information from previous connections and packets belonging to the same connection (Figure 5-34).

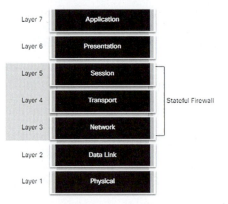

Figure 5-34   Stateful Firewall

■ *Application gateway firewall (proxy firewall)*: Filters information at Layers 3, 4, 5, and 7 of the OSI reference model. Most of the firewall control and filtering is done in software. When a client needs to access a remote server, it connects to a proxy server. The proxy server connects to the remote server on behalf of the client. Therefore, the server only sees a connection from the proxy server (Figure 5-35).

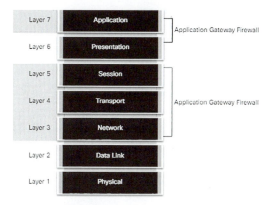

Figure 5-35   Application Gateway Firewall

Other methods of implementing firewalls include:

- **Host-based (server and personal) firewall:** A PC or server with firewall software running on it.

- **Transparent firewall:** Filters IP traffic between a pair of bridged interfaces.

- **Hybrid firewall:** A combination of the various firewall types. For example, an application inspection firewall combines a stateful firewall with an application gateway firewall.

Packet Filtering Firewalls (5.2.1.4)

Packet filtering firewalls are usually part of a router firewall, which permits or denies traffic based on Layer 3 and Layer 4 information. They are stateless firewalls that use a simple policy table lookup that filters traffic based on specific criteria, as shown in Figure 5-36.

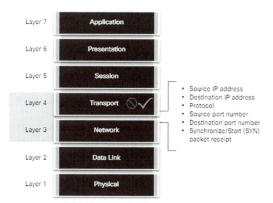

Figure 5-36   Packet Filtering Firewall

For example, SMTP servers listen to port 25 by default. An administrator can configure the packet filtering firewall to block port 25 from a specific workstation to prevent it from broadcasting an email virus.

Stateful Firewalls (5.2.1.5)

Stateful firewalls are the most versatile and the most common firewall technologies in use. Stateful firewalls provide stateful packet filtering by using connection information maintained in a state table. Stateful filtering is a firewall architecture that is classified at the network layer. It also analyzes traffic at OSI Layer 4 and Layer 5, as shown in Figure 5-37.

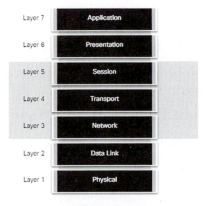

Figure 5-37 Stateful Firewalls and the OSI Model

Next-Generation Firewalls (5.2.1.6)

Next-generation firewalls go beyond stateful firewalls by providing

- Standard firewall capabilities like stateful inspection
- Integrated intrusion prevention
- Application awareness and control to see and block risky apps
- Upgrade paths to include future information feeds
- Techniques to address evolving security threats

Activity 5.2.1.7: Identify the Type of Firewall

Refer to the online course to complete this Activity.

Intrusion Protection and Detection Devices (5.2.1.8)

A networking architecture paradigm shift is required to defend against fast-moving and evolving attacks. This must include cost-effective detection and prevention systems, such as intrusion detection systems (IDS) or the more scalable *intrusion prevention systems (IPS)*. The network architecture integrates these solutions into the entry and exit points of the network.

When implementing IDS or IPS, it is important to be familiar with the types of systems available, host-based and network-based approaches, the placement of these systems, the role of signature categories, and possible actions that a Cisco IOS router can take when an attack is detected.

IDS and IPS technologies share several characteristics, as shown in Figure 5-38.

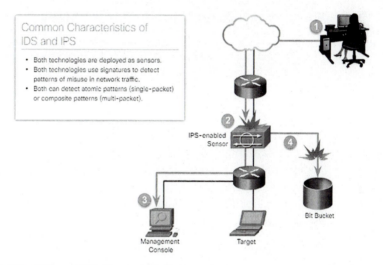

Figure 5-38   IDS and IPS Characteristics

IDS and IPS technologies are both deployed as sensors. An IDS or IPS sensor can be in the form of several different devices:

- A router configured with Cisco IOS IPS software

- A device specifically designed to provide dedicated IDS or IPS services

- A network module installed in a Cisco Adaptive Security Appliance (ASA), switch, or router

IDS and IPS technologies use signatures to detect patterns in network traffic. A signature is a set of rules that an IDS or IPS uses to detect malicious activity. Signatures can be used to detect severe breaches of security, to detect common network attacks, and to gather information. IDS and IPS technologies can detect atomic signature patterns (single-packet) or composite signature patterns (multi-packet).

Advantages and Disadvantages of IDS and IPS (5.2.1.9)

A list of the advantages and disadvantages of IDS and IPS is shown in Table 5-3.

Table 5-3 Comparing IDS and IPS Solutions

	Advantages	**Disadvantages**
IDS	No impact on network (latency, jitter).	Response action cannot stop trigger packets.
	No network impact if there is a sensor failure.	Correct tuning required for response actions.
	No network impact if there is a sensor overload.	More vulnerable to network security evasion.
IPS	Stops trigger packets.	Sensor issues might affect network traffic.
	Can use stream normalization techniques.	Sensor overloading impacts the network.
		Some impact on network (latency, jitter).

IDS Advantages and Disadvantages

A primary advantage of an IDS platform is that it is deployed in offline mode. Because the IDS sensor is not inline, it has no impact on network performance. It does not introduce latency, jitter, or other traffic flow issues. In addition, if a sensor fails it does not affect network functionality. It only affects the ability of the IDS to analyze the data.

However, there are many disadvantages of deploying an IDS platform. An IDS sensor is primarily focused on identifying possible incidents, logging information about the incidents, and reporting the incidents. The IDS sensor cannot stop the trigger packet and is not guaranteed to stop a connection. The trigger packet alerts the IDS to a potential threat. IDS sensors are also less helpful in stopping email viruses and automated attacks, such as worms.

Users deploying IDS sensor response actions must have a well-designed security policy and a good operational understanding of their IDS deployments. Users must spend time tuning IDS sensors to achieve expected levels of intrusion detection.

Finally, because IDS sensors are not inline, an IDS implementation is more vulnerable to network security evasion techniques in the form of various network attack methods.

IPS Advantages and Disadvantages

An IPS sensor can be configured to perform a packet drop to stop the trigger packet, the packets associated with a connection, or packets from a source IP address. Additionally, because IPS sensors are inline, they can use stream normalization. Stream normalization is a technique used to reconstruct the data stream when the attack occurs over multiple data segments.

A disadvantage of IPS is that (because it is deployed inline) errors, failure, and overwhelming the IPS sensor with too much traffic can have a negative effect on network performance. An IPS sensor can affect network performance by introducing latency and jitter. An IPS sensor must be appropriately sized and implemented so that time-sensitive applications, such as VoIP, are not adversely affected.

Deployment Considerations

Using one of these technologies does not negate the use of the other. In fact, IDS and IPS technologies can complement each other. For example, an IDS can be implemented to validate IPS operation because the IDS can be configured for deeper packet inspection offline. This allows the IPS to focus on fewer but more critical traffic patterns inline.

Deciding which implementation to use is based on the security goals of the organization as stated in their network security policy.

Types of IPS (5.2.1.10)

There are two primary kinds of IPSs available: host-based and network-based. These IPSs are compared in Table 5-4.

Table 5-4   Comparing Host-Based and Network-Based IPS Solutions

	Advantages	Disadvantages
Host-Based IPS	Provides protection specific to a host operating system	Operating system dependent
	Provides operating system and application level protection	Must be installed on all hosts
	Protects the host after the message is decrypted	
Network-Based IPS	Cost effective	Cannot examine encrypted traffic
	Operating system independent	Must stop malicious traffic prior to arriving at host

Host-based IPS

A *host-based IPS (HIPS)* is software installed on a single host to monitor and analyze suspicious activity. A significant advantage of HIPS is that it can monitor and protect operating system and critical system processes that are specific to that host. With detailed knowledge of the operating system, HIPS can monitor abnormal activity and prevent the host from executing commands that do not match typical behavior. This suspicious or malicious behavior might include unauthorized registry updates, changes to the system directory, executing installation programs, and activities that cause buffer overflows. Network traffic can also be monitored to prevent the host from participating in a denial-of-service (DoS) attack or being part of an illicit FTP session.

A HIPS can be thought of as a combination of antivirus software, antimalware software, and firewall. Combined with a network-based IPS, a HIPS is an effective tool in providing additional protection for the host.

A disadvantage of a HIPS is that it operates only at a local level. It does not have a complete view of the network, or coordinated events that might be happening across the network. To be effective in a network, a HIPS must be installed on every host and have support for every operating system.

Network-based IPS

A network-based IPS can be implemented using a dedicated or non-dedicated IPS device. Network-based IPS implementations are a critical component of intrusion prevention. There are host-based IDS/IPS solutions, but these must be integrated with a network-based IPS implementation to ensure a robust security architecture.

Sensors detect malicious and unauthorized activity in real time and can take action when required. Sensors are deployed at designated network points (Figure 5-39) that enable security managers to monitor network activity while it is occurring, regardless of the location of the attack target.

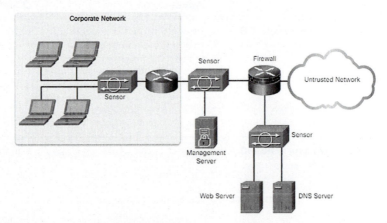

Figure 5-39   Sample IPS Sensor Deployment

Specialized Security Appliances (5.2.1.11)

Cisco Advanced Malware Protection (AMP) is an enterprise-class advanced malware analysis and protection solution. It provides comprehensive malware protection for organizations before, during, and after an attack:

- Before an attack, AMP strengthens defenses and protects against known and emerging threats.

- During an attack, AMP identifies and blocks policy-violating file types, exploit attempts, and malicious files from infiltrating the network.

- After an attack, or after a file is initially inspected, AMP goes beyond point-in-time detection capabilities and continuously monitors and analyzes all file activity and traffic, regardless of disposition, searching for any indications of malicious behavior. If a file with an unknown or previously deemed "good" disposition starts behaving badly, AMP will detect it and instantly alert security teams with an indication of compromise. It then provides visibility into where the malware originated, what systems were affected, and what the malware is doing.

AMP accesses the collective security intelligence of the Cisco Talos Security Intelligence and Research Group. Talos detects and correlates threats in real time using the largest threat-detection network in the world.

Cisco Web Security Appliance (WSA) is a secure web gateway that combines leading protections to help organizations address the growing challenges of securing and controlling web traffic. WSA protects the network by automatically blocking risky sites and testing unknown sites before allowing users to access them. WSA provides malware protection, application visibility and control, acceptable use policy controls, insightful reporting, and secure mobility.

While WSA protects the network from malware intrusion, it does not provide protection for users who want to connect to the Internet directly outside of the protected network, such as at a public Wi-Fi service. In this instance, the user's PC can be infected with malware, which can then spread to other networks and devices. To help protect user PCs from these types of malware infections there is Cisco Cloud Web Security (CWS).

CWS together with WSA provides comprehensive protection against malware and the associated impacts. The Cisco CWS solution enforces secure communication to and from the Internet and provides remote workers the same level of security as onsite employees when using a laptop issued by Cisco. Cisco CWS incorporates two main functions, web filtering and web security, and both are accompanied by extensive, centralized reporting.

Cisco Email Security Appliance (ESA)/Cisco Cloud Email Security help to mitigate email-based threats. The Cisco ESA defends mission-critical email systems. The Cisco

ESA is constantly updated by real-time feeds from Cisco Talos, which detects and correlates threats using a worldwide database monitoring system. These are some of the main features of ESA:

- **Global threat intelligence:** Cisco Talos provides a 24-hour view into global traffic activity. It analyzes anomalies, uncovers new threats, and monitors traffic trends.

- **Spam blocking:** A multilayered defense combines an outer layer of filtering based on the reputation of the sender and an inner layer of filtering that performs a deep analysis of the message.

- **Advanced malware protection:** Includes AMP that takes advantage of the vast cloud security intelligence network of Sourcefire. It delivers protection across the attack continuum before, during, and after an attack.

- **Outbound message control:** Controls outbound messages to help ensure that important messages comply with industry standards and are protected in transit.

Interactive Graphic

Activity 5.2.1.12: Compare IDS and IPS Characteristics

Refer to the online course to complete this Activity.

Security Services (5.2.2)

In this topic, you will learn how network services enhance network security.

Video

Video Tutorial 5.2.2.1: Security Services

Refer to the online course to view this video.

Traffic Control with ACLs (5.2.2.2)

An *access control list (ACL)* is a series of commands that control whether a device forwards or drops packets based on information found in the packet header. When configured, ACLs perform the following tasks:

- They limit network traffic to increase network performance. For example, if corporate policy does not allow video traffic on the network, ACLs that block video traffic could be configured and applied. This would greatly reduce the network load and increase network performance.

- They provide traffic flow control. ACLs can restrict the delivery of routing updates to ensure that the updates are from a known source.

- They provide a basic level of security for network access. ACLs can allow one host to access a part of the network and prevent another host from accessing the same area. For example, access to the Human Resources network can be restricted to authorized users.

- They filter traffic based on traffic type. For example, an ACL can permit email traffic, but block all Telnet traffic.

- They screen hosts to permit or deny access to network services. ACLs can permit or deny a user to access file types, such as FTP or HTTP.

In addition to either permitting or denying traffic, ACLs can be used for selecting types of traffic to be analyzed, forwarded, or processed in other ways. For example, ACLs can be used to classify traffic to enable priority processing. This capability is similar to having a VIP pass at a concert or sporting event. The VIP pass gives selected guests privileges not offered to general admission ticket holders, such as priority entry or being able to enter a restricted area.

Figure 5-40 shows a sample topology with ACLs applied to routers R1, R2, and R3.

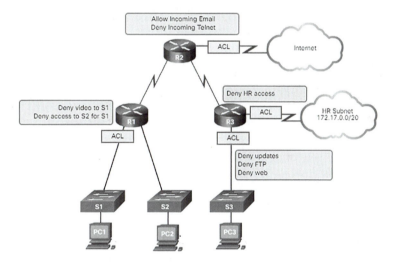

Figure 5-40   What Is an ACL?

ACLs: Important Features (5.2.2.3)

Two types of Cisco IPv4 ACLs are standard and extended. Standard ACLs can be used to permit or deny traffic only from source IPv4 addresses. The destination of the packet and the ports involved are not evaluated.

Extended ACLs filter IPv4 packets based on several attributes that include:

- Protocol type
- Source IPv4 address

- Destination IPv4 address

- Source TCP or UDP ports

- Destination TCP or UDP ports

- Optional protocol type information for finer control

Standard and extended ACLs can be created using either a number or a name to identify the ACL and its list of statements.

Using numbered ACLs is an effective method for determining the ACL type on smaller networks with more homogeneously defined traffic. However, a number does not provide information about the purpose of the ACL. For this reason, a name can be used to identify a Cisco ACL.

By configuring ACL logging, an ACL message can be generated and logged when traffic meets the permit or deny criteria defined in the ACL.

Cisco ACLs can also be configured to only allow TCP traffic that has an ACK or RST bit set, so that only traffic from an established TCP session is permitted. This can be used to deny any TCP traffic from outside the network that is trying to establish a new TCP session.

Packet Tracer 5.2.2.4: ACL Demonstration

In this activity, you will observe how an access control list (ACL) can be used to prevent a ping from reaching hosts on remote networks. After removing the ACL from the configuration, the pings will be successful.

SNMP (5.2.2.5)

Simple Network Management Protocol (SNMP) allows administrators to manage end devices, such as servers, workstations, routers, switches, and security appliances, on an IP network. It enables network administrators to monitor and manage network performance, find and solve network problems, and plan for network growth.

SNMP is an application layer protocol that provides a message format for communication between managers and agents. The SNMP system consists of three elements, as shown in Figure 5-41:

- **SNMP manager:** Runs SNMP management software

- **SNMP agents:** The nodes being monitored and managed

- **Management Information Base (MIB):** A database on the agent that stores data and operational statistics about the device

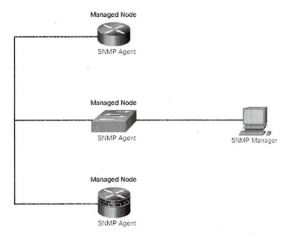

Figure 5-41   SNMP Topology

NetFlow (5.2.2.6)

NetFlow is a Cisco IOS technology that provides statistics on packets flowing through a Cisco router or multilayer switch. While SNMP attempts to provide a very wide range of network management features and options, NetFlow is focused on providing statistics on IP packets flowing through network devices.

NetFlow provides data to enable network and security monitoring, network planning, traffic analysis to include identification of network bottlenecks, and IP accounting for billing purposes. For example, in Figure 5-42, PC1 connects to PC2 using an application such as HTTPS. NetFlow can monitor that application connection, tracking byte and packet counts for that individual application flow. It then pushes the statistics over to an external server called a NetFlow collector.

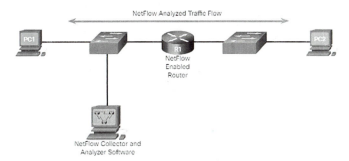

Figure 5-42   NetFlow in the Network

NetFlow technology has seen several generations that provide more sophistication in defining traffic flows, but "original NetFlow" distinguished flows using a combination of seven fields. Should one of these fields vary in value from another packet, the packets could be safely determined to be from different flows:

- Source IP address
- Destination IP address
- Source port number
- Destination port number
- Layer 3 protocol type
- Type of Service (ToS) marking
- Input logical interface

The first four of the fields NetFlow uses to identify a flow should be familiar. The source and destination IP addresses, plus the source and destination ports, identify the connection between source and destination application. The Layer 3 protocol type identifies the type of header that follows the IP header (usually TCP or UDP, but other options include ICMP). The ToS byte in the IPv4 header holds information about how devices should apply quality of service (QoS) rules to the packets in that flow.

Port Mirroring (5.2.2.7)

A *packet analyzer* (also known as a packet sniffer or traffic sniffer) is typically software that captures packets entering and exiting the network interface card (NIC). It is not always possible or desirable to have the packet analyzer on the device that is being monitored. Sometimes it is better on a separate station designated to capture the packets.

Because network switches can isolate traffic, traffic sniffers or other network monitors, such as IDS, cannot access all the traffic on a network segment. *Port mirroring* is a feature that allows a switch to make duplicate copies of traffic passing through a switch, and then send it out a port with a network monitor attached. The original traffic is forwarded in the usual manner. An example of port mirroring is illustrated in Figure 5-43.

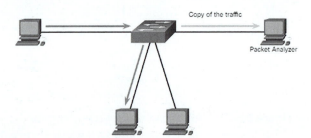

Figure 5-43   Traffic Sniffing Using a Switch

Syslog Servers (5.2.2.8)

When certain events occur on a network, networking devices have trusted mechanisms to notify the administrator with detailed system messages. These messages can be either noncritical or significant. Network administrators have a variety of options for storing, interpreting, and displaying these messages, and for being alerted to those messages that could have the greatest impact on the network infrastructure.

The most common method of accessing system messages is to use a protocol called syslog.

Many networking devices support *syslog*, including routers, switches, application servers, firewalls, and other network appliances. The syslog protocol allows networking devices to send their system messages across the network to syslog servers as shown in Figure 5-44.

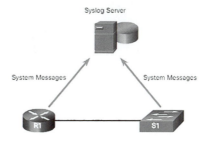

Figure 5-44   Syslog

The syslog logging service provides three primary functions:

- The ability to gather logging information for monitoring and troubleshooting
- The ability to select the type of logging information that is captured
- The ability to specify the destination of captured syslog messages

NTP (5.2.2.9)

It is important to synchronize the time across all devices on the network because all aspects of managing, securing, troubleshooting, and planning networks require accurate and consistent timestamping. When the time is not synchronized between devices, it will be impossible to determine the order of the events that have occurred in different parts of the network.

Typically, the date and time settings on a network device can be set using one of two methods:

- Manual configuration of the date and time
- Configuring the *Network Time Protocol (NTP)*

As a network grows, it becomes difficult to ensure that all infrastructure devices are operating with synchronized time. Even in a smaller network environment, the manual method is not ideal. If a device reboots, how will it get an accurate date and timestamp?

A better solution is to configure NTP on the network. This protocol allows routers on the network to synchronize their time settings with an NTP server. A group of NTP clients that obtain time and date information from a single source have more consistent time settings. When NTP is implemented in the network, it can be set up to synchronize to a private master clock or it can synchronize to a publicly available NTP server on the Internet.

NTP networks use a hierarchical system of time sources. Each level in this hierarchical system is called a stratum. The stratum level is defined as the number of hop counts from the authoritative source. The synchronized time is distributed across the network using NTP. Figure 5-45 displays a sample NTP network.

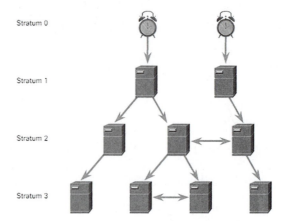

Figure 5-45   NTP Stratum Labels

NTP servers are arranged in three levels known as strata:

- **Stratum 0:** An NTP network gets the time from authoritative time sources. These authoritative time sources, also referred to as stratum 0 devices, are high-precision timekeeping devices assumed to be accurate and with little or no delay associated with them.

- **Stratum 1:** The stratum 1 devices are directly connected to the authoritative time sources. They act as the primary network time standard.

- **Stratum 2 and lower:** The stratum 2 servers are connected to stratum 1 devices through network connections. Stratum 2 devices, such as NTP clients, synchronize their time using the NTP packets from stratum 1 servers. They could also act as servers for stratum 3 devices.

Smaller stratum numbers indicate that the server is closer to the authorized time source than larger stratum numbers. The larger the stratum number, the lower the stratum level. The max hop count is 15. Stratum 16, the lowest stratum level, indicates that a device is unsynchronized. Time servers on the same stratum level can be configured to act as a peer with other time servers on the same stratum level for backup or verification of time.

AAA Servers (5.2.2.10)

AAA is an architectural framework for configuring a set of three independent security functions:

- **Authentication:** Users and administrators must prove that they are who they say they are. Authentication can be established using username and password combinations, challenge and response questions, token cards, and other methods. For example: "I am user 'student' and I know the password to prove it." AAA authentication provides a centralized way to control access to the network.

- **Authorization:** After the user is authenticated, authorization services determine which resources the user can access and which operations the user is allowed to perform. An example is "User 'student' can access host serverXYZ using SSH only."

- **Accounting and auditing:** Accounting records what the user does, including what is accessed, the amount of time the resource is accessed, and any changes that were made. Accounting keeps track of how network resources are used. An example is "User 'student' accessed host serverXYZ using SSH for 15 minutes."

Terminal Access Controller Access-Control System Plus (TACACS+) and *Remote Authentication Dial-In User Service (RADIUS)* are both authentication protocols that are used to communicate with AAA servers. Whether TACACS+ or RADIUS is selected depends on the needs of the organization.

While both protocols can be used to communicate between a router and AAA servers, TACACS+ is considered the more secure protocol. This is because all TACACS+ protocol exchanges are encrypted, while RADIUS only encrypts the user's password. RADIUS does not encrypt usernames, accounting information, or any other information carried in the RADIUS message. Table 5-5 shows differences between the two protocols.

Table 5-5   TACACS+ versus RADIUS

	TACACS+	**RADIUS**
Functionality	Separates AAA according to the AAA architecture, allowing modularity of the security server implementation	Combines authentication and authorization but separates accounting, allowing less flexibility in implementation than TACACS+
Standard	Mostly Cisco supported	Open/RFC standard
Transport Protocol	TCP	UDP
CHAP	Bidirectional challenge and response as used in Challenge Handshake Authentication Protocol (CHAP)	Unidirectional challenge and response from the RADIUS security server to the RADIUS client
Confidentiality	Entire packet encrypted	Password encrypted
Customization	Provides authorization of router commands on a per-user or per-group basis	Has no option to authorize router commands on a per-user or per-group basis
Accounting	Limited	Extensive

VPN (5.2.2.11)

A *virtual private network (VPN)* is a private network that is created over a public network, usually the Internet, as shown in Figure 5-46.

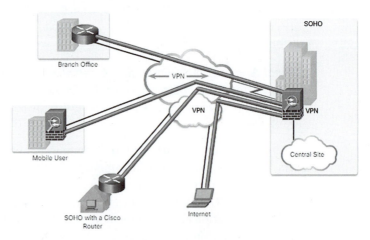

Figure 5-46   Virtual Private Networks

Instead of using a dedicated physical connection, a VPN uses virtual connections routed through the Internet from the organization to the remote site. The first VPNs were strictly IP tunnels that did not include authentication or encryption of the data. For example, *Generic Routing Encapsulation (GRE)* is a tunneling protocol developed by Cisco that can encapsulate a wide variety of network layer protocol packet types inside IP tunnels. This creates a virtual point-to-point link to Cisco routers at remote points over an IP internetwork.

A VPN is virtual in that it carries information within a private network, but that information is actually transported over a public network. A VPN is private in that the traffic is encrypted to keep the data confidential while it is transported across the public network.

A VPN is a communications environment in which access is strictly controlled to permit peer connections within a defined community of interest. Confidentiality is achieved by encrypting the traffic within the VPN. Today, a secure implementation of VPN with encryption is what is generally equated with the concept of virtual private networking.

In the simplest sense, a VPN connects two endpoints, such as a remote office to a central office, over a public network, to form a logical connection. The logical connections can be made at either Layer 2 or Layer 3. Common examples of Layer 3 VPNs are GRE, Multiprotocol Label Switching (MPLS), and IPsec. Layer 3 VPNs can be point-to-point site connections, such as GRE and IPsec, or they can establish any-to-any connectivity to many sites using MPLS.

IPsec is a suite of protocols developed with the backing of the IETF to achieve secure services over IP packet-switched networks, as shown in Figure 5-47.

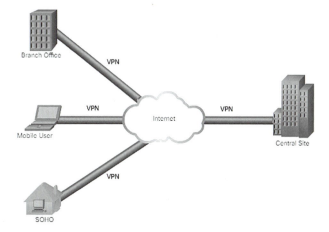

Figure 5-47   IPsec VPN

IPsec services allow for authentication, integrity, access control, and confidentiality. With IPsec, the information exchanged between remote sites can be encrypted and verified. Both remote-access and site-to-site VPNs can be deployed using IPsec.

Activity 5.2.2.12: Identify the Network Security Device or Service

Refer to the online course to complete this Activity.

Network Representations (5.3)

In this section, you will learn how networks and network topologies are represented.

Network Topologies (5.3.1)

In this topic, you will learn how network designs are represented by interconnected symbols.

Overview of Network Components (5.3.1.1)

The path that a message takes from source to destination can be as simple as a single cable connecting one computer to another, or as complex as a collection of networks that literally spans the globe. This network infrastructure provides the stable and reliable channel over which these communications occur.

The network infrastructure contains three categories of network components:

- Devices (Figure 5-48)
- Media (Figure 5-49)
- Services (Figure 5-50)

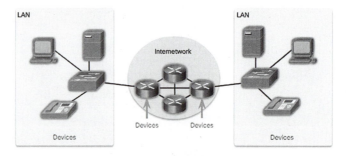

Figure 5-48   Components of a Network: Devices

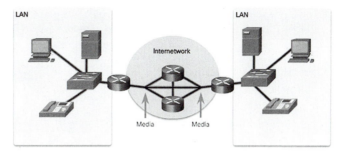

Figure 5-49   Components of a Network: Media

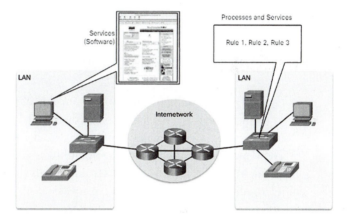

Figure 5-50   Components of a Network: Services and Processes

Devices and media are the physical elements, or hardware, of the network. Hardware is often the visible components of the network platform such as a laptop, PC, switch, router, wireless access point, or the cabling used to connect the devices.

Services include many of the common network applications people use every day, like email hosting services and web hosting services. Processes provide the functionality that directs and moves the messages through the network. Processes are less obvious to us but are critical to the operation of networks.

Physical and Logical Topologies (5.3.1.2)

The topology of a network is the arrangement or relationship of the network devices and the interconnections between them. LAN and wide area network (WAN) topologies can be viewed in two ways:

- *Physical topology*: Refers to the physical connections and identifies how end devices and infrastructure devices such as routers, switches, and wireless access points are interconnected (Figure 5-51).

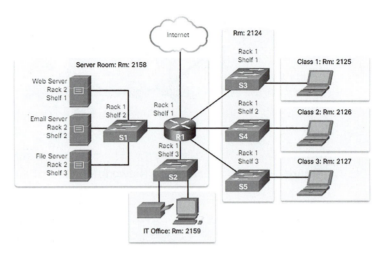

Figure 5-51   Physical Topology

■ *Logical topology*: Refers to the way a network transfers frames from one node to the next. This arrangement consists of virtual connections between the nodes of a network. These logical signal paths are defined by data link layer protocols. The logical topology of point-to-point links is relatively simple, while shared media offers different access control methods (Figure 5-52).

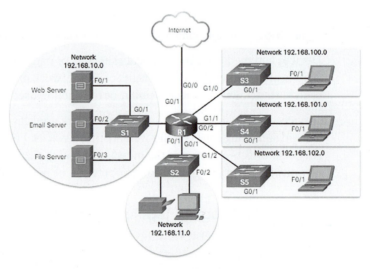

Figure 5-52   Logical Topology

The data link layer "sees" the logical topology of a network when controlling data accesses the media. It is the logical topology that influences the type of network framing and media access control used.

WAN Topologies (5.3.1.3)

WANs are commonly interconnected using the following physical topologies:

- **Point-to-point:** This is the simplest topology. It consists of a permanent link between two endpoints. For this reason, this is a very popular WAN topology.

- **Hub and spoke:** This topology is a WAN version of the star topology in which a central site interconnects branch sites using point-to-point links.

- **Mesh:** This topology provides high availability, but requires that every end system be interconnected to every other system. Therefore, the administrative and physical costs can be significant. Each link is essentially a point-to-point link to the other node.

The three common physical WAN topologies are illustrated in Figure 5-53.

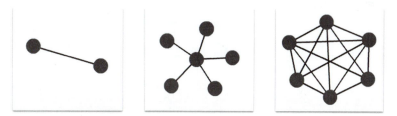

Figure 5-53   WAN Physical Topologies

A hybrid is a variation or combination of any of the above topologies. For example, a partial mesh is a hybrid topology in which some, but not all, end devices are interconnected.

LAN Topologies (5.3.1.4)

Physical topology defines how the end systems are physically interconnected. In shared media LANs, end devices can be interconnected using the following physical topologies:

- **Star:** End devices are connected to a central intermediate device. Early star topologies interconnected end devices using Ethernet hubs. However, star topologies now use Ethernet switches. The star topology is easy to install, very scalable (easy to add and remove end devices), and easy to troubleshoot.

- **Extended star:** In an extended star topology, additional Ethernet switches interconnect other star topologies. An extended star is an example of a hybrid topology.

- **Bus:** All end systems are chained to each other and terminated in some form on each end. Infrastructure devices such as switches are not required to interconnect the end devices. Bus topologies using coaxial cables were used in legacy Ethernet networks because it was inexpensive and easy to set up.

- **Ring:** End systems are connected to their respective neighbors, forming a ring. Unlike the bus topology, the ring does not need to be terminated. Ring topologies were used in legacy Fiber Distributed Data Interface (FDDI) and Token Ring networks.

Figure 5-54 illustrates how end devices are interconnected on LANs.

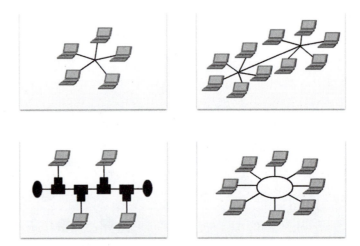

Figure 5-54   LAN Physical Topologies

The Three-Layer Network Design Model (5.3.1.5)

The campus wired LAN uses a hierarchical design model to break the design up into modular groups or layers. Breaking the design up into layers allows each layer to implement specific functions, which simplifies the network design and, therefore, the deployment and management of the network.

The campus wired LAN enables communications between devices in a building or group of buildings, as well as interconnection to the WAN and Internet edge at the network core.

A hierarchical LAN design includes the following three layers, as shown in Figure 5-55:

- *Access layer*: Provides endpoints and users direct access to the network

- *Distribution layer*: Aggregates access layers and provides connectivity to services

- *Core layer*: Provides connectivity between distribution layers for large LAN environments

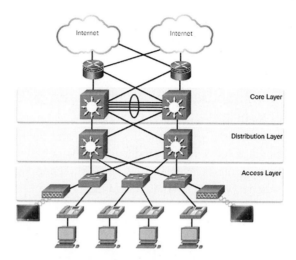

Figure 5-55   Hierarchical Design Model

User traffic is initiated at the access layer and passes through the other layers if the functionality of those layers is required. Even though the hierarchical model has three layers, some smaller enterprise networks may implement a two-tier hierarchical design. In a two-tier hierarchical design, the core and distribution layers are collapsed into one layer, reducing cost and complexity, as shown in Figure 5-56.

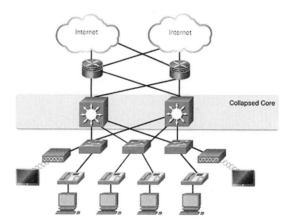

Figure 5-56   Collapsed Core

In flat or meshed network architectures, changes tend to affect a large number of systems. Hierarchical design helps constrain operational changes to a subset of the network, which makes it easy to manage as well as improve resiliency. Modular structuring of the network into small, easy-to-understand elements also facilitates resiliency via improved fault isolation.

Video Tutorial 5.3.1.6: Three-Layer Network Design

Refer to the online course to view this video.

Common Security Architectures (5.3.1.7)

Firewall design is primarily about device interfaces permitting or denying traffic based on the source, the destination, and the type of traffic. Some designs are as simple as designating an outside network and inside network, which are determined by two interfaces on a firewall. As shown in Figure 5-57, the public network (or outside network) is untrusted, and the private network (or inside network) is trusted.

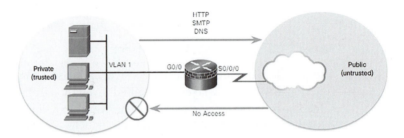

Figure 5-57   Private and Public Networks

Typically, a firewall with two interfaces is configured as follows:

- Traffic originating from the private network is permitted and inspected as it travels toward the public network. Inspected traffic returning from the public network and associated with traffic that originated from the private network is permitted.

- Traffic originating from the public network and traveling to the private network is generally blocked.

A *demilitarized zone (DMZ)* is a firewall design where there is typically one inside interface connected to the private network, one outside interface connected to the public network, and one DMZ interface, as shown in Figure 5-58.

- Traffic originating from the private network is inspected as it travels toward the public or DMZ network. This traffic is permitted with little or no restriction. Inspected traffic returning from the DMZ or public network to the private network is permitted.

- Traffic originating from the DMZ network and traveling to the private network is usually blocked.

- Traffic originating from the DMZ network and traveling to the public network is selectively permitted based on service requirements.

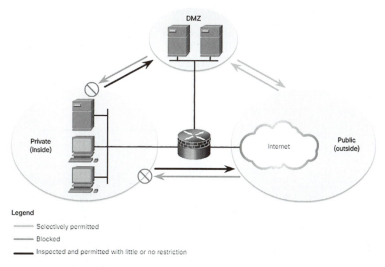

Figure 5-58   Permitted, Blocked, and Inspected Traffic

■ Traffic originating from the public network and traveling toward the DMZ is selectively permitted and inspected. This type of traffic is typically email, DNS, HTTP, or HTTPS traffic. Return traffic from the DMZ to the public network is dynamically permitted.

■ Traffic originating from the public network and traveling to the private network is blocked.

Zone-based policy firewalls (ZPFs) use the concept of zones to provide additional flexibility. A zone is a group of one or more interfaces that have similar functions or features. Zones help you specify where a Cisco IOS firewall rule or policy should be applied. In Figure 5-59, security policies for LAN 1 and LAN 2 are similar and can be grouped into a zone for firewall configurations. By default, the traffic between interfaces in the same zone is not subject to any policy and passes freely. However, all zone-to-zone traffic is blocked. In order to permit traffic between zones, a policy allowing or inspecting traffic must be configured.

The only exception to this default deny any policy is the router self zone. The self zone is the router itself and includes all the router interface IP addresses. Policy configurations that include the self zone would apply to traffic destined to and sourced from the router. By default, there is no policy for this type of traffic. Traffic that should be considered when designing a policy for the self zone includes management plane and control plane traffic, such as SSH, SNMP, and routing protocols.

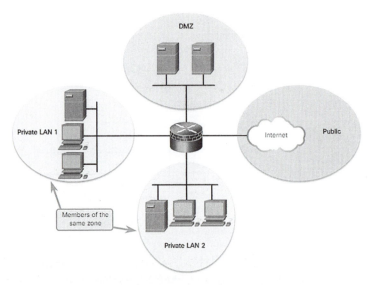

Figure 5-59   Zone-Based Policy Firewalls

Activity 5.3.1.8: Identify the Network Topology

Refer to the online course to complete this Activity.

Activity 5.3.1.9: Identify the Network Design Terminology

Refer to the online course to complete this Activity.

Packet Tracer 5.3.1.10: Identify Packet Flow

In this Packet Tracer activity, you will observe packet flow in a LAN and WAN topology. You will also observe how the packet flow path may change when there is a change in the network topology.

Summary (5.4)

In this chapter, you learned the basic operation of the network infrastructure. Routers are network layer devices and use the process of routing to forward data packets between networks or subnetworks. Switches segment a LAN into separate collision domains, one for each switch port. A switch makes forwarding decisions based on Ethernet MAC addresses. Multilayer switches (also known as Layer 3 switches) not only perform Layer 2 switching, but also forward frames based on Layer 3 and 4 information. Wireless networking devices, such as an AP or WLC, use the 802.11 standard instead of the 802.3 standard to connect wireless devices to the network.

Various types of firewalls enable network security, including

- **Packet filtering (stateless) firewall:** This provides Layer 3 and sometimes Layer 4 filtering.

- **Stateful firewall:** A stateful inspection firewall allows or blocks traffic based on state, port, and protocol.

- **Application gateway firewall (proxy firewall):** This filters information at Layers 3, 4, 5, and 7.

Network security services enhance network security through the use of the following:

- **ACLs:** These are a series of commands that control whether a device forwards or drops packets based on information found in the packet header.

- **SNMP:** This service enables network administrators to monitor and manage network performance, find and solve network problems, and plan for network growth.

- **NetFlow:** This provides statistics on packets flowing through a Cisco router or multilayer switch.

- **Port mirroring:** This is a feature that allows a switch to make duplicate copies of traffic passing through a switch, and then send it out a port with a network monitor attached.

- **Syslog server:** Use this to access the system messages generated by networking devices.

- **NTP:** This will synchronize the time across all devices on the network to ensure accurate and consistent timestamping of system messages.

- **AAA:** This is a framework for configuring user authentication, authorization, and accounting services.

- **VPN:** This is a private network created between two endpoints across a public network.

Network topologies are typically represented as physical networks and logical networks. A physical network topology refers to the physical connections and identifies how end devices are connected. A logical topology refers to the standards and protocols that devices use to communicate. Most topologies are a combination of both, showing how devices are physically and logically connected.

When looking at a topology that has access to outside or public networks, you should be able to determine the security architecture. Some designs are as simple as designating an outside network and inside network, which are determined by two interfaces on a firewall. Networks that require public access to services will often include a DMZ that the public can access, while strictly blocking access to the inside network. ZPFs use the concept of zones to provide additional flexibility. A zone is a group of one or more interfaces that have similar functions or features.

Practice

The following activities provide practice with the topics introduced in this chapter. The Packet Tracer Activities are available in the companion *CCNA Cybersecurity Operations Lab Manual* (ISBN: 9781587134388). The PKA files are found in the online course.

Packet Tracer Activities

Packet Tracer 5.2.2.4: ACL Demonstration

Packet Tracer 5.3.1.10: Identify Packet Flow

Check Your Understanding

Complete all the review questions listed here to test your understanding of the topics and concepts in this chapter. The appendix "Answers to 'Check Your Understanding' Questions" lists the answers.

1. What specialized network device is responsible for enforcing access control policies between networks?

   A. Bridge

   B. Switch

   C. Firewall

   D. IDS

2. What information does an Ethernet switch examine and use to build its address table?

   A. Source IP address

   B. Destination IP address

   C. Source MAC address

   D. Destination MAC address

3. Which device is an intermediary device?

   A. Smart device

   B. PC

   C. Server

   D. Firewall

4. Which statement describes a difference between RADIUS and TACACS+?

   A. RADIUS uses TCP, whereas TACACS+ uses UDP.

   B. RADIUS is supported by the Cisco Secure ACS software, whereas TACACS+ is not.

   C. RADIUS encrypts only the password, whereas TACACS+ encrypts all communication.

   D. RADIUS separates authentication and authorization, whereas TACACS+ combines them as one process.

5. Which wireless parameter refers to the frequency bands used to transmit data to a wireless access point?

   A. SSID

   B. Security mode

   C. Scanning mode

   D. Channel settings

6. What specialized network device uses signatures to detect patterns in network traffic?

   A. Bridges

   B. Switches

   C. IDS

   D. Firewalls

7. What type of physical topology can be created by connecting all Ethernet cables to a central device?

A. Star

B. Bus

C. Ring

D. Mesh

8. Which network service synchronizes the time across all devices on the network?

A. NetFlow

B. Syslog

C. NTP

D. SNMP

9. Which network service allows administrators to monitor and manage network devices?

A. NTP

B. SNMP

C. Syslog

D. NetFlow

## CHAPTER 6

Principles of Network Security

Objectives

Upon completion of this chapter, you will be able to answer the following questions:

- What is the evolution of network security?
- What are the various types of attack tools used by threat actors?
- What is malware?
- What are some common network attacks?

Key Terms

This chapter uses the following key terms. You can find the definitions in the Glossary.

virus   page 306

Trojan horse   page 306

worms   page 307

social engineering   page 309

spyware   page 310

adware   page 310

scareware   page 310

phishing   page 310

reconnaissance   page 312

access attacks   page 314

pass-the-hash   page 315

man-in-the-middle attack   page 315

spoofing   page 315

pretexting   page 318

quid pro quo   page 318

tailgating   page 318

baiting   page 318

visual hacking   page 318

spear phishing   page 319

whaling   page 319

pharming   page 319

watering hole   page 319

vishing   page 319

smishing   page 319

zombies   page 321

bots   page 321

botnet   page 321

handlers   page 321

botmaster   page 321

buffer overflow attack   page 322

Introduction (6.0)

The motivation for attacking networks can be financial gain, corporate- or state-sponsored espionage, activism, or simply malicious intent. The people and groups that engage in attacks on our network infrastructures are commonly referred to as threat actors.

This chapter covers the variety of tools and methods threat actors use to launch network attacks.

Attackers and Their Tools (6.1)

In this section, you will learn how networks are attacked.

Who Is Attacking Our Network (6.1.1)

In this topic, you will learn about the evolution of network security.

Threat, Vulnerability, and Risk (6.1.1.1)

We are under attack and attackers want access to our assets. Assets are anything of value to an organization such as data and other intellectual property, servers, computers, smart phones, tablets, and more.

To better understand any discussion of network security, it is important to know the following terms:

- *Threat*: A potential danger to an asset such as data or the network itself.

- *Vulnerability*: A weakness in a system or its design that could be exploited by a threat.

- *Attack surface*: The total sum of the vulnerabilities in a given system that is accessible to an attacker. The attack surface describes different points where an attacker could get into a system, and where they could get data out of the system. For example, your operating system and web browser could both need security patches. They are each vulnerable to attacks. Together, they create an attack surface the threat actor can exploit.

- *Exploit*: The mechanism that is used to leverage a vulnerability to compromise an asset. Exploits may be remote or local. A remote exploit is one that works over the network without any prior access to the target system. The attacker does not need an account in the end system to exploit the vulnerability. In a local exploit, the threat actor has some type of user or administrative access to the end system. A local exploit does not necessarily mean that the attacker has physical access to the end system.

- *Risk*: The likelihood that a particular threat will exploit a particular vulnerability of an asset and result in an undesirable consequence.

Risk management is the process that balances the operational costs of providing protective measures with the gains achieved by protecting the asset. There are four common ways to manage risk:

- *Risk acceptance*: This is when the cost of risk management options outweighs the cost of the risk itself. The risk is accepted without action.

- *Risk avoidance*: This is an action that avoids any exposure to the risk. This is usually the most expensive risk mitigation option.

- *Risk limitation*: This limits a company's risk exposure by taking some action. It is a strategy employing a bit of risk acceptance along with a bit of risk avoidance. It is the most commonly used risk mitigation strategy.

- *Risk transfer*: The risk is transferred to a willing third party such as an insurance company.

Other commonly used network security terms include

- *Countermeasure*: The protection solution that mitigates a threat or risk.

- *Impact*: The resulting damage to the organization that is caused by the threat.

> **Note**
>
> A local exploit requires inside network access such as a user with an account on the network. A remote exploit does not require an account on the network to exploit that network's vulnerability.

Hacker vs. Threat Actor (6.1.1.2)

As we know, *hacker* is a common term used to describe a threat actor. However, the term "hacker" has a variety of meanings:

- A clever programmer capable of developing new programs and coding changes to existing programs to make them more efficient

- A network professional who uses sophisticated programming skills to ensure that networks are not vulnerable to attack

- A person who tries to gain unauthorized access to devices on the Internet

- Individuals who run programs to prevent or slow network access to a large number of users, or corrupt or wipe out data on servers

The following terms are often used to describe hackers:

- *White hat hackers*: These are ethical hackers who use their programming skills for good, ethical, and legal purposes. White hat hackers may perform network penetration tests in an attempt to compromise networks and systems by using their knowledge of computer security systems to discover network vulnerabilities. Security vulnerabilities are reported to developers for them to fix before the vulnerabilities can be threatened. Some organizations award prizes or bounties to white hat hackers when they inform them of a vulnerability.

- *Gray hat hackers*: These are individuals who commit crimes and do arguably unethical things, but not for personal gain or to cause damage. An example would be someone who compromises a network without permission and then discloses the vulnerability publicly. A gray hat hacker may disclose a vulnerability to the affected organization after having compromised their network. This allows the organization to fix the problem.

- *Black hat hackers*: These are unethical criminals who violate computer and network security for personal gain, or for maliciousness reasons such as attacking networks. Black hat hackers exploit vulnerabilities to compromise computer and network systems.

Good or bad, hacking is an important aspect of network security. In this course, the term threat actor is used when referring to those individuals or groups that could be classified as gray or black hat hackers.

Evolution of Threat Actors (6.1.1.3)

Hacking started in the 1960s with phone freaking, or phreaking, which refers to using various audio frequencies to manipulate phone systems. At that time, telephone switches used various tones, or tone dialing, to indicate different functions. Early threat actors realized that by mimicking a tone using a whistle, they could exploit the phone switches to make free long-distance calls.

In the mid-1980s, computer dial-up modems were used to connect computers to networks. Threat actors wrote "war dialing" programs which dialed each telephone number in a given area in search of computers, bulletin board systems, and fax machines. When a phone number was found, password-cracking programs were used to gain access. Since then, general threat actor profiles and motives have changed quite a bit.

Modern threat actor terms include the following:

- *Script kiddies*: Started in the 1990s and are usually teenagers running existing scripts, tools, and exploits to cause harm, but typically not for profit.

- *Vulnerability brokers*: These are usually gray hat hackers who attempt to discover exploits and report them to vendors, sometimes for prizes or rewards.

- *Hacktivists*: These are gray hat hackers who rally and protest against different political and social ideas. Hacktivists publicity protest against organizations or governments by posting numerous articles and videos, leaking sensitive information, and performing distributed denial-of-service (DDoS) attacks.

- *Cybercriminals*: These are black hat hackers who are either self-employed or working for large cybercrime organizations. Each year, cybercriminals are responsible for stealing billions of dollars from consumers and businesses.

- *State-sponsored hackers*: Depending on a person's perspective, these are either white hat or black hat hackers who steal government secrets, gather intelligence, and sabotage networks. Their targets are foreign governments, terrorist groups, and corporations. Most countries in the world participate to some degree in state-sponsored hacking.

Cybercriminals (6.1.1.4)

Cybercriminals are threat actors who are motivated to make money using any means necessary. While sometimes cybercriminals work independently, they are more often financed and sponsored by criminal organizations. It is estimated that globally, cybercriminals steal billions of dollars from consumers and businesses every year.

Cybercriminals operate in an underground economy where they buy, sell, and trade exploits and tools. They also buy and sell the private information and intellectual property they steal from victims. Cybercriminals target small businesses and consumers, as well as large enterprises and industries.

Cybersecurity Tasks (6.1.1.5)

Threat actors do not discriminate. They target the vulnerable end devices of home users and small-to-medium sized businesses, as well as large public and private organizations.

To make the Internet and networks safer and more secure, we must all develop good cybersecurity awareness. Cybersecurity is a shared responsibility which all users must practice. For example, we must report cybercrime to the appropriate authorities, be aware of potential threats in email and the web, and guard important information from theft.

Organizations must take action and protect their assets, users, and customers.

Cyber Threat Indicators (6.1.1.6)

Many network attacks can be prevented by sharing information about *attack indicators*. Each attack has unique identifiable attributes. These are known as cyber threat indicators or simply attack indicators.

For instance, a user receives an email claiming they have won a big prize. Clicking on the link in the email results in an attack. The attack indicators could include the fact the user did not enter that contest, the IP address of the sender, the email subject line, the included link to click, or an attachment to download, among others.

Governments are now actively promoting cybersecurity. For instance, the U.S. Department of Homeland Security (DHS) and U.S. Computer Emergency Readiness Team (US-CERT) are leading efforts to automate the sharing of cybersecurity information with public and private organizations at no cost. DHS and US-CERT use a system called Automated Indicator Sharing (AIS). AIS enables the sharing of attack indicators between the U.S. government and the private sector as soon as the threat is verified.

The DHS also promotes cybersecurity to all users. For instance, they have an annual campaign in October called "Cybersecurity Awareness Month." This campaign was developed to promote and raise awareness about cybersecurity. The DHS also promotes the "Stop. Think. Connect." campaign to encourage all citizens to be safer and more secure online. The campaign provides material on a wide variety of security topics, including:

- Best Practices for Creating a Password
- Best Practices for Using Public Wi-Fi
- Five Every Day Steps Towards Online Safety
- How to Recognize and Prevent Cybercrime
- Five Steps to Protecting Your Digital Home

Interactive Graphic

Activity 6.1.1.7: What Color Is My Hat?

Refer to the online course to complete this Activity.

Threat Actor Tools (6.1.2)

In this topic, you will learn about the various types of attack tools used by threat actors.

Introduction of Attack Tools (6.1.2.1)

To exploit a vulnerability, an attacker must have a technique or tool that can be used. Over the years, attack tools have become more sophisticated, and highly automated, requiring less technical knowledge to use them than in the past.

Figures 6-1 and 6-2 compare the sophistication of attack tools versus the technical knowledge required to use them in 1985 and today.

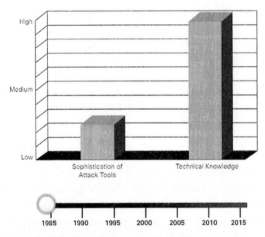

Figure 6-1   Comparing Attack Tools and Technical Knowledge—1985

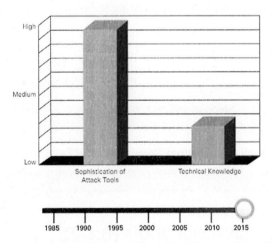

Figure 6-2   Comparing Attack Tools and Technical Knowledge—Today

Evolution of Security Tools (6.1.2.2)

Ethical hacking involves many different types of tools to test and keep the network and its data secure. To validate the security of a network and its systems, many network penetration testing tools have been developed. However, many of these tools can also be used by threat actors for exploitation.

Threat actors have also created various hacking tools. These tools are explicitly written for nefarious reasons. Cybersecurity personnel must also know how to use these tools when performing network penetration tests.

The following list highlights categories of common network penetration testing tools. Notice how some tools are used by white hats and black hats. Keep in mind that the list is not exhaustive as new tools are continually being developed.

- **Password crackers**: Passwords are the most vulnerable security threat. Password cracking tools are often referred to as password recovery tools and can be used to crack or recover the password. This is accomplished either by removing the original password, after bypassing the data encryption, or by outright discovery of the password. Password crackers repeatedly make guesses in order to crack the password and access the system. Examples of password cracking tools include John the Ripper, Ophcrack, L0phtCrack, THC Hydra, RainbowCrack, and Medusa.

- **Wireless hacking tools**: Wireless networks are more susceptible to network security threats. Wireless hacking tools are used to intentionally hack into a wireless network to detect security vulnerabilities. Examples of wireless hacking tools include Aircrack-ng, Kismet, InSSIDer, KisMAC, Firesheep, and NetStumbler.

- **Network scanning and hacking tools**: Network scanning tools are used to probe network devices, servers, and hosts for open TCP or UDP ports. Examples of scanning tools include Nmap, SuperScan, Angry IP Scanner, and NetScanTools.

- **Packet crafting tools**: These tools are used to probe and test a firewall's robustness using specially crafted forged packets. Examples of such tools include Hping, Scapy, Socat, Yersinia, Netcat, Hping, Nping, and Nemesis.

- **Packet sniffers**: These tools are used to capture and analyze packets within traditional Ethernet LANs or WLANs. Tools include Wireshark, Tcpdump, Ettercap, Dsniff, EtherApe, Paros, Fiddler, Ratproxy, and SSLstrip.

- **Rootkit detectors**: These tools are directory and file integrity checkers used by white hats to detect installed root kits. Example tools include AIDE, Netfilter, and PF OpenBSD Packet Filter.

- **Fuzzers to search vulnerabilities**: Fuzzers are tools used by hackers when attempting to discover a computer system's security vulnerabilities. Examples of fuzzers include Skipfish, Wapiti, and W3af.

- **Forensic tools**: These tools are used by white hat hackers to sniff out any trace of evidence existing in a particular computer system. Example of tools include Sleuth Kit, Helix, Maltego, and EnCase.

- *Debuggers*: These tools are used by black hats to reverse engineer binary files when writing exploits. They are also used by white hats when analyzing malware. Debugging tools include GDB, WinDbg, IDA Pro, and Immunity Debugger.

- *Hacking operating systems*: These are specially designed operating systems preloaded with tools and technologies optimized hacking. Examples of specially designed hacking operating systems include Kali Linux, Backtrack 5r3, SELinux, Knoppix, and BackBox Linux

- *Encryption tools*: These tools safeguard the contents of an organization's data at rest and data in motion. Encryption tools use algorithm schemes to encode the data to prevent unauthorized access to the encrypted data. Examples of these tools include TrueCrypt, OpenSHH, OpenSSL, Tor, OpenVPN, and Stunnel.

- *Vulnerability exploitation tools*: These tools identify whether a remote host is vulnerable to a security attack. Examples of vulnerability exploitation tools include Metasploit, Core Impact, Sqlmap, Social Engineer Toolkit, and Netsparker.

- *Vulnerability scanners*: These tools scan a network or system to identify open ports. They can also be used to scan known vulnerabilities and scan virtual machines (VMs), BYOD devices, and client databases. Examples of tools include Nipper, Secunia PSI, Core Impact, Nessus v6, SAINT, and Open VAS.

Note

Many of these tools are UNIX or Linux based; therefore, a security professional should have a strong UNIX and Linux background.

Categories of Attacks (6.1.2.3)

Threat actors can use the previously mentioned tools or a combination of tools to create various attacks. The following list of attacks is not exhaustive as new ways to attack networks are continually discovered.

- **Eavesdropping attack:** This is when a hacker captures and "listens" to network traffic. This attack is referred to as sniffing or snooping.

- **Data modification attack:** If hackers have captured enterprise traffic, they can alter the data in the packet without the knowledge of the sender or receiver.

- **IP address spoofing attack:** A hacker constructs an IP packet that appears to originate from a valid address inside the corporate intranet.

- **Password-based attacks:** If hackers discover a valid user account, the attackers have the same rights as the real user. Hackers could obtain lists of valid user and computer names and network information. They could also modify server and network configurations, and modify, reroute, or delete data.

- **Denial-of-service (DoS) attack:** A DoS attack prevents normal use of a computer or network by valid users. After gaining access to your network, a DoS attack can crash applications or network services, flood a computer, or flood the entire network with traffic until a shutdown occurs because of the overload. A DoS attack can also block traffic, which results in a loss of access to network resources by authorized users.

- **Man-in-the-middle attack:** This attack occurs when hackers have positioned themselves between a source and destination. They can now actively monitor, capture, and control the communication transparently.

- **Compromised-key attack:** If a hacker obtains a secret key, that key is referred to as a compromised key. A compromised key can be used to gain access to a secured communication without the sender or receiver being aware of the attack.

- **Sniffer attack:** A sniffer is an application or device that can read, monitor, and capture network data exchanges and read network packets. If the packets are not encrypted, a sniffer provides a full view of the data inside the packet. Even encapsulated (tunneled) packets can be broken open and read unless they are encrypted and the attacker does not have access to the key.

It is important to understand that threat actors use a variety of security tools to carry out these attacks.

Interactive Graphic

Activity 6.1.2.4: Classify Hacking Tools

Refer to the online course to complete this Activity.

Common Threats and Attacks (6.2)

In this section, you will learn the various types of threats and attacks.

Malware (6.2.1)

In this topic, you will learn about malware.

Types of Malware (6.2.1.1)

End devices are especially prone to malware attacks. Malware is short for malicious software or malicious code. It is code or software that is specifically designed to damage, disrupt, steal, or generally inflict some other "bad" or illegitimate action on data, hosts, or networks. It is important to know about malware because threat actors and online criminals frequently try to trick users into installing malware to help exploit security gaps. In addition, malware morphs so rapidly that malware-related security incidents are extremely common because antimalware software cannot be updated quickly enough to stop the new threats.

The three most common types of malware are viruses, worms, and Trojan horse attacks, as shown in Figure 6-3.

The primary vulnerabilities for end-user workstations are virus, worm, and Trojan Horse attacks.

Figure 6-3   Types of Malware

Viruses (6.2.1.2)

A *virus* is a type of malware that propagates by inserting a copy of itself into another program. Viruses then spread from one computer to another, infecting the computers. Most viruses require human help to spread. For example, when someone connects an infected USB drive to their PC, the virus will enter the PC. The virus may then infect a new USB drive, and spread to new PCs. Viruses can lay dormant for an extended period and then activate at a specific time and date.

A simple virus may install itself at the first line of code in an executable file. When activated, the virus might check the disk for other executables so that it can infect all the files it has not yet infected. Viruses can be harmless, such as those that display a picture on the screen, or they can be destructive, such as those that modify or delete files on the hard drive. Viruses can also be programmed to mutate to avoid detection.

Most viruses are now spread by USB memory drives, CDs, DVDs, network shares, and email. Email viruses are now the most common type of virus.

Trojan Horses (6.2.1.3)

The term *Trojan horse* originated from Greek mythology. Greek warriors offered the people of Troy (the Trojans) a giant hollow wooden horse as a gift. The Trojans brought the giant horse into their walled city, unaware that it contained many Greek warriors. At night, after most Trojans were asleep, the warriors burst out of the horse, opened the city gates, and allowed a sizeable force to enter and take over the city.

Trojan horse malware is software that appears to be legitimate, but it contains malicious code which exploits the privileges of the user that runs it. Often, Trojans are found attached to online games.

Users are commonly tricked into loading and executing the Trojan horse on their systems. While playing the game, the user will not notice a problem. In the background, the Trojan horse has been installed on the user's system. The malicious code from the Trojan horse continues operating even after the game has been closed.

The Trojan horse concept is flexible. It can cause immediate damage, provide remote access to the system, or provide access through a back door. It can also perform actions as instructed remotely, such as "send me the password file once per week." This tendency of malware to send data back to the cybercriminal highlights the need to monitor outbound traffic for attack indicators.

Custom-written Trojan horses, such as those with a specific target, are difficult to detect.

Trojan Horse Classification (6.2.1.4)

Trojan horses are usually classified according to the damage that they cause, or the manner in which they breach a system:

- **Remote-access Trojan horse:** This enables unauthorized remote access.

- **Data-sending Trojan horse:** This provides the threat actor with sensitive data, such as passwords.

- **Destructive Trojan horse:** This corrupts or deletes files.

- **Proxy Trojan horse:** This will use the victim's computer as the source device to launch attacks and perform other illegal activities.

- **FTP Trojan horse:** This enables unauthorized file transfer services on end devices.

- **Security software disabler Trojan horse:** This stops antivirus programs or firewalls from functioning.

- **DoS Trojan horse:** This slows or halts network activity through a denial of service (DoS) attack.

Worms (6.2.1.5)

Computer *worms* are similar to viruses because they replicate and can cause the same type of damage. Specifically, worms replicate themselves by independently exploiting vulnerabilities in networks. Worms can slow down networks as they spread from system to system.

Whereas a virus requires a host program to run, worms can run by themselves. Other than the initial infection, they no longer require user participation. After a host is infected, the worm is able to spread very quickly over the network.

Worms are responsible for some of the most devastating attacks on the Internet. In 2001 the Code Red worm had infected 658 servers. Within 19 hours, the worm had infected over 300,000 servers.

The initial infection of the SQL Slammer worm, known as the worm that ate the Internet, was a DoS attack that exploited a buffer overflow bug in Microsoft's SQL Server. At its peak, the number of infected servers doubled in size every 8.5 seconds. This is why it was able to infect 250,000+ hosts within 30 minutes. When it was released on the weekend of January 25, 2003, it disrupted the Internet, financial institutions, ATM cash machines, and more. Ironically, a patch for this vulnerability had been released 6 months earlier. The infected servers did not have the updated patch applied. This was a wake-up call for many organizations to implement a security policy requiring that updates and patches be applied in a timely fashion.

Worms share similar characteristics. They all exploit an enabling vulnerability, have a way to propagate themselves, and contain a payload.

Worm Components (6.2.1.6)

Despite the mitigation techniques that have emerged over the years, worms have continued to evolve and pose a persistent threat. Worms have become more sophisticated over time, but they still tend to be based on exploiting weaknesses in software applications.

Most worm attacks consist of the following three components:

- **Enabling vulnerability:** A worm installs itself using an exploit mechanism, such as an email attachment, an executable file, or a Trojan horse, on a vulnerable system.

- **Propagation mechanism:** After gaining access to a device, the worm replicates itself and locates new targets.

- **Payload:** Any malicious code that results in some action is a payload. Most often this is used to create a backdoor that allows a threat actor access to the infected host or to create a DoS attack.

Worms are self-contained programs that attack a system to exploit a known vulnerability. Upon successful exploitation, the worm copies itself from the attacking host to the newly exploited system and the cycle begins again. Their propagation mechanisms are commonly deployed in a way that is difficult to detect.

Figure 6-4 displays the propagation technique used by the Code Red worm.

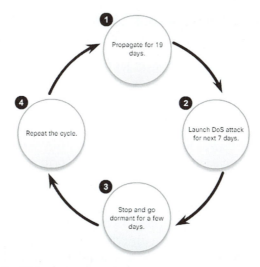

Figure 6-4   Code Red Worm Propagation

Ransomware (6.2.1.7)

Threat actors have used viruses, worms, and Trojan horses to carry their payloads and for other malicious reasons. However, malware continues to evolve.

Currently, the most dominating malware is ransomware. Ransomware is malware that denies access to the infected computer system or its data. The cybercriminals then demand payment to release the computer system.

Ransomware has evolved to become the most profitable malware type in history. In the first half of 2016, ransomware campaigns targeting both individual and enterprise users became more widespread and potent.

There are dozens of ransomware variants. Ransomware frequently uses an encryption algorithm to encrypt system files and data. The majority of known ransomware encryption algorithms cannot be easily decrypted, leaving victims with little option but to pay the asking price. Payments are typically paid in bitcoin because users of bitcoin can remain anonymous. Bitcoin is an open source, digital currency that nobody owns or controls.

Email and malicious advertising, also known as malvertising, are vectors for ransomware campaigns. *Social engineering* is also used, such as when cybercriminals who identify themselves as security technicians call homes and persuade users to connect to a website that downloads the ransomware to the user's computer.

Other Malware (6.2.1.8)

These are some examples of the varieties of modern malware:

- *Spyware*: This malware is used to gather information about a user and send the information to another entity without the user's consent. Spyware can be a system monitor, Trojan horse, Adware, tracking cookies, or key loggers, or a combination of these tools.

- *Adware*: This malware typically displays annoying pop-ups to generate revenue for its author. The malware may analyze user interests by tracking the websites visited. It can then send pop-up advertising pertinent to those sites.

- *Scareware*: This malware includes scam software which uses social engineering to shock or induce anxiety by creating the perception of a threat. It is generally directed at an unsuspecting user and attempts to persuade the user to infect a computer by taking action to address the bogus threat.

- *Phishing*: This malware attempts to convince people to divulge sensitive information. Examples include receiving an email from their bank asking users to divulge their account and PIN numbers.

- **Rootkit**: This malware is installed on a compromised system. After it is installed, it continues to hide its intrusion and provide privileged access to the threat actor.

This list will continue to grow as the Internet evolves. New malware will always be developed. A major goal of cybersecurity operations is to learn about new malware and how to promptly mitigate it.

Common Malware Behaviors (6.2.1.9)

Cybercriminals continually modify malware code to change how it spreads and infects computers. However, most produce similar symptoms that can be detected through network and device log monitoring.

Computers infected with malware often exhibit one or more of the following symptoms:

- Appearance of strange files, programs, or desktop icons

- Antivirus and firewall programs are turning off or reconfiguring settings

- Computer screen is freezing or system is crashing

- Emails are spontaneously being sent without your knowledge to your contact list

- Files have been modified or deleted

- Increased CPU and/or memory usage

- Problems connecting to networks

- Slow computer or web browser speeds

- Unknown processes or services running

- Unknown TCP or UDP ports open

- Connections are made to hosts on the Internet without user action

- Strange computer behavior

Note

Malware behavior is not limited to the preceding list.

Activity 6.2.1.10: Identify the Malware Type

Refer to the online course to complete this Activity.

Lab 6.2.1.11: Anatomy of Malware

In this lab, you will research and analyze some recent malware.

Common Network Attacks (6.2.2)

In this topic, you will learn about common network attacks.

Types of Network Attacks (6.2.2.1)

Malware is a means to get a payload delivered. When it is delivered and installed, the payload can be used to cause a variety of network-related attacks from the inside. Threat actors can also attack the network from outside.

Why do threat actors attack networks? There are many motives, including money, greed, revenge, or political, religious, or sociological beliefs. Network security professionals must understand the types of attacks used to counter these threats to ensure the security of the LAN.

To mitigate attacks, it is useful to first categorize the various types of attacks. By categorizing network attacks, it is possible to address types of attacks rather than individual attacks.

Although there is no standardized way of categorizing network attacks, the method used in this course classifies attacks in three major categories.

- Reconnaissance attacks
- Access attacks
- DoS attacks

Reconnaissance Attacks (6.2.2.2)

Reconnaissance is known as information gathering. It is analogous to a thief surveying a neighborhood by going door-to-door pretending to sell something. What the thief is actually doing is looking for vulnerable homes to break into such as unoccupied residences, residences with easy-to-open doors or windows, and those residences without security systems or security cameras.

Threat actors use reconnaissance (or recon) attacks to do unauthorized discovery and mapping of systems, services, or vulnerabilities. When directed at an endpoint on the network, such as PCs and servers, a recon attack is also called host profiling. This is because the attacker can get a profile of the system, including operating system type and version. If a system is not fully patched, the attacker will then look for known vulnerabilities to exploit.

Recon attacks precede intrusive access attacks or DoS attacks, and often employ the use of widely available tools.

Sample Reconnaissance Attacks (6.2.2.3)

These are some of the techniques used by malicious threat actors conducting reconnaissance attacks:

- **Perform an information query of a target:** The threat actor is looking for initial information about a target. Readily available tools are used including a Google search of the organization's website. Public information about the target network is available from DNS registries using **dig**, **nslookup**, and **whois** utilities.

- **Initiate a ping sweep of the target networks:** The threat actor initiates a ping sweep of the target networks revealed by the previous DNS queries to identify target network addresses. The ping sweep identifies which IP addresses are active. This allows creation of a logical topology of the target network.

- **Initiate a port scan of active IP addresses:** The threat actor then initiates port scans on the live hosts identified by the ping sweep to determine which ports or services are available. Port scanning tools such as Nmap, SuperScan, Angry IP Scanner, and NetScanTools initiate connections to the target hosts by scanning for ports that are open on the target computers.

- **Run vulnerability scanners:** The threat actor uses a vulnerability scanning tool such as Nipper, Secuna PSI, Core Impact, Nessus v6, SAINT, or Open VAS to query the identified ports. The goal is to identify potential vulnerabilities on the target hosts.

- **Run exploitation tools:** The threat actor now attempts to exploit the identified vulnerabilities in the system. The threat actor uses vulnerability exploitation tools such as Metasploit, Core Impact, Sqlmap, Social Engineer Toolkit, and Netsparker.

Figure 6-5 shows an example of a threat actor using the **whois** command to find information about a target.

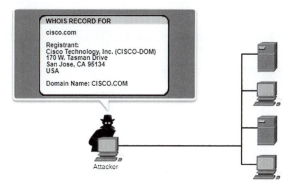

Figure 6-5   Internet Information Queries

Figure 6-6 shows an example of a threat actor doing a ping sweep of the target's network address space to discover live and active IP addresses.

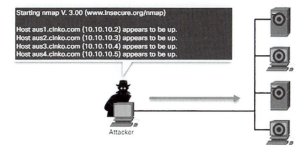

Figure 6-6   Performing Ping Sweeps

Figure 6-7 shows an example of a threat actor performing a port scan on the discovered active IP addresses using Nmap.

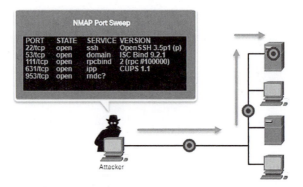

Figure 6-7   Performing Port Scans

Access Attacks (6.2.2.4)

Access attacks exploit known vulnerabilities in authentication services, FTP services, and web services to gain entry to web accounts, confidential databases, and other sensitive information. The goal of the threat actor may be to steal information or to remotely control the inside host.

There are at least three reasons that threat actors would use access attacks on networks or systems:

- To retrieve data

- To gain access to systems

- To escalate access privileges

Figure 6-8 shows an example of a threat actor using an access attack to gain root privileges to an FTP server.

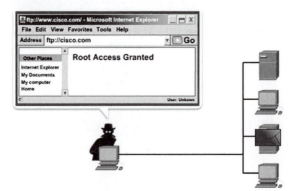

Figure 6-8   Access Attack on an FTP Server

Types of Access Attacks (6.2.2.5)

There are several common types of access attacks:

- **Password attack:** Threat actors attempt to discover critical system passwords using various methods such as phishing attacks, dictionary attacks, brute-force attacks, network sniffing, or social engineering techniques. Brute-force password attacks involve repeated attempts using tools such as Ophcrack, L0phtCrack, THC Hydra, RainbowCrack, and Medusa.

- *Pass-the-hash*: The threat actor already has access to the user's machine and uses malware to gain access to the stored password hashes. The threat actor then uses the hashes to authenticate to other remote servers or devices without using brute force. Hashing is discussed in more detail later in the course.

- **Trust exploitation:** Threat actors use a trusted host to gain access to network resources. For example, an external host that accesses an internal network over VPN is trusted. If that host is attacked, the attacker may use the trusted host to gain access to the internal network.

- **Port redirection:** This is when a threat actor uses a compromised system as a base for attacks against other targets.

- *Man-in-the-middle attack*: The threat actor is positioned in between two legitimate entities in order to read, modify, or redirect the data that passes between the two parties.

- **IP, MAC, DHCP** *spoofing*: Spoofing attacks are attacks in which one device attempts to pose as another by falsifying address data. There are multiple types of spoofing attacks. For example, MAC address spoofing occurs when one computer accepts data packets based on the MAC address of another computer that is the actual destination for the data.

Figures 6-9 through 6-11 show an example of trust exploitation.

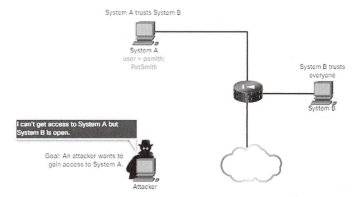

Figure 6-9 Trust Exploitation: Attacker Cannot Access System A

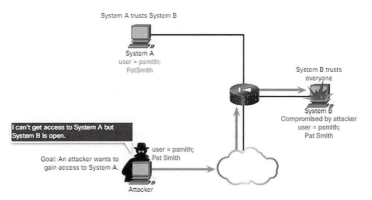

Figure 6-10   Trust Exploitation: Attacker Can Access System B

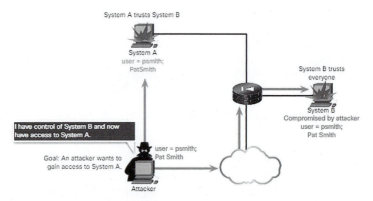

Figure 6-11   Trust Exploitation: Attacker Uses System B to Access System A

The port redirection example in Figure 6-12 displays a threat actor using SSH to connect to compromised Host A. Host A is trusted by Host B; therefore, the threat actor is allowed to use Telnet to access it.

Figure 6-13 displays an example of a man-in-the-middle attack.

The steps in Figure 6-13 are as follows:

Step 1.   When a victim requests a web page, the request is directed to the attacker's computer.

Step 2.   The attacker's computer receives the request and retrieves the real page from the legitimate website.

Step 3.   That attacker can alter the legitimate web page and apply transformations to the data.

Step 4.   The attacker forwards the requested page to the victim.

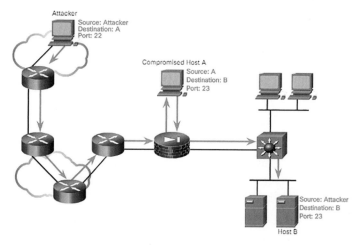

Figure 6-12 Port Redirection Example

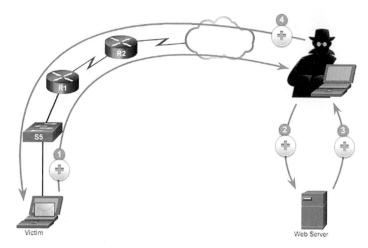

Figure 6-13 Man-in-the-Middle Attack Example

Social Engineering Attacks (6.2.2.6)

Social engineering is a type of access attack that attempts to manipulate individuals into performing actions or divulging confidential information such as passwords and usernames. It typically involves the use of social skills to manipulate inside network users to divulge information needed to access the network.

Social engineers often rely on people's willingness to be helpful. They also prey on people's weaknesses. For example, a threat actor could call an authorized employee with an urgent problem that requires immediate network access. The threat actor could appeal to the employee's vanity, invoke authority using name-dropping techniques, or appeal to the employee's greed.

Examples of social engineering attacks include

- *Pretexting*: This is when a threat actor calls an individual and lies to them in an attempt to gain access to privileged data. An example involves a threat actor who pretends to need personal or financial data in order to confirm the identity of the recipient.

- **Spam:** Threat actors may use spam email to trick a user into clicking an infected link, or downloading an infected file.

- **Phishing:** There are many variations of this social engineering technique. A common version is the threat actor sends enticing custom-targeted spam email to individuals with the hope the target users click a link or download malicious code.

- **Something for something (*quid pro quo*):** This is when a threat actor requests personal information from a party in exchange for something like a free gift.

- *Tailgating*: This is when a threat actor quickly follows an authorized person with a corporate badge into a badge-secure location. The threat actor then has access to a secure area.

- *Baiting*: This is when a threat actor leaves a malware-infected physical device, such as a USB flash drive, in a public location such as a corporate washroom. The finder finds the device and inserts it into their computer. On a Windows host, the autoplay feature may automatically install the malware.

- *Visual hacking*: This is where a threat actor physically observes the victim entering credentials such as a workstation login, an ATM PIN, or the combination on a physical lock. This practice is also referred to as "shoulder surfing."

Phishing Social Engineering Attacks (6.2.2.7)

Phishing is a common social engineering technique that threat actors use to send emails that appear to be from a legitimate organization (such as a bank). The goal is to get the victim to submit personal or sensitive information such as usernames, passwords, account information, financial information, and more. The email could also attempt to trick the recipient into installing malware on their device.

Variations of phishing attacks include

- *Spear phishing*: This is a targeted phishing attack tailored for a specific individual or organization and is more likely to successfully deceive the target.

- *Whaling*: This is similar to spear phishing but is focused on big targets such as top executives of an organization.

- *Pharming*: This attack compromises domain name services by injecting entries into local host files. Pharming also includes poisoning the DNS by compromising the DHCP servers that specify DNS servers to their clients.

- ■ *Watering hole*: This attack first determines websites that a target group visits regularly. Next, the threat actor attempts to compromise those websites by infecting them with malware that can identify and target only members of the target group.

- ■ *Vishing*: This is a phishing attack using voice and the phone system instead of email.

- ■ *Smishing*: This is a phishing attack using SMS texting instead of email.

The Social Engineering Toolkit (SET) was designed by TrustedSec to help white hat hackers and other network security professionals create social engineering attacks to test their own networks.

Strengthening the Weakest Link (6.2.2.8)

Cybersecurity is only as strong as its weakest link. Since computers and other Internet-connected devices have become an essential part of our lives, they no longer seem new or different. People have become very casual in their use of these devices and rarely think about network security. The weakest link in cybersecurity can be the personnel within an organization, with social engineering as a major security threat. Because of this, one of the most effective security measures that an organization can take is to train its personnel and create a "security-aware culture."

Lab 6.2.2.9: Social Engineering

In this lab, you will research examples of social engineering and identify ways to recognize and prevent it.

Denial-of-Service Attacks (6.2.2.10)

Denial-of-service (DoS) attacks are highly publicized network attacks. A DoS attack results in some sort of interruption of service to users, devices, or applications.

There are two major sources of DoS attacks:

- ■ **Overwhelming quantity of traffic:** This is when a network, host, or application is unable to handle an enormous quantity of data, causing the system to crash or become extremely slow.

- ■ **Maliciously formatted packets:** This is when maliciously formatted packets are forwarded to a host or application and the receiver is unable to handle an unexpected condition. A buffer overflow attack is a method used in this type of DoS attack. For example, a threat actor forwards packets containing errors that cannot be identified by the application, or forwards improperly formatted packets. This causes the receiving device to crash or run very slowly.

Figure 6-14 shows an example of a DoS attack.

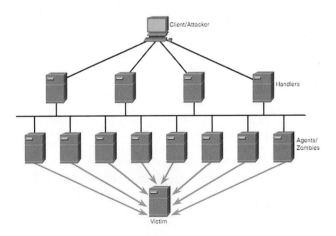

Figure 6-14 DoS Attack

DoS attacks are considered a major risk because they can easily interrupt business processes or essential network services, and cause significant loss. These attacks are relatively simple to conduct, even by an unskilled threat actor.

DDoS Attacks (6.2.2.11)

If threat actors can compromise many hosts, they can perform a distributed DoS (DDoS) attack. DDoS attacks are similar in intent to DoS attacks, except that a DDoS attack increases in magnitude because it originates from multiple, coordinated sources, as shown in Figure 6-15. A DDoS attack can use hundreds or thousands of sources, as in IoT-based DDoS attacks.

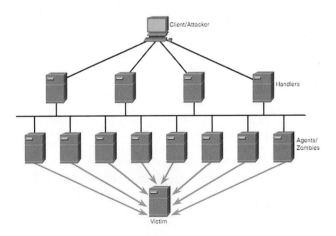

Figure 6-15 Components of a DoS Attack

The following terms are used to describe components of a DDoS attack:

- *Zombies*: Refers to a group of compromised hosts (i.e., agents). These hosts run malicious code referred to as robots (i.e., bots). The zombie malware continually attempts to self-propagate like a worm.

- *Bots*: Bots are malware that are designed to infect a host and communicate with a handler system. Bots can also log keystrokes, gather passwords, capture and analyze packets, and more.

- *Botnet*: Refers to a group of zombies that have been infected using self-propagating malware (i.e., bots) and are controlled by handlers.

- *Handlers*: Refers to a master command-and-control (CnC or C2) server controlling groups of zombies. The originator of a botnet can use Internet Relay Chat (IRC) or a web server on the C2 server to remotely control the zombies.

- *Botmaster*: This is the threat actor in control of the botnet and handlers.

Note

There is an underground economy where botnets can be bought (and sold) for a nominal fee. This can provide threat actors with botnets of infected hosts ready to launch a DDoS attack.

Example DDoS Attack (6.2.2.12)

As an example, a DDoS attack could proceed as follows:

1. The threat actor builds or purchases a botnet of zombie hosts.

2. Zombie computers continue to scan and infect more targets to create more zombies.

3. When ready, the botmaster uses the handler systems to make the botnet of zombies carry out the DDoS attack on the chosen target.

Figures 6-16 and 6-17 show an example of a DDoS attack.

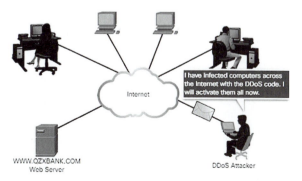

Figure 6-16   DDoS Attack: Infecting Zombies

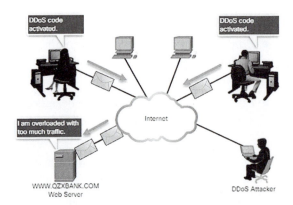

Figure 6-17   DDoS Attack: Zombies Flood Victim Server

Buffer Overflow Attack (6.2.2.13)

The goal of a threat actor when using a ***buffer overflow attack*** is to find a system memory-related flaw on a server and exploit it. Exploiting the buffer memory by overwhelming it with unexpected values usually renders the system inoperable, creating a DoS attack.

For example, a threat actor enters input that is larger than expected by the application running on a server. The application accepts the large amount of input and stores it in memory. The result is that it may consume the associated memory buffer and potentially overwrite adjacent memory, eventually corrupting the system and causing it to crash.

An early example of using malformed packets was the Ping of Death. In this legacy attack, the threat actor sent a ping of death, which was an echo request in an IP packet larger than the maximum packet size of 65,535 bytes. The receiving host would not be able to handle a packet of that size and it would crash, as shown in Figure 6-18.

Figure 6-18   Buffer Overflow

Buffer overflow attacks are continually evolving. For instance, a remote DoS attack vulnerability was recently discovered in Microsoft Windows 10. Specifically, a threat actor created malicious code to access out-of-scope memory. When this code is accessed by the Windows AHCACHE.SYS process, it attempts to trigger a system crash, denying service to the user.

Note

It is estimated that one-third of malicious attacks are the result of buffer overflows.

Evasion Methods (6.2.2.14)

Threat actors learned long ago that "to hide is to thrive." This means their malware and attack methods are most effective when they are undetected. For this reason, many attacks use stealthy evasion techniques to disguise an attack payload. Their goal is to prevent detection by network and host defenses.

Some of the evasion methods used by threat actors include:

- **Encryption and tunneling:** This evasion technique uses tunneling to hide the content, or encryption to scramble its contents, making it difficult for many security detection techniques to detect and identify the malware.

- **Resource exhaustion:** This evasion technique keeps the host too busy to properly use security detection techniques.

- **Traffic fragmentation:** This evasion technique splits a malicious payload into smaller packets to bypass network security detection. After the fragmented packets bypass the security detection system, the malware is reassembled and may begin sending sensitive data out of the network.

- **Protocol-level misinterpretation:** This evasion technique occurs when network defenses do not properly handle features of a PDU like a checksum or TTL value. This can trick a firewall into ignoring packets that it should check.

- **Traffic substitution:** In this evasion technique, the threat actor attempts to trick the IPS by obfuscating the data in the payload. This is done by encoding it in a different format. For example, the threat actor could use encoded traffic in Unicode instead of ASCII. The IPS does not recognize the true meaning of the data, but the target end system can read the data.

- **Traffic insertion:** Similar to traffic substitution, but the threat actor inserts extra bytes of data in a malicious sequence of data. The IPS rules miss the malicious data, accepting the full sequence of data.

- **Pivoting:** This technique assumes the threat actor has compromised an inside host and wants to expand their access further into the compromised network.

An example is a threat actor who has gained access to the administrator password on a compromised host and is attempting to log in to another host using the same credentials.

■ **Rootkits:** A rootkit is a complex attacker tool used by experienced threat actors. It integrates with the lowest levels of the operating system. When a program attempts to list files, processes, or network connections, the rootkit presents a sanitized version of the output, eliminating any incriminating output. The goal of the rootkit is to completely hide the activities of the attacker on the local system.

New attack methods are constantly being developed. Network security personnel must be aware of the latest attack methods in order to detect them.

Interactive Graphic

Activity 6.2.2.15: Identify the Types of Network Attack

Refer to the online course to complete this Activity.

Interactive Graphic

Activity 6.2.2.16: Components of a DDoS Attack

Refer to the online course to complete this Activity.

Summary (6.3)

In this chapter, you learned how networks are attacked. You learned the types of threats and attacks used by threat actors. Threat actors are gray or black hat hackers who attempt to gain unauthorized access to our networks. They may also run programs that prevent or slow network access for others. Cybercriminals are threat actors who are motivated solely by financial gain.

Threat actors use a variety of tools, including

- Password crackers
- Wireless hacking tools
- Network scanning and hacking tools
- Packet crafting tools
- Packet sniffers
- Rootkit detectors
- Forensic tools
- Debuggers
- Hacking operating systems
- Encryption tools
- Vulnerability exploitation tools
- Vulnerability scanners

These tools can be used to launch a variety of attacks, including

- Eavesdropping
- Data modification
- IP address spoofing
- Password cracking
- Denial of service
- Man-in-the-middle
- Compromised key
- Network sniffing

Malware, or malicious code, is software that is specifically designed to damage, disrupt, steal, or generally inflict some other "bad" or illegitimate action on data, hosts, or networks. The three most common types of malware are viruses, worms, and Trojan horses:

- A virus is a type of malware that propagates by inserting a copy of itself into another program.

- Worms are similar to viruses because they replicate and can cause the same type of damage. Whereas a virus requires a host program to run, worms can run by themselves.

- A Trojan horse is software that appears to be legitimate, but it contains malicious code which exploits the privileges of the user that runs it.

Malware continues to evolve. The most dominant attack currently is ransomware. Ransomware is malware that denies access to the infected computer system or its data until the owner pays the cybercriminal.

All the various types of tools threat actors use to launch network attacks can be classified as one or more of the following:

- **Reconnaissance:** This is unauthorized discovery and mapping of systems, services, or vulnerabilities.

- **Access attacks:** These exploit known vulnerabilities to gain entry to web accounts, confidential databases, and other sensitive information.

- **Social engineering:** This is an attempt to manipulate individuals into performing actions or divulging confidential information such as passwords and usernames.

- **Denial of service:** This occurs by overwhelming the network with a large quantity of traffic, or maliciously formatting packets that the receiver is unable to handle, causing the device to run very slowly or even crash.

- **Buffer overflow:** This uses a system memory–related flaw on a server to overwhelm it with unexpected values. The goal is to render it inoperable.

To stay hidden and continue their attack, threat actors use a variety of evasion methods, including:

- Encryption and tunneling

- Resource exhaustion

- Traffic fragmentation

- Protocol-level misinterpretation

- Traffic substitution

- Traffic insertion
- Pivoting
- Rootkits

Practice

The following activities provide practice with the topics introduced in this chapter. The Labs are available in the companion *CCNA Cybersecurity Operations Lab Manual* (ISBN: 9781587134388).

Labs

Lab 6.2.1.11: Anatomy of Malware

Lab 6.2.2.9: Social Engineering

Check Your Understanding

Complete all the review questions listed here to test your understanding of the topics and concepts in this chapter. The appendix "Answers to 'Check Your Understanding' Questions" lists the answers.

1. What type of attack uses zombies?

    A. Trojan horse

    B. SEO poisoning

    C. Spear phishing

    D. DDoS

2. What is the best description of Trojan horse malware?

    A. It is the most easily detected form of malware.

    B. It appears as useful software but hides malicious code.

    C. It is malware that can only be distributed over the Internet.

    D. It is software that causes annoying but not fatal computer problems.

3. What is the purpose of a rootkit?

    A. To masquerade as a legitimate program

    B. To deliver advertisements without user consent

    C. To replicate itself independently of any other programs

    D. To gain privileged access to a device while concealing itself

4. When describing malware, what is a difference between a virus and a worm?

   A. A virus focuses on gaining privileged access to a device, whereas a worm does not.

   B. A virus replicates itself by attaching to another file, whereas a worm can replicate itself independently.

   C. A virus can be used to launch a DoS attack (but not a DDoS), but a worm can be used to launch both DoS and DDoS attacks.

   D. A virus can be used to deliver advertisements without user consent, whereas a worm cannot.

5. What is an example of "hacktivism"?

   A. Criminals use the Internet to attempt to steal money from a banking company.

   B. A country tries to steal defense secrets from another country by infiltrating government networks.

   C. A teenager breaks into the web server of a local newspaper and posts a picture of a favorite cartoon character.

   D. A group of environmentalists launch a denial-of-service attack against an oil company that is responsible for a large oil spill.

6. What is the purpose of a reconnaissance attack on a computer network?

   A. To steal data from the network servers

   B. To prevent users from accessing network resources

   C. To redirect data traffic so that it can be monitored

   D. To gather information about the target network and system

7. Which tool is used to provide a list of open ports on network devices?

   A. Nmap

   B. Ping

   C. Whois

   D. Tracert

8. Which type of attack allows an attacker to use a brute-force approach?

   A. Packet sniffing

   B. Social engineering

   C. Denial of service

   D. Password cracking

9. Which term is used to describe the act of sending an email message in an attempt to divulge sensitive information from someone?

   A. Phishing

   B. DoS attack

   C. Hacktivisim

   D. Script kiddie

10. What is the significant characteristic of worm malware?

   A. A worm can execute independently of the host system.

   B. Worm malware disguises itself as legitimate software.

   C. A worm must be triggered by an event on the host system.

   D. Once installed on a host system, a worm does not replicate itself.

11. A network administrator detects unknown sessions involving port 21 on the network. What could be causing this security breach?

   A. An FTP Trojan horse is executing.

   B. A reconnaissance attack is occurring.

   C. A denial-of-service attack is occurring.

   D. Cisco Security Agent is testing the network.

12. Which example illustrates how malware might be concealed?

   A. A botnet of zombies carry personal information back to the hacker.

   B. An attack is launched against the public website of an online retailer with the objective of blocking its response to visitors.

   C. A hacker uses techniques to improve the ranking of a website so that users are redirected to a malicious site.

   D. An email is sent to the employees of an organization with an attachment that looks like an antivirus update, but the attachment actually consists of spyware.

13. Which type of security threat can be described as software that attaches itself to another program to execute a specific unwanted function?

   A. Worm

   B. Virus

   C. Proxy Trojan horse

   D. Denial-of-service Trojan horse

## CHAPTER 7

Network Attacks: A Deeper Look

Objectives

Upon completion of this chapter, you will be able to answer the following questions:

- What is the importance of network monitoring?

- How is network monitoring conducted?

- How do IP vulnerabilities enable network attacks?

- How do TCP and UDP vulnerabilities enable network attacks?

- What are the IP vulnerabilities?

- How do network application vulnerabilities enable network attacks?

Key Terms

This chapter uses the following key terms. You can find the definitions in the Glossary.

Introduction (7.0)

Cybersecurity analysts use a variety of tools to identify attacks. A solid understanding of protocol vulnerabilities is essential to using these tools.

This chapter first covers the importance of traffic monitoring and how it is conducted. This is followed by an in-depth discussion of the vulnerabilities to network protocols and services including IP, TCP, UDP, ARP, DNS, DHCP, HTTP, and email.

Class Activity 7.0.1.2: What's Going On?

In this activity, you will identify the processes running on a computer, the protocol they are using, and their local and remote port addresses.

Network Monitoring and Tools (7.1)

In this section, you will learn about network traffic monitoring.

Introduction to Network Monitoring (7.1.1)

In this topic, you will learn the importance of network monitoring.

Network Security Topology (7.1.1.1)

"All networks are targets" is a common adage used to describe the current landscape of network security. Therefore, to mitigate threats, all networks must be secured and protected as best as possible.

This requires a defense-in-depth approach. It requires using proven methods and secure infrastructure consisting of firewalls, intrusion detection systems (IDSs)/intrusion prevention systems (IPSs), and endpoint security software. These methods and technologies are used to introduce automated monitoring to the network, creating alerts or even automatically blocking offensive devices when something goes wrong.

However, for large networks, an extra layer of protection must be added. Devices such as firewalls and IPSs operate based on preconfigured rules. They monitor traffic and compare it against the configured rules. If there is a match, the traffic is handled according to the rule. This works relatively seamlessly, but sometimes, legitimate traffic is mistaken for unauthorized traffic. Called false positives, these situations require human eyes to see and evaluate them before they can be validated. An important part of the job of the security analyst is to review all alerts generated by network devices and validate their nature. Was that file downloaded by user X really malware? Is that website visited by user Y really malicious? Is the printer on the third floor really compromised because it is trying to connect to a server that is out on the Internet? All these questions are commonly asked by security analysts daily. It is their job to determine the correct answers.

Monitoring the Network (7.1.1.2)

The day-to-day operation of a network consists of common patterns of traffic flow, bandwidth usage, and resource access. Together, these patterns identify the normal network behavior. Security analysts must be intimately familiar with the normal network behavior because abnormal network behavior typically indicates a problem.

To discover the normal network behavior, network monitoring must be implemented. Various tools are used to help discover normal network behavior including IDS, packet analyzers, SNMP, NetFlow, and others.

Some of these tools require captured network data. There are two common methods used to capture traffic and send it to network monitoring devices:

- Network Terminal Access Points (TAPs)

- Traffic mirroring using Switched Port Analyzer (SPAN)

Both of these methods are discussed in this chapter.

Network TAPs (7.1.1.3)

A *network TAP* is typically a passive splitting device implemented inline between a device of interest and the network. A TAP forwards all traffic including physical layer errors to an analysis device.

Figure 7-1 displays a sample topology displaying a TAP installed between a network firewall and the internal router.

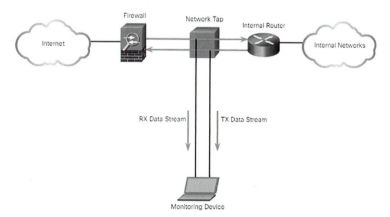

Figure 7-1   Implementing a TAP in a Sample Network

Notice how the TAP simultaneously sends both the transmit (TX) data stream from the internal router and the receive (RX) data stream to the internal router on separate, dedicated channels. This ensures that all data arrives at the monitoring device in real time. Therefore, network performance is not affected or degraded by monitoring the connection.

TAPs are also typically fail-safe, which means if it fails or loses power, traffic between the firewall and internal router is not affected.

Traffic Mirroring and SPAN (7.1.1.4)

Network switches segment the network by design, limiting the amount of traffic visible by the network monitoring device. Because data capturing for network monitoring requires all traffic to be captured, special techniques must be employed to bypass the network segmentation imposed by network switches. *Port mirroring* is one of these techniques. Supported by many enterprise switches, port mirroring enables the switch to copy frames of one or more ports to a *Switch Port Analyzer (SPAN)* port connected to an analysis device.

SPAN terminology includes

- **Ingress traffic:** Traffic that enters the switch.

- **Egress traffic:** Traffic that leaves the switch.

- **Source (SPAN) port:** A port that is monitored as traffic enters it before being replicated (mirrored) to the destination ports.

- **Destination (SPAN) port:** A port that mirrors source ports. Destination SPAN ports often connect to analysis devices such as a packet analyzer or an IDS.

Figure 7-2 displays a sample topology that shows a switch interconnecting two hosts. The switch will forward ingress traffic on F0/1 and egress traffic on F0/2 to the destination SPAN port G0/1 connecting to an IDS.

The association between source ports and a destination port is called a SPAN session. In a single session, one or multiple ports can be monitored. On some Cisco switches, session traffic can be copied to more than one destination port. Alternatively, a source VLAN can be specified in which all ports in the source VLAN become sources of SPAN traffic. Each SPAN session can have ports or VLANs as sources, but not both.

> **Note**
>
> A variation of SPAN called Remote SPAN (RSPAN) enables a network administrator to use the flexibility of VLANs to monitor traffic on remote switches.

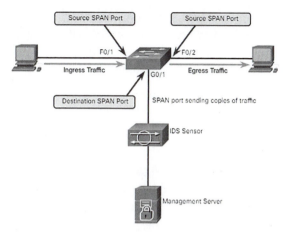

Figure 7-2   SPAN Operation

Introduction to Network Monitoring Tools (7.1.2)

In this topic, you will learn how network monitoring is conducted.

Network Security Monitoring Tools (7.1.2.1)

Common tools used for network security monitoring include:

- Network protocol analyzers (Wireshark and **tcpdump**)
- NetFlow
- Security information and event management (SIEM) systems

It is also common for security analysts to rely on log files and Simple Network Management Protocol (SNMP) to discover normal network behavior.

Practically all systems generate log files to communicate and record their operations. By closely monitoring log files, a security analyst can gather extremely valuable information.

SNMP allows analysts to ask for and receive information about the operation of network devices, and is another good tool for monitoring the behavior of a network.

Security analysts must be familiar with all of these tools.

Network Protocol Analyzers (7.1.2.2)

Network protocol analyzers (or "packet sniffer" applications) are programs used to capture traffic. Often including a graphical interface, protocol analyzers show what is happening on the network. Analysts can use these applications to see network exchanges down to the packet level. If a computer has been infected with malware and is currently attacking other computers in the network, the analyst can see that clearly by capturing real-time network traffic and analyzing the packets.

Not only used for security analysis, network protocol analyzers are also very useful for network troubleshooting, software and protocol development, and education. For instance, in security forensics, a security analyst may attempt to reconstruct an incident from relevant packet captures.

Wireshark, shown in Figure 7-3, has become a very popular network protocol analyzer tool that is used in Windows, Linux, and Mac OS environments. Captured frames are saved in a PCAP file. PCAP files contain the frame information, interface information, packet length, and timestamps.

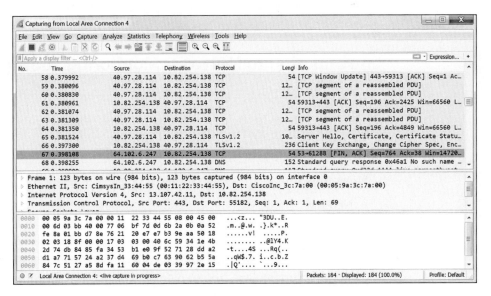

Figure 7-3 Sample Wireshark Output

Performing a long-term packet capture produces large PCAP files.

Wireshark can also open files that contain captured traffic from other software such as the **tcpdump** utility. Popular among UNIX-like systems such as Linux, **tcpdump** is a powerful utility with numerous command-line options. Example 7-1 displays a sample **tcpdump** capture of ping packets.

Example 7-1   Sample **tcpdump** Output

```
[root@secOps analyst]# tcpdump -i h1-eth0 -n

tcpdump: verbose output suppressed, use -v or -vv for full protocol decode
listening on h1-eth0, link-type EN10MB (Ethernet), capture size 262144 bytes
10:42:19.841549 IP 10.0.0.12 > 10.0.0.11: ICMP echo request, id 2279, seq 5,
  length 64
10:42:19.841570 IP 10.0.0.11 > 10.0.0.12: ICMP echo reply, id 2279, seq 5,
  length 64
10:42:19.854287 IP 10.0.0.12 > 10.0.0.11: ICMP echo request, id 2279, seq 6,
  length 64
10:42:19.854304 IP 10.0.0.11 > 10.0.0.12: ICMP echo reply, id 2279, seq 6,
  length 64
10:42:19.867446 IP 10.0.0.12 > 10.0.0.11: ICMP echo request, id 2279, seq 7,
  length 64
10:42:19.867468 IP 10.0.0.11 > 10.0.0.12: ICMP echo reply, id 2279, seq 7,
  length 64
^C
6 packets captured
6 packets received by filter
0 packets dropped by kernel

[root@secOps analyst]#
```

Note

windump is a Microsoft Windows variant of **tcpdump**, and **tshark** is Wireshark command-line tool similar to **tcpdump**.

NetFlow (7.1.2.3)

NetFlow is a Cisco IOS technology that provides 24x7 statistics on packets flowing through a Cisco router or multilayer switch. NetFlow is the standard for collecting IP operational data in IP networks. NetFlow is now supported on non-Cisco platforms.

NetFlow can be used for network and security monitoring, network planning, and traffic analysis. It provides a complete audit trail of basic information about every IP flow forwarded on a device. This information includes the source and destination device IP information, the time of the communication, and the amount of data transferred. NetFlow does not capture the actual content on the flow. NetFlow functionality is often compared to a telephone bill. The bill identifies the destination number and the time and duration of the call. However, it does not display the content of the telephone conversation.

Although NetFlow stores flow information in a local cache on the device, it should always be configured to forward data to a NetFlow collector such as Cisco Stealthwatch.

For example, in Figure 7-4, PC1 connects to PC2 using an application such as HTTPS. NetFlow can monitor that application connection, tracking byte and packet counts for that individual application flow. It then pushes the statistics over to an external server called a NetFlow collector.

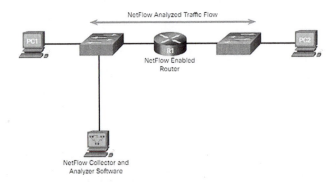

Figure 7-4   NetFlow in the Network

NetFlow collectors like Cisco Stealthwatch can also perform advanced functions including:

- **Flow stitching:** It groups individual entries into flows.

- **Flow deduplication:** It filters duplicate incoming entries from multiple NetFlow clients.

- **NAT stitching:** It simplifies flows with NAT entries.

Cisco Stealthwatch has many more features than just NetFlow.

SIEM (7.1.2.4)

Security information and event management (SIEM) is a technology used in enterprise organizations to provide real-time reporting and long-term analysis of security events.

SIEM includes the following essential functions:

- **Forensic analysis:** Provides the ability to search logs and event records from sources throughout the organization. It provides more complete information for forensic analysis.

- **Correlation:** Examines logs and events from different systems or applications, speeding detection of and reaction to security threats.

- **Aggregation:** Reduces the volume of event data by consolidating duplicate event records.

- **Reporting:** Presents the correlated and aggregated event data in real-time monitoring and long-term summaries.

SIEM provides details on the source of suspicious activity:

- User information such as username, authentication status, location

- Device information such as manufacturer, model, OS version, MAC address, network connection method, and location

- Posture information such as whether the device is compliant with the security policy, has up-to-date antivirus files, and is updated with latest OS patches

Using this information, network security analysts can quickly and accurately assess the significance of any security event and answer the critical questions, such as:

- Who is associated with this event?

- Does the user have access to other sensitive resources?

- Does this event represent a potential compliance issue?

- Is it an important user with access to intellectual property or sensitive information?

- Is the user authorized to access that resource?

- What kind of device is being used?

SIEM Systems (7.1.2.5)

Several SIEM systems exist. Splunk is one of the more popular proprietary SIEM systems used by Security Operation Centers.

As an open source option, this course uses the ELK suite for SIEM functionality. ELK is an acronym for three open source products from Elastic:

- **Elasticsearch:** Document-oriented, full-text search engine

- **Logstash:** Pipeline processing system that connects "inputs" to "outputs" with optional "filters" in between

- **Kibana:** Browser-based analytics and search dashboard for Elasticsearch

Interactive Graphic

Activity 7.1.2.6: Identify the Network Monitoring Tool

Refer to the online course to complete this Activity.

Packet Tracer 7.1.2.7: Logging Network Activity

In this activity, you will intercept credentials using a sniffer device, while observing an FTP session. An exchange of syslog messages will also be intercepted by a sniffer device.

Attacking the Foundation (7.2)

In this section, you will learn how TCP/IP vulnerabilities enable network attacks.

IP Vulnerabilities and Threats (7.2.1)

In this topic, you will learn how IP vulnerabilities enable network attacks.

IPv4 and IPv6 (7.2.1.1)

IP was designed as a connectionless protocol. It provides the necessary functions to deliver a packet from a source host to a destination host over an interconnected system of networks. The protocol was not designed to track and manage the flow of packets. These functions, if required, are performed primarily by TCP at Layer 4.

IP makes no effort to validate whether the source IP address contained in a packet actually came from that source. For this reason, threat actors can send packets using a spoofed source IP address. In addition, threat actors can tamper with the other fields in the IP header to carry out their attacks. Therefore, it is important for security analysts to understand the different fields in both the IPv4 and IPv6 headers.

The IPv4 Packet Header (7.2.1.2)

There are ten fields in the IPv4 packet header, as shown in Figure 7-5:

- **Version:** Contains a 4-bit binary value set to 0100 that identifies this as an IPv4 packet.

- **Internet Header Length:** A 4-bit field containing the length of the IP header. The minimum length of an IP header is 20 bytes.

- **Differentiated Services or DiffServ (DS):** Formerly called the Type of Service (ToS) field, the DS field is an 8-bit field used to determine the priority of each packet. The 6 most significant bits of the DiffServ field are the Differentiated Services Code Point (DSCP). The last 2 bits are the Explicit Congestion Notification (ECN) bits.

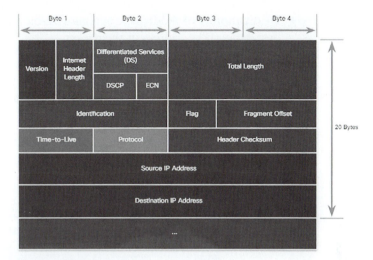

Figure 7-5   IPv4 Packet Header

- **Total Length:** Specifies the length of the IP packet that includes the IP header and the user data. The Total Length field is 2 bytes, so the maximum size of an IP packet is 65,535 bytes.

- **Identification, Flag, and Fragment Offset:** As an IP packet moves through the Internet, it might need to cross a route that cannot handle the size of the packet. The packet will be divided, or fragmented, into smaller packets and reassembled later. These fields are used to fragment and reassemble packets.

- **Time-to-Live (TTL):** Contains an 8-bit binary value that is used to limit the lifetime of a packet. The packet sender sets the initial TTL value, and it is decreased by a value of 1 each time the packet is processed by a router. If the TTL field decrements to 0, the router discards the packet and sends an Internet Control Message Protocol (ICMP) Time Exceeded message to the source IP address.

- **Protocol:** Used to identify the next-level protocol. This 8-bit binary value indicates the data payload type that the packet is carrying, which enables the network layer to pass the data to the appropriate upper-layer protocol. Common values include ICMP (1), TCP (6), and UDP (17).

- **Header Checksum:** A value that is calculated based on the contents of the IP header. Used to determine if any errors have been introduced during transmission.

- **Source IPv4 Address:** Contains a 32-bit binary value that represents the source IPv4 address of the packet. The source IPv4 address is always a unicast address.

- **Destination IPv4 Address:** Contains a 32-bit binary value that represents the destination IPv4 address of the packet.

- **Options and Padding:** This is a field that varies in length from 0 to a multiple of 32 bits. If the option values are not a multiple of 32 bits, 0s are added or padded to ensure that this field contains a multiple of 32 bits.

The IPv6 Packet Header (7.2.1.3)

There are eight fields in the IPv6 packet header, as shown Figure 7-6:

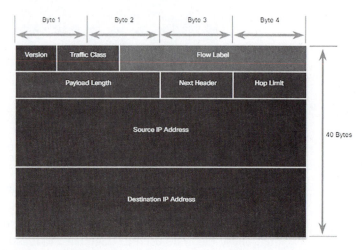

Figure 7-6 IPv6 Packet Header

- **Version:** This field contains a 4-bit binary value set to 0110 that identifies this as an IPv6 packet.

- **Traffic Class:** This 8-bit field is equivalent to the IPv4 Differentiated Services (DS) field.

- **Flow Label:** This 20-bit field suggests that all packets with the same flow label receive the same type of handling by routers.

- **Payload Length:** This 16-bit field indicates the length of the data portion or payload of the IPv6 packet.

- **Next Header:** This 8-bit field is equivalent to the IPv4 Protocol field. It indicates the data payload type that the packet is carrying, enabling the network layer to pass the data to the appropriate upper-layer protocol.

- **Hop Limit:** This 8-bit field replaces the IPv4 TTL field. This value is decremented by a value of 1 by each router that forwards the packet. When the counter reaches 0, the packet is discarded, and an ICMPv6 Time Exceeded message is forwarded to the sending host, indicating that the packet did not reach its destination because the hop limit was exceeded.

- **Source IPv6 Address:** This 128-bit field identifies the IPv6 address of the sending host.

- **Destination IPv6 Address:** This 128-bit field identifies the IPv6 address of the receiving host.

An IPv6 packet may also contain extension headers (EHs), which provide optional network layer information. Extension headers are optional and are placed between the IPv6 header and the payload. EHs are used for fragmentation, security, to support mobility, and more.

Unlike IPv4, routers do not fragment routed IPv6 packets.

IP Vulnerabilities (7.2.1.4)

There are different types of attacks targeting IP. These are some of the more common IP-related attacks:

- **ICMP attacks:** Threat actors use ICMP echo packets (pings) to discover subnets and hosts on a protected network, to generate DoS flood attacks, and to alter host routing tables.

- **Denial-of-service (DoS) attacks:** Threat actors attempt to prevent legitimate users from accessing information or services.

- **Distributed DoS (DDoS) attacks:** Similar to a DoS attack, but features a simultaneous, coordinated attack from multiple source machines.

- **Address spoofing attacks:** Threat actors spoof the source IP address in an IP packet to perform blind spoofing or non-blind spoofing.

- **Man-in-the-middle (MITM) attacks:** Threat actors position themselves between a source and destination to transparently monitor, capture, and control the communication. They could simply eavesdrop by inspecting captured packets or alter packets and forward them to their original destination.

- *Session hijacking*: Threat actors gain access to the physical network, and then use an MITM attack to hijack a session.

ICMP Attacks (7.2.1.5)

ICMP was developed to carry diagnostic messages and to report error conditions when routes, hosts, and ports are unavailable. ICMP messages are generated by devices when a network error or outage occurs. The **ping** command is a user-generated ICMP message, called an Echo Request, used to verify connectivity to a destination.

Threat actors use ICMP for reconnaissance and scanning attacks. This enables them to launch information-gathering attacks to map out a network topology, discover which hosts are active (reachable), identify the host operating system (*OS fingerprinting*), and determine the state of a firewall.

Threat actors also use ICMP for DoS attacks, as shown in the ICMP flood attack in Figure 7-7.

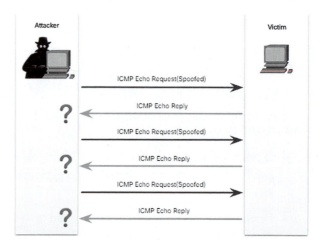

Figure 7-7   ICMP Flood

Note

ICMP for IPv4 (ICMPv4) and ICMP for IPv6 (ICMPv6) are susceptible to similar types of attacks.

Common ICMP messages of interest to threat actors include:

- **ICMP Echo Request and Echo Reply:** These are used to perform host verification and DoS attacks.

- **ICMP Unreachable:** This is used to perform network reconnaissance and scanning attacks.

- **ICMP Mask Reply:** This is used to map an internal IP network.

- **ICMP Redirect:** This is used to lure a target host into sending all traffic through a compromised device and create an MITM attack.

- **ICMP Router discovery:** This is used to inject bogus route entries into the routing table of a target host.

Networks should have strict ICMP access control list (ACL) filtering on the network edge to avoid ICMP probing from the Internet. Security analysts should be able to detect ICMP-related attacks by looking at captured traffic and log files. In the case of large networks, security devices such as firewalls and IDSs should detect such attacks and generate alerts to the security analysts.

DoS Attacks (7.2.1.6)

DoS is one of the most common type of attacks. The goal of a DoS attack is to prevent legitimate users from gaining access to websites, email, online accounts, and other services.

There are two major sources of DoS attacks:

- **Maliciously formatted packets:** Threat actors craft a maliciously formatted packet and forward it to a susceptible host, causing it to crash or become extremely slow.

- **Overwhelming quantity of traffic:** Threat actors overwhelm a target network, host, or application, causing it to crash or become extremely slow.

A DDoS attack combines multiple DoS attacks. In Figure 7-8, the attacker first infects computers to create zombies.

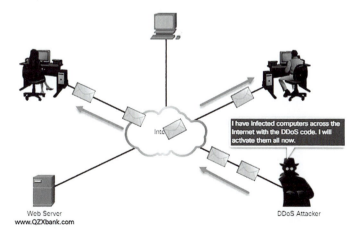

Figure 7-8 DDoS Attack: Activating Zombies

Then, in Figure 7-9, the attacker activates the zombies to attack the victim server.

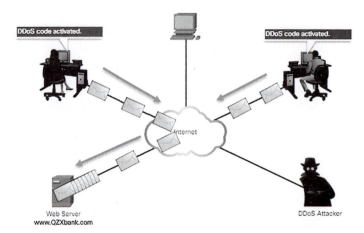

Figure 7-9   DDoS Attack: Zombies Attack Target

ICMP is often used to create DoS attacks. For example, threat actors use ICMP messages to significantly saturate and slow down the target device.

Amplification and Reflection Attacks (7.2.1.7)

Threat actors often use ***amplification and reflection techniques*** to create DoS attacks. The example in Figure 7-10 illustrates how an amplification and reflection technique called a Smurf attack is used to overwhelm a target host:

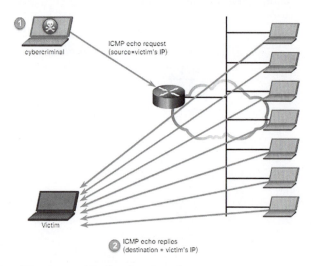

Figure 7-10   Amplification and Reflection Attack

1. **Amplification:** The threat actor forwards ICMP echo request messages that contain the source IP address of the victim to a large number of hosts.

2. **Reflection:** These hosts all reply to the spoofed IP address of the victim to overwhelm it.

Note

Newer forms of amplification and reflection attacks are now being used, such as DNS-based reflection and amplification attacks and Network Time Protocol (NTP) amplification attacks.

Threat actors also use resource exhaustion attacks to consume the resources of a target host to crash it or to consume the resources of a network to adversely affect its operation.

DDoS Attacks (7.2.1.8)

A DDoS attack is similar in intent to a DoS attack, except that a DDoS attack increases in magnitude because it originates from multiple, coordinated sources. DDoS attacks also introduce new terms such as botnet, handler systems, and zombie computers.

A DDoS attack could proceed as follows:

1. The threat actor (botmaster) builds or purchases the use of a botnet of zombie hosts. The command-and-control (CnC) server communicates with zombies over a covert channel using IRC, P2P, DNS, HTTP, or HTTPS.

2. Zombie computers continue to scan and infect more targets to create more zombies.

3. When ready, the botmaster uses the handler systems to make the botnet of zombies carry out the DDoS attack on the chosen target.

In Figure 7-11, the threat actor communicates with the zombies using the CnC server to launch a DDoS attack against the victim's infrastructure.

Bots have a worm-like ability to self-propagate but they can also be used to log keystrokes, gather passwords, capture and analyze packets, gather financial information, launch DoS attacks, relay spam, and open back doors on the infected host.

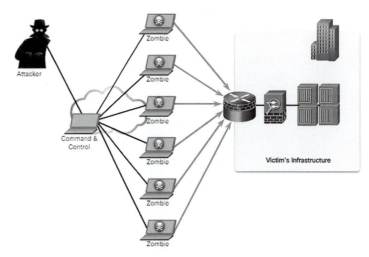

Figure 7-11   DDoS Attack

There are many potential sources of DoS and DDoS attacks. While DDoS attacks are very easy to detect, they are hard to combat. Insecure IoT devices have been exploited to exponentially increase the size of botnets. There are a few countermeasures that can be used to fight these attacks:

- Implement firewalls and IPS monitoring

- Rate-limit incoming and outgoing traffic to normal baseline settings

- Maximize the memory and harden all devices

Address Spoofing Attacks (7.2.1.9)

IP address spoofing attacks occur when a threat actor creates packets with false source IP address information to either hide the identity of the sender or to pose as another legitimate user. The attacker can then gain access to otherwise inaccessible data or circumvent security configurations. Spoofing is usually incorporated into another attack such as a Smurf attack.

Spoofing attacks can be conducted as follows:

- *Non-blind spoofing*: The threat actor can see the traffic that is being sent between the host and the target. Non-blind spoofing is used by the threat actor to inspect the reply packet from the target victim. Reasons for non-blind spoofing include determining the state of a firewall, sequence-number prediction, or hijacking an authorized session.

- *Blind spoofing*: The threat actor cannot see the traffic that is being sent between the host and the target. Blind spoofing is used in DoS attacks.

MAC address spoofing attacks are used when threat actors have access to the internal network. Threat actors alter the MAC address of their host to match another known MAC address of a target host, as shown in Figure 7-12.

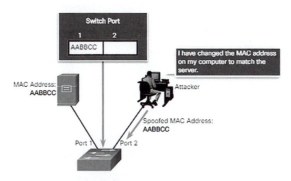

Figure 7-12   Attacker Spoofs a Server's MAC Address

The attacking host then sends a frame throughout the network with the newly configured MAC address. When the switch receives the frame, it examines the source MAC address. The switch overwrites the current CAM table entry and assigns the MAC address to the new port, as shown in Figure 7-13. It then forwards frames destined for the target host to the attacking host.

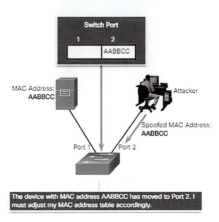

Figure 7-13   Switch Updates CAM Table with Spoofed Address

Application or service spoofing is another spoofing example. A threat actor can connect a rogue DHCP server to create an MITM condition.

Activity 7.2.1.10: Identify the IP Vulnerability

Refer to the online course to complete this Activity.

Lab 7.2.1.11: Observing a DDoS Attack

In this lab, you will simulate and observe a DoS and DDoS attack.

TCP and UDP Vulnerabilities (7.2.2)

In this topic, you will learn how TCP and UDP vulnerabilities enable network attacks.

TCP (7.2.2.1)

Like IP, TCP is also vulnerable. TCP segment information appears immediately after the IP header. The fields of the TCP segment and the flags for the Control Bits field are displayed in Figure 7-14.

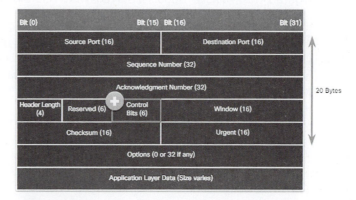

Figure 7-14   TCP Segment

The control bits are as follows:

- **URG:** Urgent pointer field significant
- **ACK:** Acknowledgment field significant
- **PSH:** Push function
- **RST:** Reset the connection
- **SYN:** Synchronize sequence numbers
- **FIN:** No more data from sender

TCP provides the following services:

- **Reliable delivery:** Reliable communication is the largest benefit of TCP. TCP incorporates acknowledgments to guarantee delivery, instead of relying on upper-layer protocols to detect and resolve errors. If a timely acknowledgment is not received, the sender retransmits the data. But requiring acknowledgments of received data can cause substantial delays.

- **Flow control:** TCP implements flow control to address the delay issue. Rather than acknowledge one segment at a time, multiple segments can be acknowledged with a single acknowledgment segment.

- **Stateful communication:** TCP stateful communication between two parties happens by way of a TCP three-way handshake. Before data can be transferred using TCP, a three-way handshake opens the TCP connection as shown in Figure 7-15. If both sides agree to the TCP connection, data can be sent and received by both parties using TCP.

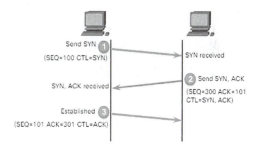

Figure 7-15   Establishing a TCP Connection

Examples of application layer protocols that make use of TCP reliability include HTTP, SSL/TLS, FTP, DNS zone transfers, and others.

TCP Attacks (7.2.2.2)

Though TCP is a connection-oriented and reliable protocol, it still has vulnerabilities that can be exploited.

The TCP protocol is vulnerable to port scanning. Network applications use TCP or UDP ports. Threat actors conduct port scans of target devices to discover which services they offer.

The TCP SYN flood attack exploits the TCP three-way handshake. As illustrated in Figure 7-16, the threat actor continually sends TCP SYN session request packets with a randomly spoofed source IP address to an intended target.

The target device replies with a TCP SYN-ACK packet to the spoofed IP address and waits for a TCP ACK packet. Those responses never arrive. Eventually the target host is overwhelmed with half-open TCP connections and denies TCP services (e.g., email, file transfer, or http) to legitimate users.

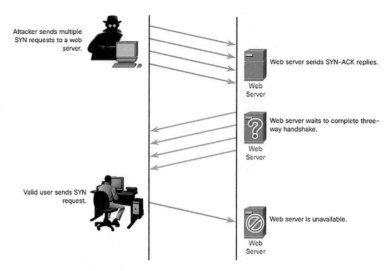

Figure 7-16   Sample TCP SYN Flood Attack

A TCP reset attack can be used to terminate a TCP communication between two hosts. Figure 7-17 displays how TCP uses a four-way exchange to close the TCP connection using a pair of FIN and ACK segments from each TCP endpoint.

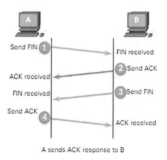

Figure 7-17   Terminating a TCP Connection

A TCP connection can also be torn down when it receives an RST bit. This is an abrupt way to tear down the TCP connection and inform the receiving host to immediately stop using the TCP connection. A threat actor could do a TCP reset attack and send a spoofed packet containing a TCP RST to one or both endpoints.

TCP session hijacking is another TCP vulnerability. Although difficult to conduct, it enables a threat actor to overtake an already-authenticated host as it communicates with the target. The threat actor would have to spoof the IP address of one host, predict the next sequence number, and send an ACK to the other host. If successful, the threat actor could send data to, but not receive data from, the target device.

UDP and UDP Attacks (7.2.2.3)

UDP is a simple protocol that provides the basic transport layer functions. UDP is commonly used by DNS, TFTP, NFS, and SNMP. It is also used with real-time applications such as media streaming or VoIP. UDP is a connectionless transport layer protocol. It has much lower overhead than TCP because it is not connection-oriented and does not offer the sophisticated retransmission, sequencing, and flow control mechanisms that provide reliability. The UDP segment structure is much smaller than TCP's segment structure, and is shown in Figure 7-18.

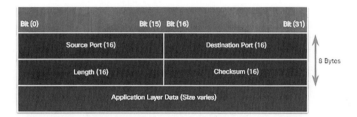

Figure 7-18   UDP Data Structure

This does not mean that applications that use UDP are always unreliable, nor does it mean that UDP is an inferior protocol. It means that these functions are not provided by the transport layer protocol and must be implemented elsewhere if required.

The low overhead of UDP makes it very desirable for protocols that make simple request and reply transactions. For example, using TCP for DHCP would introduce unnecessary network traffic. If there is a problem with a request or a reply, the device simply sends the request again if no response is received.

UDP is not protected by any encryption. It is possible to add encryption to UDP, but it is not available by default. The lack of encryption allows anyone to look at the traffic, change it, and send it on to its destination. Changing the data in the traffic will alter the 16-bit checksum, but the checksum is optional and not always used. When the checksum is used, the attacker can create a new checksum based on the new data payload, and record it in the header as a new checksum. The destination device will find that the checksum matches the data without knowing the data has been altered.

This type of attack is not the most widely used. It is more common to see a UDP attack where all of the resources on a network are consumed. This is called a UDP flood attack. To do this, the attacker must use a tool like UDP Unicorn or Low Orbit Ion Cannon (LOIC) that sends a flood of UDP packets, often from a spoofed host, to a server on the subnet. The program will sweep through all of the known ports trying to find closed ports. This will cause the server to reply with an ICMP port unreachable message. Because there are so many closed ports on the server, this causes so much traffic on the segment that almost all of the bandwidth gets used. The result is very similar to a DoS attack.

Lab 7.2.2.4: Observing TCP Anomalies

In this lab, you will complete the following objectives:

- Load Mininet and Start Services
- Enable Wireshark to Capture and Observe Normal Traffic Packets
- Use Wireshark to Capture SYN Flood Attack Packets
- Stopping Mininet

Attacking What We Do (7.3)

In this section, you will learn how common network applications and services are vulnerable to attack.

IP Services (7.3.1)

In this topic, you will learn about IP vulnerabilities.

ARP Vulnerabilities (7.3.1.1)

Hosts broadcast an ARP Request to other hosts on the segment to determine the MAC address of a host with a particular IP address. All hosts on the subnet receive and process the ARP Request. The host with the matching IP address in the ARP Request (Figure 7-19) sends an ARP Reply (Figure 7-20).

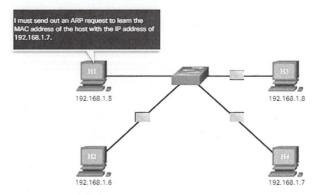

Figure 7-19 The ARP Process: ARP Request

Any client can send an unsolicited ARP Reply called a "gratuitous ARP." This is often done when a device first boots up to inform all other devices on the local network of the new device's MAC address. When a host sends a gratuitous ARP, other hosts on the subnet store the MAC address and IP address contained in the gratuitous ARP in their ARP tables.

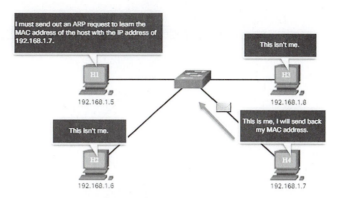

Figure 7-20   The ARP Process: ARP Reply

However, this feature of ARP also means that any host can claim to be the owner of any IP/MAC they choose. A threat actor can poison the ARP cache of devices on the local network, creating an MITM attack to redirect traffic. The goal is to target a victim host and have it change its default gateway to the threat actor's device. This positions the threat actor in between the victim and all other systems outside of the local subnet.

ARP Cache Poisoning (7.3.1.2)

To see how *ARP cache poisoning* works, consider the following example. In Figure 7-21, PC-A requires the MAC address of its default gateway (R1) and therefore sends an ARP Request for the MAC address of 192.168.10.1.

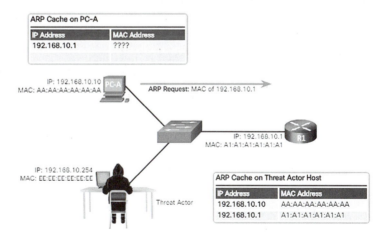

Figure 7-21   PC-A Sends an ARP Request to the Default Gateway

In Figure 7-22, R1 updates its ARP cache with the IP and MAC addresses of PC-A and sends an ARP Reply to PC-A, which then updates its ARP cache with the IP and MAC addresses of R1.

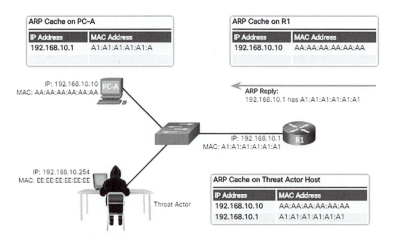

Figure 7-22 R1 Sends ARP Reply

In Figure 7-23, the threat actor sends two spoofed gratuitous ARP Replies using its own MAC address for the indicated destination IP addresses. PC-A updates its ARP cache with its default gateway now pointing to the threat actor's host MAC. R1 also updates its ARP cache with the IP address of PC-A pointing to the threat actor's MAC address.

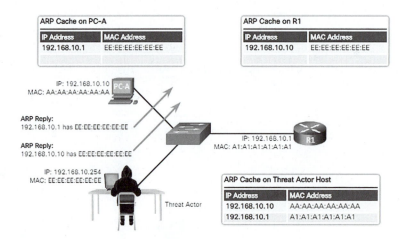

Figure 7-23 Threat Actor Sends Spoofed Gratuitous Replies

The threat actor's host is now doing an ARP poisoning attack.

Note

There are many tools available on the Internet to create ARP MITM attacks, including dsniff, Cain & Abel, Ettercap, Yersinia, and others.

The ARP poisoning attack can be

- **Passive:** Threat actors steal confidential information.

- **Active:** Threat actors modify data in transit or inject malicious data.

DNS Attacks (7.3.1.3)

The Domain Name Service (DNS) protocol defines an automated service that matches resource names with the required numeric network address. It includes the format for queries, responses, and data and uses resource records (RRs) to identify the type of DNS response.

Securing DNS is often overlooked. However, it is crucial to the operation of a network and should be secured accordingly.

Many organizations use the services of publicly open DNS servers such as Google DNS (8.8.8.8) to provide responses to queries. This type of DNS server is called an open resolver. A DNS open resolver answers queries from clients outside of its administrative domain.

DNS open resolvers are vulnerable to multiple malicious activities, including

- **DNS cache poisoning attacks:** Threat actors send spoofed, falsified RR information to a DNS resolver to redirect users from legitimate sites to malicious sites. DNS cache poisoning attacks can all be used to inform the DNS resolver to use a malicious name server that is providing RR information for malicious activities.

- **DNS amplification and reflection attacks:** Threat actors use DNS open resolvers to increase the volume of attacks and to hide the true source of an attack. This technique is used in DoS or DDoS attacks. These attacks are possible because the open resolver will respond to queries from anyone asking a question. Threat actors send DNS messages to the open resolvers using the IP address of a target host (victim).

- **DNS resource utilization attacks:** Threat actors launch a DoS attack that consumes the resources of the DNS open resolvers. Examples of such resources include CPU, memory, and socket buffers. This DoS attack consumes all the available resources to negatively affect the operations of the DNS open resolver. The impact of this DoS attack may require the DNS open resolver to be rebooted or services to be stopped and restarted.

To hide their identity, threat actors also use the following DNS stealth techniques to carry out their attacks:

- *Fast flux*: Threat actors use this technique to hide their phishing and malware delivery sites behind a quickly changing network of compromised DNS hosts.

The DNS IP addresses are continuously changed within minutes. Botnets often employ fast flux techniques to effectively hide (i.e., cloak) malicious servers from being detected.

- *Double IP flux*: Threat actors use this technique to rapidly change the hostname to IP address mappings and to also change the authoritative name server. This increases the difficulty of identifying the source of the attack.

- *Domain generation algorithms*: Threat actors use this technique in malware to randomly generate domain names that can then be used as rendezvous points to their command and control (CnC) servers.

Other threats to DNS include DNS shadowing attacks and DNS tunneling. DNS tunneling is discussed next. Domain shadowing involves the threat actor compromising a parent domain and creating multiple subdomains to be used during the attacks.

DNS Tunneling (7.3.1.4)

Botnets have become a popular attack method of threat actors. Most often, botnets are used to spread malware or launch DDoS and phishing attacks.

DNS in the enterprise is sometimes overlooked as a protocol which can be used by botnets. Because of this, when DNS traffic is determined to be part of an incident, the attack is already over. It is necessary for the security analyst to be able to detect when an attacker is using **DNS tunneling** to steal data, and prevent and contain the attack. To accomplish this, the security analyst must implement a solution that can block the outbound communications from the infected hosts.

Threat actors who use DNS tunneling place non-DNS traffic within DNS traffic. This method often circumvents security solutions. For the threat actor to use DNS tunneling, the different types of DNS records such as TXT, MX, SRV, NULL, A, or CNAME are altered. For example, the TXT record can store the most commands for sending to the infected hosts over DNS replies. A DNS tunneling attack using TXT works like this:

1. The data is split into multiple encoded chunks.

2. Each chunk is placed into a lower level domain name label of the DNS query.

3. Because there is no response from the local or networked DNS for the query, the request is sent to the ISP's recursive DNS servers.

4. The recursive DNS service forwards the query to the attacker's authoritative name server.

5. The process is repeated until all of the queries containing the chunks are sent.

6. When the attacker's authoritative name server receives the DNS queries from the infected devices, it sends responses for each DNS query, which contain the encapsulated, encoded commands.

7. The malware on the compromised host recombines the chunks and executes the commands hidden within.

To be able to stop DNS tunneling, a filter that inspects DNS traffic must be used. Pay particular attention to DNS queries that are longer than average, or those that have a suspicious domain name. Also, DNS solutions, like Cisco OpenDNS, block much of the DNS tunneling traffic by identifying suspicious domains.

DHCP (7.3.1.5)

DHCP servers dynamically provide IP configuration information including IP address, subnet mask, default gateway, DNS servers, and more to clients. The typical sequence of DHCP message exchange between client and server is displayed in Figure 7-24.

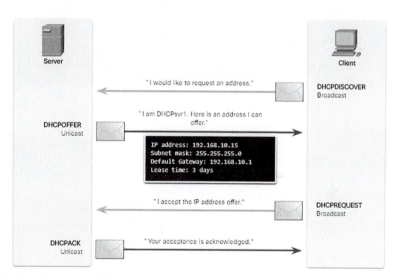

Figure 7-24   Normal DHCP Operation

DHCP is vulnerable to DHCP spoofing attacks. A DHCP spoofing attack occurs when a rogue DHCP server is connected to the network and provides false IP configuration parameters to legitimate clients. A rogue server can provide a variety of misleading information:

- **Wrong default gateway:** The threat actor provides an invalid gateway or the IP address of its host to create an MITM attack. This may go entirely undetected as the intruder intercepts the data flow through the network.

- **Wrong DNS server:** The threat actor provides an incorrect DNS server address pointing the user to a malicious website.

■ **Wrong IP address:** The threat actor provides an invalid IP address, invalid default gateway IP address, or both invalid IP address and default gateway. The threat actor then creates a DoS attack on the DHCP client.

Figures 7-25 through 7-28 illustrate a DHCP spoofing attack. Assume a threat actor has successfully connected a rogue DHCP server to a switch port on the same subnet as the target clients. The goal of the rogue server is to provide clients with false IP configuration information.

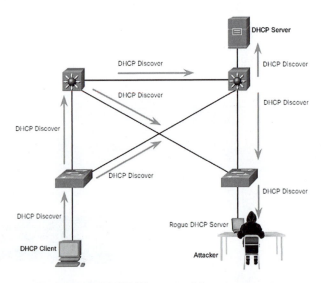

Figure 7-25   Client Broadcasts DHCP Discovery Messages

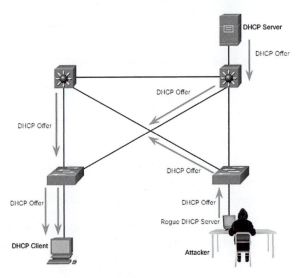

Figure 7-26   Legitimate and Rogue DHCP Reply

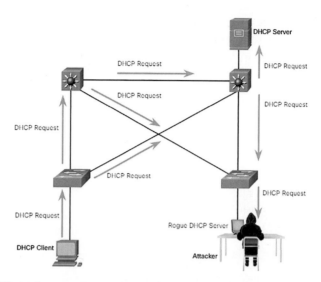

Figure 7-27   Client Accepts Rogue DHCP Offer

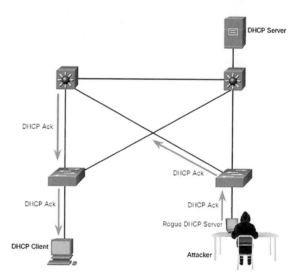

Figure 7-28   Rogue Acknowledges

In Figure 7-25, a legitimate client connects to the network and requires IP configuration parameters. Therefore, the client broadcasts a DHCP Discover request looking for a response from a DHCP server. Both servers will receive the message. Figure 7-26 illustrates how the legitimate and rogue DHCP servers each respond with valid IP configuration parameters. The client will reply to the first offer received.

In this scenario, the client received the rogue offer first. It broadcasts a DHCP request accepting the parameters from the rogue server as shown in Figure 7-27. The legitimate and rogue server will receive the request. However, as shown in Figure 7-28, only the rogue server unicasts a reply to the client to acknowledge its request. The legitimate server will cease communicating with the client.

DHCP is also vulnerable to a DHCP starvation attack. The goal of this attack is to create a DoS for connecting clients. DHCP starvation attacks require an attack tool such as Gobbler. Gobbler forwards DHCP discovery messages with bogus MAC addresses in an attempt to lease the entire pool of addresses.

Lab 7.3.1.6: Exploring DNS Traffic

In this lab, you will complete the following objectives:

- Capture DNS Traffic
- Explore DNS Query Traffic
- Explore DNS Response Traffic

Enterprise Services (7.3.2)

In this topic, you will learn how network application vulnerabilities enable network attacks.

HTTP and HTTPS (7.3.2.1)

Internet browsers are used by almost everyone. Blocking web browsing completely is not an option because businesses need access to the web, without undermining web security.

To investigate web-based attacks, security analysts must have a good understanding of how a standard web-based attack works. These are the common stages of a typical web attack:

1. The victim unknowingly visits a web page that has been compromised by malware.

2. The compromised web page redirects the user, often through many compromised servers, to a site containing malicious code.

3. The user visits this site with malicious code and their computer becomes infected. This is known as a drive-by download. When the user visits the site, an exploit kit scans the software running on the victim's computer, including the OS, Java, and Flash player, looking for an exploit in the software. The exploit kit

is often a PHP script and provides the attacker with a management console to manage the attack.

4. After identifying a vulnerable software package running on the victim's computer, the exploit kit contacts the exploit kit server to download code that can use the vulnerability to run malicious code on the victim's computer.

5. After the victim's computer has been compromised, it connects to the malware server and downloads a payload. This could be malware, or a file download service that downloads other malware.

6. The final malware package is run on the victim's computer.

Independent of the type of attack being used, the main goal of the threat actor is to ensure the victim's web browser ends up on the threat actor's web page, which then serves out the malicious exploit to the victim.

Some malicious sites take advantage of vulnerable plugins or browser vulnerabilities to compromise the client's system. Larger networks rely on IDSs to scan downloaded files for malware. If detected, the IDSs issue alerts and records the event to log files for later analysis.

Server connection logs can often reveal information about the type of scan or attack. The different types of connection status codes are listed here:

- **Informational 1xx:** A provisional response, consisting only of the Status-Line and optional headers. It is terminated by an empty line. There are no required headers for this class of status code. Servers MUST NOT send a 1xx response to an HTTP/1.0 client except under experimental conditions.

- **Successful 2xx:** The client's request was successfully received, understood, and accepted.

- **Redirection 3xx:** Further action must be taken by the user agent to fulfill the request. A client SHOULD detect infinite redirection loops, because these loops generate network traffic for each redirection.

- **Client Error 4xx:** For cases in which the client seems to have erred. Except when responding to a HEAD request, the server SHOULD include an entity containing an explanation of the situation, and if it is temporary. User agents SHOULD display any included entity to the user.

- **Server Error 5xx:** For cases where the server is aware that it has erred, or it cannot perform the request. Except when responding to a HEAD request, the server SHOULD include an entity containing an explanation of the error situation, and if it is temporary. User agents SHOULD display any included entity to the user.

To defend against web-based attacks, the following countermeasures should be used:

- Always update the OS and browsers with current patches and updates.

- Use a web proxy like Cisco Cloud Web Security or Cisco Web Security Appliance to block malicious sites.

- Use the best security practices from the Open Web Application Security Project (OWASP) when developing web applications.

- Educate end users by showing them how to avoid web-based attacks.

Malicious iFrames

Threat actors often make use of malicious inline frames (iFrames). An *iFrame* is an HTML element that allows the browser to load another web page from another source. iFrame attacks have become very common, as they are often used to insert advertisements from other sources into the page. In some instances, the iFrame page that is loaded consists of only a few pixels. This makes it very hard for the user to see. Because the iFrame is run in the page, it can be used to deliver a malicious exploit.

These are some of the ways to prevent or reduce malicious iFrames:

- Use a web proxy like Cisco Cloud Web Security or Cisco Web Security Appliance to block malicious sites.

- Because attackers often change the source of the iFrame in a compromised website, make sure web developers do not use iFrames to isolate any content from third parties from a website.

- Use a service such as Cisco OpenDNS to prevent users from navigating to websites that are known to be malicious.

- Make sure the end user understands what an IFrame is and that threat actors have been using this method often in web-based attacks.

HTTP 302 Cushioning

Another type of HTTP attack is the *HTTP 302 cushioning* attack. Threat actors use the 302 Found HTTP response status code to direct the user's web browser to the new location. Threat actors often use legitimate HTTP functions such as HTTP redirects to carry out their attacks. HTTP allows servers to redirect a client's HTTP request to a different server. HTTP redirection is used, for example, when web content has moved to a different URL or domain name. This allows old URLs and bookmarks to continue to function. Therefore, security analysts should understand how a function such as HTTP redirection works and how it can be used during attacks.

When the response from the server is a 302 Found status, it also provides the URL in the location field. The browser believes that the new location is the URL provided in the header. The browser is invited to request this new URL. This redirect function can be used multiple times until the browser finally lands on the page that contains the exploit. The redirects may be difficult to detect due to the fact that legitimate redirects frequently occur on the network.

These are some ways to prevent or reduce HTTP 302 cushioning attacks:

- Use a web proxy like Cisco Cloud Web Security or Cisco Web Security Appliance to block malicious sites.

- Use a service such as Cisco OpenDNS to prevent users from navigating to websites that are known to be malicious.

- Make sure the end user understands how the browser is redirected through a series of HTTP 302 redirections.

Domain Shadowing

When a threat actor wishes to create a *domain shadowing* attack, they must first compromise a domain. Then they must create multiple subdomains of that domain to be used for the attacks. Hijacked domain registration logins are then used to create the many subdomains needed. After these subdomains have been created, attackers can use them as they wish even if they are found out to be malicious domains. They can simply make more from the parent domain. The following sequence is typically used by threat actors:

1. The website becomes compromised.

2. HTTP 302 cushioning is used.

3. Domain shadowing is used.

4. An exploit kit landing page is created.

5. Malware is spread through its payload.

These are some ways to prevent or reduce domain shadowing attacks:

- Secure all domain owner accounts. Use strong passwords and use two-factor authentication to secure these powerful accounts.

- Use a web proxy like Cisco Cloud Web Security or Cisco Web Security Appliance to block malicious sites.

- Use a service such as Cisco OpenDNS to prevent users from navigating to websites that are known to be malicious.

- Make sure that domain owners validate their registration accounts and look for any subdomains that they have not authorized.

Email (7.3.2.2)

Over the past 25 years, email has evolved from a tool used primarily by technical and research professionals to become the backbone of corporate communications. Each day, more than 100 billion corporate email messages are exchanged. As the level of use rises, security becomes a greater priority. The way that users access email today also increases the opportunity for the threat of malware to be introduced. It used to be that corporate users accessed text-based email from a corporate server. The corporate server was on a workstation that was protected by the company's firewall. Today, HTML messages are accessed from many different devices that are often not protected by the company's firewall. HTML allows more attacks because of the amount of access that can sometimes bypass different security layers.

The following are examples of email threats:

- **Attachment-based attacks:** Threat actors embed malicious content in business files such as an email from the IT department. Legitimate users open malicious content. Malware is used in broad attacks often targeting a specific business vertical to seem legitimate, enticing users working in that vertical to open attachments, or click embedded links.

- **Email spoofing:** Threat actors create email messages with a forged sender address that is meant to fool the recipient into providing money or sensitive information. For example, a bank sends you an email asking you to update your credentials. When this email displays the identical bank logo as mail you have previously opened that was legitimate, it has a higher chance of being opened, having attachments opened and links clicked. The spoofed email may even ask you to verify your credentials so that the bank is assured that you are you, exposing your login information.

- **Spam email:** Threat actors send unsolicited email containing advertisements or malicious files. This type of email is sent most often to solicit a response, telling the threat actor that the email is valid and a user has opened the spam.

- **Open mail relay server:** Threat actors take advantage of enterprise servers that are misconfigured as open mail relays to send large volumes of spam or malware to unsuspecting users. The open mail relay is an SMTP server that allows anybody on the Internet to send mail. Because anyone can use the server, they are vulnerable to spammers and worms. Very large volumes of spam can be sent by using an open mail relay. It is important that corporate email servers are never set up as an open relay. This will considerably reduce the amount of unsolicited emails.

■ *Homoglyphs*: Threat actors can use text characters that are very similar or even identical to legitimate text characters. These can be used in phishing emails to make them look very convincing. In DNS, these characters are very different from the real thing. When the DNS record is searched, a completely different URL is found when the link with the homoglyph is used in the search.

Just like any other service that is listening to a port for incoming connections, SMTP servers also may have vulnerabilities. Always keep SMTP software up to date with security and software patches and updates. To further prevent threat actors from completing their task of fooling the end user, implement countermeasures. Use a security appliance specific to email such as the Cisco Email Security Appliance. This will help to detect and block many known types of threats such as phishing, spam, and malware. Also, educate the end user. When attacks make it by the security measures in place, and they will sometimes, the end user is the last line of defense. Teach them how to recognize spam, phishing attempts, suspicious links and URLs, and homoglyphs, and teach them to never open suspicious attachments.

Web-Exposed Databases (7.3.2.3)

Web applications commonly connect to a relational database to access data. Because relational databases often contain sensitive data, databases are a frequent target for attacks.

Command Injection

Attackers are able to execute commands on a web server's OS through a web application that is vulnerable. This might occur if the web application provides input fields to the attacker for entering malicious data. The attacker's commands that are executed through the web application have the same permissions as the web application. This type of attack is used because often there is insufficient validation of input. SQL injection and XSS are two different types of command injection.

SQL Injection

SQL is the language used to query a relational database. Threat actors use SQL injections to breach the relational database, create malicious SQL queries, and obtain sensitive data from the relational database.

One of the most common database attacks is the *SQL injection* attack. The SQL injection attack consists of inserting a SQL query via the input data from the client to the application. A successful SQL injection exploit can read sensitive data from the database, modify database data, execute administration operations on the database, and, sometimes, issue commands to the operating system.

Unless an application uses strict input data validation, it will be vulnerable to the SQL injection attack. If an application accepts and processes user-supplied data without any input data validation, a threat actor could submit a maliciously crafted input string to trigger the SQL injection attack.

Security analysts should be able to recognize suspicious SQL queries in order to detect if the relational database has been subjected to SQL injection attacks. They need to be able to determine which user ID was used by the threat actor to log in, then identify any information or further access the threat actor could have leveraged after a successful login.

Cross-Site Scripting

Not all attacks are initiated from the server side. *Cross-site scripting (XSS)* is where web pages that are executed on the client side, within their own web browser, are injected with malicious scripts. These scripts can be used by Visual Basic, JavaScript, and others to access a computer, collect sensitive information, or deploy more attacks and spread malware. As with SQL injection, this is often due to the attacker posting content to a trusted website with a lack of input validation. Future visitors to the trusted website will be exposed to the content provided by the attacker.

These are the two main types of XSS:

- **Stored (persistent):** This is permanently stored on the infected server and is received by all visitors to the infected page.

- **Reflected (non-persistent):** This only requires that the malicious script is located in a link and visitors must click the infected link to become infected.

These are some ways to prevent or reduce command injection attacks:

- Use the items listed in the OWASP XSS prevention cheat sheet for web application developers.

- Use an IPS implementation to detect and prevent malicious scripts.

- Use a web proxy like Cisco Cloud Web Security or Cisco Web Security Appliance to block malicious sites.

- Use a service such as Cisco OpenDNS to prevent users from navigating to websites that are known to be malicious.

- As with all other security measures, be sure to educate end users. Teach them to identify phishing attacks and notify infosec personnel when they are suspicious of anything security-related.

Lab 7.3.2.4: Attacking a MySQL Database

In this lab, you will view a PCAP file from a previous attack against a SQL database.

Lab 7.3.2.5: Reading Server Logs

In this lab, you will complete the following objectives:

- Reading Log Files with Cat, More, and Less
- Log Files and Syslog
- Log Files and Journalctl

Summary (7.4)

In this chapter, you learned the importance of network monitoring and the tools used by cybersecurity analysts. These tools include port mirroring, protocol analyzers, and SIEMs.

You also learned about the inherent vulnerabilities in network protocols and services.

IP is vulnerable to a variety of attacks, including:

- ICMP attacks
- DoS attacks
- DDoS attacks
- Address spoofing attacks
- Man-in-the-middle attack (MITM)
- Session hijacking

TCP is also vulnerable to TCP SYN flood attacks, TCP reset attacks, and TCP session hijacking attacks. UDP is vulnerable to checksum modification attacks and UDP flood attacks.

IP services have a several of vulnerabilities, including:

- ARP cache poisoning
- DNS attacks, including poisoning, amplification and reflection, resource utilization, and stealth attacks
- DNS tunneling for botnets and other malicious activity
- DHCP spoofing and starvation attacks
- Web attacks through unsecure HTTP, iFrames, and HTTP 302 cushioning
- SQL injection attacks
- Cross-site scripting attacks

Practice

The following activities provide practice with the topics introduced in this chapter. The Labs and Class Activities are available in the companion *CCNA Cybersecurity Operations Lab Manual* (ISBN: 9781587134388). The Packet Tracer Activity instructions are also in the *Labs & Study Guide*. The PKA files are found in the online course.

Class Activities

Class Activity 7.0.1.2: What's Going On?

Labs

Lab 7.2.1.11: Observing a DDoS Attack

Lab 7.2.2.4: Observing TCP Anomalies

Lab 7.3.1.6: Exploring DNS Traffic

Lab 7.3.2.4: Attacking a MySQL Database

Lab 7.3.2.5: Reading Server Logs

Packet Tracer
☐ Activity

Packet Tracer Activities

Packet Tracer 7.1.2.7: Logging Network Activity

Check Your Understanding

Complete all the review questions listed here to test your understanding of the topics and concepts in this chapter. The appendix "Answers to 'Check Your Understanding' Questions" lists the answers.

1. Which technology is a proprietary SIEM system?

    A. SNMP agent

    B. Splunk

    C. Stealthwatch

    D. NetFlow collector

2. Which term is used to describe legitimate traffic that is mistaken for unauthorized traffic by firewalls and IPSs?

    A. True positive

    B. True negative

    C. False positive

    D. False negative

3. Which monitoring technology mirrors traffic flowing through a switch to an analysis device connected to another switch port?

   A. SNMP

   B. SIEM

   C. SPAN

   D. NetFlow

4. Which network monitoring tool saves captured network frames in PCAP files?

   A. NetFlow

   B. Wireshark

   C. SNMP

   D. SIEM

5. Which language is used to query a relational database?

   A. SQL

   B. C++

   C. Python

   D. Java

6. Which network monitoring tool is in the category of network protocol analyzers?

   A. SNMP

   B. SPAN

   C. Wireshark

   D. SIEM

7. Which SIEM function is associated with examining the logs and events of multiple systems to reduce the amount of time of detecting and reacting to security events?

   A. Retention

   B. Aggregation

   C. Correlation

   D. Forensic analysis

8. Which network technology uses a passive splitting device that forwards all traffic, including Layer 1 errors, to an analysis device?

   A. IDS

   B. SNMP

   C. NetFlow

   D. Network TAP

9. What technique is a security attack that depletes the pool of IP addresses available for legitimate hosts?

   A. DHCP spoofing

   B. DHCP snooping

   C. DHCP starvation

   D. Reconnaissance attack

10. In what type of attack is a cybercriminal attempting to prevent legitimate users from accessing network services?

    A. DoS

    B. MITM

    C. Session hijacking

    D. Address spoofing

11. Which network monitoring technology collects IP operational data on packets flowing through Cisco routers and multilayer switches?

    A. SNMP

    B. SIEM

    C. NetFlow

    D. Wireshark

## CHAPTER 8

Protecting the Network

Objectives

Upon completion of this chapter, you will be able to answer the following questions:

- How is the defense-in-depth strategy used to protect networks?

- What are common security policies, regulations, and standards?

- What are access control policies?

- How is AAA used to control network access?

- What information sources are used to communicate emerging network security threats?

- What threat intelligence is used to identify threats and vulnerabilities?

Key Terms

This chapter uses the following key terms. You can find the definitions in the Glossary.

Introduction (8.0)

Protecting our networks will continue to be a challenge. Millions of new devices are joining our networks every year as the Internet of Things (IoT) continues to expand. In addition, with wireless capabilities those devices can be almost anywhere. Threat actors will continue to look for vulnerabilities that can be exploited.

We use a variety of methods to protect our networks, devices, and data. This chapter covers approaches to network security defense, access control methods, and the various sources cybersecurity analysts rely on for threat intelligence.

Understanding Defense (8.1)

In this section, you will learn about a variety of approaches to network security defense.

Defense-in-Depth (8.1.1)

In this topic, you will learn how the defense-in-depth strategy is used to protect networks.

Assets, Vulnerabilities, Threats (8.1.1.1)

Cybersecurity analysts must prepare for any type of attack. It is their job to secure the assets of the organization's network. To do this, cybersecurity analysts must first identify:

- *Asset*: Anything of value to an organization that must be protected, including servers, infrastructure devices, end devices, and the greatest asset, data.

- **Vulnerability:** A weakness in a system or its design that could be exploited by a threat.

- **Threat:** Any potential danger to an asset.

Identify Assets (8.1.1.2)

As an organization grows, so do its assets. Consider the number of assets a large organization would have to protect. It may also acquire other assets through mergers with other companies. The result is that many organizations only have a general idea of the assets that need to be protected.

The collection of all the devices and information owned or managed by the organization are the assets. The assets constitute the attack surface that threat actors could target. These assets must be inventoried and assessed for the level of protection needed to thwart potential attacks.

Asset management consists of inventorying all assets, and then developing and implementing policies and procedures to protect them. This task can be daunting considering many organizations must protect internal users and resources, mobile workers, and cloud-based and virtual services.

Further, organizations need to identify where critical information assets are stored, and how access is gained to that information. Information assets vary, as do the threats against them. For example, a retail business may store customer credit card information. An engineering firm will store competition-sensitive designs and software. A bank will store customer data, account information, and other sensitive financial information. Each of these assets can attract different threat actors who have different skill levels and motivations.

Identify Vulnerabilities (8.1.1.3)

Threat identification provides an organization with a list of likely threats for a particular environment. When identifying threats, it is important to ask several questions:

- What are the possible vulnerabilities of a system?

- Who may want to exploit those vulnerabilities to access specific information assets?

- What are the consequences if system vulnerabilities are exploited and assets are lost?

For example, as highlighted in Figure 8-1, threat identification for an e-banking system would include:

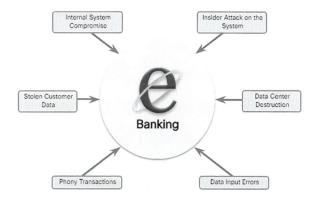

Figure 8-1   Identified Electronic Banking Threats

- **Internal system compromise:** The attacker uses the exposed e-banking servers to break into an internal bank system.

- **Stolen customer data:** An attacker steals the personal and financial data of bank customers from the customer database.

- **Phony transactions from an external server:** An attacker alters the code of the e-banking application and makes transactions by impersonating a legitimate user.

- **Phony transactions using a stolen customer PIN or smart card:** An attacker steals the identity of a customer and completes malicious transactions from the compromised account.

- **Insider attack on the system:** A bank employee finds a flaw in the system from which to mount an attack.

- **Data input errors:** A user inputs incorrect data or makes incorrect transaction requests.

- **Data center destruction:** A cataclysmic event severely damages or destroys the data center.

Identifying vulnerabilities on a network requires an understanding of the important applications that are used, as well as the different vulnerabilities of those applications and the network hardware. This can require a significant amount of research on the part of the network administrator.

Identify Threats (8.1.1.4)

Organizations must use a defense-in-depth approach to identify threats and secure vulnerable assets. This approach uses multiple layers of security at the network edge, within the network, and on network endpoints.

For example, Figure 8-2 displays a simple topology of a defense-in-depth approach:

A router first screens the traffic before forwarding it to a dedicated firewall appliance, for example, the Cisco ASA.

Figure 8-2   Defense-in-Depth Approach

- *Edge router:* The first line of defense is known as an edge router (R1 in Figure 8-2). The edge router has a set of rules specifying which traffic it allows or denies. It passes all connections that are intended for the internal LAN to the firewall.

- **Firewall:** A second line of defense is the firewall. The firewall is a checkpoint device that performs additional filtering and tracks the state of the connections. It denies the initiation of connections from the outside (untrusted) networks to the inside (trusted) network while enabling internal users to establish two-way connections to the untrusted networks. It can also perform user authentication (authentication proxy) to grant external remote users access to internal network resources.

- **Internal router:** Another line of defense is the internal router (R2 in Figure 8-2). It can apply final filtering rules on the traffic before it is forwarded to its destination.

Routers and firewalls are not the only devices that are used in a defense-in-depth approach. Other security devices include intrusion prevention systems (IPSs), advanced malware protection (AMP), web and email content security systems, identity services, network access controls, and more.

In the layered defense-in-depth security approach, the different layers work together to create a security architecture in which the failure of one safeguard does not affect the effectiveness of the other safeguards.

Security Onion and Security Artichoke Approaches (8.1.1.5)

A common analogy used to describe a defense-in-depth approach is called the *security onion*. As illustrated in Figure 8-3, a threat actor would have to peel away at a network's defense mechanisms in a manner similar to peeling an onion.

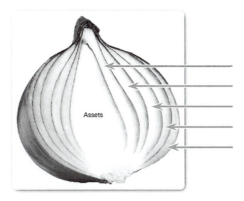

Assets

Figure 8-3   Security Onion Layers

However, the changing landscape of networking, such as the evolution of borderless networks, has changed this analogy to the *security artichoke*, which benefits the threat actor. As illustrated in Figure 8-4, threat actors no longer have to peel away each layer.

Figure 8-4   Security Artichoke Leaves

They only need to remove certain "artichoke leaves." The bonus is that each "leaf" of the network may reveal sensitive data that is not well secured. For example, it's easier for a threat actor to compromise a mobile device than it is to compromise an internal computer or server that is protected by layers of defense. Each mobile device is a leaf. And leaf after leaf, it all leads the hacker to more data. The heart of the artichoke is where the most confidential data is found. Each leaf provides a layer of protection while simultaneously providing a path to attack.

Not every leaf needs to be removed in order to get at the heart of the artichoke. The hacker chips away at the security armor along the perimeter to get to the "heart" of the enterprise.

While Internet-facing systems are usually very well protected and boundary protections are typically solid, persistent hackers, aided by a mix of skill and luck, do eventually find a gap in that hard-core exterior through which they can enter and go where they please.

Note

The security onion described on this page is a way of visualizing defense-in-depth. This is not to be confused with the Security Onion suite of network security tools.

Security Policies (8.1.2)

In this topic, you will learn about security policies, regulations, and standards.

Business Policies (8.1.2.1)

Business policies are the guidelines developed by an organization to govern its actions. The policies define standards of correct behavior for the business and its employees. In networking, policies define the activities that are allowed on the network. This sets a baseline of acceptable use. If behavior that violates business policy is detected on the network, it is possible that a security breach has occurred.

An organization may have several guiding policies:

- *Company policies*: These policies establish the rules of conduct and the responsibilities of both employees and employers. Policies protect the rights of workers as well as the business interests of employers. Depending on the needs of the organization, various policies and procedures establish rules regarding employee conduct, attendance, dress code, privacy, and other areas related to the terms and conditions of employment.

- *Employee policies*: These policies are created and maintained by human resources staff to identify employee salary, pay schedule, employee benefits, work schedule, vacations, and more. They are often provided to new employees to review and sign.

- *Security policies*: These policies identify a set of security objectives for a company, define the rules of behavior for users and administrators, and specify system requirements. These objectives, rules, and requirements collectively ensure the security of a network and the computer systems in an organization. Much like a continuity plan, a security policy is a constantly evolving document based on changes in the threat landscape, vulnerabilities, and business and employee requirements.

Security Policy (8.1.2.2)

A comprehensive security policy has a number of benefits:

- Demonstrates an organization's commitment to security

- Sets the rules for expected behavior

- Ensures consistency in system operations, software and hardware acquisition and use, and maintenance

- Defines the legal consequences of violations

- Gives security staff the backing of management

Security policies are used to inform users, staff, and managers of an organization's requirements for protecting technology and information assets. A security policy also specifies the mechanisms that are needed to meet security requirements and provides a baseline from which to acquire, configure, and audit computer systems and networks for compliance.

A security policy may include the following:

- **Identification and authentication policy:** Specifies authorized persons that can have access to network resources and identity verification procedures.

- **Password policy:** Ensures passwords meet minimum requirements and are changed regularly.

- *Acceptable use policy (AUP)*: Identifies network applications and uses that are acceptable to the organization. It may also identify ramifications if this policy is violated.

- **Remote access policy:** Identifies how remote users can access a network and what is accessible via remote connectivity.

- **Network maintenance policy:** Specifies network device operating systems and end user application update procedures.

- **Incident handling procedures:** Describes how security incidents are handled.

One of the most common security policy components is an acceptable use policy (AUP). This can also be referred to as an appropriate use policy. This component defines what users are allowed and not allowed to do on the various system components. This includes the type of traffic that is allowed on the network. The AUP should be as explicit as possible to avoid misunderstanding. For example, an AUP might list specific websites, newsgroups, or bandwidth-intensive applications that are prohibited from being accessed by company computers or from the company network. Every employee should be required to sign an AUP, and the signed AUPs should be retained for the duration of employment.

BYOD Policies (8.1.2.3)

Many organizations must now also support *Bring Your Own Device (BYOD)*. This enables employees to use their own mobile devices to access company systems, software, networks, or information. BYOD provides several key benefits to enterprises, including increased productivity, reduced IT and operating costs, better mobility for employees, and greater appeal when it comes to hiring and retaining employees.

However, these benefits also bring an increased information security risk, because BYOD can lead to data breaches and greater liability for the organization.

A BYOD security policy should be developed to accomplish the following:

- Specify the goals of the BYOD program.

- Identify which employees can bring their own devices.

- Identify which devices will be supported.

- Identify the level of access employees are granted when using personal devices.

- Describe the rights to access and activities permitted to security personnel on the device.

- Identify which regulations must be adhered to when using employee devices.

- Identify safeguards to put in place if a device is compromised.

The following BYOD security best practices help mitigate BYOD risks:

- **Password protect access:** Use unique passwords for each device and account.

- **Manually control wireless connectivity:** Turn off Wi-Fi and Bluetooth connectivity when not in use. Connect only to trusted networks.

- **Keep updated:** Always keep the device OS and other software updated. Updated software often contains security patches to mitigate against the latest threats or exploits.

- **Back up data:** Enable backup of the device in case it is lost or stolen.

- **Enable "Find my Device":** Subscribe to a device locator service with remote wipe feature.

- **Provide antivirus software:** Provide antivirus software for approved BYOD devices.

- **Use Mobile Device Management (MDM) software:** MDM software enables IT teams to implement security settings and software configurations on all devices that connect to company networks.

Regulatory and Standard Compliance (8.1.2.4)

There are also external regulations regarding network security. Network security professionals must be familiar with the laws and codes of ethics that are binding on Information Systems Security (INFOSEC) professionals.

Many organizations are mandated to develop and implement security policies. Compliance regulations define what organizations are responsible for providing and the liability if they fail to comply. The compliance regulations that an organization is obligated to follow depend on the type of organization and the data that the organization handles. Specific compliance regulations will be discussed later in the course.

Access Control (8.2)

In this section, you will learn about access control as a method of protecting a network.

Access Control Concepts (8.2.1)

In this topic, you will learn about access control policies.

Communications Security: CIA (8.2.1.1)

Information security deals with protecting information and information systems from unauthorized access, use, disclosure, disruption, modification, or destruction.

As shown in Figure 8-5, the CIA triad consists of three components of information security:

Figure 8-5 CIA Triad

- *Confidentiality*: Only authorized individuals, entities, or processes can access sensitive information.

- *Integrity*: Refers to the protection of data from unauthorized alteration.

- *Availability*: Authorized users must have uninterrupted access to important resources and data.

Network data can be encrypted (made unreadable to unauthorized users) using various cryptography applications. The conversation between two IP phone users can be encrypted. The files on a computer can also be encrypted. These are just a few examples. Cryptography can be used almost anywhere that there is data communication. In fact, the trend is toward all communication being encrypted.

Access Control Models (8.2.1.2)

An organization must implement proper access controls to protect its network resources, information system resources, and information.

A security analyst should understand the different basic access control models to have a better understanding of how attackers can break the access controls.

- *Mandatory access control (MAC)*: Applies the strictest access control and is typically used in military or mission-critical applications. It assigns security level labels to information and enables users with access based on their security level clearance.

- *Discretionary access control (DAC)*: Allows users to control access to their data as owners of that data. DAC may use ACLs or other methods to specify which users or groups of users have access to the information.

- *Non-discretionary access control*: Access decisions are based on an individual's roles and responsibilities within the organization, also known as role-based access control (RBAC).

- *Attribute-based access control (ABAC)*: Allows access based on attributes of the object (resource) to be accessed, the subject (user) accessing the resource, and environmental factors regarding how the object is to be accessed, such as time of day.

Another access control model is the principle of least privilege, which specifies a limited, as-needed approach to granting user and process access rights to specific information and tools. The principle of least privilege states that users should be granted the minimum amount of access required to perform their work function.

A common exploit is known as *privilege escalation*. In this exploit, vulnerabilities in servers or access control systems are exploited to grant an unauthorized user, or software process, higher levels of privilege than they should have. After the privilege is granted, the threat actor can access sensitive information or take control of a system.

Interactive Graphic

Activity 8.2.1.3: Identify the Access Control Model

Refer to the online course to complete this Activity.

AAA Usage and Operation (8.2.2)

In this topic, you will learn how AAA is used to control network access.

AAA Operation (8.2.2.1)

A network must be designed to control who is allowed to connect to it and what they are allowed to do when they are connected. These design requirements are identified in the network security policy. The policy specifies how network administrators, corporate users, remote users, business partners, and clients access network resources. The network security policy can also mandate the implementation of an accounting system that tracks who logged in and when and what they did while logged in. Some compliance regulations may specify that access must be logged and the logs retained for a set period of time.

The *Authentication, Authorization, and Accounting (AAA)* protocol provides the necessary framework to enable scalable access security.

Network and administrative AAA security has several functional components:

- **Authentication:** Users and administrators must prove that they are who they say they are. Authentication can be established using username and password combinations, challenge and response questions, token cards, and other methods. For example: "I am user 'student'. I know the password to prove that I am user 'student'."

- **Authorization:** After the user is authenticated, authorization services determine which resources the user can access and which operations the user is allowed to perform. An example is "User 'student' can access host serverXYZ using Telnet only."

- **Accounting and auditing:** Accounting records what the user does and when they do it, including what is accessed, the amount of time the resource is accessed, and any changes that were made. Accounting keeps track of how network resources are used. An example is "User 'student' accessed host serverXYZ using Telnet for 15 minutes."

This concept is similar to the use of a credit card, as indicated by Figure 8-6. The credit card identifies who can use it, identifies how much that user can spend, and keeps account of what items the user spent money on.

AAA Authentication (8.2.2.2)

AAA authentication can be used to authenticate users for administrative access or it can be used to authenticate users for remote network access. Cisco provides two common methods of implementing AAA services.

Local AAA Authentication

This method is sometimes known as self-contained authentication because it authenticates users against locally stored usernames and passwords, as shown in Figure 8-7. Local AAA is ideal for small networks.

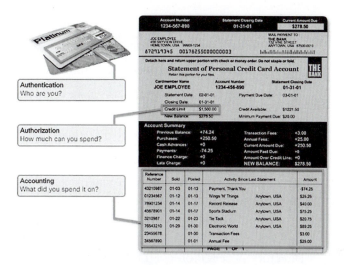

Figure 8-6   The AAA Concept Is Similar to Using a Credit Card

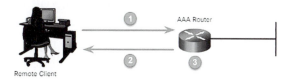

Figure 8-7   Local AAA Authentication

In Figure 8-7...

1. The client establishes a connection with the router.

2. The AAA router prompts the user for a username and password.

3. The router authenticates the username and password using the local database and the user is authorized to access the network based on information in the local database.

Server-Based AAA Authentication

This method authenticates against a central AAA server that contains the usernames and passwords for all users, as shown in Figure 8-8. Server-based AAA authentication is appropriate for medium-to-large networks.

Figure 8-8   Server-Based AAA Authentication

In Figure 8-8...

1. The client establishes a connection with the router.

2. The AAA router prompts the user for a username and password.

3. The router authenticates the username and password using a remote AAA server such as a Cisco Secure ACS Server.

4. The user is authorized to access the network based on information on the remote AAA Server.

Centralized AAA is more scalable and manageable than local AAA authentication and, therefore, is the preferred AAA implementation.

A centralized AAA system may independently maintain databases for authentication, authorization, and accounting. It can leverage Active Directory or Lightweight Directory Access Protocol (LDAP) for user authentication and group membership, while maintaining its own authorization and accounting databases.

Devices communicate with the centralized AAA server using either the Remote Authentication Dial-In User Service (RADIUS) or Terminal Access Controller Access Control System Plus (TACACS+) protocols.

The following are specifics of the RADIUS protocol:

- RADIUS uses UDP ports 1812 and 1813, or 1645 and 1646.

- RADIUS combines authentication and authorization.

- RADIUS encrypts only the password in the access-request packet from the client to the server. The remainder of the packet is unencrypted, leaving the username, authorized services, and accounting unprotected.

The following are specifics of the TACACS+ protocol:

- TACACS+ uses TCP port 49.

- TACACS+ separates authentication, authorization, and accounting.

- TACACS+ encrypts the entire body of the packet but leaves a standard TACACS+ header.

AAA Accounting Logs (8.2.2.3)

Centralized AAA also enables the use of the accounting method. Accounting records from all devices are sent to centralized repositories, enabling simplified auditing of user actions.

AAA accounting collects and reports usage data in AAA logs. These logs are useful for security auditing. The collected data might include the start and stop connection times, executed commands, number of packets, and number of bytes.

One widely deployed use of accounting is to combine it with AAA authentication. This helps with managing access to internetworking devices by network administrative staff. Accounting provides more security than just authentication. The AAA servers keep a detailed log of exactly what the authenticated user does on the device, as shown in Figure 8-9.

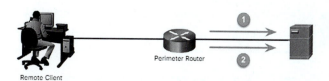

Figure 8-9   AAA Accounting

In Figure 8-9...

1. When a user has been authenticated, the AAA accounting process generates a start message to begin the accounting process.

2. When the user finishes, a stop message is recorded and the accounting process ends.

This includes all EXEC and configuration commands issued by the user. The log contains numerous data fields, including the username, the date and time, and the actual command that was entered by the user. This information is useful when troubleshooting devices. It also provides evidence against individuals who perform malicious actions.

The various types of accounting information that can be collected include:

- **Network accounting:** Network accounting captures information for all Point-to-Point Protocol (PPP) sessions, including packet and byte counts.

- **Connection accounting:** Connection accounting captures information about all outbound connections made from the AAA client, such as Telnet or SSH.

- **EXEC accounting:** EXEC accounting captures information about user EXEC terminal sessions (user shells) on the network access server, including username, date, start and stop times, and the access server IP address.

- **System accounting:** System accounting captures information about all system-level events (for example, when the system reboots or when accounting is turned on or off).

- **Command accounting:** Command accounting captures information about the EXEC shell commands for a specified privilege level that are being executed on a network access server. Each command accounting record includes a list of the commands executed for that privilege level, as well as the date and time each command was executed, and the user who executed it.

■ **Resource accounting:** The Cisco implementation of AAA accounting captures "start" and "stop" record support for calls that have passed user authentication. The additional feature of generating "stop" records for calls that fail to authenticate as part of user authentication is also supported. Such records are necessary for users employing accounting records to manage and monitor their networks.

Interactive Graphic

Activity 8.2.2.4: Identify the Characteristic of AAA

Refer to the online course to complete this Activity.

Threat Intelligence (8.3)

In this section, you will learn how to use various intelligence sources to locate current security threats.

Information Sources (8.3.1)

In this topic, you will learn how information sources are used to communicate emerging network security threats.

Network Intelligence Communities (8.3.1.1)

To effectively protect a network, security professionals must stay informed and gain network intelligence. There are many security organizations which provide network intelligence. They provide resources, workshops, and conferences to help security professionals. These organizations often have the latest information on threats and vulnerabilities.

Figure 8-10 shows a few important network security organizations, described here:

Figure 8-10   Network Security Organizations

- **CERT:** Computer Emergency Response Team (CERT) is a U.S. federally funded initiative chartered to work with the Internet community in detecting and resolving computer security incidents. The CERT Coordination Center (CERT/CC) coordinates communication among experts during security emergencies to help prevent future incidents. CERT also responds to major security incidents and analyzes product vulnerabilities. CERT manages changes relating to progressive intruder techniques and to the difficulty of detecting attacks and catching attackers. It also develops and promotes the use of appropriate technology and systems management practices to resist attacks on networked systems, to limit damage, and to ensure continuity of services.

- **SANS:** SysAdmin, Audit, Network, Security (SANS) Institute resources are largely free upon request and include the popular Internet Storm Center, the Internet's early warning system; NewsBites, the weekly news digest; @RISK, the weekly vulnerability digest; flash security alerts; and more than 1,200 award-winning, original research papers. SANS also develops security courses.

- **MITRE:** The MITRE Corporation maintains a list of Common Vulnerabilities and Exposures (CVE) used by prominent security organizations.

- **(ISC)²:** International Information Systems Security Certification Consortium (ISC)² provides vendor-neutral education products and career services in more than 135 countries, to 75,000+ certified industry professionals. Their mission is to make the cyber world a safer place by elevating information security to the public domain, and supporting and developing network security professionals around the world. They also provide information security certifications including the Certified Information Systems Security Professional (CISSP).

- **INFOSYSSEC:** Information Systems Security (InfoSysSec) is a network security organization that hosts a security news portal, providing the latest breaking news pertaining to alerts, exploits, and vulnerabilities.

- **FIRST:** Forum of Incident Response and Security Teams (FIRST) is a security organization that brings together a variety of computer security incident response teams from government, commercial, and educational organizations to foster cooperation and coordination in information sharing, incident prevention, and rapid reaction.

- **MS-ISAC:** The Multi-State Information Sharing & Analysis Center (MS-ISAC) is the focal point for cyberthreat prevention, protection, response, and recovery for the nation's state, local, tribal, and territorial (SLTT) governments. The MS-ISAC 24x7 cybersecurity operations center provides real-time network monitoring, early cyberthreat warnings and advisories, vulnerability identification and mitigation, and incident response.

To remain effective, a network security professional must:

- **Keep abreast of the latest threats:** This includes subscribing to real-time feeds regarding threats, routinely perusing security-related websites, following security blogs and podcasts, and more.

- **Continue to upgrade skills:** This includes attending security-related training, workshops, and conferences.

Note

Network security has a very steep learning curve and requires a commitment to continuous professional development.

Cisco Cybersecurity Reports (8.3.1.2)

A resource to help security professionals stay abreast of the latest threats is the Cisco Annual Cybersecurity Report, and the Mid-Year Cybersecurity Report. These reports provide an update on the state of security preparedness, expert analysis of top vulnerabilities, factors behind the explosion of attacks using adware and spam, and more.

Cybersecurity analysts should subscribe to and read these reports to learn how threat actors are targeting their networks, and what can be done to mitigate these attacks.

Security Blogs and Podcasts (8.3.1.3)

Another method for keeping up-to-date on the latest threats is to read blogs and listen to podcasts. Blogs and podcasts also provide advice, research, and recommended mitigation techniques.

There are several security blogs and podcasts available that a cybersecurity analyst should follow to learn about the latest threats, vulnerabilities, and exploits.

Search the Internet for Cisco's podcast and blog from the Cisco Talos group.

Threat Intelligence Services (8.3.2)

In this topic, you will learn how to use threat intelligence to identify threats and vulnerabilities.

Cisco Talos (8.3.2.1)

Threat intelligence services allow the exchange of threat information such as vulnerabilities, indicators of compromise (IOCs), and mitigation techniques. This information is shared not only with personnel, but also with security systems. As threats emerge, threat intelligence services create and distribute firewall rules and IOCs to the devices that have subscribed to the service.

One such service is the Cisco Talos group. Talos is a world-leading threat intelligence team with a goal to help protect enterprise users, data, and infrastructure from active adversaries. The Talos team collects information about active, existing, and emerging threats. Talos then provides comprehensive protection against these attacks and malware to its subscribers.

Cisco Security products can use Talos threat intelligence in real time to provide fast and effective security solutions.

Cisco Talos also provides free software, services, resources, and data.

FireEye (8.3.2.2)

FireEye is another security company that offers services to help enterprises secure their networks. FireEye uses a three-pronged approach combining security intelligence, security expertise, and technology.

The FireEye Malware Analysis product blocks attacks across web and email threat vectors, and latent malware that resides on file shares. It can block advanced malware that easily bypasses traditional signature-based defenses and compromises the majority of enterprise networks. It addresses all stages of an attack lifecycle with a signature-less engine utilizing stateful attack analysis to detect zero-day threats.

Automated Indicator Sharing (8.3.2.3)

The U.S. Department of Homeland Security (DHS) offers a free service called Automated Indicator Sharing (AIS). AIS enables the real-time exchange of cyberthreat indicators (e.g., malicious IP addresses, the sender address of a phishing email, etc.) between the U.S. federal government and the private sector.

AIS creates an ecosystem where, as soon as a threat is recognized, it is immediately shared with the community to help them protect their networks from that particular threat.

Common Vulnerabilities and Exposures Database (8.3.2.4)

The U.S. government sponsored the MITRE Corporation to create and maintain a catalog of known security threats called Common Vulnerabilities and Exposures (CVE). The CVE serves as a dictionary of common names (i.e., CVE Identifiers) for publicly known cybersecurity vulnerabilities.

The MITRE Corporation defines unique CVE Identifiers for publicly known information-security vulnerabilities to make it easier to share data.

Threat Intelligence Communication Standards (8.3.2.5)

Network organizations and professionals must share information to increase knowledge about threat actors and the assets they want to access. Several intelligence sharing open standards have evolved to enable communication across multiple networking platforms. These standards enable the exchange of cyberthreat intelligence (CTI) in an automated, consistent, and machine-readable format.

Two common threat intelligence sharing standards include

- **Structured Threat Information Expression (STIX):** This is a set of specifications for exchanging cyberthreat information between organizations. The Cyber Observable Expression (CybOX) standard has been incorporated into STIX.

- **Trusted Automated Exchange of Indicator Information (TAXII):** This is the specification for an application layer protocol that allows the communication of CTI over HTTPS. TAXII is designed to support STIX.

These open standards provide the specifications that aid in the automated exchange of cyberthreat intelligence information in a standardized format.

Interactive Graphic

Activity 8.3.2.6: Identify the Threat Intelligence Information Source

Refer to the online course to complete this Activity.

Summary (8.4)

In this chapter, you learned the importance of protecting our networks, devices, and data from threat actors.

Organizations must use a defense-in-depth approach to identify threats and secure vulnerable assets. This approach uses multiple layers of security at the network edge, within the network, and on network endpoints.

Organizations must also have a set of policies that define the activities that are allowed on the network. These include business policies, security policies, BYOD policies, and policies that ensure the organization complies with governmental regulations.

Access control methods are used to protect the confidentiality, integrity, and availability of our networks, devices, and data. Access control models include:

- Mandatory access control

- Discretionary access control

- Non-discretionary access control

- Attribute-based access control

AAA security provides the necessary framework to enable scalable access security:

- **Authentication:** Users and administrators must prove that they are who they say they are.

- **Authorization:** After the user is authenticated, authorization services determine which resources the user can access and which operations the user is allowed to perform.

- **Accounting:** Records what the user does and when they do it, including what is accessed, the amount of time the resource is accessed, and any changes that were made.

Security experts and cybersecurity analysts rely on various information sources to keep abreast of the latest threats and continue to upgrade their skills. Threat intelligences services, such as Cisco Talos, FireEye, DHS AIS, and the CVE database, allow the exchange of threat information such as vulnerabilities, indicators of compromise (IOCs), and mitigation techniques. These services are guided by the threat intelligence sharing standards STIX and TAXII.

Practice

The chapter does not have any Labs or Packet Tracer activities.

Check Your Understanding Questions

Complete all the review questions listed here to test your understanding of the topics and concepts in this chapter. The appendix "Answers to 'Check Your Understanding' Questions" lists the answers.

1. With the evolution of borderless networks, which vegetable is now used to describe a defense-in-depth approach?

    A. Artichoke

    B. Lettuce

    C. Onion

    D. Cabbage

2. What is a characteristic of a layered defense-in-depth security approach?

    A. Three or more devices are used.

    B. Routers are replaced with firewalls.

    C. When one device fails, another one takes over.

    D. One safeguard failure does not affect the effectiveness of other safeguards.

3. Passwords, passphrases, and PINs are examples of which security term?

    A. Identification

    B. Authorization

    C. Authentication

    D. Access

4. What is privilege escalation?

    A. Someone is given rights because she or he has received a promotion.

    B. Vulnerabilities in systems are exploited to grant higher levels of privilege than someone or some process should have.

    C. A security problem occurs when high-ranking corporate officials demand rights to systems or files that they should not have.

    D. Everyone is given full rights by default to everything and rights are taken away only when someone abuses privileges.

5. What are two characteristics of the RADIUS protocol? (Choose two.)

   A. Encryption of the entire body of the packet

   B. The use of TCP port 49

   C. The use of UDP ports for authentication and accounting

   D. Encryption of the password only

   E. The separation of the authentication and authorization processes

6. Which component of AAA is used to determine which resources a user can access and which operations the user is allowed to perform?

   A. Auditing

   B. Accounting

   C. Authorization

   D. Authentication

7. Which type of business policy establishes the rules of conduct and the responsibilities of employees and employers?

   A. Company

   B. Data

   C. Employee

   D. Security

8. Which component of AAA allows an administrator to track individuals who access network resources and any changes that are made to those resources?

   A. Accessibility

   B. Accounting

   C. Authentication

   D. Authorization

9. Which of the following offers a free service called Automated Indicator Sharing that enables the real-time exchange of cyberthreat indicators?

   A. FireEye

   B. Department of Homeland Security

   C. The MITRE Corporation

   D. Talos

10. The security policy of an organization allows employees to connect to the office intranet from their homes. Which type of security policy is this?

    A. Acceptable use

    B. Incident handling

    C. Network maintenance

    D. Remote access

11. During the AAA process, when will authorization be implemented?

    A. Immediately after successful authentication against an AAA data source

    B. Immediately after AAA accounting and auditing receives detailed reports

    C. Immediately after an AAA client sends authentication information to a centralized server

    D. Immediately after the determination of which resources a user can access

## CHAPTER 9

Cryptography and the Public Key Infrastructure

Objectives

Upon completion of this chapter, you will be able to answer the following questions:

- How is cryptography used to secure communications?

- What is the role of cryptography in ensuring the integrity and authenticity of data?

- How do cryptographic approaches enhance data confidentiality?

- What is public key cryptography?

- How does the Public Key Infrastructure function?

- How does the use of cryptography affect cybersecurity operations?

Key Terms

This chapter uses the following key terms. You can find the definitions in the Glossary.

Introduction (9.0)

When Internet standards were first drafted, no one was thinking that data would need to be protected from threat actors. As you have seen in previous chapters, the protocols of the TCP/IP protocol suite are vulnerable to a variety of attacks.

To address these vulnerabilities, we use a variety of cryptographic technologies to keep our data private and secure. However, cryptography is a double-edged sword in that threat actors can also use it to hide their actions. This chapter covers the impact of cryptography on network security monitoring.

Class Activity 9.0.1.2: Creating Codes

Secret codes have been used for thousands of years. Ancient Greeks and Spartans used a scytale (rhymes with Italy) to encode messages. Romans used a Caesar cipher to encrypt messages. A few hundred years ago, the French used the Vigenère cipher to encode messages. Today, there are many ways that messages can be encoded.

In this lab, you will create and encrypt messages using online tools.

Cryptography (9.1)

In this section, you will learn how tools are used to encrypt and decrypt data.

What Is Cryptography? (9.1.1)

In this topic, you will learn how cryptography is used to secure communications.

Securing Communications (9.1.1.1)

To ensure secure communications across both public and private networks, the first goal is to secure devices, including routers, switches, servers, and hosts.

For example, the topology in Figure 9-1 displays a number of secure devices indicated by the padlock or red brick firewall icon.

Network infrastructure devices and hosts are secured using a variety of techniques:

- Device hardening
- AAA (Authentication, Authorization, and Accounting) access control
- Access control lists (ACLs)
- Firewalls
- Monitoring threats using an intrusion prevention system (IPS)

- Securing endpoints using Cisco Advanced Malware Protection (AMP)

- Enforcing email and web security using the Cisco Email Security Appliance (ESA) and Cisco Web Security Appliance (WSA)

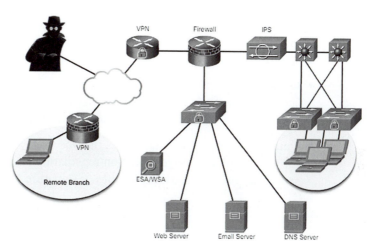

Figure 9-1   Secure Network Topology

The next goal is to secure the data as it travels across various links. This may include internal traffic, but of greater concern is protecting the data that travels outside of the organization to branch sites, telecommuter sites, and partner sites.

Secure communications consists of four elements, as summarized in Figure 9-2:

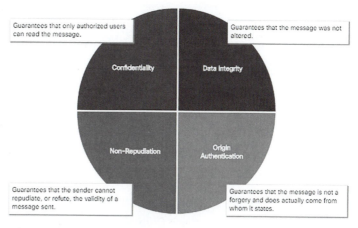

Figure 9-2   Elements of Secure Communications

- **Data confidentiality:** Guarantees that only authorized users can read the message. If the message is intercepted, it cannot be deciphered within a reasonable amount of time. Data confidentiality is implemented using symmetric and asymmetric encryption algorithms.

- **Data integrity:** Guarantees that the message was not altered. Any changes to data in transit will be detected. Integrity is ensured by implementing either Message Digest version 5 (MD5) or Secure Hash Algorithm (SHA) hash-generating algorithms.

- **Origin authentication:** Guarantees that the message is not a forgery and does actually come from whom it states. Many modern networks ensure authentication with protocols, such as hash message authentication code (HMAC).

- **Data non-repudiation:** Guarantees that the sender cannot repudiate, or refute, the validity of a message sent. Non-repudiation relies on the fact that only the sender has the unique characteristics or signature for how that message is treated.

Note

MD5, SHA, and HMAC are discussed in more detail later in the chapter.

Cryptology (9.1.1.2)

Cryptology is used to secure communications. Cryptology is the science of making and breaking secret codes.

As shown in Figure 9-3, cryptology combines two separate disciplines:

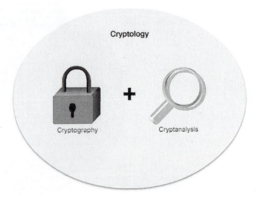

Figure 9-3   Cryptology = Cryptography + Cryptanalysis

- *Cryptography*: This is the development and use of codes that are used for communicating privately. Specifically, it is the practice and study of techniques to secure communications. Historically, cryptography was synonymous with encryption.

- *Cryptanalysis*: This is the breaking of those codes. Specifically, it is the practice and study of determining and exploiting weaknesses in cryptographic techniques.

There is a symbiotic relationship between the two disciplines because each makes the other one stronger. National security organizations employ practitioners of both disciplines and put them to work against each other.

There have been times when one of the disciplines has been ahead of the other. For example, during the Hundred Years War between France and England, the cryptanalysts were leading the cryptographers. France mistakenly believed that the Vigenère cipher was unbreakable, and then the British cracked it. Some historians believe that the successful cracking of encrypted codes and messages had a major impact on the outcome of World War II.

Currently, it is believed that cryptographers have the advantage.

Cryptography: Ciphers (9.1.1.3)

Over the centuries, various cryptography methods, physical devices, and aids have been used to encrypt and decrypt text. The following historical ciphering examples are in displayed in Figure 9-4:

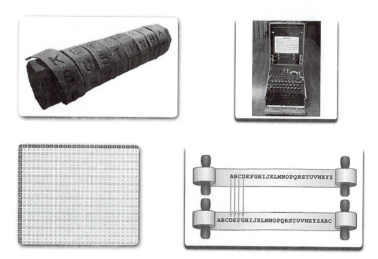

Figure 9-4   Example of Ciphers

- Scytale (top left)

- Enigma machine (top right)

- Vigenère cipher (bottom left)

- Caesar cipher (bottom right)

Each of these encryption methods uses a specific algorithm, called a cipher. A *cipher* is an algorithm that consists of a series of well-defined steps that can be followed as a procedure when encrypting and decrypting messages.

The following are types of ciphers that have been used over the years:

- **Substitution cipher:** Substitution ciphers retain the letter frequency of the original message. The Caesar cipher was a simple substitution cipher. For example, refer to the plaintext message in Figure 9-5. If the key used was 3, the letter A was moved three letters to the right to become D, as shown in Figure 9-6. The resulting ciphertext is displayed in Figure 9-7.

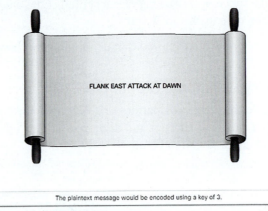

FLANK EAST ATTACK AT DAWN

The plaintext message would be encoded using a key of 3.

Figure 9-5   Plaintext Message

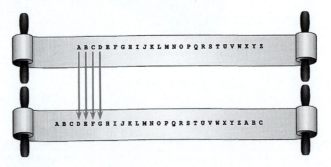

ABCDEFGHIJKLMNOPQRSTUVWXYZ

ABCDEFGHIJKLMNOPQRSTUVWXYZABC

Shift the top scroll over by three characters (key of 3), an A becomes D, B becomes E, and so on.

Figure 9-6   Encrypting Using the Caesar Substitution Cipher

IODQN HDVW DWWDFN DW GDZQ

The appearance of the text after encryption.

Figure 9-7   Resulting Ciphertext

- **Transposition cipher:** In transposition ciphers, no letters are replaced; they are simply rearranged. An example is taking the FLANK EAST ATTACK AT DAWN message and reversing it to read NWAD TAKCATTA TSAE KNALF. Another example of a transposition cipher is known as the rail fence cipher. For example, refer to the plaintext message in Figure 9-8. Figure 9-9 displays how to transpose the message using a rail fence cipher with a key of 3. The key specifies that three lines are required when creating the encrypted code. The resulting ciphertext is displayed in Figure 9-10.

FLANK EAST

ATTACK AT DAWN

The plaintext message would be encoded using a key of 3.

Figure 9-8   Plaintext Message

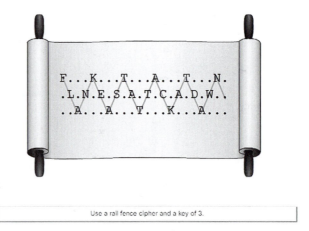

Use a rail fence cipher and a key of 3.

Figure 9-9 Encrypting Using the Rail Fence Transposition Cipher

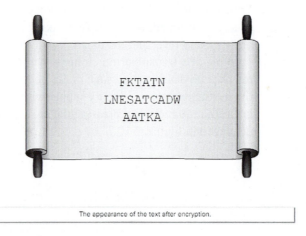

The appearance of the text after encryption.

Figure 9-10 Resulting Ciphertext

- **Polyalphabetic ciphers:** Polyalphabetic ciphers are based on substitution, using multiple substitution alphabets. The famous Vigenère cipher is an example, shown in Figure 9-11. That cipher uses a series of different Caesar ciphers that are based on the letters of a keyword. It is a simple form of polyalphabetic substitution and is therefore invulnerable to frequency analysis.

Cryptanalysis: Code Breaking (9.1.1.4)

Cryptanalysis is often used by cybercriminals to decipher encrypted messages. While cryptanalysis is often linked to mischievous purposes, it is actually a necessity.

Cryptanalysis is also used by governments in military and diplomatic surveillance, and by enterprises in testing the strength of security procedures. Enterprises and governments employ the services of mathematicians, scholars, security forensic experts, and cryptanalysts for these purposes.

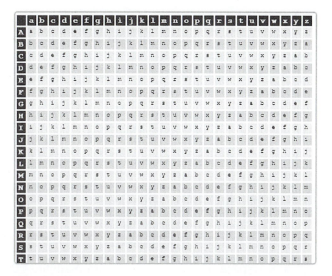

Figure 9-11   Vigenère Cipher

Cryptanalysts are individuals who perform cryptanalysis to crack secret codes. Several methods are used in cryptanalysis:

- **Brute-force method:** The cryptanalyst tries every possible key, knowing that eventually one of them will work. All algorithms are vulnerable to brute force. If every possible key is tried, one of the keys has to work.

- **Ciphertext method:** The cryptanalyst has the ciphertext of several encrypted messages but no knowledge of the underlying plaintext.

- **Known-plaintext method:** The cryptanalyst has access to the ciphertext of several messages and knows something about the plaintext underlying that ciphertext.

- **Chosen-plaintext method:** The cryptanalyst chooses which data the encryption device encrypts and observes the ciphertext output.

- **Chosen-ciphertext method:** The cryptanalyst can choose different ciphertext to be decrypted and has access to the decrypted plaintext.

- **Meet-in-the-middle method:** The cryptanalyst knows a portion of the plaintext and the corresponding ciphertext.

Note

The actual processes of these cryptanalysis methods are beyond the scope of this course.

No algorithm is unbreakable. It is an ironic fact of cryptography that it is impossible to prove that any algorithm is secure. It can only be proven that it is not vulnerable to known cryptanalytic attacks.

Keys (9.1.1.5)

Authentication, integrity, and data confidentiality are implemented in many ways, using various protocols and algorithms. The choice of protocol and algorithm varies based on the level of security required to meet the goals of the network security policy.

Old encryption algorithms, such as the Caesar cipher or the Enigma machine, were based on the secrecy of the algorithm to achieve confidentiality.

With modern technology, security of encryption lies in the secrecy of the keys, not the algorithm.

Two terms that are used to describe keys are:

- **Key length:** Also called the key size, this is measured in bits. In this course, we will use the term key length.

- **Keyspace:** This is the number of possibilities that can be generated by a specific key length.

As key length increases, the keyspace increases exponentially. The keyspace of an algorithm is the set of all possible key values. A key that has n bits produces a keyspace that has 2^n possible key values:

- A 2-bit (2^2) key length = a keyspace of 4 because there are four possible keys (00, 01, 10, and 11).

- A 3-bit (2^3) key length = a keyspace of 8, because there are eight possible keys (000, 001, 010, 011, 100, 101, 110, 111).

- A 4-bit (2^4) key length = a keyspace of 16 possible keys.

- A 40-bit (2^{40}) key length = a keyspace of 1,099,511,627,776 possible keys.

By adding one bit to the key, the keyspace is effectively doubled, as shown in Figure 9-12.

Longer keys are more secure. However, they are also more resource intensive. Caution should be exercised when choosing longer keys because handling them could add a significant load to the processor in lower-end products.

Lab 9.1.1.6: Encrypting and Decrypting Data Using OpenSSL

In this lab, you will complete the following objectives:

- Encrypting Messages with OpenSSL

- Decrypting Messages with OpenSSL

DES Key	Keyspace	# of Possible Keys
56-bit	2^{56} 11111111 11111111 11111111 11111111 11111111 11111111 11111111	72,000,000,000,000,000
57-bit	2^{57} 11111111 11111111 11111111 11111111 11111111 11111111 11111111 1	144,000,000,000,000,000
58-bit	2^{58} 11111111 11111111 11111111 11111111 11111111 11111111 11111111 11	288,000,000,000,000,000
59-bit	2^{59} 11111111 11111111 11111111 11111111 11111111 11111111 11111111 111	576,000,000,000,000,000
60-bit	2^{60} 11111111 11111111 11111111 11111111 11111111 11111111 11111111 1111	1,152,000,000,000,000,000

Figure 9-12   Double the Keyspace with Every Bit

Lab 9.1.1.7: Encrypting and Decrypting Data Using a Hacker Tool

In this lab, you will complete the following objectives: .

- Setup Scenario
- Create and Encrypt Files
- Recover Encrypted Zip File Passwords

Lab 9.1.1.8: Examining Telnet and SSH in Wireshark

In this lab, you will complete the following objectives:

- Examine a Telnet Session with Wireshark
- Examine an SSH Session with Wireshark

Integrity and Authenticity (9.1.2)

In this topic, you will learn the role of cryptography in ensuring the integrity and authenticity of data.

Cryptographic Hash Functions (9.1.2.1)

Hashes are used to verify and ensure data integrity. Hashing is based on a one-way mathematical function that is relatively easy to compute, but significantly harder to reverse. Grinding coffee is a good analogy of a one-way function. It is easy to grind coffee beans, but it is almost impossible to put all of the tiny pieces back together to rebuild the original beans. The cryptographic hashing function can also be used to verify authentication.

As shown in Figure 9-13, a hash function takes a variable block of binary data, called the message, and produces a fixed-length, condensed representation, called the hash. The resulting hash is also sometimes called the message digest, digest, or digital fingerprint.

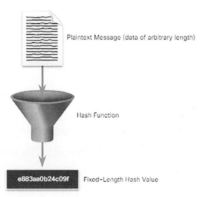

Figure 9-13 Creating a Hash

With hash functions, it is computationally infeasible for two different sets of data to come up with the same hash output. Every time the data is changed or altered, the hash value also changes. Because of this, cryptographic hash values are often called digital fingerprints. They can be used to detect duplicate data files, file version changes, and similar applications. These values are used to guard against an accidental or intentional change to the data, or accidental data corruption.

In Table 9-1, the config.txt and config-bk.txt files have the same hash value. This means that the content of these files is identical. The cryptographic hash function is applied in many different situations for entity authentication, data integrity, and data authenticity purposes.

Table 9-1 Creating a Hash

Date	Filename	Size	Hash
3/28/2017	topology.png	71 KB	d4a02c1520fb999b90fb5906a070130f
4/3/2017	config.txt	1 KB	aea9d4bb8c9457e37838db26bfe4a56e
4/10/2017	dev-gui.htm	53 KB	ee5b9602fd98414d3a2a051cb16a815a
4/12/2017	dev-image.zip	348,512 KB	f3b911b2dab14dfbc6f5a3a8c664033b
4/15/2017	config_bk.txt	1 KB	aea9d4bb8c9457e37838db26bfe4a56e

Cryptographic Hash Operation (9.1.2.2)

Mathematically, the equation $b = H(x)$ is used to explain how a hash algorithm operates. As shown in Figure 9-14, a hash function H takes an input x and returns a fixed-size string hash value b.

Figure 9-14 summarizes the mathematical process.

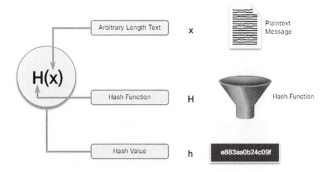

Figure 9-14 Hashing Formula

A cryptographic hash function should have the following properties:

- The input can be any length.
- The output has a fixed length.
- $H(x)$ is relatively easy to compute for any given x.
- $H(x)$ is one way and not reversible.
- $H(x)$ is collision free, meaning that two different input values will result in different hash values.

If a hash function is hard to invert, it is considered a one-way hash. Hard to invert means that given a hash value of b, it is computationally infeasible to find an input for x such that $b = H(x)$.

MD5 and SHA (9.1.2.3)

Hash functions are used to ensure the integrity of a message. They ensure data has not changed accidentally or intentionally.

In Figure 9-15, the sender is sending a $100 money transfer to Alex.

Pay to Alex	$100.00		Pay to Jeremy	$1000.00

One Hundred and 00/100 Dollars

One Thousand and 00/100 Dollars

4ehiDx67NMop9 ←— Different —→ 12ehqPx67NMoX

Starting Hash   Ending Hash

Figure 9-15 Hash Algorithms

The sender wants to ensure that the message is not altered on its way to the receiver.

1. The sending device inputs the message into a hashing algorithm and computes its fixed-length hash of 4ehiDx67NMop9.

2. This hash is then attached to the message and sent to the receiver. Both the message and the hash are in plaintext.

3. The receiving device removes the hash from the message and inputs the message into the same hashing algorithm. If the computed hash is equal to the one that is attached to the message, the message has not been altered during transit. If the hashes are not equal, as shown in Figure 9-15, then the integrity of the message can no longer be trusted.

There are three well-known hash functions:

- *Message Digest 5 (MD5)* **with 128-bit digest:** Developed by Ron Rivest and used in a variety of Internet applications, MD5 is a one-way function that produces a 128-bit hashed message, as shown in Figure 9-16. MD5 is considered to be a legacy algorithm and should be avoided, and used only when no better alternatives are available. It is recommended that SHA-2 be used instead.

Plaintext Message

MD5 Hash Function

128-bit Hashed Message

Figure 9-16 MD5 Hashing Algorithm

- *Secure Hash Algorithm 1 (SHA-1)*: Developed by the U.S. National Institute of Standards and Technology (NIST) in 1994 and is very similar to the MD5 hash functions, as shown in Figure 9-17. Several versions exist. SHA-1 creates a 160-bit hashed message and is slightly slower than MD5. SHA-1 has known flaws and is a legacy algorithm.

Figure 9-17   SHA Hashing Algorithm

- *Secure Hash Algorithm 2 (SHA-2)*: Developed by NIST and includes SHA-224 (224 bit), SHA-256 (256 bit), SHA-384 (384 bit), and SHA-512 (512 bit). SHA-256, SHA-384, and SHA-512 are next-generation algorithms and should be used whenever possible.

While hashing can be used to detect accidental changes, it cannot be used to guard against deliberate changes. There is no unique identifying information from the sender in the hashing procedure. This means that anyone can compute a hash for any data, as long as they have the correct hash function.

For example, when the message traverses the network, a potential attacker could intercept the message, change it, recalculate the hash, and append it to the message. The receiving device will only validate against whatever hash is appended.

Therefore, hashing is vulnerable to man-in-the-middle attacks and does not provide security to transmitted data. To provide integrity and origin authentication, something more is required.

Hash Message Authentication Code (9.1.2.4)

To add authentication to integrity assurance, a *keyed-hash message authentication code* (*HMAC*; also sometimes abbreviated as KHMAC) is used. To add authentication, HMAC uses an additional secret key as input to the hash function.

As shown in Figure 9-18, an HMAC is calculated using a specific algorithm (e.g., MD5 or SHA-1) that combines a cryptographic hash function with a secret key. Hash functions are the basis of the protection mechanism of HMACs.

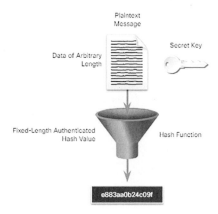

Figure 9-18   HMAC Hashing Algorithm

Only the sender and the receiver know the secret key, and the output of the hash function now depends on the input data and the secret key. Only parties who have access to that secret key can compute the digest of an HMAC function. This characteristic defeats man-in-the-middle attacks and provides authentication of the data origin.

If two parties share a secret key and use HMAC functions for authentication, a properly constructed HMAC digest of a message that a party has received indicates that the other party was the originator of the message. This is because the other party possesses the secret key.

As shown in Figure 9-19, the sending device inputs data (such as Terry Smith's pay of $100 and the secret key) into the hashing algorithm and calculates the fixed-length HMAC digest. This authenticated digest is then attached to the message and sent to the receiver.

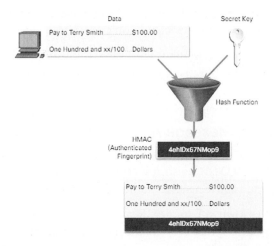

Figure 9-19   Creating the HMAC Value

In Figure 9-20, the receiving device removes the digest from the message and uses the plaintext message with its secret key as input to the same hashing function.

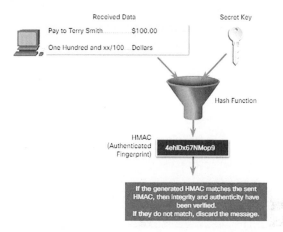

Figure 9-20   Verifying the HMAC Value

If the digest that is calculated by the receiving device is equal to the digest that was sent, the message has not been altered. Additionally, the origin of the message is authenticated because only the sender possesses a copy of the shared secret key. The HMAC function has ensured the authenticity of the message.

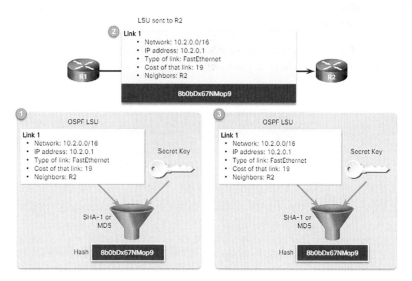

Figure 9-21   Verifying the HMAC Value: Details

Figure 9-21 illustrates how HMACs are used by Cisco routers configured to use Open Shortest Path First (OSPF) routing authentication. R1 is sending a link state update (LSU) regarding a route to network 10.2.0.0/16:

1. R1 calculates the hash value using the LSU message and the secret key.

2. The resulting hash value is sent with the LSU to R2.

3. R2 calculates the hash value using the LSU and its secret key. R2 accepts the update if the hash values match. Otherwise, R2 discards the update.

Lab 9.1.2.5: Hashing Things Out

In this lab, you will complete the following objectives:

- Creating Hashes with OpenSSL

- Verifying Hashes

Confidentiality (9.1.3)

In this topic, you will learn how cryptographic approaches enhance data confidentiality.

Encryption (9.1.3.1)

There are two classes of encryption used to provide data confidentiality. These two classes differ in how they use keys:

- *Symmetric encryption* **algorithms:** Encryption algorithms that use the same key to encrypt and decrypt data. They are based on the premise that each communicating party knows the pre-shared key.

- *Asymmetric encryption* **algorithms:** Encryption algorithms that use different keys to encrypt and decrypt data. They are based on the assumption that the two communicating parties have not previously shared a secret and must establish a secure method to do so. Asymmetric algorithms are resource intensive and slower to execute.

The following summarizes some differences between each encryption algorithm method.

Symmetrical Encryption

- Uses the same key to encrypt and decrypt data.

- Key lengths are short (40 bits to 256 bits).

- Faster than asymmetrical encryption.

- Commonly used for encrypting bulk data such as in VPN traffic.

Asymmetrical Encryption

- Uses different keys to encrypt and decrypt data.

- Key lengths are long (512 bits to 4096 bits)

- Computationally tasking and therefore slower than symmetrical encryption.

- Commonly used for quick data transactions such as HTTPS when accessing your bank data.

Symmetric Encryption (9.1.3.2)

Symmetric algorithms use the same pre-shared key to encrypt and decrypt data. A pre-shared key, also called a secret key, is known by the sender and receiver before any encrypted communications can take place.

To help illustrate how symmetric encryption works, consider an example where Alice and Bob live in different locations and want to exchange secret messages with one another through the mail system. In this example, Alice wants to send a secret message to Bob.

In Figure 9-22, Alice and Bob have identical keys to a single padlock.

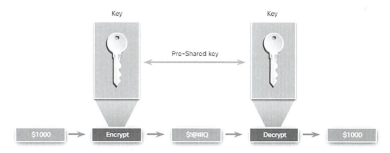

Figure 9-22   Symmetric Encryption Example

These keys were exchanged prior to sending any secret messages. Alice writes a secret message and puts it in a small box that she locks using the padlock with her key. She mails the box to Bob. The message is safely locked inside the box as the box makes its way through the post office system. When Bob receives the box, he uses his key to unlock the padlock and retrieve the message. Bob can use the same box and padlock to send a secret reply back to Alice.

Today, symmetric encryption algorithms are commonly used with VPN traffic. This is because symmetric algorithms use less CPU than asymmetric encryption algorithms, which are discussed later. This allows the encryption and decryption of data to be fast when using a VPN. When using symmetric encryption algorithms, like any other type of encryption, the longer the key, the longer it will take for someone to discover the key. Most encryption keys are between 112 and 256 bits. To ensure that the encryption is safe, a minimum key length of 128 bits should be used. Use a longer key for more secure communications.

Symmetric Encryption Algorithms (9.1.3.3)

Encryption algorithms are often classified as a block cipher or stream cipher:

- *Block ciphers*: Block ciphers transform a fixed-length block of plaintext into a common block of ciphertext of 64 or 128 bits, as shown in Figure 9-23. Common block ciphers include DES with a 64-bit block size and AES with a 128-bit block size.

Figure 9-23   Block Cipher

- *Stream ciphers*: Stream ciphers encrypt plaintext one byte or one bit at a time, as shown in Figure 9-24. Stream ciphers are basically a block cipher with a block size of one byte or bit. Stream ciphers are typically faster than block ciphers because data is continuously encrypted. Examples of stream ciphers include RC4 and A5, the latter of which is used to encrypt GSM cell phone communications. Data Encryption Standard (DES) can also be used in stream cipher mode.

Figure 9-24   Stream Cipher

Well-known symmetric encryption algorithms include

- *Data Encryption Standard (DES)*: This is an older legacy symmetric encryption algorithm. It can be used in stream cipher mode but usually operates in block mode by encrypting data in 64-bit block size. Table 9-2 summarizes DES.

Table 9-2   DES Scorecard

DES Characteristics	
Description	Data Encryption Standard
Timeline	Standardized 1976
Type of algorithm	Symmetric
Key size	56 bits
Speed	Medium
Time to crack (assuming a computer could try 255 keys per second)	Days (6.4 days by the COPACABANA machine, a specialized cracking device)
Resource consumption	Medium

- **3DES (Triple DES)**: This is a newer version of DES, but it repeats the DES algorithm process three times. It is more computationally taxing than DES. The basic algorithm has been well tested in the field for more than 35 years and is therefore considered very trustworthy when implemented using very short key lifetimes. Table 9-3 summarizes 3DES.

Table 9-3   3DES Scorecard

3DES Characteristics	
Description	Triple Data Encryption Standard
Timeline	Standardized 1977
Type of algorithm	Symmetric
Key size	112 and 168 bits
Speed	Low
Time to crack (assuming a computer could try 255 keys per second)	4.6 billion years with current technology
Resource consumption	Medium

- **Advanced Encryption Standard (AES)**: Based on the Rijndael cipher, it is a popular and recommended symmetric encryption algorithm. It offers nine combinations of key and block length by using a variable key length of 128-, 192-, or 256-bit key to encrypt data blocks that are 128, 192, or 256 bits long. AES is a secure and more efficient algorithm than 3DES. Table 9-4 summarizes AES. AES counter mode (AES-CTR) is the preferred encryption algorithm for SSHv2. It can use any of the AES key lengths, such as AES256-CTR.

Table 9-4   AES Scorecard

AES Characteristics

Description	Advanced Encryption Standard
Timeline	Official standard since 2001
Type of algorithm	Symmetric
Key size	128, 192, and 256 bits
Speed	High
Time to crack (assuming a computer could try 255 keys per second)	149 trillion years
Resource consumption	Low

- *Software-Optimized Encryption Algorithm (SEAL)*: SEAL is a fast, alternative symmetric encryption algorithm to DES, 3DES, and AES. It is a stream cipher that uses a 160-bit encryption key. SEAL has a lower impact on the CPU compared to other software-based algorithms but is still considered unproven. Table 9-5 summarizes SEAL.

Table 9-5   SEAL Scorecard

SEAL Characteristics

Description	Software-Optimized Encryption Algorithm
Timeline	First published in 1994; current version is 3.0 (1997)
Type of algorithm	Symmetric
Key size	160 bits
Speed	High
Time to crack (assuming a computer could try 255 keys per second)	Unknown but considered very safe
Resource consumption	Low

- *Rivest ciphers (RC)* series algorithms (includes RC2, RC4, RC5, and RC6): This was developed by Ron Rivest. Several variations have been developed, but RC4 is the most prevalent in use. RC4 is a stream cipher and is used to secure web traffic in SSL and TLS. Table 9-6 summarizes the RC algorithms.

Table 9-6   RC Algorithms Summary

RC Algorithms	Timeline	Type of Algorithm	Key Size in Bits
RC2	1987	Block cipher	40 and 64
RC4	1987	Stream cipher	1 to 256
RC5	1994	Block cipher	0 to 2048
RC6	1998	Block cipher	128, 192, or 256

Note

There are many other symmetric encryption algorithms, such as Blowfish, Twofish, Threefish, and Serpent. However, these algorithms are beyond the scope of this course.

Asymmetric Encryption Algorithms (9.1.3.4)

Asymmetric algorithms, also called public key algorithms, are designed so that the key that is used for encryption is different from the key that is used for decryption, as shown in Figure 9-25. The decryption key cannot, in any reasonable amount of time, be calculated from the encryption key and vice versa.

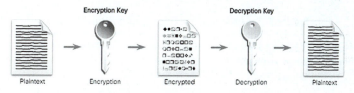

Figure 9-25   Asymmetric Encryption Example

Asymmetric algorithms use a public key and a private key. Both keys are capable of the encryption process, but the complementary paired key is required for decryption. The process is also reversible in that data encrypted with the public key requires the private key to decrypt.

This process enables asymmetric algorithms to achieve confidentiality, authentication, and integrity.

Because neither party has a shared secret, very long key lengths must be used. Asymmetric encryption can use key lengths between 512 to 4,096 bits. Key lengths greater than or equal to 1,024 bits can be trusted, while shorter key lengths are considered unreliable.

Examples of protocols that use asymmetric key algorithms include

- **Internet Key Exchange (IKE):** This is a fundamental component of IPsec VPNs.

- **Secure Sockets Layer (SSL):** This is now implemented as IETF standard Transport Layer Security (TLS).

- **Secure Shell (SSH):** This is a protocol that provides a secure remote access connection to network devices.

- **Pretty Good Privacy (PGP):** This is a computer program that provides cryptographic privacy and authentication. It is often used to increase the security of email communications.

Asymmetric algorithms are substantially slower than symmetric algorithms. Their design is based on computational problems, such as factoring extremely large numbers or computing discrete logarithms of extremely large numbers.

Because they lack speed, asymmetric algorithms are typically used in low-volume cryptographic mechanisms, such as digital signatures and key exchange. However, the key management of asymmetric algorithms tends to be simpler than symmetric algorithms, because usually one of the two encryption or decryption keys can be made public.

Common examples of asymmetric encryption algorithms are described in Table 9-7.

Table 9-7   Asymmetric Encryption Algorithms

Asymmetric Encryption Algorithm	Key Length (in Bits)	Description
Diffie-Hellman (DH)	512, 1024, 2048, 3072, or 4096	The Diffie-Hellman algorithm is a public key algorithm invented in 1976 by Whitfield Diffie and Martin Hellman. It allows two parties to agree on a key that they can use to encrypt messages they want to send to each other. The security of this algorithm depends on the assumption that it is easy to raise a number to a certain power, but difficult to compute which power was used given the number and the outcome.
Digital Signature Standard (DSS) **and** *Digital Signature Algorithm (DSA)*	512 to 1024	DSS was created by NIST and specifies DSA as the algorithm for digital signatures. DSA is a public key algorithm based on the ElGamal signature scheme. Signature creation speed is similar with RSA, but is 10 to 40 times as slow for verification.

Asymmetric Encryption Algorithm	Key Length (in Bits)	Description
RSA **encryption algorithms**	512 to 2048	Developed by Ron Rivest, Adi Shamir, and Leonard Adleman at MIT in 1977, RSA is an algorithm for public key cryptography that is based on the current difficulty of factoring very large numbers. It is the first algorithm known to be suitable for signing as well as encryption, and one of the first great advances in public key cryptography. It is widely used in electronic commerce protocols, and is believed to be secure given sufficiently long keys and the use of up-to-date implementations.
ElGamal	512 to 1024	An asymmetric key encryption algorithm for public key cryptography which is based on the Diffie-Hellman key agreement. It is described by Taher ElGamal in 1984 and is used in GNU Privacy Guard software, PGP, and other cryptosystems. A disadvantage of the ElGamal system is that the encrypted message becomes very big, about twice the size of the original message, and for this reason ElGamal is only used for small messages such as secret keys.
Elliptical curve **techniques**	160	Elliptic curve cryptography was invented by Neil Koblitz and Victor Miller in the mid 1980s. Can be used to adapt many cryptographic algorithms, such as Diffie-Hellman or ElGamal. The main advantage of elliptic curve cryptography is that the keys can be much smaller.

Asymmetric Encryption: Confidentiality (9.1.3.5)

Asymmetric algorithms are used to provide confidentiality without pre-sharing a password. The confidentiality objective of asymmetric algorithms is initiated when the encryption process is started with the public key.

The process can be summarized using the formula:

Public Key (Encrypt) + Private Key (Decrypt) = Confidentiality

When the public key is used to encrypt the data, the private key must be used to decrypt the data. Only one host has the private key; therefore, confidentiality is achieved.

If the private key is compromised, another key pair must be generated to replace the compromised key.

For example, in Figure 9-26, Alice requests and obtains Bob's public key.

Figure 9-26   Alice Acquires Public Key

In Figure 9-27, Alice uses Bob's public key to encrypt a message using an agreed-upon algorithm.

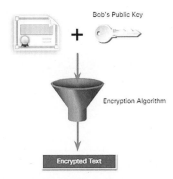

Figure 9-27   Alice Encrypts Message Using Bob's Public Key

Alice sends the encrypted message to Bob. Bob then uses his private key to decrypt the message as shown in Figure 9-28.

Figure 9-28   Bob Decrypts the Message Using His Private Key

Asymmetric Encryption: Authentication (9.1.3.6)

The authentication objective of asymmetric algorithms is initiated when the encryption process is started with the private key.

The process can be summarized using the formula:

Private Key (Encrypt) + Public Key (Decrypt) = Authentication

When the private key is used to encrypt the data, the corresponding public key must be used to decrypt the data. Because only one host has the private key, only that host could have encrypted the message, providing authentication of the sender. Typically, no attempt is made to preserve the secrecy of the public key, so any number of hosts can decrypt the message. When a host successfully decrypts a message using a public key, it is trusted that the private key encrypted the message, which verifies who the sender is. This is a form of authentication.

For example, in Figure 9-29, Alice encrypts a message using her private key.

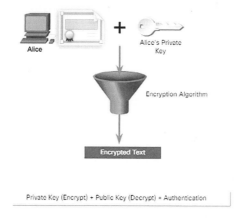

Figure 9-29 Alice Encrypts the Message Using Her Private Key

Alice sends the encrypted message to Bob. Bob needs to authenticate that the message did, indeed, come from Alice. Therefore, in Figure 9-30, Bob requests Alice's public key.

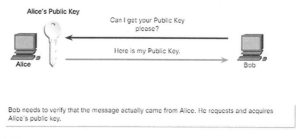

Figure 9-30 Bob Requests Alice's Public Key

In Figure 9-31, Bob uses Alice's public key to decrypt the message.

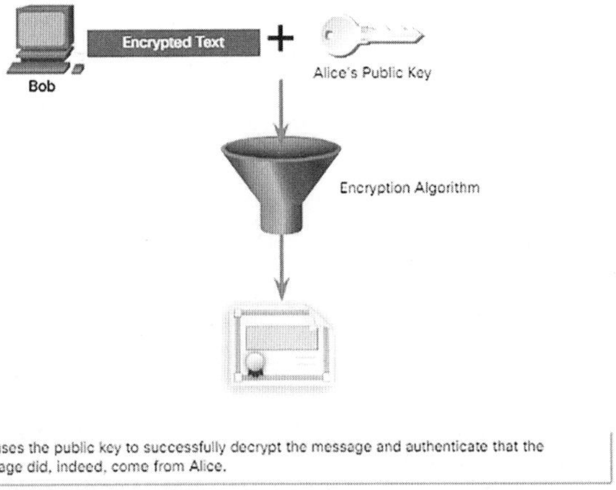

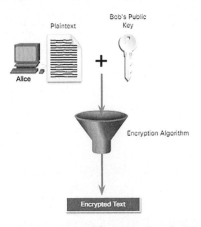

Figure 9-31   Bob Deciphers the Message Using the Public Key

Asymmetric Encryption: Integrity (9.1.3.7)

Combining the two asymmetric encryption processes provides message confidentiality, authentication, and integrity.

The following example will be used to illustrate this process. In this example, a message will be ciphered using Bob's public key and a ciphered hash will be encrypted using Alice's private key to provide confidentiality, authenticity, and integrity.

The process in Figure 9-32 provides confidentiality. Alice wants to send a message to Bob, ensuring that only Bob can read the document. In other words, Alice wants to ensure message confidentiality. Alice uses the public key of Bob to cipher the message. Only Bob will be able to decipher it using his private key.

Figure 9-32   Alice Encrypts a Message Using Bob's Public Key

Alice also wants to ensure message authentication and integrity. Authentication ensures Bob that the document was sent by Alice, and integrity ensures that it was not modified. In Figure 9-33, Alice uses her private key to cipher a hash of the message. Alice sends the encrypted message with its encrypted hash to Bob.

Figure 9-33   Alice Encrypts a Hash Using Alice's Private Key

In Figure 9-34, Bob uses Alice's public key to verify that the message was not modified. The received hash is equal to the locally determined hash based on Alice's public key. Additionally, this verifies that Alice is definitely the sender of the message because nobody else has Alice's private key.

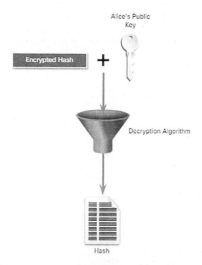

Figure 9-34   Bob Uses Alice's Public Key to Decrypt the Hash

Finally, in Figure 9-35, Bob uses his private key to decipher the message.

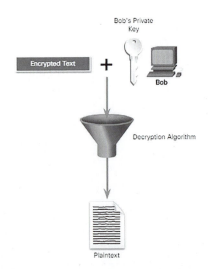

Figure 9-35   Bob Uses His Private Key to Decrypt Message

Diffie-Hellman (9.1.3.8)

Diffie-Hellman (DH) is an asymmetric mathematical algorithm that allows two computers to generate an identical shared secret without having communicated before. The new shared key is never actually exchanged between the sender and receiver. However, because both parties know it, the key can be used by an encryption algorithm to encrypt traffic between the two systems.

Here are three examples of instances when DH is commonly used:

- Data is exchanged using an IPsec VPN.

- Data is encrypted on the Internet using either SSL or TLS.

- SSH data is exchanged.

To help illustrate how DH operates, refer to Figure 9-36. Colors are used instead of complex long numbers to simplify the DH key agreement process. The DH key exchange begins with Alice and Bob agreeing on an arbitrary common color that does not need to be kept secret. The agreed on color in our example is yellow.

Next, Alice and Bob will each select a secret color. Alice chose red while Bob chose blue. These secret colors will never be shared with anyone. The secret color represents the chosen secret private key of each party.

Alice and Bob now mix the shared common color (yellow) with their respective secret color to produce a private color. Therefore, Alice will mix the yellow with her red color to produce a private color of orange. Bob will mix the yellow and the blue to produce a private color of green.

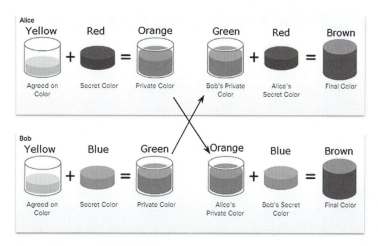

Figure 9-36   DH Operation Simplified

Alice sends her private color (orange) to Bob and Bob sends his private color (green) to Alice.

Alice and Bob each mix the color they received with their own, original secret color (red for Alice and blue for Bob). The result is a final brown color mixture that is identical to the partner's final color mixture. The brown color represents the resulting shared secret key between Bob and Alice.

The security of DH is based on the fact that it uses unbelievably large numbers in its calculations. For example, a DH 1,024-bit number is roughly equal to a decimal number of 309 digits. Considering that 1 billion is 10 decimal digits (1,000,000,000), one can easily imagine the complexity of working with not one, but multiple 309-digit decimal numbers.

Unfortunately, asymmetric key systems are extremely slow for any sort of bulk encryption. This is why it is common to encrypt the bulk of the traffic using a symmetric algorithm, such as 3DES or AES, and use the DH algorithm to create keys that will be used by the encryption algorithm.

Interactive Graphic

Activity 9.1.3.9: Classify the Encryption Algorithms

Refer to the online course to complete this Activity.

Public Key Infrastructure (9.2)

In this section, you will learn how the public key infrastructure (PKI) supports network security.

Public Key Cryptography (9.2.1)

In this topic, you will learn about public key cryptography.

Using Digital Signatures (9.2.1.1)

Digital signatures are a mathematical technique used to provide three basic security services:

- **Authenticity:** Provides authenticity of digitally signed data. Digital signatures authenticate a source, proving that a certain party has seen and signed the data in question.

- **Integrity:** Provides integrity of digitally signed data. Digital signatures guarantee that the data has not changed from the time it was signed.

- **Non-repudiation:** Provides non-repudiation of the transaction. The recipient can take the data to a third party, and the third party accepts the digital signature as a proof that this data exchange did take place. The signing party cannot repudiate that it has signed the data.

Digital signatures have the following properties that enable entity authentication and data integrity:

- **Signature is authentic:** The signature is not forgeable and provides proof that the signer, and no one else, signed the document.

- **Signature is not reusable:** The signature is part of the document and cannot be moved to a different document.

- **Signature is unaltered:** After a document is signed, it cannot be altered.

- **Signature cannot be repudiated:** For legal purposes, the signature and the document are considered physical things. Signers cannot claim later that they did not sign it.

Digital signatures are commonly used in the following two situations:

- **Code signing:** This is used for data integrity and authentication purposes. Code signing is used to verify the integrity of executable files downloaded from a vendor website. It also uses signed digital certificates to authenticate and verify the identity of the site.

- **Digital certificates:** These are similar to a virtual ID card and used to authenticate the identity of the system with a vendor website and establish an encrypted connection to exchange confidential data.

There are three Digital Signature Standard (DSS) algorithms that are used for generating and verifying digital signatures:

- **Digital Signature Algorithm (DSA):** DSA is the original standard for generating public and private key pairs, and for generating and verifying digital signatures. Table 9-8 summarizes DSA.

Table 9-8   DSA Scorecard

DSA Characteristics	
Description	Digital Signature Algorithm (DSA)
Timeline	1994
Type of algorithm	Provides digital signatures
Advantages	Signature generation is fast
Disadvantages	Signature verification is slow

- **Rivest-Shamir-Adleman Algorithm (RSA):** RSA is an asymmetric algorithm that is commonly used for generating and verifying digital signatures. Table 9-9 summarizes RSA.

Table 9-9   RSA Scorecard

RSA Characteristics	
Description	Ron Rivest, Adi Shamir, and Len Adleman
Timeline	1977
Type of algorithm	Asymmetric
Key size	512 to 2048 bits
Advantages	Signature verification is fast
Disadvantages	Signature generation is slow

- **Elliptic Curve Digital Signature Algorithm (ECDSA):** ECDSA is a newer variant of DSA and provides digital signature authentication and non-repudiation with the added benefits of computational efficiency, small signature sizes, and minimal bandwidth.

Diffie-Hellman uses different DH groups to determine the strength of the key that is used in the key agreement process. The higher group numbers are more secure, but require additional time to compute the key. The following identifies the DH groups supported by Cisco IOS Software and their associated prime number value:

- DH Group 1: 768 bits

- DH Group 2: 1024 bits

- DH Group 5: 1536 bits

- DH Group 14: 2048 bits

- DH Group 15: 3072 bits

- DH Group 16: 4096 bits

Note

A DH key agreement can also be based on elliptic curve cryptography. DH groups 19, 20, and 24, based on elliptic curve cryptography, are also supported by Cisco IOS Software.

In the 1990s, RSA Security Inc. started to publish public key cryptography standards (PKCS). There were 15 PKCS, although 1 has been withdrawn as of the time of this writing. RSA published these standards because they had the patents to the standards and wished to promote them. PKCS are not industry standards, but are well recognized in the security industry and have recently begun to become relevant to standards organizations such as the IETF and PKIX working group.

Digital Signatures for Code Signing (9.2.1.2)

Digital signatures are commonly used to provide assurance of the authenticity and integrity of software code. Executable files are wrapped in a digitally signed envelope, which allows the end user to verify the signature before installing the software.

Digitally signing code provides several assurances about the code:

- The code is authentic and is actually sourced by the publisher.

- The code has not been modified since it left the software publisher.

- The publisher undeniably published the code. This provides non-repudiation of the act of publishing.

The U.S. Government Federal Information Processing Standard (FIPS) Publication 140-3 specifies that software available for download on the Internet is to be digitally signed and verified. The purpose of digitally signed software is to ensure that the software has not been tampered with, and that it originated from the trusted source as claimed.

Refer to Figures 9-37 through 9-41 to see the properties of a file with a digitally signed certificate. Figure 9-37 displays the properties of a file that has been downloaded from the Internet. The intent of the file is to update the flash player on the host.

Figure 9-37   File Properties

Clicking the Digital Signature tab (Figure 9-38) reveals that the file is from a trusted organization, Adobe Systems.

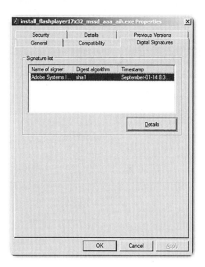

Figure 9-38   Digital Signatures Tab

Clicking the Details button opens the Digital Signature Details window (Figure 9-39), which reveals that the Symantec corporation is validating that the file has indeed originated from Adobe Systems Incorporated.

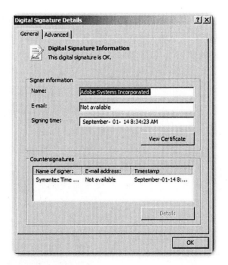

Figure 9-39   Digital Signature Details

Clicking the View Certificate button opens the details of the certificate (Figure 9-40). The certificate details display the purposes of the certificate, who it was issued to, and who is was issued by. It also displays the amount of time that this certificate is valid.

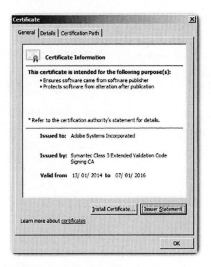

Figure 9-40   Digital Certificate Information

The Certificate Path tab (Figure 9-41) indicates that the file came from Adobe as authenticated by Symantec, which in turn is validated by VeriSign.

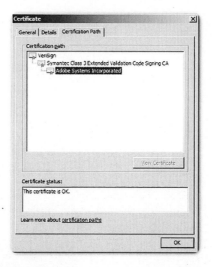

Figure 9-41   Digital Certificate Path

Digital Signatures for Digital Certificates (9.2.1.3)

A digital certificate is equivalent to an electronic passport. It enables users, hosts, and organizations to securely exchange information over the Internet. Specifically, a digital certificate is used to authenticate and verify that users sending a message are who they claim to be. Digital certificates can also be used to provide confidentiality for the receiver with the means to encrypt a reply.

Digital certificates are similar to physical certificates. For example, the paper-based Cisco Certified Network Associate Security (CCNA-S) certificate in Figure 9-42 identifies who the certificate is issued to, who authorized the certificate, and for how long the certificate is valid.

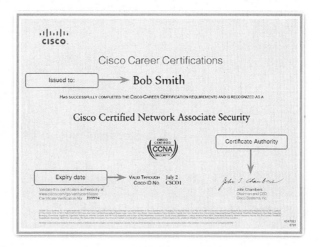

Figure 9-42   Physical CCNA Security Certificate

Notice how the digital certificate in Figure 9-43 also identifies similar elements.

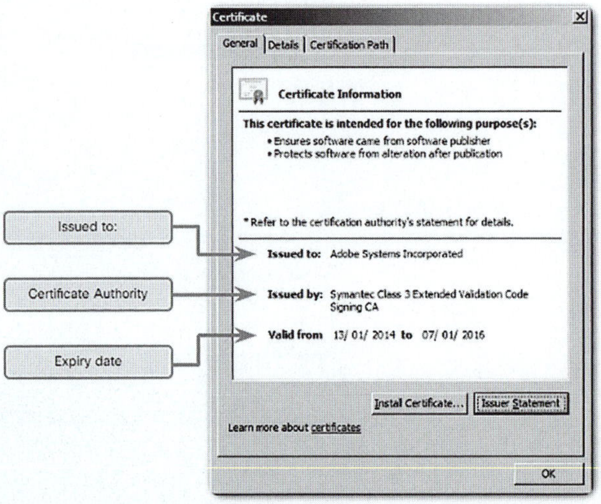

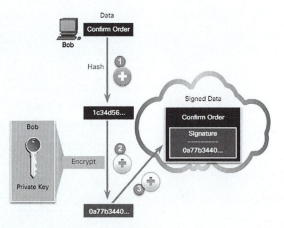

Figure 9-43   Digital Certificate Information

To help understand how a digital certificate is used, refer to Figure 9-44. In this scenario, Bob is confirming an order with Alice. The steps are as follows:

1. Bob confirms the order and his computer creates a hash of the confirmation.

2. The computer encrypts the hash with the private key of Bob.

3. The encrypted hash, known as the digital signature, is appended to the document. The order confirmation is sent to Alice over the Internet.

Figure 9-44   Sending a Digital Certificate

Figure 9-45 shows how Alice will use the digital certificate:

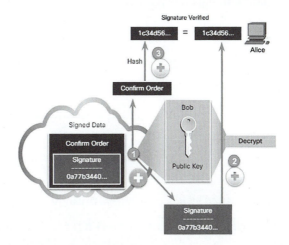

Figure 9-45   Receiving a Digital Certificate

1. Alice's receiving device accepts the order confirmation with the digital signature and obtains Bob's public key.

2. Her computer then decrypts the signature using Bob's public key. This step reveals the assumed hash value of the sending device.

3. Alice's computer creates a hash of the received document, without its signature, and compares this hash to the decrypted signature hash. If the hashes match, the document is authentic. This means it authenticates that it was sent by Bob and that it has not changed since it was signed.

Authorities and the PKI Trust System (9.2.2)

In this topic, you will learn how the public key infrastructure functions.

Public Key Management (9.2.2.1)

Internet traffic consists of traffic between two parties. When establishing an asymmetric connection between two hosts, the hosts will exchange their public key information. There are trusted third parties on the Internet that validate the authenticity of these public keys using digital certificates. The trusted third party does an in-depth investigation prior to the issuance of credentials. After this in-depth investigation, the third party issues credentials (i.e., digital certificate) that are difficult to forge. From that point forward, all individuals who trust the third party simply accept the credentials that the third party issues.

These trusted third parties provide services similar to governmental licensing bureaus. Figure 9-46 illustrates how a driver's license is analogous to a digital certificate.

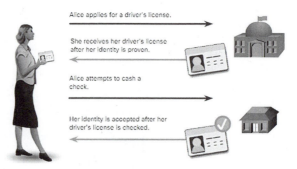

Figure 9-46 Driver's License PKI Analogy

The *Public Key Infrastructure (PKI)* is an example of a trusted third-party system referred to as certificate authority (CA). The CA provides a service similar to governmental licensing bureaus. The PKI is the framework used to securely exchange information between parties. The CA issues digital certificates that authenticate the identity of organizations and users. These certificates are also used to sign messages to ensure that the messages have not been tampered with.

The Public Key Infrastructure (9.2.2.2)

PKI is needed to support large-scale distribution and identification of public encryption keys. The PKI framework facilitates a highly scalable trust relationship.

It consists of the hardware, software, people, policies, and procedures needed to create, manage, store, distribute, and revoke digital certificates.

Figure 9-47 shows the main elements of the PKI:

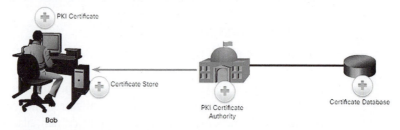

Figure 9-47 Elements of the PKI Framework

- **PKI certificate authority (CA):** The CA is a trusted third party that issues PKI certificates to entities and individuals after verifying their identity. It signs these certificates using its private key.

- **Certificate database:** The certificate database stores all certificates approved by the CA.

- **PKI certificate:** Certificates contain an entity's or individual's public key, its purpose, the CA that validated and issued the certificate, the date range during which the certificate can be considered valid, and the algorithm used to create the signature.

- **Certificate store:** The certificate store resides on a local computer and stores issued certificates and private keys.

Figure 9-48 shows an example of PKI, the steps of which are described as follows:

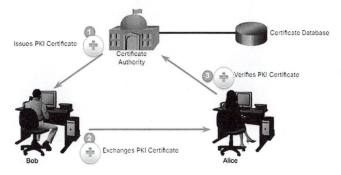

Figure 9-48   PKI Example

1. Bob initially requests a certificate from the CA. The CA authenticates Bob and stores Bob's PKI certificate in the certificate database.

2. Bob communicates with Alice using his PKI certificate.

3. Alice communicates with the trusted CA using the CA's public key. The CA refers to the certificate database to validate Bob's PKI certificate.

> **Note**
>
> Not all PKI certificates are directly received from a CA. A registration authority (RA) is a subordinate CA and is certified by a root CA to issue certificates for specific uses.

The PKI Authorities System (9.2.2.3)

Many vendors provide CA servers as a managed service or as an end-user product. Some of these vendors include Symantec Group (VeriSign), Comodo, Go Daddy Group, GlobalSign, and DigiCert, among others.

Organizations may also implement private PKIs using Microsoft Server or Open SSL.

CAs, especially those that are outsourced, issue certificates based on classes which determine how trusted a certificate is.

Table 9-10 provides a description of the classes. The class number is determined by how rigorous the procedure was that verified the identity of the holder when the certificate was issued. The higher the class number, the more trusted the certificate. Therefore, a class 5 certificate is trusted much more than a lower class certificate.

Table 9-10   Classes of Certificates

Class	Description
0	Used for testing purposes in which no checks have been performed.
1	Used for individuals with a focus on verification of email.
2	Used for organizations for which proof of identity is required.
3	Used for servers and software signing for which independent verification and checking of identity and authority is done by the issuing certificate authority.
4	Used for online business transactions between companies.
5	Used for private organizations or governmental security.

For example, a class 1 certificate might require an email reply from the holder to confirm that they wish to enroll. This kind of confirmation is a weak authentication of the holder. For a class 3 or 4 certificate, the future holder must prove identity and authenticate the public key by showing up in person with at least two official ID documents.

Some CA public keys are preloaded, such as those listed in web browsers. Figure 9-49 displays various VeriSign certificates contained in the certificate store on the host. Any certificates signed by any of the CAs in the list will be seen by the browser as legitimate and will be trusted automatically.

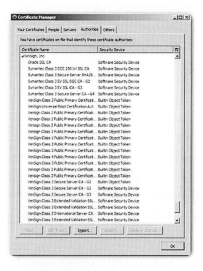

Figure 9-49   Sample VeriSign Certificates

> **Note**
>
> An enterprise can also implement PKI for internal use. PKI can be used to authenticate employees who are accessing the network. In this case, the enterprise is its own CA.

The PKI Trust System (9.2.2.4)

PKIs can form different topologies of trust. The simplest is the single-root PKI topology.

As shown in Figure 9-50, a single CA, called the root CA, issues all the certificates to the end users, which are usually within the same organization.

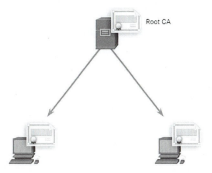

Figure 9-50   Single-Root PKI Topology

The benefit to this approach is its simplicity. However, it is difficult to scale to a large environment because it requires a strictly centralized administration, which creates a single point of failure.

On larger networks, PKI CAs may be linked using two basic architectures:

- **Cross-certified CA topologies:** As shown in Figure 9-51, this is a peer-to-peer model in which individual CAs establish trust relationships with other CAs by cross-certifying CA certificates. Users in either CA domain are also assured that they can trust each other. This provides redundancy and eliminates the single point of failure.

- **Hierarchical CA topologies:** As shown in Figure 9-52, the highest level CA is called the root CA. It can issue certificates to end users and to a subordinate CA. The sub-CAs could be created to support various business units, domains, or communities of trust. The root CA maintains the established "community of trust" by ensuring that each entity in the hierarchy conforms to a minimum set of practices. The benefits of this topology include increased scalability and manageability. This topology works well in most large organizations. However, it can be difficult to determine the chain of the signing process.

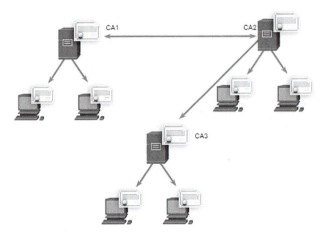

Figure 9-51 Cross-Certified CA

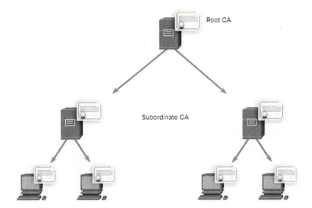

Figure 9-52 Hierarchical CA

A hierarchical and cross-certification topology can be combined to create a hybrid infrastructure. An example would be when two hierarchical communities want to cross-certify each other in order for members of each community to trust each other.

Interoperability of Different PKI Vendors (9.2.2.5)

Interoperability between a PKI and its supporting services, such as Lightweight Directory Access Protocol (LDAP) and X.500 directories, is a concern because many CA vendors have proposed and implemented proprietary solutions instead of waiting for standards to develop.

Note

LDAP and X.500 are protocols that are used to query a directory service, such as Microsoft Active Directory, to verify a username and password.

To address this interoperability concern, the IETF published the Internet X.509 Public Key Infrastructure Certificate Policy and Certification Practices Framework (RFC 2527). The X.509 version 3 (X.509v3) standard defines the format of a digital certificate.

As shown Figure 9-53, the X.509 format is already extensively used in the infrastructure of the Internet.

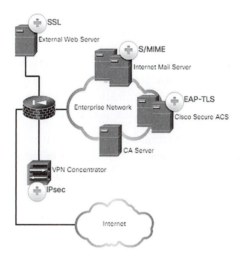

Figure 9-53   X.509v3 Applications

The applications in Figure 9-53 include the following:

- **SSL:** Secure web servers use X.509v3 for website authentication in the SSL and TLS protocols, while web browsers use X.509v3 to implement HTTPS client certificates. SSL is the most widely used certificate-based authentication.

- **S/MIME:** User mail agents that support mail protection using the Secure/Multipurpose Internet Mail Extensions (S/MIME) protocol use X.509.

- **EAP-TLS:** Cisco switches can use certificates to authenticate end devices connecting to LAN ports using 802.1X between the adjacent devices. The authentication can be proxied to a central ACS via the Extensible Authentication Protocol with TLS (EAP-TLS).

- **IPsec:** IPsec VPNs where certificates can be used as a public key distribution mechanism for IKE RSA-based authentication use X.509.

Certificate Enrollment, Authentication, and Revocation (9.2.2.6)

In the CA authentication procedure, the first step when contacting the PKI is to securely obtain a copy of the CA's public key. All systems that leverage the PKI must have the CA's public key, called the self-signed certificate. The CA public key verifies all the certificates issued by the CA and is vital for the proper operation of the PKI.

> **Note**
>
> Only a root CA can issue a self-signed certificate.

For many systems such as web browsers, the distribution of CA certificates is handled automatically. The web browser comes preinstalled with a set of public CA root certificates. Organizations also push their private CA root certificate to clients through various software distribution methods.

The certificate enrollment process is used by a host system to enroll with a PKI. To do so, CA certificates are retrieved in-band over a network, and the authentication is done out-of-band (OOB) using the telephone. The system enrolling with the PKI contacts a CA to request and obtain a digital identity certificate for itself and to get the CA's self-signed certificate. The final stage verifies that the CA certificate was authentic and is performed using an OOB method such as the Plain Old Telephone System (POTS) to obtain the fingerprint of the valid CA identity certificate.

The first part of the certificate enrollment process consists of acquiring the CA's self-signed certificate.

Figure 9-54 demonstrates how CA certificates are retrieved, as described in the following steps:

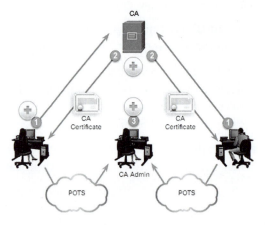

Figure 9-54   Retrieving CA Certificates

1. Alice and Bob request the CA certificate that contains the CA public key.

2. Upon receipt of the CA certificate, each requesting system verifies the validity of the certificate using public key cryptography.

3. Alice and Bob follow up the technical verification done by their system by telephoning the CA administrator and verifying the public key and serial number of the certificate.

After retrieving the CA certificate, Alice and Bob submit certificate requests to the CA, as shown in Figure 9-55 and described next:

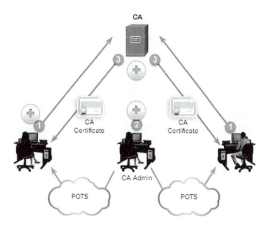

Figure 9-55   Submitting Certificate Requests to the CA

1. Both systems forward a certificate request that includes their public key along with some identifying information. All of this information is encrypted using the public key of the CA.

2. Upon the receipt of the certificate requests on the CA server, the CA administrator telephones Alice and Bob to confirm their submittal and the public key. The CA administrator issues the certificate by adding some additional data to the certificate request and digitally signing it all.

3. Either the end user manually retrieves the certificate or SCEP automatically retrieves the certificate, and the certificate is installed onto the system.

Having installed certificates signed by the same CA, Bob and Alice are now ready to authenticate each other, as shown in Figure 9-56 and described next:

1. Bob and Alice exchange certificates. The CA is no longer involved.

2. Each party verifies the digital signature on the certificate by hashing the plaintext portion of the certificate, decrypting the digital signature using the CA public key, and comparing the results. If the results match, the certificate is verified as being signed by a trusted third party and the verification by the CA that Bob is Bob and Alice is Alice is accepted.

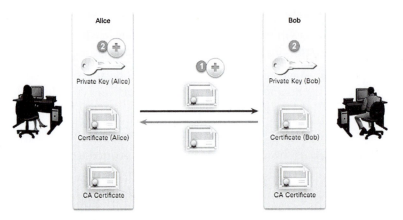

Figure 9-56   Peers Authenticate Each Other

Authentication no longer requires the presence of the CA server, and each user exchanges their certificates containing public keys.

Certificate must sometimes be revoked. For example, a digital certificate can be revoked if a key is compromised or if it is no longer needed.

Here are two of the most common methods of revocation:

- **Certificate revocation list (CRL):** A list of revoked certificate serial numbers that have been invalidated because they expired. PKI entities regularly poll the CRL repository to receive the current CRL.

- **Online Certificate Status Protocol (OCSP):** An Internet protocol used to query an OCSP server for the revocation status of an X.509 digital certificate. Revocation information is immediately pushed to an online database.

Lab 9.2.2.7: Certificate Authority Stores

In this lab, you will complete the following objectives:

- Certificates Trusted by Your Browser
- Checking for Man-In-Middle

Applications and Impacts of Cryptography (9.2.3)

In this topic, you will learn how the use of cryptography affects cybersecurity operations.

PKI Applications (9.2.3.1)

Where can PKI be used by an enterprise? The following provides a short list of common use of PKIs:

- SSL/TLS certificate-based peer authentication
- Secure network traffic using IPsec VPNs
- Secure HTTPS web traffic
- Control access to the network using 802.1X authentication
- Secure email using the S/MIME protocol
- Secure instant messaging
- Approve and authorize applications with code signing
- Protect user data with the Encrypting File System (EFS)
- Implement two-factor authentication with smart cards
- Secure USB storage devices

Encrypting Network Transactions (9.2.3.2)

A security analysis must be able to recognize and solve potential problems related to permitting PKI-related solutions on the enterprise network.

Consider how the increase of SSL/TLS traffic poses a major security risk to enterprises because the traffic is encrypted and cannot be intercepted and monitored by normal means. Users can introduce malware or leak confidential information over an SSL/TLS connection.

Threat actors can use SSL/TLS to introduce regulatory compliance violations, viruses, malware, data loss, and intrusion attempts in a network.

Other SSL/TLS-related issues may be associated with validating the certificate of a web server. When this occurs, web browsers will display a security warning. PKI-related issues that are associated with security warnings include

- **Validity date range:** The X.509v3 certificates specify "not before" and "not after" dates. If the current date is outside the range, the web browser displays a message. Expired certificates may simply be the result of administrator oversight, but they may also reflect more serious conditions.
- **Signature validation error:** If a browser cannot validate the signature on the certificate, there is no assurance that the public key in the certificate is authentic. Signature validation will fail if the root certificate of the CA hierarchy is not available in the browser's certificate store.

Figure 9-57 displays an example of a signature validation error with the Cisco AnyConnect Secure Mobility Client.

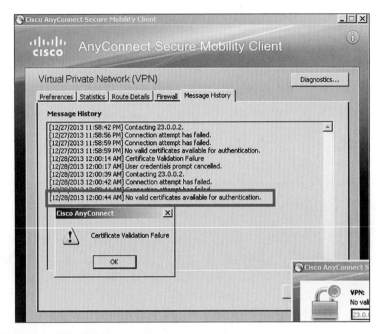

Figure 9-57 Signature Validation Error

Some of these issues can be avoided due to the fact that the SSL/TLS protocols are extensible and modular. This is known as a cipher suite. The key components of the cipher suite are the message authentication code (MAC) algorithm, the encryption algorithm, the key exchange algorithm, and the authentication algorithm. These can be changed without replacing the entire protocol. This is very helpful because the different algorithms continue to evolve. As cryptanalysis continues to reveal flaws in these algorithms, the cipher suite can be updated to patch these flaws. When the protocol versions within the cipher suite change, the version number of SSL/TLS changes as well.

Encryption and Security Monitoring (9.2.3.3)

Network monitoring becomes more challenging when packets are encrypted. However, security analysts must be aware of those challenges and address them as best as possible. For instance, when site-to-site VPNs are used, the IPS should be positioned so it can monitor unencrypted traffic.

However, the increase of HTTPS in the enterprise network introduces new challenges. Since HTTPS introduces end-to-end encrypted HTTP traffic (via TLS/SSL), it is not as easy to peek into user traffic.

Security analysts must know how to circumvent and solve these issues. Here is a list of some of the things that a security analyst could do:

- Configure rules to distinguish between SSL and non-SSL traffic, HTTPS and non-HTTPS SSL traffic.

- Enhance security through server certificate validation using CRLs and OCSP.

- Implement antimalware protection and URL filtering of HTTPS content.

- Deploy a Cisco SSL Appliance (Figure 9-58) to decrypt SSL traffic and send it to IPS appliances to identify risks normally hidden by SSL.

Cryptography is dynamic and always changing. A security analyst must maintain a good understanding of cryptographic algorithms and operations to be able to investigate cryptography-related security incidents.

Figure 9-58   Cisco SSL Appliance

There are two main ways in which cryptography impacts security investigations. First, attacks can be directed to specifically target the encryption algorithms themselves. After the algorithm has been cracked and the attacker has obtained the keys, any encrypted data that has been captured can be decrypted by the attacker and read, thus exposing private data. The security investigation is also affected because data can be hidden in plain sight by encrypting it. For example, command and control traffic that is encrypted with TLS/SSL most likely cannot be seen by a firewall. The command and control traffic between a command and control server and an infected computer in a secure network cannot be stopped if it cannot be seen and understood. The attacker would be able to continue using encrypted commands to infect more computers and possibly create a botnet. This type of traffic can be detected by decrypting the traffic and comparing it with known attack signatures, or by detecting anomalous TLS/SSL traffic. This is either very difficult and time consuming or a hit-or-miss process.

Summary (9.3)

In this chapter, you learned about the various cryptographic techniques and how their use affects network security monitoring. Securing communications with cryptography consists of four elements:

- Data confidentiality to guarantee that only authorized users can read the message
- Data integrity to guarantee that the message was not altered
- Origin authentication to guarantee that the message is not a forgery and does actually come from whom it states
- Data non-repudiation to guarantee that the sender cannot repudiate, or refute, the validity of a message sent

One of the main ways to verify and ensure data integrity is through the use of hash functions. Hash functions make it computationally infeasible for two different sets of data to come up with the same hash output. Three well-known hash functions include a;

- MD5 with a 128-bit digest
- SHA-1
- SHA-2

To include authentication along with message integrity, an HMAC is added as an input to a hash function. If two parties share a secret key and use HMAC functions for authentication, a properly constructed HMAC digest of a message that a party has received indicates that the other party was the originator of the message.

Confidentiality of the data is ensured through one of two types of encryption: symmetric or asymmetric.

Symmetric encryption uses the same key to encrypt and decrypt data. Well-known symmetric encryption algorithms include a;

- Data Encryption Standard (DES)
- 3DES (Triple DES)
- Advanced Encryption Standard (AES)
- Software-Optimized Encryption Algorithm (SEAL)
- Rivest Ciphers (RC)

Asymmetric encryption uses different keys to encrypt and decrypt data. Examples of protocols that use asymmetric key algorithms include:

- Internet Key Exchange (IKE)

- Secure Sockets Layer (SSL)

- Secure Shell (SSH)

- Pretty Good Privacy (PGP)

Diffie-Hellman (DH) is an asymmetric mathematical algorithm that allows two computers to generate an identical shared secret key without having communicated before. The new shared secret key is never actually exchanged between the sender and receiver.

The Public Key Infrastructure (PKI) relies on digital certificates. Digital certificates provide a digital signature that authenticates the source, guarantees the integrity of the data, and provides non-repudiation for the transaction. The three Digital Signature Standard (DSS) algorithms are:

- Digital Signature Algorithm (DSA)

- Rivest-Shamir-Adleman Algorithm (RSA)

- Elliptic Curve Digital Signature Algorithm (ECDSA)

Trusted third-party organizations such as VeriSign validate the authenticity of digital certificates. Digital certificates are used in a variety of PKI applications, including:

- IPsec VPNs

- HTTPS traffic

- 802.1X authentication

- Email and instant message security

- Code signing

- Encrypting File System (EFS)

- Two-factor authentication

- USB device security

Practice

The following activities provide practice with the topics introduced in this chapter. The Labs and Class Activities are available in the companion *CCNA Cybersecurity Operations Lab Manual* (ISBN: 9781587134388).

Class Activities

Class Activity 9.0.1.2: Creating Codes

Labs

Lab 9.1.1.6: Encrypting and Decrypting Data Using OpenSSL

Lab 9.1.1.7: Encrypting and Decrypting Data Using a Hacker Tool

Lab 9.1.1.8: Examining Telnet and SSH in Wireshark

Lab 9.1.2.5: Hashing Things Out

Lab 9.2.2.7: Certificate Authority Stores

Check Your Understanding

Complete all the review questions listed here to test your understanding of the topics and concepts in this chapter. The appendix "Answers to 'Check Your Understanding' Questions" lists the answers.

1. If an asymmetric algorithm uses a public key to encrypt data, what is used to decrypt it?

   A. DH

   B. A private key

   C. A digital certificate

   D. A different public key

2. Which type of attack does the use of HMACs protect against?

   A. DoS

   B. DDoS

   C. Brute force

   D. Man-in-the-middle

3. Which algorithm can ensure data confidentiality?

   A. MD5

   B. AES

   C. RSA

   D. PKI

4. What is the purpose of code signing?

   A. Data encryption

   B. Reliable transfer of data

   C. Source identity secrecy

   D. Integrity of source .EXE files

5. What are two symmetric encryption algorithms? (Choose two.)

   A. 3DES

   B. MD5

   C. AES

   D. HMAC

   E. SHA

6. What is the purpose of the DH algorithm?

   A. To provide non-repudiation support

   B. To support email data confidentiality

   C. To encrypt data traffic after a VPN is established

   D. To generate a shared secret between two hosts that have not communicated before

7. Which cryptographic technique provides both data integrity and non-repudiation?

   A. 3DES

   B. HMAC

   C. MD5

   D. SHA-1

8. In a hierarchical CA topology, where can a subordinate CA obtain a certificate for itself?

   A. From the root CA only

   B. From the root CA or from self-generation

   C. From the root CA or another subordinate CA at the same level

   D. From the root CA or another subordinate CA at a higher level

   E. From the root CA or another subordinate CA anywhere in the tree

9. Which objective of secure communications is achieved by encrypting data?

    A. Authentication

    B. Availability

    C. Confidentiality

    D. Integrity

10. Which statement describes the use of hashing?

    A. Hashing can be used to prevent both accidental and deliberate changes.

    B. Hashing can be used to detect both accidental and deliberate changes.

    C. Hashing can be used to detect accidental changes, but does not protect against deliberate changes.

    D. Hashing can be used to protect against deliberate changes, but does not detect accidental changes.

11. Which IETF standard defines the PKI digital certificate format?

    A. X.500

    B. X.509

    C. LDAP

    D. SSL/TLS

12. Which two statements correctly describe certificate classes used in the PKI? (Choose two.)

    A. A class 0 certificate is for testing purposes.

    B. A class 0 certificate is more trusted than a class 1 certificate.

    C. The lower the class number, the more trusted the certificate.

    D. A class 5 certificate is for users with a focus on verification of email.

    E. A class 4 certificate is for online business transactions between companies.

13. Alice and Bob want to use a CA authentication procedure to authenticate each other. What must be obtained first?

    A. CA self-signed certificate

    B. Self-signed certificates of two CA authorities

    C. Self-signed certificate of the other device and the CA certificate

    D. Self-signed certificate of the other device and the SCEP certificate

## CHAPTER 10

Endpoint Security and Analysis

Objectives

Upon completion of this chapter, you will be able to answer the following questions:

- What are some methods of mitigating malware?

- What are the contents of host-based IPS/IDS log entries?

- How do you use a public service to generate a malware analysis report?

- How do you classify endpoint vulnerability assessment information?

- What is the value of network and server profiling?

- How do you classify CVSS reports?

- What are the compliance frameworks and reporting methods?

- How are secure device management techniques used to protect data and assets?

- How are information security management systems used to protect assets?

Key Terms

This chapter uses the following key terms. You can find the definitions in the Glossary.

endpoint   *page 456*

antivirus/antimalware   *page 459*

host-based firewalls   *page 463*

host-based intrusion detection system (HIDS)   *page 464*

sandboxing   *page 469*

profiling   *page 470*

Payment Card Industry Data Security Standard (PCI DSS)   *page 480*

Federal Information Security Management Act of 2002 (FISMA)   *page 481*

Sarbanes-Oxley Act of 2002 (SOX)   *page 482*

Gramm-Leach-Bliley Act (GLBA)   *page 482*

Health Insurance Portability and Accountability Act (HIPAA)   *page 482*

Information Security Management System (ISMS)   *page 491*

Introduction (10.0)

Endpoints are the most numerous devices on a network; therefore, they are the targets of the majority of network attacks. A cybersecurity analyst must be familiar with the threats to endpoints, the methods for protecting endpoints from attacks, and the methods for detecting compromised endpoints.

This chapter discusses how to investigate endpoint vulnerabilities and attacks.

Endpoint Protection (10.1)

In this section, you will learn how to use a malware analysis website to generate a malware analysis report.

Antimalware Protection (10.1.1)

In this topic, you will learn how to explain methods of mitigating malware.

Endpoint Threats (10.1.1.1)

The term *endpoint* is defined in various ways. For the purpose of this course, we can define endpoints as hosts on the network that can access or be accessed by other hosts on the network. This obviously includes computers and servers, but many other devices can also access the network. With the rapid growth of the Internet of Things (IoT), other types of devices are now endpoints on the network. This includes networked security cameras, controllers, and even light bulbs and appliances. Each endpoint is potentially a way for malicious software to gain access to a network. In addition, new technologies, such as cloud, expand the boundaries of enterprise networks to include locations on the Internet for which the enterprises are not responsible.

Devices that remotely access networks through VPNs are also endpoints that need to be considered. These endpoints could inject malware into the VPN network from the public network.

The following points summarize some of the reasons why malware remains a major challenge:

- More than 75% of organizations experienced adware infections from 2015 to 2016.

- From 2016 to early 2017, global spam volume increased dramatically (Figure 10-1); 8 to 10% of this spam can be considered to be malicious (Figure 10-2).

- Malware that targets the Android mobile operating system was in the top ten most common types of malware found in 2016.

- Several common types of malware have been found to significantly change features in less than 24 hours in order to evade detection.

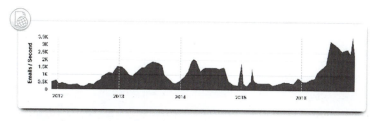

Figure 10-1 Total Spam Volume

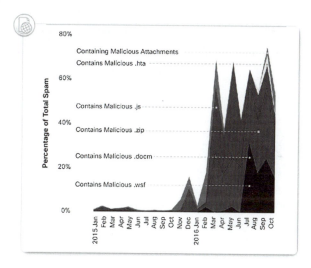

Figure 10-2 Malicious Spam Percentage

Endpoint Security (10.1.1.2)

News media commonly cover external network attacks on enterprise networks. These are some examples of such attacks:

- DoS attacks on an organization's network to degrade or even halt public access to it

- Breach of an organization's web server to deface their web presence

- Breach of an organization's data servers and hosts to steal confidential information

Various network security devices are required to protect the network perimeter from outside access. As shown in Figure 10-3, these devices could include a hardened router that is providing VPN services, a next-generation firewall (ASA in Figure 10-3), an IPS appliance, and an authentication, authorization, and accounting service (AAA server in Figure 10-3).

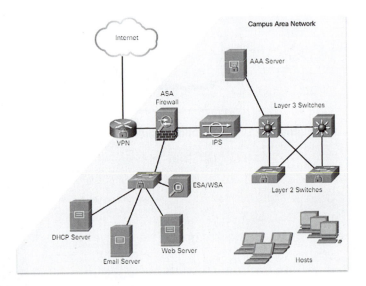

Figure 10-3   Internal LAN Elements

However, many attacks originate from inside the network. Therefore, securing an internal LAN is nearly as important as securing the outside network perimeter. Without a secure LAN, users within an organization are still susceptible to network threats and outages that can directly affect an organization's productivity and profit margin. After an internal host is infiltrated, it can become a starting point for an attacker to gain access to critical system devices, such as servers and sensitive information.

Specifically, there are two internal LAN elements to secure:

- **Endpoints:** Hosts commonly consist of laptops, desktops, printers, servers, and IP phones, all of which are susceptible to malware-related attacks.

- **Network infrastructure:** LAN infrastructure devices interconnect endpoints and typically include switches, wireless devices, and IP telephony devices. Most of these devices are susceptible to LAN-related attacks including MAC address table overflow attacks, spoofing attacks, DHCP-related attacks, LAN storm attacks, STP manipulation attacks, and VLAN attacks.

This chapter focuses on securing endpoints.

Host-Based Malware Protection (10.1.1.3)

The network perimeter is always expanding. People access corporate network resources with mobile devices that use remote access technologies such as VPN. These same devices are also used on unsecured, or minimally secured, public and home networks. Host-based antimalware/antivirus software and host-based firewalls are used to protect these devices.

Antivirus/Antimalware Software

Antivirus/antimalware is software that is installed on a host to detect and mitigate viruses and malware. Examples are Windows Defender (Figure 10-4), Norton Security, McAfee, Trend Micro, and others.

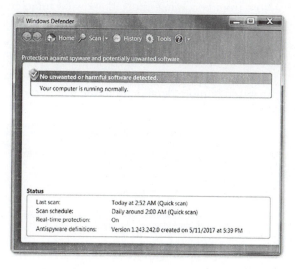

Figure 10-4   Windows Defender

Antimalware programs may detect viruses using three different approaches:

- **Signature-based:** This approach recognizes various characteristics of known malware files.

- **Heuristics-based:** This approach recognizes general features shared by various types of malware.

- **Behavior-based:** This approach employs analysis of suspicious behavior.

Many antivirus programs are able to provide real-time protection by analyzing data as it is used by the endpoint. These programs also scan for existing malware that may have entered the system prior to it being recognizable in real time.

Host-based antivirus protection is also known as agent-based. Agent-based antivirus runs on every protected machine. Agentless antivirus protection performs scans on hosts from a centralized system. Agentless systems have become popular for virtualized environments in which multiple OS instances are running on a host simultaneously. Agent-based antivirus running in each virtualized system can be a serious drain on system resources. Agentless antivirus for virtual hosts involves the use of a special security virtual appliance that performs optimized scanning tasks on the virtual hosts. An example of this is VMware's vShield.

Host-Based Firewall

This software is installed on a host. It restricts incoming and outgoing connections to connections initiated by that host only. Some firewall software can also prevent a host from becoming infected and stop infected hosts from spreading malware to other hosts. This function is included in some operating systems. For example, Windows includes Windows Defender (Figure 10-4) and Windows Firewall (Figure 10-5). Other solutions are produced by other companies or organizations. The Linux iptables and TCP Wrapper tools are examples. Host-based firewalls are discussed in more detail later in the chapter.

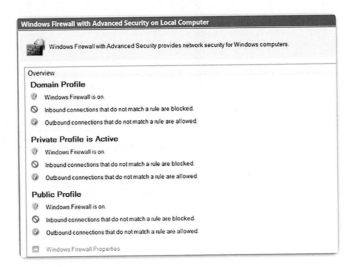

Figure 10-5   Windows Firewall

Host-Based Security Suites

It is recommended to install a host-based suite of security products on home networks as well as business networks. These host-based security suites include antivirus, anti-phishing, safe browsing, host-based intrusion prevention system, and firewall capabilities. These various security measures provide a layered defense that will protect against most common threats.

In addition to the protection functionality provided by host-based security products is the telemetry function. Most host-based security software includes robust logging functionality that is essential to cybersecurity operations. Some host-based security programs will submit logs to a central location for analysis.

There are many host-based security programs and suites available to users and enterprises. The independent testing laboratory AV-TEST, whose website is shown in Figure 10-6, provides high-quality reviews of host-based protections, as well as information about many other security products.

Figure 10-6   AV-TEST Website

Network-Based Malware Protection (10.1.1.4)

New security architectures for the borderless network address security challenges by having endpoints use network scanning elements. These devices provide many more layers of scanning than a single endpoint possibly could. Network-based malware prevention devices are also capable of sharing information among themselves to make better-informed decisions.

Protecting endpoints in a borderless network can be accomplished using both network-based and host-based techniques. The following are examples of devices and techniques that implement host protections and the network level:

- **Advanced Malware Protection (AMP):** This provides endpoint protection from viruses and malware.

- **Email Security Appliance (ESA):** This provides filtering of spam and potentially malicious emails before they reach the endpoint. An example is the Cisco ESA.

- **Web Security Appliance (WSA):** This provides filtering of websites and blacklisting to prevent hosts from reaching dangerous locations on the web. The Cisco WSA provides control over how users access the Internet and can enforce acceptable use policies, control access to specific sites and services, and scan for malware.

- **Network Admission Control (NAC):** This permits only authorized and compliant systems to connect to the network.

These technologies work in concert with each other to give more protection than host-based suites can provide, as shown in Figure 10-7.

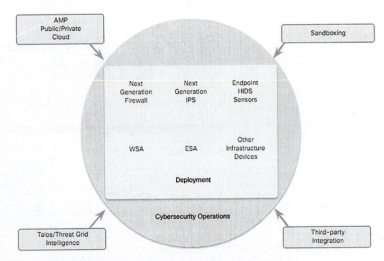

Figure 10-7 Network-Based Malware Protection Structure

Cisco Advanced Malware Protection (AMP) (10.1.1.5)

Cisco Advanced Malware Protection (AMP) addresses all phases of a malware attack, from breach prevention to detection, response, and remediation. AMP is an integrated, enterprise-class malware analysis and protection solution. It provides comprehensive protection for organizations across the attack continuum:

- **Before an attack:** AMP uses global threat intelligence from Cisco's Talos Security Intelligence and Research Group, and Threat Grid's threat intelligence feeds to strengthen defenses and protect against known and emerging threats.

- **During an attack:** AMP uses that intelligence coupled with known file signatures and Cisco Threat Grid's dynamic malware analysis technology. It identifies and blocks policy-violating file types and exploit attempts, as well as malicious files trying to infiltrate the network.

■ **After an attack:** The solution goes beyond point-in-time detection capabilities and continuously monitors and analyzes all file activity and traffic, regardless of disposition, searching for any indications of malicious behavior. This happens not only after an attack, but also after a file is initially inspected. If a file with an unknown or previously deemed "good" disposition starts behaving badly, AMP will detect it and instantly alert security teams with an indication of compromise. It then provides visibility into where the malware originated, what systems were affected, and what the malware is doing. It also provides the controls to rapidly respond to the intrusion and remediate it with a few clicks. This gives security teams the level of deep visibility and control they need to quickly detect attacks, determine the impact, and contain malware before it causes damage.

Cisco AMP is very flexible and can be deployed on endpoints, on Cisco ASA and FirePOWER firewalls, and on various other appliances, such as ESA, WSA, and Meraki MX.

Interactive Graphic

Activity 10.1.1.6: Identify Antimalware Terms and Concepts

Refer to the online course to complete this Activity.

Host-Based Intrusion Protection (10.1.2)

In this topic, you will learn how to explain host-based IPS/IDS log entries.

Host-Based Firewalls (10.1.2.1)

Host-based firewalls are stand-alone software programs that control traffic entering or leaving a computer. Firewall apps are also available for Android phones and tablets.

Host-based firewalls may use a set of predefined policies, or profiles, to control packets entering and leaving a computer. They also may have rules that can be directly modified or created to control access based on addresses, protocols, and ports. Host-based firewall applications can also be configured to issue alerts to users if suspicious behavior is detected. They can then offer the user the ability to allow an offending application to run or to be prevented from running in the future.

Logging data varies depending on the firewall application. It typically includes date and time of the event, whether the connection was allowed or denied, information about the source or destination IP addresses of packets, and the source and destination ports of the encapsulated segments. In addition, common activities such as DNS lookups and other routine events can show up in host-based firewall logs, so filtering and other parsing techniques are useful for inspecting large amounts of log data.

One approach to intrusion prevention is the use of distributed firewalls. Distributed firewalls combine features of host-based firewalls with centralized management. The management function pushes rules to the hosts and may also accept log files from the hosts.

Whether installed completely on the host or distributed, host-based firewalls are an important layer of network security along with network-based firewalls. Here are some examples of host-based firewalls:

- **Windows Firewall:** First included with Windows XP, Windows Firewall uses a profile-based approach to configuring firewall functionality. Access to public networks is assigned the restrictive Public firewall profile. The Private profile is for computers that are isolated from the Internet by other security devices, such as a home router with firewall functionality. The Domain profile is the third available profile. It is chosen for connections to a trusted network, such as a business network that is assumed to have an adequate security infrastructure. Windows Firewall has logging functionality and can be centrally managed with customized group security policies from a management server such as System Center 2012 Configuration Manager.

- **iptables:** This is an application that allows Linux system administrators to configure network access rules that are part of the Linux kernel Netfilter modules.

- **nftables:** The successor to iptables, nftables is a Linux firewall application that uses a simple virtual machine in the Linux kernel. Code is executed within the virtual machine that inspects network packets and implements decision rules regarding packet acceptance and forwarding.

- **TCP Wrapper:** This is a rule-based access control and logging system for Linux. Packet filtering is based on IP addresses and network services.

Host-Based Intrusion Detection (10.1.2.2)

The distinction between host-based intrusion detection and intrusion prevention is blurred. In fact, some sources refer to host-based intrusion detection and prevention systems (HIPDS). Because the industry seems to favor the use of the acronym HIDS, we will use it in our discussion here.

A *host-based intrusion detection system (HIDS)* is designed to protect hosts against known and unknown malware. An HIDS can perform detailed monitoring and reporting on the system configuration and application activity. It can provide log analysis, event correlation, integrity checking, policy enforcement, rootkit detection, and alerting. An HIDS will frequently include a management server endpoint, as shown in Figure 10-8.

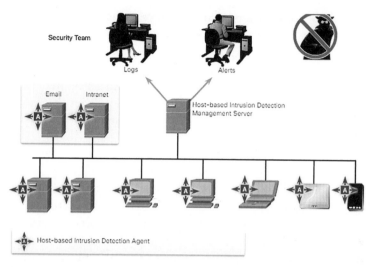

Figure 10-8   Host-Based Intrusion Detection Architecture

An HIDS is a comprehensive security application that combines the functionalities of antimalware applications with firewall functionality. An HIDS not only detects malware but also can prevent it from executing if it should reach a host. Because the HIDS software must run directly on the host, it is considered an agent-based system.

HIDS Operation (10.1.2.3)

It can be said that host-based security systems function as both detection and prevention systems because they prevent known attacks and detect unknown potential attacks. An HIDS uses both proactive and reactive strategies. An HIDS can prevent intrusion because it uses signatures to detect known malware and prevent it from infecting a system. However, this strategy is only good against known threats. Signatures are not effective against new, or zero day, threats. In addition, some malware families exhibit polymorphism. This means that variations of a type, or family, of malware may be created by attackers that will evade signature-based detections by changing aspects of the malware signature just enough so that it will not be detected. An additional set of strategies are used to detect the possibility of successful intrusions by malware that evades signature detection:

- **Anomaly-based:** Host system behavior is compared to a learned baseline model. Significant deviations from the baseline are interpreted as the result of some sort of intrusion. If an intrusion is detected, the HIDS can log details of the intrusion, send alerts to security management systems, and take action to prevent the attack. The measured baseline is derived from both user and system behavior. Because many things other than malware can cause system behavior to change, anomaly detection can create many erroneous results, which can increase the workload for security personnel and also lower the credibility of the system.

■ **Policy-based:** Normal system behavior is described by rules, or the violation of rules, that are predefined. Violation of these policies will result in action by the HIDS. The HIDS may attempt to shut down software processes that have violated the rules and can log these events and alert personnel to violations. Most HIDS software comes with a set of predefined rules. With some systems, administrators can create custom policies that can be distributed to hosts from a central policy management system.

HIDS Products (10.1.2.4)

There are a number of HIDS products on the market today. Most of them utilize software on the host and some sort of centralized security management functionality that allows integration with network security monitoring services and threat intelligence. Examples are Cisco AMP, AlienVault Unified Security Management (USM), Tripwire, and Open Source HIDS SECurity (OSSEC).

OSSEC uses a central manager server and agents that are installed on individual hosts. Currently, agents only exist for Microsoft Windows platforms. For other platforms, OSSEC can also operate as an agentless system, and can be deployed in virtual environments. The OSSEC server can also receive and analyze alerts from a variety of network devices and firewalls over syslog. OSSEC monitors system logs on hosts and also conducts file integrity checking. OSSEC can detect rootkits, and can also be configured to run scripts or applications on hosts in response to event triggers.

Interactive Graphic

Activity 10.1.2.5: Identify the Host-Based Intrusion Protection Terminology

Refer to the online course to complete this Activity.

Application Security (10.1.3)

In this topic, you will learn about attack surfaces, application blacklisting and whitelisting, and sandboxing.

Attack Surface (10.1.3.1)

Recall that a vulnerability is a weakness in a system or its design that could be exploited by a threat. An attack surface is the total sum of the vulnerabilities in a given system that is accessible to an attacker. The attack surface can consist of open ports on servers or hosts, software that runs on Internet-facing servers, wireless network protocols, and even users.

The attack surface is continuing to expand, as shown Figure 10-9.

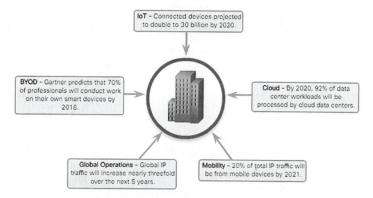

Figure 10-9 An Expanding Attack Surface

More devices are connecting to networks through the Internet of Things (IoT) and Bring Your Own Device (BYOD). Much of network traffic now flows between devices and some location in the cloud. Mobile device use continues to increase. All of these trends contribute to a prediction that global IP traffic will increase threefold in the next five years.

The SANS Institute describes three components of the attack surface:

- **Network Attack Surface:** The attack exploits vulnerabilities in networks. This can include conventional wired and wireless network protocols, as well as other wireless protocols used by smartphones or IoT devices. Network attacks also exploit vulnerabilities at the network and transport layers.

- **Software Attack Surface:** The attack is delivered through exploitation of vulnerabilities in web, cloud, or host-based software applications.

- **Human Attack Surface:** The attack exploits weaknesses in user behavior. Such attacks include social engineering, malicious behavior by trusted insiders, and user error.

Application Blacklisting and Whitelisting (10.1.3.2)

One way of decreasing the attack surface is to limit access to potential threats by creating lists of prohibited applications. This is known as blacklisting.

Application blacklists can dictate which user applications are not permitted to run on a computer, as shown in Figure 10-10. Similarly, whitelists can specify which programs are allowed to run, also shown in Figure 10-10. In this way, known vulnerable applications can be prevented from creating vulnerabilities on network hosts.

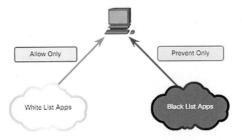

Figure 10-10   Application Blacklisting and Whitelisting

Whitelists are created in accordance with a security baseline that has been established by an organization. The baseline establishes an accepted amount of risk, and the environmental components that contribute to that level of risk. Non-whitelisted software can violate the established security baseline by increasing risk.

Figure 10-11 shows the Windows Local Group Policy Editor blacklisting and whitelisting settings.

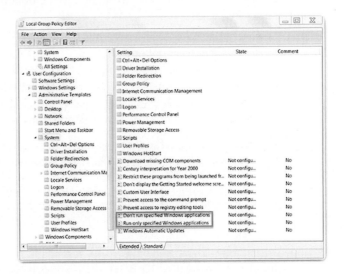

Figure 10-11   Editing Windows Local Group Policy

Figure 10-12 shows how entries can be added, in this case to the list of blacklisted applications.

Websites can also be whitelisted and blacklisted. These blacklists can be manually created, or they can be obtained from various security services. Blacklists can be continuously updated by security services and distributed to firewalls and other security systems that use them. Cisco's FireSIGHT security management system is an example of a device that can access the Cisco Talos security intelligence service to obtain blacklists. These blacklists can then be distributed to security devices within an enterprise network.

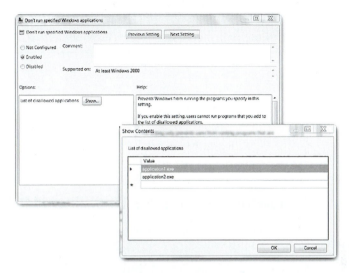

Figure 10-12   Verifying Windows Blacklisted Applications

System-Based Sandboxing (10.1.3.3)

Sandboxing is a technique that allows suspicious files to be executed and analyzed in a safe environment. Automated malware analysis sandboxes offer tools that analyze malware behavior. These tools observe the effects of running unknown malware so that features of malware behavior can be determined and then used to create defenses against it.

As mentioned previously, polymorphic malware changes frequently and new malware appears regularly. Malware will enter the network despite the most robust perimeter and host-based security systems. HIDS and other detection systems can create alerts on suspected malware that may have entered the network and executed on a host. Systems such as Cisco AMP can track the trajectory of a file through the network, and can "roll back" network events to obtain a copy of the downloaded file. This file can then be executed in a sandbox, such as Cisco Threat Grid Glovebox, and the activities of the file documented by the system. This information can then be used to create signatures to prevent the file from entering the network again. The information can also be used to create detection rules and automated plays that will identify other systems that have been infected.

Cuckoo Sandbox is a free malware analysis system sandbox. It can be run locally and have malware samples submitted to it for analysis.

A number of online public sandboxes also exist. These services allow malware samples to be uploaded for analysis. Some of these services are VirusTotal, Payload Security VxStream Sandbox, and Malwr.

Video

Video Demonstration 10.1.3.4: Using a Sandbox to Launch Malware

Refer to the online course to view this video.

Endpoint Vulnerability Assessment (10.2)

In this section, you will learn how to classify endpoint vulnerability assessment information.

Network and Server Profiling (10.2.1)

In this topic, you will learn how to explain the value of network and server profiling.

Network Profiling (10.2.1.1)

In order to detect serious security incidents, it is important to understand, characterize, and analyze information about normal network functioning. Networks, servers, and hosts all exhibit typical behavior for a given point in time. Network and device *profiling* can provide a baseline that serves as a reference point. Unexplained deviations from the baseline may indicate a compromise.

Increased utilization of WAN links at unusual times can indicate a network breach and exfiltration of data. Hosts that begin to access obscure Internet servers, resolve domains that are obtained through dynamic DNS, or use protocols or services that are not needed by the system user can also indicate compromise. Deviations in network behavior are difficult to detect if normal behavior is not known.

Tools like NetFlow and Wireshark can be used to characterize normal network traffic characteristics. Because organizations can make different demands on their networks depending on the time of day or day of the year, network baselining should be carried out over an extended period of time. Some questions to ask when establishing a network baseline, as shown Figure 10-13, address important elements of the network profile:

- **Session duration:** This is the time between the establishment of a data flow and its termination.

- **Total throughput:** This is the amount of data passing from a given source to a given destination in a given period of time.

- **Ports used:** This is a list of TCP or UDP processes that are available to accept data.

- **Critical asset address space:** These are the IP addresses or the logical location of essential systems or data.

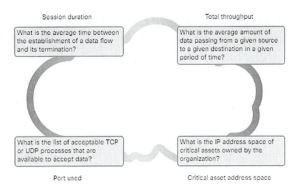

Session duration

What is the average time between the establishment of a data flow and its termination?

Total throughput

What is the average amount of data passing from a given source to a given destination in a given period of time?

What is the list of acceptable TCP or UDP processes that are available to accept data?

What is the IP address space of critical assets owned by the organization?

Port used

Critical asset address space

Figure 10-13 Elements of a Network Profile

In addition, a profile of the types of traffic that typically enter and leave the network is an important tool in understanding network behavior. Malware can use unusual ports that may not be typically seen during normal network operation. Host-to-host traffic is another important metric. Most network clients communicate directly with servers, so an increase of traffic between clients can indicate that malware is spreading laterally through the network. Finally, changes in user behavior, as revealed by AAA, server logs, or a user profiling system like Cisco Identity Services Engine (ISE), is another valuable indicator. Knowing how individual users typically use the network leads to detection of potential compromise of user accounts. A user who suddenly begins logging in to the network at strange times from a remote location should raise alarms if this behavior is a deviation from a known norm.

Server Profiling (10.2.1.2)

Server profiling is used to establish the accepted operating state of servers. A server profile is a security baseline for a given server. It establishes the network, user, and application parameters that are accepted for a specific server.

In order to establish a server profile, it is important to understand the function that a server is intended to perform in a network. From there, various operating and usage parameters can be defined and documented. A server profile may establish the following:

- **Listening ports:** These are the TCP and UDP daemons and ports that are allowed to be open on the server.

- **User accounts:** These are the parameters defining user access and behavior.

- **Service accounts:** These are the definitions of the type of service that an application is allowed to run on a given host.

- **Software environment:** This contains the tasks, processes, and applications that are permitted to run on the server.

Network Anomaly Detection (10.2.1.3)

Network behavior is described by a large amount of diverse data such as the features of packet flow, features of the packets themselves, and telemetry from multiple sources. One approach to detection of network attacks is the analysis of this diverse, unstructured data using Big Data analytics techniques.

This entails the use of sophisticated statistical and machine learning techniques to compare normal performance baselines with network performance at a given time. Significant deviations can be indicators of compromise.

Anomaly detection can recognize network congestion caused by worm traffic that exhibits scanning behavior. Anomaly detection also can identify infected hosts on the network that are scanning for other vulnerable hosts.

Figure 10-14 illustrates a simplified version of an algorithm designed to detect an unusual condition at the border routers of an enterprise.

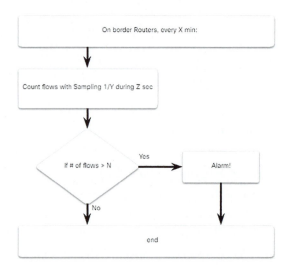

Figure 10-14   Example of a Simple Anomaly Detection Algorithm

For example, the cybersecurity analyst could provide the following values:

- $X = 5$
- $Y = 100$
- $Z = 30$
- $N = 500$

Now, the algorithm can be interpreted as "Every 5th minute, get a sampling of 1/100th of the flows during second 30. If the number of flows is greater than 500, generate an alarm. If the number of flows is less than 500, do nothing." This is a simple example of using a traffic profile to identify the potential for data loss.

Network Vulnerability Testing (10.2.1.4)

Most organizations connect to public networks in some way due to the need to access the Internet. These organizations must also provide Internet-facing services of various types to the public. Because of the vast number of potential vulnerabilities, and the fact that new vulnerabilities can be created within an organization network and its Internet-facing services, periodic security testing is essential. Network security can be tested using a variety of tools and services. Various types of tests can be performed:

- **Risk analysis:** This is a discipline in which analysts evaluate the risk posed by vulnerabilities to a specific organization. A risk analysis includes assessment of the likelihood of attacks, identifies types of likely threat actors, and evaluates the impact of successful exploits on the organization.

- **Vulnerability assessment:** This test employs software to scan Internet-facing servers and internal networks for various types of vulnerabilities. These vulnerabilities include unknown infections, weaknesses in web-facing database services, missing software patches, unnecessary listening ports, etc. Tools for vulnerability assessment include the open source OpenVAS platform, Microsoft Baseline Security Analyzer, Nessus, Qualys, and FireEye Mandiant services. Vulnerability assessment includes, but goes beyond, port scanning.

- **Penetration testing:** This type of test uses authorized simulated attacks to test the strength of network security. Internal personnel with hacker experience, or professional ethical hackers, identify assets that could be targeted by threat actors. A series of exploits is used to test security of those assets. Simulated exploit software tools are frequently used. Penetration testing does not only verify that vulnerabilities exist, it actually exploits those vulnerabilities to determine the potential impact of a successful exploit. An individual penetration test is often known as a pen test. Metasploit is a tool used in penetration testing. Core Impact offers penetration testing software and services.

Interactive Graphic

Activity 10.2.1.5: Identify the Elements of Network Profiling

Refer to the online course to complete this Activity.

Common Vulnerability Scoring System (CVSS) (10.2.2)

In this topic, you will learn how to classify CVSS reports.

CVSS Overview (10.2.2.1)

The Common Vulnerability Scoring System (CVSS) is a risk assessment designed to convey the common attributes and severity of vulnerabilities in computer hardware and software systems. The third revision, CVSS 3.0, is a vendor-neutral, industry-standard, open framework for weighting the risks of a vulnerability using a variety of metrics. These weights combine to provide a score of the risk inherent in a vulnerability. The numeric score can be used to determine the urgency of the vulnerability, and the priority of addressing it. The benefits of the CVSS can be summarized as follows:

- It provides standardized vulnerability scores that should be meaningful across organizations.

- It provides an open framework with the meaning of each metric openly available to all users.

- It helps prioritize risk in a way that is meaningful to individual organizations.

The Forum of Incident Response and Security Teams (FIRST) has been designated as the custodian of the CVSS to promote its adoption globally. Version 3.0 was under development for 3 years, and Cisco and other industry partners contributed to the standard.

CVSS Metric Groups (10.2.2.2)

Before performing a CVSS assessment, it is important to know key terms that are used in the assessment instrument.

Many of the metrics address the role of what the CVSS calls an authority. An authority is a computer entity, such as a database, operating system, or virtual sandbox, which grants and manages access and privileges to users.

As shown Figure 10-15, the CVSS uses three groups of metrics to assess vulnerability: Base, Temporal, and Environmental.

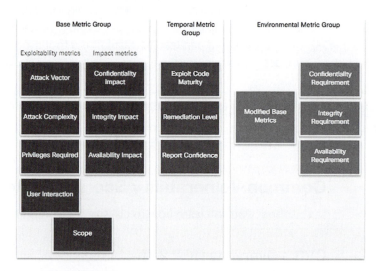

Figure 10-15 CVSS Metric Groups

Base Metric Group

This represents the characteristics of a vulnerability that are constant over time and across contexts. It has two classes of metrics:

- **Exploitability:** These are features of the exploit such as the vector, complexity, and user interaction required by the exploit.

- **Impact:** The impacts of the exploit are rooted in the CIA triad of confidentiality, integrity, and availability.

Temporal Metric Group

This measures the characteristics of a vulnerability that may change over time, but not across user environments. Over time, the severity of a vulnerability will change as it is detected and measures to counter it are developed. The severity of a new vulnerability may be high, but will decrease as patches, signatures, and other countermeasures are developed.

Environmental Metric Group

This measures the aspects of a vulnerability that are rooted in a specific organization's environment. These metrics help to guide consequences within an organization and also allow adjustment of metrics that are less relevant to what an organization does.

CVSS Base Metric Group (10.2.2.3)

The Base metric group Exploitability metrics include the following:

- **Attack Vector (AV):** This is a metric that reflects the proximity of the threat actor to the vulnerable component. The more remote the threat actor is to the component, the higher the severity. Threat actors close to your network or inside your network are easier to detect and mitigate.

- **Attack Complexity (AC):** This is a metric that expresses the number of components, software, hardware, or networks that are beyond the attacker's control and that must be present in order for a vulnerability to be successfully exploited.

- **Privileges Required (PR):** This is a metric that captures the level of access that is required for a successful exploit of the vulnerability.

- **User Interaction (UI):** This metric expresses the presence or absence of the requirement for user interaction in order for an exploit to be successful.

- **Scope (S):** This metric expresses whether multiple authorities must be involved in an exploit. This is expressed as whether the initial authority changes to a second authority during the exploit.

The Base metric group Impact metrics increase with the degree or consequence of loss due to the impacted component. Impact metrics include:

- **Confidentiality Impact (C):** This is a metric that measures the impact to confidentiality due to a successfully exploited vulnerability. Confidentiality refers to the limiting of access to only authorized users.

- **Integrity Impact (I):** This is a metric that measures the impact to integrity due to a successfully exploited vulnerability. Integrity refers to the trustworthiness and authenticity of information.

- **Availability Impact (A):** This is a metric that measures the impact to availability due to a successfully exploited vulnerability. Availability refers to the accessibility of information and network resources. Attacks that consume network bandwidth, processor cycles, or disk space all impact the availability.

The CVSS Process (10.2.2.4)

The CVSS Base metric group is designed as a way to assess security vulnerabilities found in software and hardware systems. It describes the severity of a vulnerability based on the characteristics of a successful exploit of the vulnerability. The other metric groups modify the base severity score by accounting for how the base severity rating is affected by time and environmental factors.

The CVSS process uses a tool called the CVSS v3.0 Calculator, shown in Figure 10-16.

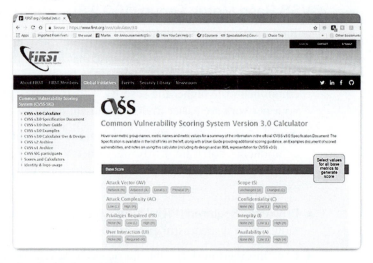

Figure 10-16   CVSS Calculator

The calculator is similar to a questionnaire in which choices are made that describe the vulnerability for each metric group. After all choices are made, a score is generated. Pop-up text that offers an explanation for each metric and metric value are displayed by hovering a mouse over each. Choices are made by choosing one of the values for the metric. Only one choice can be made per metric.

A detailed user guide that defines metric criteria, examples of assessments of common vulnerabilities, and the relationship of metric values to the final score is available to support the process.

After the Base metric group is completed, the numeric severity rating is displayed, as shown in Figure 10-17.

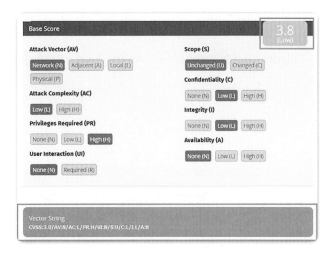

Figure 10-17   Example of a Base Score Calculation

A vector string is also created that summarizes the choices made. If other metric groups are completed, those values are appended to the vector string. The string consists of the initial(s) for the metric, and an abbreviated value for the selected metric value separated by a colon. The metric-value pairs are separated by slashes. An example vector for the Base metric group is shown in the Figure 10-18. The vector strings allow the results of the assessment to be easily shared and compared.

In order for a score to be calculated for the Temporal or Environmental metric groups, the Base metric group must first be completed. The Temporal and Environmental metric values then modify the Base metric results to provide an overall score. The interaction of the scores for the metric groups is shown in Figure 10-19.

CVSS:3.0/AV:N/AC:L/PR:H/UI:N/S:U/C:L/I:L/A:N

Metric Name	Initials	Possible Values	Values
Attack Vector	AV	[N,A,L,P]	N = network A = adjacent L = local P = physical
Attack Complexity	AC	[L,H]	L = low H = high
Privileges Required	PR	[N,L,H]	N = none L = low H = high
User Interaction	UI	[N,R]	N = none R= required
Scope	S	[U,C]	U = unchanged C = changed
Confidentiality Impact	C	[H,L,N]	H = high L = low N = none
Integrity Impact	I	[H,L,N]	H = high L = low N = none
Availability Impact	A	[H,L,N]	H = high L = low

Metric Name	Values
Attack Vector, AV	Network
Attack Complexity, AC	Low
Privileges Required, PR	High
User Interaction, UI	None
Scope, S	Unchanged
Confidentiality Impact, C	Low
Integrity Impact, I	Low
Availability Impact, A	None

Figure 10-18   Example of a Vector for the Base Group Metric

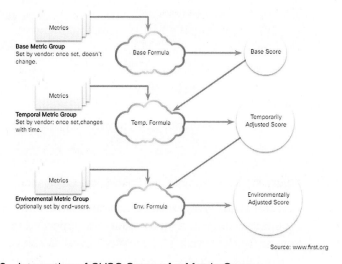

Figure 10-19   Interaction of CVSS Scores for Metric Groups

CVSS Reports (10.2.2.5)

The ranges of scores and the corresponding qualitative meaning are shown in Table 10-1.

Table 10-1 CVSS Qualitative Scores for Ranges

Rating	CVSS Score
None	0
Low	0.1 to 3.9
Medium	4.0 to 6.9
High	7.0 to 8.9
Critical	9.0 to 10.0

Frequently, the Base and Temporal metric group scores will be supplied to customers by the application or security vendor in whose product the vulnerability has been discovered. The affected organization completes the Environmental metric group to tailor the vendor-supplied scoring to the local context.

The resulting score serves to guide the affected organization in the allocation of resources to address the vulnerability. The higher the severity rating, the greater the potential impact of an exploit and the greater the urgency in addressing the vulnerability. While not as precise as the numeric CVSS scores, the qualitative labels are very useful for communicating with stakeholders who are unable to relate to the numeric scores.

In general, any vulnerability that exceeds 3.9 should be addressed. The higher the rating level, the greater the urgency for remediation.

Other Vulnerability Information Sources (10.2.2.6)

There are other important vulnerability information sources. These work together with the CVSS to provide a comprehensive assessment of vulnerability severity. There are two systems that operate in the United States: CVE and NVD.

Common Vulnerabilities and Exposures (CVE)

This is a dictionary of common names, in the form of CVE Identifiers, for known cybersecurity vulnerabilities. The CVE Identifier provides a standard way to research a reference to vulnerabilities. When a vulnerability has been identified, CVE Identifiers can be used to access fixes. In addition, threat intelligence services use CVE Identifiers, and they appear in various security system logs. The CVE Details website (https://www.cvedetails.com/) provides a linkage between CVSS scores and CVE information. It allows browsing of CVE vulnerability records by CVSS severity rating.

National Vulnerability Database (NVD)

This database utilizes CVE identifiers and supplies additional information on vulnerabilities such as CVSS threat scores, technical details, affected entities, and resources for further investigation. The database was created and is maintained by the U.S. National Institute of Standards and Technology (NIST) agency.

Activity 10.2.2.7: Identify CVSS Metrics

Refer to the online course to complete this Activity.

Compliance Frameworks (10.2.3)

In this topic, you will learn how to explain compliance frameworks and reporting.

Compliance Regulations (10.2.3.1)

Recent history is full of instances in which sensitive information has been lost to threat actors. Recent security breaches at large retailers have resulted in the loss of personally identifiable information (PII) for millions of people. Corporations have lost valuable intellectual property which has resulted in the loss of millions of dollars in revenue. In addition, security breaches have resulted in the loss of sensitive information related to national security.

To prevent similar losses, a number of security compliance regulations have emerged. The regulations offer a framework for practices that enhance information security while also stipulating incidence response actions and penalties for failure to comply. Organizations can verify compliance through the process of compliance assessment and audit. Assessments verify compliance or noncompliance for informational purposes. Audits also verify compliance but can result in consequences, such as financial penalties or loss of business opportunity.

This topic will discuss and differentiate the important and far reaching compliance regulations.

Overview of Regulatory Standards (10.2.3.2)

There are five major regulatory compliance regulations.

Payment Card Industry Data Security Standard (PCI DSS)

PCI DSS is a proprietary, non-governmental standard maintained by the Payment Card Industry Security Standards Council, which was formed by the five major credit card companies. The standard specifies requirements for the secure handling of customer credit card data by merchants and service providers. It dictates standards for how credit card information is to be stored and transmitted, and when customer information must be removed from storage systems.

PCI DSS applies to any entity that stores, processes, and/or transmits data about credit cardholders. As shown in Figure 10-20, cardholder data includes

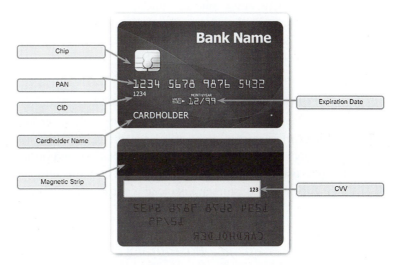

Figure 10-20   Bank Cardholder Data

- Cardholder name

- Primary account number (PAN)

- Expiration date

- Service Code (part of the magnetic strip)

- Card Verification Code (CVC), Card Verification Value (CVV), Card Security Code (CSC)

- Card Identification Code (CID)

- Sensitive data stored on magnetic strip or chip

Many network management platforms include compliance reporting in their security management–related functionalities.

Federal Information Security Management Act of 2002 (FISMA)

FISMA was established by NIST by an act of the U.S. Congress. FISMA regulations specify security standards for U.S. government systems and contractors to the U.S. government. FISMA also provides standards for the categorization of information and information systems according to a range of risk levels, and requirements for the security of information in each risk category.

Sarbanes-Oxley Act of 2002 (SOX)

SOX set new or expanded requirements for all U.S. public company boards, management, and public accounting firms regarding the way in which corporations control and disclose financial information. The act is designed to ensure the integrity of financial practices and reporting. It also dictates controls for access to financial information and information systems.

Gramm-Leach-Bliley Act (GLBA)

GLBA established that financial institutions must ensure the security and confidentiality of customer information; protect against any anticipated threats or hazards to the security or integrity of such information; and protect against unauthorized access to or use of customer information that could result in substantial harm or inconvenience to any customer. Financial institutions are considered to be banks, brokerages, insurance companies, etc.

Health Insurance Portability and Accountability Act (HIPAA)

HIPAA requires that all patient personally identifiable healthcare information be stored, maintained, and transmitted in ways that ensure patient privacy and confidentiality. HIPAA stipulates controlled access policies and data encryption of patient information. HIPAA specifies detailed administrative safeguards and implementation specifications in the areas of security management, workforce security, and information access management, among others.

Interactive Graphic

Activity 10.2.3.3: Identify Regulatory Standards

Refer to the online course to complete this Activity.

Secure Device Management (10.2.4)

In this topic, you will learn how secure device management techniques are used to protect data and assets.

Risk Management (10.2.4.1)

Risk management involves the selection and specification of security controls for an organization. It is part of an ongoing organization-wide information security program that involves the management of the risk to the organization or to individuals associated with the operation of a system.

Risk management is an ongoing, multistep, cyclical process, as shown in Figure 10-21.

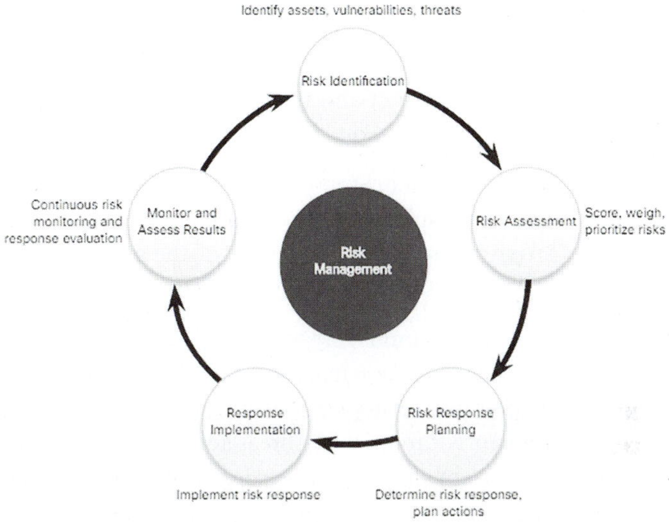

Figure 10-21   Risk Management

Risk is determined as the relationship between threat, vulnerability, and the nature of the organization. It first involves answering the following questions as part of a risk assessment:

- Who are the threat actors who want to attack us?

- What vulnerabilities can threat actors exploit?

- How would we be affected by attacks?

- What is the likelihood that different attacks will occur?

NIST Special Publication 800-30 describes risk assessment as:

> …the process of identifying, estimating, and prioritizing information security risks. Assessing risk requires the careful analysis of threat and vulnerability information to determine the extent to which circumstances or events could adversely impact an organization and the likelihood that such circumstances or events will occur.

A mandatory activity in risk assessment is the identification of threats and vulnerabilities and the matching of threats with vulnerabilities in what is often called threat-vulnerability (T-V) pairing. The T-V pairs can then be used as a baseline to indicate risk before security controls are implemented. This baseline can then be compared to ongoing risk assessments as a means of evaluating risk management effectiveness. This part of risk assessment is referred to as determining the inherent risk profile of an organization.

After the risks are identified, they may be scored or weighted as a way of prioritizing risk reduction strategies. For example, vulnerabilities that are found to have corresponded with multiple threats can receive higher ratings. In addition, T-V pairs that map to the greatest institutional impact will also receive higher weightings.

There are four potential ways to respond to risks that have been identified, based on their weightings or scores:

■ **Risk avoidance:** Stop performing the activities that create risk. It is possible that as a result of a risk assessment, it is determined that the risk involved in an activity outweighs the benefit of the activity to the organization. If this is found to be true, then it may be determined that the activity should be discontinued.

■ **Risk reduction:** Decrease the risk by taking measures to reduce vulnerability. This involves implementing management approaches discussed earlier in this chapter. For example, if an organization uses server operating systems that are frequently targeted by threat actors, risk can be reduced through ensuring that the servers are patched as soon as vulnerabilities have been addressed.

■ **Risk sharing:** Shift some of the risk to other parties. For example, a risk-sharing technique might be to outsource some aspects of security operations to third parties. Hiring a security as a service (SECaaS) CSIRT to perform security monitoring is an example. Another example is to buy insurance that will help to mitigate some of the financial losses due to a security incident.

■ **Risk retention:** Accept the risk and its consequences. This strategy is acceptable for risks that have low potential impact and relatively high cost of mitigation or reduction. Other risks that may be retained are those that are so dramatic that they cannot realistically be avoided, reduced, or shared.

Interactive Graphic

Activity 10.2.4.2: Identify the Risk Response

Refer to the online course to complete this Activity.

Vulnerability Management (10.2.4.3)

According to NIST, vulnerability management is a security practice designed to proactively prevent the exploitation of IT vulnerabilities that exist within an organization. The expected result is to reduce the time and money spent dealing with vulnerabilities and the exploitation of those vulnerabilities. Proactively managing vulnerabilities of systems will reduce or eliminate the potential for exploitation, and involve considerably less time and effort than responding after an exploitation has occurred.

Vulnerability management requires a robust means of identifying vulnerabilities based on vendor security bulletins and other information systems such as CVE.

Security personnel must be competent in assessing the impact, if any, of vulnerability information they have received. Solutions should be identified with effective means of implementing and assessing the unanticipated consequences of implemented solutions. Finally, the solution should be tested to verify that the vulnerability has been eliminated.

The steps in the Vulnerability Management Life Cycle, shown in Figure 10-22, are described below:

Figure 10-22   Vulnerability Management Life Cycle

- **Discover:** Inventory all assets across the network and identify host details, including operating systems and open services, to identify vulnerabilities. Develop a network baseline. Identify security vulnerabilities on a regular automated schedule.

- **Prioritize assets:** Categorize assets into groups or business units, and assign a business value to asset groups based on their criticality to business operations.

- **Assess:** Determine a baseline risk profile to eliminate risks based on asset criticality, vulnerability, threats, and asset classification.

- **Report:** Measure the level of business risk associated with your assets according to your security policies. Document a security plan, monitor suspicious activity, and describe known vulnerabilities.

- **Remediate:** Prioritize according to business risk and address vulnerabilities in order of risk.

- **Verify:** Verify that threats have been eliminated through follow-up audits.

Asset Management (10.2.4.4)

Asset management involves the implementation of systems that track the location and configuration of networked devices and software across an enterprise. As part of any security management plan, organizations must know what equipment accesses the network, where that equipment is within the enterprise and logically on the network, and what software and data those systems store or can access. Asset management not only tracks corporate assets and other authorized devices, but also can be used to identify devices that are not authorized on the network.

In publication NISTIR 8011 Volume 2, NIST specifies the detailed records that should be kept for each relevant device. NIST describes potential techniques and tools for operationalizing an asset management process:

- Automated discovery and inventory of the actual state of devices
- Articulation of the desired state for those devices using policies, plans, and procedures in the organization's information security plan
- Identification of noncompliant authorized assets
- Remediation or acceptance of device state, possible iteration of desired state definition
- Repeat the process at regular intervals, or ongoing

Figure 10-23 provides an overview of this process.

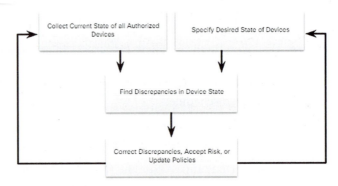

Figure 10-23   An Operational Concept for Asset Management

Mobile Device Management (10.2.4.5)

Mobile device management (MDM), especially in the age of BYOD, presents special challenges to asset management. Mobile devices cannot be physically controlled on the premises of an organization. They can be lost, stolen, or tampered with, putting data and network access at risk. Part of an MDM plan is taking action when devices leave the custody of the responsible party. Measures that can be taken include disabling the lost device, encrypting the data on the device, and enhancing device access with more robust authentication measures.

Due to the diversity of mobile devices, it is possible that some devices that will be used on the network are inherently less secure than others. Network administrators should assume that all mobile devices are untrusted until they have been properly secured by the organization.

MDM systems, such as Cisco Meraki Systems Manager, shown in Figure 10-24, allow security personnel to configure, monitor, and update a very diverse set of mobile clients from the cloud.

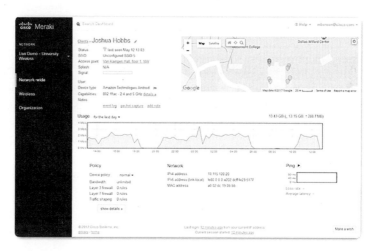

Figure 10-24   Cisco Meraki Systems Manager

Configuration Management (10.2.4.6)

Configuration management addresses the inventory and control of hardware and software configurations of systems. Secure device configurations reduce security risk. For example, an organization provides many computers and laptops to its workers. This enlarges the attack surface for the organization, because each system may be vulnerable to exploits. To manage this, the organization may create baseline software images and hardware configurations for each type of machine. These images may include a basic package of required software, endpoint security software, and customized security policies that control user access to aspects of the system configuration that could be made vulnerable. Hardware configurations may specify the permitted types of network interfaces and the permitted types of external storage.

Configuration management extends to the software and hardware configuration of networking devices and servers as well. As defined by NIST, configuration management "comprises a collection of activities focused on establishing and maintaining the integrity of products and systems, through control of the processes for initializing, changing, and monitoring the configurations of those products and systems."

For internetworking devices, software tools are available that will back up configurations, detect changes in configuration files, and enable bulk change of configurations across a number of devices.

With the advent of cloud data centers and virtualization, management of numerous servers presents special challenges. Configuration management tools like Puppet, Chef, Ansible, and SaltStack were developed to allow efficient management of servers that enable cloud-based computing.

Enterprise Patch Management (10.2.4.7)

Patch management is related to vulnerability management. Vulnerabilities frequently appear in critical client, server, and networking device operating systems and firmware. Application software, especially Internet applications and frameworks like Acrobat, Flash, and Java, also are frequently discovered to have vulnerabilities. Patch management involves all aspects of software patching, including identifying required patches, acquiring, distributing, and installing required patches, and verifying that the patches are installed on all required systems. Installing patches is frequently the most effective way to mitigate software vulnerabilities. Sometimes, it is the only way to do so.

Patch management is required by some security compliance regulations, such as SOX and HIPAA. Failure to implement patches in a systematic and timely manner could result in audit failure and penalties for noncompliance. Patch management depends on asset management data to identify systems that are running software that requires patching. Figure 10-25 shows a screenshot of the SolarWinds Patch Manager tool.

Patch Management Techniques (10.2.4.8)

At the enterprise level, patch management is most efficiently run from a patch management system. Most patch management systems incorporate a client-centralized server architecture, as do other end point–related security systems. There are three patch management technologies:

■ **Agent-based:** This requires a software agent to be running on each host to be patched. The agent reports whether vulnerable software is installed on the host. The agent communicates with the patch management server, determines if patches exist that require installation, and installs the patches (Figure 10-26). The agent runs with sufficient privileges to allow it to install the patches. Agent-based approaches are the preferred means of patching mobile devices.

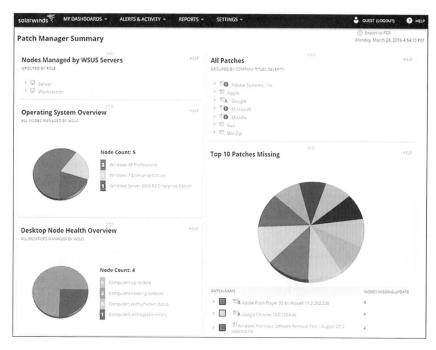

Figure 10-25   SolarWinds Patch Manager

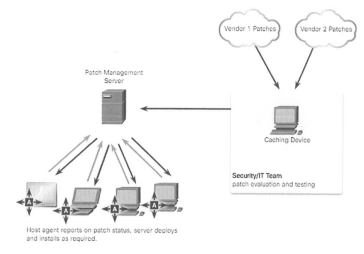

Figure 10-26   Agent-Based Patch Management

- **Agentless scanning:** Patch management servers scan the network for devices that require patching. The server determines which patches are required and installs those patches on the clients (Figure 10-27). Only devices that are on scanned network segments can be patched in this way. This can be a problem for mobile devices.

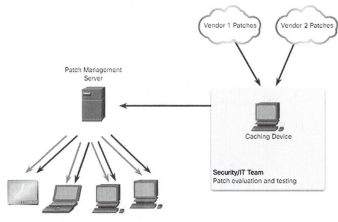

Figure 10-27   Agentless Scanning Patch Management

■ **Passive network monitoring:** Devices requiring patching are identified through the monitoring of traffic on the network (Figure 10-28). This approach is only effective for software that includes version information in its network traffic.

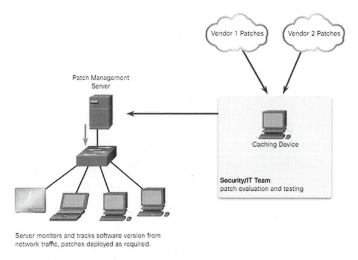

Figure 10-28   Passive Network Monitoring Patch Management

Interactive Graphic

Activity 10.2.4.9: Identify Device Management Activities

Refer to the online course to complete this Activity.

Information Security Management Systems (10.2.5)

In this topic, you will learn how information security management systems are used to protect assets.

Security Management Systems (10.2.5.1)

An *Information Security Management System (ISMS)* consists of a management framework through which an organization identifies, analyzes, and addresses information security risks. ISMSs are not based in servers or security devices. Instead, an ISMS consists of a set of practices that are systematically applied by an organization to ensure continuous improvement in information security. ISMSs provide conceptual models that guide organizations in planning, implementing, governing, and evaluating information security programs.

ISMSs are a natural extension of the use of popular business models, such as Total Quality Management (TQM) and Control Objectives for Information and Related Technologies (COBIT), into the realm of cybersecurity.

An ISMS is a systematic, multilayered approach to cybersecurity. The approach includes people, processes, technologies, and the cultures in which they interact in a process of risk management.

An ISMS often incorporates the "plan-do-check-act" framework, known as the Deming cycle, from TQM. It is seen as an elaboration on the process component of the People-Process-Technology-Culture model of organizational capability, as shown in Figure 10-29.

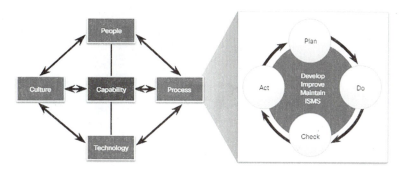

Figure 10-29 A General Model for Organizational Capability

ISO-27001 (10.2.5.2)

ISO is the International Organization for Standardization. ISO's voluntary standards are internationally accepted and facilitate business conducted between nations.

ISO partnered with the International Electrotechnical Commission (IEC) to develop the ISO/IEC 27000 family of specifications for ISMSs, as shown in Table 10-2.

Table 10-2   ISO/IEC 27000 Family of Standards

Standard	Title and Description
ISO/IEC 27000	*Information security management systems – Overview and vocabulary*. Introduction to the standards family, overview of ISMS, essential vocabulary.
ISO/IEC 27001	*Information security management systems – Requirements*. Provides an overview of ISMS and the essentials of ISMS processes and procedures.
ISO/IEC 27003	*Information security management systems – Guidance*. Critical factors necessary for successful design and implementation of ISMS. All specification up to the production of implementation plans.
ISO/IEC 27004	*Information security management – Monitoring, measurement, analysis and evaluation*. Discussion of metrics and measurement procedures to assess effectiveness of ISMS implementation.
ISO/IEC 27005	*Information security risk management*. Supports the implementation of ISMS based on a risk-centered management approach.

The ISO 27001 Certification is a global, industry-wide specification for an ISMS. Figure 10-30 illustrates the relationship of actions stipulated by the standard with the plan-do-check-act cycle.

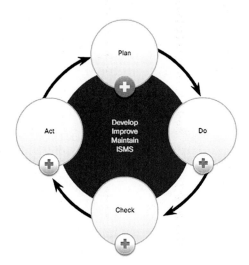

Figure 10-30   ISO 27001 ISMS Plan–Do–Check-Act Cycle

The details of each action are as follows:

Plan

- Understand relevant business objectives
- Define scope of activities
- Access manage support
- Assess and define risk
- Perform asset management and vulnerability assessment

Do

- Create and implement risk management plan
- Establish and enforce risk management policies and procedures
- Train personnel, allocate resources

Check

- Monitor implementation
- Compile reports
- Support external certification audit

Act

- Continually audit processes
- Continual process improvement
- Take corrective action
- Take preventive action

Certification means an organization's security policies and procedures have been independently verified to provide a systematic and proactive approach for effectively managing security risks to confidential customer information.

NIST Cybersecurity Framework (10.2.5.3)

NIST is very effective in the area of cybersecurity, as we have seen in this chapter. More NIST standards will be discussed later in the course.

NIST has developed the Cybersecurity Framework, which, like ISO/IEC 27000, is a set of standards designed to integrate existing standards, guidelines, and practices to help better manage and reduce cybersecurity risk. The Framework was first issued in February 2014 and continues to undergo development.

The Framework consists of a set of activities suggested to achieve specific cybersecurity outcomes, and references examples of guidance to achieve those outcomes. The core functions, defined in Table 10-3, are split into major categories and subcategories.

Table 10-3   NIST Cybersecurity Framework Core and Functions

Core Function	Description
Identify	Develop an organizational understanding to manage cybersecurity risk to systems, assets, data, and capabilities.
Protect	Develop and implement appropriate safeguards to ensure delivery of critical infrastructure services.
Detect	Develop and implement appropriate activities to identify the occurrence of a cybersecurity event.
Respond	Develop and implement appropriate activities to take action regarding a detected cybersecurity incident.
Recover	Develop and implement appropriate activities to maintain plans for resilience and to restore any capabilities or services that were impaired due to a cybersecurity incident.

The major categories provide an understanding of the types of activities related to each function, as shown in Table 10-4.

Table 10-4   NIST Cybersecurity Framework Core and Activities

Core Function	Activity
Identify	Asset Management
	Business Environment
	Risk Assessment
	Risk Management Strategy
Protect	Access Control
	Data Security
	Information Protection Processes and Procedures
	Maintenance
	Protective Technology
Detect	Anomalies and Events
	Security Continuous Monitoring
	Detection Processes

Core Function	Activity
Respond	Response Planning
	Communications
	Analysis
	Mitigation
	Improvements
Recover	Recovery Planning
	Improvements
	Communications

Organizations of many types are using the Framework in a number of ways. Many have found it helpful in raising awareness and communicating with stakeholders within their organization, including executive leadership. The Framework is also improving communications across organizations, allowing cybersecurity expectations to be shared with business partners, suppliers, and among sectors. By mapping the Framework to current cybersecurity management approaches, organizations are learning and showing how they match up with the Framework's standards, guidelines, and best practices. Some parties are using the Framework to reconcile internal policy with legislation, regulation, and industry best practice. The Framework also is being used as a strategic planning tool to assess risks and current practices.

Interactive Graphic

Activity 10.2.5.4: Identify the ISO 27001 Activity Cycle

Refer to the online course to complete this Activity.

Interactive Graphic

Activity 10.2.5.5: Identify the Stages in the NIST Cybersecurity Framework

Refer to the online course to complete this Activity.

Summary (10.3)

In this chapter, you learned how to investigate endpoint vulnerabilities and attacks. Antimalware for network devices and hosts provides a method for mitigating the impact of attacks. Host-based personal firewalls are stand-alone software programs that control traffic entering or leaving a computer. A host-based intrusion detection system (HIDS) is designed to protect hosts against known and unknown malware. A HIDS is a comprehensive security application that combines the functionalities of antimalware applications with firewall functionality. Host-based security solutions are essential to protecting the expanding attack surfaces.

Cybersecurity analysts and security experts use a variety of tools to perform endpoint vulnerability assessments. Network and device profiling provide a baseline that serves as a reference point for identifying deviations from normal operations. Similarly, server profiling is used to establish the accepted operating state of servers. Network security can be evaluated using a variety of tools and services, including:

- Risk analysis to evaluate the risk posed by vulnerabilities to a specific organization

- Vulnerability assessment, which uses software to scan Internet-facing servers and internal networks for various types of vulnerabilities

- Penetration testing, which uses authorized simulated attacks to test the strength of network security

The Common Vulnerability Scoring System (CVSS) is a risk assessment designed to convey the common attributes and severity of vulnerabilities in computer hardware and software systems. The benefits of CVSS include:

- Standardized vulnerability scores that should be meaningful across organizations

- Open framework with the meaning of each metric openly available to all users

- Prioritization of risk in a way that is meaningful to individual organizations

A number of security compliance regulations have emerged, including:

- **Federal Information Security Management Act of 2002 (FISMA):** This provides security standards for U.S. government systems and contractors to the U.S. government.

- **Sarbanes-Oxley Act of 2002 (SOX):** This provides the requirements for the way in which U.S. corporations control and disclose financial information.

- **Gramm-Leach-Bliley Act (GLBA):** This states that financial institutions must secure customer information, protect against threats to customer information, and protect against unauthorized access to customer information.

- **Health Insurance Portability and Accountability Act (HIPAA):** This requires that all patient personally identifiable healthcare information be stored, maintained, and transmitted in ways that ensure patient privacy and confidentiality.

- **Payment Card Industry Data Security Standard (PCI DSS):** This is a proprietary, non-governmental standard for the secure handling of customer credit card data.

Risk management involves the selection and specification of security controls for an organization. There are four potential ways to respond to risks that have been identified, based on their weightings or scores:

- Risk avoidance, if it is determined that the activity should be discontinued

- Risk reduction, by implementing management approaches to reduce vulnerability

- Risk sharing, to shift risk by outsourcing some aspects of security operations to third parties

- Risk retention and acceptance, for risks that have low potential impact and/or relatively high cost of mitigation or reduction

Risk management tools include:

- Vulnerability management

- Asset management

- Mobile device management

- Configuration management

- Enterprise patch management

Organizations can use an Information Security Management System (ISMS) to identify, analyze, and address information security risks. Standards for managing cybersecurity risk are available from ISO and NIST.

Practice

There are no Labs or Packet Tracer activities in this chapter.

Check Your Understanding

Complete all the review questions listed here to test your understanding of the topics and concepts in this chapter. The appendix "Answers to 'Check Your Understanding' Questions" lists the answers.

1. Which HIDS is an open source product?

   A. Tripwire

   B. OSSEC

   C. Cisco AMP

   D. AlienVault USM

2. In Windows Firewall, when is the Domain profile applied?

   A. When the host accesses the Internet

   B. When the host checks emails from an enterprise email server

   C. When the host is connected to a trusted network such as an internal business network

   D. When the host is connected to an isolated network from the Internet by another security device

3. Which function does CVSS provide?

   A. Risk assessment

   B. Penetration testing

   C. Vulnerability assessment

   D. Central security management service

4. In addressing an identified risk, which strategy aims to decrease the risk by taking measures to reduce vulnerability?

   A. Risk sharing

   B. Risk retention

   C. Risk reduction

   D. Risk avoidance

5. Which regulatory compliance regulation specifies security standards for U.S. government systems and contractors to the U.S. government?

   A. Gramm-Leach-Bliley Act (GLBA)

   B. Sarbanes-Oxley Act of 2002 (SOX)

   C. Health Insurance Portability and Accountability Act (HIPAA)

   D. Federal Information Security Management Act of 2002 (FISMA)

6. Which three devices are possible examples of network endpoints? (Choose three.)

    A. Router

    B. Sensor

    C. Wireless AP

    D. IoT controller

    E. VPN appliance

    F. Network security camera

7. Which antimalware software approach can recognize various characteristics of known malware files to detect a threat?

    A. Routing-based

    B. Behavior-based

    C. Signature-based

    D. Heuristics-based

8. As described by the SANS Institute, which attack surface includes the exploitation of vulnerabilities in wired and wireless protocols used by IoT devices?

    A. Human Attack Surface

    B. Internet Attack Surface

    C. Network Attack Surface

    D. Software Attack Surface

9. In profiling a server, what defines what an application is allowed to do or run on a server?

    A. User accounts

    B. Listening ports

    C. Service accounts

    D. Software environment

10. Which class of metric in the CVSS Basic metric group defines the features of the exploit such as the vector, complexity, and user interaction required by the exploit?

    A. Impact

    B. Exploitability

    C. Modified Base

    D. Exploit Code Maturity

11. Which step in the Vulnerability Management Life Cycle performs inventory of all assets across the network and identifies host details, including operating system and open services?

    A. Assess

    B. Discover

    C. Remediate

    D. Prioritize assets

12. In network security assessments, which type of test is used to evaluate the risk posed by vulnerabilities to a specific organization, including assessment of the likelihood of attacks and the impact of successful exploits on the organization?

    A. Risk analysis

    B. Port scanning

    C. Penetration testing

    D. Vulnerability assessment

## CHAPTER 11

Security Monitoring

Objectives

Upon completion of this chapter, you will be able to answer the following questions:

- What is the behavior of common network protocols in the context of security monitoring?

- How do security technologies affect the ability to monitor common network protocols?

- What are the types of data used in security monitoring?

- What are the elements of an end device log file?

- What are the elements of a network device log file?

Key Terms

This chapter uses the following key terms. You can find the definitions in the Glossary.

Introduction (11.0)

Network security monitoring (NSM) uses various types of data to detect, verify, and contain exploits. The primary task of the cybersecurity analyst is to verify successful or attempted exploits using NSM data and tools.

In this chapter, you will learn about the security technologies and log files used in security monitoring.

Technologies and Protocols (11.1)

In this section, you will learn how security technologies affect security monitoring.

Monitoring Common Protocols (11.1.1)

In this topic, you will learn the behavior of common network protocols in the context of security monitoring.

Syslog and NTP (11.1.1.1)

Various protocols that commonly appear on networks have features that make them of special interest in security monitoring. For example, syslog and Network Time Protocol (NTP) are essential to the work of the cybersecurity analyst.

The syslog standard is used for logging event messages from network devices and endpoints, as shown in Figure 11-1.

Figure 11-1   Syslog Operation

The standard allows for a system-neutral means of transmitting, storing, and analyzing messages. Many types of devices from many different vendors can use syslog to send log entries to central servers that run a syslog daemon. This centralization of log collection helps to make security monitoring practical. Servers that run syslog typically listen on UDP port 514.

Because syslog is so important to security monitoring, syslog servers may be a target for threat actors. Some exploits, such as those involving data exfiltration, can take a long time to complete due to the very slow ways in which data is secretly stolen from the network. Some attackers may try to hide the fact that exfiltration is occurring. They attack syslog servers that contain the information that could lead to detection of the exploit. Hackers may attempt to block the transfer of data from syslog clients to servers, tamper with or destroy log data, or tamper with software that creates and transmits log messages. The next generation (ng) syslog implementation, known as syslog-ng, offers enhancements that can help prevent some of the exploits that target syslog.

NTP (11.1.1.2)

Syslog messages are usually timestamped. This allows messages from different sources to be organized by time to provide a view of network communication processes. Because the messages can come from many devices, it is important that the devices share a consistent time clock. One way that this can be achieved is for the devices to use Network Time Protocol (NTP). NTP uses a hierarchy of authoritative time sources to share time information between devices on the network, as shown in Figure 11-2. In this way, device messages that share consistent time information can be submitted to the syslog server. NTP operates on UDP port 123.

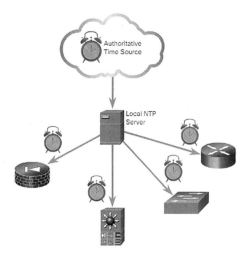

Figure 11-2   NTP Operation

Because events that are connected to an exploit can leave traces across every network device on their path to the target system, timestamps are essential for detection. Threat actors may attempt to attack the NTP infrastructure in order to corrupt time information used to correlate logged network events. This can serve to obfuscate traces of ongoing exploits. In addition, threat actors have been known to use NTP systems to direct DDoS attacks through vulnerabilities in client or server software. While these attacks do not necessarily result in corrupted security monitoring data, they can disrupt network availability.

DNS (11.1.1.3)

Domain Name Service (DNS) is used by millions of people daily. Because of this, many organizations have less stringent policies in place to protect against DNS-based threats than they have to protect against other types of exploits. Attackers have recognized this and commonly encapsulate different network protocols within DNS to evade security devices. DNS is now used by many types of malware. Some varieties of malware use DNS to communicate with command-and-control (CnC) servers and to exfiltrate data in traffic disguised as normal DNS queries. Various types of encoding, such as Base64, 8-bit binary, and Hex, can be used to camouflage the data and evade basic data loss prevention (DLP) measures.

For example, malware could encode stolen data as the subdomain portion of a DNS lookup for a domain where the name server is under control of an attacker. A DNS lookup for "long-string-of-exfiltrated-data.example.com" would be forwarded to the name server of example.com, which would record "long-string-of-exfiltrated-data" and reply to the malware with a coded response. This use of the DNS subdomain is shown in Figure 11-3. The exfiltrated data is the encoded text shown in the box. The threat actor collects this encoded data, decodes and combines it, and now has access to an entire data file, such as a username/password database.

Figure 11-3 DNS Exfiltration

It is likely that the subdomain part of such requests would be much longer than usual requests. Cyberanalysts can use the distribution of the lengths of subdomains within DNS requests to construct a mathematical model that describes normality. They can then use this to compare their observations and identify an abuse of the DNS query process. For example, it would not be normal to see a host on your network sending a query to aW4gcGxhY2UgdG8gcHJvdGVjdC.example.com.

DNS queries for randomly generated domain names, or extremely long random-appearing subdomains, should be considered suspicious, especially if their occurrence spikes dramatically on the network. DNS proxy logs can be analyzed to detect these conditions. Alternatively, services such as the Cisco Umbrella passive DNS service can be used to block requests to suspected CnC and exploit domains.

HTTP and HTTPS (11.1.1.4)

Hypertext Transfer Protocol (HTTP) is the backbone protocol of the World Wide Web. However, all information carried in HTTP is transmitted in plaintext from the source computer to the destination on the Internet. HTTP does not protect data from alteration or interception by malicious parties, which is a serious threat to privacy, identity, and information security. All browsing activity should be considered to be at risk.

A common exploit of HTTP is called iFrame (inline frame) injection. Most web-based threats consist of malware scripts that have been planted on web servers. These web servers then direct browsers to infected servers by loading iFrames. In iFrame injection, a threat actor compromises a web server and plants malicious code that creates an invisible iFrame on a commonly visited web page. When the iFrame loads, malware is downloaded, frequently from a different URL than the web page that contains the iFrame code. Network security services, such as Cisco Web Reputation filtering, can detect when a website attempts to send content from an untrusted website to the host, even when sent from an iFrame, as shown in Figure 11-4.

Figure 11-4   HTTP iFrame Injection Exploit

To address the alteration or interception of confidential data, many commercial organizations have adopted HTTPS or implemented HTTPS-only policies to protect visitors to their websites and services.

HTTPS adds a layer of encryption to the HTTP protocol by using Secure Sockets Layer (SSL)/Transport Layer Security (TLS), as shown in Figure 11-5. This makes the HTTP data unreadable as it leaves the source computer until it reaches the server. Note that HTTPS is not a mechanism for web server security. It only secures HTTP protocol traffic while it is in transit.

Note

Although you may still encounter SSL implemented in some websites, the Internet Engineering Task Force (IETF) deprecated it in June 2015 in RFC 7568. Any version of TLS is more secure than SSL.

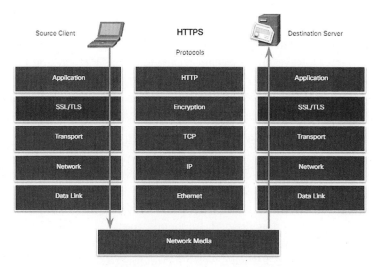

Figure 11-5 HTTPS Protocol Diagram

Unfortunately, the encrypted HTTPS traffic complicates network security monitoring. Some security devices include SSL decryption and inspection; however, this can present processing and privacy issues. In addition, HTTPS adds complexity to packet captures due to the additional messaging involved in establishing the encrypted connection. This process is summarized in Figure 11-6 and represents additional overhead on top of HTTP.

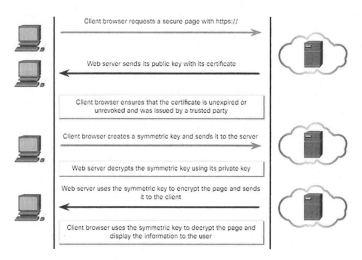

Figure 11-6 HTTPS Transactions

Email Protocols (11.1.1.5)

Email protocols such as SMTP, POP3, and IMAP can be used by threat actors to spread malware, exfiltrate data, or provide channels to malware CnC servers, as shown in Figure 11-7.

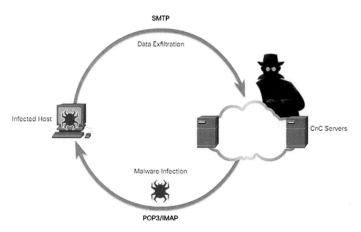

Figure 11-7   Email Protocol Threats

SMTP sends data from a host to a mail server and between mail servers. Like DNS and HTTP, it is a common protocol to see leaving the network. Because there is so much SMTP traffic, it is not always monitored. However, SMTP has been used in the past by malware to exfiltrate data from the network. In the 2014 hack of Sony Pictures, one of the exploits used SMTP to exfiltrate user details from compromised hosts to CnC servers. This information may have been used to help develop exploits of secured resources within the Sony Pictures network. Security monitoring could reveal this type of traffic based on features of the email message.

IMAP and POP3 are used to download email messages from a mail server to the host computer. For this reason, they are the application protocols that are responsible for bringing malware to the host. Security monitoring can identify when a malware attachment entered the network and which host it first infected. Retrospective analysis can then track the behavior of the malware from that point forward. In this way, the malware behavior can better be understood and the threat identified. Security monitoring tools may also allow recovery of infected file attachments for submission to malware sandboxes for analysis.

ICMP (11.1.1.6)

Internet Control Message Protocol (ICMP) has many legitimate uses. However, the ICMP functionality has been used to craft a number of types of exploits. ICMP can be used to identify hosts on a network, map the structure of a network, and determine the operating systems at use on the network. It can also be used as a vehicle for various types of DoS attacks.

ICMP can also be used for data exfiltration. Because of the concern that ICMP can be used to surveil or deny service from outside of the network, ICMP traffic from inside the network is sometimes overlooked. However, some varieties of malware use crafted ICMP packets to transfer files from infected hosts to threat actors using this method, which is known as ICMP tunneling.

A number of tools exist for crafting tunnels, such as Hans and Ping Tunnel.

Interactive Graphic

Activity 11.1.1.7: Identify the Monitored Protocol

Refer to the online course to complete this Activity.

Security Technologies (11.1.2)

In this topic, you will learn how security technologies affect the ability to monitor common network protocols.

ACLs (11.1.2.1)

Many technologies and protocols can have impacts on security monitoring. Access control lists (ACLs) are among these technologies. ACLs can give a false sense of security if they are overly relied upon. ACLs, and packet filtering in general, are technologies that contribute to an evolving set of network security protections.

Figure 11-8, Example 11-1, and Example 11-2 illustrate the use of ACLs to permit only specific types of ICMP traffic.

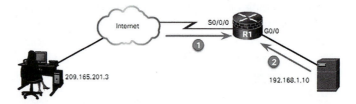

Figure 11-8   Mitigating ICMP Abuse

Example 11-1   Rules on R1 for ICMP Traffic from the Internet

```
access-list 112 permit icmp any any echo-reply
access-list 112 permit icmp any any source-quench
access-list 112 permit icmp any any unreachable
access-list 112 deny icmp any any
access-list 112 permit ip any any
```

Example 11-2   Rules of R1 for ICMP Traffic from Inside the Network

```
access-list 114 permit icmp 192.168.1.0 0.0.0.255 any echo
access-list 114 permit icmp 192.168.1.0 0.0.0.255 any parameter-problem
access-list 114 permit icmp 192.168.1.0 0.0.0.255 any packet-too-big
access-list 114 permit icmp 192.168.1.0 0.0.0.255 any source-quench
access-list 114 deny icmp any any
access-list 114 permit ip any any
```

The server at 192.168.1.10 is part of the inside network and is allowed to send ping requests to the outside host at 209.165.201.3. The outside host's return ICMP traffic is allowed if it is an ICMP reply, source quench (tells the source to reduce the pace of traffic), or any ICMP unreachable message. All other ICMP traffic types are denied. For example, the outside host cannot initiate a ping request to the inside host. The outbound ACL is allowing ICMP messages that report various problems. This will allow ICMP tunneling and data exfiltration.

Attackers can determine which IP addresses, protocols, and ports are allowed by ACLs. This can be done either by port scanning or penetration testing, or through other forms of reconnaissance. Attackers can craft packets that use spoofed source IP addresses. Applications can establish connections on arbitrary ports. Other features of protocol traffic can also be manipulated, such as the established flag in TCP segments. Rules cannot be anticipated and configured for all emerging packet manipulation techniques.

To detect and react to packet manipulation, more sophisticated behavior and context-based measures need to be taken. Cisco Next-Generation Firewalls (NGFW), Advanced Malware Protection (AMP), and Email and Web Security Appliances (ESA and WSA) can address the shortcomings of rule-based security measures.

NAT and PAT (11.1.2.2)

Network Address Translation (NAT) and Port Address Translation (PAT) can complicate security monitoring. Multiple IP addresses are mapped to one or more public addresses that are visible on the Internet, hiding the individual IP addresses that are inside the network (inside addresses).

Figure 11-9 illustrates the relationship between internal and external addresses that are used as source addresses (SA) and destination addresses (DA).

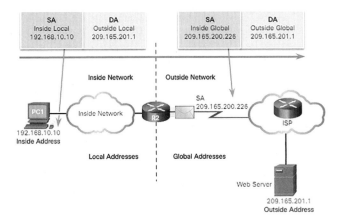

Figure 11-9   NAT Example

These internal and external addresses are in a network that is using NAT to communicate with a destination on the Internet. If PAT is in effect, and all IP addresses leaving the network use the 209.165.200.226 inside global address for traffic to the Internet, it could be difficult to log the specific inside device that is requesting and receiving the traffic when it enters the network.

This problem can be especially relevant with NetFlow data. NetFlow flows are unidirectional and are defined by the addresses and ports that they share. NAT will essentially break a flow that passes a NAT gateway, making flow information beyond that point unavailable. Cisco offers security products that will "stitch" flows together even if the IP addresses have been replaced by NAT.

NetFlow is discussed in more detail later in the chapter.

Encryption, Encapsulation, and Tunneling (11.1.2.3)

As mentioned with HTTPS, encryption can present challenges to security monitoring by making packet details unreadable. Encryption is part of VPN technologies. In VPNs, a commonplace protocol like IP is used to carry encrypted traffic. The encrypted traffic essentially establishes a virtual point-to-point connection between networks over public facilities. Encryption makes the traffic unreadable to any other devices but the VPN endpoints.

A similar technology can be used to create a virtual point-to-point connection between an internal host and threat actor devices. Malware can establish an encrypted tunnel that rides on a common and trusted protocol, and use it to exfiltrate data from the network. A similar method of data exfiltration was discussed previously for DNS.

Peer-to-Peer Networking and Tor (11.1.2.4)

In peer-to-peer (P2P) networking, shown in Figure 11-10, hosts can operate in both client and server roles.

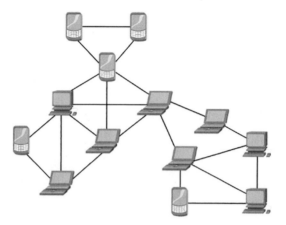

Figure 11-10 P2P Topology Example

Three types of P2P applications exist: file sharing, processor sharing, and instant messaging. In file-sharing P2P, files on a participating machine are shared with members of the P2P network. Examples of this are the once-popular Napster and Gnutella. Bitcoin is a P2P operation that involves the sharing of a distributed database, or ledger, that records Bitcoin balances and transactions. BitTorrent is a P2P file-sharing network.

Any time that unknown users are provided access to network resources, security is a concern. File-sharing P2P applications should not be allowed on corporate networks. P2P network activity can circumvent firewall protections and is a common vector for the spread of malware. P2P is inherently dynamic. It can operate by connecting to numerous destination IP addresses, and it can also use dynamic port numbering. Shared files are often infected with malware, and threat actors can position their malware on P2P clients for distribution to other users.

Processor-sharing P2P networks donate processor cycles to distributed computational tasks. Cancer research, searching for extraterrestrials, and scientific research use donated processor cycles to distribute computational tasks.

Instant messaging (IM) is also considered to be a P2P application. IM has legitimate value within organizations that have geographically distributed project teams. In this case, specialized IM applications are available, such as the *Cisco Jabber* platform, which are more secure than IM that uses public servers.

Tor is a software platform and network of P2P hosts that function as Internet routers on the Tor network. The Tor network allows users to browse the Internet anonymously. Users access the Tor network by using a special browser. When a browsing session is begun, the browser constructs a layered end-to-end path across the Tor server network that is encrypted, as shown in Figure 11-11.

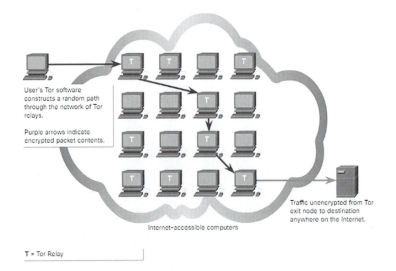

Figure 11-11   Tor Operation

Each encrypted layer is "peeled away" like the layers of an onion (hence "onion routing") as the traffic traverses a Tor relay. The layers contain encrypted next-hop information that can only be read by the router that needs to read the information. In this way, no single device knows the entire path to the destination, and routing information is readable only by the device that requires it. Finally, at the end of the Tor path, the traffic reaches its Internet destination. When traffic is returned to the source, an encrypted layered path is again constructed.

Tor presents a number of challenges to cybersecurity analysts. First, Tor is widely used by criminal organizations on the "dark net." In addition, Tor has been used as a communications channel for malware CnC. Because the destination IP address of Tor traffic is obfuscated by encryption, with only the next-hop Tor node known, Tor traffic avoids blacklists that have been configured on security devices.

Load Balancing (11.1.2.5)

Load balancing involves the distribution of traffic between devices or network paths to prevent overwhelming network resources with too much traffic. If redundant resources exist, a load balancing algorithm or device will work to distribute traffic between those resources, as shown in Figure 11-12.

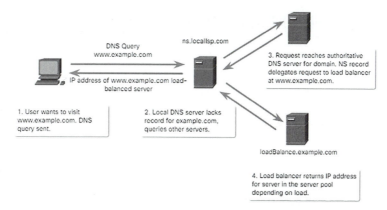

DNS Query
www.example.com

ns.locallsp.com

3. Request reaches authoritative DNS server for domain. NS record delegates request to load balancer at www.example.com.

IP address of www.example.com load-balanced server

1. User wants to visit www.example.com. DNS query sent.

2. Local DNS server lacks record for example.com, queries other servers.

loadBalance.example.com

4. Load balancer returns IP address for server in the server pool depending on load.

Figure 11-12   Load Balancing with DNS Delegation

One way this is done on the Internet is through various techniques that use DNS to send traffic to resources that have the same domain name but multiple IP addresses. In some cases, the distribution may be to servers that are distributed geographically. This can result in a single Internet transaction being represented by multiple IP addresses on the incoming packets. This may cause suspicious features to appear in packet captures. In addition, some load balancing manager (LBM) devices use probes to test for the performance of different paths and the health of different resources. For example, an LBM may send probes to the different servers that it is load balancing traffic to in order to detect that the servers are operating. This is done to avoid sending traffic to a resource that is not available. These probes can appear to be suspicious traffic if the cybersecurity analyst is not aware that this traffic is part of the operation of the LBM.

Interactive Graphic

Activity 11.1.2.6: Identify the Impact of the Technology on Security and Monitoring

Refer to the online course to complete this Activity.

Log Files (11.2)

In this section, you will learn the types of log files used in security monitoring

Types of Security Data (11.2.1)

In this topic, you will learn the types of data used in security monitoring.

Alert Data (11.2.1.1)

Alert data consists of messages generated by intrusion prevention systems (IPSs) or intrusion detection systems (IDSs) in response to traffic that violates a rule or matches the signature of a known exploit. A network-based IDS (NIDS), such as *Snort*, comes configured with rules for known exploits. Alerts are generated by Snort and are made readable and searchable by applications such as Snorby and Sguil, which are part of the Security Onion suite of NSM tools.

A testing site that is used to determine whether Snort is operating is www.testmyids.com. It consists of a web page that displays only the text **uid=0(root) gid=0(root) groups=0(root)**. If Snort is operating correctly and a host visits this site, a signature will be matched and an alert will be triggered. This is an easy and harmless way to verify that the NIDS is running.

The Snort rule that is triggered is

```
alert ip any any -> any any (msg:"GPL ATTACK_RESPONSE id check returned root";
    content:"uid=0|28|root|29|"; fast_pattern:only; classtype:bad-unknown;
    sid:2100498; rev:8;)
```

This rule generates an alert if any IP address in the network receives data from an external source that contains the text matching the pattern of **uid=0(root)**. The alert contains the message **GPL ATTACK_RESPONSE id check returned root**. The ID of the Snort rule that was triggered is **2100498**.

Figure 11-13 illustrates a series of alerts that have been accessed and displayed on the Security Onion console application *Sguil*.

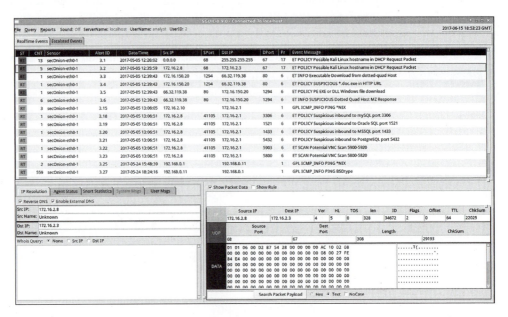

Figure 11-13 Sguil Console Showing Alert Event Data

Session and Transaction Data (11.2.1.2)

Session data is a record of a conversation between two network endpoints, often a client and a server. The server could be inside the enterprise network or at a location accessed over the Internet. Session data is data about the session, not the data retrieved and used by the client. Session data will include identifying information such as the five tuples of source and destination IP addresses, source and destination port numbers, and the IP code for the protocol in use. Data about the session typically includes a session ID, the amount of data transferred by source and destination, and information related to the duration of the session.

Bro is a network security monitoring tool you will use in labs later in the course. Figure 11-14 shows a partial output for three HTTP sessions from a Bro connection log.

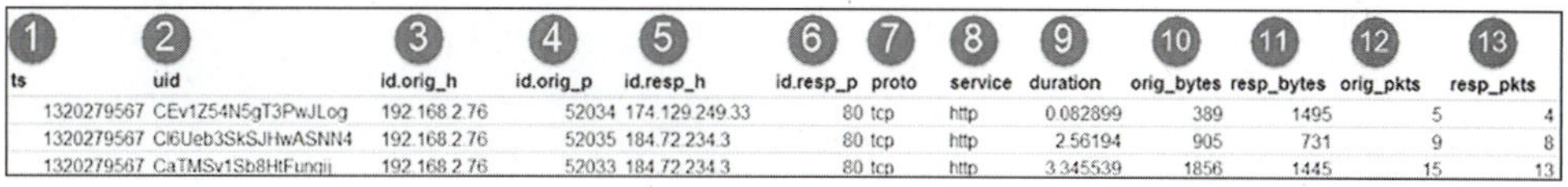

① ts	② uid	③ id.orig_h	④ id.orig_p	⑤ id.resp_h	⑥ id.resp_p	⑦ proto	⑧ service	⑨ duration	⑩ orig_bytes	⑪ resp_bytes	⑫ orig_pkts	⑬ resp_pkts
1320279567	CEv1Z54N5gT3PwJLog	192.168.2.76	52034	174.129.249.33	80	tcp	http	0.082899	389	1495	5	4
1320279567	Ci6Ueb3SkSJHwASNN4	192.168.2.76	52035	184.72.234.3	80	tcp	http	2.56194	905	731	9	8
1320279567	CaTMSv1Sb8HtFunqji	192.168.2.76	52033	184.72.234.3	80	tcp	http	3.345539	1856	1445	15	13

Figure 11-14   Bro Session Data: Partial Display

The following describes each field in Figure 11-14:

1. session start timestamp in Unix epoch format

2. unique session ID

3. IP address of host originating the session (source address)

4. protocol port for the originating host (source port)

5. IP address of host responding to originating host (destination address)

6. protocol for responding host (destination port)

7. transport layer protocol for session

8. application layer protocol

9. duration of session

10. bytes from originating host

11. bytes from responding host

12. packets from originating host

13. packets from responding host

Transaction data consists of the messages that are exchanged during network sessions. These transactions can be viewed in packet capture transcripts. Device logs kept by servers also contain information about the transactions that occur between clients and servers. For example, a session might include the downloading of content from a web server, as shown in Figure 11-15. The transactions representing the requests and replies would be logged in an access log on the server or by a NIDS like Bro. The session is all traffic involved in making up the request, and the transaction is the request itself.

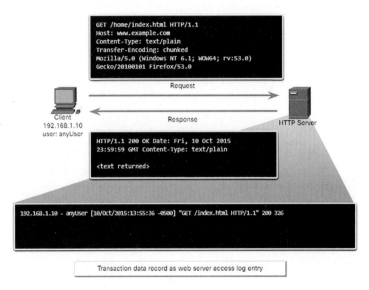

Figure 11-15   Transaction Data

Full Packet Captures (11.2.1.3)

Full packet captures are the most detailed network data that is generally collected. Because of the amount of detail, they are also the most storage- and retrieval-intensive types of data used in NSM. Full packet captures contain not only data about network conversations, such as session data, but also the actual contents of the conversations themselves. Full packet captures contain the text of email messages, the HTML in web pages, and the files that enter or leave the network. Extracted content can be recovered from full packet captures and analyzed for malware or user behavior that violates business and security policies. The familiar tool Wireshark is very popular for viewing full packet captures and accessing the data associated with network conversations.

Figure 11-16 illustrates the interface for the Network Analysis Monitor component of Cisco Prime Infrastructure system, which, like Wireshark, can display full packet captures.

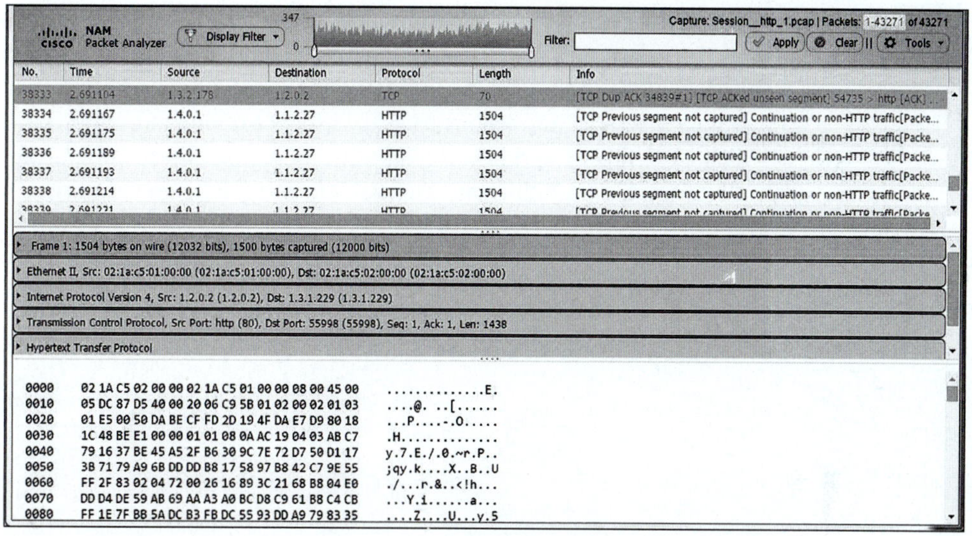

Figure 11-16   Cisco Prime Network Analysis Module: Full Packet Capture

Statistical Data (11.2.1.4)

Like session data, *statistical data* is about network traffic. Statistical data is created through the analysis of other forms of network data. From these analyses, conclusions can be made that describe or predict network behavior. Statistical characteristics of normal network behavior can be compared to current network traffic in an effort to detect anomalies. Statistics can be used to characterize normal amounts of variation in network traffic patterns in order to identify network conditions that are significantly outside of those ranges. Statistically significant differences should raise alarms and prompt investigation.

Network Behavior Analysis (NBA) and Network Behavior Anomaly Detection (NBAD) are approaches to network security monitoring that use advanced analytical techniques to analyze NetFlow or Internet Protocol Flow Information Export (IPFIX) network telemetry data. Techniques such as predictive analytics and artificial intelligence perform advanced analyses of detailed session data to detect potential security incidents.

Note

IPFIX is the open standard version of Cisco's NetFlow.

An example of an NSM tool that utilizes statistical analysis is Cisco Cognitive Threat Analytics. It is able to find malicious activity that has bypassed security controls, or entered through unmonitored channels (including removable media), and is operating inside an organization's environment. Cognitive Threat Analytics is a cloud-based product that uses machine learning and statistical modeling of networks. It creates a baseline of the traffic in a network and identifies anomalies. It analyzes user and device behavior, and web traffic, to discover command-and-control communications, data exfiltration, and potentially unwanted applications operating in the infrastructure. Figure 11-17 illustrates an architecture for Cisco Cognitive Threat Analytics.

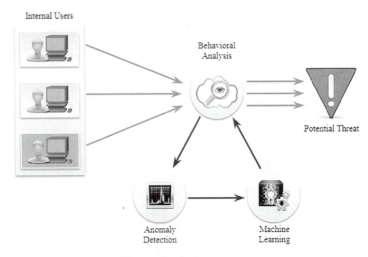

Figure 11-17   Cisco Cognitive Threat Analytics

Interactive Graphic

Activity 11.2.1.5: Identify Types of Network Monitoring Data

Refer to the online course to complete this Activity.

End Device Logs (11.2.2)

In this topic, you will learn the elements of an end device log file.

Host Logs (11.2.2.1)

As previously discussed, host-based intrusion detection (HIDS) runs on individual hosts. HIDS not only detects intrusions, but, in the form of host-based firewalls, can also prevent intrusion. This software creates logs and stores them on the host. This can make it difficult to get a view of what is happening on hosts in the enterprise, so many host-based protections have a way to submit logs to centralized log management servers. In this way, the logs can be searched from a central location using NSM tools.

HIDS systems can use agents to submit logs to management servers. *OSSEC*, a popular open source HIDS, includes a robust log collection and analysis functionality. Microsoft Windows includes several methods for automated host log collection and analysis. Tripwire, a HIDS for Linux, includes similar functionality. All can scale to larger enterprises.

Microsoft Windows host logs are visible locally through Event Viewer. Event Viewer keeps four types of logs:

- **Application logs:** These contain events logged by various applications.

- **System logs:** These include events regarding the operation of drivers, processes, and hardware.

- **Setup logs:** These record information about the installation of software, including Windows updates.

- **Security logs:** These record events related to security, such as logon attempts and operations related to file or object management and access.

Various logs can have different event types. Table 11-1 lists the Windows host log event types.

Table 11-1   Windows Host Log Event Types

Event Type	Description
Error	An event that indicates a significant problem such as loss of data or loss of functionality. For example, if a service fails to load during startup, an Error event is logged.
Warning	An event that is not necessarily significant, but may indicate a possible future problem. For example, when disk space is low, a Warning event is logged. If an application can recover from an event without loss of functionality or data, it can generally classify the event as a Warning event.
Information	An event that describes the successful operation of an application, driver, or service. For example, when a network driver loads successfully, it may be appropriate to log an Information event. Note that it is generally inappropriate for a desktop application to log an event each time it starts.
Success Audit	An event that records an audited security access attempt that is successful. For example, a user's successful attempt to log on to the system is logged as a Success Audit event.
Failure Audit	An event that records an audited security access attempt that fails. For example, if a user tries to access a network drive and fails, the attempt is logged as a Failure Audit event.

Security logs consist only of audit success or failure messages. On Windows computers, security logging is carried out by the Local Security Authority Subsystem Service (LSASS), which is also responsible for enforcing security policies on a Windows host. LSASS runs as lsass.exe. It is frequently faked by malware. It should be running from the Windows System32 directory. If a file with this name, or a camouflaged name, such as 1sass.exe, is running or running from another directory, it could be malware.

Syslog (11.2.2.2)

Syslog includes specifications for message formats, a client-server application structure, and network protocol. Many different types of network devices can be configured to use the syslog standard to log events to centralized syslog servers.

Syslog is a client/server protocol. Syslog was defined within the Syslog working group of the IETF (RFC 5424) and is supported by a wide variety of devices and receivers across multiple platforms.

The syslog sender sends a small (less than 1 KB) text message to the syslog receiver. The syslog receiver is commonly called "syslogd," "syslog daemon," or "syslog server." Syslog messages can be sent via UDP (port 514) and/or TCP (typically, port 5000). While there are some exceptions, such as SSL wrappers, this data is typically sent in plaintext over the network.

The full format of a syslog message seen on the wire has three distinct parts, as shown in Figure 11-18:

- PRI (priority)

- HEADER

- MSG (message text)

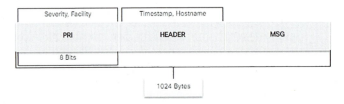

Figure 11-18   Syslog Packet Format

The PRI consists of two elements, the Facility and Severity of the message, which are both integer values, as shown in Figure 11-19.

Integer	Severity
0	**Emergency**: System is unusable
1	**Alert**: Action must be taken immediately
2	**Critical**: Critical conditions
3	**Error**: Error conditions
4	**Warning**: Warning conditions
5	**Notice**: Normal but significant condition
6	**Informational**: Informational messages
7	**Debug**: Debug-level messages

Integer	Facility
0	**kern**: Kernel messages
1	**user**: User-level messages
2	**mail**: Mail system
3	**daemon**: System daemons
4	**auth**: Security/authorization messages
5	**syslog**: Messages generated internally by Syslogd
6	**lpr**: Line printer subsystem
7	**news**: Network news subsystem
8	**uucp**: Unix-to-Unix copy subsystem
9	Clock daemon
10	**authpriv**: Security/authorization messages
11	**ftp**: FTP daemon
12	NTP subsystem
13	Log audit
14	Log alert
15	**cron**: Clock daemon

$$\text{Priority} = (\text{Facility} \times 8) + \text{Severity}$$

Figure 11-19   Syslog Severity and Facility

The Facility consists of broad categories of sources that generated the message, such as the system, process, or application. The Facility value can be used by logging servers to direct the message to the appropriate log file. The Severity is a value from 0 to 7 that defines the severity of the message. The Priority (PRI) value is calculated by multiplying the Facility value by 8, and then adding it to the Severity value:

Priority = (Facility * 8) + Severity

The Priority value is the first value in a packet and occurs between angle brackets (<>).

The HEADER section of the message contains the timestamp in MMM DD HH:MM:SS format. If the timestamp is preceded by the period (.) or asterisk (*) symbols, a problem is indicated with NTP. The HEADER section also includes the hostname or IP address of the device that is the source of the message.

The MSG portion contains the meaning of the syslog message. This can vary between device manufacturers and can be customized. Therefore, this portion of the message is the most meaningful and useful to the cybersecurity analyst.

Server Logs (11.2.2.3)

Server logs are an essential source of data for network security monitoring. Network application servers such as email and web servers keep access and error logs. Especially important are DNS proxy server logs, which document all the DNS queries and responses that occur on the network. DNS proxy logs are useful for identifying hosts that may have visited dangerous websites and for identifying DNS data exfiltration and connections to malware command-and-control servers. Many UNIX and Linux servers use syslog. Others may use proprietary logging. The contents of log file events depend on the type of server.

Two important log files to be familiar with are the Apache HTTP Server access logs and Microsoft Internet Information Services (IIS) access logs. Examples of each are shown in Example 11-3 and Example 11-4.

Example 11-3 Apache Access Log

```
203.0.113.127 - dsmith [10/Oct/2016:10:26:57 -0500] "GET /logo_sm.gif HTTP/1.0"
   200 2254 ""http://www.example.com/links.html"" "Mozilla/5.0 (Windows NT 6.1;
   Win64; x64; rv:47.0) Gecko/20100101 Firefox/47.0"
```

Example 11-4 IIS Access Log

```
6/14/2016, 16:22:43, 203.0.113.24, -, W3SVC2, WEB3, 198.51.100.10, 80, GET, /home.
   htm, -, 200, 0, 15321, 159, 15, HTTP/1.1, Mozilla/5.0 (compatible; MSIE 9.0;
   Windows Phone OS 7.5; Trident/5.0; IEMobile/9.0), -, http://www.example.com
```

Apache HTTP Server Access Logs (11.2.2.4)

Apache HTTP Server access logs record the requests for resources from clients to the server. The logs can be in two formats. The first is common log format (CLF), and the second is combined log format, which is CLF with the addition of the Referrer and User Agent fields, as shown in the figure.

The fields in the Apache access log (Example 11-3) in CLF are as follows:

- **IP address of requesting host:** In Example 11-3, the address is 203.0.113.127.

- **Identity of client:** This is unreliable, and is frequently replaced by the hyphen (-) placeholder, which is used to represent missing or unavailable data.

- **User ID:** If the user is authenticated to the web server, this is the username for the account. Much access to web servers is anonymous, so this value will frequently be replaced by a hyphen.

- **Timestamp:** The time the request was received in DD/MMM/YYYY:HH:MM:SS (+I-) zone format.

- **Request:** The request method, the requested resource, and the request protocol.

- **Status code:** Three-digit numeric code representing the status of request. Codes beginning with 2 represent success, such as the 200 in Example 11-3. Codes that begin with a 3 represent redirection. Codes that begin with a 4 represent client errors. Codes that begin with a 5 represent server errors.

- **Size of the response:** Size, in bytes, of data returned to the client.

  The combined log format adds the following two fields:

- **Referrer:** The URL of the resource from which the request was made. If the request is made directly by the user typing the URL into the browser, from a bookmark, or from a URL in a document, the value will normally be a hyphen.

- **User agent:** The identifier for the browser that made the request.

Table 11-2 identifies the value of each field in Example 11-3.

Table 11-2 Apache Access Log Entry Explanation

Field	Name	Description	Example
1	Client IP Address	IP address of requesting client	`203.0.113.127`
2	Client Identity	Client userid, frequently omitted	`-`
3	User ID	Username of authenticated user, if any	`dsmith`
4	Timestamp	Date and time of request	`[10/Oct/2016:10:26:57 -0500]`
5	Request	Request method and requested resource	`GET /logo_sm.gif HTTP/1.0`
6	Status Code	HTTP status code	`200`
7	Size of Response	Bytes returned to client	`2254`
8	Referrer	Location, if any, from which the client reached the resource	`http://www.example.com/ links.html`
9	User Agent	Browser used by client	`Mozilla/5.0 (Windows NT 6.1; Win64; x64; rv:47.0) Gecko/20100101 Firefox/47.0`

Note

The terms Uniform Resource Identifier (URI) and Uniform Resource Locator (URL) are not the same. A URI is a compact method of referring to a source such as example.com. A URL specifies the method for accessing the resource, such as https://www.example.com or ftp://www.example.com.

IIS Access Logs (11.2.2.5)

Microsoft IIS creates access logs that can be viewed from the server with Event Viewer. Event Viewer makes viewing the native IIS log format much easier. An explanation of each field in Example 11-4 is provided in Table 11-3. The native IIS log format is not customizable. However, IIS can log in more standard formats such as W3C Extended format, which does allow customization.

Table 11-3   IIS Access Log Entry Explanation

Item	Field	Explanation	Example
Date	date	Date on which the activity occurred	6/14/2016
Time	time	UTC time at which the activity occurred	16:22:22
Client IP Address	c-ip	IP address of the client that made the request	203.0.113.24
User Name	cs-username	Authenticated username	-
Service Name and Instance Number	s-sitename	Internet service name and instance number	W3SVC2
Server Name	s-computername	Name of the server that generated the log entry	WEB3
Server IP Address	s-ip	IP address of the server	198.51.100.10
Server Port	s-port	Server port for the service	80
Method	cs-method	Requested action (HTTP method)	GET
URI Stem	cs-uri-stem	Target of the action	/home.htm
URI Query	cs-uri-query	The query the client was trying to perform	-
HTTP Status	sc-status	HTTP status code	200
Win32 Status	sc-win32-status	Windows status code	0
Bytes Sent	sc-bytes	Bytes that the server sent	15321
Bytes Received	cs-bytes	Bytes that the server received	159
Time Taken	time-taken	Length of time that the action took, in milliseconds	15
Protocol Version	cs-version	The protocol version	HTTP/1.1
User Agent	cs(User-Agent)	Browser type that the client used	Mozilla/5.0 (compatible; MSIE 9.0; Windows Phone OS 7.5; Trident/5.0; IEMobile/9.0)
Cookie	cs(Cookie)	The content of the cookie sent or received, if any	-
Referrer	cs(Referrer)	Site that provided a link to the current site	http://www.example.com

SIEM and Log Collection (11.2.2.6)

Security Information and Event Management (SIEM) technology is used in many organizations to provide real-time reporting and long-term analysis of security events, as shown in Figure 11-20.

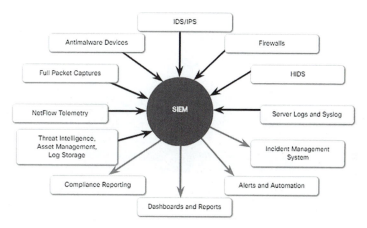

Figure 11-20 SIEM Components

SIEM combines the essential functions of security event management (SEM) and security information management (SIM) tools to provide a comprehensive view of the enterprise network using the following functions:

- **Log collection:** These event records from sources throughout the organization provide important forensic information and help to address compliance reporting requirements.

- **Normalization:** This maps log messages from different systems into a common data model, enabling the organization to connect and analyze related events, even if they are initially logged in different source formats.

- **Correlation:** This links logs and events from disparate systems or applications, speeding detection of and reaction to security threats.

- **Aggregation:** This reduces the volume of event data by consolidating duplicate event records.

- **Reporting:** This presents the correlated, aggregated event data in real-time monitoring and long-term summaries, including graphical interactive dashboards.

- **Compliance:** This is reporting to satisfy the requirements of various compliance regulations.

A popular SIEM is *Splunk*, which is made by a Cisco partner. Figure 11-21 shows the Splunk Botnet Dashboard. Splunk is widely used in SOCs. Another popular and open source SIEM solution is ELK, which consists of the integrated Elasticsearch, Logstash, and Kibana applications.

Figure 11-21   Splunk Botnet Dashboard

Interactive Graphic

Activity 11.2.2.7: Identify Information in Logged Events

Refer to the online course to complete this Activity.

Network Logs (11.2.3)

In this topic, you will learn the elements of a network device log file.

Tcpdump (11.2.3.1)

The *tcpdump* command line tool is a very popular packet analyzer. It can display packet captures in real time or write packet captures to a file. It captures detailed packet protocol and content data. Wireshark is a GUI built on **tcpdump** functionality.

The structure of **tcpdump** captures varies depending on the protocol captured and the fields requested.

NetFlow (11.2.3.2)

NetFlow is a protocol that was developed by Cisco as a tool for network trouble-shooting and session-based accounting. NetFlow efficiently provides an important set of services for IP applications, including network traffic accounting, usage-based network billing, network planning, security, denial of service monitoring capabilities, and network monitoring. NetFlow provides valuable information about network users and applications, peak usage times, and traffic routing.

NetFlow does not capture the entire contents of a packet as does full packet capture. Instead, NetFlow records information about the packet flow. For example, a full packet capture is viewed in Wireshark or **tcpdump**. NetFlow collects metadata, or data about the flow, not the flow data itself.

Cisco invented NetFlow and then allowed it to be used as a basis for an IETF standard called IPFIX. IPFIX is based on Cisco NetFlow Version 9.

NetFlow information can be viewed with tools such as the **nfdump** tool. Similar to **tcpdump**, **nfdump** provides a command line utility for viewing NetFlow data from the **nfcapd** capture daemon, or collector. Tools exist that add GUI functionality to viewing flows. Figure 11-22 shows a screen from the open source FlowViewer tool. The Cisco/Lancope StealthWatch technology enhances the use of NetFlow data for NSM.

Traditionally, an IP flow is based on a set of five, and up to seven, IP packet attributes flowing in a single direction. A flow consists of all packets transmitted until the TCP conversation terminates. IP packet attributes used by NetFlow are:

- IP source address
- IP destination address
- Source port
- Destination port
- Layer 3 protocol type
- Class of service
- Router or switch interface

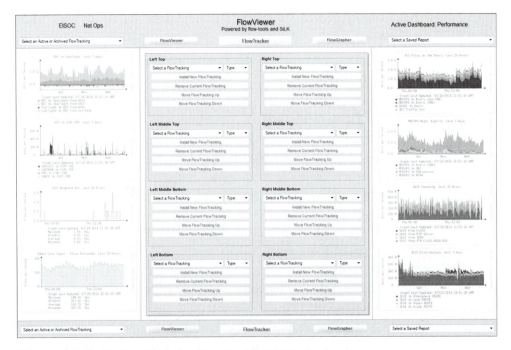

Figure 11-22   NetFlow Session Data Dashboard: FlowViewer

All packets with the same source/destination IP address, source/destination ports, protocol interface, and class of service are grouped into a flow, and then packets and bytes are tallied. This methodology of fingerprinting or determining a flow is scalable because a large amount of network information is condensed into a database of NetFlow information called the NetFlow cache.

All NetFlow flow records will contain the first five items in the preceding list and flow start and end timestamps. The additional information that may appear is highly variable and can be configured on the NetFlow exporter. Exporters are devices that can be configured to create flow records and transmit those flow records for storage on a NetFlow collector device. An example of a basic NetFlow flow record, in two different presentations, is shown in Example 11-5.

Example 11-5   Simple NetFlow Version 5 Flow Record

```
Traffic Contribution: 8% (3/37)


Flow information:
IPV4 SOURCE ADDRESS:         10.1.1.2
IPV4 DESTINATION ADDRESS:    13.1.1.2
INTERFACE INPUT:             Se0/0/1
TRNS SOURCE PORT:            8974
```

```
TRNS DESTINATION PORT:      80
IP TOS:                     0x00
IP PROTOCOL:                6
FLOW SAMPLER ID:            0
FLOW DIRECTION:             Input
ipv4 source mask:           /0
ipv4 destination mask:      /8
counter bytes:              205
ipv4 next hop address:      13.1.1.2
tcp flags:                  0x1b
interface output:           Fa0/0
counter packets:            5
timestamp first:            00:09:12.596
timestamp last:             00:09:12.606
ip source as:               0
ip destination as:          0
```

A large number of attributes for a flow are available. The IANA registry of IPFIX entities lists several hundred, with the first 128 being the most common.

Although NetFlow was not initially conceived as tool for network security monitoring, it is seen as a useful tool in the analysis of network security incidents. It can be used to construct a timeline of compromise, understand individual host behavior, or to track the movement of an attacker or exploit from host to host within a network.

Application Visibility and Control (11.2.3.3)

The Cisco Application Visibility and Control (AVC) system, depicted in Figure 11-23, combines multiple technologies to recognize, analyze, and control over 1000 applications. These include voice and video, email, file sharing, gaming, peer-to-peer (P2P), and cloud-based applications. AVC uses Cisco Next-Generation Network-Based Application Recognition (NBAR2) to discover and classify the applications in use on the network. The NBAR2 application recognition engine supports over 1000 network applications.

To truly understand the importance of this technology, consider Figure 11-24. Identification of network applications by port provides very little granularity and visibility into user behavior. However, application visibility through the identification of application signatures identifies what users are doing, whether it be teleconferencing or downloading movies to their phones.

A management and reporting system, such as Cisco Prime, analyzes and presents the application analysis data into dashboard reports for use by network monitoring personnel. Application usage can also be controlled through quality of service classification and policies based on the AVC information.

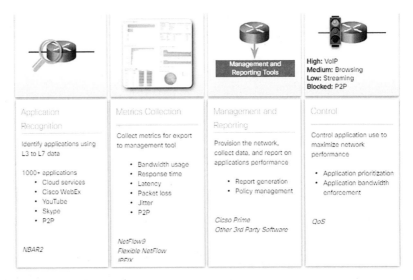

Figure 11-23 Cisco Application Visibility and Control

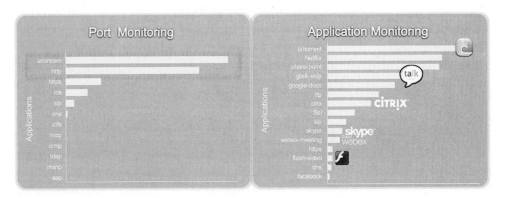

Figure 11-24 Cisco Application Visibility and Control Example

Content Filter Logs (11.2.3.4)

Devices that provide content filtering, such as the Cisco Email Security Appliance (ESA) and the Cisco Web Security Appliance (WSA), provide a wide range of functionalities for security monitoring. Logging is available for many of these functionalities.

The ESA, for example, has more than 30 logs that can be used to monitor most aspects of email delivery, system functioning, antivirus, antispam operations, and blacklist and whitelist decisions. Most of the logs are stored in text files and can be collected on syslog servers, or can be pushed to FTP or SCP servers. In addition, alerts regarding the functioning of the appliance itself and its subsystems can be monitored by email to administrators who are responsible for monitoring and operating the device.

WSA devices offer a similar depth of functioning. WSA effectively acts as a web proxy, meaning that it logs all inbound and outbound transaction information for HTTP traffic. These logs can be quite detailed and are customizable. They can be configured in a W3C compatibility format. The WSA can be configured to submit the logs to a server in various ways, including syslog, FTP, and SCP.

Other logs that are available to the WSA include ACL decision logs, malware scan logs, and web reputation filtering logs.

Figure 11-25 illustrates the "drill-down" dashboards available from Cisco content filtering devices.

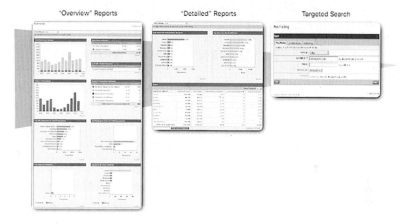

Figure 11-25   Cisco Content Filtering Dashboards

Logging from Cisco Devices (11.2.3.5)

Cisco security devices can be configured to submit events and alerts to security management platforms using SNMP or syslog. Figure 11-26 illustrates a syslog message generated by a Cisco ASA device and a syslog message generated by a Cisco IOS device.

Note that there are two meanings used for the term Facility in Cisco syslog messages. The first is the standard set of Facility values that were established by the syslog standards. These values are used in the PRI message part of the syslog packet to calculate the message priority. Cisco uses some of the values between 15 and 23 to identify Cisco log Facilities, depending on the platform. For example, Cisco ASA devices use syslog Facility 20 by default, which corresponds to local4. The other Facility value is assigned by Cisco, and occurs in the MSG part of the syslog message.

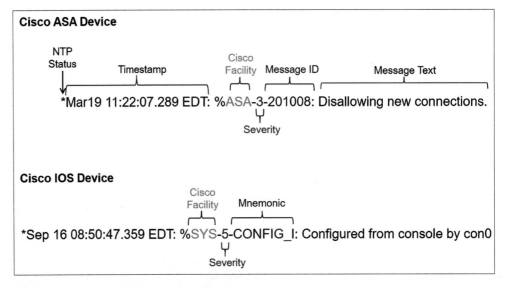

Figure 11-26   Cisco Syslog Message Formats

Cisco devices may use slightly different syslog message formats, and may use mnemonics instead of message IDs, as shown in Figure 11-26.

Proxy Logs (11.2.3.6)

Proxy servers, such as those used for web and DNS requests, contain valuable logs that are a primary source of data for network security monitoring.

Proxy servers are devices that act as intermediaries for network clients. For example, an enterprise may configure a web proxy to handle web requests on the behalf of clients. Instead of requests for web resources being sent directly to the server from the client, the request is sent to a proxy server first. The proxy server requests the resources and returns them to the client. The proxy server generates logs of all requests and responses. These logs can then be analyzed to determine which hosts are making the requests, to assess whether the destinations are safe or potentially malicious, and to gain insights into the kind of resources that have been downloaded.

Web Proxies

Web proxies provide data that help determine whether responses from the web were generated in response to legitimate requests or have been manipulated to appear to be responses but are in fact exploits. It is also possible to use web proxies to inspect outgoing traffic as a means of data loss prevention (DLP). DLP involves scanning outgoing traffic to detect whether the data that is leaving the web contains sensitive, confidential, or secret information. Examples of popular web proxies are Squid, CCProxy, Apache Traffic Server, and WinGate.

Example 11-6 illustrates an example of a Squid web proxy log in the Squid-native format. Explanations of the field values are provided in Table 11-4.

Example 11-6   Squid Web Proxy Log: Native Format

```
1265939281.764     19478 172.16.167.228 TCP_MISS/200 864 GET http://www.example.com//
  images/home.png - NONE/- image/png
```

Table 11-4   Squid Web Proxy Log Explanation

Field	Description
1265939282	**Time:** In UNIX epoch timestamp format, with milliseconds
19478	**Duration:** The elapsed time received, request, and response from Squid
172.16.31.7	**Client IP address:** The IP address of the client that made the request
TCP_MISS/200	**Result codes:** Squid result code and HTTP status code separated by a slash
864	**Size in bytes:** The size/amount of data delivered to client
GET	**Request method:** Request method made by client
http://www.example.com//images/home.png	**URI/URL:** Address of requested resource
-	**Client identity:** RFC 1413 value of the client that made the request; not used by default
NONE/-	**Peering code/peer host:** Neighbor cache server consulted
image/png	**Type:** MIME content type from Content-Type value in the response HTTP header

Note

Open web proxies, which are proxies that are available to any Internet user, can be used to obfuscate threat actor IP addresses. Open proxy addresses may be used in blacklisting Internet traffic.

OpenDNS

OpenDNS, a Cisco company, offers a hosted DNS service that extends the capability of DNS to include security enhancements. Rather than organizations hosting and maintaining blacklisting, phishing protection, and other DNS-related security, OpenDNS provides these protections on their own DNS service. OpenDNS is able to apply many more resources to managing DNS than most organizations can afford. OpenDNS functions in part as a DNS super proxy in this regard. The OpenDNS suite of security products apply real-time threat intelligence to managing DNS access and the security of DNS records. DNS access logs are available from OpenDNS for the subscribed enterprise. Example 11-7 shows an example of an OpenDNS proxy log. Table 11-5 has an explanation of each field. Instead of using local or ISP DNS servers, an organization can choose to subscribe to OpenDNS for DNS services.

Example 11-7   OpenDNS Web Proxy Log

```
@40000000573b4e1a11876764 9.2 192.168.1.11 192.168.1.11 203.0.113.200 normal 0 -
   www.example.com. 1 0 18e7e3b69b 0 800000 0 com m7.dfx
```

Table 11-5   OpenDNS Web Proxy Log Explanation

Field	Example	Explanation
Timestamp	@40000000573b4e1a11876764	Log file entry timestamp in TAI64N format
Version	9.2	Version of the log format
remoteIP	192.168.1.11	Address of original requestor, same as the client address if no proxy is involved
client	192.168.1.11	Client address
server	203.0.113.200	DNS server IP address
handling	normal	Normal operation or other action such as redirection, blocking, etc.
origin_id	0	Device ID that applied policy
other origin IDs	-	List of additional origin devices
qname	www.example.com	Resource queried
qtype	1	Type of query
rcode	0	Response code
dlink	18e7e3b69b	Device ID
blocked categories	0	Associated category that resulted in blocking of request
categories	8000000	Category or request resource
flags	0	Transaction-specific flags for the stats system
public suffix	com	Top-level domain suffix
host	m6.dfw	First two components of hostname that generated log entry

NextGen IPS (11.2.3.7)

NextGen IPS (NGIPS) devices extend network security beyond IP addresses and Layer 4 port numbers to the application layer and beyond. NextGen IPS devices are advanced devices that provided much more functionality than previous generations of network security devices. One of those functionalities is reporting dashboards with interactive features that allow quick point-and-click reports on very specific information without the need for SIEM or other event correlators.

Features of Cisco's line of NGIPS devices is shown in Figure 11-27.

Figure 11-27   Cisco Next-Generation IPS Major Functionalities

Cisco NGIPSs use FirePOWER services to consolidate multiple security layers into a single platform. This helps to contain costs and simplify management. FirePOWER services include application visibility and control, FirePOWER NGIPS, reputation- and category-based URL filtering, and Advanced Malware Protection (AMP). FirePOWER devices allow monitoring network security through a web-enabled GUI called Event Viewer.

Common NGIPS events include:

- **Connection events:** Connection logs contain data about sessions that are detected directly by the NGIPS. Connection events include basic connection properties such as timestamps, source and destination IP addresses, and metadata about why the connection was logged, such as which access control rule logged the event.

- **Intrusion events:** The system examines the packets that traverse the network for malicious activity that could affect the availability, integrity, and confidentiality of a host and its data. When the system identifies a possible intrusion, it generates an intrusion event, which is a record of the date, time, type of exploit, and contextual information about the source of the attack and its target.

■ **Host or endpoint events:** When a host appears on the network, the system can detect it and log details of the device hardware, IP addressing, and the last known presence on the network.

■ **Network discovery events:** Network discovery events represent changes that have been detected in the monitored network. These changes are logged in response to network discovery policies that specify the kinds of data to be collected, the network segments to be monitored, and the hardware interfaces of the device that should be used for event collection.

■ **NetFlow events:** Network discovery can use a number of mechanisms, one of which is to use exported NetFlow flow records to generate new events for hosts and servers.

Interactive Graphic

Activity 11.2.3.8: Identify the Security Technology from the Data Description

Refer to the online course to complete this Activity.

Interactive Graphic

Activity 11.2.3.9: Identify the NextGen IPS Event Type

Refer to the online course to complete this Activity.

Packet Tracer ☐ Activity

Packet Tracer 11.2.3.10: Explore a NetFlow Implementation

In this Packet Tracer activity, you will explore an implementation of NetFlow.

Packet Tracer ☐ Activity

Packet Tracer 11.2.3.11: Logging from Multiple Sources

In this activity, you will use Packet Tracer to compare network data generated by multiple sources including syslog, AAA, and NetFlow.

Summary (11.3)

In this chapter, you learned how cybersecurity analysts use various tools and techniques to identify network security alerts. Syslog is a common monitoring protocol that can log a variety of events. NTP is used to timestamp these events. Protocols that are particularly vulnerable, such as DNS, HTTP, email protocols, and ICMP, should be actively monitored by the cybersecurity analyst.

Security technologies used to protect the privacy of our data also make it more difficult for security monitoring. ACLs can give a false sense of security if they are overly relied upon. NAT and PAT can complicate security monitoring, hiding the individual IP addresses that are inside the network. Encrypted traffic is difficult to monitor because the data is unreadable to any other devices but the VPN endpoints. P2P network activity can circumvent firewall protections, is difficult to monitor, and is a common vector for the spread of malware.

Log files are the data used by cybersecurity analysts to monitor the security of the network. Security data includes:

- Alert data
- Session and transaction data
- Full packet captures
- Statistical data

The sources for these security data include a variety of logs:

- Host logs
- Syslog
- Server logs
- Web logs
- Network logs

 Lab 11.3.1.1: Set Up a Multi-VM Environment

In this lab, you will set up a virtual network environment by connecting multiple virtual machines in VirtualBox. This environment will be used for the rest of the labs in this course.

Practice

The following activities provide practice with the topics introduced in this chapter. The Labs and are available in the companion *CCNA Cybersecurity Operations Lab Manual* (ISBN: 9781587134388). The Packet Tracer Activity instructions are also in the *Labs & Study Guide*. The PKA files are found in the online course.

Labs

Lab 11.3.1.1: Set Up a Multi-VM Environment

Packet Tracer Activities

Packet Tracer 11.2.3.10: Explore a NetFlow Implementation

Packet Tracer 11.2.3.11: Logging from Multiple Sources

Check Your Understanding

Complete all the review questions listed here to test your understanding of the topics and concepts in this chapter. The appendix "Answers to 'Check Your Understanding' Questions" lists the answers.

1. Which statement describes the **tcpdump** tool?

   A. It is a command line packet analyzer.

   B. It is used to control multiple TCP-based applications.

   C. It accepts and analyzes data captured by Wireshark.

   D. It can be used to analyze network log data in order to describe and predict network behavior.

2. Which Windows host log event type describes the successful operation of an application, driver, or service?

   A. Error

   B. Warning

   C. Information

   D. Success Audit

3. A NIDS/NIPS has identified a threat. Which type of security data will be generated and sent to a logging device?

   A. Alert

   B. Session

   C. Statistical

   D. Transaction

4. What is the purpose of Tor?

   A. To donate processor cycles to distributed computational tasks in a processor-sharing P2P network

   B. To allow users to browse the Internet anonymously

   C. To securely connect to a remote network over an unsecure link such as an Internet connection

   D. To inspect incoming traffic and look for any that violates a rule or matches the signature of a known exploit

5. Which statement describes an operational characteristic of NetFlow?

   A. NetFlow captures the entire contents of a packet.

   B. NetFlow can provide services for user access control.

   C. NetFlow flow records can be viewed by the **tcpdump** tool.

   D. NetFlow collects metadata about the packet flow, not the flow data itself.

6. Which type of security data can be used to describe or predict network behavior?

   A. Alert

   B. Session

   C. Statistical

   D. Transaction

7. What type of server can threat actors use DNS to communicate with?

   A. CnC

   B. Database

   C. NTP

   D. Web

8. In a Cisco AVC system, in which module is NBAR2 deployed?

   A. Control

   B. Metrics Collection

   C. Application Recognition

   D. Management and Reporting

9. A security analyst reviews network logs. The data shows user network activities such as username, IP addresses, web pages accessed, and timestamp. Which type of data is the analyst reviewing?

   A. Alert

   B. Session

   C. Application

   D. Transaction

10. Which type of server daemon accepts messages sent by network devices to create a collection of log entries?

    A. SSH

    B. NTP

    C. Syslog

    D. AAA

11. Which Windows tool can be used to review host logs?

    A. Services

    B. Event Viewer

    C. Task Manager

    D. Device Manager

12. Which two protocols may devices use in the application process that sends email? (Choose two.)

    A. HTTP

    B. SMTP

    C. POP

    D. IMAP

    E. DNS

    F. POP3

## CHAPTER 12

Intrusion Data Analysis

Objectives

Upon completion of this chapter, you will be able to answer the following questions:

- What is the structure of alerts?

- How are alerts classified?

- How is data prepared for use in a network security monitoring (NSM) system?

- How do you use Security Onion tools to investigate network security events?

- Which network monitoring tools enhance workflow management?

- What is the role of the digital forensic processes?

Key Terms

This chapter uses the following key terms. You can find the definitions in the Glossary.

Introduction (12.0)

Now that you have spent some time learning about security monitoring and the types of data cybersecurity analysts work with on a daily basis, it is time to turn your attention to data analysis.

This chapter discusses how network security alerts are reported, evaluated, escalated, and preserved as evidence.

> **Note**
>
> At the end of the last chapter, you had the opportunity to install the multi-VM environment that will be used in this chapter. While reading this chapter, you may find it useful to have the Security Onion VM running so that you can become more familiar with the interface.

Evaluating Alerts (12.1)

In this section, you will learn the process for evaluating alerts.

Sources of Alerts (12.1.1)

In this topic, you will learn how to identify the structure of alerts.

Security Onion (12.1.1.1)

Security Onion is an open source suite of network security monitoring (NSM) tools for evaluating alerts, providing three core functions to the cybersecurity analyst:

- Full packet capture and data types
- Network-based and host-based intrusion detection systems
- Alert analysis tools

Security Onion runs on an Ubuntu Linux distribution and can be installed as a stand-alone installation or as a sensor and server platform. Some components of Security Onion are owned and maintained by corporations, such as Cisco and Riverbend Technologies, but are made available as open source.

> **Note**
>
> In some resources, you may see Security Onion abbreviated as SO. In this course, we will use Security Onion.

Detection Tools for Collecting Alert Data (12.1.1.2)

Security Onion contains many components. It is an integrated environment which is designed to simplify the deployment of a comprehensive NSM solution. Figure 12-1 illustrates a simplified view of the way in which some of the components of Security Onion work together.

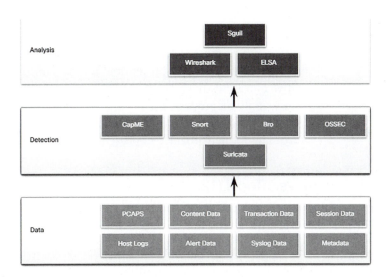

Figure 12-1   A Security Onion Architecture

Previously in the course you have learned about the diverse types of data that are available for NSM. These data types, shown in the bottom of Figure 12-1, are collected by detection tools, which are shown in the middle of Figure 12-1:

- *CapME*: This is a web application that allows viewing of pcap transcripts rendered with the tcpflow or Bro tools. CapME can be accessed from the Enterprise Log Search and Archive (ELSA) tool. CapME provides the cybersecurity analyst with an easy-to-read means of viewing an entire Layer 4 session. CapME acts as a plugin to ELSA and provides access to relevant pcap files that can be opened in Wireshark.

- **Snort:** This is a network-based intrusion detection system (NIDS). It is an important source of the alert data that is indexed in the Sguil analysis tool. Snort uses rules and signatures to generate alerts. Snort can automatically download new rules using the PulledPork component of Security Onion. Snort and PulledPork are open source tools that are sponsored by Cisco.

- **Bro:** This is an NIDS that uses more of a behavior-based approach to intrusion detection. Rather than using signatures or rules, Bro uses policies, in the form of scripts that determine what data to log and when to issue alert notifications.

Bro can also submit file attachments for malware analysis, block access to malicious locations, and shut down a computer that appears to be violating security policies.

- *OSSEC*: This is a host-based intrusion detection system (HIDS) that is integrated into Security Onion. It actively monitors host system operations, including conducting file integrity monitoring, local log monitoring, system process monitoring, and rootkit detection. OSSEC alerts and log data are available to Sguil and ELSA. OSSEC requires an agent to be running on the Windows computers in the enterprise.

- *Suricata*: This is a NIDS that uses a signature-based approach. It can also be used for inline intrusion prevention. It is similar to Bro; however, Suricata uses native multithreading, which allows the distribution of packet stream processing across multiple processor cores. It also includes some additional features such as reputation-based blocking and support for graphics processing unit (GPU) multithreading for performance improvement.

Analysis Tools (12.1.1.3)

Security Onion integrates these various types of data and IDS logs into a single platform through the following tools:

- **Sguil:** This provides a high-level cybersecurity analysts' console for investigating security alerts from a wide variety of sources. Sguil serves as a starting point in the investigation of security alerts. A wide variety of data sources are available to the cybersecurity analyst through pivoting directly from Sguil to other tools.

- *ELSA*: This provides an interface to a wide variety of NSM data logs. Logging sources such as HIDS, NIDS, firewalls, syslog clients and servers, domain services, and others can be configured to make their logs available to ELSA databases. ELSA is configured to normalize logs from diverse sources so that the logs can be represented, stored, and accessed by following a common schema. ELSA search functionality is directly linked to Sguil alert records. ELSA right-click menus allow the cybersecurity analyst to easily search NSM data for details of an alert.

- **Wireshark:** This is a packet capture application that is integrated into the Security Onion suite. It can be opened directly from other tools and will display full-packet captures relevant to an analysis.

Alert Generation (12.1.1.4)

Security alerts are notification messages that are generated by NSM tools, systems, and security devices. Alerts can come in many forms depending on the source. For example, syslog provides support for severity ratings which can be used to alert cybersecurity analysts regarding events that require attention.

In Security Onion, Sguil provides a console that integrates alerts from multiple sources into a timestamped queue. A cybersecurity analyst can work through the security queue investigating, classifying, escalating, or retiring alerts. In lieu of a dedicated workflow management system such as Request Tracker for Incident Response (RTIR), a cybersecurity analyst would use the output of an application like Sguil to orchestrate an NSM investigation.

Alerts will generally include five-tuples information when available, as well as timestamps and information identifying which device or system generated the alert. Five-tuples includes the following information for tracking a conversation between a source and destination application:

- **SrcIP:** The source IP address for the event

- **SPort:** The source (local) Layer 4 port for the event

- **DstIP:** The destination IP for the event

- **DPort:** The destination Layer 4 port for the event

- **Pr:** The IP protocol number for the event

Additional information could be whether a permit or deny decision was applied to the traffic, some captured data from the packet payload, a hash value for a downloaded file, or any of a variety of data.

Figure 12-2 shows the Sguil application window with the queue of alerts in the top portion that are waiting to be investigated.

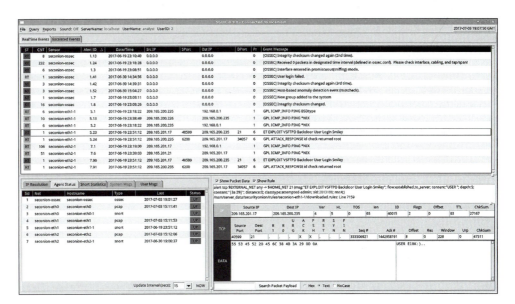

Figure 12-2   Sguil Window

The fields available for the real-time events are as follows:

- **ST:** This is the status of the event. RT means real time. The event is color-coded by priority. The priorities are based on the category of the alert. There are four priority levels; very low, low, medium, and high. The colors range from light yellow to red as the priority increases.

- **CNT:** This is the count for the number of times this event has been detected for the same source and destination IP address. The system has determined that this set of events is correlated. Rather than reporting each in a potentially long series of correlated events in this window, the event is listed once with the number of times it has been detected in this column. High numbers here can represent a security problem or the need for tuning of the event signatures to limit the number of potentially spurious events that are being reported.

- **Sensor:** This is the agent reporting the event. The available sensors and their identifying numbers can be found in the Agent Status tab of the pane which appears below the events window on the left. These numbers are also used in the Alert ID column. From the Agent Status pane we can see that OSSEC, pcap, and Snort sensors are reporting to Sguil. In addition, we can see the default hostnames for these sensors, which includes the monitoring interface. Note that each monitoring interface has both pcap and Snort data associated with it.

- **Alert ID:** This two-part number represents the sensor reporting the problem and the event number for that sensor. We can see from Figure 12-2 that the largest number of events displayed are from the OSSEC sensor. The OSSEC sensor has reported eight sets of correlated events. Of these events, 232 have been reported with event ID 1.24.

- **Date/Time:** This is the timestamp for the first event in a correlated series of events.

- **Event Message:** This is the identifying text for the event. This is configured in the rule that triggered the alert. The associated rule can be viewed in the right-hand pane, just above the packet data. To do so, click the Show Rule checkbox.

Depending on the security technology, alerts can be generated based on rules, signatures, anomalies, or behaviors. No matter how they are generated, the conditions that trigger an alert must be predefined in some manner.

Rules and Alerts (12.1.1.5)

Alerts can come from a number of sources:

- **NIDS:** Snort, Bro and Suricata

- **HIDS:** OSSEC

- **Asset management and monitoring:** Passive Asset Detection System (PADS)

- **HTTP, DNS, and TCP transactions:** Recorded by Bro and pcaps

- **Syslog messages:** Multiple sources

The information found in the alerts displayed in Sguil will differ in message format because they come from different sources.

The Sguil alert in Figure 12-3 was triggered by a rule that was configured in Snort.

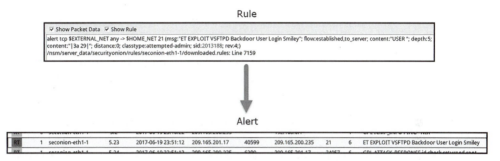

Figure 12-3   Sguil Alert and Associated Rule

It is important for the cybersecurity analyst to be able to interpret what triggered the alert so that the alert can be investigated. For this reason, the cybersecurity analyst should understand the components of Snort rules, which are a major source of alerts in Security Onion.

Snort Rule Structure (12.1.1.6)

Snort rules consist of two sections, as shown in Example 12-1 and Table 12-1: the rule header and the rule options.

Example 12-1   Snort Rule

```
alert ip any any -> any any (msg:"GPL ATTACK_RESPONSE id check returned root";
  content:"uid=0|28|root|29|"; fast_pattern:only; classtype:bad-unknown;
  sid:2100498; rev:8;)
/nsm/server_data/securityonion/rules/seconion-eth1-1/downloaded.rules:Line 692
```

Table 12-1   Snort Rule Structure

Component	Explanation
Rule header	Contains action to be taken, source and destination addresses and ports, and direction of traffic
Rule options	Includes the message to be displayed, details of packet content, alert type, and source ID and details, such as a reference for the rule
Rule location	Added by Sguil to indicate where the rule is in the SO file structure and in the specified rule file

The rule header contains the action, protocol, source and destination IP addresses and netmasks, and the source and destination port information. In Example 12-1, the rule header is

```
alert ip any any -> any any
```

The rule options section contains alert messages and information on which parts of the packet should be inspected to determine if the rule action should be taken. In Example 12-1, the rule action is enclosed within the parentheses:

```
(msg:"GPL ATTACK_RESPONSE id check returned root"; content:"uid=0|28|root|29|";
    fast_pattern:only; classtype:bad-unknown; sid:2100498; rev:8;)
```

Rule location is sometimes added by Sguil. Rule location is the path to the file that contains the rule and the line number at which the rule appears so that it can be found and modified, or eliminated, if required. In Example 12-1, the rule location is

```
/nsm/server_data/securityonion/rules/seconion-eth1-1/downloaded.rules:Line 692
```

The Rule Header

Table 12-2 shows the structure for the rule header in Example 12-1.

Table 12-2   Snort Rule Header Structure

Component	Explanation
alert	The action to be taken is to issue an alert; other actions are log and pass.
ip	The protocol.
any any	The specified source is any IP address and any Layer 4 port.
->	The direction of flow is from the source to the destination.
any any	The specified destination is any IP address and any Layer 4 port.

The rule header contains the action, protocol, addressing, and port information. In addition, the direction of flow that triggered the alert is indicated. The structure of the header portion is consistent between Snort alert rules.

Snort can be configured to use variables to represent internal and external IP addresses. These variables, **$HOME_NET** and **$EXTERNAL_NET**, appear in the Snort rules. They simplify the creation of rules by eliminating the need to specify specific addresses and masks for every rule. The values for these variables are configured in the snort.conf file. Snort also allows individual IP addresses, blocks of addresses, or lists of either to be specified in rules. Ranges of ports can be specified by separating the upper and lower values of the range with a colon. Other operators are also available.

The Rule Options

The structure of the options section of the rule is variable. Table 12-3 shows the structure for the rule options in Example 12-1.

Table 12-3   Snort Rule Options Structure

Component	Explanation
msg:	Text that describes the alert.
content:	Refers to content of the packet. In this case, an alert will be sent if the literal text "uid=0(root)" appears anywhere in the packet data. Values specifying the location of the text in the data payload can also be provided.
reference:	This is not present in all rules. It is often a link to a URL that provides more information about the rule. In this case, the sid is hyperlinked to the source of the rule on the Internet.
classtype:	A category for the attack. Snort includes a set of default categories that have one of four priority values.
sid:	A unique numeric rule identifier for the rule.
rev:	The revision of the rule that is represented by the sid.

The rule options section contains the text message that identifies the alert. It also contains metadata about the alert, such as a URL that provides reference information for the alert. Other information can be included, such as the type of rule and a unique numeric identifier for the rule and the rule revision. In addition, features of the packet payload can be specified in the options.

Snort rule messages may include the source of the rule. Three common sources for Snort rules are

- **GPL:** Older Snort rules that were created by Sourcefire and distributed under a GPLv2. The GPL ruleset is not Cisco Talos certified. It includes Snort SIDs 3464 and below. The GPL is included in Security Onion.

- **ET:** Snort rules from Emerging Threats. Emerging Threats is a collection point for Snort rules from multiple sources. ET rules are open source under a BSD license. The ET ruleset contains rules from multiple categories. A set of ET rules is included with Security Onion.

- **VRT:** These rules are immediately available to subscribers and are released to registered users 30 days after they were created, with some limitations. They are now created and maintained by Cisco Talos.

Rules can be downloaded automatically from Snort.org using the PulledPork rule management utility that is included with Security Onion.

Alerts not generated by Snort rules are identified by the OSSEC or PADS tags, among others. In addition, custom local rules can be created.

Lab 12.1.1.7: Snort and Firewall Rules

Different security appliances and software perform different functions and record different events. As a consequence, the alerts that are generated by different appliances and software will also vary.

In this lab, to get familiar with firewall rules and IDS signatures, you will:

- Perform live-monitoring of IDS and events.
- Configure your own customized firewall rule to stop internal hosts from contacting a malware-hosting server.
- Craft a malicious packet and launch it against an internal target.
- Create a customized IDS rule to detect the customized attack and issue an alert based on it.

Overview of Alert Evaluation (12.1.2)

In this topic, you will learn how alerts are classified.

The Need for Alert Evaluation (12.1.2.1)

The threat landscape is constantly changing as new vulnerabilities are discovered and new threats evolve. As user and organizational needs change, so too does the attack surface. Threat actors have learned how to quickly vary features of their exploits in order to evade detection.

It is impossible to design measures to prevent all exploits. Exploits will inevitably evade protection measures, no matter how sophisticated they may be. Sometimes, the best that can be done is to detect exploits during or after they have occurred. Detection rules should be overly conservative. In other words, having alerts that are sometimes generated by innocent traffic is better than having rules that miss malicious traffic. For this reason, it is necessary to have skilled cybersecurity analysts investigate alerts to determine if an exploit has actually occurred.

Tier 1 cybersecurity analysts will typically work through queues of alerts in a tool like Sguil. As shown in Figure 12-4, from Sguil, the analyst can pivot to tools like Bro, Wireshark, and ELSA to verify that an alert represents an actual exploit.

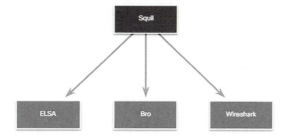

Figure 12-4 Primary Tools for the Tier 1 Cybersecurity Analyst

Evaluating Alerts (12.1.2.2)

Security incidents are classified using a scheme borrowed from medical diagnostics. This classification scheme is used to guide actions and to evaluate diagnostic procedures. For example, when a patient visits a doctor for a routine examination, one of the doctor's tasks is to determine whether the patient is sick. One of the outcomes can be a correct determination that disease is present and the patient is sick. Another outcome can be that there is no disease and the patient is healthy.

The concern is that either diagnosis can be accurate, or true, or inaccurate, or false. For example, the doctor could miss the signs of disease and make the incorrect determination that the patient is well when they are in fact sick. Another possible error is to rule that a patient is sick when that patient is in fact healthy. False diagnoses are either costly or dangerous.

In network security analysis, the cybersecurity analyst is presented with an alert. This is similar to a patient going to the doctor and saying, "I am sick." The cybersecurity analyst, like the doctor, needs to determine if this diagnosis is true. The cybersecurity analyst asks, "The system says that an exploit has occurred. Is this true?"

Table 12-4 shows the classification of alerts.

Table 12-4 Classification of Alerts

	TRUE	**FALSE**
Positive (alert exists)	Incident occurred	No incident occurred
Negative (no alert exists)	No incident occurred	Incident occurred

Alerts can be classified as follows:

- *True positive*: The alert has been verified to be an actual security incident.

- *False positive*: The alert does not indicate an actual security incident.

An alternative situation is that an alert was not generated. The absence of an alert can be classified as:

- *True negative*: No security incident has occurred.
- *False negative*: An undetected incident has occurred.

True positives are the desired type of alert. They mean that the rules that generate alerts have worked.

False positives are not desirable. Although they do not indicate that an undetected exploit has occurred, they are costly because cybersecurity analysts musts investigate false alarms; therefore, time is taken away from investigation of alerts that indicate true exploits.

True negatives are also desirable. They indicate that normal traffic is correctly ignored and erroneous alerts are not being issued.

False negatives are dangerous. They indicate that exploits are not being detected by the security systems that are in place. These incidents could go undetected for a long time, and ongoing data loss and damage could result.

When true positives are suspected, a Tier 1 cybersecurity analyst is sometimes required to escalate the alert to a cybersecurity investigator who is working at Tier 2. The Tier 2 cybersecurity analyst will move forward with the investigation in order to confirm the incident and identify any potential damage that may have been caused. This information will be used by more senior security personnel who will work to isolate the damage, address vulnerabilities, mitigate the threat, and deal with reporting requirements.

A cybersecurity analyst may also be responsible for informing security personnel that false positives are occurring to the extent that the cybersecurity analyst's time is seriously impacted. This situation indicates that security systems need to be tuned to become more efficient. Legitimate changes in the network configuration or newly downloaded detection rules could result in a sudden spike in false positives.

False negatives may be discovered well after an exploit has occurred. This can happen through retrospective security analysis (RSA). RSA can occur when newly obtained rules or other threat intelligence is applied to archived network security data. For this reason, it is important to monitor threat intelligence to learn of new vulnerabilities and exploits and to evaluate the likelihood that the network was vulnerable. In addition, the exploit needs to be evaluated regarding the potential damage that the enterprise could suffer. It may be determined that adding new mitigation techniques is sufficient, or that a more detailed analysis should be conducted.

Deterministic Analysis and Probabilistic Analysis (12.1.2.3)

Statistical techniques can be used to evaluate the risk that exploits will be successful in a given network. This type of analysis can help decision makers to better evaluate the cost of mitigating a threat with the damage that an exploit could cause.

Two general approaches used to do this are deterministic and probabilistic analysis, which can be summarized as follows:

- *Deterministic analysis*: For an exploit to be successful, all prior steps in the exploit must also be successful. The cybersecurity analyst knows the steps for a successful exploit

- *Probabilistic analysis*: Use statistical techniques to predict the probability that an exploit will occur based on the likelihood that prior events will occur.

Deterministic analysis evaluates risk based on what is known about a vulnerability. It assumes that for an exploit to be successful all prior steps in the exploit process must also be successful. This type of risk analysis can only describe the worst case. However, many threat actors, although aware of the process to carry out an exploit, may lack the knowledge or expertise to successfully complete each step on the path to a successful exploit. This can give the cybersecurity analyst an opportunity to detect the exploit and stop it before it proceeds any further.

Probabilistic analysis estimates the potential success of an exploit by estimating the likelihood that if one step in an exploit has successfully been completed that the next step will also be successful. Probabilistic analysis is especially useful in real-time network security analysis in which numerous variables are at play and a given threat actor can make unknown decisions as an exploit is pursued.

Probabilistic analysis relies on statistical techniques that are designed to estimate the probability that an event will occur based on the likelihood that prior events will occur. Using this type of analysis, the most likely paths that an exploit will take can be estimated and the attention of security personnel can be focused on preventing or detecting the most likely exploit.

In a deterministic analysis, all of the information to accomplish an exploit is assumed to be known. The characteristics of the exploit, such as the use of specific port numbers, are known either from other instances of the exploit, or because standardized ports are in use. In probabilistic analysis, it is assumed that the port numbers that will be used can only be predicted with some degree of confidence. In this situation, an exploit that uses dynamic port numbers, for example, cannot be analyzed deterministically. Such exploits have been optimized to avoid detection by firewalls that use static rules.

Interactive Graphic

Activity 12.1.2.4: Identify Deterministic and Probabilistic Scenarios

Refer to the online course to complete this Activity.

Interactive Graphic

Activity 12.1.2.5: Identify the Alert Classification

Refer to the online course to complete this Activity.

Working with Network Security Data (12.2)

In this section, you will learn how to interpret data to determine the source of an alert.

A Common Data Platform (12.2.1)

In this topic, you will learn how data is prepared for use in an NSM system.

ELSA (12.2.1.1)

ELSA stands for Enterprise Log Search and Archive. As the name implies, ELSA is an enterprise-level tool for searching and archiving of NSM data that originates from multiple sources. ELSA is able to normalize log file entries into a common schema that can then be displayed in the ELSA web interface. Search follows a simple syntax and also more complex regular expression-based patterns for searching and filtering, if required. ELSA is capable of indexing, archiving, and searching large amounts of NSM data.

ELSA receives logs over syslog-ng, stores logs in MySQL databases, and indexes using Sphinx Search. The data is served by a web server process and accessed by users through a browser. ELSA is designed to handle a high volume of data and is fast and scalable.

Searches can be executed by "pivoting" from Sguil to ELSA, or ELSA may be opened on its own. A large set of premade queries is available when ELSA is opened on its own, and searches can be constructed as well. Figure 12-5 shows the ELSA interface with example query results.

The frame on the left side of the browser window contains a list of the types of pre-made queries available. Each type of search can be expanded to reveal a variety of queries that can suit the general needs of a cybersecurity analyst.

Data Reduction (12.2.1.2)

The amount of network traffic that is collected by packet captures and the number of log file entries and alerts that are generated by network and security devices can be enormous. Even with recent advances in Big Data, processing, storing, accessing, and archiving NSM-related data is a daunting task. For this reason, it is important to identify the network data that should be gathered. Not every log file entry, packet, and alert needs to be gathered. By limiting the volume of data, tools like ELSA will be far more useful, as shown in Figure 12-6.

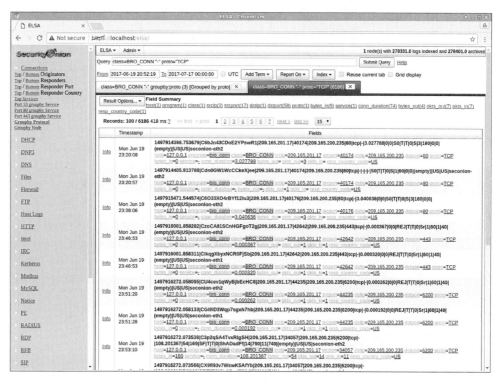

Figure 12-5   ELSA Interface

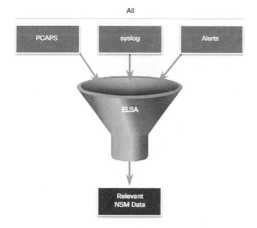

Figure 12-6   Data Reduction

Some network traffic has little value to NSM. Encrypted data, such as IPsec or SSL traffic, is largely unreadable. Some traffic, such as that generated by routing protocols or STP, is routine and can be excluded. Other broadcast and multicast protocols can usually be eliminated from packet captures, as can traffic from other protocols that generate a lot of routine traffic.

In addition, alerts that are generated by a HIDS, such as Windows security auditing or OSSEC, should be evaluated for relevance. Some are informational or of low potential security impact. These messages can be filtered from NSM data. Similarly, syslog may store messages of very low severity that should be disregarded to diminish the quantity of NSM data to be handled.

Data Normalization (12.2.1.3)

Data normalization is the process of combining data from a number of data sources into a common format. ELSA provides a series of plugins that process security data and transform it before it is added to ELSA databases. Additional plugins can be created to suit the needs of the organization.

A common schema will specify the names and formats for the required data fields. Formatting of the data fields can vary widely between sources. However, if searching is to be effective, the data fields must be consistent. For example, IPv6 addresses, MAC addresses, and date and time information can be represented in varying formats, as shown below:

IPv6 Address Formats

- 2001:db8:acad:1111:2222::33
- 2001:DB8:ACAD:1111:2222::33
- 2001:DB8:ACAD:1111:2222:0:0:33
- 2001:DB8:ACAD:1111:2222:0000:0000:0033

MAC Address Formats

- A7:03:DB:7C:91:AA
- A7-03-DB-7C-91-AA
- A70.3DB.7C9.1AA

Date Formats

- Monday, July 24, 2017 7:39:35pm
- Mon, 24 Jul 2017 19:39:35 +0000
- 2017-07-24T19:39:35+00:00
- 1500925254

Similarly, subnet masks, DNS records, and so on can vary in format between data sources.

Data normalization is required to simplify searching for correlated events. If differently formatted values exist in the NSM data for IPv6 addresses, for example, a separate query term would need to be created for every variation in order for correlated events to be returned by the query.

When ELSA displays a log file entry, the original entry is shown in bold, and the normalized entry appears below it with the ELSA field identifiers and their values, as shown in Figure 12-7.

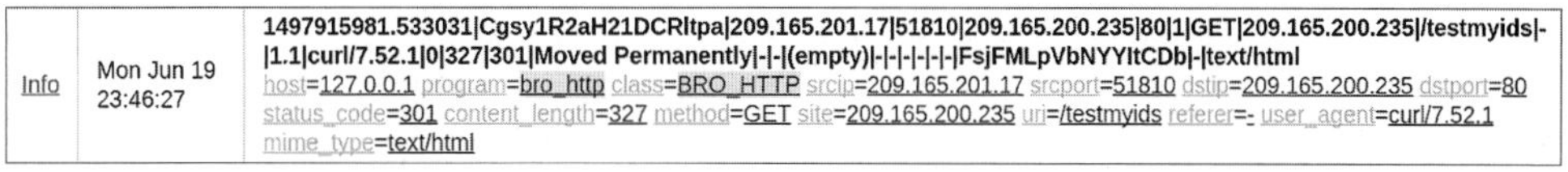

| Info | Mon Jun 19 23:46:27 | **1497915981.533031\|Cgsy1R2aH21DCRltpa\|209.165.201.17\|51810\|209.165.200.235\|80\|1\|GET\|209.165.200.235\|/testmyids\|-\|1.1\|curl/7.52.1\|0\|327\|301\|Moved Permanently\|-\|-\|(empty)\|-\|-\|-\|-\|-\|FsjFMLpVbNYYltCDb\|-\|text/html** host=127.0.0.1 program=bro_http class=BRO_HTTP srcip=209.165.201.17 srcport=51810 dstip=209.165.200.235 dstport=80 status_code=301 content_length=327 method=GET site=209.165.200.235 uri=/testmyids referer=- user_agent=curl/7.52.1 mime_type=text/html |

Figure 12-7   ELSA Normalizes Log Records

Table 12-5 shows how the Bro log entry in Figure 12-7 is normalized by ELSA.

Table 12-5   ELSA Log Structure

Bro Log Format Fields	Normalized and Labeled ELSA Log Format Fields
1497915982	Mon Jun 19
	23:46:27

Bro Log Format Fields	Normalized and Labeled ELSA Log Format Fields
|209.165.201.17|51810|209.165.200.235|80|	srcip=209.165.201.17 srcport=51810 dstip=209.165.200.235 dstport=80
|327|301|	status_code=301 content_length=327
|GET|209.165.200.235|/testmyids|	method=GET site=209.165.200.235 uri=/testmyids

Data Archiving (12.2.1.4)

Everyone would love the security of collecting and saving everything, just in case. However, retaining NSM data indefinitely is not feasible due to storage and access issues. It should be noted that the retention period for certain types of network security information may be specified by compliance frameworks. For example, the Payment Card Industry Data Security Standard (PCI DSS) requires that an audit trail of user activities related to protected information be retained for one year.

Security Onion has different data retention periods for different types of NSM data. For pcaps and raw Bro logs, a value assigned in the **securityonion.conf** file controls the percentage of disk space that can be used by log files. By default, this value is set to 90%. For ELSA, retention of archived logs is dependent on values set in the **elsa_node.conf** file. These values are related to the amount of storage space that is available. By default, Security Onion is configured with a log size limit of 3 GB. The guideline is that this value should be 90 to 95% of the total disk space that ELSA is using. By default, ELSA will use 33% of the configured log size limit for archived logs. ELSA can optionally be configured to retain data for a period of time. The provided value for this in the configuration file is 90 days.

Sguil alert data is retained for 30 days by default. This value is set in the **securityonion.conf** file.

Security Onion is known to require a lot of storage and RAM to run properly. Depending on the size of the network, multiple terabytes of storage may be required. Of course, Security Onion data can always be archived to external storage by a data archive system, depending on the needs and capabilities of the organization.

> **Note**
>
> The storage locations for the different types of Security Onion data will vary based on the Security Onion implementation.

Lab 12.2.1.5: Convert Data into a Universal Format

Log entries are generated by network devices, operating systems, applications, and various types of programmable devices. A file containing a time-sequenced stream of log entries is called a log file.

By nature, log files record events that are relevant to the source. The syntax and format of data within log messages are often defined by the application developer.

Therefore, the terminology used in the log entries often varies from source to source. For example, depending on the source, the terms login, logon, authentication event, and user connection may all appear in log entries to describe a successful user authentication to a server.

It is often desirable to have a consistent and uniform terminology in logs generated by different sources. This is especially true when all log files are being collected by a centralized point.

The term *normalization* refers to the process of converting parts of a message, in this case a log entry, to a common format.

In this lab, you will use command line tools to manually normalize log entries. In Part 2, the timestamp field must be normalized. In Part 3, the IPv6 field is the one that requires normalization.

Investigating Network Data (12.2.2)

In this topic, you will learn how to use Security Onion tools to investigate network security events.

Working in Sguil (12.2.2.1)

The primary duty of a cybersecurity analyst is the verification of security alerts. Depending on the organization, the tools used to do this will vary. For example, a ticketing system may be used to manage task assignment and documentation. In Security Onion, the first place that a cybersecurity analyst will go to verify alerts is Sguil.

Sguil automatically correlates similar alerts into a single line and provides a way to view correlated events represented by that line. In order to get a sense of what has been happening in the network, it may be useful to sort on the CNT column to display the alerts with the highest frequency.

Right-clicking the CNT value and selecting View Correlated Events opens a tab displaying all the correlated events. This can help the cybersecurity analyst understand the time frame during which the correlated events were received by Sguil. Note that each event receives a unique event ID. Only the first event ID in the series of correlated events is displayed in the RealTime tab. Figure 12-8 shows Sguil alerts sorted on CNT with the View Correlated Events menu open.

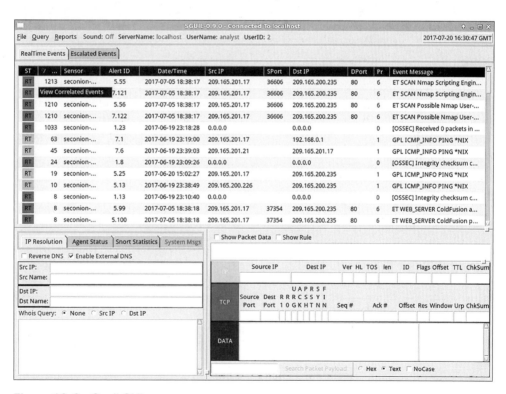

Figure 12-8   Sguil GUI

Note

In Figure 12-8, the title of the CNT column is hidden. The CNT column is between the ST and Sensor columns.

Sguil Queries (12.2.2.2)

Queries can be constructed in Sguil using the Query Builder. It simplifies constructing queries to a certain degree, but the cybersecurity analyst must know the field names and some issues with field values. For example, Sguil stores IP addresses in an integer representation. In order to query on an IP address in dotted decimal notation, the IP address value must be placed within the **INET_ATON()** function. Query Builder is opened from the Sguil Query menu. Select **Query Event Table** to search active events.

Table 12-6 shows the names of the Event Table fields that can be queried directly.

Table 12-6   Event Table Fields

Field Name	Type	Description
sid	int	The unique ID of this sensor.
cid	int	The sensor's unique event number.
signature	varchar	The human-readable name of the event (e.g., "WEB-IIS view source via translate header").
timestamp	datetime	The time the event occurred on the sensor.
status	int	The Sguil classification assigned to this event. Unclassified events are priority 0.
src_ip	int	The event's source IP address. Use the **INET_ATON()** function to convert the address to the database's integer representation.
dst_ip	int	The event's destination IP address. See entry above.
src_port	int	The source port of the packet that triggered the event.
dst_port	int	The destination port of the packet that triggered the event.
ip_proto	int	IP protocol type of the packet (6 = TCP, 17 = UDP, 1 = ICMP, but others are possible).

Selecting Show DataBase Tables from the Query menu displays a reference to the field names and types for each of the tables that can be queried. Figure 12-9 shows a simple timestamp and IP address query made in the Query Builder window. Note the use of the **INET_ATON()** function to simplify entering an IP address.

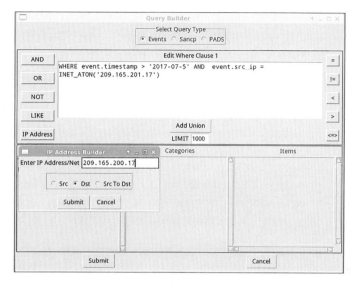

Figure 12-9   Sguil Query Builder

In Figure 12-10, the cybersecurity analyst is investigating a source port 40754 that is associated with an Emerging Threats alert.

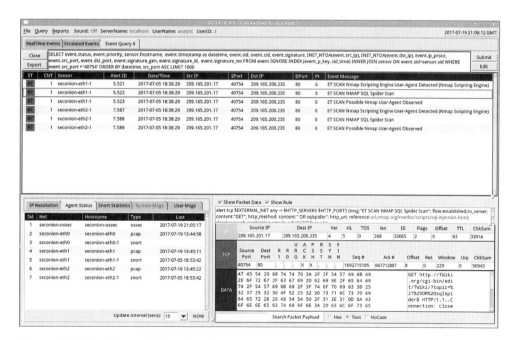

Figure 12-10   Query Builder Results

Toward the end of the query, the **WHERE event.src_port = '40754'** portion was created by the user in Query Builder. The remainder of the Query is supplied automatically by Sguil and concerns how the data that is associated with the events is to be retrieved, displayed, and presented.

Pivoting from Sguil (12.2.2.3)

Sguil provides the ability for the cybersecurity analyst to pivot to other information sources and tools. Log files are available in ELSA, relevant packet captures can be displayed in Wireshark, and transcripts of TCP sessions and Bro information are also available. The menu shown in Figure 12-11 was opened by right-clicking an Alert ID. Selecting from this menu will open information about the alert in other tools, which provides rich, contextualized information to the cybersecurity analyst.

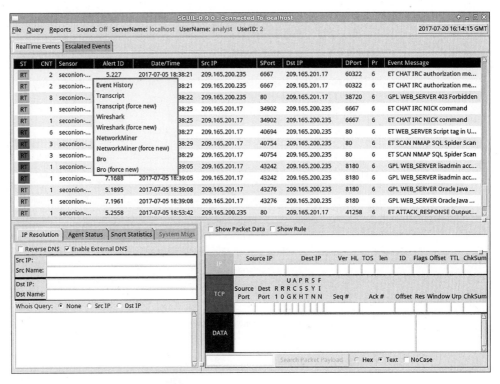

Figure 12-11   Pivoting from Sguil

Additionally, Sguil can provide pivots to Passive Real-time Asset Detection System (PRADS) and Security Analyst Network Connection Profiler (SANCP) information.

PRADS gathers network profiling data, including information about the behavior of assets on the network. PRADS is an event source, like Snort and OSSEC. It can also be queried through Sguil when an alert indicates that an internal host may have been compromised. Executing a PRADS query out of Sguil can provide information about the services, applications, and payloads that may be relevant to the alert. In addition, PRADS detects when new assets appear on the network.

> **Note**
>
> The Sguil interface refers to PADS instead of PRADS. PADS was the predecessor to PRADS. PRADS is the tool that is actually used in Security Onion. PRADS is also used to populate SANCP tables. In Security Onion, the functionalities of SANCP have been replaced by PRADS, however, the term SANCP is still used in the Sguil interface. PRADS collects the data, and a SANCP agent records the data in a SANCP data table.

The SANCP functionalities concern collecting and recording statistical information about network traffic and behavior. SANCP provides a means of verifying that network connections are valid. This is done through the application of rules that indicate which traffic should be recorded and the information with which the traffic should be tagged.

Event Handling in Sguil (12.2.2.4)

Finally, Sguil is not only a console that facilitates investigation of alerts. It is also a tool for addressing alerts. Three tasks can be completed in Sguil to manage alerts. First, alerts that have been found to be false positives can be expired. This can be done by using the right-click menu or by pressing the F8·key. An expired event disappears from the queue. Second, if the cybersecurity analyst is uncertain how to handle an event, pressing the F9 key escalates it. The alert will be moved to the Sguil Escalated Events tab. Finally, an event can be categorized. Categorization is for events that have been identified as true positives.

Sguil includes seven prebuilt categories that can be assigned by using the menu, which is shown in Figure 12-12, or by pressing the corresponding function key.

For example, an event would be categorized as Cat I by pressing the F1 key. In addition, criteria can be created that will automatically categorize an event. Categorized events are assumed to have been handled by the cybersecurity analyst. When an event is categorized, it is removed from the list of RealTime Events. The event remains in the database, however, and it can be accessed by queries that are issued by category.

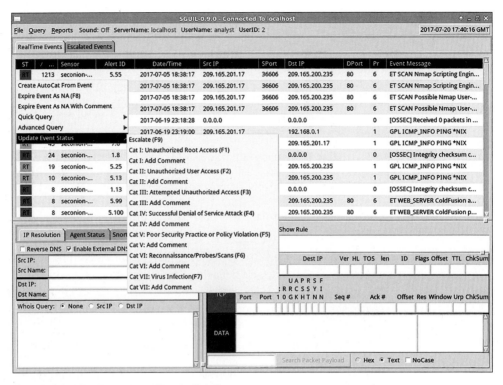

Figure 12-12 Event Handling in Sguil

Working in ELSA (12.2.2.5)

ELSA provides access to a large number of log file entries. Because the number of logs that could be displayed in ELSA is so large, several default values have been set to minimize the number of records that ELSA displays when it is launched. It is important to know that ELSA will only retrieve the first 100 records for the previous 48 hours. If no records have been generated for that period (unlikely in a production network) the ELSA window will be empty. To increase the number of records displayed, the directive **limit:1000** can be added to the query. This specifies the limit for the number of records to be returned by the query, in this case 1000.

To see log file records for a different period of time, the From and To dates in the ELSA query can be changed by clicking **From** or **To** and using the calendar pop-up menus, or by entering dates and times manually. Figure 12-13 shows the calendar pop-up menu. In addition, ELSA must have a query submitted in order to display records. Changing the dates is not enough to refresh the list of log file entries.

The easiest way to see information in ELSA is to issue the built-in queries that appear to the left of the ELSA window and then adjust the dates and resubmit the query using the Submit Query button. There are many useful searches available. When clicked, the queries appear in the query field and can be edited there if necessary.

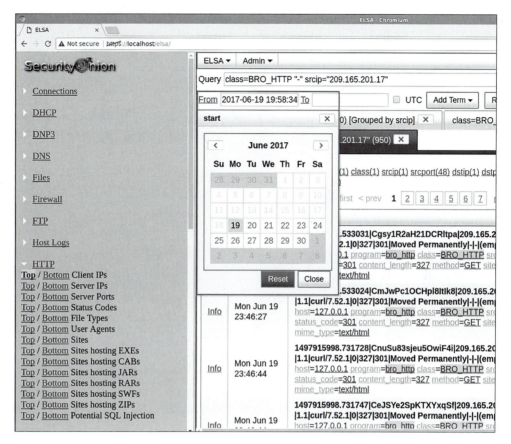

Figure 12-13   Adjusting Search Scope by Date

Queries in ELSA (12.2.2.6)

Constructing queries is very simple in ELSA. There are many shortcuts available for refining queries without doing any typing. ELSA uses a very natural syntax roughly based on Google Search syntax. A query consisting of just an IP address will work. However, because of the large numbers of records that are potentially returned, various operators and directives exist for narrowing searches and stipulating which records should be displayed.

Note

Advanced ELSA queries are beyond the scope of this course. In the labs, you will be provided with the complex query statements, if necessary.

Figure 12-14 shows a query executed on an IP address. This will result in all records that contain the IP address for the given time and date range being returned. This is not very useful. However, it is easy to narrow the query by clicking an entry in the Field Summary list that summarizes the search results.

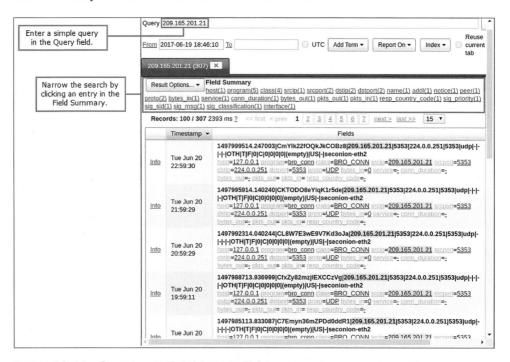

Figure 12-14 Querying an IP Address in ELSA

Clicking an entry will display a summary screen with bar graphs that depict all of the unique values and their frequencies that appear for the results of the query, as shown in Figure 12-15. Clicking an entry in the Value column will display the query with the value added to the previous query. This process can be repeated to narrow down search results easily. In this way, queries can be constructed for the five-tuples and a wide range of other values.

ELSA provides field summary and value information for every field that is indexed in the query results. This permits refining queries based on a wide range of values. In addition, queries can be created by simply clicking a value or attribute in the ELSA-normalized portion of a log file entry.

ELSA queries can also use regular expressions to create advanced patterns for matching specific packet contents. Regular expressions are executed in ELSA using the grep function. Grep serves as a transform in ELSA queries. This means it is used to process the results from a query. The grep transform serves as a text-based filter that tells ELSA which records should be displayed. The grep function is passed the field name to match, and a regular expression pattern to apply, as in **grep**(*field*,*pattern*). UNIX-like pipes, using the | symbol, can be used to direct the output of ELSA queries through ELSA plugins and transforms.

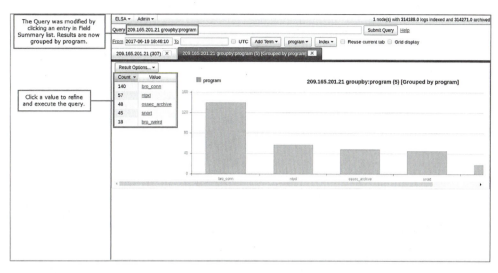

Figure 12-15   ELSA Query Results

ELSA queries may be saved as named macros. These queries can then be called in the query box by entering the name of the query preceded by the dollar sign symbol (**$**). Query macros can also be combined with other query elements.

Investigating Process or API Calls (12.2.2.7)

Application programs interact with an operating system (OS) through system calls to the OS application programming interface (API), as shown in Figure 12-16.

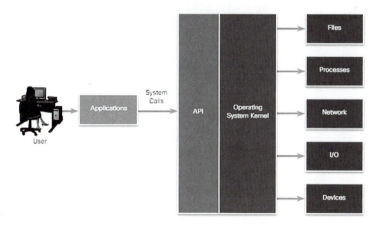

Figure 12-16   APIs Connect Applications to the Operating System

These system calls allow access to many aspects of system operation such as:

■ Software process control

■ File management

- Device management

- Information management

- Communication

Malware can also make system calls. If malware can fool an OS kernel into allowing it to make system calls, many exploits are possible.

HIDS software tracks the operation of a host OS. OSSEC rules detect changes in host-based parameters like the execution of software processes, changes in user privileges, and registry modifications, among many others. OSSEC rules will trigger an alert in Sguil. Pivoting to ELSA on the host IP address allows you to choose the type of alert based on the program that created it. Choosing OSSEC as the source program in ELSA results in a view of the OSSEC events that occurred on the host, including indicators that malware may have interacted with the OS kernel.

Investigating File Details (12.2.2.8)

When ELSA is opened directly, a query shortcut exists for Files. By opening the **Files** queries and selecting **Mime Types** in the menu, a list of the types of files that have been downloaded, and their frequencies, is displayed, as shown in Figure 12-17.

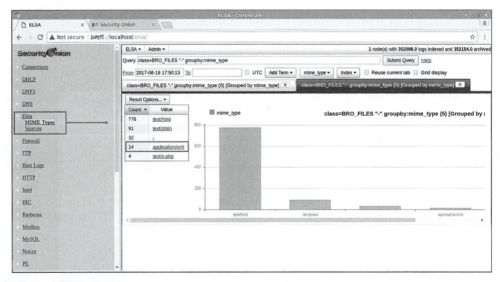

Figure 12-17 Query for Files Grouped by MIME Type

If the cybersecurity analyst is interested in the executable files, clicking **application/ xml** will display records for all logged instances in which executable files were downloaded during the time scope of the query.

Figure 12-18 shows details of a record returned by this query.

| Info | Wed Jul 05 18:38:20 | 1499279898.845537\|FUbg3K3NNhTu0ncL8g\|209.165.201.17\|209.165.200.235\|Cyroe61xUnLOz4Upih\|HTTP\|0\|MD5,SHA1\|application/xml\|-\|0.000000\|T\|T\|86\|86\|0\|0\|F\|-\|d3f95e87a5531c708ed1e4507af5c88f\|2121db20cf1aa9cc6588650754ecdbad4866fd6d\|-\|-host=127.0.0.1 program=bro_files class=BRO_FILES seen_bytes=86 total_bytes=86 missing_bytes=0 tx_hosts=209.165.201.17 rx_hosts=209.165.200.235 source=HTTP mime_type=application/xml md5=d3f95e87a5531c708ed1e4507af5c88f sha1=2121db20cf1aa9cc6588650754ecdbad4866fd6d |

Figure 12-18   ELSA Shows Properties of Downloaded File

File details, such as the file size, sending and receiving hosts, and protocol used to download the file, are displayed. In addition, the MD5 and SHA-1 hashes for the file have been calculated and are as follows:

- md5 = d3f95e87a5531c708ed1e4507af5c88f

- sha1 = 2121db20cf1aa9cc6588650754ecdbad4866fd6d

If the cybersecurity analyst is suspicious of the file, the hash value can be submitted to an online site, such as *VirusTotal*, to determine if the file is known malware. The hash value can be submitted from the Search tab on the VirusTotal page found here: https://www.virustotal.com/.

Lab 12.2.2.9: Regular Expression Tutorial

A regular expression (regex) is a pattern of symbols that describes data to be matched in a query or other operation. Regular expressions are constructed similarly to arithmetic expressions, by using various operators to combine smaller expressions. There are two major standards of regular expression, POSIX and Perl.

In this lab, you will use an online tutorial to explore regular expressions. You will also describe the information that matches given regular expressions.

Lab 12.2.2.10: Extract an Executable from a PCAP

Looking at logs is very important but it is also important to understand how network transactions happen at the packet level.

In this lab, you will analyze the traffic in a previously captured pcap file and extract an executable from the file.

Enhancing the Work of the Cybersecurity Analyst (12.2.3)

In this topic, you will learn about network monitoring tools that enhance workflow management.

Dashboards and Visualizations (12.2.3.1)

Dashboards provide a combination of data and visualizations designed to improve the access of individuals to large amounts of information. Dashboards are usually interactive. They allow cybersecurity analysts to focus on specific details and information by clicking elements of the dashboard. For example, clicking a bar in a bar chart could provide a breakdown of the information for the data represented by that bar. ELSA includes the capability of designing custom dashboards. In addition, other tools that are included in Security Onion, such as Squert, provide a visual interface to NSM data.

Workflow Management (12.2.3.2)

Because of the critical nature of network security monitoring, it is essential that workflows are managed. This enhances efficiency of the cyberoperations team, increases the accountability of staff, and ensures that all potential alerts are treated properly. In large security organizations, it is conceivable that thousands of alerts will be received daily. Each alert should be systematically assigned, processed, and documented by cyberoperations staff.

Runbook automation, or workflow management systems, provide the tools necessary to streamline and control processes in a cybersecurity operations center. Sguil provides basic workflow management. However, it is not a good choice for large operations with many employees. Instead, third-party workflow management systems are available that can be customized to suit the needs of cybersecurity operations.

In addition, automated queries are useful for adding efficiency to the cyberoperations workflow. These queries, sometimes known as plays, or playbooks, automatically search for complex security incidents that may evade other tools. For example, an ELSA query can be configured as an alert rule that can be run regularly. ELSA can notify cybersecurity analysts by email, or other means, that a suspected exploit has been detected by the query. Playbooks can also be created in a scripting language such as Python and integrated into workflow management systems to ensure that the alerts are processed, documented, and reported along with other alerts.

Digital Forensics (12.3)

In this section, you will learn how the cybersecurity analyst handles digital forensics and evidence to ensure proper attack attribution.

Evidence Handling and Attack Attribution (12.3.1)

In this topic, you will learn the role of the digital forensic processes.

Digital Forensics (12.3.1.1)

Now that you have investigated and identified valid alerts, what do you do with the evidence? The cybersecurity analyst will inevitably uncover evidence of criminal activity. In order to protect the organization and to prevent cybercrime, it is necessary to identify threat actors, report them to the appropriate authorities, and provide evidence to support prosecution. Tier 1 cybersecurity analysts are usually the first to uncover wrongdoing. Cybersecurity analysts must know how to properly handle evidence and attribute it to threat actors.

Digital forensics is the recovery and investigation of information found on digital devices as it relates to criminal activity. This information could be data on storage devices, data in volatile computer memory, or the traces of cybercrime that are preserved in network data, such as pcaps and logs.

Cybercriminal activity can be broadly characterized as originating from inside of or outside of the organization. Private investigations are concerned with individuals inside the organization. These individuals could simply be behaving in ways that violate user agreements or constitute other prohibited but noncriminal conduct. When individuals are suspected of involvement in criminal activity involving the theft or destruction of intellectual property, an organization may choose to involve law enforcement authorities, in which case the investigation becomes public. Internal users could also have used the organization's network to conduct other criminal activities that are unrelated to the organizational mission but are in violation of various legal statutes. In this case, public officials will carry out the investigation.

When an external attacker has exploited a network and stolen or altered data, evidence needs to be gathered to document the scope of the exploit. Various regulatory bodies specify a range of actions that an organization must take when various types of data have been compromised. The results of forensic investigation can help to identify the actions that need to be taken.

For example, under HIPAA, if a data breach has occurred that involves patient information, notification of the breach must be made to the affected individuals. If the breach involves more than 500 individuals in a state or jurisdiction, the media, as well as the affected individuals, must be notified. Digital forensic investigation must be used to determine which individuals were affected, and to certify the number of affected individuals so that appropriate notification can be made in compliance with HIPAA regulations.

It is possible that the organization itself could be the subject of an investigation. Cybersecurity analysts may find themselves in direct contact with digital forensic evidence that details the conduct of members of the organization. Analysts must know the requirements regarding the preservation and handling of such evidence. Failure to do so could result in criminal penalties for the organization and even the cybersecurity analyst if the intention to destroy evidence is established.

The Digital Forensics Process (12.3.1.2)

It is important that an organization develop well-documented processes and procedures for digital forensic analysis. Regulatory compliance may require this documentation, and this documentation may be inspected by authorities in the event of a public investigation.

NIST Special Publication 800-86, *Guide to Integrating Forensic Techniques into Incident Response*, is a valuable resource for organizations that require guidance in developing digital forensics plans.

NIST describes the digital forensics process as involving four steps, as shown in Figure 12-19:

Figure 12-19   The Forensics Process

1. **Data collection:** This is the identification of potential sources of forensic data and acquisition, handling, and storage of that data. This stage is critical because special care must be taken not to damage, lose, or omit important data.

2. **Examination:** This entails assessing and extracting relevant information from the collected data. This may involve decompression or decryption of the data. Information that is irrelevant to the investigation may need to be removed. Identifying actual evidence in large collections of data can be very difficult and time-consuming.

3. **Analysis:** This entails drawing conclusions from the data. Salient features, such as people, places, times, events, and so on, should be documented. This step may also involve the correlation of data from multiple sources.

4. **Reporting:** This entails preparing and presenting information that resulted from the analysis. Reporting should be impartial and alternative explanations should be offered if appropriate. Limitations of the analysis and problems encountered should be included. Suggestions for further investigation and next steps should also be made.

In Figure 12-19, note the transition from media, to data, to information, to evidence that occurs during the forensics process.

Types of Evidence (12.3.1.3)

In legal proceedings, evidence is broadly classified as either direct or indirect. Direct evidence is evidence that was indisputably in the possession of the accused, or is eyewitness evidence from someone who observed criminal behavior.

Evidence is further classified as follows:

- *Best evidence*: This is evidence that is in its original state. This evidence could be storage devices used by an accused, or archives of files that can be proven to be unaltered.

- *Corroborating evidence*: This is evidence that supports an assertion that is developed from best evidence.

- *Indirect evidence*: This is evidence that, in combination with other facts, establishes a hypothesis. This is also known as circumstantial evidence. For example, evidence that an individual has committed similar crimes can support the assertion that the person committed the crime of which they are accused.

Evidence Collection Order (12.3.1.4)

IETF *RFC 3227* provides guidelines for the collection of digital evidence. It describes an order for the collection of digital evidence based on the volatility of the data, as shown in Figure 12-20.

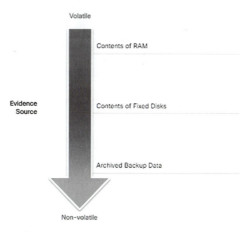

Figure 12-20   Evidence Collection Priority

Data stored in RAM is the most volatile, and it will be lost when the device is turned off. In addition, important data in volatile memory could be overwritten by routine machine processes. Therefore, the collection of digital evidence should begin with the most volatile evidence and proceed to the least volatile. An example of most volatile to least volatile evidence collection order is as follows:

1. Memory registers, caches

2. Routing table, ARP cache, process table, kernel statistics, RAM

3. Temporary file systems

4. Non-volatile media, fixed and removable

5. Remote logging and monitoring data

6. Physical interconnections and topologies

7. Archival media, tape or other backups

Details of the systems from which the evidence was collected, including who has access to those systems and at what level of permissions, should be recorded. Such details should include hardware and software configurations for the systems from which the data was obtained.

Chain of Custody (12.3.1.5)

Although evidence may have been gathered from sources that support attribution to an accused individual, it can be argued that the evidence could have been altered or fabricated after it was collected. In order to counter this argument, a rigorous *chain of custody* must be defined and followed.

Chain of custody involves the collection, handling, and secure storage of evidence. Detailed records should be kept of the following:

- Who discovered and collected the evidence.

- All details about the handling of evidence including times, places, and personnel involved.

- Who has primary responsibility for the evidence, when responsibility was assigned, and when custody changed.

- Who has physical access to the evidence while it was stored. Access should be restricted to only the most essential personnel.

Data Integrity and Preservation (12.3.1.6)

When collecting data, it is important that it is preserved in its original condition. Timestamping of files should be preserved. For this reason, the original evidence should be copied, and analysis should be conducted only on copies of the original. This is to avoid accidental loss or alteration of the evidence. Because timestamps may be part of the evidence, opening files from the original media should be avoided.

The process used to create copies of the evidence that is used in the investigation should be recorded. Whenever possible, the copies should be direct bit-level copies of the original storage volumes. Volatile memory could contain forensic evidence, so special tools should be used to preserve that evidence before the device is shut down and evidence is lost. Users should not disconnect, unplug, or turn off infected machines unless explicitly told to do so by security personnel.

Attack Attribution (12.3.1.7)

After the extent of the cyberattack has been assessed and evidence collected and preserved, incident response can move to identifying the source of the attack. As we know, a wide range of threat actors exist, ranging from disgruntled individuals, hackers, cybercriminals and criminal gangs, or nation states. Some criminals act from inside the network, while others can be on the other side of the world. Sophistication of cybercrime varies as well. Nation-states may employ large groups of highly trained individuals to carry out an attack and hide their tracks, while other threat actors may openly brag about their criminal activities.

Attack attribution refers to the act of determining the individual, organization, or nation responsible for a successful intrusion or attack incident.

Identifying responsible threat actors should occur through the principled and systematic investigation of the evidence. While it may be useful to also speculate as to the identity of threat actors by identifying potential motivations for an incident, it is important not to let this bias the investigation. For example, attributing an attack to a commercial competitor may lead the investigation away from the possibility that a criminal gang or nation state was responsible.

In an evidence-based investigation, the incident response team correlates Tactics, Techniques, and Procedures (TPP) that were used in the incident with other known exploits. Cybercriminals, much like other criminals, have specific traits that are common to most of their crimes. Threat intelligence sources can help to map the TTP identified by an investigation to known sources of similar attacks. However, this highlights a problem with threat attribution. Evidence of cybercrime is seldom direct evidence. Identifying commonalities between TTPs for known and unknown threat actors is circumstantial evidence.

Some aspects of a threat that can aid in attribution are the location of originating hosts or domains, features of the code used in malware, the tools used, and other techniques. Sometimes, at the national security level, threats cannot be openly attributed because doing so would expose methods and capabilities that need to be protected.

For internal threats, asset management plays a major role. Uncovering the devices from which an attack was launched can lead directly to the threat actor. IP addresses,

MAC addresses, and DHCP logs can help track the addresses used in the attack back to a specific device. AAA logs are very useful in this regard, as they track who accessed what network resources at what time.

Interactive Graphic

Activity 12.3.1.8: Identify the Type of Evidence

Refer to the online course to complete this Activity.

Interactive Graphic

Activity 12.3.1.9: Identify the Forensic Technique Terminology

Refer to the online course to complete this Activity.

Summary (12.4)

In this chapter, you learned how to work with the Security Onion suite of applications and analyze intrusion data. You also learned about the proper handling of evidence in a digital forensics investigation.

Security Onion contains a variety of detection and analysis tools, including

- CapME
- Snort
- Bro
- OSSEC
- Suricata
- Wireshark
- Elsa
- Sguil

After completing all the labs in this chapter and working with your multi-VM environment, you should now be familiar with these tools, their uses, and their importance to the cybersecurity analyst. Some organizations use a variety of other tools and supplement Security Onion with additional tools. However, basic understanding of Security Onion should transfer easily during your training period in your new job.

Lab 12.4.1.1: Interpret HTTP and DNS Data to Isolate Threat Actor

MySQL is a popular database used by numerous web applications. Unfortunately, SQL injection is a common web hacking technique. It is a code injection technique where an attacker executes malicious SQL statements to control a web application's database server.

Domain Name System (DNS) traffic can be used to exfiltrate data.

In this lab, you will perform a SQL injection to access the SQL database on the server. You will also use the DNS service to facilitate data exfiltration.

Lab 12.4.1.2: Isolate Compromised Host Using 5-Tuple

In this lab, you will exploit a vulnerable server using known exploits. You will also review the logs to determine the compromised hosts and file using the 5-tuples.

Practice

The following activities provide practice with the topics introduced in this chapter. The Labs are available in the companion *CCNA Cybersecurity Operations Lab Manual* (ISBN: 9781587134388).

Labs

Lab 12.1.1.7: Snort and Firewall Rules

Lab 12.2.1.5: Convert Data into a Universal Format

Lab 12.2.2.9: Regular Expression Tutorial

Lab 12.2.2.10: Extract an Executable from a PCAP

Lab 12.4.1.1: Interpret HTTP and DNS Data to Isolate Threat Actor

Lab 12.4.1.2: Isolate Compromised Host Using 5-Tuple

Check Your Understanding

Complete all the review questions listed here to test your understanding of the topics and concepts in this chapter. The appendix "Answers to 'Check Your Understanding' Questions" lists the answers.

1. Which two technologies are used in the ELSA tool? (Choose two.)

   A. MySQL

   B. CapME

   C. Suricata

   D. Sphinx Search

   E. Security Onion

2. What is the host-based intrusion detection tool that is integrated into Security Onion?

   A. OSSEC

   B. Snort

   C. Sguil

   D. Wireshark

3. According to NIST, which step in the digital forensics process involves drawing conclusions from data?

   A. Data collection

   B. Examination

C. Analysis

D. Reporting

4. Which two strings will be matched by the regular expression **[24]**? (Choose two.)

A. Level1

B. Level2

C. Level3

D. Level4

E. Level5

5. Which alert classification indicates that exploits are not being detected by installed security systems?

A. False negative

B. True negative

C. True positive

D. False positive

6. A cybersecurity analyst is going to verify security alerts using the Security Onion. Which tool should the analyst visit first?

A. Bro

B. Sguil

C. ELSA

D. CapME

7. What is the purpose for data normalization?

A. To reduce the amount of alert data

B. To make the alert data transmission fast

C. To simplify searching for correlated events

D. To enhance the secure transmission of alert data

8. Which term describes evidence that is in its original state?

A. Corroborating evidence

B. Best evidence

C. Indirect evidence

D. Direct evidence

## CHAPTER 13

Incident Response and Handling

Objectives

Upon completion of this chapter, you will be able to answer the following questions:

- What are the steps in the Cyber Kill Chain?

- How do you classify an intrusion event using the Diamond Model?

- How do you apply the VERIS schema to an incident?

- What are the various goals of a given CSIRT?

- How do you apply the NIST 800-61r2 incident handling procedures to a given incident scenario?

Key Terms

This chapter uses the following key terms. You can find the definitions in the Glossary.

Introduction (13.0)

In cybersecurity, threat actors are always developing new techniques. New threats constantly emerge that must be detected and contained so that assets and communication are restored as quickly as possible. Many attackers use extortion, fraud, and identity theft for financial gain. The need to consistently defend against these attacks led to the creation of several incident response models.

This chapter covers incident response and handling models and procedures. These include the Cyber Kill Chain, the Diamond Model, the VERIS schema, and NIST guidelines for the structure of Computer Security Incident Response Teams (CSIRTs) and processes for handling an incident.

Incident Response Models (13.1)

In this section, you will learn how to apply incident response models to an intrusion event.

The Cyber Kill Chain (13.1.1)

In this topic, you will learn to identify the steps in the Cyber Kill Chain.

Steps of the Cyber Kill Chain (13.1.1.1)

The *Cyber Kill Chain* was developed by Lockheed Martin to identify and prevent cyber intrusions. As Figure 13-1 shows, there are seven steps to the Cyber Kill Chain, which help analysts understand the techniques, tools, and procedures of threat actors.

Figure 13-1   The Cyber Kill Chain

When responding to an incident, the objective is to detect and stop the attack as early as possible in the kill chain progression. The earlier the attack is stopped, the less damage is done and the less the attacker learns about the target network.

The Cyber Kill Chain specifies what an attacker must complete to accomplish their goal. The steps in the Cyber Kill Chain are as follows:

1. Reconnaissance

2. Weaponization

3. Delivery

4. Exploitation

5. Installation

6. Command & Control (CnC)

7. Action on Objectives

If the attacker is stopped at any stage, the chain of attack is broken. Breaking the chain means the defender successfully thwarted the threat actor's intrusion. Threat actors are successful only if they reach Step 7.

Note

Threat actor is the term used throughout this course to refer to the party instigating the attack. However, Lockheed Martin uses the term "adversary" in its description of the Cyber Kill Chain. The two terms, adversary and threat actor, are used interchangeably in this topic.

Reconnaissance (13.1.1.2)

Reconnaissance is when the threat actor performs research, gathers intelligence, and selects targets. This will inform the threat actor if the attack is worth performing. Any public information may help to determine what attack could be performed, where it could be performed, and how it could be performed. There is a lot of publicly available information, especially for larger organizations, including news articles, websites, conference proceedings, and public-facing network devices. Increasing amounts of information surrounding employees is available through social media outlets.

The threat actor will choose targets that have been neglected or unprotected because they will have a higher likelihood of becoming penetrated and compromised. All information obtained by the threat actor is reviewed to determine its importance and if it reveals possible additional avenues of attack.

Table 13-1 outlines some of the tactics and defenses used during this step.

Table 13-1 Examples of Reconnaissance Tactics and Defenses

Adversary Tactics	SOC Defenses
Plan and conduct research: ■ Harvest email addresses. ■ Identify employees on social media networks. ■ Collect all public relations information (press releases, awards, conferences attendees, etc.). ■ Discover Internet-facing servers.	Discover adversary's intent: ■ Investigate web log alerts and historical searching data. ■ Data mine browser analytics. ■ Build playbooks for detecting browser behavior that indicates recon activity. ■ Prioritize defense around technologies and people that recon activity is targeting.

Weaponization (13.1.1.3)

The goal of *weaponization* is to use the information from the earlier reconnaissance to develop a weapon against specific targeted systems in the organization. To develop this weapon, the designer will use the vulnerabilities of the assets that were discovered and build them into a tool that can be deployed. After the tool has been used, it is expected that the threat actor has achieved their goal of gaining access into the target system or network, degrading the health of a target, or the entire network. The threat actor will further examine network and asset security to expose additional weaknesses, gain control over other assets, or deploy additional attacks.

It is not difficult to choose a weapon for the attack. The threat actor needs to look at what attacks are available for the vulnerabilities they have discovered. There are many attacks that have already been created and tested at large. One problem is that because these attacks are so well known, they are most likely also known by the defenders. It is often more effective to use a zero-day attack to avoid detection methods. The threat actor may wish to develop their own weapon that is specifically designed to avoid detection, using the information about the network and systems that they have learned.

Table 13-2 summarizes some of the tactics and defenses used during this step.

Table 13-2 Examples of Weaponization Tactics and Defenses

Adversary Tactics	SOC Defenses
Prepare and stage the operation: ■ Obtain an automated tool to deliver the malware payload (weaponizer). ■ Select or create a document to present to the victim.	Detect and collect weaponization artifacts: ■ Conduct full malware analysis. ■ Build detections for the behavior of known weaponizers.

Adversary Tactics	SOC Defenses
■ Select backdoor and command and control infrastructure.	■ Determine whether malware is old, "off the shelf," or new malware that might indicate a tailored attack. ■ Collect files and metadata for future analysis. ■ Determine which weaponizer artifacts are common to which APT campaigns.

Delivery (13.1.1.4)

During this step, the weapon is transmitted to the target using a delivery vector. This may be through the use of a website, removable USB media, or an email attachment. If the weapon is not delivered, the attack will be unsuccessful. The threat actor will use many different methods to increase the odds of delivering the payload such as encrypting communications, making the code look legitimate, or obfuscating the code. Security sensors are so advanced that they will detect the code as malicious unless it is altered to avoid detection. The code may be altered to seem innocent, yet still perform the necessary actions, even though it may take longer to execute.

Table 13-3 summarizes some of the tactics and defenses used during this step.

Table 13-3 Examples of Delivery Tactics and Defenses

Adversary Tactics	SOC Defenses

Launch malware at target:
■ Directly against web servers
■ Indirect delivery through:
  ■ Malicious email
  ■ Malware on USB stick
  ■ Social media interactions
  ■ Compromised websites
	Block delivery of malware:
	■ Analyze the infrastructure path used for delivery.
	
	■ Understand targeted servers, people, and data available to attack.
	
	■ Infer intent of the adversary based on targeting.
	
	■ Collect email and web logs for forensic reconstruction.

Exploitation (13.1.1.5)

After the weapon has been delivered, the threat actor uses it to break the vulnerability and gain control of the target. The most common exploit targets are applications, operating system vulnerabilities, and users. The attacker must use an exploit that gains the effect they desire. This is very important because if the wrong exploit is conducted, obviously the attack will not work, but unintended side effects such as a DoS or multiple system reboots will cause undue attention that could easily inform cybersecurity analysts of the attack and the threat actor's intentions.

Table 13-4 summarizes some of the tactics and defenses used during this step.

Table 13-4   Examples of Exploitation Tactics and Defenses

Adversary Tactics	SOC Defenses
Initiate zero-day exploit: ■ Directly against web servers ■ Indirect delivery through: 　■ Malicious email 　■ Malware on USB stick 　■ Social media interactions 　■ Compromised websites	Train employees, secure code, and harden devices: ■ Conduct employee awareness training and email testing. ■ Conduct web developer training for securing code. ■ Perform regular vulnerability scanning and penetration testing. ■ Implement endpoint hardening measures. ■ Perform endpoint auditing to forensically determine origin of exploit.

Installation (13.1.1.6)

This step is where the threat actor establishes a backdoor into the system to allow for continued access to the target. To preserve this backdoor, it is important that remote access does not alert cybersecurity analysts or users. The access method must survive through antimalware scans and rebooting of the computer to be effective. This persistent access can also allow for automated communications, especially effective when multiple channels of communication are necessary when commanding a botnet.

Table 13-5 summarizes some of the tactics and defenses used during this step.

Table 13-5   Examples of Installation Tactics and Defenses

Adversary Tactics	SOC Defenses
Install persistent backdoor: ■ Install web shell on web server for persistent access. ■ Create point of persistence by adding services, AutoRun keys, etc. ■ Modify the timestamp of the malware to make it appear as part of the operating system.	Detect, log, and analyze installation activity: ■ Use a HIPS to alert or block on common installation paths. ■ Determine if malware requires admin privileges or only user privileges. ■ Perform endpoint auditing to discover abnormal file creations. ■ Determine if malware is a known threat or a new variant.

Command and Control (13.1.1.7)

In this step, the goal is to establish *command and control (CnC or C2)* with the target system. Compromised hosts usually beacon out of the network to a controller on the Internet. This is because most malware requires manual interaction in order to exfiltrate data from the network. CnC channels are used by the threat actor to issue commands to the software that they installed on the target. The cybersecurity analyst must be able to detect CnC communications in order to discover the compromised host. This may be in the form of unauthorized Internet Relay Chat (IRC) traffic or excessive traffic to suspect domains.

Table 13-6 summarizes some of the tactics and defenses used during this step.

Table 13-6 Examples of Command & Control (CnC) Tactics and Defenses

Adversary Tactics	SOC Defenses
Open two-way communications channel to CnC infrastructure for target manipulation: ■ Most common CnC channels are over web, DNS, and email protocols. ■ CnC infrastructure may be adversary owned or another victim network itself.	Last chance to block operation: ■ Research possible new CnC infrastructures. ■ Discover CnC infrastructure thorough malware analysis. ■ Prevent impact by blocking or disabling CnC channel. ■ Consolidate number of Internet points of presence. ■ Customize blocks of CnC protocols on web proxies.

Actions on Objectives (13.1.1.8)

The final step of the Cyber Kill Chain describes the threat actor achieving their original objective. This may be data theft, performing a DDoS attack, or using the compromised network to create and send spam. At this point the threat actor is deeply rooted in the systems of the organization, hiding their moves and covering their tracks. It is extremely difficult to remove the threat actor from the network.

Table 13-7 summarizes some of the tactics and defenses used during this step.

Table 13-7 Examples of Actions on Objectives Tactics and Defenses

Adversary Tactics	SOC Defenses
Reap the rewards of successful attack: ■ Collect user credentials. ■ Escalate privileges. ■ Conduct internal reconnaissance. ■ Move laterally through environment. ■ Collect and exfiltrate data. ■ Destroy systems. ■ Overwrite, modify, or corrupt data.	Detect by using forensic evidence: ■ Establish incident response playbook. ■ Detect data exfiltration, lateral movement, and unauthorized credential usage. ■ Ensure immediate analyst response of all alerts. ■ Conduct forensic analysis of endpoints for rapid triage. ■ Capture network packets to re-create activity. ■ Conduct damage assessment.

Interactive Graphic

Activity 13.1.1.9: Identify the Kill Chain Step

Refer to the online course to complete this Activity.

The Diamond Model of Intrusion (13.1.2)

In this topic, you will learn to classify an intrusion event using the Diamond Model.

Diamond Model Overview (13.1.2.1)

The *Diamond Model* was developed by Sergio Caltagirone, Andrew Pendergast, and Christopher Betz from the Center for Cyber Threat Intelligence and Threat Research. The Diamond Model is made up of four parts and represents a security incident or event, as shown Figure 13-2.

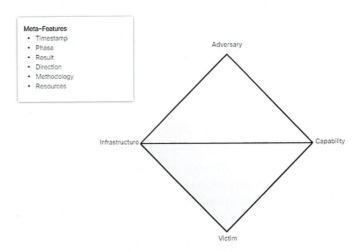

Figure 13-2   The Diamond Model

In the Diamond Model, an event is a time-bound activity restricted to a specific step where an adversary uses a capability over some infrastructure against a victim to achieve a specific result.

The four core features of an intrusion event are adversary, capability, infrastructure, and victim:

- **Adversary:** This is the party responsible for the intrusion.

- **Capability:** This is a tool or technique that the adversary uses to attack the victim.

- **Infrastructure:** This is the network path or paths that the adversary uses to establish and maintain command and control over their capabilities.

- **Victim:** This is the target of the attack. However, a victim might be the target initially and then used as part of the infrastructure to launch other attacks.

The adversary uses capabilities over infrastructure to attack the victim. Each line in the model shows how each part reached the other. For example, a capability like malware might be used over email by an adversary to attack a victim.

Meta-features expand the model slightly to include the following important elements:

- **Timestamp:** This indicates the start and stop time of an event and is an integral part of grouping malicious activity.

- **Phase:** This is analogous to steps in the Cyber Kill Chain; malicious activity includes two or more steps executed in succession to achieve the desired result.

- **Result:** This delineates what the adversary gained from the event. Results can be documented as one or more of the following: confidentiality compromised, integrity compromised, and availability compromised.

- **Direction:** This indicates the direction of the event across the Diamond Model. These include Adversary-to-Infrastructure, Infrastructure-to-Victim, Victim-to-Infrastructure, and Infrastructure-to-Adversary.

- **Methodology:** This is used to classify the general type of event, such as port scan, phishing, content delivery attack, syn flood, etc.

- **Resources:** These are one or more external resources used by the adversary for the intrusion event, such as software, adversary's knowledge, information (e.g., username/passwords), and assets to carry out the attack (hardware, funds, facilities, network access).

Pivoting Across the Diamond Model (13.1.2.2)

As a cybersecurity analyst, you may be called on to use the Diamond Model to diagram a series of intrusion events. The Diamond Model is ideal for illustrating how the adversary pivots from one event to the next.

For example, in Figure 13-3 an employee reports that his computer is acting abnormally.

A host scan by the security technician indicates that the computer is infected with malware. An analysis of the malware reveals that the malware contains a list of CnC domain names. These domain names resolve to a list of IP addresses. These IP addresses are then used to identify the adversary, as well as investigate logs to determine if other victims in the organization are using the CnC channel.

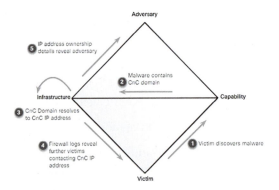

Figure 13-3   Diamond Model Pivoting Example

The Diamond Model and the Cyber Kill Chain (13.1.2.3)

Adversaries do not operate in just a single event. Instead, events are threaded together in a chain in which each event must be successfully completed before the next event. This thread of events can be mapped to the Cyber Kill Chain previously discussed in the chapter.

The following example, shown in Figure 13-4, illustrates the end-to-end process of an adversary as they vertically traverse the Cyber Kill Chain, use a compromised host to horizontally pivot to another victim, and then begin another activity thread:

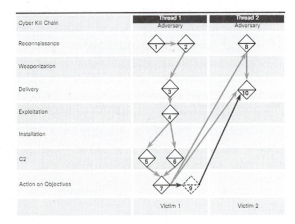

Figure 13-4   Activity Thread Example

1. Adversary conducts a web search for victim company Gadgets, Inc., receiving as part of the results their domain gadgets.com.

2. Adversary uses the newly discovered domain gadets.com for a new search "network administrator gadgets.com" and discovers forum postings from users claiming to be network administrators of gadgets.com. The user profiles reveal their email addresses.

3. Adversary sends phishing emails with a Trojan horse attached to the network administrators of gadgets.com.

4. One network administrator (NA1) of gadgets.com opens the malicious attachment. This executes the enclosed exploit, allowing for further code execution.

5. NA1's compromised host sends an HTTP POST message to an IP address, registering it with a CnC controller. NA1's compromised host receives an HTTP response in return.

6. It is revealed from reverse engineering that the malware has additional IP addresses configured which act as a back-up if the first controller does not respond.

7. Through a CnC HTTP response message sent to NA1's host, the malware begins to act as a proxy for new TCP connections.

8. Through the proxy established on NA1's host, Adversary does a web search for "most important research ever" and finds Victim 2, Interesting Research Inc.

9. Adversary checks NA1's email contact list for any contacts from Interesting Research Inc. and discovers the contact for the Interesting Research Inc. Chief Research Officer.

10. Chief Research Officer of Interesting Research Inc. receives a spear-phish email from Gadgets, Inc.'s NA1's email address, sent from NA1's host with the same payload as observed in Event 3.

The adversary now has two compromised victims from which additional attacks can be launched. For example, the adversary could mine the Chief Research Officer's email contacts for additional potential victims. The adversary might also set up another proxy to exfiltrate all of the Chief Research Officer's files.

> **Note**
>
> This example is a modification of the U.S. Department of Defense's example in the publication "The Diamond Model of Intrusion Analysis."

Interactive Graphic

Activity 13.1.2.4: Identify the Diamond Model Features

Refer to the online course to complete this Activity.

The VERIS Schema (13.1.3)

In this topic, you will learn how to apply the VERIS Schema to an Incident.

What Is the VERIS Schema? (13.1.3.1)

Designed by Verizon and placed on the GitHub community coding site, the *Vocabulary for Event Recording and Incident Sharing (VERIS)* is a set of metrics designed to create a way to describe security incidents in a structured and repeatable way. VERIS was created to share quality information about security events to the community, anonymously. The VERIS Community Database (VCDB) is an open and free collection of publicly reported security incidents in VERIS format. You can use unformatted, raw data or the dashboard to find VERIS entries. The VCDB is a central location for the security community to learn from experience and help with decision making, before, during, and after a security incident.

In the VERIS schema, risk is defined as the intersection of four landscapes of Threat, Asset, Impact, and Control, as shown in Figure 13-5. Information from each landscape helps to understand the level of risk to the organization. VERIS helps to determine these landscapes using real security incidents to help risk management assessment.

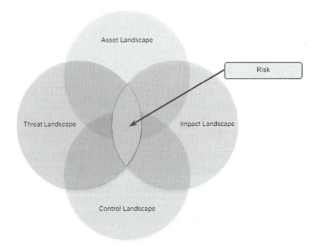

Figure 13-5 Risk at the Intersection of Four Landscapes

Create a VERIS Record (13.1.3.2)

When creating records to add to the database, start with the basic facts about the incident. It is helpful to use the VERIS elements outlined by the community. Table 13-8 shows the most basic record that can exist. The framework does not need to be complicated. The only required fields in the record are those where the attribute is present. As more is known about the incident, data can be added.

Table 13-8   A Basic VERIS Record

Variable	Value
timeline.incident.year	2017
schema_version	1.3
incident_id	1
security_incident	Confirmed
discovery_method	Unknown
action	Unknown
asset	Unknown
actor	Unknown
attribute	Unknown

When an incident is recorded, it is most likely that you will have more specific information than just the year when the incident occurred. For example, the month and day can be documented by adding VERIS labels to the existing record, as shown in Table 13-9. The way the incident was discovered, a summary of what happened, and any other notes about the type of incident should also be recorded using VERIS labels. Any variable, data, or text can be recorded as part of the VERIS record using VERIS labels. For example, in Table 13-9 variables were added to document that Debbie in Sales reported that her computer was infected with malware. It was determined, through an interview with Debbie and a scan of her computer, that a rootkit was installed via an infected USB drive.

Table 13-9   Adding Information to the VERIS Record

Variable	Value
timeline.incident.year	2017
timeline.incident.month	6
timeline.incident.day	20
summary	computer was infected with malware
discovery.notes	Reported by Debbie in sales
malware.notes	rootkit was found on Debbie's computer
social.notes	Debbie brought in an infected USB drive and used it on her company laptop.

After the initial records are created, additional details should be added to aid in data analysis. The only two required in the VERIS schema are whether the incident was a real security incident, and how the incident was discovered. Most ticketing systems will allow new fields to be added to forms. To add more details to the record, just add a new field and designate a VERIS enumeration for it. A Word document, Excel spreadsheet, or other software can be used to create these records as well. You could also create a dedicated reporting tool for incident recording.

After the major details have been recorded, even more detail can be added as you continue to document the incident. Every bit of information that can be entered into the record may be helpful to your organization and others who respond to the incident and may help to prevent and detect future incidents of this type. The more data available to the community, the better chance there is of preventing future incidents.

VERIS can record the details of the organization that was affected such as industry, number of employees, or the country of the organization. This information can be useful in the overall picture when multiple organizations have a record of a similar incident. This demographic information can be shared without revealing specific, private information about the affected organization.

Top-Level and Second-Level Elements (13.1.3.3)

There are five top-level elements of the VERIS schema, each of which provides a different aspect of the incident. Each top-level element contains several second-level elements, as shown in Figure 13-6. These elements are useful for classifying data that has been collected about an incident.

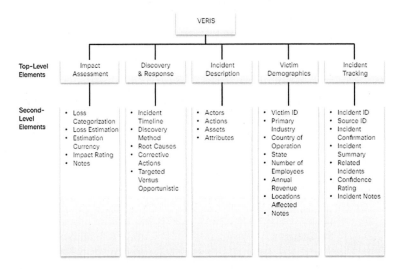

Figure 13-6   VERIS Schema Elements

Impact Assessment

For any incident, there is impact, whether it is minor or widespread. It is often very difficult to determine the scope of the impact until well after an incident has occurred, or even after it has been remediated. The second-level elements used for impact assessment are as follows:

- **Loss Categorization:** Identifies the types of losses that occurred due to the incident.

- **Loss Estimation:** This is an estimate of the total losses that were incurred because of the incident.

- **Estimation Currency:** Uses the same currency when multiple types are involved.

- **Impact Rating:** This is a rating that indicates the overall impact of the incident. It could be a number between 1 and 100, or another scale such as a grading scale.

- **Notes:** Additional details that may be of use are recorded here.

Discovery and Response

This section is for recording the timeline of events, the method of incident discovery, and what the response was to the incident, including how it was remediated. The second-level elements used for discovery and response are as follows:

- **Incident Timeline:** The timeline of all events from the discovery of the incident to the time the incident has been contained or restored to a fully functional state. This section is very important for gathering metrics such as readiness, the actions of the threat actors, and the response of the affected organization, along with many others.

- **Discovery Method:** Identifies the way in which the incident was discovered. This may be accidental or by design.

- **Root Causes:** Identifies any weakness or failure in security allowing the incident to take place.

- **Corrective Actions:** This variable is for recording what will be done to detect or prevent this type of incident in the future.

- **Targeted vs. Opportunistic:** Identifies if the incident was a deliberate, targeted attack, or if it was a random incident, based on a found opportunity by an attacker.

Incident Description

To describe an incident completely, VERIS uses the A4 threat model that was developed by the RISK team at Verizon. The second-level elements used for incident description, also known as the 4 As, are as follows:

- **Actors:** Whose actions affected the asset?

- **Actions:** What actions affected the asset?

- **Assets:** Which assets were affected?

- **Attributes:** How was the asset affected?

Each of these elements should be further refined through the use of their associated subelements by answering the questions in Table 13-10.

Table 13-10   Incident Description for Subelements

Actors

Variable	Question
actor.external	Was there an external threat actor?
actor.internal	Was there an internal threat actor?
actor.partner	Was there a partner threat actor?
actor.unknown	Was there a threat actor but you don't know what kind?

Actions

Variable	Question
action.hacking	Was there evidence of hacking?
action.malware	Was there evidence of malware?
action.social	Was there evidence of social engineering?
action.misuse	Was there evidence of misuse of privileges?
action.error	Was there an error that lead to the incident?
action.physical	Was there evidence of physical attack?
action.environmental	Was there an act of God that lead to the incident?
action.unknown	Are we unsure what happened?

Attributes

Variable	Question
attribute.confidentiality	Is it possible that confidential information was exposed?
attribute.integrity	Was the integrity of any system affected?
attribute.availability	Was there an availability loss?
attribute.unknown	Are we unsure what was affected?

Assets	
Variable	**Question**
asset.assets.server	Was a server affected by the incident?
asset.assets.network	Was a network device affected?
asset.assets.user	Were any end-user devices affected?
asset.assets.terminal	Were any terminal devices affected (e.g., ATM, Kiosk, etc.)?
asset.assets.media	Did the incident affect any paper documents, or storage media?
asset.assets.people	Were any people compromised (e.g., Social Engineering)?
asset.assets.unknown	Are we unsure what was affected?

Victim Demographics

This section is for describing the organization that has experienced the incident. The characteristics of the organization can be compared to other organizations to determine if there are aspects of an incident that are common. The second-level elements used for victim demographics are as follows:

- **Victim ID:** Identifies incidents with the organization that experienced them.

- **Primary Industry:** Identifies the industry in which the affected organization conducts business. The six-digit North American Industry Classification System (NAICS) code is entered here.

- **Country of Operation:** Used to record the country where the primary location of the organization operates.

- **State:** Only used when the organization operates in the United States.

- **Number of Employees:** This is for recording the size of the entire organization, not a department or branch.

- **Annual Revenue:** This variable can be rounded for privacy.

- **Locations Affected:** Identifies any additional regions or branches that were affected by the incident.

- **Notes:** Additional details that may be of use are recorded here.

Incident Tracking

This is for recording general information about the incident so organizations can identify, store, and retrieve incidents over time. The second-level elements used for incident tracking are as follows:

- **Incident ID:** This is a unique identifier for storage and tracking.

- **Source ID:** Identifies the incident in the context of who reported it.

- **Incident Confirmation:** Differentiates the incident from those that are known or suspected as being non-incidents.

- **Incident Summary:** Provides a short description of the incident.

- **Related Incidents:** Allows the incident to be associated with similar incidents.

- **Confidence Rating:** Provides a rating as to how accurate the reported incident information is.

- **Incident Notes:** Allows recording of any information not captured in other VERIS fields.

The VERIS Community Database (13.1.3.4)

There are some organizations that collect data for security incidents, but either the data is not available to the public for free or it is not in a format that allows for manipulation or transformation that may be required to make it useful. This makes it difficult for researchers who study security incident trends and organizations to make reliable risk management calculations.

This is where the VERIS Community Database (VCDB) is useful. Through the proper use of the VERIS schema and a willingness to participate, organizations can submit security incident details to the VCDB for the community to use. The larger and more robust the VCDB becomes, the more useful it will be in prevention, detection, and remediation of security incidents. It will also become a very useful tool for risk management, saving organizations data, time, effort, and money.

Like any database, it can be used to determine answers to questions. It can also be used to find out how one organization compares to another when it is of the same approximate size and operating in the same kind of industry.

Interactive Graphic

Activity 13.1.3.5: Apply the VERIS Schema to an Incident

Refer to the online course to complete this Activity.

Incident Handling (13.2)

In this section, you will learn how to apply standards specified in NIST 800-61r2 to a computer security incident.

CSIRTs (13.2.1)

In this topic, you will learn the various goals of a given CSIRT.

CSIRT Overview (13.2.1.1)

A computer security incident can be defined differently across organizations. Generally, a computer security incident is any malicious or suspicious act which violates a security policy or any event that threatens the security, confidentiality, integrity, or availability of an organization's assets, information systems, or data network. Although this definition may be considered vague, these are some common computer security incidents:

- Malicious code

- Denial of service

- Unauthorized entry

- Device theft

- Malicious scans or probes

- Security breach

- Violation of any security policy item

When a security incident takes place, an organization needs a way to respond. A *Computer Security Incident Response Team (CSIRT)* is an internal group commonly found within an organization that provides services and functions to secure the assets of that organization. A CSIRT does not necessarily only respond to incidents that have already happened. A CSIRT may also provide proactive services and functions such as penetration testing, intrusion detection, or even security awareness training. These types of services can help to prevent incidents, but also increase response time and mitigate damage. In the case where a security incident needs to be contained and mitigated, the CSIRT coordinates and oversees these efforts.

Types of CSIRTs (13.2.1.2)

In larger organizations, the CSIRT will focus on investigating computer security incidents. Information security teams (InfoSec) will focus on implementing security policies and monitoring for security incidents. Many times in smaller organizations, the CSIRT will handle the tasks of the InfoSec team. Every organization is different. The goals of the CSIRT must be in alignment with the goals of the organization. There are many different types of CSIRTs and related organizations:

- **Internal CSIRT:** Provides incident handling for the organization in which the CSIRT resides. Any organization, such as a hospital, bank, university, or construction company, can have an internal CSIRT.

- **National CSIRT:** Provides incident handling for a country.

- **Coordination center:** Coordinates incident handling across multiple CSIRTs. One example is US-CERT. US-CERT responds to major incidents, analyzes threats, and exchanges information with other cybersecurity experts and partners around the world.

- **Analysis center:** Uses data from many sources to determine incident activity trends. Trends help to predict future incidents and provide early warning to prevent and mitigate damages as quickly as possible. The VERIS community is an example of an analysis center.

- **Vendor team:** Provides remediation for vulnerabilities in an organization's software or hardware. These teams often handle customer reports concerning security vulnerabilities. A vendor team may also act as the internal CSIRT for an organization.

- **Managed security service provider (MSSP):** Provides incident handling to other organizations as a fee-based service. Cisco, Symantec, Verizon, and IBM are all examples of managed security service providers.

CERT (13.2.1.3)

Computer Emergency Response Teams (CERTs) are similar to CSIRTs, but are not the same. CERT is a trademarked acronym owned by Carnegie Mellon University. A CSIRT is an organization responsible for receiving, reviewing, and responding to security incidents. A CERT provides security awareness, best practices, and security vulnerability information to their populations. CERTs do not directly respond to security incidents.

Many countries have asked for permission to use the CERT acronym. These are some of the more prominent CERTs:

- US-CERT: https://www.us-cert.gov

- Japan CERT Coordination Center: http://www.jpcert.or.jp/english/

- Indian Computer Emergency Response Team: http://www.cert-in.org.in

- Singapore Computer Emergency Response Team: https://www.csa.gov.sg/singcert

- CERT Australia: https://www.cert.gov.au

Activity 13.2.1.4: Match the CSIRT with the CSIRT Goal

Refer to the online course to complete this Activity.

NIST 800-61r2 (13.2.2)

In this topic, you will learn how to apply the *NIST 800-61r2* incident handling procedures to a given incident scenario.

Establishing an Incident Response Capability (13.2.2.1)

The NIST recommendations for incident response are detailed in Special Publication 800-61, revision 2, entitled *Computer Security Incident Handling Guide*.

> **Note**
>
> Although this chapter summarizes much of the content in the NIST 800-61r2 standard, you should also read the entire publication as it covers six major exam topics for the Cybersecurity CCNA SECOPS exam. Search the Internet for **"NIST 800-61r2"**, download the PDF, and study it.

The NIST 800-61r2 standard provides guidelines for incident handling, particularly for analyzing incident-related data and determining the appropriate response to each incident. The guidelines can be followed independently of particular hardware platforms, operating systems, protocols, or applications.

The first step for an organization is to establish a computer security incident response capability (CSIRC). NIST recommends creating policies, plans, and procedures for establishing and maintaining a CSIRC.

Policy

An incident response policy details how incidents should be handled based on the organization's mission, size, and function. The policy should be reviewed regularly to adjust it to meet the goals of the roadmap that has been laid out. Policy elements are as follows:

- Statement of management commitment
- Purpose and objectives of the policy
- Scope of the policy
- Definition of computer security incidents and related terms
- Organizational structure and definition of roles, responsibilities, and levels of authority

- Prioritization or severity ratings of incidents

- Performance measures

- Reporting and contact forms

Plan Elements

A good incident response plan helps to minimize damage caused by an incident. It also helps to make the overall incident response program better by adjusting it according to lessons learned. It will ensure that each party involved in the incident response has a clear understanding of not only what they will be doing, but what others will be doing as well. Plan elements are as follows:

- Mission

- Strategies and goals

- Senior management approval

- Organizational approach to incident response

- How the incident response team will communicate with the rest of the organization and with other organizations

- Metrics for measuring the incident response capability and its effectiveness

- Roadmap for maturing the incident response capability

- How the program fits into the overall organization

Procedure Elements

The procedures that are followed during an incident response should follow the incident response plan. Procedures such as following technical processes, using techniques, filling out forms, and following checklists are standard operating procedures (SOPs). These SOPs should be detailed so that the mission and goals of the organization are in mind when these procedures are followed. SOPs minimize errors that may be caused by personnel who are under stress while participating in incident handling. It is important to share and practice these procedures, making sure that they are useful, accurate, and appropriate.

Incident Response Stakeholders (13.2.2.2)

Other groups and individuals within the organization may also be involved with incident handling. It is important to ensure that they will cooperate before an incident is underway. Their expertise and abilities can help the CSIRT to handle the incident quickly and correctly. These are some of the stakeholders that may be involved in handing a security incident:

- **Management:** Managers create the policies that everyone must follow. They also design the budget and are in charge of staffing all of the departments. Management must coordinate the incident response with other stakeholders and minimize the damage of an incident.

- **Information Assurance:** This group may need to be called in to change things such as firewall rules during some stages of incident management such as containment or recovery.

- **IT Support:** This is the group that works with the technology in the organization and understands it the most. Because IT support has a deeper understanding, it is more likely that they will perform the correct action to minimize the effectiveness of the attack or preserve evidence properly.

- **Legal Department:** It is a best practice to have the legal department review the incident policies, plans, and procedures to make sure that they do not violate any local or federal guidelines. Also, if any incident has legal implications, a legal expert will need to become involved. This might include prosecution, evidence collection, or lawsuits.

- **Public Affairs and Media Relations:** There are times when the media and the public might need to be informed of an incident, such as when their personal information has been compromised during an incident.

- **Human Resources:** The human resources department might need to perform disciplinary measures if an incident caused by an employee occurs.

- **Business Continuity Planning:** Security incidents may alter an organization's business continuity. It is important that those in charge of business continuity planning are aware of security incidents and the impact they have had on the organization as a whole. This will allow them to make any changes in plans and risk assessments.

- **Physical Security and Facilities Management:** When a security incident happens because of a physical attack, such as tailgating or shoulder surfing, these teams might need to be informed and involved. It is also their responsibility to secure facilities that contain evidence from an investigation.

NIST Incident Response Life Cycle (13.2.2.3)

NIST defines four steps in the incident response process life cycle, as shown in Figure 13-7.

Figure 13-7   Incident Response Life Cycle

- **Preparation:** The members of the CSIRT are trained in how to respond to an incident.

- **Detection and analysis:** Through continuous monitoring, the CSIRT quickly identifies, analyzes, and validates an incident.

- **Containment, eradication, and recovery:** The CSIRT implements procedures to contain the threat, eradicate the impact on organizational assets, and use backups to restore data and software. This phase may cycle back to detection and analysis to gather more information, or to expand the scope of the investigation.

- **Post-incident activities:** The CSIRT then documents how the incident was handled, recommends changes for future response, and specifies how to avoid a reoccurrence.

The incident response life cycle is meant to be a self-reinforcing learning process whereby each incident informs the process for handling future incidents. Each of these phases is discussed in more detail in this topic.

Preparation (13.2.2.4)

The preparation phase is when the CSIRT is created and trained. This phase is also when the tools and assets that will be needed by the team to investigate incidents are acquired and deployed. The following list has examples of actions that also take place during the preparation phase:

- Organizational processes are created to address communication between people on the response team. This includes such things as compiling contact information for stakeholders, other CSIRTs, and law enforcement, establishing an issue tracking system, and distributing smartphones, encryption software, etc.

- Facilities to host the response team and the SOC are created.

- Necessary hardware and software for incident analysis and mitigation are acquired. This may include forensic software, spare computers, servers and network devices, backup devices, packet sniffers, and protocol analyzers.

- Risk assessments are used to implement controls that will limit the number of incidents.

- Validation of security hardware and software deployment is performed on end-user devices, servers, and network devices.

- User security awareness training materials are developed.

Additional incident analysis resources might be required. Examples of these resources are a list of critical assets, network diagrams, port lists, hashes of critical files, and baseline readings of system and network activity. Mitigation software is also an important item when preparing to handle a security incident. An image of a clean OS and application installation files may be needed to recover a computer from an incident.

Often, the CSIRT may have a jump kit prepared. This is a portable box with many of the items listed above to help in establishing a swift response. Some of these items may be a laptop with appropriate software installed, backup media, and any other hardware, software, or information to help in the investigation. It is important to inspect the jump kit on a regular basis to install updates and make sure that all the necessary elements are available and ready for use. It is helpful to practice deploying the jump kit with the CSIRT to ensure that the team members know how to use its contents properly.

Detection and Analysis (13.2.2.5)

Because there are so many different ways in which a security incident can occur, it is impossible to create instructions that completely cover each step to follow to handle them. Different types of incidents will require different responses.

Attack Vectors

An organization should be prepared to handle any incident, but should focus on the most common types of incidents so that they can be dealt with swiftly. These are some of the more common types of attack vectors:

- **Web:** Any attack that is initiated from a website or application hosted by a website.

- **Email:** Any attack that is initiated from an email or email attachment.

- **Loss or theft:** Any equipment that is used by the organization such as a laptop, desktop, or smartphone can provide the required information for someone to initiate an attack.

- **Impersonation:** When something or someone is replaced for the purpose of malicious intent.

- **Attrition:** Any attack that uses brute force to attack devices, networks, or services.

- **Media:** Any attack that is initiated from external storage or removable media.

Detection

Some incidents are easy to detect, while others may go undetected for months. The detection of security incidents might be the most difficult phase in the incident response process. Incidents are detected in many different ways and not all of these ways are very detailed or provide detailed clarity. There are automated ways of detection such as antivirus software or an IDS. There are also manual detections through user reports.

It is important to accurately determine the type of incident and the extent of the effects. There are two categories for the signs of an incident:

- **Precursor:** This is a sign that an incident might occur in the future. When precursors are detected, an attack might be avoided by altering security measures to specifically address the type of attack detected. Examples of precursors are log entries that show a response to a port scan, or a newly discovered vulnerability to an organization's web server.

- **Indicator:** This is a sign that an incident might already have occurred or is currently occurring. Some examples of indicators are a host that has been infected with malware, multiple failed logins from an unknown source, or an IDS alert.

Analysis

Incident analysis is difficult because not all of the indicators are accurate. In a perfect world, each indicator should be analyzed to find out if it is accurate. This is nearly impossible due to the number and variety of logged and reported incidents. The use of complex algorithms and machine learning often help to determine the validity of security incidents. This is more prevalent in large organizations that have thousands or even millions of incidents daily. One method that can be used is network and system profiling. Profiling is measuring the characteristics of expected activity in networking devices and systems so that changes to it can be more easily identified.

When an indicator is found to be accurate, it does not necessarily mean that a security incident has occurred. Some indicators happen for other reasons besides security. A server that continually crashes, for example, may have bad RAM instead of being the target of a buffer overflow attack. To be safe, even ambiguous or contradictory symptoms must be analyzed to determine if a legitimate security incident has taken place. The CSIRT must react quickly to validate and analyze incidents. This is performed by following a predefined process and documenting each step.

Scoping

When the CSIRT believes that an incident has occurred, it should immediately perform an initial analysis to determine the incident's scope, such as which networks, systems, or applications are affected, who or what originated the incident, and how the incident is occurring. This scoping activity should provide enough information for the team to prioritize subsequent activities, such as containment of the incident and deeper analysis of the effects of the incident.

Incident Notification

When an incident is analyzed and prioritized, the incident response team needs to notify the appropriate individuals so that all who need to be involved will play their roles. Examples of parties that are typically notified include:

- Chief Information Officer (CIO)
- Head of information security
- Local information security officer
- Other incident response teams within the organization
- External incident response teams (if appropriate)
- System owner
- Human resources (for cases involving employees, such as harassment through email)
- Public affairs (for incidents that may generate publicity)
- Legal department (for incidents with potential legal ramifications)
- US-CERT (required for federal agencies and systems operated on behalf of the federal government)
- Law enforcement (if appropriate)

Containment, Eradication, and Recovery (13.2.2.6)

After a security incident has been detected and sufficient analysis has been performed to determine that the incident is valid, it must be contained in order to determine what to do about it. Strategies and procedures for incident containment need to be in place before an incident occurs and implemented before there is widespread damage.

Containment Strategy

For every type of incident, a containment strategy should be created and enforced. These are some conditions to determine the type of strategy to create for each incident type:

- How long it will take to implement and complete a solution?
- How much time and how many resources will be needed to implement the strategy?
- What is the process to preserve evidence?

- Can an attacker be redirected to a sandbox so that the CSIRT can safely document the attacker's methodology?

- What will be the impact to the availability of services?

- What is the extent of damage to resources or assets?

- How effective is the strategy?

During containment, additional damage may be incurred. For example, it is not always advisable to unplug the compromised host from the network. The malicious process could notice this disconnection to the CnC controller and trigger a data wipe or encryption on the target. This is where experience and expertise can help to contain an incident beyond the scope of the containment strategy.

Evidence

During an incident, evidence must be gathered to resolve it. Evidence is also important for subsequent investigation by authorities. Clear and concise documentation surrounding the preservation of evidence is critical. For evidence to be admissible in court, evidence collection must conform to specific regulations. After evidence collection, it must be accounted for properly. This is known as the chain of custody. These are some of the most important items to log when documenting evidence used in the chain of custody:

- Location of the recovery and storage of all evidence

- Any identifying criteria for all evidence such as serial number, MAC address, hostname, or IP address

- Identification information for all of the people who participated in collecting or handling the evidence

- Time and date that the evidence was collected and each instance it was handled

It is vital to educate anyone involved in evidence handling on how to preserve evidence properly.

Attacker Identification

Identifying attackers is secondary to containing, eradicating, and recovering hosts and services. However, identifying attackers will minimize the impact to critical business assets and services. These are some of the most important actions to perform to attempt to identify an attacking host during a security incident:

- Use incident databases to research related activity. This database may be in-house or located at organizations that collect data from other organizations and consolidate it into incident databases such as the VERIS community database.

- Validate the attacker's IP address to determine if it is a viable one. The host may or may not respond to a request for connectivity. This may be because it has been configured to ignore the requests, or the address has already been reassigned to another host.

- Use an Internet search engine to gain additional information about the attack. Another organization or individual may have released information about an attack from the identified source IP address.

- Monitor the communication channels that some attackers use, such as IRC. Because users can be disguised or anonymized in IRC channels, they may talk about their exploits in these channels. Often, the information gathered from this type of monitoring is misleading, and should be treated as leads and not facts.

Eradication, Recovery, and Remediation

After containment, the first step to eradication is identifying all of the hosts that need remediation. All of the effects of the security incident must be eliminated. This includes malware infections and user accounts that have been compromised. All of the vulnerabilities that were exploited by the attacker must also be corrected or patched so that the incident does not occur again.

To recover hosts, use clean and recent backups, or rebuild them with installation media if no backups are available or they have been compromised. Also, fully update and patch the operating systems and installed software of all hosts. Change all host passwords and passwords for critical systems in accordance with the password security policy. This may be a good time to validate and upgrade network security, backup strategies, and security policies. Attackers often attack the systems again, or use a similar attack to target additional resources, so be sure to prevent this as best as possible. Focus on what can be fixed quickly while prioritizing critical systems and operations.

Post-Incident Activities (13.2.2.7)

After incident response activities have eradicated the threats and the organization has begun to recover from the effects of the attack, it is important to take a step back and periodically meet with all of the parties involved to discuss the events that took place and the actions of all of the individuals while handling the incident. This will provide a platform to learn what was done right, what was done wrong, what could be changed, and what should be improved upon.

Lessons-Based Hardening

After a major incident has been handled, the organization should hold a "lessons learned" meeting to review the effectiveness of the incident handling process and identify necessary hardening needed for existing security controls and practices. Examples of good questions to answer during the meeting include the following:

- Exactly what happened, and at what times?

- How well did the staff and management perform while dealing with the incident?

- Were the documented procedures followed? Were they adequate?

- What information was needed sooner?

- Were any steps or actions taken that might have inhibited the recovery?

- What would the staff and management do differently the next time a similar incident occurs?

- How could information sharing with other organizations be improved?

- What corrective actions can prevent similar incidents in the future?

- What precursors or indicators should be watched for in the future to detect similar incidents?

- What additional tools or resources are needed to detect, analyze, and mitigate future incidents?

Incident Data Collection and Retention (13.2.2.8)

By having "lessons learned" meetings, the collected data can be used to determine the cost of an incident for budgeting reasons, as well as to determine the effectiveness of the CSIRT and identify possible security weaknesses throughout the system. The collected data needs to be actionable. Only collect data that can be used to define and refine the incident handling process.

A higher number of incidents handled can show that something in the incidence response methodology is not working properly and needs to be refined. It could also show incompetence in the CSIRT. A lower number of incidents might show that network and host security has been improved. It could also show a lack of incident detection. Separate incident counts for each type of incident may be more effective at showing strengths and weakness of the CSIRT and implemented security measures. These subcategories can help to target where a weakness resides, rather than whether there is a weakness at all.

The time of each incident provides insight into the total amount of labor used and the total time of each phase of the incident response process. The time until the first response is also important, as well as how long it took to report the incident and escalate it beyond the organization, if necessary.

It is important to perform an objective assessment of each incident. The response to an incident that has been resolved can be analyzed to determine how effective it was.

NIST 800-61r2 provides the following examples of performing an objective assessment of an incident:

- Reviewing logs, forms, reports, and other incident documentation for adherence to established incident response policies and procedures

- Identifying which precursors and indicators of the incident were recorded to determine how effectively the incident was logged and identified

- Determining whether the incident caused damage before it was detected

- Determining whether the actual cause of the incident was identified, and identifying the vector of attack, the vulnerabilities exploited, and the characteristics of the targeted or victimized systems, networks, and applications

- Determining whether the incident is a recurrence of a previous incident

- Calculating the estimated monetary damage from the incident (e.g., information and critical business processes negatively affected by the incident)

- Measuring the difference between the initial impact assessment and the final impact assessment

- Identifying which measures, if any, could have prevented the incident

Subjective assessment of each incident requires that incident response team members assess their own performance, as well as that of other team members and of the entire team. Another valuable source of input is the owner of a resource that was attacked, in order to determine if the owner thinks the incident was handled efficiently and if the outcome was satisfactory.

There should be a policy in place in each organization that outlines how long evidence of an incident should be retained. Evidence is often retained for many months or many years after an incident has taken place. These are some of the determining factors for evidence retention:

- **Prosecution:** When an attacker will be prosecuted because of a security incident, the evidence should be retained until after all legal actions have been completed. This may be several months or many years. In legal actions, no evidence should be overlooked or considered insignificant. An organization's policy may state that any evidence surrounding an incident that has been involved with legal actions must never be deleted or destroyed.

- **Data Retention:** An organization may specify that specific types of data should be kept for a specific period of time. Items such as email or text may only need to be kept for 90 days. More important data such as that used in an incident response (that has not had legal action), may need to be kept for three years or more.

- **Cost:** If there is a lot of hardware and storage media that needs to be stored for a long time, storage management can become costly. Remember also that as technology changes, functional devices that can use outdated hardware and storage media must be stored as well.

Reporting Requirements and Information Sharing (13.2.2.9)

Governmental regulations should be consulted by the legal team to determine precisely the organization's responsibility for reporting the incident. In addition, management will need to determine what additional communication is necessary with other stakeholders, such as customers, vendors, partners, etc.

Beyond the legal requirements and stakeholder considerations, NIST recommends that an organization coordinate with organizations to share details for the incident. For example, the organization could log the incident in the VERIS community database.

The critical recommendations from NIST for sharing information are as follows:

- Plan incident coordination with external parties before incidents occur.

- Consult with the legal department before initiating any coordination efforts.

- Perform incident information sharing throughout the incident response life cycle.

- Attempt to automate as much of the information sharing process as possible.

- Balance the benefits of information sharing with the drawbacks of sharing sensitive information.

- Share as much of the appropriate incident information as possible with other organizations.

Interactive Graphic

Activity 13.2.2.10: Identify the Incident Response Plan Elements

Refer to the online course to complete this Activity.

Interactive Graphic

Activity 13.2.2.11: Identify the Incident Handling Term

Refer to the online course to complete this Activity.

Interactive Graphic

Activity 13.2.2.12: Identify the Incident Handling Step

Refer to the online course to complete this Activity.

Lab 13.2.2.13: Incident Handling

In this lab, you will apply your knowledge of security incident handling procedures to formulate questions about given incident scenarios.

Summary (13.3)

In this chapter, you learned about incident response models commonly used by cybersecurity analysts to manage network security incidents.

The Cyber Kill Chain specifies the steps that an attacker must complete to accomplish their goal. The steps in the Cyber Kill Chain are as follows:

1. Reconnaissance

2. Weaponization

3. Delivery

4. Exploitation

5. Installation

6. Command and Control

7. Action on Objectives

If the attacker is stopped at any stage, the chain of attack is broken.

The Diamond Model of intrusion is made up of four parts and represents a security incident or event: adversary, capability, infrastructure, and victim. As a cybersecurity analyst, you may be called on to use the Diamond Model to diagram a series of intrusion events. The Diamond Model is ideal for illustrating how the adversary pivots from one event to the next.

In the VERIS schema, risk is defined as the intersection of four landscapes of Threat, Asset, Impact, and Control. Through the proper use of the VERIS schema and a willingness to participate, organizations can submit security incident details to the VCDB for the community to use.

Generally, a computer security incident is any malicious or suspicious act which violates a security policy, or any event that threatens the security, confidentiality, integrity, or availability of an organization's assets, information systems, or data network.

A CSIRT is an internal group commonly found within an organization that provides services and functions to respond to security incidents.

The types of CSIRTs are

- Internal CSIRT

- National CSIRT

- Coordination centers

- Analysis centers
- Vendor teams
- Managed security service providers

Unlike CSIRTs, CERTs provide security awareness, best practices, and security vulnerability information to their populations. CERTs do not directly respond to security incidents.

NIST 800-61r2 defines four phases in the incident response process life cycle:

- Preparation
- Detection and analysis
- Containment, eradication, and recovery
- Post-incident activities

Practice

The following Lab provides practice with the topics introduced in this chapter. All the Labs, Class Activities, and Packet Tracer Activities are available in the companion *CCNA Cybersecurity Operations Lab Manual* (ISBN: 9781587134388). The PKA files are found in the online course.

Labs

Lab 13.2.2.13: Incident Handling

Check Your Understanding

Complete all the review questions listed here to test your understanding of the topics and concepts in this chapter. The appendix "Answers to 'Check Your Understanding' Questions" lists the answers.

1. In the NIST incident response process life cycle, which type of attack vector involves the use of brute force against devices, networks, or services?

   A. Media

   B. Impersonation

   C. Attrition

   D. Loss or theft

2. Which NIST incident response life cycle phase includes continuous monitoring by the CSIRT to quickly identify and validate an incident?

    A. Detection and analysis

    B. Preparation

    C. Containment, eradication, and recovery

    D. Post-incident activities

3. Which NIST incident response life cycle phase includes training for the computer security incident response team on how to respond to an incident?

    A. Post-incident activities

    B. Containment, eradication, and recovery

    C. Detection and analysis

    D. Preparation

4. Which three aspects of a target system are most likely to be exploited after a weapon is delivered? (Choose three.)

    A. Applications

    B. User accounts

    C. OS vulnerabilities

    D. Existing backdoors

    E. Domain name space

    F. DHCP configurations

5. Which meta-feature element in the Diamond Model describes tools and information (such as software, black hat knowledge base, and username and password) that the adversary uses for the intrusion event?

    A. Results

    B. Direction

    C. Resources

    D. Methodology

6. Which activity is typically performed by a threat actor in the installation phase of the Cyber Kill Chain?

    A. Harvest email addresses of user accounts.

    B. Obtain an automated tool to deliver the malware payload.

    C. Open a two-way communication channel to the CnC infrastructure.

    D. Install a web shell on the target web server for persistent access.

7. Which top-level element of the VERIS schema would allow a company to document the incident timeline?

   A. Discovery and Response

   B. Incident Description

   C. Incident Tracking

   D. Victim Demographics

8. When dealing with a security threat and using the Cyber Kill Chain model, which two approaches can an organization use to help block potential exploitations on a system? (Choose two.)

   A. Conduct full malware analysis.

   B. Train web developers to secure code.

   C. Collect email and web logs for forensic reconstruction.

   D. Build detections for the behavior of known weaponizers.

   E. Perform regular vulnerability scanning and penetration testing.

9. What is a chain of custody?

   A. The documentation surrounding the preservation of evidence related to an incident

   B. A list of all of the stakeholders that were exploited by an attacker

   C. The disciplinary measures an organization may perform if an incident is caused by an employee

   D. A plan ensuring that each party involved in an incident response understands how to collect evidence

10. What type of CSIRT organization is responsible for determining trends to help predict and provide warning of future security incidents?

    A. Analysis center

    B. Vendor team

    C. Coordination center

    D. National CSIRT

11. Which approach can help block potential malware delivery methods, as described in the Cyber Kill Chain model, on an Internet-facing web server?

    A. Build detections for the behavior of known malware.

    B. Collect malware files and metadata for future analysis.

    C. Analyze the infrastructure path used for files.

    D. Audit the web server to forensically determine the origin of exploit.

12. According to NIST standards, which incident response stakeholder is responsible for coordinating an incident response with other stakeholders to minimize the damage of an incident?

    A. IT support

    B. Management

    C. Legal department

    D. Human resources

13. After a threat actor completes a port scan of the public web server of an organization and identifies a potential vulnerability, what is the next phase for the threat actor in order to prepare and launch an attack as defined in the Cyber Kill Chain?

    A. Exploitation

    B. Weaponization

    C. Reconnaissance

    D. Action on objectives

Answers to the "Check Your Understanding" Questions

Chapter 1

1. C. Ransomware commonly encrypts data on a computer and makes the data unavailable until the computer user pays a specific sum of money.

2. D. Cyberwarfare is a subset of information warfare (IW). Its objective is to disrupt (availability), corrupt (integrity), or exploit (confidentiality or privacy). It can be directed against military forces, critical infrastructures, or other national interests, such as economic targets. It involves several teams that work together. A botnet might be one of several tools used for launching the attack.

3. A. A security information and event management system (SIEM) combines data from multiple sources to help SOC personnel collect and filter data, detect and classify threats, analyze and investigate threats, and manage resources to implement preventive measures.

4. C, D, F. Technologies in a SOC should include the following:

   - Event collection, correlation, and analysis

   - Security monitoring

   - Security control

   - Log management

   - Vulnerability assessment

   - Vulnerability tracking

   - Threat intelligence

   Proxy server, user authentication, and intrusion prevention systems (IPS) are security devices and mechanisms deployed in the network infrastructure and managed by the network operations center (NOC).

5. C. The term is used to describe gray hat hackers who rally and protect for a cause.

6. A. (ISC)^2 is an international nonprofit organization that offers the CISSP certification.

7. B. An incident responder is a Tier 2 security professional in an SOC. If the responder cannot resolve the incident ticket, the incident ticket should be escalated to the next-tier support, a Tier 3 subject matter expert. A Tier 3 SME would further investigate the incident.

8. A. In a typical SOC, the Tier 1 personnel are called alert analysts, also known as cyberoperations analysts.

9. D. A rogue wireless hotspot is a wireless access point running in a business or an organization without the official permission from the business or organization.

Chapter 2

1. B. The master boot record (MBR) contains a small program that is responsible for locating and loading the operating system. The BIOS executes this code and the operating system starts to load.

2. A. The **net** command is a very important command in Windows. Some common **net** commands include the following:

   - **net accounts:** Sets password and logon requirements for users

   - **net session:** Lists or disconnects sessions between a computer and other computers on the network

   - **net share:** Creates, removes, or manages shared resources

   - **net start:** Starts a network service or lists running network services

   - **net stop:** Stops a network service

   - **net use:** Connects, disconnects, and displays information about shared network resources

   - **net view:** Shows a list of computers and network devices on the network

3. C. An automatic startup will start the service automatically when the PC starts. The manual startup process will occur when the application is launched by a user. There is no boot, start, or startup service type that can be configured.

4. D. The types of commands that PowerShell can execute include the following:

   - **Cmdlets:** Perform an action and return an output or object to the next command that will be executed

   - **PowerShell scripts:** Files with a .ps1 extension that contain PowerShell commands that are executed

   - **PowerShell functions:** Pieces of code that can be referenced in a script

5. B. The registry contains information about applications, users, hardware, network settings, and file types. The registry also contains a unique section for every user, which contains the settings configured by that particular user.

6. B. There are more than 20 releases and versions of the Windows operating system. The Windows XP release introduced 64-bit processing to Windows computing.

7. D. If the ping from one host to another host on a remote network is successful, this indicates that the default gateway is operational. In this scenario, if a ping from one host to the default gateway failed, it is possible that some security features are applied to the router interface, preventing it from responding to ping requests.

8. C. The **nslookup** command was created to allow a user to manually query a DNS server to resolve a given host name. The **ipconfig /displaydns** command only displays previously resolved DNS

entries. The **tracert** command was created to examine the path that packets take as they cross a network and can resolve a hostname by automatically querying a DNS server. The **net** command is used to manage network computers, servers, printers, and network drives.

9. B. CLI commands are typed into the Command Prompt window of the Windows operating system. The **cd** command is used to change the directory to the Windows root directory.

10. A. A 32-bit operating system is capable of supporting approximately 4 GB of memory. This is because 2^32 is approximately 4 GB.

11. C. Network applications have specific TCP or UDP ports that can be left open or blocked in Windows Firewall. Disabling automatic IP address assignment may result in the computer not being able to connect to the network at all. Enabling MAC address filtering is not possible in Windows and would only block specific network hosts, not applications. Changing default usernames and passwords will secure the computer from unauthorized users, not from applications.

12. A. The Windows Task Manager utility includes a Users tab from which the system resources consumed by each user can be displayed

Chapter 3

1. B. The **man** command is short for manual and is used to obtain documentation about a Linux command. The command **man man** would provide documentation about how to use the manual.

2. C. Linux is an open source operating system and any person can access the source code, inspect it, modify it, and recompile it. Linux distributions are maintained by a community of programmers, are designed to be connected to a network, and do not have to provide free support.

3. D. In Linux, services are managed using configuration files. When the service starts, it looks for its configuration files, loads them into memory, and adjusts itself according to the settings in the files.

4. B. A graphical user interface (GUI) is considered to be more user-friendly because it presents the operating system with an interface and icons that make it easy to locate applications and complete tasks.

5. B. The Quicklist is accessed by right-clicking any application hosted on the Launcher. Quicklist allows access to a few tasks for the specific application.

6. C. A process is a running instance of a computer program. Multitasking operating systems can execute multiple processes at the same time. A process ID (PID) is used to identify a process. The **ps** or **top** command can be used to see what processes are currently running on a computer.

7. B. PenTesting is known as penetration testing and includes tools that are used to search for vulnerabilities in a network or computer by attacking it.

8. B. The basic best practices for device hardening are as follows:
   - Ensure physical security.
   - Minimize installed packages.

- Disable unused services.

- Use SSH and disable the root account login over SSH.

- Keep the system updated.

- Disable USB auto-detection.

- Enforce strong passwords.

- Force periodic password changes.

- Keep users from reusing old passwords.

- Review logs regularly.

9. B. The file permissions are always displayed in the User, Group, and Other order. In the example displayed, the file has the following permissions:

- The dash (-) means that this is a file. For directories, the first dash would be replaced with a "d".

- The first set of characters is for user permission (**rwx**). The user, **sales**, who owns the file can read, write, and execute the file.

- The second set of characters is for group permissions (**rw-**). The group, **staff**, who owns the file can read and write to the file.

- The third set of characters is for any other user or group permissions (**r--**). Any other user or group on the computer can only read the file.

Chapter 4

1. B. When the client receives the DHCPOFFER from the server, it sends back a DHCPREQUEST broadcast message. On receiving the DHCPREQUEST message, the server replies with a unicast DHCPACK message.

2. B. The transport layer of the OSI model has several responsibilities. One of the primary responsibilities is to segment data into blocks that can be reassembled in proper sequence at the destination device.

3. C. When a network device has to communicate with a device on another network, it broadcasts an ARP request asking for the default gateway MAC address. The default gateway (RT1) unicasts an ARP reply with its MAC address.

4. D. ARP, or the Address Resolution Protocol, works by mapping a destination MAC address to a destination IPv4 address. The host knows the destination IPv4 address and uses ARP to resolve the corresponding destination MAC address.

5. A. FTP is a client/server protocol. FTP requires two connections between the client and the server and uses TCP to provide reliable connections. With FTP, data transfer can happen in either direction. The client can download (pull) data from the server or upload (push) data to the server.

6. B, C. The OSI transport layer is functionally equivalent to the TCP/IP transport layer, and the OSI network layer is equivalent to the TCP/IP Internet layer. The OSI data link and physical layers together are equivalent to the TCP/IP network access layer. The OSI session layer (with the presentation layer) is included within the TCP/IP application layer.

7. A. The TCP/IP Internet layer provides the same function as the OSI network layer. The transport layer of both the TCP/IP and OSI models provides the same function. The TCP/IP application layer includes the same functions as OSI Layers 5, 6, and 7.

8. D. The IPv6 address 2001:0000:0000:abcd:0000:0000:0000:0001 in its most compressed format would be 2001:0:0:abcd::1. The first two hextets of zeros would each compress to a single zero. The three consecutive hextets of zeros can be compressed to a double colon ::. The three leading zeros in the last hextet can be removed. The double colon :: can only be used once in an address.

9. B, C, D. DNS, DHCP, and FTP are all application layer protocols in the TCP/IP protocol suite. ARP and PPP are network access layer protocols, and NAT is an Internet layer protocol in the TCP/IP protocol suite.

10. D. A default gateway is only required to communicate with devices on another network. The absence of a default gateway does not affect connectivity between devices on the same local network.

11. D. When all devices need to receive the same message simultaneously, the message would be delivered as a broadcast. Unicast delivery occurs when one source host sends a message to one destination host. The sending of the same message from a host to a group of destination hosts is multicast delivery. Duplex communications refers to the ability of the medium to carry messages in both directions.

Chapter 5

1. C. Firewalls are used to permit or block traffic between networks according to access control policies.

2. C. An Ethernet switch examines the source MAC address of an incoming frame. If the source MAC address is not in the MAC address table, the switch will add it to the table with the associated ingress Ethernet port.

3. D. An intermediary device sends network messages toward a final destination. Examples of intermediary devices include a firewall, router, switch, multilayer switch, and wireless router.

4. C. TACACS+ uses TCP, encrypts the entire packet (not just the password), and separates authentication and authorization into two distinct processes. Both protocols are supported by the Cisco Secure ACS software.

5. D. An access point can be manually set to a specific frequency band or channel in order to avoid interference with other wireless devices in the area.

6. C. Intrusion detection systems (IDSs) use a set of rules, referred to as signatures, to identify malicious traffic on the network.

7. A. Devices connected to the Ethernet star topology connect to either a hub or a switch.

8. C. There are two methods that can be used to set date and time settings on network devices. Manual configuration and automatically using the Network Time Protocol (NTP). NTP keeps the time across all devices synchronized by using a hierarchical system of sources.

9. B. SNMP is an application layer protocol that allows administrators to manage and monitor devices on the network such as routers, switches, and servers.

Chapter 6

1. D. The hacker infects multiple machines (zombies), creating a botnet. Zombies launch the distributed denial-of-service (DDoS) attack.

2. B. The best description of Trojan horse malware, and what distinguishes it from viruses and worms, is that it appears as useful software but hides malicious code. Trojan horse malware may cause annoying computer problems, but can also cause fatal problems. Some Trojan horses may be distributed over the Internet, but they can also be distributed by USB memory sticks and other means. Specifically targeted Trojan horse malware can be some of the most difficult malware to detect.

3. D. Malware can be classified as follows:

   - Virus (self replicates by attaching to another program or file)

   - Worm (replicates independently of another program)

   - Trojan horse (masquerades as a legitimate file or program)

   - Rootkit (gains privileged access to a machine while concealing itself)

   - Spyware (collects information from a target system)

   - Adware (delivers advertisements with or without consent)

   - Bot (waits for commands from the hacker)

   - Ransomware (holds a computer system or data captive until payment is received)

4. B. Malware can be classified as follows:

   - Virus (self-replicates by attaching to another program or file)

   - Worm (replicates independently of another program)

- Trojan horse (masquerades as a legitimate file or program)
- Rootkit (gains privileged access to a machine while concealing itself)
- Spyware (collects information from a target system)
- Adware (delivers advertisements with or without consent)
- Bot (waits for commands from the hacker)
- Ransomware (holds a computer system or data captive until payment is received)

5. D. Hacktivism is a term used to describe cyberattacks carried out by people who are considered political or ideological extremists. Hacktivists attack people or organizations that they believe are enemies to the hacktivist agenda.

6. Preventing users from accessing network resources is a denial-of-service attack. Being able to steal data from the network servers may be the objective after a reconnaissance attack gathers information about the target network and system. Redirecting data traffic so it can be monitored is a man-in-the-middle attack.

7. A. The Nmap tool is a port scanner that is used to determine which ports are open on a particular network device. A port scanner is used before launching an attack.

8. D. Common ways used to crack Wi-Fi passwords include social engineering, brute-force attacks, and network sniffing.

9. A. Phishing uses deception to convince people to divulge information. Hactivism is hacking done for a specific cause such as political or social reasons. A script kiddie is an inexperienced hacker who uses free scripts, software, and tools. A denial-of-service (DoS) attack causes one or more services to be inaccessible or not work.

10. A. Worm malware can execute and copy itself without being triggered by a host program. It is a significant network and Internet security threat.

11. A. Network security personnel must be familiar with port numbers in order to identify the service being attacked. Well-known port number 21 is used to initiate an FTP connection to an FTP server. Well-known port 20 is then used to transfer data between the two devices. If the device connecting to the FTP server is unknown and launching an attack, the type of attack might be an FTP Trojan horse.

12. D. An email attachment that appears as valid software but actually contains spyware shows how malware might be concealed. An attack to block access to a website is a DoS attack. A hacker uses search engine optimization (SEO) poisoning to improve the ranking of a website so that users are directed to a malicious site that hosts malware or uses social engineering methods to obtain information. A botnet of zombie computers is used to launch a DDoS attack.

13. B. Viruses can be malicious and destructive or simply change something about the computer, such as words or images, and not necessarily cause the computer to malfunction. Viruses can be spread through shared media such as CDs or memory sticks, but can also be delivered via the Internet and email.

Chapter 7

1. B. Security information event management (SIEM) is a technology that is used in enterprise organizations to provide real-time reporting and long-term analysis of security events. Splunk is a proprietary SIEM system.

2. C. Network security devices such as firewalls and intrusion prevention systems (IPSs) use preconfigured rules to identify malicious traffic on the network. Sometimes legitimate traffic is mistakenly identified as unauthorized or malicious. When legitimate traffic is incorrectly identified as unauthorized, it is known as a false positive.

3. C. When enabled on a switch, SPAN, or port mirroring, copies frames sent and received by the switch and forwards them to another port, known as a Switch Port Analyzer port, which has an analysis device attached.

4. B. Wireshark is a network protocol analyzer used to capture network traffic. The traffic captured by Wireshark is saved in PCAP files and includes interface information and timestamps.

5. A. Cybercriminals use SQL injections to breach a relational database, create malicious SQL queries, and obtain sensitive data.

6. C. Wireshark is a network protocol analyzer used to capture network traffic. The traffic captured by Wireshark is saved in PCAP files and includes interface information and timestamps.

7. C. SIEM provides administrators with details on sources of suspicious activity such as user information, device location, and compliance with security policies. One of the essential functions of SIEM is correlation of logs and events from different systems in order to speed the detection and reaction to security events.

8. D. A network TAP is a common technology that is used to capture traffic for monitoring the network. The TAP is typically a passive splitting device implemented inline on the network and that forwards all traffic, including physical layer errors, to an analysis device.

9. C. DHCP starvation attacks create a denial of service for network clients. The attacker sends DHCP discovery messages that contain fake MAC addresses in an attempt to lease all of the IP addresses. In contrast, DHCP spoofing occurs when a cybercriminal configures a rogue DHCP server to provide network clients with incorrect IP configuration information.

10. A. In a DoS, or denial-of-service, attack, the goal of the attacker is to prevent legitimate users from accessing network services.

11. C. NetFlow is a Cisco technology that runs on Cisco routers and multilayer switches and that gathers statistics on forwarded packets.

Chapter 8

1. A. The artichoke is now used to provide a visual analogy to describe a defense-in-depth security approach. The onion used to be descriptive because the attacker would "peel away" each layer of the network defense mechanisms. Now the artichoke is used because a single petal or leaf can be moved or removed to reveal sensitive information.

2. D. When a layered defense-in-depth security approach is used, layers of security are placed through the organization—at the edge, within the network, and on endpoints. The layers work together to create the security architecture. In this environment, a failure of one safeguard does not affect the effectiveness of other safeguards.

3. C. Authentication methods are used to strengthen access control systems. It is important to understand the available authentication methods.

4. B. With privilege escalation, vulnerabilities are exploited to grant higher levels of privilege. After the privilege is granted, the threat actor can access sensitive information or take control of the system.

5. C, D. RADIUS is an open-standard AAA protocol using UDP port 1645 or 1812 for authentication and UDP port 1646 or 1813 for accounting. It combines authentication and authorization into one process.

6. C. One of the components in AAA is authorization. After a user is authenticated through AAA, authorization services determine which resources the user can access and which operations the user is allowed to perform.

7. A. Business policies set a baseline of acceptable use. Company policies establish the rules and conduct and the responsibilities of both employees and the employer. Company policies protect the rights of the workers as well as the business interests of the company.

8. B. One of the components in AAA is accounting. After a user is authenticated through AAA, AAA servers keep a detailed log of exactly what actions the authenticated user takes on the device.

9. B. The U.S. Department of Homeland Security (DHS) offers a free service called Automated Indicator Sharing (AIS). AIS enables the real-time exchange of cyberthreat indicators (e.g., malicious IP addresses, the sender address of a phishing email, etc.) between the U.S. federal government and the private sector.

10. D. The remote access policy section of a corporate security policy identifies how remote users can access a network and what is accessible via remote connectivity.

11. A. AAA authorization is implemented immediately after the user is authenticated against a specific AAA data source.

Chapter 9

1. A. When an asymmetric algorithm is used, public and private keys are used for the encryption. Either key can be used for encryption, but the complementary matched key must be used for the decryption. For example, if the public key is used for encryption, then the private key must be used for the decryption.

2. D. Because only the sender and receiver know the secret key, only parties that have access to that key can compute the digest of an HMAC function. This defeats man-in-the-middle attacks and provides authentication of where the data originated.

3. B. Data confidentiality is ensured through symmetric encryption algorithms, including DES, 3DES, and AES.

4. D. Code signing is used to verify the integrity of executable files downloaded from a vendor website. Code signing uses digital certificates to authenticate and verify the identity of a website.

5. A, C. MD5, HMAC, and SHA are hashing algorithms.

6. D. DH is an asymmetric mathematical algorithm that allows two computers to generate an identical shared secret, without having communicated before. Asymmetric key systems are extremely slow for any sort of bulk encryption. It is common to encrypt the bulk of the traffic using a symmetric algorithm such as DES, 3DES, or AES, and use the DH algorithm to create keys that will be used by the symmetric encryption algorithm.

7. B. A Keyed-hash message authentication code (HMAC and KHMAC) is a type of message authentication code that uses an additional secret key as input to the hash function. This adds authentication to integrity assurance. When two parties share a secret key and use HMAC functions for authentication, the received HMAC digest of a message indicates that the other party was the originator of the message (non-repudiation), because it is the only other entity possessing the secret key. 3DES is an encryption algorithm, and MD5 and SHA-1 are hashing algorithms.

8. D. In a hierarchical CA topology, CAs can issue certificates to end users and to subordinate CAs, which in turn issue their certificates to end users, other lower level CAs, or both. In this way, a tree of CAs and end users is built in which every CA can issue certificates to lower level CAs and end users. Only the root CA can issue a self-signing certificate in a hierarchical CA topology.

9. C. When data is encrypted, it is scrambled to keep the data private and confidential so that only authorized recipients can read the message. A hash function is another way of providing confidentiality.

10. C. Hashing can be used to detect accidental changes only. It is possible for an attacker to intercept a message, change it, recalculate the hash, and append it to the message. The receiving device would validate the appended hash.

11. B. To address the interoperability of different PKI vendors, IETF published the Internet X.509 Public Key Infrastructure Certificate Policy and Certification Practices Framework (RFC 2527). The standard defines the format of a digital certificate.

12. A, E. A digital certificate class is identified by a number. The higher the number, the more trusted the certificate. The classes include the following:

   - Class 0 is for testing purposes in which no checks have been performed.

   - Class 1 is for individuals with a focus on verification of email.

   - Class 2 is for organizations for which proof of identity is required.

   - Class 3 is for servers and software signing for which independent verification and checking of identity and authority is done by the issuing certificate authority.

   - Class 4 is for online business transactions between companies.

   - Class 5 is for private organizations or governmental security.

13. A. In the CA authentication procedure, the first step when contacting the PKI is to obtain a copy of the public key of CA itself, called the self-signed certificate. The CA public key verifies all the certificates issued by the CA.

Chapter 10

1. B. The Open Source HIDS SECurity (OSSEC) software is an open source HIDS that uses a central manager server and agents that are installed on the hosts that are to be monitored.

2. C. The Domain profile in Windows Firewall configuration is for connections to a trusted network, such as a business network, that is assumed to have an adequate security infrastructure.

3. A. The Common Vulnerability Scoring System (CVSS) is a risk assessment tool to convey the common attributes and severity of vulnerabilities in computer hardware and software systems.

4. C. There are four potential strategies for responding to risks that have been identified:

   - **Risk avoidance:** Stop performing the activities that create risk.

   - **Risk reduction:** Decrease the risk by taking measures to reduce vulnerability.

   - **Risk sharing:** Shift some of the risk to other parties.

   - **Risk retention:** Accept the risk and its consequences.

5. D. The major regulatory compliance options include:

   - **Federal Information Security Management Act of 2002 (FISMA):** Specifies security standards for U.S. government systems and contractors to the U.S. government.

   - **Sarbanes-Oxley Act of 2002 (SOX):** Sets new or expanded requirements for all U.S. public company boards, management, and public accounting firms regarding the way in which corporations control and disclose financial information.

- **Gramm-Leach-Bliley Act (GLBA):** Established that financial institutions must ensure the security and confidentiality of customer information; protect against any anticipated threats or hazards to the security or integrity of such information; and protect against unauthorized access to or use of customer information that could result in substantial harm or inconvenience to any customer.

- **Health Insurance Portability and Accountability Act (HIPAA):** Requires that all patient personally identifiable healthcare information be stored, maintained, and transmitted in ways that ensure patient privacy and confidentiality.

6. B, D, F. IoT components, such as sensors, controllers, and network security cameras, are network endpoints when they are connected to a network. Routers, VPN appliances, and wireless access points are examples of intermediate devices.

7. C. Antimalware programs may detect viruses using three different approaches:

   - Signature-based, by recognizing various characteristics of known malware files

   - Heuristics-based, by recognizing general features shared by various types of malware

   - Behavior-based, through analysis of suspicious activities

8. C. The SANS Institute describes three components of the attack surface:

   - **Network Attack Surface:** Exploitation of vulnerabilities in networks

   - **Software Attack Surface:** Exploitation of vulnerabilities in web, cloud, or host-based software applications

   - **Human Attack Surface:** Exploitation of weaknesses in user behavior

9. C. The service accounts element of a server profile defines the type of service that an application is allowed to run on a given host.

10. B. The Base metric group of CVSS represents the characteristics of a vulnerability that are constant over time and across contexts. It contains two classes of metrics:

    - **Exploitability metrics:** Features of the exploit such as the vector, complexity, and user interaction required by the exploit

    - **Impact metrics:** The impacts of the exploit rooted in the CIA triad of confidentiality, integrity, and availability

11. B. The steps in the Vulnerability Management Life Cycle include these:

    - **Discover:** Inventory all assets across the network and identify host details, including operating systems and open services to identify vulnerabilities.

    - **Prioritize assets:** Categorize assets into groups or business units, and assign a business value to asset groups based on their criticality to business operations.

- **Assess:** Determine a baseline risk profile to eliminate risks based on asset criticality, vulnerability threats, and asset classification.

- **Report:** Measure the level of business risk associated with your assets according to your security policies. Document a security plan, monitor suspicious activity, and describe known vulnerabilities.

- **Remediate:** Prioritize according to business risk and fix vulnerabilities in order of risk.

- **Verify:** Verify that threats have been eliminated through follow-up audits.

12. A. A risk analysis includes assessment of the likelihood of attacks, identifies types of likely threat actors, and evaluates the impact of successful exploits on the organization.

Chapter 11

1. A. The **tcpdump** command line tool is a popular packet analyzer. It can display packet captures in real time or write packet captures to a file.

2. C. Various Windows host logs can have different event types. The Information event type records an event that describes the successful operation of an application, driver, or service.

3. A. Alert data is generated by IPS or IDS devices in response to traffic that violates a rule or matches the signature of a known security threat.

4. B. Tor is a software platform and network of peer-to-peer (P2P) hosts that function as routers. Users access the Tor network by using a special browser that allows them to browse anonymously.

5. D. NetFlow does not capture the entire contents of a packet. Instead, NetFlow collects metadata, or data about the flow, not the flow data itself. NetFlow information can be viewed with tools such as **nfdump** and FlowViewer.

6. C. Statistical data is created through the analysis of other forms of network data. Conclusions from these analyses can be used to describe or predict network behavior.

7. A. Some malware uses DNS to communicate with command-and-control (CnC) servers to exfiltrate data in traffic that is disguised as normal DNS query traffic.

8. C. AVC uses Cisco Next-Generation Network-Based Application Recognition (NBAR2) to discover and classify the applications in use on the network.

9. D. Transaction data focuses on the results of network sessions as reflected by the device logs kept by server processes, such as the details of a user's visit to a website.

10. C. Syslog is important to security monitoring because network devices send periodic messages to the syslog server. These logs can be examined to detect inconsistencies and issues within the network.

11. B. Event Viewer in Windows can be used to review entries in various logs.

12. B, E. POP, POP3, and IMAP are protocols that are used to retrieve email from servers. SMTP is the default protocol that is used to send email. DNS may be used by the sender email server to find the address of the destination email server. HTTP is a protocol for send and receiving web pages.

Chapter 12

1. A, D. Enterprise Log Search and Archive (ELSA) is an enterprise-level tool for allowing searching and archiving of NSM data that originates from multiple sources. ELSA receives logs over Syslog-NG, stores logs in MySQL databases, and indexes using Sphinx Search.

2. A. Integrated into the Security Onion, OSSEC is a host-based intrusion detection system (HIDS) that can conduct file integrity monitoring, local log monitoring, system process monitoring, and rootkit detection.

3. C. NIST describes the digital forensics process as involving the following four steps:

- **Data collection:** The identification of potential sources of forensic data and acquisition, handling, and storage of that data.

- **Examination:** Assessing and extracting relevant information from the collected data. This may involve decompression or decryption of the data.

- **Analysis:** Drawing conclusions from the data. Salient features, such as people, places, times, events, and so on, should be documented.

- **Reporting:** Preparing and presenting information that resulted from the analysis. Reporting should be impartial and alternative explanations should be offered if appropriate.

4. B, D. Regular expressions allow forensics analysts to search through large quantities of text information for patterns of data. Some common operators used in regular expressions are the following:

- $ End of a line

- [] Any single value within the square brackets

- * Preceding sub-expression zero or more times

- [^1] Any character except those bound by the [^ and the]

5. A. A false negative classification indicates that a security system has not detected an actual exploit.

6. B. The primary duty of a cybersecurity analyst is the verification of security alerts. In the Security Onion, the first place that a cybersecurity analyst will go to verify alerts is Sguil because it provides a high-level console for investigating security alerts from a wide variety of sources.

7. C. With data normalization various sources of data are combined into a common display format, which simplifies the searching for similar or relevant events.

8. B. Evidence can be classified as follows:

   ■ **Best evidence:** This is evidence that is in its original state. It might be storage devices used by an accused or archives of files that can be proven to be unaltered.

   ■ **Corroborating evidence:** This is evidence that supports a proposition already supported by initial evidence, therefore confirming the original proposition.

   ■ **Indirect evidence:** This evidence acts in combination with other facts to establish a hypothesis.

Chapter 13

1. C. Common attack vectors include media, attrition, impersonation, and loss or theft. Attrition attacks are any attacks that use brute force. Media attacks are those initiated from storage devices. Impersonation attacks occur when something or someone is replaced for the purpose of the attack, and loss or theft attacks are initiated by equipment inside the organization.

2. A. It is in the detection and analysis phase of the NIST incident response life cycle that the CSIRT identifies and validates incidents through continuous monitoring. The NIST defines four stages of the incident response life cycle.

3. D. It is in the preparation phase of the NIST incident response life cycle phase that the CSIRT is trained on how to respond to an incident.

4. A, B, C. The most common exploit targets, once a weapon is delivered, are applications, operating system vulnerabilities, and user accounts. Threat actors will use an exploit that gains the effect they desire, does it quietly, and avoids detection.

5. C. The resources element in the Diamond Model is used to describe one or more external resources used by the adversary for the intrusion event. The resources include software, knowledge gained by the adversary, information (e.g., username/passwords), and assets to carry out the attack.

6. D. In the installation phase of the Cyber Kill Chain, the threat actor establishes a backdoor into the system to allow for continued access to the target.

7. A. The Discovery and Response element is used to record the timeline of events, the method of incident discovery, and what the response was to the incident. Incident Tracking is for recording general information about the incident.

8. B, E. The most common exploit targets, once a weapon is delivered, are applications, operating system vulnerabilities, and user accounts. Among other measures, such as regular vulnerability scanning and penetration testing, training web developers in securing code can help block potential exploitations on systems.

9. A. A chain of custody refers to the documentation of evidence collected about an incident that is used by authorities during an investigation.

10. A. There are many different types of CSIRTs and related information security organizations. Analysis centers use data from many sources to determine security incident trends that can help predict future incidents and provide early warning. This helps to mitigate the damages that incidents can cause.

11. C. A threat actor may send the weapon through web interfaces to the target server, either in file uploads or coded web requests. By analyzing the infrastructure storage path used for files, security measures can be implemented to monitor and detect malware deliveries through these methods.

12. B. The management team creates the policies, designs the budget, and is in charge of staffing all departments. Management is also responsible for coordinating the incident response with other stakeholders and minimizing the damage of an incident.

13. B. The Cyber Kill Chain specifies seven steps (or phases) and sequences that a threat actor must complete to accomplish an attack:

    1. **Reconnaissance:** The threat actor performs research, gathers intelligence, and selects targets.

    2. **Weaponization:** The threat actor uses the information from the reconnaissance phase to develop a weapon against specific targeted systems.

    3. **Delivery:** The weapon is transmitted to the target using a delivery vector.

    4. **Exploitation:** The threat actor uses the weapon delivered to break the vulnerability and gain control of the target.

    5. **Installation:** The threat actor establishes a backdoor into the system to allow for continued access to the target.

    6. **Command and Control (CnC):** The threat actor establishes command and control (CnC) with the target system.

    7. **Action on Objectives:** The threat actor is able to take action on the target system, thus achieving the original objective.

Glossary

3DES (Triple DES) Newer version of DES that repeats the DES algorithm process three times.

A

acceptable use policy (AUP) Identifies network applications and uses that are acceptable to the organization as well as ramifications for violating the policy.

access attacks Attacks that exploit known vulnerabilities in authentication services, FTP services, and web services to gain entry to web accounts, confidential databases, and other sensitive info.

access control list (ACL) A series of commands that control whether a device forwards or drops packets based on information found in the packet header.

access layer Provides endpoints and users direct access to the network.

Address Resolution Protocol (ARP) Provides dynamic address mapping between an IP address and a hardware address.

Advanced Encryption Standard (AES) Currently recommended symmetric encryption algorithm that offers nine combinations of key and block length.

adware Malware that typically displays annoying pop-ups to generate revenue for its author.

Alternate Data Streams (ADSs) Sometimes used by applications that are storing additional information about a file and can be used by threat actors to store malicious code.

amplification and reflection techniques A DoS attack in which the threat actor forwards packets, such as ICMP echo requests, that contain the source IP address of the victim to a large number of hosts (amplification), which in turn reply with ICMP echo replies (reflection), overwhelming the victim with traffic.

antivirus/antimalware Software that is installed on a host to detect and mitigate viruses and malware.

application gateway firewall (proxy firewall) Filters information at Layers 3, 4, 5, and 7; the proxy server connects to the remote server on behalf of the client.

Application layer OSI layer that contains protocols used for process-to-process communications.

ARP cache poisoning Attack in which the threat actor replies to ARP requests, spoofing the IP and MAC address of a desired device, such as the default gateway, in order to have the victim forward traffic to the threat actor instead of the legitimate default gateway.

ARP spoofing A technique used by an attacker to reply to an ARP request for an IPv4 address belonging to another device, such as the default gateway.

asset   Anything of value to an organization that must be protected, including servers, infrastructure devices, end devices, and data.

asymmetric encryption   Uses different keys to encrypt and decrypt data.

attack attribution   Determining the individual, organization, or nation responsible for a successful intrusion or attack incident.

attack indicators   The uniquely identifiable attributes of an attack.

attack surface   Different points where an attacker could get into a system, and where they could get data out of the system.

attribute-based access control (ABAC)   Access control model that allows access based on attributes of the object (resource) be to accessed, the subject (user) accessing the resource, and environmental factors regarding how the object is to be accessed.

Authentication, Authorization, and Accounting (AAA)   An architectural framework for configuring a set of three independent security functions. Authentication confirms the identity of the user or device. Authorization determines what the user or device is allowed to do. Accounting records information about access attempts, including inappropriate requests.

authoritative server   A DNS server that responds to query messages with information stored in Resource Records (RRs) for a domain name space stored on the server.

availability   Element of the CIA triad (confidentiality, integrity, availability) that states authorized users must have uninterrupted access to important resources and data.

B

baiting   Social engineering attack in which a threat actor leaves a malware-infected physical device with the hopes that someone will find it and insert it into a computer.

Basic Input-Output System (BIOS)   Older version of a computer firmware that is responsible for hardware initialization, the power on self-test (POST), and locating the master boot record (MBR). *See also* Unified Extensible Firmware Interface (UEFI).

best evidence   Evidence that is in its original state and can be proven to be unaltered.

black hat hackers   Unethical criminals who violate computer and network security for personal gain, or for maliciousness reasons such as attacking networks.

blind spoofing   Spoofing attack in which the threat actor cannot see the traffic that is being sent between the host and the target, such as in DoS attacks.

block ciphers   Transform a fixed-length block of plaintext into a common block of ciphertext.

Boot Configuration Database (BCD)   Contains any additional code needed to start the computer, along with an indication of whether this is a cold start or the computer is coming out of hibernation.

Bootstrap Protocol (BOOTP)   Enables a diskless workstation to discover its own IP address, the IP address of a BOOTP server on the network, and a file to be loaded into memory to boot the machine. BOOTP is being superseded by Dynamic Host Configuration Protocol (DHCP).

botmaster   A threat actor in control of the botnet and handlers.

botnet   A group of zombies that have been infected using self-propagating malware and are controlled by handlers.

bots   Malware that is designed to infect a host and communicate with a handler system.

Bring Your Own Device (BYOD)   A policy that allows employees to use their own mobile devices to access company systems, software, networks, or information.

Bro   An open source network security monitoring tool included in Security Onion.

broadcast   A one-to-all delivery option where all hosts on the network are the destination for the message.

buffer overflow attack   An attack that exploits a system's buffer memory by overwhelming it with unexpected values usually rendering the system inoperable, creating a DoS attack.

C

CapME   Web application that allows viewing of pcap transcripts rendered with the tcpflow or Bro tools.

chain of custody   The documentation of the collection, handling, and secure storage of evidence.

cipher   A secret way of encoding a message.

clients   A program or application designed to communicate with a specific server.

command and control (CnC or C2)   A threat actor's online server to which compromised hosts (zombies) beacon out of the network to establish a channel of communications for launching other attacks or exfiltrating data.

command line interface (CLI)   A text-based interface to the operating system that enables a user to enter commands to run programs, navigate the file system, and manage files and folders.

Compact Disc File System (CDFS)   A file system created specifically for optical disk media.

Company policies   Policies that protect the rights of workers as well as the business interests of employers.

Computer Emergency Response Teams (CERTs)   Provides security awareness, best practices, and security vulnerability information to their populations. CERT is a trademarked acronym owned by Carnegie Mellon University.

Computer Security Incident Response Team (CSIRT)   An internal group commonly found within an organization that provides services and functions to secure the assets of that organization.

confidentiality   Element of the CIA triad (confidentiality, integrity, availability) that states only authorized individuals, entities, or processes should access sensitive information.

configuration files   Used to manage the services offered by a server and can usually only be activated or modified by the administrator.

connectionless   No dedicated end-to-end connection is created before data is sent.

content addressable memory (CAM)   Similar to a MAC table, a special type of memory on a switch used in high-speed searching applications.

core layer   Provides connectivity between distribution layers for large LAN environments.

corroborating evidence   Evidence that supports an assertion that is developed from best evidence.

countermeasure   A protection solution that mitigates a threat or risk.

cross-site scripting (XSS)   An attack in which web pages that are executed on the client side, within their own web browser, are injected with malicious scripts.

cryptanalysis   The practice and study of determining and exploiting weaknesses in cryptographic techniques.

cryptography   The development and use of codes that are used for communicating privately.

cryptology   The science of making and breaking secret codes.

CSMA/CA   Carrier sense multiple access with collision avoidance; a media-access mechanism that defines how devices decide when they can send, with a goal of avoiding collisions as much as possible. IEEE WLANs use CSMA/CA.

CSMA/CD   Carrier sense multiple access with collision detection; a media-access mechanism in which devices ready to transmit data first check the channel for a carrier. If no carrier is sensed for a specific period of time, a device can transmit. If two devices transmit simultaneously, a collision occurs and is detected by all colliding devices. This collision subsequently delays retransmissions from those devices for some random length of time.

cybercriminals   Black hat hackers who are either self-employed or working for large cybercrime organizations.

Cyber Kill Chain   A method, developed by Lockheed Martin, for identifying and preventing cyber intrusions. Specifies seven steps that an attacker must complete to accomplish their goal.

D

daemon   A background process that runs without the need for user interaction.

dashboards   An interactive interface that provides a combination of data and visualizations designed to improve the access of individuals to large amounts of information.

Data Encryption Standard (DES)   An older legacy symmetric encryption algorithm that usually operates in block mode by encrypting data in 64-bit block size.

Data Link layer   Uses protocols that describe methods for exchanging data frames between devices over a common media.

data normalization   The process of combining data from a number of data sources into a common format.

debuggers   Tools used to reverse engineer binary files when writing exploits or analyzing malware.

default gateway   The local gateway that a device can use to reach remote networks.

demilitarized zone (DMZ)   A firewall design where there is typically one inside interface connected to the private network, one outside interface connected to the public network, and one DMZ interface.

destination port   Transport layer field value in the segment header which tells the destination server what service is being requested.

deterministic analysis   An analysis approach in which all the steps for a successful exploit are known by the analyst and all steps must be done in sequence for the exploit to be successful.

device hardening   Methods of securing a device and protecting its administrative access.

Diamond Model   A model that breaks down an intrusion into for core features: adversary, capability, infrastructure, and victim.

Diffie-Helman (DH)   Public key algorithm that allows two parties to agree on a key that they can use to encrypt messages they want to send to each other.

digital forensics   The recovery and investigation of information found on digital devices as it relates to criminal activity.

Digital Signature Algorithm (DSA)   A public key algorithm based on the ElGamal signature scheme.

Digital Signature Standard (DSS)   Uses the Digital Signature Algorithm (DSA) for digital signatures.

discretionary access control (DAC)   Access control model that allows users to control access to their data as owners of that data.

Disk Operating System (DOS)   An operating system that the computer uses to enable data storage devices to read and write files.

distributed denial of service (DDoS)   A type of denial of service (DoS) attack whose goal is to cause problems by preventing legitimate users from being able to access services, thereby preventing the normal operation of computers and networks. In a DDoS attack, as opposed to a DoS attack, the attack traffic originates from many sources.

distribution layer   Aggregates access layers and provides connectivity to services.

distros   A Linux distribution that includes the Linux kernel and customized tools and software packages.

DNS tunneling   An attack in which threat actors place non-DNS traffic within DNS traffic as a way to exfiltrate stolen data.

DNS zone   A database that contains information about the domain name space stored on an authoritative server.

domain   Network service where all of the users, groups, computers, peripherals, and security settings are stored on and controlled by a database.

domain controllers (DCs)   Stores all the domain databases and is used to authenticate users and computers and applies the security settings for each session.

domain generation algorithms   Technique used in malware to randomly generate domain names that can then be used as rendezvous points to the threat actor's command and control (CnC) servers.

Domain Name System (DNS)   Translates domain names, such as cisco.com, into IP addresses.

domain shadowing   A threat actor first compromises a domain and then creates multiple subdomains to be used to launch attacks.

dotted-decimal   Four octets represented as a decimal value and separated by a decimal point.

double IP flux   Technique used by threat actors to rapidly change the hostname-to-IP address mappings and to also change the authoritative name server.

Duplicate Address Detection (DAD)   Ensures that a host's assigned IPv6 address is unique. The host sends an NS message with its own IPv6 address as the destination IPv6 address. If another device on the network has this address, it will respond with an NA message.

Dynamic DNS (DDNS)   Allows the IP address associated with a domain name to be changed and then dynamically propagated throughout the DNS hierarchy almost instantaneously.

Dynamic Host Configuration Protocol (DHCP)   Dynamically assigns IP addresses to client stations at start-up. Allows the addresses to be reused when no longer needed.

dynamic routing protocol   Protocol that exchanges network reachability information between routers and dynamically adapts to network changes.

E

edge router   A router with basic permit and deny rules as a first line of defense that then passes all connections that are permitted to the internal network to the firewall.

ElGamal   An asymmetric key encryption algorithm for public key cryptography which is based on the Diffie-Hellman key agreement.

Elliptical curve   Used to adapt many cryptographic algorithms, such as Diffie-Hellman or ElGamal, so that the keys can be much smaller.

ELSA   Enterprise Log Search and Archive, a tool that provides an interface to a wide variety of network security monitoring (NSM) data logs including logs from HIDS, NIDS, firewalls, syslog, etc.

employee policies   Policies created and maintained by human resources staff to identify employee salary, pay schedule, benefits, work schedule, vacations, and more.

encryption   Applying a specific algorithm to data to alter the appearance of the data, making it incomprehensible to those who are not authorized to see the information.

encryption tools   Tools that use algorithm schemes to encode the data to prevent unauthorized access to the encrypted data.

endpoint   A host on the network that can access or be accessed by other hosts on the network.

Enhanced Interior Gateway Routing Protocol (EIGRP)   Cisco proprietary routing protocol that uses composite metric based on bandwidth, delay, load, and reliability.

Ethernet   A computer network architecture of the OSI Physical and Data Link layers that defines the rules for wiring and signaling standards of the network access layer.

Event Viewer   Windows security tool that logs the history of application, security, and system events.

exploit   Mechanism used to leverage a vulnerability to compromise an asset.

ext2   Second extended file system, the default Linux file system until replaced by ext3; still used in flash-based storage media.

ext3   Third extended file system, designed to improve ext2; added a journaling feature.

ext4   Fourth extended file system, created based on a series of extensions to ext3.

Extended FAT (exFAT)   An extended version of FAT that has even fewer restrictions than FAT32, but is not supported very well outside of the Windows ecosystem.

Extended File System (EXT)   A file system used with Linux-based computers.

F

false negative   An alert classification that means that an undetected incident has occurred.

false positive   An alert classification that means the alert does not indicate an actual security incident.

fast flux   Technique used by threat actors to hide their phishing and malware delivery sites behind a quickly changing network of compromised DNS hosts.

Federal Information Security Management Act of 2002 (FISMA)   Security standards established by NIST for U.S. government systems and contractors to the U.S. government.

File Allocation Table (FAT)   A simple file system supported by many different operating systems that has limitations to the number of partitions, partition sizes, and file sizes that it can address.

File Transfer Protocol (FTP)   Sets rules that enable a user on one host to access and transfer files to and from another host over a network. A reliable, connection-oriented, and acknowledged file delivery protocol.

firewall   A device that forwards packets between the less secure and more secure parts of the network, applying rules that determine which packets are allowed to pass, and which are not.

flow control   The amount of data that the destination can receive and process reliably.

forensic tools   Tools used to sniff out any trace of evidence existing in a particular computer system.

forking   Method to allow a process to create a copy of itself.

fully qualified domain name (FQDN)   The absolute name of a device within the distributed DNS database.

fuzzers   Tools used by hackers when attempting to discover a computer system's security vulnerabilities.

G

Generic Routing Encapsulation (GRE)   A tunneling protocol developed by Cisco that can encapsulate a wide variety of network layer protocol packet types inside IP tunnels.

Gramm-Leach-Bliley Act (GLBA)   Requires financial institutions to ensure the security and confidentiality of customer information.

gray hat hackers   Hackers who do arguably unethical things, not for personal gain or to cause damage, but to expose vulnerabilities.

H

hacker Common term used to describe a threat actor but also includes other meanings such as gray hat hacker and white hat hacker.

hacking operating systems Specially designed operating systems preloaded with tools and technologies optimized hacking.

hacktivists Gray hat hackers who rally and protest against different political and social ideas by posting numerous articles and videos, leaking sensitive information, and performing DDoS attacks.

handler A master command-and-control (CnC or C2) server controlling groups of zombies.

hard link In Linux, a link that creates another version of a file with a different name linked to the same place in the file system (called an inode). *See also* symbolic link.

hardware abstraction layer (HAL) Windows code that handles all of the communication between the hardware and the kernel.

hashes A unidirectional process (rather than a reversible algorithm) that takes a variable-sized input and creates a fixed-size output.

Health Insurance Portability and Accountability Act (HIPAA) Requires that all patient personally identifiable healthcare information be stored, maintained, and transmitted in ways that ensure patient privacy and confidentiality.

hextet A segment of an IPv6 address that is made up of 16 bits and usually represented as four hexadecimal values.

Hierarchical File System Plus (HFS+) A file system used on macOS X computers that allows much longer filenames, file sizes, and partition sizes than previous file systems.

homoglyphs Text characters that are similar to legitimate text characters, used by threat actors to spoof legitimate domain names, company names, and so on.

host-based firewalls Stand-alone software program that controls traffic entering or leaving a computer; examples include Windows Firewall, iptables, nftables, and TCP Wrapper.

host-based intrusion detection system (HIDS) Software designed to protect hosts against known and unknown malware; examples include Cisco AMP, AlienVault USM, Tripwire, and Open Source HIDS SECurity (OSSEC).

host-based intrusion prevention system (HIPS) Software installed on a single host to monitor and analyze suspicious activity.

HTTP 302 cushioning Attack in which threat actors use the 302 Found HTTP response status code to direct the user's web browser to the new location.

Hypertext Transfer Protocol (HTTP) Set of rules for exchanging text, graphic images, sound, video, and other multimedia files on the World Wide Web.

I

iFrame An HTML element that allows the browser to load another web page from another source.

impact The damage to the organization that is caused by the threat.

indirect evidence   Evidence that, in combination with other facts, establishes a hypothesis; also known as circumstantial evidence.

Information Security Management System (ISMS)   A management framework through which an organization identifies, analyzes, and addresses information security risks.

integrity   Element of the CIA triad (confidentiality, integrity, availability) that refers to the protection of data from unauthorized alteration.

intermediary device   A device that connects end devices to the network, connects multiple individual networks to form an internetwork, and provides connectivity to ensure that data flows across the network.

Internet Control Message Protocol (ICMP)   Provides feedback from a destination host to a source host about errors in packet delivery.

Internet Message Access Protocol (IMAP)   Enables clients to access email stored on a mail server. Maintains email on the server.

Internet Protocol (IP)   Receives message segments from the transport layer. Packages messages into packets. Addresses packets for end-to-end delivery over an internetwork.

intrusion detection systems (IDSs)   A security function that examines more complex traffic patterns against a list of both known attack signatures and general characteristics of how attacks may be carried out, rating each perceived threat and reporting the threats.

intrusion prevention systems (IPS)   A security function that primarily uses signature matching, can alert administrators about an attack on the network, and can prevent the initial packet from entering the network.

J

journal   A logging technique that keeps track of all changes made to the file system; used to minimize the risk of file system corruption in the event of sudden power loss.

K

Kali Linux   A Linux distribution created to group many penetration tools.

kernel   Core of the operating system that handles all of the input and output requests, memory, and peripherals connected to the computer.

Kernel Mode Code Signing (KMCS)   Ensures that the drivers are digitally signed and safe to load as the Windows computer starts.

hash message authentication code (HMAC)   Used to verify data integrity and authenticity of a message.

L

lightweight APs (LWAPs)   An AP that is connected to a wireless LAN controller (WLC) and only forwards data between the WLAN and WLC.

Linux   An operating system that is open source, fast, reliable, and small. It requires very little hardware resources to run, and is highly customizable.

load balancing   Distributing traffic between devices or network paths to prevent overwhelming network resources with too much traffic.

log files   Records that a computer stores to keep track of important events.

Logical Link Control (LLC) sublayer Data link sublayer that is responsible for communication with the network layer.

logical topology A depiction of the way a network transfers frames from one node to the next and includes addressing information.

M

malware Malicious software that is intended to gain unauthorized access to computers or computer systems.

mandatory access control (MAC) Access control model that has the strictest access control, typically used in military or mission-critical applications.

man-in-the-middle attack A threat actor positioned between two legitimate entities in order to read, modify, or redirect the data that passes between the two parties.

master boot record (MBR) Contains a small program that is responsible for locating and loading the operating system.

Master File Table (MFT) A table that contains the locations of all the files and directories on the partition, including file attributes such as security information and timestamps.

maximum transmission unit (MTU) The maximum size of the protocol data unit (PDU) that each medium can transport.

Media Access Control (MAC) sublayer Data link sublayer that is responsible for encapsulating the IP packet into a frame, converting the frame into bits, and sending the bits out on the media.

Message Digest 5 (MD5) Cryptographic function with a 128-bit hash.

mounting Assigning a directory to a specific partition so that it can be accessed.

MS-DOS A disk operating system (DOS) created by Microsoft.

multicast A one-to-many delivery option where there is more than one destination for the message.

multilayer switches Also known as a Layer 3 switch, this device not only performs Layer 2 switching, but also forwards frames based on Layer 3 and 4 information.

multiplexing Many different conversations interleaved on the network.

N

Neighbor Advertisement (NA) IPv6 message sent by a host to reply to an NS message and includes the host's MAC address; similar to an ARP reply in IPv4.

Neighbor Discovery Protocol (ND or NDP) A protocol that is part of the IPv6 protocol suite, used to discover and exchange information about devices on the same subnet (neighbors). In particular, it replaces the IPv4 ARP protocol.

Neighbor Solicitation (NS) IPv6 message sent by a host to determine the MAC address for a destination; similar to an ARP request in IPv4.

NetFlow Cisco IOS technology that provides statistics on packets flowing through a Cisco router or multilayer switch.

netstat Command that displays all of the active TCP connections and can be used to look for inbound or outbound connections that are not authorized.

Network Address Translation (NAT) Translates IP addresses from a private network into globally unique public IP addresses.

Network File System (NFS)   A network-based file system, allowing file access over the network.

Network layer   Provides services to exchange the individual pieces of data over the network between identified end devices.

network protocols   Dictates the message encoding, formatting, encapsulation, size, timing, and delivery options.

network scanning tools   Tools used to probe network devices, servers, and hosts for open TCP or UDP ports.

network TAP   A passive splitting device, implemented inline between a device of interest and the network, that forwards all traffic including physical layer errors to an analysis device.

Network Time Protocol (NTP)   Allows routers on the network to synchronize their time settings with an NTP server.

New Technology File System (NTFS)   Most commonly used file system when installing Windows.

NextGen IPS   Extends network security beyond IP addresses and Layer 4 port numbers to the application layer and beyond.

NIST 800-61r2   NIST standard that provides guidelines for incident handling and can be followed independently of particular hardware platforms, operating systems, protocols, or applications.

non-blind spoofing   Spoofing attack in which the threat actor can see the traffic that is being sent between the host and the target and can inspect the reply packet from the target victim.

non-discretionary access control   Access control model in which access decisions are based on an individual's roles and responsibilities within the organization.

O

octet   An 8-bit byte.

Open Shortest Path First (OSPF)   Link-state routing protocol. Hierarchical design based on areas. Open standard interior routing protocol.

Open Systems Interconnection (OSI) model   A network architectural model developed by the ISO. The model consists of seven layers, each of which specifies particular network functions, such as addressing, flow control, error control, encapsulation, and reliable message transfer.

OS fingerprinting   The process of using a variety of tools to identify the target's operating system.

OSSEC   Open Source SECurity; host-based intrusion detection system (HIDS) that is integrated into Security Onion.

P

packet analyzer   Software that captures packets entering and exiting the network interface card (NIC).

packet crafting tools   Tools used to probe and test a firewall's robustness using specially crafted forged packets.

packet filtering (stateless) firewall   Typically a router with the capability to filter some packet content, such as Layer 3 and sometimes Layer 4 information, according to a set of configured rules.

packet forwarding   The process of switching that a router uses to accept a packet on one interface and forward it out of another interface.

packet sniffers   Tools used to capture and analyze packets within traditional Ethernet LANs or WLANs.

Partition Boot Sector   The first 16 sectors of the drive that contains the location of the Master File Table (MFT).

pass-the-hash   An attack in which a threat actor with access to a user's machine uses malware to gain access to the stored password hashes and then uses the hashes to authenticate to other remote servers or devices without using brute force.

password cracker   A tool that repeatedly makes guesses in order to discover the password and access the system.

patches   An operating system update released periodically to address known vulnerabilities.

path determination   The process by which a router builds and maintains a routing table of known networks and uses it to decide the path to forward a packet.

Payment Card Industry Data Security Standard (PCI DSS)   Proprietary, non-governmental standard that specifies requirements for the secure handling of customer credit card data by merchants and service providers.

penetration testing   A penetration test; it is the process of looking for vulnerabilities in a network or computer by attacking it.

personally identifiable information (PII)   Any information that can be used to positively identify an individual.

pharming   An attack that compromises domain name services by injecting entries into local host files.

phishing   Social engineering attack in which a threat actor sends enticing custom-targeted spam email to individuals with the hope the target user clicks a link or downloads malicious code.

Physical layer   Uses protocols that describe the mechanical, electrical, functional, and procedural means to activate, maintain, and deactivate physical connections for bit transmission to and from a network device.

physical topology   A depiction of the physical connections and how end devices and infrastructure devices such as routers, switches, and wireless access points are interconnected.

ping   A testing utility that uses ICMP echo request and echo reply messages to test connectivity between hosts.

piping   Chaining commands together, feeding the output of one command into the input of another.

Point-to-Point Protocol (PPP)   Provides a means of encapsulating packets for transmission over a serial link.

port   A reserved network resource used by a service.

Port Address Translation (PAT)   The process of mapping many internal addresses to a single public address by using port numbers to keep track of each conversation.

port mirroring   Allows a switch to make duplicate copies of traffic passing through a switch, and then send it out a port with a network monitor attached.

Post Office Protocol version 3 (POP3) Enables clients to retrieve email from a mail server. Downloads email from the mail server to the desktop.

PowerShell An integrated program within Windows that provides a CLI for initiating commands.

Presentation layer Provides for common representation of the data transferred between application layer services.

pretexting Social engineering attack in which a threat actor calls an individual and lies to them in an attempt to gain access to privileged data.

private IPv4 address An address that is not unique, can be used by any internal network, and cannot be routed on the Internet.

privilege escalation An attack in which vulnerabilities in servers or access control systems are exploited to grant an unauthorized user, or software process, higher levels of privilege than they should have.

probabilistic analysis An analysis approach that uses statistical techniques to predict the probability that an exploit will occur based on the likelihood that prior events will occur.

processes An instance of an application that is being executed.

profiling Providing a baseline to serve as a reference point such as for a device's or network's expected performance.

protected health information (PHI) A subset of PII created by the medical community and regulated in the United States by the Health Insurance Portability and Accountability Act

(HIPAA) and in the EU by the regulation called Data Protection.

protocol data unit (PDU) The form that an encapsulated piece of data takes at each layer of the OSI model.

protocol suite A set of protocols that work together to provide comprehensive network communication services.

public IPv4 address A unique address that can be globally routed on the Internet.

Public Key Infrastructure (PKI) A scalable architecture that includes software, hardware, people, and procedures used to securely exchange information between parties.

Q

quid pro quo Social engineering attack in which a threat actor requests personal information from a party in exchange for something like a free gift.

R

ransomware A type of malware that compromises a system and then often demands a ransom from the victim to pay the attacker in order for the malicious activity to cease or for the malware to be removed from the affected system.

reconnaissance An attack used by threat actors to discover and map systems, services, and vulnerabilities.

recursion The action taken when a DNS server is asked to query on behalf of a DNS resolver.

recursive resolver   A DNS server that recursively queries for the information asked in the DNS query.

registry   A large database in which Windows stores all of the information about hardware, applications, users, and system settings.

Remote Authentication Dial-In User Service (RADIUS)   An open AAA standard that provides the means for a router or switch to communicate with a AAA server.

resolver   A DNS client that sends DNS messages to obtain information about the requested domain name space.

Resource Monitor   Windows tool that provides more detailed information about the computer than the Task Manager, including process IDs, number of threads, memory, disk processes, and network processes.

resource record (RR)   A format used in DNS messages that is composed of the following fields: NAME, TYPE, CLASS, TTL, RDLENGTH, and RDATA.

risk   The likelihood that a particular threat will exploit a particular vulnerability of an asset and result in an undesirable consequence.

risk acceptance   A decision that the cost of risk management options outweighs the cost of the risk itself.

risk avoidance   An action that avoids any exposure to the risk.

risk limitation   A strategy employing a bit of risk acceptance along with a bit of risk avoidance to limit a company's risk exposure.

risk transfer   Risk is transferred to a willing third party such as an insurance company.

Rivest ciphers (RC)   A series of stream cipher encryption algorithms (RC2, RC4, RC5, and RC6) used to secure web traffic in SSL and TLS.

rootkit   A set of software tools designed to increase a threat actor's privileges, or grant access to portions of the software that should not normally be allowed.

rootkit detectors   Directory and file integrity checkers used to detect installed rootkits.

round-trip time (RTT)   The time a packet takes to reach the remote host and for the response from the host to return.

routed port   A pure Layer 3 interface similar to a physical interface on a Cisco IOS router.

routers   A device that operates at the network layer and uses the process of routing to forward data packets between networks.

Router Advertisement (RA)   IPv6 message sent by routers to provide addressing information to hosts using Stateless Address Autoconfiguration (SLAAC).

Router Solicitation (RS)   IPv6 message sent by hosts configured to use SLAAC requesting the addressing information sent in an RA message.

RSA   An algorithm for public key cryptography, developed by Ron Rivest, Adi Shamir, and Leonard Adleman, based on the current difficulty of factoring very large numbers.

S

sandboxing   A technique that allows suspicious files to be executed and analyzed in a safe environment.

Sarbanes-Oxley Act of 2002 (SOX)   Designed to ensure the integrity of financial practices and reporting for all U.S. public company boards, management, and public accounting firms.

scareware   Malware that includes scam software which uses social engineering to shock or induce anxiety by creating the perception of a threat.

script kiddies   Amateur hackers who have little or no skill and use existing tools or instructions found on the Internet to launch attacks.

Secure Hash Algorithm 1 (SHA-1)   Algorithm developed by the U.S. National Institute of Standards and Technology (NIST) that uses a 160-bit hashed message.

Secure Hash Algorithm 2 (SHA-2)   More secure than SHA-1; includes next-generation algorithms such as SHA-256, SHA-384, and SHA-512.

security artichoke   A defense-in-depth approach that considers the borderless nature of today's networks in which attackers only have to peel away a few leaves to get at a target, such as a remote worker who has VPN access to the corporate network.

security information and event management system (SIEM)   A specialized device or software for security event management. It typically includes logs collection, normalization, aggregation and correlation capabilities, and built-in reporting.

security onion   A defense-in-depth approach that applies layers of defense that a threat actor must peel away to gain access to the assets of the organization

Security Onion   An open source suite of network security monitoring (NSM) tools for evaluating alerts.

Security Operations Center (SOC)   Provides a broad range of services, from monitoring and management, to comprehensive threat solutions and hosted security that can be customized to meet customer needs.

security policies   Policies that identify a set of security objectives for a company, define the rules of behavior for users and administrators, and specify system requirements.

segmentation   Dividing data into smaller, more manageable pieces to send over the network.

servers   A computer with software that enables it to provide services to other computers.

Server Message Block (SMB)   A client/server file sharing protocol that describes the structure of shared network resources, such as directories, files, printers, and serial ports.

service set identifier (SSID)   A text value used in wireless LANs to uniquely identify a single WLAN.

services   Programs that run in the background to support the operating system and applications.

session data   A record of a conversation between two network endpoints.

session hijacking   An attack in which a threat actor gains access to the physical network, and then uses a man-in-the-middle attack to hijack a session.

Session layer   Provides services to the presentation layer to organize its dialogue and to manage data exchange.

Session Manager Subsystem (SMSS)   Reads the registry to create the user environment, start the Winlogon service, and prepare each user's desktop as they log on.

Sguil   An open source console application for viewing alerts from IDSs, such as Snort.

Simple Mail Transfer Protocol (SMTP)   Enables clients to send email to a mail server. Enables servers to send email to other servers.

Simple Network Management Protocol (SNMP)   Allows administrators to manage end devices, such as servers, workstations, routers, switches, and security appliances, on an IP network.

smishing   A phishing attack using SMS texting instead of email.

Snort   An open source network-based intrusion detection system (NIDS) configured with rules for known exploits.

SOC Manager   Professional who manages all the resources of the SOC and serves as the point of contact for the larger organization or customer.

social engineering   A type of access attack that attempts to manipulate individuals into performing actions or divulging confidential information such as passwords and usernames.

socket   The combination of the source IP address and source port number, or the destination IP address and destination port number.

Software-Optimized Encryption Algorithm (SEAL)   A fast, alternative symmetric encryption algorithm to DES, 3DES, and AES that uses a 160-bit encryption key, has a lower impact on the CPU, but is still considered unproven.

source port   Transport layer field value in the segment header dynamically generated by the sending device to identify a conversation between two devices.

Spanning Tree Protocol (STP)   A protocol defined by IEEE standard 802.1d that allows switches and bridges to create a redundant LAN, with the protocol dynamically causing some ports to block traffic, so that the bridge/switch forwarding logic will not cause frames to loop indefinitely around the LAN.

spear phishing   A phishing attack tailored for a specific individual or organization.

spoofing   An attack in which one device attempts to pose as another by falsifying address data, such as an IP or MAC address, or spoofing a DHCP message.

spyware   Malware used to gather information about a user and send the information to another entity without the user's consent.

SQL injection   An attack that consists of inserting a SQL query via the input data from the client to the application. A successful SQL injection exploit can read sensitive data from the database, modify database data, execute administration operations on the database, and sometimes issue commands to the operating system.

stateful firewall   A firewall that allows or blocks traffic based on state, port, and protocol.

Stateless Address Autoconfiguration (SLAAC)   A feature of IPv6 in which a host or router can be assigned an IPv6 unicast address without the need for a stateful DHCP server.

state-sponsored hackers   Hacking by either white hat or black hat hackers who steal government secrets, gather intelligence, and sabotage networks. Their targets are foreign governments, terrorist groups, and corporations.

static route   A route manually entered in a router's routing table.

statistical data   Data created through the analysis of other forms of network data.

stream ciphers   Encrypt plaintext one byte or one bit at a time.

subnet mask   Used to identify the network/host portion of the IPv4 address.

subnetting   The process of reducing the size of a network broadcast domain into a number of smaller broadcast domains.

superuser   Administrator user in Linux who has absolute control over all aspects of the computer. Also known as the root user.

Suricata   Network-based intrusion detection system (NIDS) that uses a signature-based approach.

swap file system   Used by a Linux system to free up random access memory (RAM) by moving inactive RAM content to the swap partition on the disk.

Switch Port Analyzer (SPAN)   Cisco version of port mirroring that is configured on the switch to select traffic of interest from an ingress port, copy it, and then forward it out the egress port.

switch virtual interface (SVI)   A virtual VLAN interface for inter-VLAN routing. In other words, SVIs are the virtual-routed VLAN interfaces.

symbolic link   Similar to a hard link; however, deleting a symbolic link will not delete the underlying file.

symmetric encryption   Uses the same key to encrypt and decrypt data.

syslog protocol   Allows networking devices to send their system messages across the network to syslog servers.

System Files   Hidden files that store information about other volumes and file attributes.

T

tailgating   A threat actor quickly follows an authorized person with a corporate badge into a badge-secure location.

Task Manager   Windows tool that provides information about the current general performance of the computer.

tcpdump   A command line packet analyzer that displays packet captures in real time or writes packet captures to a file.

TCP/IP protocol suite   A common name for the suite of protocols developed by the U.S. Department of Defense in the 1970s to support the construction of worldwide internetworks. TCP and IP are the two best-known protocols in the suite.

Terminal Access Controller Access-Control System Plus (TACACS+)   Cisco proprietary AAA standard that provides the means for a router or switch to communicate with a AAA server; considered more secure than RADIUS.

terminal emulator   An application that provides the user access to the command line interface (CLI).

thread   The smallest part of a process that is currently being executed by the computer.

threat   A potential danger to an asset such as data or the network itself.

threat actor   A person or entity that is responsible for the impact of a cybersecurity incident.

Tier 1 Alert Analyst   A professional who monitors incoming alerts, verifies that a true incident has occurred, and forwards tickets to Tier 2, if necessary.

Tier 2 Incident Responder   A professional who is responsible for deep investigation of incidents and advises remediation or action to be taken.

Tier 3 Subject Matter Expert (SME)/ Hunter   A professional who has expert-level skill in network, endpoint, threat intelligence, and malware reverse engineering. These professionals are experts at tracing the processes of the malware to determine its impact and how it can be removed. They are also deeply involved in hunting for potential threats and implementing threat detection tools.

Time to Live (TTL)   A field in a packet which is decremented by one at each hop as the packet is routed from source to destination; if the value of the field reaches zero, the router drops the packet.

Tor   A software platform and network of peer-to-peer (P2P) hosts that function as Internet routers and allows users to browse the Internet anonymously.

traceroute   A utility that generates a list of hops that were successfully reached along the path from source to destination.

transaction data   Consists of the messages that are exchanged during network sessions.

Transmission Control Protocol (TCP)   Enables reliable communication between processes running on separate hosts. Provides reliable, acknowledged transmissions that confirm successful delivery.

Transport layer   Defines services to segment, transfer, and reassemble the data for individual communications between the end devices.

Trivial File Transfer Protocol (TFTP)   A simple, connectionless file transfer protocol. A best-effort, unacknowledged file delivery protocol. Utilizes less overhead than FTP.

Trojan horse   Software that appears to be legitimate but contains malicious code which exploits the privileges of the user who runs it.

true negative   An alert classification that means that no security incident has occurred.

true positive   An alert classification that means the alert has been verified to be an actual security incident.

U

unicast   A one-to-one delivery option where there is only a single destination for the message.

Unified Extensible Firmware Interface (UEFI)   Designed to replace the Basic Input-Output System (BIOS) firmware.

unreliable   Describes a protocol that does not have the capability to manage and recover from undelivered or corrupt data.

User Datagram Protocol (UDP)   Enables a process running on one host to send packets to a process running on another host. Does not confirm successful datagram transmission.

V

virtual LANs (VLANs)   A group of devices connected to one or more switches that are grouped into a single broadcast domain through configuration. VLANs allow switch administrators to place the devices connected to the switches in separate VLANs without requiring separate physical switches. This creates design advantages of separating the traffic without the expense of buying additional hardware.

virtual private network (VPN)   A set of security protocols that, when implemented by two devices on either side of an unsecure network such as the Internet, can allow the devices to send data securely. VPNs provide privacy, device authentication, anti-replay services, and data integrity services.

virus   A type of malware that propagates by inserting a copy of itself into another program.

vishing   A phishing attack using voice and the phone system instead of email.

visual hacking   Also called shoulder surfing, a social engineering attack in which a threat actor physically observes the victim entering credentials such as a workstation login, an ATM PIN, or the combination on a physical lock.

Vocabulary for Event Recording and Incident Sharing (VERIS)   A set of metrics designed to create a way to describe security incidents in a structured and repeatable way.

vulnerability   A weakness in a system or its design that could be exploited by a threat.

vulnerability brokers   Usually gray hat hackers who attempt to discover exploits and report them to vendors, sometimes for prizes or rewards.

vulnerability exploitation tools   Tools that identify whether a remote host is vulnerable to a security attack.

vulnerability scanners   Tools that scan a network or system to identify open ports or known vulnerabilities.

W

watering hole   An attack in which the threat actor determines websites that a target group visits regularly and then attempts to compromise those websites by infecting them with malware that can identify and target only members of the target group.

weaponization   Embedding the vulnerabilities of a victim's assets into a tool that can be deployed.

whaling   A spear phishing attack focused on big targets such as top executives of an organization.

white hat hackers   Ethical hackers who use their programming skills for good, ethical, and legal purposes such as network penetration tests.

WHOIS   A TCP-based protocol that is used to identify the owners of Internet domains through the DNS system.

window size   The number of bytes that the destination device of a TCP session can accept and process at one time.

Windows Defender   A suite of protection tools built into Windows.

Windows Management Instrumentation (WMI)   Management infrastructure that can retrieve information about computer components, display hardware and software statistics, and monitor the health of remote computers.

wireless access point (AP)   A device that connects wireless devices to a WLAN.

wireless hacking tools   Tools used to intentionally hack into a wireless network to detect security vulnerabilities.

wireless LAN controller (WLC)   Centralizes the administration of multiple APs and WLANs.

wireless LANs (WLANs)   Uses radio frequencies (RF) instead of cables at the physical layer and MAC sublayer of the data link layer to connect wireless devices to the network.

worms   Similar to a virus, replicates itself by independently exploiting vulnerabilities in networks.

X, Y, Z

X Window System   Graphical interface used in most Linux distros.

zombies   A group of compromised hosts that run malicious code and continually attempts to self-propagate like a worm.

zone-based policy firewalls (ZPFs)   Uses the concept of zones, which is a group of one or more interfaces that have similar functions or features.

C

G

M

S

T

V

X-Y

Z

REGISTER YOUR PRODUCT at CiscoPress.com/register
Access Additional Benefits and SAVE 35% on Your Next Purchase

- Download available product updates.
- Access bonus material when applicable.
- Receive exclusive offers on new editions and related products.
  (Just check the box to hear from us when setting up your account.)
- Get a coupon for 35% for your next purchase, valid for 30 days.
  Your code will be available in your Cisco Press cart. (You will also find
  it in the Manage Codes section of your account page.)

Registration benefits vary by product. Benefits will be listed on your account page under Registered Products.

CiscoPress.com – Learning Solutions for Self-Paced Study, Enterprise, and the Classroom
Cisco Press is the Cisco Systems authorized book publisher of Cisco networking technology, Cisco certification self-study, and Cisco Networking Academy Program materials.

At **CiscoPress.com** you can

- Shop our books, eBooks, software, and video training.
- Take advantage of our special offers and promotions (ciscopress.com/promotions).
- Sign up for special offers and content newsletters (ciscopress.com/newsletters).
- Read free articles, exam profiles, and blogs by information technology experts.
- Access thousands of free chapters and video lessons.

Connect with Cisco Press – Visit CiscoPress.com/community
Learn about Cisco Press community events and programs.

Cisco Press